5e
AUDIT ing
& ASSURANCE SERVICES

DAVID N. RICCHIUTE
UNIVERSITY OF NOTRE DAME

SOUTH-WESTERN College Publishing

An International Thomson Publishing Company

Team Director: Richard K. Lindgren
Senior Acquisitions Editor: David L. Shaut
Marketing Manager: Matt Filimonov
Developmental Editor: Mignon Worman
Production Editor: Marci Dechter
Internal Design: Craig LaGesse Ramsdell
Cover Designer: Michael H. Stratton
Cover Photography: FPG International Corp. and SuperStock, Inc.
Manufacturing Coordinator: Gordon Woodside

ISBN: 0-538-86952-6

4 5 6 7 8 9 D 5 4 3 2 1 0 9

Printed in the United States of America

Library of Congress Cataloging-in-Publication Data

Ricchiute, David N.
    Auditing and assurance services / David N. Ricchiute. -- 5th ed.
      p.   cm.
    Rev. ed. of: Auditing. 4th ed. c1995.
    Includes bibliographical references and index.
    ISBN 0-538-86952-6 (alk. paper)
    1. Auditing.   I. Ricchiute, David N.   Auditing.   II. Title.
HF5667.R58 1997
657'.45--dc21
                                              97-12700
                                                 CIP

I(T)P®
International Thomson Publishing
South-Western is an ITP Company. The ITP trademark is used under license.

Preface

ABOUT THE AUTHOR

David N. Ricchiute, Deloitte & Touche Professor of Accountancy, University of Notre Dame, has published articles in *The Accounting Review*, the *Journal of Accounting Research*, *Accounting Organizations & Society*, the *Journal of Applied Psychology*, *Organizational Behavior and Human Decision Processes*, *Issues in Accounting Education*, the *Journal of Accountancy*, and *The CPA Journal*, among others. Formerly on the audit staff of Price Waterhouse and a visiting professor at the University of Michigan, Ann Arbor, he has served as Director of Research of the Audit Section of the American Accounting Association (AAA), on the editorial boards of accounting and auditing journals, as an educational and professional consultant to public accounting firms and state audit agencies throughout the country, and on committees of the AICPA and the AAA, including the AAA Audit Section's Task Force on Future Audit, Attestation, and Assurance Services. His teaching awards include Outstanding Teacher of the Year, College of Business Administration, University of Notre Dame.

TO THE INSTRUCTOR

Consistent with the work of the *Accounting Education Change Commission* and the AICPA *Special Committee on Assurance Services*, auditing education is undergoing dramatic changes in at least two ways:

- An awakening that practitioners have a comparative advantage in offering professional services that transcend the **boundaries** of industrial era financial statements, and
- A transition away from first-person delivery by classroom instructors only and toward third-person **discovery** by students both inside and outside the classroom.

Each has influenced the fifth edition. To transcend the *boundaries* of financial statements, *Auditing and Assurance Services* exposes students both to the demand for and the supply of the profession's flagship service, *financial statement audits*, and to the nature of the value-added *assurance* services decision makers demand in the information age. For example, on the supply of auditing, the text explains how auditors leverage off of publicly available data sources to assemble information about a client in the pharmaceutical industry (Chapter 6). On the nature of assurance services, the text illustrates how Consumers Union and Underwriters Laboratories have captured so completely the markets they serve (Chapters 1, 2, 3, and 5), and how Deloitte & Touche LLP and Gradient Technologies have partnered to offer services on Internet security (Chapter 7).

To encourage *discovery* learning, the fifth edition integrates academic research, illustrates with real companies, links class discussion and key assignments to student skills, offers working paper review cases, and proposes research projects that expose students to databases, annual reports, and the professional literature. For example, the text explains what research has revealed about time budget pressure, auditor-client disagreements, and management discretion in earnings manipulation. And a research project asks the question, why wouldn't a client correct the circumstances that give rise to a qualified opinion? Accounting education at the turn of the century demands that educators expose students both to auditing services and to market opportunities in assurance and attestation services. The expanding scope of knowledge in the information age demands that students take responsibility for life-long, discovery learning.

TO THE STUDENT

Auditing and Assurance Services conveys experience about professional services for which most students will have little or no prior understanding—a limitation that places students' comprehension at risk. Prose fiction presents a similar hurdle, but the fiction writer's task is different, in part because much of the writer's craft centers on narrative properties that set a story in motion by accessing plausible scenes from a reader's existing memories. In auditing and assurance services education, however, students typically have no prescripted scenes about practice, since they've had little prior exposure to information systems, evidence, and the like, thereby providing few memories on which the learning experience might draw. But the limitation of no prior understanding also presents an opportunity: the student comes to the material with no biases or expectations that limit the boundaries of understanding, providing the textbook and the instructor with a unique opportunity to shape professional practice into insight and to make seemingly sterile professional tasks come to life. I urge you as a student to exploit the material presented in this text by allowing its chapters to awaken in you a curiosity about auditing and assurance services and about how practitioners come to some of the complex decisions and judgment processes inherent in practice today.

FEATURES

NEW TO THE FIFTH EDITION

Assurance Services
Consistent with the work of the AICPA *Special Committee on Assurance Services* (Elliot Committee), the fifth edition integrates assurance and attestation services throughout the text. For example, the text introduces assurance services offered by *Consumers Union* (Chapters 1, 3, 5), by *Underwriters Laboratories* (Chapters 2 and 5), and by a number of public accounting firms (Chapters 1-4, 7, 10, 12, 15, 16, and 18), and also introduces attestation services offered by public accounting firms, including services by *Coopers and Lybrand LLP* for Wilson Sporting Good's assertions (Chapters 1 and 2), *Price Waterhouse LLP* for

Stanley H. Kaplan's *SAT* improvement assertions (Chapter 1), *KPMG Peat Marwick LLP* on ethics management (Chapter 4), *Ernst & Young LLP* for CoreStates Financial's internal control assertions (Chapter 7), and the *Deloitte & Touche LLP/Gradient Technologies* partnered service on Internet security (Chapter 7), among a host of others in Chapter 18.

Real World Illustrations

To ground otherwise abstract issues in reality, the fifth edition offers numerous examples of real world applications in practice. For example, in addition to audit report illustrations (Chapter 3) and legal liability cases (Chapter 5), some of the companies and issues illustrated include Chapter 1: *Ben & Jerry's Home-made Inc.* (management's incentives in an initial public offering), *Alyesko Pipe-line Service Co.* (operational auditing), *Harper-Collins* (information services consulting); Chapter 4: *PTL Club* (unethical business practices); Chapter 6: *Merck & Co.* (auditing in the pharmaceutical industry); Chapter 7: *Levi Straus & Co.*, *Lockheed Martin* (Internet technology), *Bell Atlantic* (home page manage-ment and global markets); Chapter 10: *Baltimore Orioles*, *Texas Rangers* (location and marketing services consulting); Chapter 11: *Taco Bell, Burger King* (area franchise fees); Chapter 12: *Bank of America* (purchase consulting services), *Camp Fire Girls & Boys, General Motors* (outsourced information services); Chapter 13: *Westinghouse, Columbia Gas System Inc.* (Superfund compliance costs); Chapter 14: *Boeing Company* (postretirement health care disclosures); Chapter 15: *IBM, AT&T, Battle Mountain Gold Company* (impaired assets); Chapter 18: *Marriott, PepsiCo, Xerox* (health care provider quality), *Lucent Technologies* (letters for underwriters).

Management Discretion and Earnings Manipulation

In addition to mapping financial statement assertions to audit procedures and explaining the procedures in detail, the fifth edition incorporates key account-ing issues into each of the five chapters devoted to substantive tests of account balances (Chapters 11, 13, 14, 15, and 16), and addresses crucial questions about each: For example, what are management's incentives and how can those incentives be impounded into earnings manipulation? and What are the legal liability and ethical implications of the issue? The accounting issues addressed are earnings manipulation and revenue recognition (Chapter 11), accounting for environmental liabilities (Chapter 13), accounting for postretirement health care obligations (Chapter 14), accounting for impaired assets (Chapter 15), and accounting for financial instruments (Chapter 16).

Integration of Computer Information Systems

Computers pervade contemporary practice, largely because most all audit and assurance service clients are computerized. As a result, rather than address computers as a free-standing chapter, the fifth edition:

- Integrates computer information systems and internal control in Chapter 7, introducing systems such as microcomputers, local area networks, tele-communications, end user computing, service bureaus, and Internet tech-nology; and computer assisted audit techniques such as base case system evaluation, test data, integrated test facilities, parallel simulation, audit hooks, audit modules, and transaction tagging.

- Introduces automated working papers, database management systems software, spreadsheet software, and text retrieval software in Chapter 6.
- Illustrates computer-assisted audit techniques in Chapters 10, 11, 12, 13, and 15.

Integration of Academic Research

Consistent with recommendations of the *Accounting Education Change Commission* (AECC), the fifth edition incorporates the results of relevant academic research. For example: Chapter 2: *independence, audit risk, materiality*; Chapter 3: *auditor changes, predicting audit qualifications, financial distress, market reaction to bankruptcy filings*; Chapter 7: *heuristics and biases, audit committee effectiveness, auditor-client disagreements, communication between predecessor and successor auditors, time-budget pressure, analytical procedures, evidence planning, the review process*; Chapter 11: *management incentives, share prices and management changes, predicting takeover targets, qualified opinions and share prices*; Chapter 15: *discretionary write-downs*; Chapter 14: *the choice of alternatives affecting health care obligations*; Chapter 18: *the voluntary purchase of quarterly reviews*.

Working Paper Review

The center of gravity in an auditor's early-career employment evaluations rests squarely on his or her performance in preparing audit working papers. To help equip students to *prepare* working papers, the fifth edition incorporates working paper *review* cases. The working papers are realistic, replicate papers and issues illustrated in the text, and are designed to lend insight into what reviewers are likely to look for. The cases appear in Chapters 6, 11, 13, 15, and 16, and include common early-career audit areas, such as *accounts receivable front summary schedules, receivables confirmations, intercompany and interbank transfers, bank reconciliations, accounts payable, accrued property taxes, physical inventory observations, fixed assets and accumulated depreciation*, and *marketable securities*.

Research Projects

The fifth edition includes over thirty end-of-chapter research projects linked to the professional literature, publicly available data sources, and annual reports of the student's/instructor's choice. The projects are intended as out-of-class, discovery-learning exercises that do not necessarily lend themselves to unambiguous solutions. For example, the research projects address issues such as *becoming familiar with the profession's controversies, self regulation and the Public Oversight Board, reporting on financial distress, unethical business practices, litigation against public accounting firms, tort reform, using the Internet to understand a client's industry, managing change in a selected industry, management discretion in earnings manipulation, internal control and transaction cycles in a selected industry, annual reports and the audit process, assurance services and retail electronic commerce*, and *internal auditing in selected industries*.

RETAINED (AND UPDATED) FROM THE FOURTH EDITION

Risk and Evidence

The text, particularly Chapter 2 and Parts II (Technology) and III (Method), explicitly incorporates the audit risk model from *SAS No. 47*, "Audit Risk and

Materiality in Conducting an Audit," and the financial statement assertions from *SAS No. 31*, "Evidential Matter." The fifth edition devotes seven chapters to tests of controls and to substantive tests within four major transaction cycles: the revenue/receipt cycle (Chapters 10 and 11), the expenditure/disbursement cycle (Chapters 12, 13, and 14), the conversion cycle (Chapter 15), and the financing cycle (Chapter 16).

Professional Literature and Articles

The text provides extensive discussion of, and references to, the professional literature, including the Auditing Standards Board's *Statements on Auditing Standards* and *Statements on Standards for Attestation Services*; contemporary articles from magazines, journals, and newspapers such as the *Journal of Accountancy, Auditing: A Journal of Practice & Theory, The Accounting Review, The Wall Street Journal, Accounting Today, Public Accounting Report* and *Business Week*, and important reports and monographs such as *Internal Control: Integrated Framework* (the COSO Report), and Mautz and Sharaf's *The Philosophy of Auditing*.

Edit/ Update

All of the chapters have been edited for clarity of exposition (every sentence, every word) and updated for, among other things:

- The work of the AICPA *Special Committee on Assurance Services* (Chapters 1, 2, and 18);
- The report of the Committee of Sponsoring Organizations of the Treadway Commission (COSO), *Internal Control: Integrated Framework* (Chapter 7);
- The Osbourne (*Bily v. Arthur Young & Co.*), Security Pacific (*Security Pacific v. Peat Marwick*) and Cherry (*Cherry v. Joseph S. Herbert & Co.*) cases, which together reaffirm both the privity concept established in *Ultramares* and the linkage test in *Credit Alliance* (Chapter 5); and
- Recent *Statements on Auditing Standards* and *Statements on Standards for Attestation Engagements* on fraud, internal control, internal auditing, letters for underwriters, using specialists, compliance auditing, and compliance attestation, among others.

Sampling (optional)

Depending on the objectives of a course, instructors may choose to cover Chapters 8 and 9 (which introduce attributes estimation, sequential sampling, discovery sampling, probability proportional to size, difference and ratio estimation, mean-per-unit estimation, and nonstatistical sampling) and/or may selectively cover sections in Chapters 10 through 13, which illustrate audit sampling applications in tests of controls over billing, accounts receivable, cash disbursements, and accounts payable.

END-OF-CHAPTER MATERIALS

The end of each chapter includes:

- Key terms (referenced to the chapter page on which the term is introduced and to a comprehensive Glossary at the end of the book)

- Extensive references to
  - Authoritative literature (*SASs, SSAEs*)
  - Professional reports
  - Articles and books
  - Review questions
  - Multiple choice questions
  - Problems and discussion cases
  - Research projects

A comprehensive case—*"YOU'RE AHEAD*SM*" A Long Distance Cost Savings Initiative*—a review of the first seven chapters, appears at the end of Chapter 7.

SUPPLEMENTAL MATERIALS

Several teaching and learning aids are new to this edition or substantially revised:

FOR THE INSTRUCTOR (COMPUTER AND HARD COPY)

- **Auditing and Assurance Services: A Course Guide** A *complete* guide for a course in auditing and assurance services that includes:
  - Day-by-day *teaching plans* and accompanying *teaching notes* tied to six key skills for students: *oral communication, written communication, group processing, critical thinking, research,* and *computers*.
  - Day-by-day *PowerPoint presentations* and *class handouts*.
  - Course *syllabus*.
  - Group *cases*.
  - Quick *cases*.
  - Description of key *assignments*.
  - Annotated *bibliography*.
- **Instructor's Resource Manual**
  - Test bank
  - Transparency masters
  - Solutions to all review questions, multiple choice questions, and problems and discussion cases

FOR THE STUDENT

- **Study Guide** A student supplement that includes note-taking templates for Instructors' Power Point presentations.
- **Integrated Audit Case** A case consisting of seven integrated units relating to new client acceptance, engagement planning, internal control, computer auditing, tests of controls, substantive tests, and completing the audit. The units are designed for assignment throughout the course and emphasize the role of professional judgment in each phase of an audit. The case provides opportunities for students to develop writing skills and to practice working paper preparation.

ORGANIZATION

The fifth edition of *Auditing and Assurance Services* is organized in four parts.

PART 1: PROFESSIONAL RESPONSIBILITIES

Chapters 1 through 5 introduce assurance, attestation, and audit services; professional standards; reports; and practitioners' responsibilities for ethical behavior and legal liability. Chapter 1, an overview of the public accounting profession, distinguishes among consulting, assurance, attestation, and audit services; addresses the demand for financial statement audits; raises the suspicion that financial statement audits may be obsolete; and introduces operational audits and compliance audits. Chapter 2, "Professional Standards," introduces the need for assurance standards, the AICPA's *generally accepted auditing standards* (GAAS) and *attestation standards*, the role of materiality and risk, and the standards of quality control and quality (peer) review in monitoring the performance of public accounting firms. Chapter 3, "Reports," introduces reports on assurance and attestation services, the standard audit report, the required circumstances and wording for modifications to a standard report, and reporting requirements for comparative financial statements and for financial statements prepared for use in a foreign country. Chapter 4, "Professional Ethics," focuses on the principles and rules of conduct underlying the AICPA's *Code of Professional Conduct*, and the formal mechanisms used to enforce the AICPA and state society codes of conduct. Chapter 5, "Legal Liability," identifies the major issues central to the legal liability cases involving independent auditors; describes an auditor's potential liability under common law, the *Securities Act of 1933*, and the *Securities Exchange Act of 1934*; and explains an auditor's responsibility to detect and report fraud and illegal acts.

PART 2: TECHNOLOGY

Chapters 6 and 7 introduce the evidence-gathering process and the consideration of internal control in a financial statement audit. Chapter 6, "Evidence," addresses evidence and its relationship to financial statement assertions and procedures; the cognitive biases that can interfere with interpreting evidence; the nature of tests of controls, substantive tests, and analytical procedures; the major activities in the audit process (including the decision to accept an engagement, planning, and interim and year-end audit work); and the purpose and content of working papers. Chapter 7, "Internal Control and Computer Information Systems," discusses information systems, the components of internal control (the control environment, risk assessment, control activities, information and communication, and monitoring), how an auditor considers internal controls when planning and performing a financial statement audit, and computer applications in auditing that are then illustrated in Chapters 10, 11, 12, 13, and 15.

Chapters 8 and 9, optional chapters, address the role of sampling in audit tests. Chapter 8, "Sampling in Tests of Controls," introduces and illustrates three sampling for attributes plans—attribute estimation, sequential (stop-or-go) sampling, and discovery sampling—and a nonstatistical sampling plan. Chapter 9, "Sampling in Substantive Tests," addresses four statistical sampling plans for variables—difference estimation, ratio estimation, mean-per-unit estimation, and probability-proportional-to-size (PPS) sampling—and a nonstatistical sampling plan.

PART 3: METHOD

Chapters 10 through 17 introduce, discuss, and illustrate the detailed tests of controls and substantive tests used in contemporary audit practice, and also identify opportunities for assurance and attestation services. Chapters 10 and 11 address the revenue/receipt cycle, sales and cash receipts transactions, accounts receivable, cash balances, and management discretion and earnings manipulation in revenue recognition. Chapters 12, 13, and 14 turn attention to the expenditure/disbursement cycle, including purchases and cash disbursement transactions, accounts payable, prepaid expenses, accrued liabilities, personnel and payroll, and management discretion in accounting for environmental liabilities and for postretirement health care benefits. Chapters 15 and 16 introduce tests of controls and substantive tests applicable to inventory, fixed assets, investments, debt, equity, and management discretion in accounting for impaired assets and for financial instruments.

Chapter 17 completes the discussion of procedures, addressing a practitioner's considerable responsibilities when completing an engagement, for example, auditing accounting estimates, the review for subsequent events, communicating with the audit committee, inquiries of a client's legal counsel, management representation letters, and forming an opinion on financial statements.

PART 4: ATTESTATION ENGAGEMENTS, COMPLIANCE AND INTERNAL AUDITING

Chapters 18 and 19 focus on engagements other than financial statement audits and two additional, and highly prominent, types of auditing in the United States. Chapter 18, "Assurance and Attestation Services," discusses examples of assurance services for the 21st century and a variety of contemporary attestation services, including reviews of financial statements, interim financial information, internal control, letters for underwriters, personal financial statements, financial forecasts and projections, and the application of accounting principles. Chapter 19, "Compliance Auditing and Internal Auditing," introduces the governmental auditor's compliance audit under generally accepted government auditing standards, the GAO's "Yellow Book," and the *Single Audit Act Amendment of 1996*, and discusses the internal auditor's operational audit.

ACKNOWLEDGMENTS

I gratefully acknowledge the following people for comments and suggestions: Michael Akers, Marquette University; Joyce Allen, Xavier University; Barbara Apostolou, Louisiana State University; Joseph Botana, Lakeland College; Edmund Boyle, The University of Rhode Island; David Davidson, California State University at Long Beach; John Delaney, Southwestern University; Rajib Doogar, University of Notre Dame; Phillip Driscoll, Syracuse University; John Edwards, Louisiana Tech University; Keith Ehrenreich, California State University at Pomona; Robert Eskew, Purdue University; Stephen Goldberg, Purdue

University; David Kerr, Texas A&M University; Ronald King, Washington University; Mark Kovarik, Price Waterhouse; Stanley Lewis, The University of Southern Mississippi; Donald Loster, University of California at Santa Barbara; William Messier, Jr., University of Florida; Frederick Neumann, University of Illinois; Bill Nichols, University of Notre Dame; Dave Nichols, University of Mississippi; Marshall Pitman, The University of Texas at San Antonio; Doug Prawitt, Brigham Young University; Sri Ramamoorti, University of Illinois at Urbana-Champaign; Alan Reinstein, Wayne State University; John Rigsby, Mississippi State University; Robert Rouse, College of Charleston; Michael Ruble, Western Washington University; Glen Sanderson, Illinois State University; Brian Shapiro, University of Arizona; Glen Sumners, Louisiana State University; Donald Tidrick, University of Texas at Austin; Dieter Weiss, Ferris State University; H. James Williams, Delaware State University; and James Yardley, Virginia Polytechnic Institute and State University.

David N. Ricchiute
University of Notre Dame

Brief Contents

Contents

PART 1

PROFESSIONAL RESPONSIBILITIES

1

An Introduction to Assurance Services

Major topics discussed in this chapter are the:

- **Nature of consulting and assurance services.**
- **Types of attestation services performed in the U.S.**
- **Demand for financial statement audits.**
- **Standard setting process.**
- **Relationship between, and organizations that influence, accounting and auditing.**
- **Suspicion held by some observers that financial statement audits may become obsolete.**
- **Nature of operational audits, compliance audits, and nonattest services.**

The scope of services offered by public accounting firms is expanding in the information age, partly because some observers[1] view the profession's flagship service, financial statement audits, as a remnant of a long past industrial age. Traditional financial statements issued after the close of an entity's fiscal year are less timely, and therefore less relevant, to decision makers in the information age. For example, large-block traders in equity securities often base investment decisions on far more timely alternate forms of information, such as analysts' forecasts, among other readily available information sources. Financial statement audits are likely to be demanded well into the 21st century. However, the survival of the public accounting profession as a major player in the financial community may depend crucially on the profession's willingness and ability to design value-added services which, like the financial statement audit of the mid-20th century, will be viewed by decision makers as utterly essential to *their* survival.

This chapter introduces the intuition underlying assurance, attestation, and audit services. The chapter begins by distinguishing between consulting and assurance services, and by describing attestation and auditing, two types of assurance services. Next, the chapter motivates the demand for independent financial statement audits, and describes audit standard setting and the organizations that influence practice. In turn, the chapter addresses a question

---

1   See, for example, R. K. Elliott. "The Third Wave Breaks on the Shores of Accounting," *Accounting Horizons* (June 1992), pp. 62-85; P. F. Drucker. "We Need to Measure, Not Count," *The Wall Street Journal* (July 17, 1993), p. B6.

troubling the highest levels of the profession: Will financial statement audits become obsolete? The chapter concludes by introducing operational audits, compliance audits, and other nonattest services.

CONSULTING AND ASSURANCE SERVICES

Figure 1-1 compares *assurance* and *consulting* services, two major categories of services offered today by professional firms that traditionally have been called *public accounting firms*. Many public accounting firms are organized as **limited liability partnerships (LLPs)**. LLPs limit the extent of a partner's liability for claims against the firm to his or her investment in the firm, although litigants can make claims against a partner's personal assets for liability linked to his or her own actions. The professional staffs of public accounting firms include **certified public accountants (CPAs)** and consultants with expertise in areas as diverse as actuarial science, organizational design, government regulation, information processing, employee benefits, and human resource management. The *Big Six* firms are: Arthur Andersen Worldwide LLP, Coopers & Lybrand LLP, Deloitte & Touche LLP, Ernst & Young LLP, KPMG Peat Marwick LLP, and Price Waterhouse LLP. Other international firms include BDO Seidman LLP and Grant Thornton LLP. Prominent regional firms, some with international

Figure 1-1: The Relationship Among Assurance, Attestation, Audit, and Consulting Services

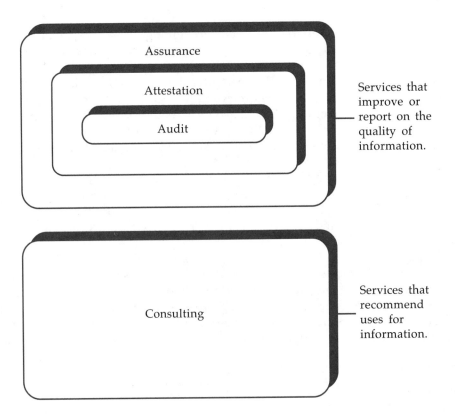

affiliations, include Baird Kurtz & Dobson LLP, Crowe Chizek LLP, McGladrey & Pullen LLP, and Moss Adams LLP.

Many **consulting services** are *two-party contracts* in which a consultant recommends *uses for information*. Consultants include international, multiservice firms such as the McKinsey Group, the Boston Consulting Group, and the Big Six firms, and smaller consulting firms devoted to niche markets. For example, the Summit Group, an information services consulting firm with principal offices in the Midwest, entered into a long-term, two-party contract with HarperCollins, a publishing house, to recommend nationwide textbook distribution routes that would minimize transportation costs. HarperCollins' information processing system captures all the data relevant to textbook distribution. However, owing to constraints on expertise and time, HarperCollins chose to outsource the textbook distribution plan rather than hire additional planning staff. The Summit Group's task was to recommend how HarperCollins could minimize costs given information HarperCollins provided about warehouse locations, inventory quantities, delivery deadlines, available transportation modes, and shipment destinations. Like other typical consulting projects, the Summit Group recommended *how* HarperCollins could use internal information, but lent no assurances about the quality of the information from which the recommendations were made. For example, unbeknown to HarperCollins, the inventory quantities may have been incorrect. Consulting projects typically focus on the use of information, not on the quality of the information used.

In contrast, many **assurance services** are *three-party contracts* in which assurers improve or report on the *quality of information*. Assurers include public accounting firms, consulting firms, and independent nonprofit institutions, among others. For example, one independent institution, Consumers Union, has long performed independent tests of consumer products, such as home appliances, and reported product quality ratings in *Consumer Reports*, a monthly periodical devoted exclusively to product comparisons. Home appliance manufacturers, such as Whirlpool and KitchenAide, provide product performance information in promotional pamphlets and advertising copy. But, the information may be unreliable because manufacturers have incentives to misrepresent quality. Consumers Union (the first party to the implied three-party contract) receives revenue from *Consumer Reports* subscribers (the second party), but accepts no advertising or other fees from product manufacturers (the third party). Consumers value the product performance assurances reported in *Consumer Reports* because Consumers Union receives no revenue from—and therefore is independent of—product manufacturers.

Some public accounting firms have been rather aggressive in offering assurance services. For example, Price Waterhouse assures the Academy Awards balloting, Crowe Chizek assures a drug monitoring program to an athletic oversight authority,[2] and several firms assure statewide lotteries. However, unlike Consumers Union, the public accounting profession has not fully exploited its reputation for independence, integrity, and objectivity in the market for value-added assurance services. In response, the American Institute of Certified Public Accountants (AICPA) established a *Special Committee on*

---

2   R. Telberg. "CPAs Cautioned on Assurance Services," *Accounting Today* (January 22-February 11, 1996), 1, 34.

Assurance Services, chaired by Robert K. Elliott (the Elliott Committee), a KPMG Peat Marwick partner, to develop a strategic plan for the profession's further penetration into the market. The plan, introduced in Chapter 18, is crucial not only because the assurance market is potentially lucrative, but because the market for accounting services, currently a major revenue producer for public accounting firms, ". . . seems saturated; there is overcapacity and price competition; and the inherent reliability of accounting data has increased with improvements in business information systems."[3]

In addressing market opportunities, the Committee speculated that in the future the consumers of information—rather than the providers—will have the power to decide the content of the information they'll consume.[4] For example, although newspaper editors once held exclusive domain over the news reported to readers, a reader today can access on-line news services that report what the reader demands. There's no reason to believe that information technology won't also affect the economic information that consumers demand. For example, although investors once relied passively on information reported by management in financial statements, some investors today actively demand information *not* reported traditionally in financial statements—such as social and ecological awareness, market share and back order data, and management's decisions to invest in politically repressed countries. The profession's task is to predict what information decision makers will demand, and to design assurance services that will improve the quality of the information demanded—i.e., value-added assurance services.

The profession's entry into the assurance services market is not without barriers.[5] For example, the marketplace views CPAs as the preferred providers for financial statement services, but may be less willing to equate a CPA's core competencies with, say, a major consulting firm for services unrelated to financial statements. For this among other reasons, some observers are suspicious of the profession's move into the assurance services market. For example, the New York State Society of CPAs sponsored a symposium that addressed the work of the Elliott Committee. Some of the panelists supported the committee's work, including AICPA vice chair Robert Mednick, who argued that, "The future of the profession lies to a large extent on the future of this project."[6] But others were less forgiving. For example, David Costello, president of the National Association of State Boards of Accountancy, questioned a public accounting firm's comparative advantage over a consulting firm: "Are CPAs any better at doing organizational design, or engineering design, or some other kind of work, than any other company?"[7] What's clear is that there is a demand for assurance services. For example, witness the well-respected work of Consumers Union. What's unclear is whether the market will view the public accounting profession as the first-stop supplier of assurance services in quite

---

3   R. K. Elliott. "The Future of Assurance Services: Implications for Academia," *Accounting Horizons* (December 1995), p. 118.
4   AICPA. *Interim Report of the Special Committee on Assurance Services* (The Elliott Committee). New York: AICPA (1995), p. 1.
5   See, for example, AICPA. *Interim Report of the Special Committee on Assurance Services* (The Elliott Committee). New York: AICPA (1995), p. 6.
6   R. Telberg. "CPAs Cautioned on Assurance Services," *Accounting Today* (January 22-February 11, 1996), p. 34.
7   Ibid., p. 1.

the same way that the financial community views the profession as *the* supplier of attestation and auditing services.

ATTESTATION SERVICES

As illustrated in Figure 1-1, some assurance services are called *attestations*, and some attestations are called *audits*. **Attestation services** are a type of assurance service in which the attester offers assurance about another party's *written assertions*. For example, in written agreements with college applicants, Stanley H. Kaplan, Inc., a test preparation firm, asserts that prior Kaplan-prepared applicants improved their College Entrance Examination Board (CEEB) *Scholastic Assessment Test (SAT)* scores by 115 points over their most recent *SAT* (or Preliminary *SAT*) scores. Kaplan guarantees that Kaplan applicants who fail to improve their scores by 115 points can repeat the test preparation course free. To lend credibility to the claim, Kaplan engaged Price Waterhouse to attest to Kaplan's written assertion about the test performance of prior Kaplan-trained applicants. Kaplan appealed to college applicants with a written assertion backed by the reputation of a major firm.

Although accountants are trained in financial and managerial accounting, notice that Price Waterhouse's attestation service for Kaplan did not involve accounting. Rather, Price Waterhouse, like other accounting firms, has a comparative advantage in gathering and evaluating evidence. Sometimes the evidence may bear on assertions about economic transactions, but other times the evidence may bear on disclosures about commodities. For example, the Wilson Sporting Goods Co., a unit of Finland's Amer Group, introduced the Wilson Ultra golf ball and asserted in writing that the Ultra outdistances the competition by an average of 5.7 yards per drive. To justify the claim, Wilson engaged Coopers & Lybrand to attest to Wilson's assertion about the yards by which amateurs' Ultra drives outdistance the competition.[8] Over the years, accounting firms have attested to a variety of written assertions unrelated to accounting, including the reliability of software specifications and insurance claims, and representations about market feasibility and shopping mall shelf space.

To capture additional market share, Stanley H. Kaplan and Wilson Sporting Goods, respectively, supplied Price Waterhouse's and Coopers & Lybrand's attestations to the public without prompting. However, in some cases, entities supply attestations in order to recapture lost market share. Consider two examples. First, in the early 1990s, two thirty-five-year-olds paid a considerable sum to access a database that a dating service asserted in writing would include the names of one hundred, mid-thirties professionals in the Los Angeles area. They paid, accessed the database, found few, and sued. Owing to demand from other potential clients, the dating service hired a firm in southern California to attest that management's service assertions were reliable. Second, a retired steelworker invested in a cash management fund that offered exceptional investment returns. The actual five-year rate-of-return having been half the range of rates asserted, the retiree's investment underperformed, and he sued. The *Public Accounting Report*, a bimonthly newsletter, reported that twenty-one

---

8   L. Berton. "After This, CPAs May Take Over Instant-Replay Duties for Football," *The Wall Street Journal* (July 9, 1991), p. B1.

of the twenty-six largest U.S. investment companies have hired accounting firms to attest that assertions about rate-of-return are reliably consistent with performance-presentation standards sanctioned by the Association for Investment Management and Research. In both examples, a party (a dating service, a cash management fund) made a written assertion (names, rate-of-return) that another party (two purchasers, a retired steelworker) relied on to his or her detriment. Both the dating service and the cash management fund attempted to regain market share by leveraging off of the accounting profession's reputation for independence.

Two attestation services are actually quite common in practice: agreed-upon procedures engagements and review engagements. First, in an *agreed-upon procedures* engagement, the attester is engaged to examine an item using procedures agreed upon by the contracting parties. For example, the Federal Depository Insurance Corporation (FDIC) *Improvement Act of 1991*, a response to the savings and loan industry debacle of the 1980s, requires insured depository institutions to have independent accountants perform agreed-upon procedures that test a bank's compliance with the FDIC's "safety and soundness" laws and regulations. The FDIC laws and regulations relate primarily to loans made to insiders and to dividend requirements. The agreed-upon procedures were developed jointly by representatives of the AICPA and the banking profession. Research reveals that other common attestation services include debt covenant compliance, financial forecasts and projections, descriptions of accounting information systems, inventory quantities and locations, and contract costs.[9] Second, a common attestation service for financial statements, called a *review*, is a service in which a public accounting firm gives limited assurance about whether an entity's financial statements conform with generally accepted accounting principles (GAAP). Review services are usually purchased by small, privately owned businesses whose creditors are willing to rely on limited assurances, rather than to demand that a business purchase a more expensive financial statement audit (discussed next). In practice, public accounting firms offer two types of attestation services for financial statements: a *review*, which provides limited (sometimes called "negative") assurance, and a financial statement *audit*, which provides positive assurance. The difference in the level of assurance between reviews and financial statement audits corresponds to the difference in the amount of effort required to perform each service. (Incidentally, accounting firms also perform a financial statement service, mostly for small companies, that offers no assurance at all: a *compilation* of financial statements, which merely compiles financial information into proper form.)

AUDIT SERVICES

As illustrated in Figure 1-1, some attestations are called *audits*. Among audit services, the most common is a **financial statement audit** performed by certified public accountants in public accounting firms. A *financial statement audit* is an attestation service in which an auditor offers assurances about management's written financial statement assertions. For example, in the

---

9   K. S. Brackney and G. L. Helms. "A Survey of Attestation Practices," *Auditing: A Journal of Practice & Theory* (Fall 1996), pp. 85-98.

financial statement disclosure "Inventory . . . . $2,000,000," management makes no less than five assertions: Inventory physically exists, includes all products on hand, is represented by rights of ownership, is stated at the lower-of-cost-or-market, and is classified properly as a current asset.

THE DEMAND FOR FINANCIAL STATEMENT AUDITS

To illustrate why audit services are demanded, consider the case of Ben & Jerry's Homemade, Inc., a high-profile producer of superpremium ice cream, low-fat frozen yogurt, and ice cream novelties. In the 1990s, Ben & Jerry's received no less than $33.5 million in an initial public offering (IPO) of Class A common shares. Does it weigh on you that Ben & Jerry's had compelling incentives to overstate their financial position (for example, by overstating inventory), thereby biasing investors' decisions to purchase the securities and Goldman Sachs' decision to underwrite the public offering? Unlike the dating list purchasers (and the retired steelworker) mentioned previously, neither a competent investor nor Goldman Sachs would likely have participated in Ben & Jerry's IPO without a written assurance (called an *audit report*) from an independent party (an **independent auditor**) that the assertions embodied within Ben & Jerry's financial statements were reliable. An audit provides Ben & Jerry's with a singularly valuable service: Lacking an audit, Ben & Jerry's cost of obtaining capital in the IPO would have been much higher, since investors would have demanded compensation (e.g., a lower stock price) for *information risk*, the risk that Ben & Jerry's financial information was misstated.

In addition to the investors and Goldman Sachs, Ben & Jerry's financial statement disclosures reveal other parties who have a need, and therefore have established a demand, for an audit. Examples include Class B common shareholders, employee pension and profit plan participants, creditors representing an Urban Development Action Grant and a Vermont Industrial Development Authority loan, and Edy's Grand Ice Cream, Inc., a participant with Ben & Jerry's in a long-term manufacturing and warehousing agreement. Other parties not named in the financial statements include labor unions, suppliers, stock exchanges, regulatory agencies (e.g., the SEC), and tax authorities (e.g., the IRS, state sales tax agencies), all of whom are at risk if Ben & Jerry's financial statements are misstated. Internal users, such as management, financial officers, and sales executives also rely on audit reports.

None of the parties who demand an audit are positioned to obtain private information about a company from anyone other than the company's management, placing them at a comparative disadvantage when negotiating contracts with the company. As a result, all of these parties are at risk if management manipulates private information into misleading financial statements. For example, assume that Fleet Mortgage Group, a Boston based lending institution, loaned Ben & Jerry's $5 million, and stipulated that the five-year loan would be payable immediately if Ben & Jerry's current ratio (current assets/current liabilities) fell below one-to-one (called a *debt covenant*). Because the incentives of Ben & Jerry's management (e.g., profit sharing, growth in shareholder wealth) differs from those of Fleet (e.g., loan repayment, protection of principal), management has incentives to misstate the financial statements for their own self interest. For example, at the end of the loan period's first year, management could deliberately understate current liabilities, thereby inflating the current ratio and masking the debt-covenant violation.

To minimize the risk of materially misstated financial statements, users demand that an unbiased monitor (an independent auditor) report on whether the assertions embodied within management's financial statements are reliable. In the U.S. (and in some foreign countries), audits are not only demanded by users but they are required by law as a prerequisite for listing on a stock exchange. The *Securities Exchange Act of 1934*, which regulates the trading of securities, requires that a publicly traded company file *Form 10-K* annually with the Securities and Exchange Commission. Apart from nonfinancial information about the company, management, and the directors, *Form 10-K* also includes an independent auditor's report and audited financial statements. Companies that fail to file *Form 10-K* by the fifteenth day of the third month following the close of their fiscal year can be de-listed from the stock exchange on which shares are traded, effectively precluding the company from obtaining capital in regulated U.S. markets.

Financial statements are audited by independent auditors, but the statements are the representations and responsibility of management, not the auditor. An independent auditor is responsible for expressing an opinion on management's financial statements, but management is responsible for the assertions embodied within the financial statements. For example, management, not the auditor, is responsible to ensure that all recorded assets and liabilities exist, that all recorded transactions occurred, that no transactions are omitted, that assets are the rights and liabilities the obligations of the entity, that all disclosed amounts are appropriate, and that the financial statements are properly classified and disclosed.

Even though auditors audit management's financial statements, management, ironically, is not the auditor's client. The client in the audit of a publicly traded corporation is the corporation's board of directors, the body elected by shareholders to protect their interests. Although this has never been unclear, the Public Oversight Board, introduced later in the chapter as an independent monitor of the public's confidence in the audit process, recently reiterated the relationship among auditors, management, and the board of directors:

. . . it is essential for the auditing profession to bring greater clarity to the issue of who is their client. The board of directors, as the representative of the shareholders, should be the client, not corporate management. Corporate boards . . . should make this clear to auditors.[10]

FINANCIAL STATEMENT AUDITS AND THE SCIENTIFIC METHOD OF INQUIRY

Some years ago, the American Accounting Association's *Committee on Basic Auditing Concepts* drafted a definition of auditing that offers some insight into the audit process:

Auditing is a systematic process of objectively obtaining and evaluating evidence regarding assertions about economic actions and events to ascertain the degree of correspondence between those assertions and established criteria and communicating the results to interested users.[11]

10   Public Oversight Board. *Directors, Management, and Auditors: Allies in Protecting Shareholder Interests.* Stamford, CT: POB (1995), p. 4.
11   Committee on Basic Auditing Concepts. "A Statement of Basic Auditing Concepts," *The Accounting Review* (Supplement to Vol. 47, 1972), p. 18.

The definition implies that auditing involves both an investigation and a report. *Investigation* means gathering and evaluating evidence as a basis for *reporting* an opinion about whether management's financial statement assertions correspond in all material respects with GAAP. The opinion conveyed in an audit report may indicate that the financial statements present fairly financial position, results of operations, and cash flows in conformity with GAAP; that the statements present fairly *except for* a matter revealed in the report; or that the statements are not presented fairly. Alternatively, the auditor may not report an opinion, for example, if sufficient evidence cannot be obtained to support or refute management's assertions.

The audit process begins when an entity engages an independent auditor and ends with an audit report. A similar process—the *scientific method of inquiry*—occurs when a scientist confronts a research problem. Like the audit process, the scientific method of inquiry is a framework for reaching reasoned, defendable conclusions. Cohen and Nagel, in *An Introduction to Logic and Scientific Method*, capture the essence of the scientific method:

Scientific method . . . is the persistent application of logic as the common feature of all reasoned knowledge . . . but in essence scientific method is simply the pursuit of truth as determined by logical considerations.[12]

If the words "scientific method" were replaced by "auditing," Cohen and Nagel would capture the essence of auditing as well.

To illustrate the similarities between the scientific method of inquiry and a financial statement audit, Figure 1-2 equates each step in the scientific method to the steps in the audit process. As the illustration implies, auditing can be thought of as a special application of the scientific method of inquiry.

Figure 1-2: Auditing and the Scientific Method of Inquiry

Scientific Method	Financial Statement Audit
Observe a problem.	Entity requests an opinion on whether financial statements present fairly in all material respects financial position, results of operations, and cash flows.
Formulate a hypothesis.	Hypothesis: Financial statements present fairly . . .
Gather evidence.	Assess risk, design audit procedures.
Evaluate evidence and conclude.	Evaluate whether evidence supports, refutes, or is inconclusive about the hypothesis.

AUDIT STANDARD SETTING

Several organizations and authoritative bodies influence audit practice today, including: (1) the American Institute of Certified Public Accountants (AICPA), the

12   M. R. Cohen and E. Nagel. *An Introduction to Logic and Scientific Method*. New York: Harcourt, Brace, and Company (1934), p. 192.

national trade association of CPAs; (2) the Securities and Exchange Commission (SEC), a federal agency empowered to protect securities traders; (3) the Auditing Standards Board, a senior technical body of the AICPA, designated to issue authoritative pronouncements for attestation and audit services; (4) the Accounting and Review Services Committee (ARSC), another senior technical body of the AICPA, designated to issue authoritative pronouncements for accounting and review services; and (5) the Public Oversight Board, an autonomous arm of the AICPA's SEC Practice Section.

THE AMERICAN INSTITUTE OF CERTIFIED PUBLIC ACCOUNTANTS

The **American Institute of Certified Public Accountants (AICPA)** is a professional trade association with over 400,000 members. Although all voting members are CPAs, not all offer assurance services. For example, some hold positions in industry or government (as CEOs, CFOs, controllers, financial officers, and internal auditors), others teach in colleges and universities, and still others serve in the executive and legislative branches of federal, state, and local governments. Since organizing in the late nineteenth century, the AICPA has had a marked influence on accounting and auditing thought. For example, the Institute actively lobbies Congress on legislation relevant to its membership, and publishes authoritative pronouncements about accounting, auditing, attestation, professional ethics, management advisory services, and taxes. Studies conducted by or for the AICPA have resulted in publications such as *Audit and Accounting Guides, Auditing Procedures Studies*, and *Auditing Research Monographs*, none of which are binding on members, but all of which are available to guide practice. The AICPA publishes a monthly periodical, *The Journal of Accountancy*, regarded by many as the leading professional publication devoted to current developments in accounting.

THE SECURITIES AND EXCHANGE COMMISSION

The **Securities and Exchange Commission (SEC)** was created by Congress in 1934 to regulate the registration and exchange of securities under the *Securities Act of 1933* and the *Securities Exchange Act of 1934*. The SEC is not empowered to issue authoritative auditing pronouncements per se, but does issue publications that govern publicly traded corporations in periodic filings to the SEC, including *Form 10-K*, the annual financial report; *Form 10-Q*, the quarterly financial report; and *Form 8-K*, a form filed when significant events occur, such as the sale of a subsidiary or a change in auditors. Currently, the SEC issues two types of releases that affect independent auditors: *Financial Reporting Releases*, which announce accounting and auditing matters of general interest; and *Accounting and Auditing Enforcement Releases*, which announce accounting and auditing matters related to the SEC's enforcement activities. The SEC also issues *Staff Accounting Bulletins*, unofficial interpretations that guide practitioners when applying SEC regulations.

PRIOR AUTHORITATIVE BODIES

As illustrated in Figure 1-3, since the 1930s four succeeding standard-setting bodies have been empowered by the AICPA to issue authoritative guidelines for audit, attestation, and accounting services. Two of them, the Auditing

Figure 1-3: Standard-Setting Bodies

Body	Tenure	Pronouncements
Committee on Auditing Procedure (CAP)	1939-72	Statements on Auditing Procedure (SAPs)
Auditing Standards Executive Committee (AudSEC)	1972-78	Statements on Auditing Standards (SASs)
Auditing Standards Board (ASB)	1978-	Statements on Auditing Standards (SASs) Statements on Standards for Attestation Engagements (SSAEs)
Accounting and Review Services Committee (ARSC)	1978-	Statements on Standards for Accounting and Review Services (SSARSs)

Standards Board and the Accounting and Review Services Committee, issue pronouncements today. In 1939, the AICPA appointed the **Committee on Auditing Procedure (CAP)** to ". . . examine into auditing procedure . . . in light of recent public discussions"—the "public discussions" referring to McKesson & Robbins' $19 million overstatement of inventory and accounts receivable in the mid-1930s. Although common practice today, McKesson & Robbins' auditors did not test the existence of recorded inventory or accounts receivable. In May 1939, the CAP issued a report, "Extensions of Auditing Procedure," which recommended physical inventory observations (Chapter 15) and accounts receivable confirmations (Chapter 11) as accepted audit practice. The report became the first of 54 **Statements on Auditing Procedure (SAPs)** issued by the CAP from 1939 to 1972.

In 1972, the name of the committee was changed to the **Auditing Standards Executive Committee (AudSEC)**, and the CAP's 54 SAPs were codified into *Statement on Auditing Standards (SAS) No. 1*. The title change from Statements on Auditing *Procedure* to **Statements on Auditing Standards (SASs)** suggested that the statements would interpret standards rather than merely promulgate procedures, underscoring AudSEC's role as a standard-setting body. From 1972 to 1978, AudSEC issued SAS Nos. 2 through 23, covering issues such as reports on audited financial statements, related party transactions, the auditor's responsibility for detecting fraud, and illegal acts by clients.

THE AUDITING STANDARDS BOARD AND THE
ACCOUNTING AND REVIEW SERVICES COMMITTEE

In 1978, the AICPA's independent *Commission on Auditors' Responsibilities* (the Cohen Commission) issued a 195-page report about the responsibilities of independent auditors. Section 10, "The Process of Establishing Auditing Standards," offered several criticisms of AudSEC, among them that SASs were typically published long after a controversial project first reached AudSEC's technical agenda and that most SASs were oriented toward audits of public companies to the exclusion of nonpublic companies, the major challenge of many smaller accounting firms.

As a partial response to these criticisms, the AICPA disbanded AudSEC and appointed two senior technical committees: the **Auditing Standards Board (ASB)**, designated to issue SASs and **Statements on Standards for Attestation Engagements (SSAEs)**; and the **Accounting and Review Services Committee (ARSC)**, designated to issue **Statements on Standards for Accounting and Review Services (SSARSs)**, relating to unaudited financial information for nonpublic entities. The individual pronouncements of both bodies are numbered sequentially when issued, and the provisions of all pronouncements are codified within code sections of the *AICPA Professional Standards*. For example, *SASs* are codified within the AICPA's *Codification of Statements on Auditing Standards*.[13]

The Auditing Standards Board consists of fifteen members who are compensated, reimbursed for expenses, and appointed for rotating terms with the consent of the AICPA's Directors. Although the most influential body in the audit and attestation standard-setting process, the Auditing Standards Board, like the Financial Accounting Standards Board, does not issue pronouncements without due process, including public meetings and public hearings.

An AICPA Vice President, Professional Standards and Technical Services, works closely with the Board. The VP has administrative responsibility for the Board's support staff, and works directly with the Board's chair on such matters as setting the agenda and overseeing project task forces. The VP does not vote in ASB matters, but is important to the Board's operations and, therefore, to the audit standard-setting process in the United States.

THE PUBLIC OVERSIGHT BOARD

Like the legal and medical professions, the public accounting profession is self-regulated. For example, practitioners abide by professional standards (Chapter 2) and by a *Code of Professional Conduct* (Chapter 4), and sanctions for violations are levied by the AICPA, by state societies of CPAs, and by state boards of accountancy (Chapter 4). However, few organizations have had more impact on the profession's self-regulation than the **Public Oversight Board (POB)**, an autonomous body that monitors the performance of the 1,260 public accounting firms that audit more than 15,800 U.S. publicly traded corporations. The five-member POB meets about eight times per year, oversees the peer reviews (Chapter 4) of some firms, and issues status reports that recommend improvements in the self-regulation process. For example, the POB has issued a far-reaching special report that addresses a series of issues bearing on self-regulation, among them litigation and the public's confidence in CPAs.[14]

RELATING ACCOUNTING AND AUDITING

Largely because auditing is studied in "accounting" curricula and practiced by public "accountants," it is often viewed as a subdivision of accounting.

---

13   Throughout this book, references to sections and paragraphs of the AICPA's *Codifications* are made parenthetically after the sentence or passages referenced, with "Section" abbreviated "Sec."
14   Public Oversight Board. *In the Public Interest: A Special Report by the Public Oversight Board of the SEC Practice Section of the AICPA.* Stamford, CT: POB (March 5, 1993).

However, accounting and auditing are related because auditors are accountants first, not because auditing is accounting first. Mautz and Sharaf comment:

Auditing is analytic, not constructive; it is critical, investigative, concerned with the basis for accounting measurements and assertions. Auditing emphasizes proof, the support for financial statements and data. Thus auditing has its principal roots, not in accounting which it reviews, but in logic on which it leans heavily for ideas and methods.[15]

Accounting and auditing are separate disciplines with unrelated foundations and dissimilar bodies of knowledge. However, a familiarity with audit method is not wholly sufficient to render an auditor competent. Because an auditor audits financial statements, he or she must also be familiar with generally accepted accounting principles (GAAP). As a result, the organizations that influence accounting also influence auditing. Prominent among them are the Financial Accounting Standards Board, the Governmental Accounting Standards Board, and several professional organizations.

THE FINANCIAL ACCOUNTING STANDARDS BOARD
AND THE GOVERNMENTAL ACCOUNTING STANDARDS BOARD

The Financial Accounting Standards Board (FASB) and the Governmental Accounting Standards Board (GASB) are independent standard-setting bodies that issue authoritative *Statements of Financial Accounting Standards* for nongovernmental entities and *Statements of Governmental Accounting Standards* for governmental entities, respectively. For example, the FASB has issued statements on leases and pensions for nongovernmental entities, like publicly traded corporations, and the GASB has also issued statements on leases and pensions, though for governmental entities, like state agencies. Except in rare circumstances (Chapter 4), an independent auditor is precluded from expressing an opinion that financial statements are presented in conformity with GAAP if the statements contain any material departure from accounting principles promulgated by the FASB or GASB. Thus, auditors must be familiar with the provisions of FASB and GASB Statements or risk violating GAAP.

PROFESSIONAL ORGANIZATIONS

Professional organizations that influence auditing standards and practice include the Institute of Internal Auditors (IIA), the Institute of Management Accountants (IMA), and the American Accounting Association (AAA). The Institute of Internal Auditors (IIA) is a voluntary membership organization for internal auditors. The Institute conducts and sponsors research and continuing professional education programs, sponsors the Certified Internal Auditor (CIA) examination, and publishes a bimonthly journal, *The Internal Auditor*.

The Institute of Management Accountants (IMA), an organization composed primarily of management accountants, also conducts and sponsors research and continuing education programs. The IMA publishes a monthly journal, *Management Accounting*, and sponsors the Certificate in Management Accounting (CMA) examination. Among its many and varied publications, the

15   R. K. Mautz and H. A. Sharaf. *The Philosophy of Auditing.* Sarasota: American Accounting Association (1961), p. 14.

IMA issues position papers on a variety of accounting and reporting topics. Although these papers are not binding on accountants, they do influence accounting thought.

The American Accounting Association (AAA) is an organization of accounting educators. In addition to its journals—among them, *The Accounting Review, Accounting Horizons, Auditing: A Journal of Practice & Theory*, and *Issues in Accounting Education*—the AAA also publishes research monographs and committee reports, including the *Report of the Committee on Basic Auditing Concepts* from which a definition of auditing was introduced earlier in this chapter.

WILL FINANCIAL STATEMENT AUDITS BECOME OBSOLETE?

Some products have rather limited life cycles. For example, Cabbage Patch dolls dominated two consecutive holiday-buying seasons in the 1980s, but their share of the market dwindled soon thereafter. However, first legislated in the British Joint Stock Companies Act of 1844, financial statement audits have survived for over a century. Does this suggest unusual endurance or looming obsolescence? Some would say "obsolescence." But, why they would has nothing to do with audits, and everything to do with what is audited: *industrial era* historical cost financial statements.

Balance sheets reflect the historical cost of industrial era assets, but intentionally overlook the value of information and the capacity to innovate. For example, assume you purchased a Motorola cellular phone for $100. Motorola's GAAP-based, historical cost balance sheet would have carried the cost of the phone's physical components (e.g., plastic, wiring, sand), say $5, but not the value of the information Motorola used to design and assemble the phone ($95). Of course, the income statement captures an "earnings multiple" ($5 inventory translated into a $100 sale) but, prior to the sale, the balance sheet carried no links to Motorola's stock price, which is the market's best estimate of the per share discounted present value of Motorola's future cash flows. In short, stock prices (and bank lending decisions, and earnings forecasts) are driven more by investors' (and lenders', and analysts') judgments of management's capacity to transform information into innovation, than by the data captured in financial statements.

In the information age, stakeholders are demanding information that is far more current and far more pertinent to their decision-making needs. As Peter Drucker has said:

Balance sheets were designed to show what a business would be worth if it was liquidated today. . . What managements need, however, are balance sheets that relate the enterprise's current condition to its future wealth-producing capacity. . . Financial accounting, balance sheets, profit-and-loss statements, allocations of costs, etc., are an X-ray of the enterprise's skeleton. But much as the diseases we most commonly die from—heart disease, cancer, Parkinson's—do not show up in a skeletal X-ray, a loss of market standing or a failure to innovate do not register in the accountant's figures until the damage has been done.[16]

---

16   P. F. Drucker. "We Need to Measure, Not Count," *The Wall Street Journal* (July 17, 1993), p. B6. See also, P. F. Drucker. *Post-Capitalist Society.* New York: HarperCollins (1992).

This is not to say that there is no need for financial statements. Rather, there is a need for statements that capture the value of information.

In response to claims that financial statements may no longer be relevant, the AICPA established a *Special Committee on Financial Reporting*, chaired by Edmund Jenkins (the Jenkins Committee), to recommend improvements in business reporting. Following three years of deliberations, the Committee released a series of recommendations, among them that businesses report forward-looking information. As the *Public Accounting Report* stated, reactions to the Jenkins Committee recommendations have been mixed. "The AICPA can anticipate an uphill battle toward implementation of the report's recommendation. Once harsh critics are mollified, it will take a cooperative effort between the SEC and the FASB."[17]

OTHER AUDIT SERVICES

In addition to financial statement audits, other types of audit services include *operational audits* and *compliance audits*.

OPERATIONAL AUDITS

An **operational audit** assesses the efficiency and effectiveness of management's operations, rather than the fair presentation of management's financial statements. Operational audits focus on information systems and operating procedures, not on recorded dollar amounts or reported financial information, and can address an entity's entire scope of operations or selected procedures. For example, the board of directors of Amoco Oil assigned the company's **internal auditors** to appraise policies used by the upstream extraction division and the downstream refining division to negotiate crude oil transfer prices.

Unlike independent auditors in public accounting firms, internal auditors are employed by a single entity and vary in number depending on the entity's size and sophistication. For example, a middle market company might employ just one internal auditor to perform relatively routine tasks. In contrast, Amoco Oil, a *Fortune 20* company with total assets of $35 billion, employs over one hundred internal auditors to perform challenging operational audits around the globe. To be effective, internal auditors should report to the highest levels of the organization, preferably to the board of directors, thereby maintaining independence from the personnel reviewed and allowing freedom from coercion when reporting.

Operational audits are not always performed by internal auditors. For example, built in the 1970s, the Trans-Alaska pipeline had been criticized by whistle blowers and congressional investigators for alleged repeated violations of environmental and safety regulations. In response, the U.S. Interior Department's Bureau of Land Management engaged a Kansas-based engineering consultant to audit the pipeline's operator, Alyeska Pipeline Service Co., a consortium owned by Atlantic Richfield, Exxon, and British Petroleum.[18] The

---

17   "Changes in Financial Reporting Proposed," *The Public Accounting Report* (September 30, 1994), p. 4.
18   C. McCoy. "Troubleshooter Heading Team Sent to Audit Alyeska Pipeline Practices," *The Wall Street Journal* (August 30, 1993), p. B3.

operational audit, the first in the pipeline's two-decade history, focused on Alyeska's information processing system, management's performance, and alleged violations of air pollution standards and electrical codes.

COMPLIANCE AUDITS

A **compliance audit** is similar in part to a financial statement audit, but is performed most often for not-for-profit entities such as state governmental agencies, municipalities, and school districts, and for commercial entities such as contractors that comply with federal requirements. Like an independent financial statement audit, a compliance audit can be designed to determine whether an entity's financial statements are presented fairly in accordance with GAAP. But unlike a financial statement audit, a compliance audit can also be designed to determine whether the entity has complied with applicable laws and regulations that may have a material effect on financial statements—hence the term "compliance" audits. For example, many state governmental agencies, such as Departments of Human Services or Departments of Motor Vehicles, receive direct grants from the federal government that impose requirements on how grant funds are to be disbursed by the grantee. A compliance audit for the recipient agency would focus not only on whether the agency's financial statements conform with GAAP, but also on whether the agency complied with the federal government's restrictions on disbursing grant funds.

Compliance audits are conducted either by independent auditors or by **governmental auditors**, of which there are several types, including state auditors and U.S. General Accounting Office (GAO) auditors. Each of the fifty states maintains a state audit department, which may report to the elected legislature or to the governor's office (or both) depending on the state's constitution. Generally, state auditors perform compliance audits of state agencies and local governmental units within the state. For example, the Office of the Auditor General in New York performs a compliance audit of New York City, although the city's port authority (e.g., LaGuardia and Kennedy airports) is audited by a public accounting firm. In contrast, GAO auditors, headed by the Comptroller General of the United States, report solely to Congress about the results of compliance audits of federal departments and agencies and about special audit engagements assigned by Congress. For example, in two highly publicized reports issued in the 1980s, each entitled *CPA Audit Quality*, the GAO, on special assignment by a House subcommittee, revealed an alarming number of substandard governmental audits performed by small public accounting firms.

NONATTEST SERVICES

Public accounting firms offer a variety of nonattest services to the public, some of which overlap with consulting. Examples include business valuation, financial planning, litigation support, information system design and processing, financial forecasts and projections, actuarial services, tax compliance and planning, and feasibility studies both for new product development and for business combinations and joint ventures. Some of these services have been criticized by congressional subcommittees who argue that the handsome fees generated from nonattest services may motivate auditors to compromise their objectivity when auditing the entity's financial statements. Although a rather complex issue, the crucial question distills to this: At what point does advice become managerial decision making? Advice is compatible with attest services, but making decisions for management is not.

SUMMARY

Financial statement audits are the primary assurance service offered by certified public accountants today, but may become obsolete as industrial era financial statements become less relevant to decision makers. Decision makers are demanding other, more timely, information sources that capture management's capacity to innovate and the value of information and other knowledge. The profession is entrusted with a major responsibility: monitoring the financial statements of middle market and larger entities operating in domestic and global markets. The volume, value, and complexity of the transactions involved forecast well for job opportunities in auditing. However, the viability of the public accounting profession as a promising career path in the long term may depend heavily on the profession's capacity to innovate. The innovative work of the AICPA's *Special Committee on Assurance Services* suggests that the profession recognizes the challenge and is game for the fight.

APPENDIX: BECOMING A CPA

To become a CPA, a candidate must pass the *Uniform CPA Examination*, and satisfy educational and experience requirements. The 15-hour *Uniform CPA Examination* is prepared and graded by the AICPA, and administered by the individual state boards of accountancy over a 2-day period, twice annually (May and November). The exam consists of four sections:

* Accounting and Reporting—Part A (GAAP for business enterprises),
* Accounting and Reporting—Part B (taxation and managerial, not-for-profit, and government accounting),
* Auditing, and
* Business Law and Professional Responsibilities.

A grade of 75 is required to pass a section of the exam, and conditional credit (i.e., credit for passing individual sections) is allowed in all states.

Educational requirements are not uniform among the states. However, most states require that a CPA candidate hold at least the equivalent of a baccalaureate degree with a minimum number of credit hours in accounting. The *experience requirements* to become a CPA also vary among the states. The requirements range from a high of three years of employment with a CPA firm (or equivalent: the Internal Revenue Service, a state audit department) to no experience requirements at all in some states. In most states, experience requirements can be fulfilled either before or after passing the CPA examination.

A license to practice as a CPA is granted by the state board of accountancy, a state agency empowered to regulate the practice of public accounting within a state. Because licenses to practice are granted by the states rather than a national regulatory agency, a license must be obtained from each state in which a CPA practices. However, there is reciprocity among the state boards of accountancy. A CPA can obtain a license to practice in another state assuming he or she is in good standing in all other states from which a license was issued and meets the requirements of the state granting reciprocity.

KEY TERMS

Limited liability partnerships (LLPs)   4
Certified public accountants (CPAs)   4
Consulting services   5
Assurance services   5
Attestation services   7
Audit services   8
Financial statement audit   8
Independent auditor   9
American Institute of Certified Public Accountants (AICPA)   12
Securities and Exchange Commission (SEC)   12
Committee on Auditing Procedure (CAP)   13
Statements on Auditing Procedure (SAPs)   13

Auditing Standards Executive Committee (AudSEC)   13
Statements on Auditing Standards (SASs)   13
Auditing Standards Board (ASB)   14
Statements on Standards for Attestation Engagements (SSAEs)   14
Accounting and Review Services Committee (ARSC)   14
Statements on Standards for Accounting and Review Services (SSARSs)   14
Public Oversight Board (POB)   14
Operational audit   17
Internal auditors   17
Compliance audit   18
Governmental auditors   18

REFERENCES

Professional Standards

AICPA. *Codification of Statements on Auditing Standards.* New York: AICPA (Appendix A).

Professional Reports

Accounting Education Change Commission. *Objectives of Education for Accountants: Position Statement Number One.* Torrance, CA: Accounting Education Change Commission (1990).

AICPA. *Interim Report of the Special Committee on Assurance Services (The Elliott Committee).* New York: AICPA (1995).

AICPA. *Report of the Special Committee on Financial Reporting (The Jenkins Committee),* "Improving Business Reporting: A Customer Focus: Meeting the Information Needs of Investors and Creditors" (1994).

AICPA. *Meeting the Financial Reporting Needs of the Future: A Public Commitment from the Public Accounting Profession.* New York: AICPA (1993).

AICPA. *Comparing Attestation and Consulting Services: A Guide for the Practitioner.* New York: AICPA (1993).

Arthur Andersen, Coopers & Lybrand, Deloitte & Touche, Ernst & Young, KPMG Peat Marwick, and Price Waterhouse. *The Public Accounting Profession: Meeting the Needs of a Changing World* (1991).

National Commission on Fraudulent Financial Reporting (The Treadway Commission). *Report of the National Commission on Fraudulent Financial Reporting* (1987).

Public Oversight Board. *In the Public Interest: A Special Report by the Public Oversight Board of the SEC Practice Section of the AICPA.* Stamford, CT: POB (1993).

Public Oversight Board. *Strengthening the Professionalism of the Independent Auditor.* Stamford, CT: POB (1994).

Public Oversight Board. *Directors, Management, and Auditors: Allies in Protecting Shareholder Interests.* Stamford, CT: POB (1995).

Web Site

AICPA. *Special Committee on Assurance Services* (The Elliott Committee): http://www.aicpa.org/assurance/pre/index.htm

Articles, Books

Brackney, K. S., and G. L. Helms. "A Survey of Attestation Practices," *Auditing: A Journal of Practice & Theory* (Fall 1996), pp. 85-98.

Brachel, J. Von. "Reinventing the CPA," *Journal of Accountancy* (November 1996), pp. 49-51.

Carey, J. L. *The Rise of the Accounting Profession from Technician to Professional.* New York: American Institute of Certified Public Accountants (1969).

Chapin, D. H. "U.S. General Accounting Office Perspective on Future Audit Issues," *The CPA Journal* (January 1995), pp. 32-35.

Craig, J. "Serving the Profession's Assurance Function: An Interview with AICPA Vice President Dan Guy," *The CPA Journal* (January 1994), pp. 36-40.

Elliott, R. K. "The Third Wave Breaks on the Shores of Accounting," *Accounting Horizons* (June 1992), pp. 62-85.

Elliott, R. K. "The Future of Audits," *Journal of Accountancy* (September 1994), pp. 74-82.

Elliott, R. K. "Confronting the Future: Choices for the Attest Function," *Accounting Horizons* (September 1994), pp. 106-124.

Elliott, R. K. "AICPA Assurance Services Committee: What Is the Future of Auditing?" *Journal of Corporate Accounting and Finance* (Winter 1994-95), pp. 87-97.

Elliott, R. K. "The Future of Assurance Services: Implications for Academia," *Accounting Horizons* (December 1995), pp. 118-127.

Hooks, K. L. "Diversity, Family Issues and the Big 6," *Journal of Accountancy* (July 1996), pp. 51-56.

Marxen, D. E. "The Big 6 Experience: A Retrospective Account by Alumni," *Accounting Horizons* (June 1996), pp. 73-87.

Mautz, R. K., and H. A. Sharaf. *The Philosophy of Auditing.* Sarasota: American Accounting Association (1961).

Mednick, R. "Reinventing the Audit," *Journal of Accountancy* (August 1991), pp. 71-78.

Pallais, D. "Positioning the Audit Function for Growth," *Journal of Accountancy* (July 1995), pp. 14-15.

Public Accounting Report. "Billions in Assurance Await, Elliott Says: AICPA Special Committee Outlines Practice Growth Targets" (October 31, 1996), pp. 1,5.

Read, W., and S. Tomczyk. "An Examination of Changes in Scope of Services Performed by CPA Firms," *Accounting Horizons* (September 1992), pp. 42-51.

Roy, R. H., and J. H. MacNeil. *Horizons for a Profession.* New York: American Institute of Certified Public Accountants (1967).

Saul, R. S. "What Ails the Accounting Profession?" *Accounting Horizons* (June 1996), pp. 131-137.

Wallman, S. "The Future of Accounting and Disclosure in an Evolving World: The Need for Dramatic Change," *Accounting Horizons* (September 1995), pp. 81-91.

QUESTIONS

1. Distinguish between consulting and assurance services.
2. When is an assurance service an attestation?
3. What is the scientific method of inquiry, and how does it relate to auditing?
4. Identify the major types of audits performed in the U.S. today.
5. Why is there a need for financial statement audits?
6. What services are generally provided to clients by public accounting firms?
7. Why has Congress criticized nonattest services?
8. What does management assert in the disclosure: "Trade receivables . . . $1,200,000"?
9. What roles are served by the AICPA's two standard-setting bodies for auditing and for accounting & review services?
10. How are auditing and accounting related?

MULTIPLE CHOICE QUESTIONS

1. Alexion Corp. has engaged a public accounting firm to issue a report on the accuracy of product quality specifications included in trade sales agreements. This is an example of a/an:

a.   Financial statement audit.
b.   Attestation service.
c.   Compliance audit.
d.   Operational audit.

2.   Unlike consulting services, assurance services:

a.   Make recommendations to management.
b.   Report on how to use information.
c.   Report on the quality of information.
d.   Are two-party contracts.

3.   A financial statement audit:

a.   Confirms that financial statement assertions are accurate.
b.   Lends credibility to the financial statements.
c.   Confirms that financial statements are presented fairly.
d.   Assures that fraud has been detected.

4.   Which of the following best describes why an independent auditor reports on financial statements?

a.   Independent auditors are likely to detect fraud.
b.   Competing interests may exist between management and the users of the statements.
c.   Misstated account balances are generally corrected by an independent audit.
d.   Ineffective internal controls may exist.

(AICPA Adapted)

5.   Financial statement audits:

a.   Reduce the cost of capital.
b.   Report on compliance with laws and regulations.
c.   Assess management's efficiency and effectiveness.
d.   Overlook information risk.

6.   Primary responsibility for the assertions in financial statements rests with the:

a.   Audit partner assigned to the engagement.
b.   Senior auditor in charge of field work.
c.   Staff auditor who drafts the statements.
d.   Client's management.

(AICPA Adapted)

7.   A public accounting firm's primary role in performing nonattest services is to:

a.   Hedge against declines in the firm's audit practice.
b.   Establish the firm as a consultant.
c.   Provide advice valuable to a client's effectiveness.
d.   Acclimate staff members to the client's business and industry.

8.   Which of the following types of audits is designed to determine whether a governmental entity's procurement practices are sound?

a.   A financial statement audit.
b.   An operational audit.
c.   A program audit.
d.   A compliance audit.

9. Which of the following authoritative bodies issues pronouncements relevant to attestation service engagements?

a. Accounting and Review Services Committee.
b. Auditing Standards Board.
c. Public Oversight Board.
d. AICPA.

10. The role of the Auditing Standards Board is to:

a. Define accepted auditing procedures applicable in practice.
b. Develop auditing standards for new *Statements of Financial* (or *Governmental*) *Accounting Standards* issued by the Financial (or Governmental) Accounting Standards Board.
c. Promulgate auditing standards and procedures that AICPA members must observe.
d. Lobby Congress on matters related to audit practice.

PROBLEMS AND DISCUSSION CASES

1-1 *Proposing Assurance Services*
To compete with manufacturers like Cray Research, the Singer Corporation, a manufacturer of mid-range supercomputers, makes oral claims of product superiority to engineers and scientists, their targeted end users. Some of the claims amount to little more than puffery: "the best . . . the most . . ." But others relate to performance and to market share. Two claims that are particularly important to Fred Singer, the corporation's chief operating officer, are:

• Average post-purchase user support time is 75 hours per end user.
• Three hundred fifty satisfied customers.

During the financial statement audit, Laurie Feldman, engagement partner, discovers that the performance and market share claims will be made in an upcoming advertising campaign and included in sales contracts. Feldman decides to propose an assurance service to Fred Singer.
    Required:
1. What argument could Feldman make to justify that the proposed assurance service will add value to Singer Corporation's product performance and market share claims?
2. Is the proposed assurance service an attestation? Why, or why not?
3. Use your imagination to describe what evidence Feldman would gather to test Singer's claims.

1-2 *Assurance Services and Reported SAT Scores*
The Wall Street Journal reported that the National Association of College Admissions Counselors, a professional organization for admissions officers and high school guidance counselors, had threatened sanctions against colleges that allegedly misrepresented SAT scores to bias college rankings, among them *U.S. News & World Report's* annual ranking of the top colleges in America (S. Stecklow, "Universities Face Trouble for Enhancing Guide Data," October 10, 1995, pp. B1, B11). The article reported that, "Some concerned academic leaders, meanwhile, are calling for accountant-certified disclosure statements to help verify . . . test scores . . .".
    Required:
1. What type of professional service does the quote in the article likely refer to?
2. Do you think the service represents an important assurance market for the public accounting profession? Why, or why not?

1-3 *Is There Value to an Audit?*

The Carter Wright Corporation entered into a consulting contract with Andersen Consulting to outsource Carter Wright's information processing to Andersen. The $3.5 million, multi-year contract would include the cost of computer upgrades to IBM workstations and of Microsoft Windows-dedicated software designed by Andersen. One year ago, Andersen Consulting received an ISO 9000 quality-control report from the McKinsey Group.

Required: You are the engagement partner for Carter Wright's financial statement audit. Carter Wright's board of directors has asked that you explain the value added to Carter Wright by your firm's audit. Discuss.

1-4 *Identifying Types of Audits*

Within the chapter, three different types of audits were identified:

- Financial statement audit.
- Operational audit.
- Compliance audit.

Each type of audit is designed for a particular purpose and is selected depending on the specific objectives of report users.

Required: For each of the following circumstances, indicate the type of audit required:

1. Management is interested in whether the purchasing department operates economically.
2. The state legislature is concerned that the requirements of a federal grant may have been violated.
3. A commercial bank will not approve a working capital loan without a report on whether the company's financial statements are presented fairly.
4. A state agency is not eligible for federal grants lacking a report on whether the agency's financial statements are presented fairly.
5. Management is interested in whether controls over highly sensitive inventory are reasonable and adequate.
6. Management is required to obtain a report indicating whether the objectives of a direct grant have been achieved.

1-5 *The Market for Audit Services*

During the past several decades, auditing has gained a considerable amount of attention both within the financial community and within academic curricula. For example, independent audits are now performed commonly for all publicly traded, and for many privately owned, corporations. Further, not only do undergraduate accounting curricula typically include an introductory auditing course, but many colleges and universities also offer advanced undergraduate and graduate auditing courses. There appears to be an established need for auditing.

Required: Explain why each of the following institutions needs auditing services:

1. Publicly owned corporations.
2. Privately owned corporations.
3. State and local governmental agencies.
4. Partnerships.

1-6 *Comparing Auditing to the Sciences*

One of your classmates, Kristin Lea, a chemistry major, is puzzled about what an auditor does. She says to you, "My only impression about auditors comes from Bob Cratchit, Tiny Tim's father, in Charles Dickens' *A Christmas Carol*. It sure seems to me as though there's little science in an auditor's work!"

Required: Explain the role of an auditor using terms that would be familiar to a chemistry major.

1-7 *Misconceptions About Auditing*

The following two statements are representative of attitudes and opinions sometimes encountered by independent auditors:

a. Today's audit consists of test checking, a dangerous policy since test checking depends on the auditor's judgment, which may be defective. An audit can be relied on only if every transaction is audited.

b. An audit is essentially unproductive and contributes to neither the gross national product nor the general well-being of society. Rather than create, the auditor merely checks what someone else has done.

Required: Evaluate both of the above statements, indicating:

1. Areas of agreement with the statement, if any.
2. Areas of misconception, incompleteness, or fallacious reasoning included in the statement, if any.

1-8 *Why an Audit?*

Feiler, the sole owner of a small hardware business, has been told that the business should have financial statements reported on by an independent certified public accountant. Having some bookkeeping experience, Feiler has personally prepared the company's financial statements and does not understand why the statements should be audited by a CPA. Feiler discussed the matter with Farber, a CPA, and asked Farber to explain why an audit is considered important.

Required:

1. Describe the objectives of a financial statement audit.
2. Identify ten ways in which a financial statement audit may be beneficial to Feiler.

(AICPA Adapted)

1-9 *Why Appoint an Outside Auditor?*

Marc David is an employee-stockholder of the Lexington Corporation. Because he has extensive accounting experience, Marc proposes to the other stockholders that he, rather than a public accounting firm, be appointed independent auditor for Lexington Corporation. Marc argues that because of his ownership in the company, the other owners' interests would be served best by his appointment. At a meeting of stockholders, Marc states, "I'd be much better for the job. For one thing, I can do the work and, for another, it won't cost us a small fortune."

Required: Indicate the deficiencies in Marc David's arguments. Be specific.

1-10 *Audit Standard Setting*

Appointment in 1939 of the AICPA's Committee on Auditing Procedure, the first authoritative audit standard-setting body in the U.S., was a response to public sector demands that the private sector "... examine into auditing procedure and other related questions in light of recent public discussions." As discussed in the text, the "public discussions" related in part to the McKesson & Robbins, Inc. $19 million overstatement of inventory and accounts receivable. McKesson & Robbins' auditors neither observed physical inventory on hand nor confirmed accounts receivable balances with debtors. In 1939, the Committee on Auditing Procedure responded with *Statement on Auditing Procedure No. 1*, which recommended physical inventory observation and accounts receivable confirmations, both of which have since become common practice.

Required: Do these beginnings, a response to a highly publicized fraud, have any implications for audit standard setting today, which is essentially the same with the Auditing Standards Board as it was in 1939 with the Committee on Auditing Procedure?

RESEARCH PROJECTS:

1. BECOMING FAMILIAR WITH THE PROFESSION'S CONTROVERSIES

The practice of public accounting, and the preprofessional education for certified public accountants, have both been subject to considerable controversy and change recently. The controversy stems largely from unprecedented litigation against public accounting firms and from concerns raised by accounting firms that the traditional accounting curriculum is not aptly suited to train students for the complex decisions confronting audit practitioners today. In response, two pivotal documents have been published by the Big Six public accounting firms and by the Accounting Education Change Commission (a blue-ribbon commission sanctioned to make recommendations about changing from a rules-based, lecture-driven curricula to a timeless, active learning curricula):

- Arthur Andersen, Coopers & Lybrand, Deloitte & Touche, Ernst & Young, KPMG Peat Marwick, and Price Waterhouse (The Big Six). *The Public Accounting Profession: Meeting the Needs of a Changing World* (1991).
- Accounting Education Change Commission (AECC). *Objectives of Education for Accountants: Position Statement Number One.* Torrance, CA: Accounting Education Change Commission (1990).

Required: Prepare a report that:
1. Documents the key recommendations of each report,
2. Explains whether you believe the AECC report is necessarily responsive to the Big Six report, and
3. Compares the substance and tone of each report with the substance and tone of the following article about Ronald S. Cohen, Chairman of the AICPA: Brachel, J. Von, "AICPA Chairman Lays the Foundation for the Future," *Journal of Accountancy* (November 1995), pp. 64-68.

2. ARE FINANCIAL STATEMENTS OBSOLETE?

Owing to serious criticisms of industrial era financial statements, the AICPA's *Special Committee on Financial Reporting* (The Jenkins Committee) recommended sweeping changes to financial statements in their final report: AICPA. *Report of the Special Committee on Financial Reporting* (The Jenkins Committee), "Improving Business Reporting: A Customer Focus: Meeting the Information Needs of Investors and Creditors" (1994).

However, the recommendations have received mixed reviews. For example, as reported in the September 30, 1994, *Public Accounting Report*, Dennis Beresford, FASB chair, stated that, "It is going to be a very important document for us, a real stimulus for changes and improvement in financial reporting over the next five to ten years." In contrast, Frank Borelli, the Financial Executive Institute's CFO Advisory chair, thought otherwise, stating that ". . . the committee's recommendations can be viewed as very self-serving. It looks as if they are trying to generate more services, which equates to more revenue."

Required: Select an annual report either from the annual report file in the AICPA's National Automated Accounting Research System (NAARS) or from a library, and prepare a report that:
1. Documents and criticizes the key recommendations of the Jenkins Committee report.
2. Explains how the Jenkins Committee's recommendations would bear on the annual report you selected.
3. Explains nonfinancial disclosures you think would improve the annual report given the company's industry, for example, the identity and stability of foreign crude oil supply sources in the oil & gas industry.

2

Professional Standards

Major topics discussed in this chapter are the:

- Roles of *assurance standards* and partnering in the market for new assurance services.
- Profession's *attestation standards* and *generally accepted auditing standards*, and the concepts that underlie the profession's services: independence, due care, evidence, and reporting.
- Alliance between materiality and risk in applications of professional standards.

Just as constitutional law is based on interpretations of a single document, the U.S. Constitution, so too are attestation and audit services. *Attestation standards* and *generally accepted auditing standards* are to attestation and audit services, respectively, what the Constitution is to constitutional law. In contrast, assurance services other than attestations and audits do not currently have standards to guide questions about training, independence, due care, supervision, evidence, reporting, and control. The profession has not fully exploited the assurance services market, and consumers have not granted the profession exclusive domain over the market in the same way that they have granted the profession domain over the audit market. In fact, certified public accountants are licensed exclusive domain over one market only, financial statements audits, and compete in the marketplace for some attestation services and for most assurance services.

This chapter focuses on standards, materiality, and risk. The chapter begins by discussing standards for assurance services, and the role of partnering with other professions to develop new markets. In turn, the chapter introduces the profession's eleven *attestation standards* and ten *generally accepted auditing standards* in the context of four concepts crucial to the profession's reputation: independence, due care, evidence, and reporting. Finally, the chapter addresses materiality and risk, two issues that weigh heavily on a practitioner's interpretation of standards.

ASSURANCE STANDARDS

The public accounting profession developed the standards used today in attestation and audit service engagements: In 1986, the AICPA's Auditing Standards Board and Accounting & Review Services Committee jointly developed *attestation standards.* And in 1948, the AICPA's Committee on Auditing Procedure developed *generally accepted auditing standards.* The purchasers of attestation and auditing services granted the profession permission to develop standards because all audit engagements, and many attestation engagements, measure management's performance against "rules" that were also developed largely by accountants: generally accepted accounting principles. After all, who better to prescribe standards for engagements that attest to accounting measurements than CPAs serving on senior technical committees empowered by the accounting profession's self-regulated trade association? However, although the profession may yet develop standards for assurance engagements, it is not clear that the marketplace will grant the profession permission to develop measurement rules for assurance engagements other than attestations and audits. The accounting profession is not uniquely qualified to do so. Accountants set the rules of accounting through authority granted to the Financial Accounting Standards Board and to the AICPA's Accounting Standards Executive Committee. But, accountants have neither the authority nor the market permission to set rules for other types of assurances.

The profession may be well positioned to adopt a strategy quite apart from the approach adopted for attestation and audit services: Develop assurance *standards* that complement the recommendations of the AICPA's *Special Committee on Assurance Services* (the Elliott Committee: Chapter 1), but defer the development of assurance *measurement rules* to other professions. For example, as consumers of health care services, many of us rely on word-of-mouth endorsements to select health care providers. Currently, there are no measurement rules—no "scorecards"—against which to measure the quality of hospitals, surgeons, and primary care physicians. Clearly, the accounting profession has no comparative advantage in developing a health care scorecard, but could partner with other professionals who do. For example, a CPA's comparative advantage in evaluating evidence for attestation and auditing engagements may translate into market permission to evaluate evidence about health care quality using measurement rules developed, for example, by the American Medical Association, a trade association which does have market permission in measuring health care quality. Partnering with other professions may be an important entree for accountants into the assurance services market, particularly in markets where consumers would likely demand and value the assurance.

Interestingly, partnering in assurance services is not without precedent. Underwriters Laboratories, an independent, not-for-profit provider of product safety certification and quality system registration services, has long provided assurance services using standards developed by other professional organizations. For example, Underwriters Laboratories' *Sanitation and Water Additives* product safety program evaluates drinking water treatment chemicals against standards accredited by the American National Standards Institute (ANSI), a privately funded federation that coordinates U.S. voluntary consensus standards. Called the "sleeper issue of the 1990s" by *Industry Week* magazine, marking product quality to standards may be an important value-added service for the public accounting profession to exploit, particularly since there's some evidence of demand for the service. For example, George Heilmeier, Bellcore president and CEO, has said, "Standards facilitate time-to-market. We believe that folks should take an active role in the standards process so that they can focus their resources a bit better on real problems that will enable them to differentiate their products in the marketplace."[1] In contrast to assurance services, standards for attestation and audit services are well-established and are introduced next.

ATTESTATION AND AUDITING STANDARDS

In 1941, the SEC issued *Accounting Series Release No. 21*, which required in part that an auditor report whether an audit engagement had been conducted in accordance with generally accepted auditing standards. But there were no written standards at the time. In response, the AICPA's Committee on Auditing Procedure began deliberating on a series of standards for auditing. Interrupted by World War II, the Committee did not finalize the nine original standards until 1947, in *Tentative Statement of Auditing Standards: Their Generally Accepted Significance and Scope*. The nine standards were approved by AICPA member vote in 1948, and a tenth was adopted from *Statement on Auditing Procedures No. 23* and approved in 1949. The ten generally accepted auditing standards (GAAS), presented in Figure 2-1, right column, are classified as general standards, standards of field work, and standards of reporting.

GAAS have been criticized over the years, mostly by practitioners complaining that the standards were not sufficiently specific. But others have argued that the standards were not sufficiently robust—in particular, to apply in the ever-expanding scope of services that lie outside of financial statements. Despite the criticisms, *GAAS* were not revised until the 1980s when the profession was urged to reconsider the standards by several opinion leaders, among them Robert K. Elliott, who would later become chair of the AICPA *Special Committee on Assurance Services*.[2] The Auditing Standards Board and the Accounting and Review Services Committee responded jointly in 1986 with *Statement on Standards for Attestation Engagements (SSAE) No. 1*, "Attestation Standards."[3] Like *GAAS*, the eleven attestation standards, presented in Figure 2-1, left column, are classified as general standards, standards of field work, and standards of reporting. The *attestation standards* are broader than *GAAS*, since they provide guidance for a broader range of services. However, rather than supersede any of the auditing standards, the *attestation standards* serve as an umbrella over the entire range of attest services. *GAAS* apply exclusively to one special type of attestation service: financial statement audits.

Neither the *attestation standards* nor GAAS offers step-by-step procedures (for example, would you feel comfortable approaching your very first engagement armed with nothing more than the declarative sentences in Figure 2-1?). Nor were they intended to. Standards are the guidelines from which procedures are derived, the measures of quality against which completed engagements are judged. Because they are guidelines, the standards rarely change

---

1   American National Standards Institute. *Home page* (World Wide Web).

2   Jacobson, P. D. and R. K. Elliott. "GAAS: Reconsidering the 'Ten Commandments'," *Journal of Accountancy* (May 1984), pp. 77-88.

3   In January 1989, the *Statements on Standards for Attestation Engagements (SSAEs)* entitled, "Attestation Standards," "Financial Forecasts and Projections," and "Reporting on Pro Forma Financial Information," were codified in *SSAE No. 1*, "Attestation Standards."

Figure 2-1: Attestation Standards and Auditing Standards

Attestation Standards	Auditing Standards
General Standards	
1. The engagement shall be performed by a practitioner or practitioners having **adequate technical training and proficiency** in the attest function.	1. The audit is to be performed by a person or persons having **adequate technical training and proficiency** as an auditor.
2. The engagement shall be performed by a practitioner or practitioners having **adequate knowledge** in the subject matter of the assertion.	
3. The practitioner shall perform an engagement only if he or she has reason to believe that the following two conditions exist: • The **assertion is capable of evaluation against reasonable criteria** that either have been established by a recognized body or are stated in the presentation of the assertion in a sufficiently clear and comprehensive manner for a knowledgeable reader to be able to understand them. • The assertion is **capable of reasonably consistent estimation or measurement** using such criteria.	
4. In all matters relating to the engagement, an **independence** in mental attitude shall be maintained by the practitioner or practitioners.	2. In all matters relating to the assignment, an **independence** in mental attitude is to be maintained by the auditor or auditors.
5. **Due professional care** shall be exercised in the performance of the engagement.	3. **Due professional care** is to be exercised in the performance of the audit and the preparation of the report.
Standards of Field Work	
1. The work shall be adequately **planned** and assistants, if any, shall be properly **supervised**.	1. The work is to be adequately **planned** and assistants, if any, are to be properly **supervised**.
	2. A sufficient **understanding of internal control** is to be obtained to plan the audit and to determine the nature, timing, and extent of tests to be performed.
2. Sufficient **evidence** shall be obtained to provide a reasonable basis for the conclusion that is expressed in the report.	3. Sufficient competent **evidential matter** is to be obtained through inspection, observation, inquiries, and confirmations to afford a reasonable basis for an opinion regarding the financial statements under audit.

Figure 2-1: *(continued)*

Attestation Standards	Auditing Standards

Standards of Reporting

1. The report shall identify the **assertion** being reported on and state the character of the engagement.

2. The report shall state the practitioner's conclusion about whether the assertion is presented in conformity with the **established or stated criteria** against which it was measured.

3. The report shall state all of the practitioner's **significant reservations** about the engagement and the presentation of the assertion.

1. The report shall state whether the financial statements are presented in accordance with **generally accepted accounting principles**.

2. The report shall identify those circumstances in which such **principles have not been consistently observed** in the current period in relation to the preceding period.

3. Informative **disclosures** in the financial statements are to be regarded as reasonably adequate unless otherwise stated in the report.

4. The report shall either contain an **expression of opinion** regarding the financial statements taken as a whole, or an assertion to the effect that an overall opinion cannot be expressed. When an overall opinion cannot be expressed, the reasons therefore should be stated. In all cases where an auditor's name is associated with financial statements, the report should contain a clear-cut indication of the character of the auditor's work, if any, and the degree of responsibility the auditor is taking.

4. The report on an engagement to evaluate an assertion that has been prepared in conformity with agreed-upon criteria or an engagement to apply agreed-upon procedures should contain a **statement limiting its use** to the parties who have agreed upon such criteria or procedures.

over time. For example, since enactment none of the *attestation standards* and only two of the *GAAS* have been revised significantly.[4] Procedures, in contrast, are detailed methods or techniques that change as technology changes. For example, wide-area computer networks require different auditing procedures than stand-alone desktop computers. Procedures are the means by which standards are fulfilled.

Much like engineering or economics, attestations and audits are grounded in several well-pitched concepts. Four concepts underlie both the *attestation standards* and *GAAS*: *independence* and *due care* (which underlie the general standards), *evidence* (the standards of field work), and *reporting* (the standards of reporting).

INDEPENDENCE

Independence is a state of mind, an attitude of impartiality, that underlies both an *attestation standard* (Figure 2-1, 4th general) and a *GAAS* (2nd general), and is powerfully important to the profession's acceptance as a trusted player in the assurance services market. The financial community values the reports of certified public accountants precisely because they perceive that CPAs are independent of both the information attested to and the information's preparers and users. But a state of mind cannot be observed in quite the same way as a behavior—say, a head nod—can be observed. Thus, to maintain an image of independence, a practitioner must remain free of any obligation or interest in a client that would damage the appearance of independence. For example, an auditor who owns an interest in a business might be intellectually honest when auditing the business, but would not *appear* independent to a bank loan officer, since the auditor has a financial interest in the bank's lending decision. A practitioner can accept neither an attestation engagement nor an audit engagement unless he or she is independent of the client.

The concept of independence relates both to the *actual* independence of *individual practitioners* (practitioner independence) and to the *apparent* independence of *all practitioners* collectively (profession independence). *Practitioner independence* is a state of mind that pervades a practitioner's approach to attestations and audits. Mautz and Sharaf identify three dimensions of practitioner independence that can minimize potential threats to impartiality:[5]

- *Programming independence.* Freedom from control or undue influence when selecting and applying procedures.
- *Investigative independence.* Access to all relevant information, and freedom from control or undue influence when selecting information to investigate.
- *Reporting independence.* Freedom from control or undue influence when reporting information revealed by the engagement, or when making recommendations or expressing opinions.

Practitioner independence demands that professional judgment neither be subordinated to nor influenced by stakeholders, including management, employees, or the board of directors. *Profession independence*, in contrast, is a

---

4   The second field work standard and the second reporting standard (Figure 2-1, right column) were revised in 1988 by *SAS No. 55* and *SAS No. 58*, respectively.
5   Adapted from R. K. Mautz and H. A. Sharaf. *The Philosophy of Auditing.* Sarasota: American Accounting Association (1961), p. 206.

perception held by the public about all practitioners collectively. To the extent that the public perceives that the profession lacks independence, the perceived independence of otherwise impartial practitioners may be at risk. Thus, public perceptions of profession independence have a direct impact on the reputation—and indeed the livelihood—of individual practitioners, and has been a major preoccupation of the public accounting profession for years.

In the 1970s and 1980s, a rather pointed debate surfaced over an issue sensitive to public accounting firms: nonattest consulting services. Critics argued that a firm compromises independence by accepting consulting fees from audit clients. For example, some accounting firms helped clients find and hire financial executives. Is a firm independent of financial executives they placed with audit clients? This question and the ensuing debate drove one major accounting firm to spin off its executive search practice in the 1970s, although the practice is common today. In the 1970s, the Securities and Exchange Commission responded to the nonattest services debate: *Accounting Series Release No. 250* required that public companies disclose nonaudit services and the percentage of nonaudit to audit fees in *Form 10-K*. Three years later, in 1981, the SEC rescinded *ASR No. 250*, and public disclosure of nonaudit services is no longer mandatory. Despite repeated criticisms by congressional committees and active monitoring by the SEC, research suggests that sophisticated financial information users, such as financial analysts, and educated but inexperienced readers, such as MBA students, have relatively high confidence in auditor independence, even in cases involving consulting.[6] The AICPA's *Code of Professional Conduct* offers guidance on some questions of independence faced commonly in practice and is discussed in Chapter 4.

Interestingly, as practitioners embark on new assurance services, *assurance* independence will likely raise questions quite apart from those raised by *audit* or *attest* independence, since, in some assurance services, the assurer is also the asserter! Consider Price Waterhouse's audit service for Amoco compared to their assurance service for the Academy of Motion Picture Arts & Sciences (Chapter 1: the Oscar balloting). In the audit service, Amoco management is the asserter (i.e., the preparer of financial statements) and Price Waterhouse is the attester. However, in the assurance service, Price Waterhouse is both asserter and attester, raising a unique set of questions not otherwise raised by audit services. For example, can assurers be independent of themselves? Can a public accounting firm reasonably claim independence if an audit client, say Paramount Pictures, has a movie nominated for Best Picture? These questions beg for the profession's serious reconsideration of independence—for example, an independence concept in which a practitioner has no interest in an outcome, for instance an assurance report, other than the reliability of the outcome.

DUE CARE

Due care underlies two issues within the *attestation standards* and *GAAS*: care when delivering professional services (Figure 2-1: 1st, 2nd, 3rd, and 5th general *attestation standards*; 3rd *GAAS*), and training (1st general *attestation standard*; 1st general *GAAS*).

---

6   See, for example: J. C. Corless and L. M. Parker. "The Impact of MAS on Auditor Independence: An Experiment," *Accounting Horizons* (September 1987), pp. 25-29; P. M. J. Reckers and A. J. Stagliano. "Nonaudit Services and Perceived Independence: Some New Evidence," *Auditing: A Journal of Practice & Theory* (Summer 1981), pp. 23-47.

Think of a work by a gifted artist, or a performance by a talented actor. That work, that performance, that is due professional care. The following quote, on the same topic, is from *Cooley on Torts*:

Every man who offers his service to another and is employed assumes the duty to exercise in the employment such skill as he possesses with reasonable care and diligence. In all these employments where peculiar skill is prerequisite, if one offers his service, he is understood as holding himself out to the public as possessing the degree of skill commonly possessed by others in the same employment, and, if his pretensions are unfounded, he commits a species of fraud upon every man who employs him in reliance on his public profession.

No other quote so clearly captures the essence of due care. In short, a practitioner is responsible to exercise reasonable care—and to be intellectually honest about possessing requisite skills—or risk committing an inexcusable fraud upon all who rely on his or her work.

Clearly, practitioners are not expected to be infallible. Like physicians, attorneys, and other responsible professionals, providers of attestation and audit services are subject to human error. However, also like other professionals, providers are entrusted with the responsibility to perform their duties with the degree of care expected of the *prudent practitioner*. In the legal profession, the notion of a "reasonable person" is often applied by the courts to determine the extent and limits of an individual's responsibility. The "prudent practitioner" serves a similar purpose in attestation and auditing engagements and, like the "reasonable person," is subject to judgment and interpretation. Mautz and Sharaf offer some interpretation:[7]

- The prudent practitioner will take steps to *foresee unreasonable risk or harm to others.*
- The prudent practitioner will attend to any employee, department, transaction, or resource that experience or history suggests may carry *extra risk.*
- The prudent practitioner will consider any *unusual circumstances* or relationships when planning and performing the engagement.
- The prudent practitioner must recognize *unfamiliar situations* and take precautions.
- The prudent practitioner will take all appropriate steps to *resolve doubt* or unanswered questions about matters material to his or her report.
- The prudent practitioner will *keep abreast of developments* in his or her area of competence.
- The prudent practitioner will *review the work of assistants* with the full understanding of the importance of the task.

Though not necessarily complete, Mautz and Sharaf's interpretation provides a framework for understanding the nature of professional care.

A practitioner comes to appreciate due care through formal preprofessional education (e.g., baccalaureate or graduate degrees), continuing professional education (e.g., AICPA or CPA firm-sponsored seminars) and through properly supervised on-the-job experience. Education and experience complement each other, are part of an attitude of lifelong learning, and are the basis for

---

7   Adapted from R. K. Mautz and H. A. Sharaf. *The Philosophy of Auditing*. Sarasota: American Accounting Association (1961), pp. 135-138.

a practitioner to develop what he or she sells: *professional judgment*. Underscoring the importance of professional judgment in auditing, the *Codification of Statements on Auditing Standards* includes over 100 references to the need for professional judgment in practice. For example, the *Codification* states:

- The auditor should obtain a level of knowledge of the entity's business that will enable him . . . to obtain an understanding of the events, transactions, and practices that, in his *judgment*, may have a significant effect on the financial statements.
- The auditor should plan the audit so that audit risk will be limited to a low level that is, in his *professional judgment*, appropriate for issuing an opinion on the financial statements.
- The assessment of possible error as of the balance sheet date should be based on the auditor's *judgment* of the state of the particular account(s) as of that date.

As the number of references to judgment suggests, the hallmark of audit and attestation services is neither the technology addressed in Chapters 6 through 9 nor the methods in Chapters 10 through 17. Rather, the hallmark is the sequence of complex professional judgments that constitute decision-making. Much as physicians are compensated for judgments about identifiable symptoms, probable cause, and likely diagnosis, attestation and audit service providers are compensated for complex professional judgments about the collection, interpretation, and reporting of evidence.

EVIDENCE

Evidence, the basis for decisions in all attestation and audit engagements, contemplates three issues: evidential matter (Figure 2-1: 2nd field work *attestation standard*; 3rd field work *GAAS*), planning and supervision (1st field work *attestation standard*; 1st *GAAS*), and internal control (2nd *GAAS*).

The nature and measurement of evidence varies depending on whether a practitioner is performing an attestation engagement or an audit engagement. For example, consider Coopers & Lybrand's attestation engagement for Wilson Sporting Goods' Ultra golf ball (Chapter 1), asserted by Wilson to outdistance the competition by 5.7 yards per drive. In this case, the *nature* of the evidence is a sample of drives observed by Coopers & Lybrand professionals, and the *measurement* scale is yards per drive. Compare that evidence to Coopers & Lybrand's audit engagement for Wilson Sporting Goods, in particular management's assertion that the Ultra golf ball inventory exists and is valued properly. In this case, the *nature* of the evidence is stacked golf ball cartons observed by Coopers & Lybrand professionals, and the *measurement* scale is generally accepted accounting principles.

The profession has been far more forthcoming about the nature of evidence in audit engagements than in attestation engagements. For example, *Statement on Auditing Standards No. 31*, "Evidential Matter" (AU Sec. 330), describes **audit evidence** as the underlying accounting data and all related corroborating information available to an auditor. *Underlying accounting data* includes journals, ledgers, reconciliations, and accounting manuals. *Corroborating information* includes receiving reports, invoices, contracts, and representations from third parties, such as confirmations of receivables balances with debtors (Chapter 11).

Audit decision-making is based on sufficient, competent evidential matter. *Sufficiency* refers to the quantity of audit evidence obtained, although it does not mean "the more, the better." Audit decisions must be reached within a reasonable length of time and at reasonable cost, requiring that an auditor balance the cost of obtaining additional evidence with the usefulness of the evidence obtained. In contrast, *competence* refers to the validity and relevance of evidence, both of which depend heavily on whether the evidence is obtained from independent sources, obtained directly by the auditor, or processed through reliable information systems. Following are well-established presumptions about evidence:

- Evidence obtained by an auditor from independent sources (e.g., banks, debtors) is more reliable than evidence obtained from management.
- Evidence obtained directly by an auditor through physical examination, observation, computation, and inspection is more persuasive than evidence obtained indirectly from management.
- Reliable evidence is more likely to be produced by effective, than by ineffective, systems of internal control.

Independent auditors would much prefer to obtain entirely convincing rather than merely persuasive audit evidence. However, because the cost of obtaining evidence should not exceed the usefulness of the evidence obtained, audit evidence is often persuasive rather than wholly convincing. But this is quite acceptable in audit practice, since an audit is designed to provide reasonable, not absolute, assurance about management's assertions in financial statements. The nature, types, and documentation of evidence are discussed more fully in Chapter 6.

Attestation and audit engagements should be planned by competent professional staff and the work of all assistants assigned to the engagement should be supervised. Due care demands no less. For example, an independent auditor should be appointed before (or soon after) an entity's fiscal year begins, since early appointment allows ample time to plan and to consider completing some audit field work before the balance sheet date. An auditor can accept an audit engagement near or after the balance sheet date, but should alert management that the engagement cannot be completed unless all relevant audit evidence can be accessed. For example, if appointed two months after the close of a prospective client's fiscal year, the auditor may have difficulty obtaining persuasive evidence that recorded inventory existed at the balance sheet date.

Statement on Auditing Standards No. 22, "Planning and Supervision" (AU Sec. 311), describes *planning* as the process of developing objectives and an overall strategy. The extent of an audit plan depends on the size and complexity of the entity, and the practitioner's knowledge of and experience with the entity's business. Planning considerations include the nature of the business and the industry in which the entity operates, the entity's organizational design, operating policies, preliminary estimates of materiality (discussed later in this chapter), and financial statement disclosures likely to require correcting. Above all, an auditor is best prepared to complete an audit when thoroughly familiar with the client, and the client's business and industry—that is, an audit should not be conducted in a vacuum. *Supervision* is the process of directing the efforts of assistants toward the objectives of the engagement, and determining whether the objectives are achieved. All work performed by assistants should be thoroughly reviewed, and their conclusions should be consistent with the opinion communicated in an audit report. Procedures should also be established to determine how to resolve differences of opinion among staff members about accounting and auditing issues.

Auditors often plan to conduct some auditing procedures, for example, tests of controls and analytical procedures, at interim dates prior to the balance sheet date. One purpose of interim audit work is to determine the risk that an entity's internal controls may fail to detect or prevent material misstatements in the financial statements. In fact, when controls are found to be effective, year end work may consist mainly of analytical procedures—such as comparison of current with prior year account balances—and less extensive detailed tests, assuming controls remain effective. Emphasis on tests of controls and analytical procedures is more appropriate for accounts with large numbers of transactions, and emphasis on detailed testing is more appropriate for accounts with few transactions. Extensive, time-consuming tests of controls for accounts with only a small number of transactions would be inefficient, since less audit time would be consumed by simply testing all or most of the transactions directly.

An entity's **internal controls** represent the policies and procedures that the board of directors and management have implemented to provide themselves with reasonable assurance that their objectives will be achieved. Although the *attestation standards* do not address internal control explicitly, attestation engagements about internal control are common. For example, Deloitte & Touche LLP has attested for years to an assertion the management of a West Coast client makes about the adequacy of stock transfer and shareholder servicing controls as defined by Rule 17Ad-13(a)(3) of the *Securities Exchange Act of 1934*. In contrast, *GAAS* are explicit about internal control. The second standard of field work requires that an auditor obtain an understanding of an entity's internal controls to help in planning the audit and in designing audit tests. The standard also points implicitly to an important inverse relationship between the effectiveness of an entity's internal controls and the extent of audit procedures required: As the effectiveness of an entity's internal controls increases, the amount of evidence necessary to reach an opinion on the financial statements should decrease. This relationship is based on the premise that effective internal controls can reduce the risk of materially misstated financial statements.

REPORTING

All attestation and audit engagements result in reports. Attestation reports conclude about whether a written assertion is presented in conformity with established or stated criteria, and audit reports conclude about whether financial statements are presented in accordance with **generally accepted accounting principles (GAAP)**. For example, Deloitte & Touche's *attestation report* for the stock transfer and shareholder servicing controls introduced earlier read, in part, as follows:

In our opinion, management's assertion that, during the year ended, the Company maintained an effective internal control structure, including appropriate segregation of responsibilities and duties, over the transfer agent and shareholder servicing functions . . . and that no material inadequacies existed as defined by Rule 17Ad-13(a)(3) of the Securities Exchange Act of 1934, is fairly stated, in all material respects, based upon criteria established by Rule 17Ad-13(a)(3) of the Securities Exchange Act of 1934.

Consistent with the *attestation standards* of reporting (Figure 2-1: left column), the report identifies management's assertion (". . . *maintained an effective internal control structure . . ."*) and the established criteria against which the assertion was measured *[Rule 17Ad-13(a)(3)]*.

Deloitte & Touche's *audit report* for the same company reads, in part, as follows:

In our opinion, the financial statements referred to above present fairly, in all material respects, the financial position of the company . . . , and the results of its operations and its cash flows . . . , in conformity with generally accepted accounting principles.

Consistent with the *GAAS* of reporting (Figure 2-1: right column), the report states that the financial statements comply with generally accepted accounting principles (*. . . in conformity with . . .*) and expresses an opinion (*present fairly*), but reports neither that the accounting principles were applied inconsistently nor that the disclosures were inadequate, because apparently they were not. Reporting is discussed extensively in Chapter 3.

RISK AND MATERIALITY

In Deloitte & Touche's attestation and audit reports, illustrated partly above, the firm used the terms *opinion* and *material*. The attestation report reads, "In our *opinion* . . . no *material* inadequacies," and the audit report reads, "In our *opinion* . . . in all *material* respects." The phrases imply to readers that the reports are statements of opinion, rather than statements of fact, and therefore that Deloitte & Touche *may* have unknowingly failed to modify their reports for material undetected inadequacies in internal control (attestation report) or for material undetected misstatements in financial statements (audit report). That is, despite performing the engagements in accordance with *attestation standards* and with *GAAS*, respectively, there is a **risk** that management's assertions about their internal controls (attestation) and about their financial statements (audit) may contain *material* omissions or misstatements. In both reports, **materiality** means that the magnitude of omission or misstatement would have changed or influenced the judgment of a reasonable person relying on the assertions. For example, there may be inappropriate commingling of responsibilities (attestation) or omitted disclosures (audit) that, if known, would drive the SEC to sanction management for violations of *Rule 17Ad-13(a)(3)* (attestation) or a large block trader to divest an equity investment (audit). Practitioners attempt mightily to hold risk to a relatively low level, but no practitioner can eliminate all risk completely, in part because attestation and audit engagements are designed to provide reasonable, not absolute, assurance.

Both risk and materiality are closely related to the standards of field work and reporting in attestation and audit engagements: to the field work standards because materiality and risk influence a practitioner's engagement strategy, and to the reporting standards because the terms *opinion* and *materiality* imply that practitioners take no responsibility for immaterial omissions or misstatements.

ATTESTATION RISK AND AUDIT RISK

In an attestation engagement, **attestation risk** is the probability that an attester may unknowingly fail to modify a written conclusion about an assertion that is materially misstated. For example, in Deloitte & Touche's attestation engagement, introduced earlier, the firm sustains a risk that the attestation report fails to capture undetected material misstatements in management's assertions about stock transfer and shareholder servicing controls. In contrast, in a financial statement audit, **audit risk** is the probability that an auditor may unknowingly fail to modify an opinion on financial statements that are materially misstated. For example, in the audit engagement for the same client, Deloitte & Touche sustains a risk that the audit report fails to capture undetected material misstatements in management's assertions about the financial statements. Practitioners plan engagements so that attestation risk or audit risk—whether assessed quantitatively (e.g., five percent or ten percent) or nonquantitatively (e.g., high, moderate, or low)—will be limited to a level that is low enough to issue a report confidently, without undue risk that management's assertions are materially misstated.

The professional literature about risk and materiality is not well developed for attestation services, but is quite rich for financial statement audits. Prior to the mid-1970s, many audits were driven largely by a prescribed set of procedures carried out in most all audits, with minor changes for industry differences: so-called *procedures-driven* audits. The logic of a procedures-driven audit was to cast a wide net, and to enjoy efficiencies on an engagement from year to year by learning to perform procedures quickly. More recently, procedures-driven audits have given way to *risk-driven* audits—that is, audits in which the auditor allocates proportionately more effort to the accounts or disclosures judged by the auditor to be the most risky. The logic of a risk-driven audit is that accounts or disclosures judged not risky are not worthy of significant effort, since the risk of material misstatement is below a relatively low level. What's most important to grasp is that risk management is at the center of gravity both in a financial statement audit and in an attestation engagement.

INHERENT RISK, CONTROL RISK, AND DETECTION RISK

In a financial statement audit, audit risk for any one individual account, such as Accounts Receivable or Inventory, consists of the:

- *Inherent* and *control risks* that the account contains error that could be material when combined with error in other accounts, and
- *Detection risk* that the auditor will not detect material error.

Inherent, control, and detection risk are introduced below, followed thereafter by how they translate into audit risk.

Inherent risk is the susceptibility of an account balance to error that could be material, assuming there are no related internal controls. For example, technological developments in the telecommunications industry could render some replacement parts inventory obsolete, thereby increasing the inherent risk that the carrying value of inventory is overstated. Some accounts are inherently more risky than others because of their very nature alone, rather than observable outside influences like changes in technology. For example, liquid assets such as cash and marketable securities are far more susceptible to theft, and therefore are inherently more risky, than nonliquid assets such as coal or timber. Auditors can do little to influence inherent risk. Rather, the task is to assess inherent risk completely by considering the client's business and industry (e.g., a technologically driven industry?), management's predisposition to manage earnings (do GAAP offer income-enhancing accounting alternatives in the industry?), and insights obtained from prior engagements (e.g., prior year inventory pricing errors?).

Control risk is the likelihood that error could occur and not be prevented or detected by internal controls. The more effective the internal controls are, the less control risk sustained by the auditor. In practice, auditors sometimes combine inherent and control risk, and sometimes assess the two risks separately. However, regardless of whether the risks are assessed separately or in combination, the auditor should have a basis for judging risk. For example, as a basis for assessing control risk, an auditor could use evidence gathered when documenting an entity's internal controls (under the second standard of field work). In addition, an auditor could use a specially designed technological obsolescence questionnaire to assess inherent risk for high-tech inventory. Like inherent risk, auditors assess—but can do little to influence—control risk. Instead, auditors attempt to manage inherent and control risk by controlling detection risk, the one risk auditors can influence.

Detection risk is the likelihood that error could occur and not be detected by the auditor's procedures. In practice, detection risk arises partly because auditors do not normally test one hundred percent of the transactions comprising an account balance, and partly because of other uncertainties that may arise even when testing all transactions—such as inadequately supervising the audit or poor judgment. Because auditors select and are free to change audit procedures, detection risk exists independent of inherent and control risk, neither of which are directly controllable by the auditor. As a result, detection risk bears an inverse relationship to inherent and control risk; that is, the greater the inherent and control risks, the less detection risk an auditor can accept. For example, if an entity's controls over precious metals are inadequate, an auditor would be willing to accept only a very low detection risk, primarily because: (1) precious metals are highly susceptible to theft and therefore have a higher level of inherent risk, and (2) controls are inadequate, indicating a high control risk. In this case, the auditor's procedures would have to be particularly effective to minimize detection risk.

MEASURING AUDIT RISK AND DETECTION RISK

In practice, auditors often express audit risk nonquantitatively (e.g., high, medium, or low) primarily because inherent, control, and detection risk are often difficult to judge quantitatively. However, assuming inherent, control, and detection risk can be quantified for a given audit client, an auditor could measure audit risk for particular accounts according to an expression implied in *SAS No. 47* "Audit Risk and Materiality in Conducting an Audit" (AU Sec. 312).[8]

---

8   See W. S. Waller. "Auditors' Assessments of Inherent and Control Risk in Field Settings," *The Accounting Review* (October 1993), pp. 783-803 for a review of *a priori* analyses of the audit risk model's assumptions and of auditor's risk assessments in experimental settings, and for an empirical test of the statistical association between control risk and inherent risk in practice.

$AR = IR \times CR \times DR$

Where: AR = Audit risk for an account

IR = Inherent risk

CR = Control risk

DR = Detection risk

However, in practice auditors more commonly preset audit risk at a level acceptable to the firm, evaluate the magnitude of control and inherent risk for an individual account, and then solve for an *acceptable level of detection risk* using the following, a rearrangement of the expression above:

$$DR = \frac{AR}{IR \times CR}$$

In short, because detection risk can be controlled by the auditor's procedures, detection risk is treated as the dependent variable (the variable on the left side of the equal sign). To illustrate, assume that an auditor wishes to hold audit risk to 2 percent for precious metals inventory and estimates from evidence obtained in prior years' engagements that inherent risk is 50 percent and control risk is 40 percent. The acceptable level of detection risk for inventory would be:

$$DR = \frac{.02}{.50 \times .40}$$

$$= \quad .10$$

Two observations about how to interpret an acceptable level of detection risk, in this case 10 percent: First, an auditor would use the acceptable level of detection risk to plan the *amount* of evidence he or she need gather to hold audit risk for inventory to 2 percent. The auditor's task is to gather enough evidence to feel confident that the likelihood of material undetected inventory errors does not exceed 10 percent.

Second, the acceptable level of detection risk is inversely related to the *amount* of audit evidence the auditor would plan to gather. That is, as the acceptable level of detection risk goes up, the amount of evidence gathered goes down and vice versa. For example, if audit risk for inventory in the above illustration were preset at 4 percent (rather than 2 percent), detection risk would go up to 20 percent (rather than 10 percent) and the auditor would require *less* evidence to hold audit risk for inventory to 4 percent than he or she would require to hold audit risk to 2 percent. Why? Because:

$1 - DR$ = *Level of confidence*

Level of confidence is the likelihood that the audit procedures did not fail. To illustrate, 20 percent detection risk translates to an 80 percent level of confidence that audit procedures did not fail, 10 percent detection risk translates to 90 percent confidence, and an auditor would require *less* evidence to be 80 percent confident than to be 90 percent confident. Of course, the reliability of quantitative measures of detection risk, such as 10 and 20 percent, is directly dependent on the accuracy of control, inherent, and audit risk—each of which is usually estimated qualitatively in practice.

BUSINESS RISK

Some practitioners believe that audit risk, the likelihood of unknowingly failing to modify an opinion on materially misstated financial statements, is not unrelated to business risk, the probability that a practitioner may incur damages despite issuing an appropriate report. For example, an auditor may face litigation brought by the shareholders of a bankrupt audit client even though the audit report raised substantial doubt about the entity's ability to continue as a going concern (discussed in Chapter 3). Public accounting firms vary in how they respond to business risk. Some firms argue that the level of assurance provided in a financial statement audit does not vary across engagements and therefore does not alter audit risk (or the amount of evidence gathered) in engagements for which business risk is greater than a relatively low level. In contrast, other firms argue that audit risk and business risk are inextricably related. These firms alter audit risk when factors such as those listed in Figure 2-2 suggest that business risk is greater than a relatively low level. For example, if an entity has recurring losses and negative cash flows, and prior unrelated civil convictions reveal that management may lack integrity, some auditors may be predisposed to: (1) set audit risk at a level lower than would be necessary in the absence of business risk, (2) decrease the acceptable level of detection risk, and (3) increase the amount of evidence gathered and evaluated.

Figure 2-2: Factors Affecting Business Risk

- Management is aggressive about financial reporting and disclosure.
- Management integrity or reputation is suspicious.
- Management faces conflicts of interest and regulatory problems.
- Management turnover is high.
- The entity operates in an industry that is new and unstable or mature and stagnant.
- The entity has recurring losses and negative cash flows.
- Significant debt or credit is denied or at risk.
- Material transactions are planned with related parties.
- Shares are traded publicly.
- Significant litigation is threatened or pending.
- Pending legislation challenges existing or planned markets.
- The entity has not been audited previously.

MATERIALITY

The question "What is material in what situations?" has never really been resolved with certainty, although there is consensus about what the *term* materiality means from SEC regulations, the courts, and the authoritative literature. For example, the Securities and Exchange Commission defines materiality in *Rule 1-02* of *Regulation S-X*:

The term material, when used to qualify a requirement for the furnishing of information as to any subject, limits the information required to those matters about which an average prudent investor ought reasonably to be informed.

Several court cases have also defined materiality. For example, in *Escott v. BarChris Construction Corp.*, the court defined a material fact as:

. . . a fact that if it had been correctly stated or disclosed would have deterred or tended to deter the average prudent investor from purchasing the securities in question.[9]

Similarly, the court in *SEC v. Texas Gulf Sulphur Co.* stated:

The basic test of materiality . . . is whether a reasonable man would have attached importance . . . in determining his choice of action in the transaction in question.[10]

And the FASB defined materiality as:

. . . the magnitude of an omission or misstatement of accounting information that, in the judgment of a reasonable person relying on the information, would have been changed or influenced by the omission or misstatement.[11]

Clearly, there is general agreement among the SEC, the courts, and the FASB that a transaction, event, or disclosure is material if it would affect a decision made by an average prudent investor, a reasonable person, or the like. However, although appealing on a conceptual level, these definitions provide little practical guidance about how to make materiality decisions in practice. The following sections address practical decision-making by discussing when an auditor makes materiality decisions in financial statement audits, how an auditor arrives at an overall preliminary estimate of materiality for an entire set of financial statements taken as a whole, and how an auditor might allocate the overall estimate to individual financial statement components.

MATERIALITY DECISIONS IN PRACTICE

As explained in *Statement on Auditing Standards No. 47,* "Audit Risk and Materiality in Conducting an Audit" (AU Sec. 312), there is an inverse relationship between audit risk and materiality. For example, the risk that a financial statement account, say Accounts Receivable, could be misstated by an extremely large amount might be quite low, but the risk that the account could be misstated by an extremely small amount might be quite high. Holding other things constant, either a decrease in the allowable level of audit risk or a decrease in the amount of error deemed material would cause the auditor to do one or more of the following: select more effective audit procedures, perform auditing procedures closer to the balance sheet date, or increase the extent of the procedures applied.

During a financial statement audit, an auditor considers materiality at least twice: once while planning the engagement, and again after all audit procedures have been completed. While planning an engagement, the auditor determines a *preliminary estimate of materiality* for the entire set of financial statements taken as a whole (although the preliminary estimate can be revised during the engagement—for example, for conditions not known while planning, such as a newly implemented product line). The preliminary estimate is the maximum amount by which a set of financial statements could be misstated and still not cause the auditor to believe that the decisions of reasonable users would be affected. For example, if a preliminary estimate is $100,000, then

9   *Escott et al. v. BarChris Construction Corp.,* 283 F. Supp. 681 (S.D.N.Y., 1966).
10   *SEC v. Texas Gulf Sulphur Co.,* 401 F. 2nd 849 (C.A. 2nd, 1968).
11   *Statement of Financial Accounting Concepts No. 2,* "Qualitative Characteristics of Accounting Information." Stamford: FASB (1980), par. 132.

combined misstatements of less than $100,000 for all accounts would be considered immaterial. The purpose of determining a preliminary estimate of materiality is to help the auditor plan the extent of audit evidence to accumulate during the engagement. For example, if the preliminary estimate were revised downward to $60,000, then the extent of audit procedures would increase, since the auditor would need to examine more evidence in order to find smaller misstatements.

Toward the end of an engagement, after all audit evidence has been gathered and evaluated, an auditor again considers materiality by comparing the combined misstatement for all accounts with the preliminary (or revised) estimate for the entire set of financial statements taken as a whole. If the combined misstatement exceeds the preliminary estimate, then the financial statements would be materially misstated, and the auditor could either perform additional audit procedures or request that management adjust the misstated accounts. Of course, if additional procedures are not performed and the client refuses to adjust the misstated accounts, then the auditor would issue either a "qualified" or an "adverse" opinion, as discussed in Chapter 3.

Determining a preliminary estimate of materiality is a crucial step in the audit process because it affects both the extent of audit procedures performed and, ultimately, whether combined misstatement is likely to affect users' decisions. But how do auditors determine a preliminary estimate?

PRELIMINARY ESTIMATES OF MATERIALITY

Statement on Auditing Standards No. 22, "Planning and Supervision" (AU Sec. 311), states that an auditor should consider a preliminary estimate of materiality when planning an audit engagement. The preliminary estimate need not necessarily be quantified, but many practitioners find quantification useful for assuring that all professional staff assigned to the engagement view materiality similarly. For example, if the preliminary judgment were determined by the audit partner to be *high* rather than stated numerically, not all members of the audit staff may interpret *high materiality* alike. In practice, auditors sometimes determine a preliminary estimate of materiality using decision aids and predetermined materiality criteria, as discussed next.

The Relationship Among Audit Risk, Materiality, and Audit Effort

Over the years, practicing auditors have designed and implemented various decision aids, not to supplant professional judgment, but to guide decision-making. For example, based on data from a sample of actual audit engagements, KPMG Peat Marwick developed a decision aid to guide the firm's preliminary estimates of materiality.[12]

The decision aid requires that the auditor first determine the larger of estimated revenues or assets and then calculate a preliminary estimate of materiality from a table similar to Figure 2-3. For example, if a client's estimated revenues are $22,500,000 and estimated assets are $15,750,000, then the preliminary estimate of materiality would be:

($22,500,000   .00400) + $34,600 = $124,600

---

12   R. K. Elliott. "Author's Response to 'Materiality in Audit Planning'," *Journal of Accountancy* (July 1983), p. 104.

Figure 2-3: A Materiality Decision Aid

If the Larger of Estimated Revenues or Assets Is:		Preliminary Estimate Is the Larger of Estimated Revenues or Assets:	
Over	But not over	Times	Plus
0	30,000	.05400	$ 0
30,000	100,000	.02900	750
100,000	300,000	.01800	1,850
300,000	1,000,000	.01250	3,500
1,000,000	3,000,000	.00830	7,700
3,000,000	10,000,000	.00600	14,600
10,000,000	30,000,000	.00400	34,600
30,000,000	100,000,000	.00272	73,000
100,000,000	1,000,000,000	.00190	155,000

Adapted from: R. K. Elliott. "Author's Response to 'Materiality in Audit Planning'," *Journal of Accountancy* (July 1983), p. 104.

However, this estimate is merely input—a baseline estimate—that would be revised based on the auditor's assessment of audit risk. If the auditor judged risk on the engagement to be relatively low, then the preliminary estimate could be higher, and the amount of audit effort required would be lower. Likewise, if the auditor judged audit risk to be relatively high, then the preliminary estimate would be lower, and the amount of audit effort required would be higher. That is, there is an inverse relationship between audit risk and materiality, and an inverse relationship between materiality and audit effort (measured in audit hours). For example, consider the preliminary estimate, $124,600, and assume the auditor had planned to perform the audit in 2,000 hours. If audit risk were judged to be low, then the auditor could raise the preliminary estimate, say, to $150,000. Now, since the preliminary estimate of materiality is higher, the auditor need not expend effort to detect aggregate misstatements below $150,000, and can therefore reduce budgeted audit hours to, say, 1,800 hours. This illustration reveals an important insight about the relationship between audit risk and audit effort: as risk goes down (up), audit effort goes down (up).

Quantitative Materiality Criteria

Research has identified quantitative materiality criteria often used by some practicing auditors, all of whom responded to hypothetical case studies in controlled experiments or in mail survey questionnaires:[13]

- Percentage effect on net income.
- Percentage effect on total revenues.
- Percentage effect on total assets.

13 Major studies include: J. R. Boatsman and J. C. Robertson. "Policy-Capturing on Selected Materiality Judgments," *The Accounting Review* (April 1974), pp. 342-352; M. Firth. "Consensus Views and Judgment Models in Materiality Decisions," *Accounting, Organizations and Society*, Vol. 4, No. 4 (1979), pp. 283-295; and S. Moriarity and F. Baton. "Modeling the Materiality Judgments of Audit Partners," *Journal of Accounting Research* (Autumn 1976), pp. 320-341. For a review of empirical research on materiality, see: G. L. Holstrum and W. F. Messier, Jr. "A Review and Integration of Empirical Research on Materiality," *Auditing: A Journal of Practice and Theory* (Fall 1982), pp. 45-63.

By far, the most common quantitative materiality criterion used by practicing auditors has been the *percentage effect on net income*. Auditors differ as to precisely what percentage is material, but many agree that combined error of less than five percent of net income is normally immaterial, and combined error of more than ten percent is normally material. Although used commonly in practice, effect on net income has drawbacks. For one, income is not always stable from year to year, suggesting that materiality thresholds based on net income alone could vary widely from year to year. For another, net income is subject to manipulation, in particular when accounting policies provide management with discretion. Management discretion in manipulating income, and the auditor's course of action, is discussed later in the book for four important accounting issues: revenue recognition (Chapter 11), environmental liabilities (Chapter 13), impaired assets (Chapter 15), and financial instruments (Chapter 16).

For these and other reasons, both the *percentage effect on total revenues* and the *percentage effect on total assets* are also important quantitative criteria, particularly when used in conjunction with net income. For example, if a large, publicly traded company were to report net income of $2,000,000 in one year and $1,000 in the following year, with total assets approximating $20,000,000 in both years, an auditor would be foolish to conclude in the latter year that 10 percent of net income, or $100, is material. Rather, the auditor would focus on total revenues and total assets. Unlike net income, total revenues and total assets are usually more stable and highly correlated.

Qualitative Factors

In making materiality decisions, an auditor considers not only quantitative criteria, but also qualitative factors, particularly those that may cause a quantitatively immaterial transaction to be material in a qualitative sense. One common example is a quantitatively immaterial adjustment to working capital that, if recorded, would result in the violation of a long-term debt covenant. To illustrate, assume that a client held a $1 million long-term bank loan that carried a debt covenant: The loan would become immediately due and payable if the current ratio went below 3 to 2. Toward the end of the engagement, a staff member proposes a $5,000 adjusting journal entry to reclassify credit balances in Receivables to Accounts Payable (*debit* Accounts Receivable, *credit* Accounts Payable) that, although quantitatively immaterial, reduces the current ratio to just below 3 to 2. In this case, although $5,000 is immaterial, violation of the debt covenant would require that the $1 million long-term debt be classified as a current liability, and the reclassification is more likely to be material.

A second qualitative factor, reversal of an earnings trend, is sometimes interpreted by auditors as a materiality criterion, even when the percentage effect on net income, total revenues, and total assets is immaterial. To illustrate, assume that in four consecutive years, a company's earnings per share had been $2.50, $2.75, $3.03, and $3.33, respectively—an approximate increase of ten percent per year. An otherwise quantitatively immaterial audit adjustment that altered the ten percent trend negatively might be considered material because of the potential effect on financial statement users. A commercial loan officer, for example, might consider the reversal to be the "tip of the iceberg," the beginning of a long-term downward trend. That is, the loan officer might be concerned that financial position may deteriorate over the loan repayment period, thereby reducing the likelihood of repayment. The loan officer might not necessarily deny the loan, but might require a marginally higher interest rate to compensate the bank for increased risk.

A third factor is more subtle: a quantitatively immaterial illegal payment that violates the *Foreign Corrupt Practices Act (FCPA)*, or another federal or state law. For example, assume an entity made two immaterial $5,000 payments to a foreign political official, ostensibly to secure favorable treatment in upcoming contract negotiations. In this case, disclosing the payments may be necessary for at least two reasons. First, the *FCPA* carries rather severe fines ($1 million per payment) that may result in material contingent liabilities if the Justice Department or Securities and Exchange Commission were to prosecute. Second, financial statement users may be influenced by the fact that management is apparently predisposed to making questionable or illegal payments.

ALLOCATING PRELIMINARY ESTIMATES OF MATERIALITY

Although an auditor's opinion relates to an entire set of financial statements taken as a whole, an audit is actually conducted piece-by-piece, on individual financial statement accounts, one account at a time. As a result, some firms allocate the preliminary estimate of materiality among individual financial statement accounts as a planning tool for the staff members assigned to audit the accounts.

In practice, most auditors who allocate the preliminary estimate to individual accounts choose to allocate to the balance sheet, rather than to the income statement accounts, because usually there are fewer balance sheet than income statement accounts, and most income statement errors also affect the balance sheet.

There are several approaches to allocating the preliminary estimate of materiality to individual accounts, among them allocation based on:

- The relative magnitude of financial statement accounts.
- The relative variability of financial statement accounts.
- Professional judgment.

Relative Magnitude

One method is to allocate the preliminary estimate based on the relative dollar balances in each balance sheet account. However, the allocation ignores accounts that will not be audited, such as Retained Earnings, and accounts that will be audited one hundred percent, such as Contingent Liabilities. A simplified model follows:[14]

$$\begin{array}{c}\text{Preliminary} \\ \text{estimate of} \\ \text{materiality for} \\ \text{an individual} \\ \text{balance sheet} \\ \text{account}\end{array} = \begin{array}{c}\text{Preliminary} \\ \text{estimate of} \\ \text{materiality for} \\ \text{all accounts}\end{array} \times \sqrt{\dfrac{\text{Amount of (a specific) balance sheet account}}{\begin{array}{c}\text{Sum of all balance sheet accounts,} \\ \text{less accounts not audited and} \\ \text{accounts audited 100 percent}\end{array}}}$$

14   G. R. Zuber, R. K. Elliott, W. R. Kinney, Jr., and J. J. Leisenring. "Using Materiality in Audit Planning," *Journal of Accountancy* (March 1983), p. 50.

Other, more comprehensive, models can be developed to allocate materiality more efficiently, although the cost to develop a more comprehensive model may exceed the benefits, given particularly that the model should be used to generate initial, not final, allocations. That is, rather than blindly accepting each allocation, an auditor should consider other factors affecting each account audited. For example, some balance sheet accounts, such as Cash, process relatively large volumes of transactions, but do not normally carry dollar balances representative of the volume of transactions processed. Thus, regardless of which relative magnitude model is applied, the allocation of materiality to Cash is apt to be adjusted.

Relative Variability
The relative magnitude approach, above, focuses on the dollar balance of each account, thereby presuming that there's more information in the size of an account than in the relative number of transactions processed in the account. To compensate, some auditors allocate materiality on the basis of a measure of the *variability* of the transactions processed in the balance sheet accounts— for example, the standard deviation of processed transactions—reasoning that as variability rises, so does an auditor's uncertainty and, therefore, audit risk. For example, if two balance sheet accounts, such as Receivables and Payables, each had recorded book values of $1 million, then relative magnitude would yield identical materiality allocations. However, if the standard deviation was $150 for Receivables and $950 for Payables, an auditor would likely conclude that Payables transactions were less homogeneous than Receivables transactions, and therefore might desire a lower materiality allocation for Payables.

Professional Judgment
Many auditors use subjective professional judgment, only, to assess materiality for each financial statement account, and then compare the sum of all materiality assessments with the overall preliminary estimate of materiality, revising as necessary. The essential difference between relative magnitude and relative variability on one hand, and professional judgment only on the other, is that the former approaches calculate quantitative estimates of materiality first, use them as decision aids, and then revise on the basis of other information, while the latter (judgment only) bypasses the use of a decision aid.

MATERIALITY IN AUDITING AND IN ACCOUNTING

Although both accountants and auditors use similar criteria to evaluate materiality, their ultimate thresholds often differ. In general, auditors have a higher threshold of materiality than do the accountants employed by the entity audited. For example, a $1,000 understatement of advertising expense is more apt to be material to the entity's controller than to the independent auditor. The controller may be more concerned because a division manager's annual bonus is based on net income, or the advertising department's expenditures for the period are about to exceed amounts budgeted. In contrast, an auditor may be less concerned because the decisions of users, such as creditors or shareholders, are not likely to be affected. Regardless of how an auditor makes materiality decisions, what matters most is that materiality is crucial to many, if not most, audit practice decisions and, therefore, to an auditor's compliance with *generally accepted auditing standards*.

SUMMARY

Although the profession may establish standards for assurance engagements, the marketplace is not likely to grant the profession permission to establish measurement rules for assurance engagements with quite the ready enthusiasm the market grants the profession permission to establish measurement rules for audit engagements (i.e., generally accepted accounting principles). Rather, the profession may be wise to defer the development of assurance measurement rules to other professions (say, for example, the American Medical Association), and to leverage instead off of the profession's long-established comparative advantage in evaluating evidence bearing on the measurements.

First developed in the 1940s, the AICPA's ten *generally accepted auditing standards* still stand today as the guidelines—the measures of quality—for contemporary audit practice in the U.S. But, *generally accepted auditing standards* are applicable to only one type of attestation engagement: independent financial statement audits. For other attest engagements, practitioners are guided by *attestation standards,* developed jointly in 1986 by the Auditing Standards Board and by the Accounting and Review Services Committee.

Materiality and risk affect applications both of *attestation standards* and of *generally accepted auditing standards* because they bear heavily on a practitioner's judgments about evidence and on the responsibility a practitioner assumes for the conclusions he or she reports. The truth is that a practitioner has neither the time nor the resources to examine all of the evidence that bears on management's assertions. Only the most material and risky transactions and events command the practitioner's attention.

KEY TERMS

Generally accepted auditing standards
  (GAAS) 29
General standards 29
Standards of field work 29
Standards of reporting 29
Attestation standards 29
Audit evidence 35
Internal controls 37
Generally accepted accounting
  principles (GAAP) 37

Risk 38
Materiality 38
Attestation risk 39
Audit risk 39
Inherent risk 39
Control risk 40
Detection risk 40
Business risk 42

REFERENCES

Professional Standards

AICPA. *Codification of Statements on Auditing Standards.* New York: AICPA (AU Sec. 150, 201, 210, 220, 230, 311, 312, 325, 326, 411, 431, 504).

SAS No. 22, "Planning and Supervision" (AU Sec. 311).

SAS No. 26, "Association with Financial Statements" (AU Sec. 504).

SAS No. 31, "Evidential Matter" (AU Sec. 326).

SAS No. 32, "Adequacy of Disclosure in Financial Statements" (AU Sec. 431).

SAS No. 47, "Audit Risk and Materiality in Conducting an Audit" (AU Sec. 312).

SAS No. 60, "Communication of Internal Control Structure Related Matters Noted in an Audit" (AU Sec. 325).

SAS No. 69, "The Meaning of 'Present Fairly in Conformity with Generally Accepted Accounting Principles' in the Independent Auditor's Report" (AU Sec. 411).

Professional Reports

AICPA. *The Expectation Gap Standards: Proceedings of the Expectation Gap Roundtable,* (May 11-12, 1992, Charleston, SC). New York: AICPA (1993).

Public Oversight Board. *In the Public Interest: A Special Report by the Public Oversight Board of the SEC Practice Section of the AICPA.* Stamford, CT: POB (1993).

Public Oversight Board. *Strengthening the Professionalism of the Independent Auditor.* Stamford, CT: POB (1994).

Public Oversight Board. *Directors, Management, and Auditors: Allies in Protecting Shareholder Interests.* Stamford, CT: POB (1995).

Articles, Books

Alderman, C. W., and R. H. Tabor. "The Case for Risk-Driven Audits," *Journal of Accountancy* (March 1989), pp. 55-61.

Bricker, R., A. Bailey, J. Grant, and J. Turner. "The Professionalization of Public Accounting," *Law & Policy* (Vol. 15, No. 2), pp. 95-120.

Brumfield, C., R. K. Elliott, and P. Jacobson. "Business Risk and the Audit Process," *Journal of Accountancy* (April 1983), pp. 60-68.

Colbert, G. J., and T. B. O'Keefe. "Compliance with GAAS Reporting Standards: Evidence from a Positive Enforcement Review," *Auditing: A Journal of Practice & Theory* (Fall 1995), pp. 1-16.

Jacobson, P. D., and R. K. Elliott. "GAAS: Reconsidering the 'Ten Commandments'," *Journal of Accountancy* (May 1984), pp. 77-88.

Mautz, R. K., and H. A. Sharaf. *The Philosophy of Auditing.* Sarasota: American Accounting Association (1961).

Mednick, R. "Licensure and Regulation of the Profession: A Time for Change," *Journal of Accountancy* (March 1996), pp. 33-38.

Schandl, C. W. *Theory of Auditing: Evaluation, Investigation, and Judgment.* Houston: Scholars Book Co. (1978).

Strawser, J. R. "Examination of the Effect of Risk Model Components on Perceived Audit Risk," *Auditing: A Journal of Practice & Theory* (Spring 1991), pp. 126-135.

QUESTIONS

1. Why is the market unlikely to permit the public accounting profession to develop measurement rules for assurance services when the same market granted the profession permission to develop measurement rules for audit services (generally accepted accounting principles)?

2. Briefly trace the historical development of *attestation standards* and *generally accepted auditing standards.*

3. Why is independence important to the profession's acceptance as a major player in the assurance services market?

4. Distinguish between practitioner independence and profession independence.

5. What precautions can be expected of a *prudent practitioner*?

6. Identify and describe the quantitative criteria often used by practicing auditors when making materiality decisions.

7. What approaches are available for allocating a preliminary estimate of materiality to individual financial statement accounts?

8. Identify and describe the three component risks underlying audit risk for an individual financial statement account.

MULTIPLE CHOICE QUESTIONS

1. Assurance service engagements:

a. Do not require independence.
b. Require application of all *attestation standards* and *GAAS*.
c. Are performed currently without professional standards.
d. Do not require evidence.

2. A practitioner should comply with applicable *attestation standards:*

a. On every attestation engagement, without exception.
b. On every attestation engagement, except financial statement audits.
c. On consulting engagements.
d. On all engagements that involve financial statements.

3. Which of the following best describes the purpose of *attestation standards* and *GAAS?*

a. Measures of quality for attestation and audit engagements.
b. Methods to discharge professional responsibilities in attestation and audit engagements.
c. Rules that represent the public's expectations on attestation and audit engagements.
d. Objectives used to select evidence for attestation and audit engagements.

4. What is the focus of the standards of field work for attestation and audit engagements?

a. Guidelines for training, proficiency, and due care.
b. Guidelines for the content of the practitioner's report.
c. Guidelines for planning and for gathering evidence.
d. Guidelines for maintaining an independence in mental attitude.

5. Which of the following best describes due care?

a. Tact in avoiding legal liability.
b. Requisite skill and diligence.
c. Reasonable infallibility.
d. Freedom from undue influence.

6. The validity of evidence depends ultimately on the:

a. *Attestation standards* and *GAAS.*
b. Availability of subordinate evidence.
c. Relevance of the evidence.
d. Practitioner's professional judgment.

7. Practitioner independence:

a. Minimizes risk.
b. Helps achieve public confidence.
c. Defends against liability.
d. Achieves compliance with the standards of field work.

8. Which of the following may be assessed nonquantitatively?

	Inherent Risk	*Control Risk*	*Detection Risk*
a.	Yes	Yes	No
b.	Yes	No	Yes
c.	No	Yes	Yes
d.	Yes	Yes	Yes

(AICPA Adapted)

9. Materiality is:

a. Addressed within a practitioner's attestation and audit reports.
b. Expressed in terms of dollars.
c. Measured using guidelines established by the AICPA.
d. Not applicable to attestation engagements.

PROBLEMS AND DISCUSSION CASES

2-1 *Standards for an Assurance Services Engagement*
Paul Dietz, CEO of the St. Joseph Medical Center, a two-hundred-bed hospital in northwest Indiana, has approached you, a partner in Dirksen & Co., a public accounting firm. The Medical Center's board of directors has approved a strategy to market arthroscopic surgery in alliance with Hankin Orthopedic Surgery and Sports Medicine, a group of sports medicine doctors in Gary, Indiana. Management plans a print and radio advertising campaign to compete with two major suppliers of arthroscopic surgery in the Chicago area: Northwestern Medical Facility and the University of Chicago Hospitals. Although known in medical circles for pioneering research and state-of-the-art surgical procedures, the Hankin Group is not well known by the general public. Paul Dietz proposes to you that an independent panel of American Medical Association members, drawn from the editorial boards of leading research journals, be commissioned by the Medical Center to design measures of quality for arthroscopic surgery from which Dirksen & Co. would measure the Hankin Group's quality. Dirksen & Co. would be asked to compile "scores" using the independent panel's measures of quality, and would be identified as "a public accounting firm" in print and radio ads. In discussing the proposed assurance service with your partners, one asks, "What standards would you propose we apply on this engagement?"
Required:
1. Is the proposed service an assurance service other than an attestation?
2. In advising the Medical Center, do you see a problem with the assurance service as proposed by Dietz?
3. Respond to your partner's question: What standards would you propose to apply?

2-2 *Comparing Attestation Standards and GAAS*
The AICPA's *attestation standards* and *GAAS* are classified as general standards, standards of field work, and standards of reporting, and are closely aligned with four concepts: independence, due care, evidence, and reporting. As illustrated in Figure 2-1, some of the standards match almost identically, and others are unmatched—that is, they address entirely different issues. For example, the first general standard of the *attestation standards* matches the first general *GAAS* (adequate technical training and proficiency), but the second *GAAS* of field work (internal control) has no match among the *attestation standards*.

Required: For each unmatched *attestation standard* and *GAAS* in Figure 2-1, explain why you think the Auditing Standards Board and the Accounting and Review Services Committee did not draft a matching standard.

2-3 GAAS: Obsolescence or Endurance?

Interrupted by World War II, the Committee on Auditing Procedure, forebear to today's Auditing Standards Board, responded in the late 1940s to the SEC's 1941 call for auditing standards. The first nine standards were approved by AICPA member vote in 1948, a tenth was adopted by member vote in 1949, and few changes have been made to the standards since.

Required: You are the engagement partner for the financial statement audit of a publicly traded software producer. The CFO has asked how your profession's standards—presumably, the profession's measures of quality for a financial statement audit—could possibly be responsive to an information age client, given that the standards were produced half a century ago. Discuss.

2-4 Standards v. Procedures

Generally accepted auditing standards are an auditor's guidelines for selecting and designing detailed audit procedures, and an auditor typically applies selected procedures to determine whether an entity's financial statements are presented in accordance with generally accepted accounting principles. Thus, *generally accepted auditing standards*, audit procedures, and generally accepted accounting principles are fundamentally related to one another in a financial statement audit.

Required:
1. What is the difference between: (a) *generally accepted auditing standards* and (b) auditing procedures?
2. Why is it important that an auditor's report state whether an entity's financial statements are presented "in conformity with generally accepted accounting principles"?

2-5 Training and Proficiency

Andrea Farell, a local CPA, has been approached by Whitely Corporation concerning audited financial statements for the year ended September 30, 1999. Whitely, a relatively new company, processes accounting data by computer. Not having been exposed to computers previously, Farell enrolls in professional development courses designed to provide participants with an understanding of:
a. A language identical to the one used by Whitely in dedicated software.
b. How data is processed.
c. How to test controls typically used in computers and how to use the computer to achieve compliance with *generally accepted auditing standards*.
d. Auditing problems peculiar to computers.
e. The types of system documentation typically available for computers.

Farell completes the rather extensive course and is pleased with both the quality of instruction and the depth and extent of coverage.

Required:
1. The first general standard of GAAS requires that an auditor have *adequate technical training and proficiency*. Has Farell complied with the standard? Discuss.
2. Why is training in computers necessary before Farell can accept the Whitely engagement? Discuss.

2-6 Independence

The second general standard of GAAS states: *In all matters relating to the assignment, an independence in mental attitude is to be maintained by the auditor or auditors.* In addition to Rule 101 of the AICPA's *Code of Professional Conduct* (Chapter 4) and selected Securities and Exchange Commission releases, the second general standard is the profession's primary guideline relating to independence.

Required: Discuss the importance of, and difficulties in achieving, independence in mental attitude.

2-7 *Professional Qualifications and the Scope Paragraph*

The public accounting firm, Rodgers and Burge, performed an audit of the Lexington Manufacturing Company's December 31, 1999 financial statements. The scope paragraph of the unqualified report reads as follows:

We conducted our audits in accordance with generally accepted auditing standards. Those standards require that we plan and perform the audit to obtain reasonable assurance about whether the financial statements are free of material misstatement. An audit includes examining, on a test basis, evidence supporting the amounts and disclosures in the financial statements. An audit also includes assessing the accounting principles used and significant estimates made by management, as well as evaluating the overall financial statement presentation. We believe that our audits provide a reasonable basis for our opinion.

Required: What does the scope paragraph imply about: (1) the professional qualifications of Rodgers and Burge and the quality of their work, and (2) the conduct of their audit work?

2-8 *Accepting an Engagement*

You are the managing partner of Berke & Co., CPAs. On February 2, 1999, you receive a letter from the president of Barbizon, Inc., requesting the following: "We have made arrangements with Farmers Loan and Trust to borrow $125,000 to finance the purchase of new equipment. The bank has asked us to submit audited financial statements for the fiscal year ended December 31, 1998." Barbizon has not been audited previously and requests that you perform the audit.

Required:

1. Can you accept the engagement? Explain.
2. Assuming you accept the engagement, what can be done about confirming December 31, 1998 accounts receivable balances with debtors and observing December 31, 1998 physical inventory quantities—two auditing procedures that you would have conducted if the engagement were accepted prior to December 31?

2-9 *Evidence*

The third generally accepted standard of field work requires that the auditor obtain sufficient competent evidential matter to afford a reasonable basis for an opinion on the financial statements audited. In considering what constitutes sufficient competent evidential matter, *SAS No. 31, Audit Evidence,* distinguishes between underlying accounting data and corroborating information available to the auditor.

Required:

1. Discuss the nature of evidence the auditor should gather in terms of the underlying accounting data, corroborating information, and the methods by which the auditor tests or gathers evidential matter.
2. Discuss briefly the meaning of competence in relation to audit evidence, and state the general presumptions that can be made about the validity of evidential matter.

(AICPA Adapted)

2-10 *Standards of Field Work*

You have been assigned by your firm to complete the audit of the financial statements of Carter Manufacturing Corporation. The senior accountant and an inexperienced assistant who began the engagement were hospitalized because of an accident. The engagement is about one-half completed. Your auditor's report must be delivered in three weeks, an agreement made when your firm accepted the engagement. You estimate that by utilizing the client's staff you can complete the engagement in five weeks. Your firm cannot assign an assistant to you.

The working papers show the status of work on the audit as follows:

a.   Completed: cash, plant assets, depreciation, mortgage payable, and stockholders' equity.

b.   Completed except as noted later: inventories, accounts payable, tests of purchase transactions, and payrolls.

c.   Nothing done: trade accounts receivable, inventory receiving cutoff and price testing, accrued expenses payable, unrecorded liability test, tests of sales transactions, payroll deductions test and observation of payroll check distribution, other expenses, analytical procedures, vouching of December purchase transactions, auditor's report, consideration of internal control, letter on control structure deficiencies, minutes, preparation of tax returns, procedural recommendations for management, subsequent events, supervision, and review.

Your review discloses that the assistant's working papers are incomplete and were not reviewed by the senior accountant. For example, the inventory working papers present incomplete notations, incomplete explanations, and no cross-referencing.

Required:

1.   What field work standards have been violated by the senior accountant who preceded you on the assignment? Explain why you feel the standards you list have been violated.

2.   In planning your work to complete the engagement, you should scan the working papers, schedule certain work as soon as possible, and identify work that may be postponed until after the report is issued to the client.

   a.   List the areas on which you should plan to work first—say in your first week of work—and explain why each item deserves early attention.

   b.   State which work you believe could be postponed until after the report is issued to the client, and give reasons why the work may be postponed.

(AICPA Adapted)

2-11   *Standards of Reporting*

You are engaged in the audit of the financial statements of Rapid, Inc. and the Slow Corporation, a recently acquired subsidiary. In acquiring Slow Corporation during 1999, Rapid, Inc. exchanged a large number of shares of its common stock for 90 percent of the outstanding common stock of Slow Corporation in a transaction accounted for as a pooling of interests. Rapid, Inc. is now preparing the annual report to shareholders and proposes to include in the report combined financial statements for the year ended December 31, 1999, with a footnote describing the pooling transaction. Rapid, Inc. also proposes to include in the 1999 report their prior year annual report (1998), including a five-year financial summary and your unqualified auditor's opinion.

Required:

1.   Discuss the objectives or purposes of the standard of reporting that requires the auditor's report to identify circumstances in which generally accepted accounting principles have not been applied consistently over the past two periods.

2.   Briefly discuss whether Rapid's proposed presentation of financial statements in the 1999 annual report would affect comparability.

(AICPA Adapted)

2-12   *The Effect of Reporting Standards on Audit Reports*

Leer, CPA, has discussed various reporting considerations with two audit clients. The two clients asked how the following situations would affect the audit report.

a.   A client has a loan agreement that restricts the amount of cash dividends that can be paid and requires the maintenance of a predetermined current ratio. The client complies with the terms of the agreement, and it is not likely that there will be a violation in the foreseeable future. The client believes there is no need to mention the restriction in the financial statements because it may mislead the readers.

b. During the year, a client correctly accounted for the acquisition of a majority-owned domestic subsidiary but did not properly present the minority interest in retained earnings or net income of the subsidiary in the consolidated financial statements. The client agrees with Leer that the minority interest presented in the consolidated financial statements is materially misstated, but takes the position that the minority shareholders of the subsidiary should look to that subsidiary's financial statements for information concerning their interest.

Required: Each of these situations relates to one of the four generally accepted standards of reporting. Identify and describe the applicable reporting standard in each situation, and discuss how the situation relates to the standard and to Leer's report. Organize your answer as follows:

Situation	Applicable Standard of Reporting	Discussion of Relationship of Client Situation to Standard of Reporting and to Leer's Report
1.		
2.		

(AICPA Adapted)

2-13 *Failure to Comply with GAAS*

Smith, the owner of a small company, engaged Holmes, a CPA, to perform a financial statement audit. Smith told Holmes that an audit was to be completed in time to submit audited financial statements to a bank as part of a loan application. Holmes immediately accepted the engagement and agreed to provide an auditor's report within three weeks. Smith agreed to pay Holmes a fixed fee plus a bonus if the loan was granted.

Holmes hired two accounting students to perform the audit and spent several hours telling them exactly what to do. Holmes told the students not to spend time reviewing the controls, but instead to concentrate on proving the mathematical accuracy of the accounts and summarizing the data in accounting records that support Smith's financial statements. The students followed Holmes' instructions and after two weeks gave Holmes the financial statements, which did not include footnotes. Holmes reviewed the statements and prepared an unqualified auditor's report. The report, however, did not refer to generally accepted accounting principles.

Required: Briefly describe each of the *generally accepted auditing standards* and indicate how Holmes' actions resulted in a failure to comply with each standard. Organize your answer as follows:

Brief Description of GAAS	How Holmes' Actions Resulted in Failure to Comply with GAAS

(AICPA Adapted)

2-14 *Audit Risk*

Audit risk, the probability that an auditor may unknowingly fail to modify his or her opinion on materially misstated financial statements, occurs on all audit engagements, partly because auditors do not usually test all transactions underlying an account balance and partly because of other uncertainties, such as inadequate planning and supervision.

Required:
1. Briefly describe inherent risk, control risk, and detection risk—the three component risks underlying audit risk for individual financial statement accounts.
2. Why are some financial statement accounts inherently more risky than others?
3. Explain why detection risk bears an inverse relationship to inherent and control risk.

4. Assuming inherent, control, and detection risks are judged by an auditor to be .75, .50, and .25, respectively, for Trade Accounts Receivable, what is audit risk for the account?
5. In regard to Question 4 above, assume inherent risk is revised downward to .50.
   a. What is audit risk?
   b. In comparison with Question 4 above, how will the new audit risk level affect the auditor's revised estimate of materiality for Trade Accounts Receivable?

2-15 *Effect of Audit Risk on Materiality*
In planning a December 31, 1999 year end audit, you note that for the 1998 engagement your firm's assessment of audit risk was high, and the preliminary estimate of materiality, $1,200,000, was allocated to balance sheet accounts based on the standard deviation of recorded transactions within each unaudited account. Owing to the design of a new accounting information system and improved control procedures—both supervised by your firm's management consulting division—you judge that, unlike 1998, the risk in 1999 that material errors or irregularities could occur and not be prevented by the internal control structure is now well below the maximum.
   Required:
1. In comparison to 1998, will the 1999 preliminary estimate of materiality likely be higher or lower? Discuss.
2. What is the purpose of the preliminary estimate of materiality? Discuss.

2-16 *Materiality*
The concept of materiality is important to the audit of financial statements and to an auditor's expression of an opinion on the statements.
   Required: Discuss the following:
1. How is materiality (and immateriality) related to the proper presentation of financial statements?
2. In what ways will materiality affect the auditor in:
   a. Developing an audit program?
   b. Performing auditing procedures?
3. What factors and measures should the auditor consider in assessing the materiality of an exception to financial statement presentation?
4. How will the materiality of an auditor's exceptions to the financial statements influence the type of opinion expressed?

(AICPA Adapted)

2-17 *Allocating Preliminary Estimates of Materiality*
Richard Yates, CPA, is auditing the Levitan Corporation's financial statements for the year ended December 31, 1999. In prior years, Levitan's financial statements were audited by other auditors. Levitan's unaudited Accounts Receivable, Inventory, and Plant Assets are $2,500,000, $7,750,000, and $15,000,000, respectively, and all other assets total $12,750,000. Total current liabilities are $9,900,000, and net income is expected to be $4,500,000 on $35,000,000 of total revenues. Levitan Corporation is publicly traded on a national stock exchange.
   Because Yates has not previously audited Levitan, he decides to audit all of the balance sheet accounts and to audit Accounts Payable, recorded at $3,000,000, 100 percent, since controls are not reliable, and the balance represents a small number of individual accounts.
   Required:
1. Determine a preliminary estimate of materiality for Levitan Corporation's financial statements taken as a whole.
2. What portion of the preliminary estimate of materiality should be allocated to Accounts Receivable, Inventory, and Plant Assets, assuming Yates uses the *relative magnitude* approach to determine the allocation?

2-18 *Materiality*

During the course of an audit engagement, an independent auditor gives serious consideration to the concept of materiality, a concept that is inherent in the work of the independent auditor and is important for planning, preparing, and modifying audit programs. The concept of materiality underlies the application of all the *generally accepted auditing standards*, particularly the standards of field work and reporting.

Required:

1. Briefly describe what is meant by the independent auditor's concept of materiality.
2. What are some common financial statement relationships and other considerations used by the auditor in judging materiality?
3. Describe how the planning and execution of an audit program might be affected by the independent auditor's concept of materiality.

RESEARCH PROJECTS

1. SELF-REGULATION AND THE PUBLIC OVERSIGHT BOARD

Few organizations have had more impact on the profession's self-regulatory efforts than the Public Oversight Board (POB). The POB is a five-member autonomous monitoring mechanism that provides oversight of the SEC Practice Section of the AICPA Division for CPA Firms, meets about eight times per year (with at least one member attending every SEC Practice Section meeting), and performs two specific oversight functions:

- Oversees the peer reviews of each member firm (e.g., evaluates the review team's qualifications and experience, reads the peer review report and letter of comment, and reads the reviewed firm's response letter) and directly observes the peer review of many firms, particularly firms with five or more SEC clients, and
- Oversees all inquiries by the Quality Control Inquiry Committee into alleged audit failures.

In conjunction with these responsibilities, the POB issues periodic reports on the profession's self-regulatory effort and special reports. For example, in 1993, the POB issued a special report:

- *In the Public Interest: A Special Report by the Public Oversight Board of the SEC Practice Section of the AICPA.* Stamford, CT: POB (March 1993).

which addressed litigation, self-regulation, standards (both accounting and auditing), public confidence, and professional practice. In 1994, the POB issued:

- *Strengthening the Professionalism of the Independent Auditor.* Stamford, CT: POB (September 1994).

which addressed audit risk, information technology, and auditors' failure to report early warnings of impending financial doom. And in 1995, the POB issued:

- *Directors, Management, and Auditors: Allies in Protecting Shareholder Interests.* Stamford, CT: POB (1995).

which addressed a corporate governance approach to improved financial reporting.

Required: Select a recent Public Oversight Board release (POB, One Station Place, Stamford, CT 06902, 203-353-5300), and draft a report that:

1. Describes briefly the background of each board member (board member biographies are included in an appendix to each report),
2. Explains why you think each board member has a comparative advantage in serving the public interest, and

3. Describes—and gives your reaction to—the POB's conclusions and recommendations.

2. THE WORK OF ROBERT K. ELLIOTT

Robert K. Elliott, KPMG Peat Marwick partner and chair of the AICPA's *Special Committee on Assurance Services* (the Elliott Committee), has been quite influential in awakening the profession to the obsolescence of financial statement audits and to the need for innovative value-added assurance services. In the following series of insightful and accessible articles, he has highlighted the role of information technology in the creation of post-industrial wealth, and framed the scope of potential assurance services to replace financial statement audits as a dominant revenue source for major public accounting firms.

- Elliott, R. K. "The Third Wave Breaks on the Shores of Accounting," *Accounting Horizons* (June 1992), pp. 62-85.
- ——. "The Future of Audits," *Journal of Accountancy* (September 1994), pp. 74-82.
- ——. "Confronting the Future: Choices for the Attest Function," *Accounting Horizons* (September 1994), pp. 106-124.
- ——. "AICPA Assurance Services Committee: What is the Future of Auditing," *Journal of Corporate Accounting and Finance* (Winter 1994-95), pp. 87-97.
- ——. "The Future of Assurance Services: Implications for Academia," *Accounting Horizons* (December 1995), pp. 118-127.

The work of the Elliott Committee will likely be influential both in paving the way for new assurance services and in developing assurance standards.

Required:
1. From the articles listed, explain:
   a. The role of information technology on the reporting entity and on financial report users.
   b. Why financial statement audits may become obsolete and the demand for new assurances services will increase.
   c. The likely content of assurance standards.
2. Identify and summarize articles from the business and accounting press (e.g., *The Wall Street Journal, Accounting Today*) or from the accounting literature (e.g., *Journal of Accountancy, The CPA Journal*) that contradict Elliott. For example: R. Telberg. "CPAs Cautioned on Assurance Services," *Accounting Today* (Jan. 22-Feb. 11, 1996), pp. 1, 34.

3

Reports

Major topics discussed in this chapter are:

- Reports on assurance services.
- Reports on attestation services.
- Reports on financial statement audit services.

This chapter introduces carefully phrased written reports that explain the practitioner's findings but that avoid the allure of spin and persuasion. The chapter begins by introducing and illustrating reports on assurance services (Consumers Union) and on attestation services (equivalent subscribers to a cable TV stock purchase agreement). Next, the chapter introduces standard audit reports in the U.S. (Procter & Gamble), Japan (Hitachi Zosen Corporation), and Germany (Daimler Benz) and illustrates circumstances for which an auditor would modify a standard report, among them circumstances that affected reports issued for Deere & Company, GenCorp, Munsingwear, and the Public Service Company of Indiana. For example, what special reporting problems surface when management's financial statements depart materially from generally accepted accounting principles, or when an auditor doubts an entity's ability to continue as a going concern? The chapter concludes by discussing reports on comparative financial statements (Sony Corporation) and on financial statements used in a foreign country (Kubota Corporation).

REPORTS ON ASSURANCE SERVICES

Attestation and audit reports have been guided by standards of reporting since 1986 and 1949 (Chapter 2), respectively. However, assurance services have no generally accepted standards of reporting for at least two reasons. First, the profession does not have a long history of delivering assurance services. But a second reason is far more telling: Many assurance services have not traditionally required reports. For example, consider the time-honored assurance services offered by some firms for achievement award balloting, such as the Oscars, the New York theater's Tony Awards, the Chicago theater's Jefferson Awards, and some national book awards. In these among other cases, the assurer (the public accounting firm) is also the asserter and, by tradition, there is no report apart from winners' names inscribed within envelopes. For example, on Oscar night, celebrities open envelopes on stage and announce the winners to an audience that includes the board of the Academy of Motion

Pictures Arts & Sciences. In all attestation and audit engagements, the asserter—for example, management—is aware of the assertion long before a public accounting firm issues a report.

In contrast, another assurance provider, Consumers Union, introduced in Chapters 1 and 2, has been serving, and reporting to, the public since 1936. Consumers Union's *Buying Guides* and *Consumer Reports* each carry language that captures three concepts introduced in Chapter 2 as important to the *attestation standards* and *GAAS*: *independence* from product manufacturers, *due care* in rating the products tested, and *evidence* used to test and rate products. Figure 3-1 illustrates.

Consumers Union establishes *independence* from product manufacturers by accepting no advertising or sample products, and by purchasing all products tested. To achieve *due care*, products are tested at Consumers Union's National Research and Testing Center in Yonkers, New York, under laboratory conditions controlled to assure that procedures are alike for all products tested. There is a reasonable presumption that *evidence* is competent because the products tested are the products bought and because the measurement rules (rating scales) are not influenced by product manufacturers. Consumers Union

Figure 3-1:   Excerpts from an Assurance Report

Report to Readers

Consumers Union derives its income solely from the sale of CONSUMER REPORTS and other publications. In addition, expenses of occasional public service efforts may be met, in part, by nonrestrictive, noncommercial contributions, grants, and fees. Consumers Union accepts no advertising or product samples and is not beholden in any way to any commercial interest. Its Ratings and reports are solely for the use of the readers of its publications. Neither the Ratings, nor the reports, nor any Consumers Union publications, including this book, may be used in advertising or for any commercial purpose. Consumers Union will take all steps open to it to prevent such uses of its material, its name, or the name of CONSUMER REPORTS.

Independence Statements

CONSUMER REPORTS magazine is published monthly by Consumers Union, a nonprofit independent testing organization serving consumers. We are a comprehensive source for unbiased advice about products and services. Since 1936, our mission has been to test products, inform the public, and protect consumers.

We buy all the products we test.

We test products under controlled laboratory conditions.

We survey our millions of readers to bring you information on services and on the reliability of autos and major products.

We report on issues of consumer concern, bringing you information on matters that affect your health, money, and well-being.

We accept no ads from companies. Our income is derived from the sale of CONSUMER REPORTS and other services and from nonrestrictive, noncommercial contributions, grants, and fees. The ads in CONSUMER REPORTS and the BUYING GUIDE are for our other services, which share the same aims. We don't permit use of reports or Ratings for any commercial purpose. If that happens, we take whatever steps are open to us. Reproductions of CONSUMER REPORTS is forbidden without prior written permission (and never for commercial purposes).

does not operate under general, field work, and reporting standards prescribed by an authoritative body in quite the same way that certified public accountants operate under *attestation standards* and *GAAS* prescribed by the AICPA's Auditing Standards Board and Accounting and Review Services Committee. However, the concepts of independence, due care, and evidence are evident in the work of Consumers Union, and ought be in the assurance services of public accounting firms as well.

REPORTS ON ATTESTATION SERVICES

An **attestation report** is a letter communicating management's *written* assertion(s), management's and the attester's responsibilities, and the attester's opinion. Most attestation engagements result in a three-paragraph report that uses relatively standard language drawn from *Statement on Standards for Attestation Engagements (SSAE) No. 1,* "Attestation Standards."

UNQUALIFIED OPINION

An **unqualified opinion** in an attestation report means it is the independent attester's opinion that management's written assertions are presented fairly in all material respects in conformity with some established criteria. To illustrate, consider Figure 3-2, adapted from a Big Six firm's attestation report for a

Figure 3-2:   An Attestation Report

Report of the Independent Accountants

To the Partners of
Aspen Telecommunications Company

We have examined the accompanying schedule of number of equivalent subscribers (the Schedule) of Aspen Telecommunications Company, Limited Partnership, as of August 31, 1999, pursuant to Section 1.3(a) of the Stock Purchase Agreement by and among Richard Aspenarger, Charles Hardigan, and Joseph Petrie dated February 12, 1999, and amended by the First Amendment dated August 31, 1999 (the Agreement). Our examination was made in accordance with attestation standards established by the American Institute of Certified Public Accountants and, accordingly, included such procedures as we considered necessary in the circumstances. The Schedule and the assertions on which it is based are the responsibility of Aspen Telecommunications Company management. Our responsibility is to express an opinion on the Schedule based on our examination.

In our opinion, the Schedule presents, in all material respects, the number of equivalent subscribers of Aspen Telecommunications Company as of August 31, 1999 computed in accordance with the measurement criteria set forth in Note 2 to the Schedule.

This report is intended solely for the information and use of the partners of Aspen Telecommunications Company and should not be used for any other purpose.

Cheever & Yates, LLP
September 17, 1999

private cable television company organized as a limited partnership. The intuition underlying the engagement is that a cable television company's stock purchase agreement entitles three parties—Aspenarger, Hardigan, and Petrie—to purchase shares in a limited partnership at a price derived from the number of equivalent basic subscribers. Aspen Telecommunication's management has engaged a public accounting firm, Cheever & Yates, to attest to management's written assertion about the number of equivalent basic subscribers.

The *title*, "Report of the Independent Accountants," distinguishes the attester's report from management's schedule of the number of equivalent subscribers. The *addressee*, the partners of Aspen Telecommunications, is the party that hired Cheever & Yates and to whom the *closing paragraph* limits distribution of the report. The **introductory** (first) **paragraph** identifies the assertion attested to (the number of equivalent basic subscribers), and indicates both that the assertion is management's responsibility and that the attester is responsible only for an opinion on the assertion, not for the assertion. The **opinion** (second) **paragraph** explicitly conveys an unqualified opinion that the schedule presents, in all material respects, the number of basic equivalent subscribers. The engagement partner signs the firm's name (Cheever & Yates), not his or her own name, and dates the report as of *the last day of field work*, the date that the firm completed work in Aspen's office. Implicitly, the introductory, opinion, and closing paragraphs in an unqualified opinion convey to the reader that all eleven *attestation standards* (Figure 2-1) were followed without exception.

OTHER TYPES OF OPINIONS

In an attestation engagement, an unqualified opinion can be issued only if the engagement has complied with the *attestation standards* and management's assertion complies with established criteria, such as the stock purchase agreement in the Aspen Telecommunications engagement. However, departures from either the *attestation standards* and/or the established criteria require that the attester issue a qualified opinion, an adverse opinion, or disclaim an opinion. As summarized in Figure 3-3 both for attestation engagements and for audit engagements, a **qualified opinion** means that *except for* the effects of a matter, management's assertions are presented fairly in all material respects. An **adverse opinion**, in contrast, means that management's assertions

Figure 3-3: Types of Opinions

Opinion	Interpretation
Unqualified	Management's assertions (in an attestation) or financial statements (in an audit) are *presented fairly* in all material respects . . .
Qualified	*Except for* the effects of a matter, the assertion or financial statements are presented fairly . . .
Adverse	The assertion or financial statements *do not present fairly* . . .
Disclaimer of Opinion	The attester or auditor *does not express an opinion* . . .

are *not* presented fairly. And a **disclaimer of opinion** means that the attester or auditor does not express an opinion, usually because there is insufficient evidence. All three types of opinion are illustrated below for audit engagements, but the intuition underlying each is transportable to attestation engagements as well.

REPORTS ON FINANCIAL STATEMENT AUDITS

An **audit report** is a letter communicating what was audited, management's and the auditor's responsibilities, what an audit entails, and the auditor's opinion. Most financial statement audits result in a three-paragraph **standard report** that uses uniform language stating that, in the auditor's opinion, management's financial statements present fairly, in all material respects, financial position, results of operations, and cash flows in conformity with generally accepted accounting principles (GAAP). The language in standard reports was first standardized in a 1934 pamphlet, "Audits of Corporate Reports," by George O. May, Price Waterhouse senior partner and chair of the American Institute of Accountants' (today's AICPA) *Committee on Cooperation with Stock Exchanges.* In 1949, following adoption of the ten *generally accepted auditing standards (GAAS:* Chapter 2), the AICPA revised the language to incorporate an explicit reference to standards.

Although the standard report remained essentially unchanged from 1949 to 1988, it was not without critics, among them Congress, the SEC, and the *Commission on Auditors' Responsibilities,* all of whom concluded the language was ambiguous, confusing, and a poor portrayal of the responsibilities assumed by an independent auditor. Partly in response to hearings conducted by the House *Subcommittee on Oversight and Investigations* in the 1980s, the Auditing Standards Board in 1988 reconsidered and revised the language of a standard audit report in *Statement on Auditing Standards No. 58,* "Reports on Audited Financial Statements" (AU Sec. 508). The following introduces today's standard report.

UNQUALIFIED OPINION

A standard audit report gives an unqualified opinion, which means it is the independent auditor's opinion that management's financial statements present fairly in all material respects the financial position, results of operations, and cash flows in conformity with generally accepted accounting principles (GAAP). To issue an unqualified opinion, the auditor must comply with *generally accepted auditing standards.* A departure from *GAAS* (or from GAAP) would preclude an unqualified opinion.

An unqualified opinion relates only to an entity's financial statements, not to the quality of the entity as an investment or credit risk. For example, a company experiencing a net loss and negative cash flows might prove a poor investment or credit risk, but if an audit reveals that the financial statements conform with GAAP, the auditor would issue an unqualified opinion. Figure 3-4 illustrates Deloitte & Touche's three-paragraph, unqualified opinion for The Procter & Gamble Company, and Figure 3-5 lists the report's basic elements.

Figure 3-4: Financial Statement Audit Report

Report of the Independent Accountants

To the Board of Directors and Shareholders of
The Procter & Gamble Company

We have audited the accompanying consolidated balance sheets of The Procter &
Gamble Company and subsidiaries as of June 30, 1996 and 1995, and the related
consolidated statements of earnings, retained earnings, and cash flows for each of
the three years in the period ended June 30, 1996. These financial statements are the
responsibility of the companies' management. Our responsibility is to express an
opinion on these financial statements based on our audits.

We conducted our audits in accordance with generally accepted auditing standards.
Those standards require that we plan and perform the audits to obtain reasonable
assurance about whether the financial statements are free of material misstatement.
An audit includes examining, on a test basis, evidence supporting the amounts and
disclosures in the financial statements. An audit also includes assessing the accounting principles used and significant estimates made by management, as well as
evaluating the overall financial statement presentation. We believe that our audits
provide a reasonable basis for our opinion.

In our opinion, the financial statements referred to above present fairly, in all
material respects, the financial position of the companies at June 30, 1996 and 1995,
and the results of their operations and their cash flows for each of the three years
in the period ended June 30, 1996, in conformity with generally accepted accounting
principles.

Deloitte & Touche
August 13, 1996

TITLE

The title "Report of the Independent Accountants" is included largely to distinguish an auditor's report on the financial statements from management's
accompanying financial statements, and from management's statement of
responsibility, a report that often appears on the same page as—or the page
facing—the auditor's report in an annual report to shareholders. Figure 3-6
illustrates The Procter & Gamble Company's statement of responsibility for the
financial statements. Deloitte & Touche takes no responsibility for management's
report, since the report is not part of Procter & Gamble's financial statements.

ADDRESSEE

An auditor's report for a corporation is commonly addressed to the shareholders, to the board of directors, or to both, as in the Procter & Gamble report
(Figure 3-4). Management is rarely included among the addressees, thereby
underscoring the auditor's independence from management. A report for an
unincorporated entity may be addressed to the partners, the general partners,
or the proprietor; and a report for a governmental entity may be addressed
to the taxpayers or to an oversight body such as a city council or town board.

Occasionally, an auditor is engaged by one entity to audit the financial
statements of another entity (for example, when a company contemplates

Figure 3-5: Elements of a Standard Audit Report

Opening
- A *title* that includes the word "independent."
- The *addressees*.

Introductory Paragraph
- A statement that the *financial statements were audited*.
- A statement that the financial statements are *management's responsibility*, and that the *auditor's responsibility* is to express an opinion.

Scope Paragraph
- A statement that the audit was conducted in accordance with *generally accepted auditing standards*.
- A statement that generally accepted auditing standards require planning and performing the audit to obtain *reasonable assurance* about whether the financial statements are *free of material misstatement*.
- A statement that an *audit includes:* (1) examining evidence on a test basis, (2) evaluating the accounting principles and significant estimates used by management, and (3) evaluating the overall financial statement presentation.

Opinion Paragraph
- A statement of *opinion* on whether the financial statements present fairly in all material respects the financial position, results of operations, and cash flows in conformity with generally accepted accounting principles.

Closing
- The *firm's signature*.
- The *date* of the auditor's report.

purchasing the audited company), in which case the auditor's report is generally addressed to the potential purchaser rather than to the entity whose statements were audited. Parties named as addressees do not necessarily enjoy exclusive legal rights against an auditor in the event of an audit failure, since other third parties, such as creditors, may also have a legal claim against the

Figure 3-6: Management's Statement of Responsibility

The financial statements of The Procter & Gamble Company and its subsidiaries are the responsibility of, and have been prepared by, the Company, in accordance with generally accepted accounting principles. To help assure the accuracy and integrity of its financial data, the Company has developed and maintains internal accounting controls that are designed to provide reasonable assurances that transactions are executed as authorized and accurately recorded, and that assets are properly safeguarded. These controls are monitored by an extensive program of internal audits.

The financial statements have been audited by the Company's independent public accountants, Deloitte & Touche.

The Board of Directors has an Audit Committee composed entirely of outside Directors. The Committee meets periodically with representatives of Deloitte & Touche and financial management to review accounting, control, auditing, and financial reporting matters. To help assure the independence of the public accountants, Deloitte & Touche regularly meets privately with the Audit Committee.

auditor (Chapter 5), even though they are not named as addressees in the auditor's report.

INTRODUCTORY PARAGRAPH

The introductory paragraph identifies the financial statements audited (typically the balance sheet and statements of earnings, retained earnings, and cash flows), and indicates that the statements are management's, not the auditor's, responsibility. The independent auditor is responsible only to express an opinion on the statements, not for the assertions within the statements. Thus, apart from identifying the statements audited, the role of the introductory paragraph is to differentiate management's responsibility (for the financial statements) from the auditor's responsibility (to express *an opinion* on management's financial statements). Although auditors customarily report on two years for nonpublicly traded companies, note that The Procter & Gamble Company report applies to three years, an SEC requirement for publicly held companies.

SCOPE PARAGRAPH

The scope paragraph states that the engagement complied with *GAAS* and describes briefly what an audit entails. The description uses several critical terms: reasonable assurance, free of material misstatement, and test basis, although *reasonable assurance* is the glue that holds all three together. Recall from Chapter 2 (Figure 2-1) that the third standard of field work states that an auditor should obtain "sufficient competent evidential matter . . . to afford a *reasonable basis* for an opinion . . ." Because an audit need provide only a reasonable (rather than an absolute) basis for an opinion, the scope paragraph implies that the auditor may overlook immaterial misstatements and tests samples, rather than the entire population of transactions and events underlying the financial statements. A standard scope paragraph can be used in practice when the auditor complies with each of the general and field work standards, suggesting the paragraph can be interpreted to mean:

Compliance with General Standards
The auditor:
- Was *adequately trained* and *proficient*,
- Maintained an *independence* in mental attitude, and
- Exercised *due professional care* when performing the audit and preparing the report.

Compliance with Field Work Standards
The auditor:
- *Planned* the engagement and *supervised* assistants,
- Obtained an *understanding of internal control* sufficient to plan the audit and to determine the nature, timing, and extent of audit tests, and
- Obtained *sufficient competent evidential matter* to afford a reasonable basis for an opinion on the financial statements.

Each statement must be true, without qualification, for an auditor to use the wording of a standard scope paragraph. If not, the scope paragraph is modified. Examples of departures from the wording of a standard scope paragraph are presented later in the chapter.

OPINION PARAGRAPH

The opinion paragraph appears after the scope paragraph. Like the unqualified opinion illustrated for The Procter & Gamble Company (Figure 3-4), the opinion paragraph states that the financial statements present fairly, in all material respects, the entity's financial position, results of operations, and cash flows in conformity with GAAP. When one or more prior period financial statements are presented with current period statements, both the introductory and opinion paragraphs include a reference to all prior periods. For example, The Procter & Gamble report draws attention to the 1995 financial statements even though 1996 is the current year audited. The terms *audit report* and *audit opinion* are sometimes used interchangeably, but *report* refers to the entire three paragraphs (and to the title, signature, and date) and *opinion* refers to the opinion paragraph only.

Just as the wording of a standard scope paragraph implies compliance with the general and field work standards, the wording of a standard opinion paragraph implies compliance with all four reporting standards. Thus, a standard opinion paragraph can be interpreted as follows:

Compliance with Reporting Standards
- The financial statements are *presented in accordance with GAAP.*
- Accounting principles are applied *consistently.*
- Informative *disclosures* are reasonably adequate.
- The *opinion* applies to the financial statements taken as a whole.

Each of these statements must be true, without qualification, for an auditor to use the wording of a standard opinion paragraph. However, when an opinion is based partly on the report of another auditor (for example, when one firm audits a parent company and another audits a subsidiary) or when an auditor emphasizes a matter within the report, an explanatory paragraph may be added to the standard report without distorting or detracting from the meaning of an unqualified opinion. These and other examples of departures from the wording of a standard opinion paragraph are presented later in the chapter.

Prior to the mid-1970s, auditors sometimes issued *piecemeal opinions*: reports that gave an opinion on selected accounts, but disclaimed an opinion on the financial statements taken as a whole. Piecemeal opinions were issued, for example, when scope limitations precluded auditing some accounts, such as Inventory or Accounts Receivable. However, piecemeal opinions overlook the fact that many accounts are related (for example, the *debit* sides of Receivables and Cash and the *credit* side of Sales all figure in a credit sale transaction), and none are wholly independent. As a result, *SAS No. 58*, "Reports on Audited Financial Statements" (AU Sec. 508), reiterated a long-standing prohibition against issuing piecemeal opinions under any circumstances. However, *SAS No. 58* does not prohibit auditors from issuing an opinion on an individual financial statement, such as a balance sheet or an income statement.

SIGNATURE

An audit report is signed by the engagement partner, but in the name of his or her firm. For example, the engagement partner signed "Deloitte & Touche" in the Procter & Gamble Company report, not his or her own name.

REPORT DATE

An audit report is dated as of the *last day of field work*. For example, in Figure 3-4, the Procter & Gamble report is dated August 13, 1996 because field work for the June 30, 1996 engagement was completed on August 13. Deloitte & Touche likely completed other work in their own offices after August 13 (for example, assembling working papers, drafting the report) and may not have issued the report until later in August. Nevertheless, the report is dated August 13, because the last day of field work is the last date on which the firm is responsible for detecting *subsequent events* (Chapter 17)—material events occurring between July 1, 1996 and August 13, 1996 that would require disclosure in the June 30 financial statements.

On occasion, a material subsequent event may occur, and come to an auditor's attention, after the last day of field work but before the report is released—for example, August 27, 1996 in the case of Procter & Gamble. If the financial statements are revised to disclose a subsequent event, the auditor has two alternatives for dating the report:

- *Dual date*. August 13, 1996, except for Note X, August 27, 1995.
- *Event date*. August 27, 1996.

Dual dating extends an auditor's responsibility beyond the last day of field work (from August 13 to August 27), but only for the event disclosed. In contrast, dating as of the subsequent event (August 27) extends the auditor's responsibility to *all* events occurring on or before August 27, even those unknown to the auditor.

UNQUALIFIED OPINIONS IN OTHER COUNTRIES

Cultural differences in foreign countries create some barriers to U.S. entrepreneurship overseas. For example, although bribes are common in some countries, the U.S. *Foreign Corrupt Practices Act (FCPA)* prohibits U.S. companies from unlawfully influencing foreign governments, thereby placing U.S. companies at a disadvantage competing for foreign business and some foreign countries at a disadvantage attracting U.S. capital. Likewise, cultural differences have driven different accounting standards, and different audit reports, across countries. For example, like U.S. auditors, Japanese auditors are guided by private sector accounting standards, but German auditors are guided largely by commercial law.

Figure 3-7 reproduces the standard unqualified audit report issued by a Japanese firm and by a German firm. The Ashi & Co. report for the Hitachi Zosen Corporation refers to generally accepted auditing standards and to generally accepted accounting principles, and renders an "opinion" that, like the U.S. report, uses the term "present fairly." In contrast, the KPMG Deutsche report for Daimler Benz also refers to generally accepted accounting principles but, consistent with a European Union directive on company accounts, uses the term "true and fair view," rather than "present fairly." Interestingly, prior to World War II, Japan's audit reports were more like German reports but, since the war, are now more like U.S. reports. Some differences across countries are real (e.g., the *FCPA*) and others are imagined (e.g., present fairly v. true and fair), but all point to a need for harmonization, given that the capital markets are now largely global. To that end, the SEC has worked with the

Figure 3-7: Standard Audit Reports in Foreign Countries

Japan

Hitachi Zosen Corporation
Ashi & Co., CPAs

We have examined the accompanying consolidated balance sheets of Hitachi Zosen Corporation and its consolidated subsidiaries at 31st March, 1995 and 1996, and the related consolidated statements of income and shareholders' equity for the years then ended, all expressed in Japanese yen. Our examinations were made in accordance with generally accepted auditing standards in Japan and, accordingly, included such tests of the accounting records and such other auditing procedures as we considered necessary in the circumstances.

In our opinion, the accompanying consolidated financial statements mentioned above, expressed in yen, present fairly the financial position of Hitachi Zosen Corporation and its consolidated subsidiaries at 31st March, 1995 and 1996, and the results of their operations for the years then ended, in conformity with generally accepted accounting principles in Japan applied on a consistent basis.

We have also reviewed the translation of the financial statements mentioned into U.S. dollars on the basis described in Note 1. In our opinion, such statements have been properly translated on such basis.

Germany

Daimler Benz
KPMG Deutsche Treuhand-Gesellschaft

We rendered an unqualified opinion on the consolidated financial statements and the business review report in accordance with Section 322 HGB (German Commercial Code). The translation of our opinion reads as follows:

"The consolidated financial statements, which we have audited in accordance with professional standards, comply with the legal provisions. With due regard to the generally accepted accounting principles, the consolidated financial statements give a true and fair view of the assets, liabilities, financial position and results of operations of the Daimler-Benz group. The business review report, which summarizes the state of affairs of Daimler-Benz Aktiengesellschaft and that of the group, is consistent with the financial statements of Daimler-Benz Aktiengesellschaft and the consolidated financial statements."

International Federation of Accountants and with the International Organization of Securities Commissioners to harmonize accounting standards and auditing standards.

OTHER TYPES OF OPINIONS

In an audit engagement, an unqualified opinion can be issued only if the audit has complied with *GAAS* and the financial statements comply with GAAP. Similar to attestation engagements, departures from *GAAS* and/or GAAP in an audit engagement require that an auditor issue either a qualified or an adverse opinion, or disclaim an opinion. Each is described briefly here and illustrated in the next section of the chapter. Figure 3-3 summarizes the meaning of unqualified (discussed previously), qualified, and adverse opinions, and disclaimers of opinion.

Qualified Opinion

A qualified opinion means that *except for* the effects of a matter, management's financial statements present fairly in all material respects financial position, results of operations, and cash flows in conformity with GAAP. Only the term *except for* or some variation—such as *except, exception,* or *with the exception of*— may be used to qualify an opinion. Qualified opinions are issued when financial statements depart materially from GAAP, when management is unable to justify a material change in accounting principles, or when the scope of an audit is limited materially.

Adverse Opinion

An adverse opinion means management's financial statements *do not* present fairly in all material respects the financial position, results of operations, and cash flows in conformity with GAAP. Adverse opinions are issued either when financial statements depart from GAAP or when management is unable to justify an accounting change, *and* the effect of the departure or change is so highly material that a qualified opinion is unwarranted.

Disclaimer of Opinion

A disclaimer of opinion means an auditor does not express an opinion on the financial statements. Generally, disclaimers are issued when the effects of a scope limitation are so highly material that the auditor does not have a reasonable basis to reach an opinion. An auditor also issues a disclaimer when he or she is not independent of management. Note carefully the difference between a disclaimer of opinion and an adverse opinion: An auditor disclaims when he or she does not have sufficient evidence to reach an opinion—for example, when the scope of an audit is limited by the client—and issues an adverse opinion when sufficient evidence is available to conclude that the financial statements are not presented fairly.

EXPLANATORY PARAGRAPHS AND MODIFICATIONS TO STANDARD REPORTS

Auditors in the U.S. add an explanatory paragraph, or otherwise modify the wording of standard reports, for the circumstances listed in Figure 3-8. For many of the circumstances, the type of opinion required depends on whether the effect of the circumstance is material or highly material. Figure 3-9 summarizes the report modifications required for each of the circumstances listed in Figure 3-8. Each circumstance is discussed and illustrated in the following sections.

OPINION BASED PARTLY ON THE REPORT OF ANOTHER AUDITOR

In practice, the audit of a geographically diverse company may necessitate that an auditor rely partly on the report of another auditor. For example, an East Coast, local public accounting firm might rely on a West Coast firm to report on the financial statements of a wholly owned, west coast subsidiary. Relying on another firm's report does not necessarily preclude an auditor from issuing an unqualified opinion for the combined statements, although it could if the other firm's opinion were qualified, adverse, or a disclaimer.

Figure 3-8: Modifications to Standard Reports

- *Another Auditor.* The auditor's opinion is based in part on the report of another auditor.
- *Emphasize a Matter.* The auditor wishes to emphasize a matter about the financial statements.
- *Departure from GAAP.* The financial statements are affected by a departure from generally accepted accounting principles.
- *Inconsistency.* Accounting principles have not been applied consistently.
- *Scope Limitation.* The scope of the audit is affected by conditions that preclude applying one or more necessary auditing procedures.
- *Going Concern.* The auditor has substantial doubt about an entity's ability to continue as a going concern.
- *Lack of Independence.* The auditor is not independent of the entity.

Figure 3-9: Modifications to the Wording of Standard Reports

Circumstance	Material	Highly Material	Paragraph(s) Modified	Explanatory Paragraph
Opinion Based Partly on Another Auditor	Unqualified	Unqualified	Introductory/ Opinion (optional)	No
Emphasize a Matter	Unqualified	Unqualified	—	Yes
Departure from GAAP	Qualified	Adverse	Opinion	Yes
Inconsistency: Management Justifies	Unqualified	Unqualified	—	Yes
Management Does Not Justify	Qualified	Adverse	Opinion	Yes
Scope Limitation	Qualified	—	Scope/ Opinion	Yes
	—	Disclaimer	Introductory/ Opinion (Omit Scope)	Yes
Going Concern	Unqualified	Unqualified	—	Yes
Lack of Independence	Disclaimer	Disclaimer	Omit Introductory, Scope, Opinion	Yes

When an opinion is based partly on the report of another auditor, the auditors must decide who is the **principal auditor**, considering factors such as (AU Sec. 543):

- The *materiality* of the financial statements audited by each auditor,
- The extent of each auditor's *knowledge of the overall financial statements*, and
- The significance of the financial statements audited in relation to the *combined entity taken as a whole.*

The principal auditor is responsible to report on the combined financial statements, but must decide whether to refer in his or her report to the other auditor's work. When no reference is made to another auditor's work, the principal auditor takes full responsibility. However, if the principal auditor shares responsibility, his or her audit report refers to the other auditor's work (though not typically to the other auditor's name) and clearly indicates the division of responsibility, sometimes by disclosing the assets and revenues audited by the other auditor.

For example, KPMG Peat Marwick, principal auditor of Gold Kist Inc., shared responsibility with another firm that audited Golden Peanut Company, an equity investment. KPMG Peat Marwick issued an unqualified opinion on the consolidated financial statements taken as a whole, but shared responsibility in the introductory and opinion paragraphs, as illustrated below:

Gold Kist Inc.
KPMG Peat Marwick

(Introductory Paragraph)
. . . Our responsibility is to express an opinion on these consolidated financial statements and financial statement schedules based on our audits. We did not audit the consolidated financial statements of Golden Peanut Company, a partnership investment accounted for using the equity method of accounting, as described in Note 9(b) to the consolidated financial statements. The consolidated financial statements of Golden Peanut Company were audited by other auditors whose reports have been furnished to us, and our opinion, insofar as it relates to the amounts included for Golden Peanut Company, is based solely on the report of the other auditors.

(Opinion Paragraph)
In our opinion, based on our audits and the report of the other auditors. . . , the consolidated financial statements present fairly, in all material respects, the financial position of Gold Kist Inc. . . .

EMPHASIS ON A MATTER

An auditor may emphasize a matter and still issue an unqualified opinion. For example, on March 24, 1994, Memorex Telex, emerged from bankruptcy and accounted for the effects of the reorganization under AICPA *Statement of Position 90-7*, "Financial Reporting by Entities in Reorganization Under the Bankruptcy Code." Ernst & Young emphasized the matter in an explanatory paragraph, but made no changes to the standard introductory, scope, or opinion paragraphs:

Memorex Telex N.V.
Ernst & Young

(Explanatory Paragraph)

As more fully described in Note 1 to the consolidated financial statements, effective March 24, 1994, the Company emerged from protection under Chapter 11 of the Federal Bankruptcy Code to a Prepackaged Plan of Reorganization which was confirmed by the Bankruptcy Court on March 14, 1994. In accordance with an AICPA Statement of Position, the Company adopted "Fresh Start Reporting" whereby its assets, liabilities, and new capital structure were adjusted to reflect fair values as of March 31, 1994. As a result, the consolidated balance sheet as of March 31, 1994 reflects the successor Company's new basis of accounting and, accordingly, is not comparable to the predecessor Company's pre-reorganization balance sheet.

DEPARTURE FROM GAAP

When management's financial statements depart materially from an accounting principle promulgated in an official pronouncement, such as an FASB or GASB statement, Rule 202 of the AICPA's *Code of Professional Conduct* (Chapter 4) prohibits an unqualified opinion, unless the auditor can demonstrate that, owing to rare and unusual circumstances, complying with the pronouncement would actually cause the financial statements to be misleading—for example, when a long-standing pronouncement is applied to a new industry. In those circumstances—which are both rare (with a capital *R*) and unusual (capital *U*)—the auditor issues an unqualified opinion and explains the departure, the approximate effects on the financial statements, and why compliance with the pronouncement would necessarily mislead readers. In practice, departures from GAAP arise typically when disclosures are inadequate or when management applies accounting principles inappropriately and, depending on materiality, result in a qualified or an adverse opinion.

Qualified Opinion

A material departure from GAAP requires an explanatory paragraph to disclose the misstatement and a modified opinion paragraph, but no change to the introductory or scope paragraphs. To illustrate, consider Arthur Andersen's report for the Union Bank, which, rather than record goodwill as an asset (to be amortized), charged goodwill to shareholders' equity:

Union Bank
Arthur Andersen

(Explanatory Paragraph)

As discussed in Note 2 to the financial statements, the Bank has charged goodwill to shareholders' equity. GAAP require that goodwill be recorded as an asset and amortized to expense over future periods.

(Opinion Paragraph)

In our opinion, except for the effects of the accounting treatment for goodwill as discussed in the preceding paragraph, the financial statements referred to above present fairly . . .

Research has reported several interesting findings about qualified opinions. First, companies that receive qualified opinions switch audit firms more frequently than companies that don't, but not necessarily to firms with a history of issuing proportionately fewer qualified opinions.[1] Second, in some cases, publicly available financial data (e.g., ratios) and market data (e.g., stock prices) can predict which companies will receive qualified opinions for the first time.[2] Third, a study in Australia revealed that qualified opinions were associated with delays in the issuance of corporate annual reports—the more serious the qualification, the longer the delay.[3]

ADVERSE OPINION

A departure from GAAP may be so highly material as to require an adverse opinion that includes one or more explanatory paragraphs. To illustrate, assume that a company carries Property, Plant, and Equipment at appraisal values, rather than historical costs:

(Explanatory Paragraphs)

As discussed in Note C to the financial statements, the Company carries property, plant, and equipment at appraisal values, and provides depreciation on the basis of such values. Generally accepted accounting principles require that property, plant, and equipment be stated at an amount not in excess of cost, reduced by depreciation, and that deferred income taxes be provided.

Because of the departure from generally accepted accounting principles identified above, as of December 31, 1999 and 1998, inventories have been increased $ _____ and $ _____ by inclusion in manufacturing overhead of depreciation in excess of that based on cost; property, plant, and equipment, less accumulated depreciation, is carried at $ _____ and $ _____ in excess of an amount based on the cost to the Company; and deferred income taxes of $ _____ and $ _____ have not been recorded; resulting in an increase of $ _____ and $ _____ in retained earnings and in appraisal surplus of $ _____ and $ _____, respectively. For the years ended December 31, 1999 and 1998, cost of goods sold has been increased $ _____ and $ _____, respectively, because the effects of depreciation accounting and deferred income taxes of $ _____ and $ _____ have not been provided, resulting in an increase in net income of $ _____ and $ _____, respectively.

(Opinion Paragraph)

In our opinion, because of the effects of the matter discussed in the preceding paragraphs, the financial statements referred to above do not present fairly . . .

INCONSISTENCY

If a newly adopted accounting principle is generally accepted and management justifies the change, an unqualified opinion is quite appropriate. For example,

1   C. Chow, and S. Rice, "Qualified Audit Opinions and Auditor Switching," *The Accounting Review* (April 1982), pp. 326-335.
2   N. Dopuch, R. Holthausen, and R. Leftwich. "Predicting Audit Qualifications with Financial and Market Variables," *The Accounting Review* (July 1987), pp. 431-454.
3   G. Whittred. "Audit Qualification and the Timeliness of Corporate Annual Reports," *The Accounting Review* (October 1980), pp. 563-577.

Deloitte & Touche reported in an explanatory paragraph that Deere & Company, like many other companies, had changed its method of accounting for postretirement benefits other than pensions, a change driven by the company's adopting *Statement of Financial Accounting Standards No. 106*, "Employers' Accounting for Postretirement Benefits Other than Pensions." The explanatory paragraph appeared after the opinion paragraph, largely because the matter explained did not drive a qualification and, therefore, was not prefatory to the opinion paragraph:

Deere & Company
Deloitte & Touche

(Explanatory Paragraph)
As discussed in the summary of significant accounting policies, the Company changed its accounting for postretirement benefits other than pensions.

However, a qualified or an adverse opinion is required if a newly adopted accounting principle is not generally accepted, if the accounting for the effect of the change departs from GAAP, or if management has not sufficiently justified the reason for the change. The opinion issued—qualified or adverse—depends on the materiality of the effect of the change.

Qualified Opinion

An opinion qualified for inconsistency requires an explanatory paragraph and a modified opinion paragraph, but no change to the introductory or scope paragraphs. For example, the Public Service Company of Indiana, Inc. accounted for revenues and pensions inconsistently. Arthur Andersen's modified opinion paragraph follows:

Public Service Company of Indiana, Inc.
Arthur Andersen

(Opinion Paragraph)
. . . present fairly the financial position, results of operations, changes in common stock equity and cash flows . . . in conformity with generally accepted accounting principles which, except for the effects of accounting for revenues and for pension costs, as more fully discussed in Note 4 and Note 10, respectively, were applied on a consistent basis.

Interestingly, research has found that stock price behavior does not differ significantly between companies that do and do not receive audit opinions qualified for inconsistency, suggesting that, although required, qualifications for inconsistency may not carry significant information to the capital markets.[4]

Adverse Opinion

Inconsistency may have such a highly material effect on an entity's financial statements that an adverse opinion is required. The adverse opinion requires

---

4   H. F. Mittlestaedt, P. Regier, E. Chewning, and K. Pany. "Do Consistency Modifications Provide Information to Equity Markets?" *Auditing: A Journal of Practice & Theory* (Spring 1992), pp. 83-98.

no reference in the introductory or scope paragraphs, an explanatory paragraph that discloses all substantive reasons for the opinion and the principal effects of the change, and an adverse opinion paragraph.

Continuing the previous example, assume the inconsistent accounting for revenues and pensions is so material to the Public Service Company's financial statements, that Arthur Andersen issues an adverse opinion. Although the explanatory paragraph (not illustrated) would not change, an adverse opinion paragraph would be presented, as illustrated earlier for departures from GAAP.

SCOPE LIMITATION

The scope of a financial statement audit is limited when conditions preclude an auditor from gathering evidence. Limitations may result from client-imposed restrictions, missing documents, inadequate record keeping, or when an auditor is engaged after the balance sheet date. Material scope limitations that preclude the application of one or more necessary auditing procedures ordinarily result in a qualified opinion or a disclaimer of opinion.

Qualified Opinion

Opinions qualified for scope limitations require no change to the introductory paragraph, a modified scope paragraph, an explanatory paragraph, and a modified opinion paragraph. To illustrate, consider the report Wilson, Haig & Co. issued for Advanced Monitoring Systems, Inc., a company that had not provided evidence relating to a material contingent liability. Modified scope and opinion paragraphs, and an explanatory paragraph, follow:

Advanced Monitoring Systems, Inc.
Wilson, Haig & Co.

(Scope Paragraph)
Except as discussed in the following paragraph, we conducted our audit . . .

(Explanatory Paragraph)
We were unable to obtain evidential matter supporting the Company's representations regarding the contingent liability as discussed in Note 8 to the consolidated financial statements.

(Opinion Paragraph)
In our opinion, except for the effects of such adjustments, if any, as might have been determined to be necessary had a response from the Company's legal counsel been obtained, the consolidated financial statements referred to above present fairly . . .

Disclaimer of Opinion

A scope limitation may be so highly material as to require a disclaimer of opinion. Disclaimers for scope limitations require a modified introductory paragraph, omission of the standard scope paragraph, an explanatory paragraph explaining why the audit did not comply with GAAP, and a paragraph explaining that the scope of the audit was not sufficient to warrant an opinion. For example, consider Arthur Andersen's explanatory and closing paragraphs for Sunshine Jr. Stores, a Florida company that filed for bankruptcy:

Sunshine Jr. Stores
Arthur Andersen

(Explanatory Paragraph)

The Company did not give effect to all adjustments to the carrying value of assets and classification of liabilities that might be necessary as a consequence of bankruptcy proceedings.

(Closing Paragraph)

Because of the possible material effect of the matters discussed in the preceding paragraphs, we are unable to express, and we do not express, an opinion on the financial statements referred to above. Our audits were made for the purpose of forming an opinion on the basic financial statements taken as a whole.

CONSIDERING AN ENTITY'S ABILITY TO CONTINUE AS A GOING CONCERN

The opinion paragraph of a standard audit report acknowledges GAAP, and one of the principles specific to GAAP is that financial statements be prepared assuming an entity is a going concern. But the going concern assumption is sometimes suspect for financially distressed companies that are unable to continue meeting obligations without disposing of assets or restructuring debt. As a result, *Statement on Auditing Standards No. 59*, "The Auditor's Consideration of an Entity's Ability to Continue as a Going Concern" (AU Sec. 341), requires that an auditor evaluate on every audit whether there is substantial doubt about an entity's ability to continue as a going concern. The evaluation is made for a reasonable period of time into the future, not to exceed one year beyond the date of the financial statements, and is based on the results of audit procedures performed normally, not on procedures designed to reveal financial distress. For example, inquiry of an entity's lawyer about litigation, claims, and assessments (Chapter 17) may reveal that a client has lost a judgment for substantial uninsured claims that, in the aggregate, raise serious questions about the going concern assumption. Other evidence gathered in the normal course of an audit may raise doubts as well—for example, recurring operating losses, working capital deficiencies, loan defaults, denial of credit from suppliers, work stoppages, loss of key management, and loss of principal customers or suppliers.

When evidence raises substantial doubt about continued existence, the auditor considers management's plans to alleviate the problem and whether the plans can be implemented. For example, if management plans to raise resources by disposing of some assets, the auditor should consider the apparent marketability of the assets, possible effects on operations, and whether there are restrictions on disposing of the assets, such as loan covenants or encumbrances. After considering management's plans and other evidence, an auditor may conclude that he or she does not have substantial doubt about the entity's ability to continue as a going concern. In that case, the auditor considers the need to disclose in the financial statements the principal conditions that gave rise to doubt, but would not modify the standard audit report. However, if substantial doubt remains, the auditor considers the recoverability and classification of recorded assets and the amounts and classification of liabilities, and modifies the report by adding an explanatory paragraph after the opinion paragraph. (The opinion paragraph is not modified, since an unqualified opinion remains appropriate.) To illustrate, consider Ernst & Young's report for the First Republic Corporation, which had experienced recurring losses and a net capital deficiency. Ernst & Young's explanatory paragraph follows:

First Republic Corporation
Ernst & Young

(Explanatory Paragraph)

The accompanying financial statements have been prepared assuming that the Company will continue as a going concern. As discussed in Note Q to the financial statements, the Company incurred recurring operating losses and has a net capital deficiency, which established a significant doubt about its capacity to continue as a going concern. The financial statements do not include any adjustments that might result from the outcome of this uncertainty.

Although a report modified for substantial doubt is *not* a prediction of bankruptcy, research suggests the modification may reduce some of the surprise in bankruptcy filings. For example, research reveals that modifications may increase investors' expected probability of financial failure,[5] may be useful in predicting bankruptcy (although, as stated previously, bankruptcy prediction is not the intent of a modification),[6] and may be somewhat useful in predicting bankruptcy resolution.[7] In addition, reports modified for substantial doubt may also be useful in explaining stock market reaction to bankruptcy filings. For example, a study reports that bankrupt companies which had received substantial doubt modifications experienced lower share price declines than bankrupt companies that did not receive substantial doubt modifications.[8]

The generalizeability of the results of the research cited above to the reports issued today under *SAS No. 59* is not clear, because much of the research studied audit reports issued prior to the effective date of *SAS No. 59*, which altered the language of going concern reports. However, one study[9] examined audit reports issued both before and after *SAS No. 59*, and found that auditors were more likely to issue modified reports *after SAS No. 59* than they had been before, suggesting that the Auditing Standards Board had been successful in responding to what motivated *SAS No. 59*: the financial community's call for early warnings of impending financial doom.

---

5   J. Campbell, and J. Mutchler. "The 'Expectations Gap' and Going-Concern Uncertainties," *Accounting Horizons* (March 1988), pp. 42-49.

6   W. Hopwood, J. McKeown, and J. Mutchler. "A Reexamination of Auditor Versus Model Accuracy Within the Context of the Going-Concern Opinion Decision," *Contemporary Accounting Research* (Spring 1994), pp. 409-432; W. Hopwood, J. McKeown, and J. Mutchler. "A Test of the Incremental Explanatory Power of Opinions," *The Accounting Review* (January 1989), pp. 28-48.

7   D. Kennedy, and W. Shaw. "Evaluating Financial Distress Resolution Using Prior Audit Opinions," *Contemporary Accounting Research* (Fall 1991), pp. 97-114.

8   K. Chen, and B. Church. "Going Concern Opinions and the Market's Reaction to Bankruptcy Filings," *The Accounting Review* (January 1996), pp. 117-128.

9   K. Raghunandan, and D. Rama. "Audit Reports for Companies in Financial Distress: Before and After *SAS No. 59*," *Auditing: A Journal of Practice & Theory* (Spring 1995), pp. 50-63.

LACK OF INDEPENDENCE

Statement on Auditing Standards No. 26, "Association with Financial Statements" (AU Sec. 504), requires a disclaimer of opinion when an auditor lacks independence, even if the audit has been completed and an opinion formulated. Lacking independence, an auditor's opinion would not be credible to users. The following explanatory paragraph (the report's only paragraph) disclaims an opinion:

> **(Explanatory Paragraph)**
>
> We are not independent with respect to the Trailways Company, and the accompanying balance sheet. . ., and the related statements of income, retained earnings, and cash flows for the year then ended were not audited by us. Accordingly, we do not express an opinion on them.

Note that the paragraph declares the auditor not independent, but does not explain why and does not reveal any auditing procedures that may have been performed. To do either might lead the reader to the false impression that the auditor is expressing limited assurance.

REPORTING ON COMPARATIVE FINANCIAL STATEMENTS

As illustrated in the Procter & Gamble report (Figure 3-4) and implied throughout this chapter, audit reports normally cover two or more fiscal years. In fact, *GAAS* require no less, since the language of the fourth standard of reporting (Figure 2-1)—". . . expression of opinion regarding the financial statements, *taken as a whole*"—applies not only to the current period financial statements, but also to those of the one or more prior periods presented. However, reporting on comparative periods raises the problem of having different opinions in compared years and the corresponding problem of updating a previously issued opinion. Each problem is discussed separately below.

REPORT WITH DIFFERING OPINIONS

Because circumstances may change from period to period, an auditor could issue different opinions for two different years in a single report. For example, Grant Thornton issued an unqualified opinion for the J. M. Peters Company's 1991 (and 1990) financial statements. However, owing to uncertainties about the Company's ability to continue as a going concern and about the ultimate realizations from the sale of real estate projects, Grant Thornton disclaimed an opinion for 1992. Notice three things particularly about the following report. First, the scope (second) paragraph refers only to the years 1991 and 1990, for which opinions are expressed, but not to 1992, for which one is not. Second, paragraphs five and six disclose separately both of the reasons for disclaiming in 1992. And third, notice by nothing more than the sheer volume of words in the report that, although unusual in practice, audit reports can be quite complex.

J. M. Peters Company, Inc.
Grant Thornton

We have audited the accompanying consolidated balance sheets of J. M. Peters Company, Inc., and subsidiaries (the "Company") as of February 29, 1992 and February 28, 1991, and the related consolidated statements of operations, stockholders' equity (deficit) and cash flows for the years ended February 29, 1992 and February 28, 1991 and 1990. These financial statements are the responsibility of the Company's management. Our responsibility is to express an opinion on these financial statements based on our audits.

We conducted our audits in accordance with generally accepted auditing standards. Those standards require that we plan and perform the audit to obtain reasonable assurance about whether the financial statements are free of material misstatement. An audit includes examining, on a test basis, evidence supporting the amounts and disclosures in the financial statements. An audit also includes assessing the accounting principles used and significant estimates made by management, as well as evaluating the overall financial statement presentation. We believe that our audits of the 1991 and 1990 consolidated financial statements provide a reasonable basis for our opinion.

In our opinion, the 1991 and 1990 consolidated financial statements referred to above present fairly, in all material respects, the consolidated financial position of the Company as of February 28, 1991 and 1990, and the results of its operations and its cash flows for the years then ended, in conformity with generally accepted accounting principles.

As discussed in Note 14, subsequent to year end the Company entered into a mutual release with its parent regarding $60.7 million in certain tax sharing claims.

The consolidated financial statements have been prepared assuming that the Company will continue as a going concern. As discussed in Note 2, the carrying values of the Company's real estate projects are dependent upon future economic, market and financing conditions which may cause the ultimate realizations to be materially different from amounts presently estimated. The current state of the financial markets, caused in part by the current regulatory environment, coupled with the Company's 1992 and 1991 operating losses, and the insolvency of its parent, have adversely affected the liquidity of the Company. Furthermore, the Company is in default under most of its financing agreements at February 29, 1992, all of which raises substantial doubt as to the Company's ability to achieve estimated net realizable values and to continue as a going concern. Management's plans concerning these matters are described in Note 2. The consolidated financial statements do not include any adjustments to reflect the possible future effects on the recoverability of assets and amounts of liabilities that would be necessary should the Company be unable to continue as a going concern.

As discussed in Note 1, the Company carries its real estate projects at the lower of cost or net realizable value assuming completion of development and disposition in accordance with management's current plans and intentions. Net realizable value is substantially greater than fair market value. As further discussed in Note 2, the Company's parent is engaged in active negotiations for the sale of its 85.8% interest in and loans made to the Company. Due to the potential change in the Company's ownership, coupled with the uncertainties discussed in the preceding paragraph, management may change its development and disposition plans of its real estate projects. Therefore, ultimate realizations from the sales of the Company's real estate projects may be substantially less than current carrying amounts.

Because of the potential material uncertainties discussed in the preceding two paragraphs, we are unable to and do not express an opinion on the consolidated financial statements as of February 29, 1992 and for the year then ended.

REPORT WITH AN UPDATED OPINION DIFFERENT FROM A PREVIOUS OPINION

Auditors sometimes become aware of circumstances or events that affect the financial statements reported on in a prior year. For example, resolution in the current year of a matter that caused a qualified opinion in a prior year may result in an updated opinion for the prior year within the current report. In addition to an updated opinion paragraph, the report also includes an explanatory paragraph disclosing the date of the prior report, the type of opinion expressed, the circumstances that caused a different opinion in the prior year, and the fact that the auditor's updated opinion for the prior year is now different. For example, the following, from Price Waterhouse's 1992 report for the Sony Corporation, illustrates an explanatory paragraph for a prior year departure from GAAP, updated in the current year:

Sony Corporation
Price Waterhouse

(Explanatory Paragraph)

In our report dated May 21, 1992, we expressed a qualified opinion that the company's consolidated financial statements for the years ended March 31, 1991 and 1992 did not disclose segment information concerning operations in different industries, and foreign operations and export sales, which was required by accounting principles generally accepted in the United States. As described in Note 18 to the accompanying consolidated financial statements, the company has disclosed . . . segment information for the years ended March 31, 1991 and 1992 in conformity with accounting principles generally accepted in the United States of America. Accordingly, our opinion on the consolidated financial statements for the years ended March 31, 1991 and 1992, as presented herein is different from that expressed in our previous report.

REPORTING ON FINANCIAL STATEMENTS
PREPARED FOR USE IN FOREIGN COUNTRIES

U.S. corporations ordinarily prepare financial statements in conformity with accounting principles generally accepted in the U.S., and auditors therefore audit the statements in accordance with the AICPA's *GAAS*. However, as a result of foreign investment in U.S. companies, it has become increasingly common for auditors to audit financial statements that are both prepared in conformity with accounting principles generally accepted in another country and intended for use outside the U.S. For example, the financial statements of a U.S. domestic corporation may be prepared for inclusion in the consolidated statements of a non-U.S. parent or, in contrast, they may be used to raise capital in another country. *Statement on Auditing Standards No. 51*, "Reporting on Financial Statements Prepared for Use in Other Countries" (AU Sec. 534), describes an auditor's obligation under U.S. and foreign auditing standards, and prescribes audit reports for use outside and within the United States.

GENERAL AND FIELD WORK STANDARDS

Even when auditing the financial statements of a U.S. corporation that are prepared in conformity with the accounting principles of another country, an auditor complies with U.S. general and field work standards. However, audit procedures may be modified, since the assertions embodied in financial statements prepared to conform with foreign accounting principles may differ significantly from those embodied in statements prepared to conform with U.S. accounting principles. For example, some foreign countries require that certain assets be revalued to adjust for the effects of inflation, and other countries neither require nor permit recognizing deferred taxes and related party transactions. As a result, when reporting on financial statements prepared for use in other countries, an auditor should be familiar with the accounting principles accepted in the other country and, if necessary, consult with foreign accountants.

STATEMENTS USED OUTSIDE THE U.S. ONLY

When reporting on financial statements intended for use outside the U.S. *only*, the auditor identifies the statements audited, refers to a note that describes the basis of financial statement presentation, states that the audit was made in accordance with U.S. auditing standards, and includes a paragraph expressing an opinion on whether the statements are presented fairly in conformity with the basis described. The following illustrates Deloitte Touche Tohmatau's 1994 report for the Kubota Corporation:

Kubota Corporation
Deloitte Touche Tohmatau

(Introductory Paragraph)

. . . years in the period ended March 31, 1994, all expressed in Japanese yen, . . . as described in Note 10, have been prepared on the basis of accounting generally accepted in Japan. These financial statements are the responsibility of the Company's management. Our responsibility is to express an opinion on these financial statements based on our audits.

(Scope Paragraph)

We conducted our audits in accordance with auditing standards generally accepted in the United States and Japan. Those standards require that we plan and perform the audit to obtain reasonable assurance about whether the financial statements are free of material misstatement. An audit includes examining, on a test basis, evidence supporting the amounts and disclosures in the financial statements. An audit also includes assessing the accounting principles used and significant estimates made by management, as well as evaluating the overall financial statement presentation. We believe that our audits provide a reasonable basis for our opinion.

(Opinion Paragraph)

In our opinion, the financial statements . . . present fairly, in all material respects . . . in conformity with accounting principles generally accepted in Japan.

An auditor may also use the standard report of another country, but only if the report would be used by auditors in the other country in similar circumstances, and the auditor understands—and is in a position to make—the attestations contained in the report.

STATEMENTS USED IN THE U.S.

If an auditor reports on financial statements prepared in accordance with accounting principles accepted in another country, and those statements will have more than limited distribution in the U.S., he or she uses the standard audit report illustrated earlier in this chapter, modified for departures from U.S. accounting principles. In addition, the auditor may include a separate paragraph in the report to express an opinion on whether the financial statements are presented in conformity with accounting principles generally accepted in the other country.

SUMMARY

Although the profession has not developed standards for assurance engagements, the concepts that underlie *attestation standards* and *GAAS*—independence, due care, evidence, and reporting—are generally applicable to assurance engagements (although reporting sometimes is not: e.g., achievement award balloting), and offer some insights into the role of assurance reports. For example, three of the concepts are apparent in reports issued by Consumers Union. Owing to a much richer history in attestation and audit engagements, the profession prescribes reports for both types of engagements, and the reports include several common components: a title that includes the word *independent*, an addressee, a signature in the firm's name, a date, and a series of paragraphs that explain what was attested to or audited, management's and the attester's or the auditor's responsibility, the standards the attester or the auditor complied with, and an opinion. Attestation and audit reports express any one of four types of opinions: unqualified (the assertion or financial statements are *presented fairly*), qualified (presented fairly *except for*), adverse (are *not* presented fairly), or disclaimer ("We *do not express an opinion . . .*"). The type of opinion expressed depends on the circumstances and on materiality.

KEY TERMS

Attestation report 62
Unqualified opinion 62
Introductory paragraph 63
Opinion paragraph 63
Qualified opinion 63
Adverse opinion 63

Disclaimer of opinion 64
Audit report 64
Standard report 64
Scope paragraph 67
Principal auditor 73

REFERENCES

Professional Standards

AICPA. *Codification of Statements on Auditing Standards.* New York: AICPA (AU Sec. 341, 410, 411, 420, 431, 504, 508, 530, 543, 544).

SAS No. 26, "Association with Financial Statements" (AU Sec. 504).

SAS No. 58, "Reports on Audited Financial Statements" (AU Sec. 508).

SAS No. 59, "The Auditor's Consideration of an Entity's Ability to Continue as a Going Concern" (AU Sec. 341).

SAS No. 79, "Reporting on Uncertainties."

SSAE No. 1, "Attestation Standards."

Articles

Chen, K. C. W., and B. K. Church. "Going Concern Opinions and the Market's Reaction to Bankruptcy Filings," *The Accounting Review* (January 1996), pp. 117-128.

Frost, C. A., and K. P. Ramin. "International Auditing Differences," *Journal of Accountancy* (April 1996), pp. 62-68.

Geiger, M. A. "SAS No. 58: Did the ASB Really Listen?" *Journal of Accountancy* (December 1988), pp. 55-57.

Kelly, A. S., and L. C. Mohrweis. "Bankers' and Investors' Perceptions of the Auditor's Role in Financial Statement Reporting: The Impact of SAS No. 58," *Auditing: A Journal of Practice & Theory* (Fall 1989), pp. 87-97.

Miller, J. R., S. A. Reed, and R. H. Strawser. "Bank Loan Officers' Perceptions of the New Audit Report," *Accounting Horizons* (March 1993), pp. 39-52.

Raghunandan, K., and D. V. Rama. "Audit Reports for Companies in Financial Distress: Before and After *SAS No. 59,*" *Auditing: A Journal of Practice & Theory* (Fall 1995), pp. 50-63.

Roussey, R. S., E. L. Ten Eyck, and M. Blanco-Best. "Three New SASs: Closing the Communications Gap," *Journal of Accountancy* (December 1988), pp. 44-52.

QUESTIONS

1. What does the language in Consumers Union *Buying Guides* and *Consumer Reports* have in common with reports issued by public accounting firms?
2. What message does an attestation report convey to readers?
3. Explain the significance of the audit report date.
4. What is meant by dual dating an audit report?
5. On what should an auditor base his or her opinion about compliance with GAAP?
6. Under what conditions is a qualified audit opinion issued ordinarily?
7. Under what conditions is an adverse audit opinion issued ordinarily?
8. How does a standard audit report differ from a report which, owing to a scope limitation, disclaims an opinion?
9. Departures from GAAP may result in either a qualified or an adverse opinion, depending on materiality. How does an auditor judge materiality?

MULTIPLE CHOICE QUESTIONS

1. A report issued by a public accounting firm uses the language: *In our opinion . . . the schedule presents . . . in all material respects . . .* The firm's report is likely:

a. A standard audit report.
b. A qualified audit report.
c. An attestation report.
d. A qualified attestation report.

2. Does an attester make the following representations explicitly or implicitly in an unqualified attestation report?

	Assertion is Capable of Evaluation Against Reasonable Criteria	Assertions are Management's Responsibility
a.	Explicitly	Explicitly
b.	Implicitly	Implicitly
c.	Implicitly	Explicitly
d.	Explicitly	Implicitly

3. Does an auditor make the following representations explicitly or implicitly in an unqualified audit report?

	Consistent Application of Accounting Principles	Examined Evidence on a Test Basis
a.	Implicitly	Explicitly
b.	Implicitly	Implicitly
c.	Explicitly	Explicitly
d.	Explicitly	Implicitly

(AICPA Adapted)

4. Which of the following is likely a scope limitation?

a. The auditor is reporting on the balance sheet only.
b. A subsidiary's financial statements are audited by another auditor.
c. Sufficient evidence is not available.
d. The auditor is engaged after the balance sheet date.

5. A departure from GAAP is disclosed in a note to the financial statements. The auditor should:

a. Issue an unqualified opinion, but emphasize the matter in an explanatory paragraph.
b. Issue an unqualified opinion, with no explanatory paragraph, since the departure from GAAP is disclosed.
c. Issue a qualified opinion.
d. Disclaim an opinion.

6. Management's financial statements disclose uncertainties about future events that are not susceptible to reasonable estimation. The auditor should issue:

a. An unqualified opinion.
b. A qualified opinion.
c. An adverse opinion.
d. A disclaimer of opinion.

7. The opinion paragraph of a qualified opinion should include language such as:

a. Except for.
b. When read in conjunction with the notes.
c. With the foregoing explanation.
d. Subject to the explanation above.

(AICPA Adapted)

8. An attestation or audit report should be dated as of:

a. The date of the assertion or financial statements.
b. The date the report is delivered.
c. The last date on which a subsequent event occurs.
d. The last day of field work.

9. An explanatory paragraph reads as follows: *The Company has adopted the first-in, first-out method of determining inventory costs, whereas it previously used the last-in, first-out method. Although use of the first-in, first-out method is in conformity with generally accepted accounting principles, in our opinion the Company has not provided reasonable justification for seeking a change as required by Opinion No. 20 of the Accounting Principles Board.*

The paragraph likely appears in:

a. An unqualified opinion.
b. An unqualified opinion that emphasized the matter.
c. A qualified opinion.
d. A disclaimer of opinion.

10. An audit report reads in part as follows: *The financial statements do not include any adjustments that might result from the outcome of this uncertainty.*

The sentence likely appears in:

a. An unqualified opinion.
b. An unqualified opinion that emphasized the matter.
c. A qualified opinion.
d. A disclaimer of opinion.

PROBLEMS AND DISCUSSION CASES

3-1   *The Intuition Underlying an Attestation Report*

On January 27, 2000, Sandeen & Walsh LLP issued the attestation report that appears below:

Independent Accountant's Report

As required by Article VI, Section 7(a)(4) of the Supplemental Unemployment Benefit Plan (the Plan) between North American Motors Corp. (the Company) and International Union, United Automobile, Aerospace and Agricultural Implement Workers of America and its affiliated Local Unions as designated (collectively, the Union), we have examined the following special purpose statements:

1. The amounts of maximum funding of the fund and credit unit cancellation base for the months of January to December 1999, inclusive,
2. The amounts by which the Company contribution to the Union was reduced for benefits paid and amounts of net Company contributions for the months of January to December 1999,
3. The number of hours for which employees received pay and the number of such hours with respect to which the Company shall not have made contributions to the fund (none in 1999), and the amount of Company contributions at the applicable rate for each hour for the months of January to December 1999, inclusive, and
4. The number and amount of Automatic Short-Week Benefits paid to employees and the amount of such benefits used to reduce contributions for the months of January to December 1999, inclusive.

These special purpose statements are the responsibility of the Company's management. Our responsibility is to express an opinion on these statements based on our examination.

The accompanying statements have been prepared for the purpose of complying with the provisions of Article VI, Sections 7(a)(1) and (a)(2) of the Plan.

In our opinion, the above-mentioned statements present fairly, in all material respects, the information stated therein for the months of January to December 1999, inclusive, in accordance with the provisions of Article VI, Sections 7(a)(1) and (a)(2) of the Plan.

This report is intended solely for the information and use of the Board of Directors of the Company and the Union, and should not be used for any other purpose.

Required: Discuss the economic motive—the intuition—underlying the report.

3-2 *The Economic Motive and Apparent Risk in an Attestation Engagement*
Following is an independent accountant's attestation report:

Independent Accountant's Report

Crownhill Super Computers, Inc.
4500 Columbus Way
Springfield, IL 62703

We have examined the accompanying schedule computing the average post-purchase end-user support time supplied by Crownhill Super Computers, Inc., (the Schedule) to major purchasers for the period November 1, 1998, to October 31, 1999. Our examination was made in accordance with attestation standards established by the American Institute of Certified Public Accountants and, accordingly, included such procedures as we considered necessary in the circumstances. Our responsibility is to express an opinion on the Schedule.

In our opinion, the Schedule presents, in all material respects, the average post-purchase end-user support time supplied by Crownhill Super Computers, Inc., to major purchasers for the period November 1, 1998, to October 31, 1999.

This report is intended solely for the information and use of the management of Crownhill Super Computers, Inc., and should not be used for any other purpose.

Hemphill & Noyes, LLP

Required:
1. Discuss the intuition—the economic motive—underlying the engagement.
2. What risks do you see accruing to Hemphill & Noyes from the wording of the report?

3-3 *Identifying Audit Opinions and Circumstances for Departure*
Following are excerpted sentences and phrases from audit reports issued by independent public accounting firms:

a.
(Scope Paragraph)
Except as described in the following paragraph . . .

(Explanatory Paragraph)
Because of insufficient records we were not able to examine sufficient evidence in support of dividend income received from a short-term investment and we were unable to satisfy ourselves as to the dividend income by means of other procedures.

(Opinion Paragraph)
In our opinion, except for the effect of the matter described in the preceding paragraph, the financial statements referred to above present fairly . . .

b.   **(Explanatory Paragraph)**

The accompanying financial statements have been prepared assuming that the Company will continue as a going concern. As discussed in Note 11 to the financial statements, under existing circumstances there is substantial doubt as to the ability of the Company to continue as a going concern.

c.   **(Explanatory Paragraph)**

As explained in Note 12 to the financial statements, certain adjustments have been made to the financial statements to conform to generally accepted accounting principles. These adjustments have not been recorded in the books.

d.   **(Explanatory Paragraph)**

As disclosed in Note 8 to the financial statements, the company has adopted the first-in, first-out method of determining inventory costs, whereas it previously used the last-in, first-out method. Although use of the first-in, first-out method is in conformity with generally accepted accounting principles, in our opinion the company has not provided reasonable justification for seeking a change as required by Opinion 19 of the Accounting Principles Board.

(Opinion Paragraph)

In our opinion, except for the change in accounting principles discussed in the preceding paragraph, the financial statements referred to above present fairly . . .

Required: For each report, identify the type of opinion (e.g., "qualified") and the circumstance for departing from the standard wording of an unqualified opinion (e.g., "departure from GAAP").

3-4 *Modifications to an Audit Report*

Christine Burke has completed field work for the Willingham Corporation engagement, a December 31, 1999 year end audit, and is now deciding whether to modify her report. Below are two unrelated situations that arose during the engagement:

Situation 1

In September 1999, a lawsuit was filed against Willingham requesting that the court order Willingham to install pollution control equipment at an aged production plant. Willingham's attorney has informed Burke that the outcome of the litigation cannot be predicted, and management has informed Burke that pollution control equipment is far too costly and that the plant will close if the litigation is lost. In addition, management told Burke that the production plant and equipment had only minimal resale values, and that lost production could not be recovered at other plants.

Situation 2

During 1999, Willingham paid 20 percent of its assets to purchase a franchise granting the exclusive right to produce and sell a newly patented product in the New England states, although there has been no appreciable production or sales of the product anywhere in the U.S. to date. Neither the franchisor nor any U.S. franchisee has conducted market research about the product.

Required: For each of the above two situations, discuss the issues Burke should consider (not the type of report Burke should issue). Consider each situation separately, thoroughly, and under the assumption that each is disclosed in notes to the financial statements.

(AICPA Adapted)

3-5 *Audit Report Deficiencies*
Timothy Ross completed field work on September 23, 1999, and issued the following report to the directors of The Rancho Corporation:

To the Directors of The Rancho Corporation:

We have audited the balance sheet of The Rancho Corporation as of July 31, 1999 and the related statements of income and retained earnings. In accordance with your instructions, a complete audit was conducted.

We conducted our audit in accordance with generally accepted auditing standards. An audit includes examining, on a test basis, evidence supporting the amounts and disclosures in the financial statements. We believe that our audit was appropriate in the circumstances.

In many respects, this was an unusual year for The Rancho Corporation. The weakening of the economy in the early part of the year and the strike of plant employees in the summer of 1999 led to a decline in sales and net income. After making several tests of sales records, nothing came to our attention that would indicate that sales have not been properly recorded.

In our opinion, with the explanation given above and the exception of some minor errors that are considered immaterial, the aforementioned financial statements present fairly, in all material respects, the financial position of The Rancho Corporation at July 31, 1999, and the results of its operations for the year then ended, in conformity with pronouncements of the Financial Accounting Standards Board.

Timothy Ross, CPA
September 23, 1999

Required: List and explain deficiencies and omissions in Ross's report. Do not discuss the type of opinion (unqualified, qualified, adverse, or disclaimer). Organize your answer by paragraph (introductory, scope, explanatory, and opinion).

(AICPA Adapted)

3-6 *Audit Report Deficiencies*
The following proposed audit report was drafted by a staff accountant at the completion of an engagement and submitted to the engagement partner for review. The partner reviewed the assistant's working papers thoroughly, and concluded that a scope limitation relating to inventory was sufficiently material to warrant a qualified opinion.

To Carl Corporation Controller:

We have audited the accompanying financial statements of Carl Corporation as of December 31, 1999. These financial statements are the responsibility of the Company's management. Our responsibility is to express an opinion on these financial statements based on our audit.

We conducted our audit in accordance with generally accepted auditing standards. Those standards require that we plan and perform the audit to obtain reasonable assurance about whether the financial statements are free of material misstatement. An audit includes examining, on a test basis, evidence supporting the amounts and disclosures in the financial statements. An audit also includes assessing the accounting principles used and significant estimates made by management, as well as evaluating the overall financial statement presentation. We believe that our audit provides a reasonable basis for our opinion.

On January 15, 1999, the company issued debentures in the amount of $1,000,000 for the purpose of financing plant expansion. As indicated in Note 6 to the financial statements, the debenture agreement restricts the payment of future cash dividends to earnings after December 31, 2001.

The company's unconsolidated foreign subsidiary did not close down production during the year audited for physical inventory purposes and took no physical inventory during the year. We made extensive tests of book inventory figures for accuracy of calculation and reasonableness of pricing. We did not make physical tests of inventory quantities. Because of this, we are unable to express an unqualified opinion on the financial statements taken as a whole. However, except for the scope limitation regarding inventory, in our opinion the accompanying balance sheet presents the financial position of Carl Corporation at December 31, 1999, subject to the effect of the inventory on the carrying value of the investment. The accompanying statements of income and of retained earnings present the incomes and expenses and the results of transactions affecting retained earnings in accordance with generally accepted accounting principles.

December 31, 1999
Pate & Co., CPAs

Required: Identify the deficiencies in the assistant's proposed report.

(AICPA Adapted)

3-7 *Audit Report Deficiencies*
The following audit report was drafted by a staff accountant and submitted to the engagement partner in the accounting firm of Better & Best, CPAs:

To the Audit Committee of
American Widgets, Inc.:

We have audited the consolidated balance sheets of American Widgets, Inc. and subsidiaries as of December 31, 1999 and 1998, and the related consolidated statements of income, retained earnings, and cash flows for the years then ended. These financial statements are the responsibility of the Company's management. Our responsibility is to express an opinion on these financial statements based on our audit. Other auditors examined the financial statements of certain subsidiaries and have furnished us with reports thereon containing no exceptions. Our opinion expressed herein, insofar as it relates to the amounts included for those subsidiaries, is based solely upon the reports of the other auditors.

As discussed in Note 4 to the financial statements, on January 8, 2000, the company halted the production of certain medical equipment as a result of inquiries by the Food and Drug Administration, which raised questions as to the adequacy of some of the Company's sterilization equipment and related procedures. Management is not in a position to evaluate the effect of this production halt and the ensuing litigation, which may have an adverse effect on the financial position of American Widgets, Inc.

As fully discussed in Note 7 to the financial statements, in 1999 the Company extended the use of the last-in, first-out (LIFO) method of accounting to include all inventories. In examining inventories, we engaged Dr. Irwin Same (Nobel Prize winner, 1992) to test check the technical requirements and specifications of certain items of equipment manufactured by the Company.

In our opinion, except for the effects, if any, on the financial statements of the ultimate resolution of the matter discussed in the second preceding paragraph, the financial statements referred to above present fairly, in all material respects, the financial position of American Widgets, Inc. as of December 31, 1999, and the results of operations and its cash flows for the year then ended in conformity with generally accepted accounting principles.

To be signed by
Better & Best, CPAs
March 1, 2000, except
for Note 4 as to which
the date is January 8, 2000

Required: Identify the deficiencies in the assistant's proposed report.

(AICPA Adapted)

3-8   *Drafting an Audit Report*

On January 15, 2000, Marc David, CPA, was engaged to audit Kristin Manufacturing Company's December 31, 1999 financial statements. Kristin had taken a physical inventory on December 31, 1999; the carrying value of the final priced inventory was $275,400 ($263,000 in 1998), which represented approximately 10 percent of total assets. David was unable to satisfy himself as to inventory quantities through other auditing procedures because of the condition of Kristin's inventory records.

Required: Draft an audit report assuming no other circumstances require departure from a standard audit report.

3-9   *Drafting an Opinion Paragraph*

Sturdy Corporation owns and operates a large office building in a desirable section of New York City's financial district. For many years the management of Sturdy Corporation has: (a) written up building accounts to appraisal values, and (b) accounted for depreciation expense on the basis of appraised values. Wyley, the successor auditor, was engaged to audit Sturdy's financial statements for the year ended December 31, 1999. After completing the audit, Wyley concluded that, consistent with prior years, an adverse opinion would have to be issued because of the materiality of the apparent departure from historical cost.

   Required:
1. Describe in detail what Wyley should include in an explanatory paragraph.
2. Draft the opinion paragraph.

(AICPA Adapted)

3-10   *Drafting an Audit Report*

On March 17, 2000, Ross, Sandler & Co., CPAs completed an audit of The Fairfax Corporation's December 31, 1999 financial statements. The firm issued an unqualified opinion. Because of a scope limitation arising from the inability to observe the January 1, 1998 physical inventory, the predecessor auditors, Smith, Ellis & Co., issued a report that contained an unqualified opinion on the December 31, 1998 balance sheet and a qualified opinion on the statements of income, retained earnings, and cash flows for the year then ended. The management of The Fairfax Corporation has decided to present comparative (1999 and 1998) financial statements in their annual report.

   Required: Prepare an audit report assuming the March 1, 1999 report of Smith, Ellis & Co. is not presented.

(AICPA Adapted)

3-11   *Drafting an Audit Report*

On March 15, 2000, you completed the audit of Excelsior Corporation's December 31, 1999 financial statements, the second year you've supervised the engagement. The following information came to your attention during the engagement:
a. Excelsior is presenting comparative financial statements.
b. Excelsior does not wish to present a statement of cash flows for either year.

c. During 1999, Excelsior changed its method of accounting for long-term construction contracts, reported the effect of the change in the current year's financial statements, and restated the prior year's statements. You are satisfied with Excelsior's justification for making the change, which is disclosed in Note 12.

d. Although unable to confirm accounts receivable, you used alternate procedures to satisfy yourself that receivables are presented fairly.

e. Excelsior Corporation is the defendant in a litigation, the outcome of which is highly uncertain. If the case is settled in favor of the plaintiff, Excelsior will be required to pay a substantial amount of cash, which might require the sale of some plant assets. The litigation and the possible effects are disclosed in Note 11.

f. Excelsior issued debentures on January 31, 1999, in the amount of $10,000,000. The funds obtained from the issuance were used to finance the expansion of plant facilities. The debenture agreement restricts the payment of future cash dividends to earnings after December 31, 2002. Excelsior declined to disclose this data in the notes to the financial statements.

Required: Draft an auditor's report.

(AICPA Adapted)

3-12 *The Repercussions of Substantial Doubt*

In an article entitled, "American Gaming Says Its Chairman Resigns; Audit Raises Questions," *The Wall Street Journal* (April 14, 1996, p. A6) reported that the board chairman of a publicly traded company had resigned, and that the company faced financial difficulties. On the matter of financial difficulties, the article stated, in part, ". . . the company said an independent audit by Deloitte & Touche found that American Gaming's problems—including recurring losses, negative working capital, defaults under debt agreements and uncertainty relating to the liquidation of subsidiaries—'raise substantial doubt about the ability of the company to continue as a going concern.'" The article made no link between the chairman's resignation and the auditor's opinion, but did appropriately link American Gaming's financial position to the opinion.

At a meeting between Christine Schutt, an engagement partner assigned to audit a middle-market building materials company, and the company's chief executive officer (CEO), Schutt reveals that she has substantial doubt about the company's ability to continue as a going concern and that she may have to add an explanatory paragraph to the audit report. The CEO says, "I understand your dilemma. You've explained that to me. But what you don't understand is that no supplier will give me credit, even for a week, if you claim you have substantial doubt. What's more, a statement like 'substantial doubt' may cause me to think twice about resigning. Look, if you'll say in your report that you have doubt, I'll buy that, and my creditors may too. But, if you insist on *substantial* doubt, I'll find another auditor."

Required:

1. Do you think Schutt can overlook the word "substantial"? Discuss.

2. What is the dilemma the CEO explained to Schutt? Discuss.

3-13 *Other Information in Annual Reports*

The annual reports for publicly traded companies typically include information that is not part of management's financial statements and, therefore, that is not captured in a financial statement audit. Examples include the chief executive officer's (CEO's) letter to shareholders, nonfinancial information about product lines, and summaries of significant financial results over a five- or ten-year period. Under *Statement on Auditing Standards No. 8*, "Other Information in Documents Containing Audited Financial Statements" (AU Sec. 550), an auditor is not obligated to corroborate, but should read, the other information to determine whether the information (or the way the information is presented) is inconsistent with the financial statements. For example, if the income statement report earnings per share (EPS) of $5.25, the CEO's letter should not report a higher EPS. The auditor should revise the audit report, withhold the report, or withdraw from the engagement if the client refuses to revise an inconsistency.

Required: Explain the role of *SAS No. 8,* given that an audit reports on management's financial statement assertions, and *SAS No. 8* addresses information outside of the financial statements.

3-14 *Opinion Based Partly on the Report of Another Auditor*
Lando Corporation controls two wholly owned domestic subsidiaries. Michaels, CPA, the principal auditor, has been engaged to audit the financial statements of Lando and one of the subsidiaries. Thomas, CPA, the other auditor, has audited the financial statements of the other subsidiary, an entity whose operations are material to the consolidated financial statements.

Michaels' audit work is sufficient to justify Michaels serving as the principal auditor. Michaels has not yet decided to make reference to Thomas, the other auditor.

Required: What are the reporting requirements if Michaels decides to name Thomas and make reference to the audit work Thomas did?

(AICPA Adapted)

3-15 *Financial Statement Deficiencies and Omissions*
The Maumee Corporation's August 31, 1999 financial statements are presented below.

The Maumee Corporation
Balance Sheet
August 31, 1999
(in Thousands of Dollars)

Assets

Cash		$ 103
Marketable securities,		
at cost that approximates market value		54
Trade accounts receivable (net of $65,000		
Allowance for doubtful accounts)		917
Inventories, at cost		775
Property plant, and equipment	$ 3,200	
Less accumulated depreciation	1,475	1,725
Prepayments and other assets		125
Total assets		$ 3,699

Liabilities and Stockholders' Equity

Accounts payable	$ 221	
Accrued taxes	62	
Bank loans and long-term debt	1,580	
Total liabilities		$ 1,863
Capital stock, $10 par value (authorized 50,000		
shares, issued and outstanding 42,400 shares)	$ 424	
Paid-in capital in excess of par value	366	
Retained earnings	1,046	
Total stockholders' equity		1,836
Total liabilities and stockholders' equity		$ 3,699

The Maumee Corporation
Statement of Income and Retained Earnings
For the Year Ended August 31, 1999
(in Thousands of Dollars)

Product sales (net of $850,000 Sales returns and allowances)		$ 10,700
Cost of goods sold		8,700
Gross profit on sales		$ 2,000
Operating expenses:		
Selling expenses	$ 1,500	
General and administrative expense	940	2,440
Operating loss		$ (440)
Interest expense		150
Net loss		$ (590)
Retained earnings, September 1, 1998		1,700
		$ 1,110
Dividends:		
Cash—$1 per share	$ 40	
Stock—6% of shares outstanding	24	64
Retained earnings, August 31, 1999		$ 1,046

Required: List deficiencies and omissions in the statements and discuss the probable effect of each deficiency or omission individually on the auditor's report. Assume that The Maumee Corporation is unwilling either to change the financial statements or to make additional disclosures. Organize your answers in two columns as follows within the general headings of Balance Sheet, Statement of Income and Retained Earnings, and Other:

Financial Statement   *Discussion of*
Deficiency or Omission   *Effect on Auditor's Report*

(AICPA Adapted)

RESEARCH PROJECTS

1. WHY WOULDN'T A CLIENT CORRECT THE CIRCUMSTANCE THAT GAVE RISE TO A QUALIFIED OPINION?

In the overwhelming majority of cases, independent auditors issue unqualified, rather than qualified, opinions for their publicly traded clients since it is unusual (though not rare):

- For a client's financial statements to depart materially from GAAP,
- For a client to fail to justify an accounting change, or
- For a client to impose scope limitations on the auditor,

the three circumstances at Figure 3-9 for which an auditor would issue a qualified opinion.

Before issuing a qualified opinion, an auditor will first alert the client of an impending qualification, largely because in each of the three circumstances listed above the issue that gives rise to a qualification is not only correctable by the client, but if corrected would result in an unqualified opinion. For example, to avoid a qualified opinion, the client in most cases could simply comply with GAAP, avoid the unjustified accounting change, or lift the limitation on the scope of the engagement.

Required: Using the annual report file in the AICPA's National Automated Accounting Research System (NAARS), the AICPA's *Accounting Trends and Techniques*, or copies of annual reports in a library, search for an example of one of the three circumstances requiring a qualified opinion. Draft a report that:

1. Explains the issue that gave rise to the circumstance (use both the explanatory paragraph and the footnote, if any, in the annual report), and
2. Compares the language used in the independent auditor's report to the language illustrated in the chapter, and
3. Gives your impressions of the likely tension that transpired between the client and the auditor in resolving that a qualified opinion was required. For example, why would the client decide that it was in their best interests to accept a qualified opinion rather than to correct the financial statements?

2. REPORTING ON FINANCIAL DISTRESS

Over the years, a substantial literature has been devoted to financial distress in general, and in particular to the independent auditor's decision to modify a report for substantial doubt about the ability of an entity to continue as a going concern. The literature appears within the popular financial press (e.g., *The Wall Street Journal, Business Week, Harvard Business Review)*, the professional accounting and auditing literature (e.g., *Journal of Accountancy, The CPA Journal, Financial Analysts Journal*), and the academic research literature (e.g., *Auditing: A Journal of Practice & Theory, The Accounting Review, Journal of Accounting Research*). For example, numerous articles in the financial press report financial distress coincident with an auditor's report that raises substantial doubt, articles in the professional literature report how auditors consider substantial doubt, and articles in the academic literature link stock price reaction to auditors' reports of substantial doubt.

Required: Select three articles about financial distress and the auditor's substantial doubt decision—one each from the financial press, the professional literature, and the academic literature. Draft a report that:

1. Summarizes the key issues in each article.
2. Identifies key issues common to all three articles. For example, is there a question posed in one article that is answered in part in another article?

4

Professional Ethics

Major topics discussed in this chapter are the:

- Relationship between general and professional ethics.
- AICPA *Code of Professional Conduct.*
- AICPA *Rules of Conduct.*
- Enforcement of the *Code of Professional Conduct.*
- Standards of quality control and quality review that monitor the performance of public accounting firms.

Although most of the issues faced in practice are largely technical in nature, certified public accountants also confront ethical questions related to their threefold responsibility to the public, to clients, and to their colleagues in practice. Interestingly, many ethical questions derive from the unique contractual relationship between practitioners and clients. For example, unlike lawyers, who report directly to and act as advocates for their clients, practitioners performing audit, attest, and assurance services report mostly to external users and act as independent attesters about—not advocates for—assertions made by their clients. In fact, the profession's well-established reputation for independence, integrity, and objectivity is partly why audit services have value, why the financial community continues to trust practitioners, and why the profession is well-positioned to add value in assurance service markets. In short, the profession is trusted, and the AICPA *Code of Professional Conduct* is the emblem of the profession's trust.

However, although the *Rules of Conduct* within the AICPA's *Code of Professional Conduct* are explicit, some of the temptations faced in practice have little to do with the rules and everything to do with the utility function of the practitioners who break the rules. For example, the engagement partner for the PTL club, a religious broadcast network, certainly knew that, Rules 102 (Integrity and Objectivity) and 501 (Acts Discreditable) aside, maintaining a secret check register to finance management's wildly excessive lifestyle—including a Palm Springs ranch house, a Florida condominium, luxury automobiles, and an unrecorded executive payroll—was both unethical and illegal, given particularly that his firm, the now defunct Laventhol & Horwath, would suffer immeasurably following indictment as a co-defendant in a $750 million class action suit filed by PTL contributors. Some of the rules introduced in this chapter, among them Rule 302 on contingent fees, will likely be news to you. Some others, though, will be nothing other than obvious.

This chapter considers questions of ethics in the context of the AICPA's *Code of Professional Conduct,* the standard of ethical behavior for AICPA members performing assurance, attestation, and audit services.[1] The chapter begins with a brief introduction to general and professional ethics and with an illustration of a related assurance service offered by one Big Six public accounting firm—an ethics audit. In turn, the Principles, Rules, Interpretations, and Rulings of the AICPA *Code of Professional Conduct* are discussed, and each of the Code's *Rules of Conduct* is interpreted. Finally, the joint enforcement efforts of the AICPA, state societies of CPAs, and the National Joint Trial Board are described.

GENERAL ETHICS, PROFESSIONAL ETHICS, AND ASSURANCE SERVICES

General ethics, the study of ideal conduct and behavior, is one of several fields of study in philosophy—others include aesthetics (the study of ideal form or beauty), logic (the study of ideal method in thought and research), metaphysics (the study of ultimate reality), and politics (the study of ideal social organization). As Mautz and Sharaf point out, questions of professional ethics—whether in law, medicine, or auditing—apply general ethics to the choices and consequences embedded within a particular profession:

Ethical behavior in auditing or in any other activity is no more than a special application of the general notion of ethical conduct devised by philosophers .... Ethical Conduct in auditing draws its justification and basic nature from the general theory of ethics.[2]

General ethics, then, provide a rationale for deriving, implementing, and justifying professional codes of ethics. However, unlike general ethics, professional codes of ethics do not, and cannot, require ideal standards of behavior, since minimum standards—the standard imposed by professional codes—can be enforced on practice professionals and ideal standards cannot. But, by requiring the bare minimum, professional codes of ethics risk encouraging mediocrity. And it is precisely for this reason that the reputation of a profession, particularly public accounting (a profession for which a practitioner's work product is observable but his or her work is not), rests squarely on each practitioner's willingness to reach for a standard of conduct well beyond their code: a standard worthy of the trust entrusted to that practitioner by the public, by clients, and by the profession that will bear the burden of adverse reputation effects.

Prior to the mid-1980s, some observers criticized the AICPA's then existing Code of Professional Ethics, arguing that the Code did not adequately encompass the profession's expanding scope of attestation and assurance services. Responding to the criticism, the AICPA appointed a *Special Committee on Standards of Professional Conduct,* chaired by George D. Anderson, a former AICPA chair, to evaluate the relevance of the Code to the profession's commitment to professionalism, quality, and the public interest. The committee

---

1   The Association of Government Accountants and Institute of Internal Auditors each have separate codes of ethics.
2   R. K. Mautz and H. A. Sharaf, *The Philosophy of Auditing* (Sarasota: American Accounting Association, 1961), p. 232.

recommended unprecedented reform: a mandatory quality assurance review *(QAR)* program, and a new code that would apply to *all* professional services (rather than to auditing alone) and to *all* AICPA members (rather than to members in public practice alone). In 1988, 92 percent of the voting AICPA members approved a new *QAR* program and a new *Code of Professional Conduct.*

The AICPA's *Code of Professional Conduct* applies to all services offered by AICPA members including, ironically, a contemporary service not at all common when the Code was developed in 1988: an "ethics audit." Although discussed for years, public accounting firms have only recently begun to offer services that report on management's performance in monitoring the risk of unethical behavior company-wide. For example, packaged as "ethics process management," KPMG Peat Marwick offers a service related to six risks that bear on corporate ethics: sexual harassment, environmental contamination, antitrust infractions, improper foreign payments, fraudulent financial reporting, and race discrimination. KPMG's service offers management an "ethics vulnerability risk assessment"—not an ethics scorecard, but an assessment of where management may be at risk for violating express or implied assertions about ethics. For example, based on focus group interviews with key management (e.g., "What is your policy about employees receiving gifts?") and with employees (e.g., "How often have you declined a supplier's gift?"), the firm identifies gaps where management's standards of employee behavior are unclear to employees. Professional services related to ethics are both supplied by public accounting firms and, more importantly, demanded by some corporations. On the matter of demand, *The Wall Street Journal* commented, albeit sardonically, "Think about it: Companies trying to mitigate a sentence before a crime has been committed, or found out. What more evidence did anyone need that corporate America knew it had an ethics problem and—more to the point— that it was willing to pay good money to ameliorate it?"[3]

AICPA CODE OF PROFESSIONAL CONDUCT—AN OVERVIEW

The AICPA Code of Professional Conduct consists of *Principles* and *Rules of Conduct.* In addition, the executive committee of the AICPA's professional ethics division issues *Interpretations* of, and *Ethics Rulings* about, the Rules of Conduct.

PRINCIPLES

Collectively, the six **Principles of the Code of Professional Conduct,** listed and explained in Figure 4-1 express responsibilities of all practitioners to the public, to their clients, and to their colleagues in the profession. The principles demand an uncompromising commitment to the public interest and to the highest standards of self-discipline, even at the expense of personal gain. Like general ethics, the Principles of the *Code of Professional Conduct* are *not* enforceable. Rather, they provide a framework for the *Rules of Conduct* which, like the rules of conduct in other professions, are minimum standards and therefore *are* enforceable on AICPA members.

---

3   "This Auditing Team Wants to Create a Moral Organization," *The Wall Street Journal* (January 19, 1996), p. B5.

Figure 4-1: Principles of Professional Conduct

Responsibilities
In carrying out their responsibilities as professionals, members should exercise sensitive professional and moral judgment in all their activities.

The Public Interest
Members should accept the obligation to act in a way that will serve the public interest, honor the public trust, and demonstrate commitment to professionalism.

Integrity
To maintain and broaden public confidence, members should perform all professional responsibilities with the highest sense of integrity.

Objectivity and Independence
A member should maintain objectivity and be free of conflicts of interest in discharging professional responsibilities. A member in public practice should be independent in fact and appearance when providing auditing and other attestation services.

Due Care
A member should observe the profession's technical and ethical standards, strive continually to improve competence and the quality of services, and discharge professional responsibility to the best of the member's ability.

Scope and Nature of Services
A member in public practice should observe the Code of Professional Conduct in determining the scope and nature of services to be provided.

RULES OF CONDUCT

The Rules of Conduct, discussed in detail later, govern the performance of all AICPA members—including those in public practice, industry, government, and education—in five general areas: independence, integrity, and objectivity; professional standards; responsibilities to clients; responsibilities to colleagues; and other responsibilities and practices. Figure 4-2 left column, lists the topics of the eleven *Rules of Conduct*, all of which are introduced and interpreted in the next section of the chapter. The Rules are to professional conduct what *generally accepted auditing standards* are to audit engagements and what *attestation standards* are to attest engagements: guidelines for behavior and measures of quality against which behavior is judged.

Because the *Rules of Conduct* are enforceable upon AICPA members, new or revised Rules require member approval by formal mail ballot before becoming effective. Proposals to amend the *Rules of Conduct* may be made by the professional ethics division, by the Institute's board of directors, by any 30 members of the AICPA Council, in writing by any 200 or more AICPA members, or by petition of five percent of the members. For example, in response to the profession's ever-expanding scope of attest and assurance services, the AICPA proposed and the membership approved substantial amendments to the Institute's *Rules of Conduct* in 1988.

INTERPRETATIONS AND ETHICS RULINGS

Interpretations of the Rules of Conduct are issued by the executive committee of the Institute's professional ethics division and are intended to interpret both

Figure 4-2: AICPA Rules of Conduct and Interpretations

Rule of Conduct	Related Interpretations
101 Independence	• The Effect of Transactions, Interests, or Relationships on Independence • Honorary Directorships and Trusteeships • Retired Partners and Firm Independence • Accounting Services • The Effect of Litigation on Independence • Effect on Independence of Financial Interests in Nonclients Having Investor or Investee Relationships with a Member's Client • The Meaning of Certain Independence Terminology and the Effect of Family Relationships on Independence • The Effect on Independence of Relationships with a Member's Client in the Financial Statements of a Governmental Entity
102 Integrity and Objectivity	• Knowing Misrepresentations in the Preparation of Financial Statements or Records
201 General Standards	• Competence • Definition of the Term "Engagement" in Rule 201
202 Compliance with Standards	
203 Accounting Principles	• Departure from Established Accounting Principles • Status of FASB Interpretations
301 Confidential Client Information	• Confidential Information and Technical Standards
302 Contingent Fees	• Meaning of the Phrase "The Findings of Governmental Agencies" in Rule 302
501 Acts Discreditable	• Client's Records and Accountant's Working Papers • Discrimination in Employment Practices • Failure to Follow Standards and/or Procedures or Other Requirements in Governmental Audits • Negligence in Preparing Statements or Records
502 Advertising and Other Forms of Solicitation	• False, Misleading or Deceptive Acts
503 Commissions and Referral Fees	• Fees in Payment of Services
505 Form of Practice and Name	• Investment in Commercial Accounting Corporation • Application of Rules of Conduct to Members Who Operate a Separate Business

the scope and the applicability of the *Rules of Conduct*. Figure 4-2, right column, lists the topics of major interpretations issued to date. Prior to adoption, all proposed *Interpretations* are first exposed to state societies (or associations) of CPAs, state boards of accountancy, and others for comment. **Ethics Rulings** are also issued by the ethics division's executive committee after exposure to state societies and boards of accountancy, among others. The Rulings summarize the applicability of *Rules of Conduct* and Interpretations to particular factual situations. AICPA members must justify departures from the *Rules of Conduct, Interpretations,* and *Ethics Rulings*.

RULES OF CONDUCT

Section 7 of the AICPA bylaws provides the authority for the *Code of Professional Conduct* in general and for the *Rules of Conduct* in particular. The Rules apply to all professional services rendered by AICPA members, except where the rule obviously indicates otherwise. For example, independence, the subject of Rule 101, applies to audit, attest, and assurance services, but not to consulting. Following a hearing for allegedly violating any provision of the *Rules of Conduct,* an ethics trial board may expel or suspend an offending AICPA member (for not more than two years) or impose a lesser sanction, such as a letter of admonishment. Of course, an AICPA member cannot engage a nonmember to carry out violations on his or her behalf, since acts carried out in a member's behalf are deemed to be performed by the member. The topics of the Rules and their related *Interpretations* are listed in Figure 4-2. Each Rule is discussed in the sections that follow.

INDEPENDENCE, INTEGRITY, AND OBJECTIVITY

Independence, integrity, and objectivity are the cornerstones of the profession, but they're also unobservable: One cannot observe a practitioner's independence from a client nor a practitioner's objectivity when he or she evaluates evidence. Owing to its importance in the profession's role as a trusted monitor over assertions made by management, independence has been the subject of more *Interpretations* and *Rulings* than any other Rule of the *Code of Professional Conduct.*

> **Rule 101—Independence**
> A member in public practice shall be independent in the performance of professional services as required by standards promulgated by bodies designated by Council.

Financial statement auditing is predicated upon a public accountant's independence both from the financial information audited and from the financial information's preparers and users. However, independence is required not only in financial statement audits, but in other attest services as well, such as review engagements and reports on prospective financial statements, both of which are discussed in Chapter 18.

Over the years, the AICPA's professional ethics division has issued a number of interpretations of Rule 101, all of which lend insight into issues that may detract from independence "in fact" or from independence "in appearance," both of which were introduced in Chapter 2. The following discusses the effect on independence of several potentially troublesome problems, all of which are addressed in AICPA ethics interpretations: (1) financial interests with clients, (2) providing both auditing and accounting services for the same client, (3) actual or threatened litigation by a client, and (4) serving as an honorary director or a trustee for a not-for-profit client.

Financial Interests

Can a practitioner be independent of a client in which he or she has a financial interest? Clearly, a CPA might well be intellectually honest in claiming independence in fact, but all parties who rely on his or her report have a legitimate claim that the practitioner lacks the appearance of independence, since he or she would have a vested interest in the outcome of the engagement. For example, consider the case of a CPA who audits the financial statements of a business he or she owns. Although the CPA may be unbiased in attesting to the financial position, results of operations, and cash flows of the business, a bank loan officer would likely suspect that the CPA's report lacks credibility, since the CPA has a vested interest in the outcome of the bank loan decision.

In practice, the appearance of independence is impaired if, for example, the practitioner has:

- A *direct* financial interest (e.g., owns stock) or *material indirect* financial interest (e.g., immediate family owns stock) in a client;
- A *joint, closely held business investment* with the client that is material in relation to the practitioner's (or his or her firm's) net worth; or
- Any *loan* to or from the client (other than automobile loans or leases, credit card and cash advance balances less than $5,000 in the aggregate, loans on the cash surrender value of insurance policies, and loans collateralized by cash deposits).

Although unrelated to financial interest, independence is also impaired if a practitioner (or a firm) acts as a promoter, underwriter, voting trustee, director or officer for a client, or in any other capacity equivalent either to management or to employment, or is a trustee for any pension or profit-sharing trust.

Accounting Services

Does the performance of accounting and data processing services for an audit client cause an auditor either to understate control risk or to compromise judgment about sensitive transactions, thereby impairing the auditor's independence from the data audited? In practice, the Securities and Exchange Commission specifically precludes an accountant from performing both accounting and auditing services for publicly traded clients. However, SEC regulations do not apply to privately owned companies.

For privately owned clients, an auditor can perform both accounting and audit services, but only when several conditions are met:

- The auditor must not have any *relationship* with the client or any *conflict of interest*;
- The client must accept *responsibility* for the financial statements;
- The auditor must not assume the role of *employee* or of *management* (e.g., selling products, maintaining custody of assets); and

- The auditor, in attesting to financial statements prepared from books and records that he or she has maintained completely or in part, must conform to *generally accepted auditing standards* (i.e., the fact that the auditor processed or maintained certain records does not eliminate the need to make sufficient audit tests).

Assuming a practitioner meets these requirements for a privately held client, he or she would retain the appearance of independence under the AICPA Rules of Conduct.

Actual or Threatened Litigation

If an auditor is to fulfill his or her obligation to render an informed opinion on an entity's financial statements, the relationship between the entity's management and the auditor must be characterized by complete candor, full disclosure, and an undisputed absence of bias. However, because of the expressed or implied contractual relationship between an auditor and a client, and the auditor's status as an independent contractor, clients sometimes sue auditors for allegedly failing to carry out the duties of an audit services contract—that is, for breach of contract. When client management commences or expresses an intention to commence legal action against an auditor, the auditor and client are suddenly placed in adversary positions, thereby raising questions about the client's candor and willingness to disclose, about the auditor's objectivity and self-interest, and therefore about the auditor's independence.

An *Interpretation* identifies four instances in which litigation would impair auditor independence: (1) litigation by management alleging deficiencies in audit work, (2) litigation by the auditor against management alleging management fraud or deceit, (3) an expressed intention by management to commence litigation alleging deficiencies in audit work (if the auditor concludes there is a strong possibility that a claim will be filed), and (4) litigation not related to audit work but material either to the public accounting firm's or to the client's financial statements (these nonaudit-related claims may arise, for example, out of disputes about billing for services or the results of tax or consulting services). Thus, in most instances, actual or threatened litigation would generally impair independence in appearance, if not independence in fact.

Honorary Directorships and Trusteeships

Accountants are often asked to serve as honorary directors or trustees for, and therefore to lend the prestige of their names to, not-for-profit charitable or civic organizations. The question raised is whether the accountant can serve both as an honorary trustee or director and as auditor without violating the appearance of independence. For example, wouldn't a major philanthropic organization have cause for alarm if a grant application from a local arts commission reveals that a partner in a public accounting firm serves both as an honorary trustee and as independent auditor for the commission? Doesn't the partner's joint appointment pose a conflict of interests?

The profession assumes that not-for-profit organizations that request only the prestige of an accountant's name also have sufficiently large boards to limit the accountant's participation in board activities. Therefore, under the *Code of Professional Conduct*, independence is not impaired as long as the accountant's position is purely honorary (and identified as honorary in all letterheads and circulated materials), the accountant restricts involvement to the use of his or her name, and the accountant does not vote or otherwise participate in management activities.

> ### Rule 102—Integrity and Objectivity
> In the performance of any professional service, a member shall maintain objectivity and integrity, shall be free of conflicts of interest, and shall not knowingly misrepresent facts or subordinate his or her judgment to others.

Rule 102 requires that in performing *any* professional service, not just financial statement auditing, an AICPA member remain objective—impartial with respect to the client—and perform the service with integrity, which is defined as having an attitude of uprightness, honesty, and sincerity. For example, an auditor would lack both objectivity and integrity if he or she knowingly allowed a client to overstate the carrying value of obsolete inventory. In fact, an Interpretation issued under Rule 102 specifically states that an accountant who knowingly makes—or directs another to make—false or misleading entries in an entity's records or financial statements is considered to have knowingly misrepresented facts in violation of Rule 102.

As noted earlier, auditors are independent attesters, not advocates for their audit clients. However, a public accountant could act as an advocate for tax or consulting clients without violating Rule 102. For example, an accountant could exhaustively research the Internal Revenue Code, a commercial tax service (e.g., Commerce Clearing House), and relevant court cases to support a deduction on a client's tax return. If the deduction had substantial authoritative support, the accountant could justifiably sign the tax return as preparer without infringing on Rule 102. But, if the accountant's research does not support the deduction, then signing the return as preparer would lack both objectivity and integrity, since the accountant would have subordinated his or her judgment to the client.

GENERAL AND TECHNICAL STANDARDS

The general and technical standards of the *Rules of Conduct* relate to an AICPA member's professional obligation to be competent and to be aware of, and comply with, the profession's published, authoritative standards.

> ### Rule 201—General Standards
> A member shall comply with the following standards and with any interpretations thereof by bodies designated by Council.
> A. **Professional Competence.** Undertake only those professional services that the member or the member's firm can reasonably expect to be completed with professional competence.
> B. **Due Professional Care.** Exercise due professional care in the performance of professional services.
> C. **Planning and Supervision.** Adequately plan and supervise the performance of professional services.
> D. **Sufficient Relevant Data.** Obtain sufficient relevant data to afford a reasonable basis for conclusions or recommendations in relation to any professional services performed.

Rule 201-A explicitly precludes a member from accepting engagements beyond the scope of his or her competence—competence being the technical qualifications of the practitioner, the ability to supervise and evaluate the work of subordinates, his or her knowledge and understanding of applicable standards, and sound professional judgment. However, Rule 201 does not preclude members from improving their competence (for example, through research, consultation with other practitioners, and continuing professional education courses) in order to offer new services.

Rules 201-B, -C, and -D relate to issues addressed also in *generally accepted auditing standards,* specifically the third general standard (201-B) and the first (201-C) and third (201-D) standards of field work. The *Code of Professional Conduct* reinforces the importance of these three standards to financial statement auditing, although all three rules apply equally to other professional services performed by AICPA members in public practice and to members not in public practice.

In practice, auditors and clients sometimes disagree over the type of audit opinion required, the interpretation of accounting principles, or the need for financial statement disclosure, among other things. When there are disagreements, some clients will request that competing public accounting firms provide professional advice to them on the disputed matters, thereby raising questions about Rule 201-D, sufficient relevant data, since the responding firm is likely to have only a subset of the evidence available to the engaged auditor. The *Code of Professional Conduct* does not preclude an accountant from providing advice to nonclients, but *Statement on Auditing Standards No. 50,* "Reports on the Application of Accounting Principles," recognizes that questions from nonclients are often prompted by disagreements and that the accountant should first consult with the engaged accountant before providing advice. In short, advice should not be given without first considering all of the facts and both sides of the issue. Reporting on the application of accounting principles is illustrated in Chapter 18.

Rule 202—Compliance with Standards

A member who performs auditing, review, compilation, management advisory, tax, or other professional services shall comply with standards promulgated by bodies designated by Council.

Rule 202 requires that AICPA members comply with all professional standards relevant to a service rendered. In audit and attestation engagements, respectively, *generally accepted auditing standards* (and all *Statements on Auditing Standards*) and *attestation standards* (and all *Statements on Standards for Attestation Engagements*) are the "standards promulgated by bodies designated by Council" (i.e., the Auditing Standards Board). Apart from audit and attestation services, other professional services also have standards. For example, for compilation engagements and for financial forecast and projection engagements, the standards of professional practice are included in *Statements on Standards for Accounting and Review Services* and *Standards for Forecasts and Projections*, respectively, both of which are discussed in Chapter 18. Violating a *generally accepted auditing standard,* an *attestation standard,* or the standards for any other professional service, in turn violates the *Code of Professional Conduct.*

Rule 203—Accounting Principles

A member shall not (1) express an opinion or state affirmatively that the financial statements or other financial data of any entity are presented in conformity with generally accepted accounting principles or (2) state that he or she is not aware of any such material modifications that should be made to such statements or data in order for them to be in conformity with generally accepted accounting principles, if such statements or data contain any departure from an accounting principle promulgated by bodies designated by Council to establish such principles that has a material effect on the statements or data taken as a whole. If, however, the statements or data contain such a departure and the member can demonstrate that due to unusual circumstances the financial statements or data would otherwise have been misleading, the member can comply with the rule by describing the departure, its approximate effects, if practicable, and the reasons why compliance with the principle would result in a misleading statement.

Rule 203 relates to all engagements for which financial statements or other financial data are reported on by an AICPA member. Thus, the rule applies to financial statement audits and to special engagements for which generally accepted accounting principles are reported on, such as reports on a comprehensive basis of accounting other than GAAP (e.g., cash basis statements) or reports on specified elements of a financial statement (e.g., gross sales), both of which are introduced in Chapter 18. Departures from FASB *Statements of Financial Accounting Standards*, GASB *Statements of Governmental Accounting Standards*, *Opinions of the Accounting Principles Board*, and *Accounting Research Bulletins* are prohibited under Rule 203.

There is a strong presumption that adherence to the accounting principles contained in authoritative pronouncements, like *Statements of Financial Accounting Standards*, would in nearly all instances result in financial statements that are not misleading. However, in rare and unusual circumstances, like new legislation or a creative business transaction, an accountant may believe that the literal interpretation and application of an accounting pronouncement would result in misleading financial statements. An *Interpretation* of Rule 203 recognizes that, because it is difficult for authoritative bodies to anticipate *all* of the circumstances to which accounting principles might apply, the proper accounting treatment for a transaction or event may deviate from the requirements of an official pronouncement. Applications of the *Interpretation* in practice, though, are rare; the operative word in the *Interpretation* is "unusual."

RESPONSIBILITIES TO CLIENTS

In serving the public, a practitioner is obligated to be independent and to perform the engagement with integrity and objectivity. However, an AICPA member also has an obligation to be fair to (although not compromised by) his or her client's interests as well.

Rule 301—Confidential Client Information

A member in public practice shall not disclose any confidential client information without the specific consent of the client.

This rule shall not be construed (1) to relieve a member of his or her professional obligations under rules 202 and 203, (2) to affect in any way the member's obligation to comply with a validly issued and enforceable subpoena or summons, (3) to prohibit review of a member's professional practice under AICPA or state CPA society authorization, or (4) to preclude a member from initiating a complaint with or responding to any inquiry made by a recognized investigative or disciplinary body.

Members of a recognized investigative or disciplinary body and professional practice reviewers shall not use to their own advantage or disclose any member's confidential client information that comes to their attention in carrying out their official responsibilities. However, this prohibition shall not restrict the exchange of information with a recognized investigative or disciplinary body or affect, in any way, compliance with a validly issued and enforceable subpoena or summons.

In the course of a professional engagement, a practitioner typically encounters confidential client information. For example, when reviewing for potential legal claims against a client, an auditor may learn from attorneys that a patent has been obtained by the company to manufacture a revolutionary new product. Other examples of confidential information include officers' salaries, unreleased advertising campaigns, and product cost information. Disclosing confidential information without a client's consent could be detrimental to a client's competitive position within an industry and therefore is prohibited. The purpose of Rule 301 is to encourage a client to provide information freely to an independent accountant without threat of confidential information being disclosed unnecessarily.

In the early 1990s, the AICPA's membership voted to clarify the circumstances under which confidential information would have to be disclosed. Effective in January 1992, members could disclose information to the AICPA Professional Ethics Division and to state boards of accountancy, but could not volunteer confidential client information to government agencies, such as the Internal Revenue Service. Closely related to confidentiality is the issue of privileged information. Information communicated between physicians and patients and between attorneys and clients is privileged and therefore cannot be requested even by a court of law. Information communicated between a CPA and client, however, is not privileged under common law (partly because accounting is a younger profession, and partly because auditors are independent attesters rather than advocates for their clients), but is privileged under the statutes of some states. That is, there is no right of privileged communication in federal jurisdictions, but there is in some states.

Rule 302—Contingent Fees

A member in public practice shall not:

(1) Perform for a contingent fee any professional service for, or receive such a fee from, a client for whom the member or member's firm performs: (a) an audit or review of a financial statement; or (b) a compilation of a financial statement when the member expects, or reasonably might expect that a third party will use the financial statement and the member's compilation report does not disclose a lack of independence; or (c) an examination of prospective financial information; or

(2) Prepare an original or amended tax return for a tax refund for a contingent fee for any client.

The prohibition in (1) above applies during the period in which the member or the member's firm is engaged to perform any of the services listed above and the period covered by any historical financial statements involved in any such listed services.

Except as stated in the next sentence, a contingent fee is a fee established for the performance of any service pursuant to an arrangement in which no fee will be charged unless a specified finding or result is attained, or in which the amount of the fee is otherwise dependent upon the finding or result of such service. Solely for purposes of this rule, fees are not regarded as being contingent if fixed by courts or other public authorities, or, in tax matters, if determined based on the result of judicial proceedings or the findings of governmental agencies.

A member's fees may vary depending, for example, on the complexity of services rendered.

Rule 302 prohibits fee arrangements with attestation clients whereby no fee is paid unless a particular outcome is attained (e.g., no fee unless the audit opinion is unqualified) or the fee is contingent upon a particular outcome (e.g., a fee of 10 percent of reported net income), the intent being to remove AICPA members from potentially compromising conflicts of interest. Interestingly, prior to the 1990s, the AICPA also prohibited contingent fee arrangements with nonattestation clients. However, in a 1987 letter to the National Association of State Boards of Accountancy (NASBA), the Federal Trade Commission (FTC) questioned contingent-fee prohibitions, stating that allowing contingent fees would link accountants' fees to the results of the engaged work, not to the hours engaged, thereby potentially lowering the cost, and raising the quality, of accounting services rendered. But what about the potential for conflicts of interest, the motivation for Rule 302? Since the conflict of interest pertains largely to attest engagements, such as financial statement audits or reviews, the AICPA agreed to prohibit contingent fees for attestation services (a proposal made originally by the FTC in a 1988 consent order to the AICPA), and for original and amended tax returns filed for a refund. Note, though, that some states do not allow contingent fees under any circumstances.

Rule 302 offers several opportunities for AICPA members to enter into contingent fee arrangements with nonattestation service clients. For example, a member acting as an expert witness in a legal liability case may charge a fee contingent on a plaintiff's award. Also, a fee may be dependent on the complexity of an engagement. For example, a member may charge more per hour of audit work for a complex multinational oil- and gas-producing company than for a local retail gas station that sells refined oil and gas products.

RESPONSIBILITIES TO COLLEAGUES

Every practicing accountant owes to every other practicing accountant an express obligation to remain competent and to participate intellectually in the profession through responsible contributions to professional organizations, like the AICPA and state societies, and by cooperating in the profession's self-regulation, like ethics enforcement, quality control, and quality review. Self-regulation may also require that a member testify as an expert witness in proceedings brought against another practitioner—for example, in a judicial proceeding or ethics division inquiry. In professional practice, an accountant is obligated to follow and, in the case of acting as an expert witness, to uphold the *Code of Professional Conduct.*

Although not an interpretation of the Rules of Conduct, *Statement on Auditing Standards No. 7*, "Communication Between Predecessor and Successor Auditors" (AU Sec. 315), addresses responsibilities to colleagues when a change of auditors occurs, which is sometimes called an "audit switch." The statement defines a **successor auditor** as one who has accepted an engagement or been invited to submit a proposal, and places the burden on the successor for initiating communication with the **predecessor auditor** (the auditor being replaced). The predecessor, however, must first obtain the client's permission before responding. Under Rule 301, a predecessor auditor may not disclose confidential client information without a client's specific permission.

Clearly, a practicing accountant must be competitive to develop a viable client base, and a natural by-product of competition is that some members will gain new clients and others will lose clients. Shifts in client bases, however, are healthy for the profession, since competition creates incentives for accountants to produce their services more efficiently. But competition should not be so intense that the interests of the profession as a whole are undermined. Accountants should be competitive in providing quality professional services, yet responsible to avoid unscrupulous means for attracting potential clients.

Prior to the 1990s, there were two Rules of Conduct on responsibilities to colleagues, but both were deleted by AICPA member vote.

OTHER RESPONSIBILITIES AND PRACTICES

In general, Rule 501 relates to acts not specifically covered by other Rules of Conduct. Although the term "discreditable" is not defined, three Interpretations of Rule 501 discussed below lend insight.

> ### Rule 501—Acts Discreditable
> A member shall not commit an act discreditable to the profession.

Working papers are the accountant's property: They need not be surrendered to the client. However, in some instances, accountants prepare working papers that contain information not included or recorded within the client's books and records, such as listings of cash receipts/disbursements and depreciation schedules. One *Interpretation* of Rule 501 recognizes that some working papers actually constitute part of the client's records, and copies should therefore be made available to the client upon request, even if the client disputes the auditor's fee. Examples of working papers considered part of a client's records include: (1) spreadsheets that replace books of original entry (e.g., listings of cash disbursements on spreadsheets), (2) spreadsheets used in place of the general ledger or subsidiary ledgers (e.g., job cost and equipment ledgers and depreciation records), (3) all adjusting entries and closing journal entries made by the auditor, and (4) all consolidating or combining journal entries and worksheets used in arriving at line items on the financial statements or tax returns. Any working papers developed by the accountant that do not result in changes to the client's records, or are not in themselves part of the records ordinarily maintained by the client, are not the client's property.

A second *Interpretation* of Rule 501 states that discrimination based on race, color, sex, age, or national origin in hiring, promotion, salary, or other employment practices constitutes an act discreditable to the profession in violation of Rule 501. A third *Interpretation* concludes that an accountant who negligently makes, or permits or directs another to make, false and misleading entries in the financial statements or records of a client has committed an act discreditable to the profession in violation of Rule 501.

Rule 502—Advertising and Other Forms of Solicitation

A member in public practice shall not seek to obtain clients by advertising or other forms of solicitation in a manner that is false, misleading, or deceptive. Solicitation by the use of coercion, overreaching, or harassing conduct is prohibited.

For over 50 years accountants were prohibited from advertising. However, in 1976, the Institute's professional ethics division became aware that state attorneys general, the Justice Department, and the FTC were beginning to advise several professional groups to repeal or at least not enforce prohibitions against advertising. In 1977 the U.S. Supreme Court ruled 5-4 in *Bates v. State Bar of Arizona* (97 S. Ct. 2691) that the Arizona Bar, a state agency, could not deprive attorneys of their First Amendment (free speech) rights to advertise. In response, the AICPA membership voted overwhelmingly to modify the language of Rule 502. The current version of the Rule was adopted by member vote in 1988.

As stated in Rule 502, false, misleading, or deceptive advertising is prohibited. An Interpretation of Rule 502 identifies four instances of advertising that are deceptive and therefore not in the public interest: advertising that creates false expectations of favorable results; implies an ability to influence any court or regulatory body; states a specific service will be performed for a stated fee, estimated fee, or fee range when it is likely the fee will be increased substantially; or contains any other representation that would likely cause a reasonable person to misunderstand or to be deceived.

Rule 503—Commissions and Referral Fees

(A) *Prohibited Commissions*. A member in public practice shall not for a commission recommend or refer to a client any product or service, or for a commission recommend or refer any product or service to be supplied by a client, or receive a commission, when the member or the member's firm also performs for that client:

   (a) an audit or review of a financial statement; or
   (b) a compilation of a financial statement when the member expects, or reasonably might expect, that a third party will use the financial statement and the member's compilation does not disclose a lack of independence; or
   (c) an examination of prospective financial information.

This prohibition applies during the period in which the member is engaged to perform any of the services listed above and the period covered by any historical financial statements involved in such listed services.

(B) *Disclosure of permitted commissions*. A member in public practice who is not prohibited by this rule from performing services for or receiving a commission and who is paid or expects to be paid a commission shall disclose that fact to any person or entity to whom the member recommends or refers a product or service to which the commission relates.

(C) *Referral fees.* Any member who accepts a referral fee for recommending or referring any service of a CPA to any person or entity or who pays a referral fee to obtain a client shall disclose such acceptance or payment to the client.

Owing to the potential for conflicts of interest, Rule 503 prohibits a member from receiving or paying commissions for referring services, or for recommending products, to clients for whom the member provides attestation services, such as financial statement audits or reviews. For example, if a practitioner recommends software to an audit client, the practitioner may not collect a commission either from the client for advice or from the software vendor for recommending their product. Rule 302 does not prohibit commissions or referral fees for products or services recommended to a nonattestation client—for example, a commission paid by a software vendor to a practitioner who recommended software to his or her consulting client—although the practitioner must disclose the commission or fee to the client.

Prior to the 1990s, commissions and referral fees were prohibited for all clients, attestation and nonattestation. However, the Federal Trade Commission (FTC), in the same letter to the National Association of State Boards of Accountancy (NASBA) referred to earlier for contingent fees, criticized Rule 503's prohibition of commissions, arguing that permitting commissions would allow consumers an option for "one stop financial shopping" and thereby encourage competition in the market for financial services. As with contingent fees, the AICPA agreed to prohibit commissions and referral fees for attestation clients only. Note that, like contingent fees, some states do not allow commissions under any circumstances.

Occasionally, an accounting firm will advise a client that, although the firm has begun work on an engagement, the firm realizes now that, under the first general standard of the AICPA's *generally accepted auditing standards,* or the first and second *attestation standards* (Chapter 2), they're not proficient to complete the engagement. Typically, the firm would then refer a successor firm. Rule 503 does not prohibit either the successor firm or the client from paying the referring practitioner for work completed on the engagement to date. In addition, Rule 503 does not prohibit firms from compensating staff for practice development (i.e., engaging new clients), since securing new clients does not by itself create a conflict of interest.

Rule 505—Form of Practice and Name

A member may practice public accounting only in the form of organization permitted by state law or regulation whose characteristics conform to resolutions of Council.

A member shall not practice public accounting under a firm name that is misleading. Names of one or more past partners or shareholders may be included in the firm name of a successor partnership or corporation. Also, a partner or shareholder surviving the death or withdrawal of all other partners or shareholders may continue to practice under such name which includes the name of past partners or shareholders for up to two years after becoming a sole practitioner.

> A firm may not designate itself as "Members of the American Institute of Certified Public Accountants" unless all of its partners or shareholders are members of the Institute.

A firm of certified public accountants may organize in any form permitted by state law, which in all states includes sole proprietorship (i.e., a self-employed CPA), partnership, or professional corporation, and in many states also includes a limited liability corporation.

In a *partnership,* each partner is jointly and severally liable for the partnership's debts, obligations, and wrongful acts and, under a legal concept known as "vicarious liability," each partner's personal assets are at risk regardless of the extent of their investment in the partnership or involvement in the debt, obligation, or act. A *professional corporation* represents a corporation in form, but a partnership in substance. Unlike traditional corporations, professional corporations do not provide relief from vicarious liability in some states; each shareholder in the firm is jointly and severally liable in litigation brought against the firm in those states.

Prior to 1992, Rule 505 permitted only the proprietorship, partnership, or professional corporation forms of organization. But, responding to a litigation explosion in the 1980s (Chapter 5) and to the rights afforded other practicing professionals (among them, members of the American Bar Association and the American Medical Association), AICPA members voted resoundingly in 1991 to permit CPA firms to organize in any manner permitted by state law, including a limited liability partnership (LLP). An LLP provides a CPA firm with the benefits of taxation as a partnership, thereby avoiding double taxation (i.e., corporate taxes to the professional corporation and individual taxes to the shareholders), and, as introduced in Chapter 1, limited liability, thereby providing relief from vicarious liability. For example, an individual partner's liability extends to his or her investment in the firm, except that a litigant can make claims against a partner's personal assets for liability linked to his or her own actions. In short, LLPs limit to his or her investment in the firm the liability of partners or shareholders who are not themselves involved in a negligent act done in a firm's name. Some form of LLP is available in all states.

The name of a public accounting firm can be fictitious or indicate a specialization, provided that the firm name or specialization is not misleading. For example, the firm name, "Raymond Carver, CPA, Tax Specialist," is acceptable, but "O'Hara and Shaw, CPAs" is *not* acceptable if one of the two is not a CPA. In this context, Rule 505 is consistent with Rule 502 on advertising: Only firm names or specializations that are false, misleading, or deceptive are prohibited. Also, all firm partners or shareholders must be AICPA members in order for the firm to carry the designation "Members of the AICPA."

JOINT ETHICS ENFORCEMENT

Three organizations enforce ethical conduct among CPAs: the AICPA, the state societies of CPAs (both voluntary membership organizations), and the state boards of accountancy (state regulatory agencies). The AICPA enforces the AICPA *Code of Professional Conduct,* state societies of CPAs enforce state codes, and, after a hearing, each organization can suspend or expel a violator and can publicize ethics violations. However, because the state boards of accountancy are empowered to regulate the practice of public accounting within their own states, and therefore can revoke a CPA's license to practice, state boards are the most powerful of the three organizations, since a CPA can practice regardless of membership in the AICPA or a state society but cannot practice without a license.

In an effort to standardize enforcement and disciplinary proceedings across the states and to promote communication, the AICPA and virtually all of the state societies have joined forces in a joint ethics enforcement program (JEEP). The program allows the AICPA's ethics division and state society ethics committees to act independently or to refer a case to the National Joint Trial Board. Alleged violations that involve more than one state, that involve potential litigation, or that are of national concern are handled by the AICPA's professional ethics division; others are handled by the state society ethics committee. Cases involving litigation are placed in a suspense file until settled; if convicted in court, a CPA's AICPA and state society memberships are automatically suspended on conviction and terminated upon final judgment.

Cases reach the Joint Trial Board if: (1) both the AICPA and the state society concur on their findings, yet do not issue a joint administrative reprimand, or (2) either the AICPA or the state society takes action individually and refers a case on its own. Following a disciplinary hearing, the Joint Trial Board may take any one of the following courses of action: acquittal, censure, suspension (up to two years) or expulsion of a member, or a judgment requiring continuing professional education. A member may appeal an adverse decision.

MONITORING PUBLIC ACCOUNTING FIRMS: STANDARDS OF QUALITY CONTROL AND QUALITY REVIEW

The value of an attestation or audit report rests squarely on the practitioner's impartiality, his or her freedom from the influences that may be exerted unduly by a client's management or by the report's users. But, given that a practitioner's judgment processes and his or her work product—called *working papers* in Chapter 6—are not matters of public record, how do we know that practitioners comply with *attestation standards* or with *generally accepted auditing standards*? Who audits the auditors? The answer is that the public accounting profession is self-regulated through the AICPA's Quality Review Division in general, and through pronouncements of the Institute's Quality Review Executive Committee in particular. Today, self-regulation is achieved through two means:

*   **Quality control**, the internal policies and procedures designed by a public accounting firm to assure consistent performance and achievement within the firm, and
*   **Peer review** (also called **quality review**), an independent outside review of a firm's quality control performed by practitioners not otherwise employed by the firm reviewed.

Over the past decade, quality control and peer review have become increasingly important to the management of a public accounting practice, particularly since the highly publicized audit failures reported in the savings and loan and government securities industries in the 1980s. The success and continued acceptance of self-regulation in the public accounting profession may depend heavily on the effectiveness of the quality control and peer review programs introduced here.

QUALITY CONTROL

The quality of a firm's audit practice is dependent on the quality of each of the firm's completed engagements: a whole is equal to the sum of its parts. Since *attestation standards* and *GAAS* are the measures of an attestation or audit engagement's quality, it follows that the quality of a firm's practice is therefore dependent on the application of *attestation standards* and *GAAS* to each engagement. Quality control is the vehicle used by public accounting firms to assure that *attestation standards* and *GAAS* are followed on each engagement and, as a result, that the firm maintains a quality practice. For example, as stated in *Statement on Auditing Standards No. 25,* "The Relationship of Generally Accepted Auditing Standards to Quality Control Standards" (AU Sec. 161):

- A firm should establish quality control policies and procedures to provide reasonable assurance of conformity with standards in individual engagements.
- Professional standards and quality control standards are related, and the quality control policies and procedures adopted by a firm may affect the conduct both of individual engagements and of a firm's practice as a whole.

Statement on Quality Control Standards No. 2, "System of Quality Control for a CPA Firm's Accounting and Auditing Practice," requires that a firm have a comprehensive and suitably designed quality control system, encompassing the firm's organization structure, internal policies, and procedures. The extent of a firm's system of quality control will depend on its size and organizational structure, the degree of operating autonomy vested in administrative personnel and practice offices, the nature of the practice, and the cost and expected benefits of the system. For example, a Big Six firm will have a far more extensive system than a single-office local firm. Despite the extent of a firm's quality control system, the firm should have policies and procedures that address each of the five elements of quality control identified in Figure 4-3.

PEER (QUALITY) REVIEW

Who better to monitor a CPA firm's system of quality control than peers in other CPA firms? Partly for this reason, the AICPA in the 1970s established a membership division for CPA firms, categorizing member firms as SEC practice firms or private companies practice firms, and requiring periodic peer reviews as a condition of membership. *SEC Practice Section* firms are those firms that provide services to any publicly traded client (i.e., companies whose securities are traded on national or regional stock exchanges or over the counter and therefore must file periodic financial reports with the SEC). The collective performance of all SEC Practice Section firms is monitored through an autonomous Public Oversight Board, introduced in Chapter 1, which meets and issues reports on section activities and oversights. *Private Companies Practice Section* firms serve nonpublicly traded, privately owned companies.

Figure 4-3: Elements and Examples of Quality Control Policies

Independence, Integrity, and Objectivity
Establish policies to provide reasonable assurance that all staff are independent of attest clients to the extent required by the AICPA's *Code of Professional Conduct*.

Example:
Require that all staff identify attest clients in which they own securities.

Personnel Management
Establish policies for hiring, advancement, assigning personnel to engagements, and professional development.

Example:
Designate a staff member to assign personnel to engagements. Base assignments on engagement needs and on staff career development.

Acceptance and Continuance of Clients
Establish policies to preclude accepting or continuing services for managements that lack integrity.

Example:
Outsource background checks for all proposed clients' management.

Engagement Performance
Establish policies for planning, performing, supervising, reviewing, documenting, and communicating the results of each engagement.

Example:
Assign staff to review planning memos, working papers, and reports, and designate a consulting partner for each industry the firm serves.

Monitoring
Establish policies for monitoring compliance with the firm's quality control policies and procedures.

Example:
Assign an assessment director to document quality control compliance.

Membership in the divisions and participation in periodic peer reviews had been voluntary through 1988. However, in 1988, the AICPA membership voted to require that practitioners in a firm not be permitted to renew their AICPA memberships unless the firm participates in a peer review program. And in 1990, the membership voted to require peer reviews for all public accounting firms engaged by publicly traded audit clients. A peer review may be performed by another public accounting firm (called a *firm review*), by a state CPA society, by the AICPA's Quality Review Division (a committee-appointed review team), or by a regional association of firms (called an *association review*). In all cases, a peer review team is charged with the following responsibilities:

- Study and evaluate the reviewed firm's system of quality control.
- Examine the reviewed firm's compliance with its quality control procedures.
- Examine the reviewed firm's documentation for compliance with section membership requirements.

Review teams report their findings to the reviewed firm. Deficiencies in quality control policies or in compliance with section membership requirements can result in fines, suspensions, expulsion from membership, or other actions against the reviewed member firm.

The AICPA's peer review program for participating firms is both educational and remedial, encouraging self-regulation and self-discipline within the profession by imposing practice requirements for all firms. In addition to establishing and maintaining a program of peer review for firms, the AICPA firm-membership sections are intended to improve the quality of each member firm's services to clients by sanctioning practice requirements and disciplinary action.

SUMMARY

General ethics relate to ideal conduct, choice, and the consequences of choice and are the basis for codes of ethics in the professions. The AICPA *Code of Professional Conduct* consists of two sections, *Principles* and *Rules of Conduct,* and also includes *Interpretations* and *Ethics Rulings.* Six principles underlie the Code: responsibilities, the public interest, integrity, objectivity and independence, due care, and the scope and nature of services. The *Rules of Conduct* relate to independence, integrity, and objectivity; general and technical standards; responsibilities to clients and colleagues; and other responsibilities. Like *Interpretations* and *Ethics Rulings,* the *Rules of Conduct* are enforceable by the AICPA upon members. *Interpretations* are intended to interpret the scope and applicability of specific *Rules of Conduct,* and *Ethics Rulings* are intended to summarize the applicability of Rules and *Interpretations* to specific, factual situations; both *Interpretations* and *Ethics Rulings* are issued by the AICPA's professional ethics division.

Enforcement of the AICPA and individual state society codes had been relatively ineffective prior to the 1990s. As a result, the AICPA and the states developed a joint ethics enforcement system in conjunction with the National Joint Trial Board. This system allows the AICPA and the state societies to act either independently or jointly to review complaints and to reprimand ethics violators. Who audits the auditors? Today, the monitoring of public accounting firms is achieved by the AICPA's quality control and peer review programs. In short, the public accounting profession is self-regulated, although the survival of the AICPA's programs depend heavily on public accounting firms' committing considerable resources to their own internal policies for assuring quality.

KEY TERMS

AICPA Code of Professional
  Conduct   97
Rules of Conduct   97
Principles of the Code of
  Professional Conduct   99
Interpretations of the Rules of
  Conduct   100

Ethics Rulings   102
Successor auditor   110
Predecessor auditor   110
Limited liability partnership (LLP)   113
Quality control   114
Peer (quality) review   114

REFERENCES

Professional Standards

AICPA Professional Standards, Vol. 2 (New York: AICPA).
SAS No. 7, "Communication Between Predecessor and Successor Auditors" (AU Sec. 315).
SAS No. 50, "Reports on the Application of Accounting Principles" (AU Sec. 625).
SQCS No. 2, "System of Quality Control for a CPA Firm's Accounting and Auditing Practice."
SQCS No. 3, "Monitoring a CPA Firm's Accounting and Auditing Practice."

Professional Reports

AICPA. *Standards for Performing and Reporting on Quality Reviews*. New York: AICPA.
AICPA. *Restructuring Professional Standards to Achieve Professional Excellence in a Changing Environment*. Report of the Special Committee on Standards of Professional Conduct for Certified Public Accountants. New York: AICPA, 1986.

Articles, Books

Albrecht, W. S., ed. *Ethical Issues in the Practice of Accounting*. Cincinnati: South-Western Publishing, 1992.
Arthur Andersen & Co. *Business Ethics Program: Volume 2, Accounting Materials*, 1992.
Barber, B., and K. M. Gibson. "New Standards Alter Quality Control Systems," *Journal of Accountancy* (August 1996), pp. 67-71.
Bowie, N. E., and D. F. Duska. *Business Ethics*. Englewood Cliffs: Prentice Hall, 1990.
Ehlen, C. R., and R. B. Welker. "Procedural Fairness in the Peer and Quality Review Programs," *Auditing: A Journal of Practice & Theory* (Spring 1996), pp. 38-52.
Grant, J., R. Bricker, and R. Shiptsova. "Audit Quality and Professional Self-Regulation," *Auditing: A Journal of Practice & Theory* (Spring 1996), pp. 142-256.
Jeffrey, C. "Ethical Development of Accounting Students, Non-Accounting Business Students, and Liberal Arts Students," *Issues in Accounting Education* (Spring 1993), pp. 86-96.
Mautz, R. K., and H. A. Sharaf. *The Philosophy of Auditing*. Sarasota: American Accounting Association, 1961.
McCabe, R. K., A. D. Luzi, and T. Brennan. "Managing Partners' Perceptions of Peer Review," *Auditing: A Journal of Practice & Theory* (Fall 1993), pp. 108-115.
Mintz, S. M. *Cases in Accounting Ethics and Professionalism*. New York: McGraw Hill, 1990.
Pearson, M. A. "Doing the Right Thing," *Journal of Accountancy* (June 1995), pp. 82-86.
Pearson, M. A. "The Professional Ethics Committee: Protecting the Public Interest," *Journal of Accountancy* (October 1993), pp. 128-131.
Velasquez, F. *Business Ethics*, 2nd. ed. Englewood Cliffs: Prentice Hall, 1988.
Windal, F. W. *Ethics and the Accountant: Text and Cases*. Englewood Cliffs: Prentice Hall, 1991.

QUESTIONS

1. What are general ethics, and how do they relate to professional ethics?
2. Identify and briefly describe the four components of the AICPA *Code of Professional Conduct.*
3. Relate the Principles of Professional Conduct, ideal conduct, and trust. Be specific.
4. Discuss the applicability of the AICPA *Rules of Conduct.*
5. Identify at least four examples of situations in which an AICPA member would not be deemed independent.
6. May an AICPA member serve as an attorney for an audit client? Explain.
7. What is the purpose of the general and technical standards of the AICPA *Code of Professional Conduct?*
8. Does Rule 301, "Confidential Client Information," preclude AICPA members who serve on AICPA ethics division subcommittees and members of state society ethics

committees from exchanging confidential client information that is central to an ethics investigation? Explain.

9. Who should initiate communication between predecessor and successor auditors when a change in auditors occurs? Explain. What impact does Rule 301, "Confidential Client Information," have on communication between predecessor and successor auditors?

10. Rule 502, "Advertising and Other Forms of Solicitation," precludes a member from advertising in a manner that is false, misleading, or deceptive. What is meant by "false, misleading, or deceptive" advertising?

11. When referring a client to another CPA, can an AICPA member accept a referral fee from the CPA if: (a) the amount is clearly immaterial, and (b) it merely covers the AICPA member's costs (i.e., time and expenses) of referring? Explain.

12. Explain the current national joint ethics enforcement system.

13. Briefly explain the AICPA's quality review program for public accounting firms.

14. Explain how quality control, *attestation standards,* and *generally accepted auditing standards* are related.

MULTIPLE CHOICE QUESTIONS

1. General ethics is the study of:

a. Ideal method in thought.
b. Ultimate reality.
c. Ideal conduct.
d. Ideal social organization.

2. Professional codes of ethics:

a. Are uncommon in professions other than public accounting.
b. Mandate ideal standards of behavior.
c. Are enforceable if based in standards of ideal behavior.
d. Mandate minimum standards of behavior.

3. A practitioner can perform accounting and auditing services for a privately owned client assuming that:

a. The practitioner takes responsibility for management's assertions.
b. The practitioner has a financial interest in management's assertions.
c. The practitioner is independent of assertions about management's information system.
d. The practitioner is certain the conflict of interest is immaterial to the firm and to the client.

4. According to the profession's Rules of Conduct, an auditor would be considered independent in which of the following instances?

a. The auditor's checking account is held at a client financial institution.
b. The auditor, an attorney, serves as the client's general counsel.
c. An employee of the auditor serves as the unpaid treasurer of a charitable organization that is an audit client.
d. The client owes the auditor fees for two consecutive years.

(AICPA Adapted)

5. The *Rules of Conduct* would most likely be violated if an auditor:

a. Owns a building and leases floor space to an attestation client.
b. Has an insured account with a brokerage firm audit client.
c. Is engaged by an audit client to identify potential acquisitions.
d. Screens candidates for an audit client's vacant controllership.

(AICPA Adapted)

6. Objectivity refers to a practitioner's ability:

a. To remain impartial.
b. To identify assertions that are appropriate.
c. To be unyielding in all disputes.
d. To choose independently between accounting principles and auditing standards.

7. Absent a client's consent, a practitioner is precluded from disclosing confidential client information to:

a. The Joint National Trial Board.
b. A state board of accountancy.
c. The board of directors of an audit client's investee.
d. An AICPA ethics committee.

8. Which of the following fee arrangements would violate the AICPA *Code of Professional Conduct?*

a. A fee based on the approval of a bank loan.
b. A fee based on the outcome of a bankruptcy proceeding.
c. A per hour fee that includes out-of-pocket expenses.
d. A fee based on the complexity of the engagement.

9. Which of the following published in a promotional brochure would likely violate the AICPA *Rules of Conduct?*

a. Names and addresses, telephone numbers, numbers of partners, office hours, foreign language competence, and date the firm was established.
b. Services offered and fees for such services, including hourly rates and fixed fees.
c. Educational and professional attainments, including date and place of certification, schools attended, dates of graduation, degrees received, and memberships in professional associations.
d. Names, addresses, and telephone numbers of the firm's clients, including the number of years served.

(AICPA Adapted)

10. Which of the following acts by a CPA who is not in public practice would most likely be considered a violation of the profession's *Code of Professional Conduct?*

a. Using the designation "CPA" on a report accompanying financial statements intended for external use without disclosing that the CPA is employed by the company issuing the statements.
b. Distributing business cards indicating "CPA" and the CPA's title and employer.
c. Corresponding on the CPA's employer's letterhead, which contains the CPA's designation and employment status.
d. Compiling the CPA's employer's financial statements and making reference to the CPA's lack of independence.

11. Quality control policies for the acceptance and continuance of clients are established to:

a. Enable the auditor to report on management's integrity.
b. Comply with standards established by regulatory bodies.
c. Minimize the likelihood of associating with managements that lack integrity.
d. Reduce exposure to litigation from failing to detect fraud.

(AICPA Adapted)

PROBLEMS AND DISCUSSION CASES

4-1 *Rationale for Code of Professional Conduct*
In the 1980s, the financial press raised the public consciousness by publicizing a series of audit failures and financial failures, most notably in the banking and government securities industries. The profession responded in 1988 with a new *Code of Professional Conduct* that captured the expanding scope of assurance services and imposed on practitioners a rigorous code for professional behavior.

Required: Discuss why a profession requires a code of professional conduct. Why not no code at all?

4-2 *Violations of Rule 101, Independence?*
Practitioners repeatedly face situations that call for an immediate response: Is this a violation of the *Code of Professional Conduct?* The following situations, all related to independence, are posed to a practicing CPA, a member of the AICPA.

a. A practitioner is performing an attestation service for a privately owned corporation that includes the practitioner's cousin as a minority shareholder.
b. A commercial bank in which a practitioner carries two automobile loans has approached the practitioner to perform a financial statement audit.
c. A privately owned company, that has outsourced its information processing system to a public accounting firm, approaches the firm for a financial statement review engagement.
d. Although unrelated to the audit, an audit client has initiated litigation against a public accounting firm that is immaterial to the firm but material to the client's financial statements.
e. A practitioner has been engaged to compile the financial statements of a company owned partly by his children.

Required: Discuss whether in your judgment the situation violates Rule 101 of the *Code of Professional Conduct* or, in contrast, whether the situation is inconclusive.

4-3 *Independence*
An auditor must not only be independent in fact, but must also appear independent.
  Required:
1. Explain the concept of "independence" as it applies to third-party reliance on management's assertions.
2. a. What determines whether or not a practitioner is independent in fact?
   b. What determines whether or not a practitioner appears to be independent?
3. Explain how a practitioner may be independent in fact but not appear to be independent.
4. Would a practitioner be considered independent for an audit of the financial statements of a
   a. Church for which he or she is serving as treasurer without compensation? Explain.
   b. Civic club for which the auditor's spouse is serving as treasurer-bookkeeper and the practitioner does not receive a fee for the audit? Explain.

(AICPA Adapted)

4-4 *Independence*

The attribute of independence has traditionally been associated with the CPA's function of auditing and expressing opinions on financial statements.

Required:

1. What is meant by "independence" as applied to the CPA's function of auditing and expressing opinions on financial statements? Explain.
2. CPAs have imposed upon themselves certain rules of professional conduct that induce their members to remain independent and to strengthen public confidence in their independence. Which of the rules of professional conduct are concerned with the CPA's independence? Explain.
3. The Wallydrag Company is indebted to a CPA for unpaid fees and has offered to issue to the CPA unsecured interest-bearing notes. Would acceptance of these notes have any bearing upon the CPA's independence from the Wallydrag Company? Discuss.
4. The Rocky Hill Corporation was formed on October 1, 1998, and its fiscal year will end on September 30, 1999. A CPA has audited, and issued an unqualified opinion on, the corporation's opening balance sheet. A month after submitting the report, the CPA is offered the position of secretary of the Company because of the need for a complete set of officers and for convenience in signing various documents. The CPA will have no financial interest in the company through stock ownership or otherwise, will receive no salary, will not keep the books, and will have no influence on its financial matters other than occasional advice on income tax matters and similar advice normally given a client by the CPA.
    a. Assume that the CPA accepts the offer but plans to resign the position before beginning the annual audit and to again assume the office after issuing an opinion on the statements. Is the CPA independent? Discuss.
    b. Assume that the CPA accepts the offer on a temporary basis until the corporation has gotten under way and can employ a secretary, but in any event would permanently resign the position before conducting the annual audit. Is the CPA independent? Discuss.

(AICPA Adapted)

4-5 *Independence*

Ruth Shafer, CPA, is auditing the financial statements of the Nelson Company. Her son, age 16, owns 100 shares of the 50,000 shares of the Nelson Company common stock outstanding at the balance sheet date.

Required: Discuss the effect, if any, the son's stock ownership would have on the auditor's opinion.

4-6 *Independence and Consulting*

Your audit client, Nuesel Corporation, requests that you conduct a feasibility study to advise management of the best way for the corporation to utilize computer equipment and which computer, if any, best meets the corporation's needs. You are technically competent in this area and accept the engagement. Upon completion of your study, the corporation accepts your suggestions and installs the computer and related equipment that you recommended.

Required:

1. Discuss the effect that accepting this management services engagement would have on your independence in expressing an opinion on the financial statements of the Nuesel Corporation.
2. Data Print, Inc., a local printer of data processing forms, customarily offers a commission for recommending Data Print as a supplier. The client is aware of, and suggests you accept, the commission offer. Would accepting the commission with the client's approval be proper? Discuss.

(AICPA Adapted)

4-7 *Independence and a Retired Audit Partner*
Benjamin Leon, a retired partner of your public accounting firm, has just been appointed to the board of directors of Palmer Corporation, your firm's client. Leon is also a member of your firm's income tax committee which meets monthly to discuss income tax problems of the partnership's clients. The partnership pays Leon $300 for each committee meeting he attends and a monthly retirement benefit of $5,000.

Required: Discuss the effect of Leon's appointment to the board of directors of Palmer Corporation on your firm's independence in expressing an opinion on the Palmer Corporation's financial statements.

(AICPA Adapted)

4-8 *Independence and Nonaudit Services*
Audrey Campbell, CPA, has audited the financial statements of the Grimm Company for several years. Grimm's president has now asked Campbell to install an inventory control system for the company.

Required: Discuss the factors that Campbell should consider in determining whether to accept this engagement.

(AICPA Adapted)

4-9 *Competence to Perform Professional Services*
Charles Adams, CPA, has practiced public accounting for several years, but feels uncomfortable with computers. As a result, he contemplates hiring an additional professional staff member who specializes in systems analysis and computers.

Required: Must Adams be personally able to perform all of the services that the specialist can perform in order to supervise the new hire? Explain.

4-10 *Compliance with Standards*
Paulette Martin, CPA, has been approached by a staff assistant regarding the applicability of the AICPA Rules of Conduct to unaudited financial statements. The assistant notes that Rule 202, "Compliance with Standards," does not permit an AICPA member's name to be associated with financial statements in a manner that would imply the member is acting as an independent public accountant unless he or she has complied with the applicable standards. The assistant then asks: "Since generally accepted auditing standards appear to relate to audited and not to unaudited financial statements, does Rule 202 effectively prohibit an AICPA member from being associated with unaudited financial statements?"

Required: Is the assistant's interpretation of Rule 202 correct? Explain.

4-11 *Internal Use Statements*
Donald Bowie, CPA, is the assistant controller for Aberdeen Industries, a highly diversified conglomerate operating in the U.S. and abroad. Bowie has been asked by Aberdeen's corporate controller to perform audits and to express an opinion on several of Aberdeen's more significant holdings. The opinions are for distribution to, and use by, Aberdeen's officials only.

Required: Is Bowie in violation of the AICPA Code of Professional Conduct if he conducts the audits and issues an internal-use opinion? Explain.

4-12 *Confidential Client Information*
Doris Sweeny, CPA, is engaged by the local municipal government to conduct periodic personal property tax audits of companies operating within the municipality. The property tax relates to business inventories, equipment, and machinery; thus, Sweeny will examine accounts and records related to sales, purchases, and gross profit percentages, among other things.

Ashton Manufacturing Company, a local producer of tool and die equipment, resents the fact that Sweeny is conducting the property tax audits because she also provides audit services to several competing tool and die manufacturing companies. Ashton fears that Sweeny, while conducting the property tax audit, may encounter trade secrets beneficial to some of her audit clients. As a result, Ashton approaches the Ethics Division of the AICPA arguing that it is unethical for Sweeny to conduct its property tax audit.

Required: Does Sweeny violate the AICPA Code of Professional Conduct by conducting a property tax audit of Ashton, a tool and die equipment manufacturer, and by providing audit services to competing companies within the same industry? Explain.

4-13 *Confidential Client Information*

Judy Hanlon, CPA, is engaged to prepare the federal income tax return for the Guild Corporation for the year ended December 31, 1999, Hanlon's first engagement of any kind for the Guild Corporation. In preparing the 1999 return, Hanlon finds an error on the 1998 return: Accumulated Depreciation brought forward from 1997 to 1998 was understated and, therefore, the 1997 base for declining balance depreciation was overstated, causing 1998 depreciation to be overstated significantly.

Hanlon reports the error to Guild's controller, the officer responsible for tax returns. The controller says: "Let the revenue agent find the error," and further instructs Hanlon to carry forward the material overstatement of the depreciable base to the 1999 depreciation computation. The controller notes that this error also had been made in the financial records for 1998 and 1999 and offers to furnish Hanlon with a letter assuming full responsibility for this treatment.

Required:
1. Evaluate Hanlon's action in this situation.
2. Discuss the additional action that Hanlon should now undertake.

(AICPA Adapted)

4-14 *Contingent Fees*

Certified public accountants often serve as expert witnesses in damage suits involving accounting and auditing matters. For example, accountants acting as expert witnesses could be asked to testify about appropriate auditing procedures or applicable accounting principles in given nonroutine circumstances.

Required: When acting as an expert witness in a damage suit, may a CPA receive compensation based on the amount awarded a plaintiff?

4-15 *Advertising*

Each of the following situations relates to Rule 502, "Advertising and Other Forms of Solicitation":

a. A trade association engages a CPA to analyze specific problems affecting members of the association. The results of the CPA's analysis will bear the CPA's name, be reproduced by the association, and be distributed to association members.

Required: Does Rule 502 prohibit distribution of results of the CPA's analysis? Explain.

b. A CPA is engaged by the local chapter of a national accounting association to conduct a continuing education course for its members. The CPA is identified in promotional material distributed by the association.

Required: What responsibility does the CPA have for information included within the promotional material? Explain.

c. A CPA is retained by a stock brokerage client to prepare a booklet on the tax aspects of security transactions. The client bears all printing costs and compensates the CPA for time expended on the project. A legend on the cover of the booklet states that it was prepared by the CPA. Booklets are mailed to the brokerage client's customers with end-of-month statements.

Required: Is there any objection to this practice? Explain.

4-16 *Form of Practice and Name*
Several CPAs within the firm of Harding & Co. specialize in professional services related to client acquisitions and mergers. The policy committee of Harding & Co. decides to form a separate partnership to perform acquisition and merger services. Harding & Co. believes that the separate partnership can indicate a specialization on its business stationery because the acquisition and merger partnership will not practice public accounting, per se.

Required: May the separate partnership indicate a specialization on business stationery? Explain.

4-17 *Commissions*
A CPA in public practice wishes to be a representative of a computer company that services tax practitioners. The CPA will utilize contacts with professional tax practitioners to introduce and promote use of the service. The CPA will receive a fee from the computer tax service for each tax return processed for a practitioner who was referred by the CPA.

Required: Does this arrangement violate Rule 503, "Commissions"? Explain.

4-18 *Nonaudit Services*
Tom Jencks, CPA, conducts a public accounting practice. In 1999, Jencks and Raymond Curtis, a non-CPA, organized Electro-Data Corporation to specialize in computerized bookkeeping services. Jencks and Curtis each supplied 50 percent of Electro-Data's capital, and each holds 50 percent of the capital stock. Curtis is the salaried general manager of Electro-Data. Jencks is affiliated with the corporation only as a stockholder; he receives no salary and does not participate in day-to-day management. However, he has transferred all of his bookkeeping accounts to the corporation and recommends its services whenever possible.

Required: Organizing your presentation around Jencks' involvement with Electro-Data Corporation, discuss the propriety of
1. A CPA's participation in an enterprise offering computerized bookkeeping services.
2. A CPA's transfer of bookkeeping accounts to a service company.
3. A CPA's recommendation of a particular bookkeeping service company.

(AICPA Adapted)

4-19 *Elected Office*
A CPA in public practice is considering running for the elected office of state controller. Principal functions of the state controller include maintaining control over all state fund accounts, administering disbursements, and allocating revenue among county and local governments. The CPA intends to continue practicing public accounting if elected.

Required: Can the CPA practice public accounting and serve as state controller? Explain.

4-20 *Form of Practice and Name*
Your CPA firm decides to form a partnership with Faye Reitz, a non-CPA management consultant, which would result in a "mixed partnership" of a CPA and a non-CPA.

Required: Under what circumstances, if any, would it be ethically proper for a CPA to form a "mixed partnership"? Discuss.

(AICPA Adapted)

4-21 *Form of Practice and Name*
Although not partners, two CPAs share an office, maintain joint bank accounts, and work together on each other's engagements. As a result, they decide to have a joint letterhead showing both names, their address, and the designation "Certified Public Accountants."

Required: Is the joint letterhead (including the address and the designation "Certified Public Accountants") proper? Explain.

4-22 *Dual Professional Services*
Frank Gilbert and Gloria Aponte formed a corporation called Financial Services, Inc., each taking 50 percent of the authorized common stock. Gilbert is a CPA and a member of the American Institute of CPAs; Aponte is a CPCU (Chartered Property Casualty Underwriter). The corporation performs auditing and tax services under Gilbert's direction and insurance services under Aponte's supervision. The opening of the corporation's office was announced by a three-inch, two-column "card" in the local newspaper.

   One of the corporation's first audit clients was the Grandtime Company. Grandtime had total assets of $600,000 and total liabilities of $270,000. In the course of his audit, Gilbert found that Grandtime's building with a book value of $240,000 was pledged as security for a ten-year note in the amount of $200,000. The client's statements did not mention that the building was pledged as security for the note. However, since the failure to disclose the lien did not affect either the value of the assets or the amount of the liabilities, and since his audit was satisfactory in all other respects, Gilbert issued an unqualified opinion on Grandtime's financial statements. About two months after the date of his opinion, Gilbert learned that an insurance company was planning to loan Grandtime $150,000 in the form of a first-mortgage note on the building. Realizing that the insurance company was unaware of the existing lien on the building, Gilbert had Aponte notify the insurance company of the fact that Grandtime's building was pledged as security for the note. Shortly after the events described above, Gilbert was charged with a violation of professional ethics.

   Required: Identify and discuss the ethical implications of those acts by Gilbert that were in violation of the AICPA Code of Professional Conduct.

(AICPA Adapted)

4-23 *Accepting an Engagement*
Lakeview Development Corporation was formed on January 2, 1999, to develop a vacation-recreation area on land purchased the same day by the corporation for $100,000. The corporation also purchased for $40,000 an adjacent tract of land that the corporation plans to subdivide into 50 building lots. When the area is developed, the lots are expected to sell for $10,000 each.

   The corporation borrowed a substantial portion of its funds from a bank and gave a mortgage on the land. A mortgage covenant requires that the corporation furnish quarterly financial statements.

   The quarterly financial statements prepared at March 31 and June 30 by the corporation's bookkeeper were unacceptable to the bank officials. The corporation's president now offers you the engagement of preparing unaudited quarterly financial statements. Because of limited funds, your fee would be paid in Lakeview Development Corporation common stock rather than in cash. The stock would be repurchased by the corporation when funds become available. You would not receive enough stock to be a major stockholder.

   Required:
1. Discuss the ethical implications of your accepting the engagement and the reporting requirements that are applicable if you should accept the engagement.
2. Assume that you accept the engagement to prepare the September 30, 1999 statements. What disclosures, if any, would you make of your prospective ownership of corporation stock in the quarterly financial statements?
3. The president insists that you present the 50 building lots at their expected sale price of $500,000 in the September 30 unaudited statements as was done in prior statements. The write-up was credited to Contributed Capital. How would you respond to the president's request?

4. The corporation elected to close its fiscal year September 30 and you are requested to prepare the corporation's federal income tax return. Discuss the implication of signing the return and the disclosure of your stock ownership in Lakeview Corporation (disregard the write-up of the land).

5. Assume that you accept the engagement to prepare the tax return. In the course of collecting information for the preparation of the return you find that the corporation's president paid the entire cost of a family vacation from corporate funds and listed the expense as travel and entertainment. You ascertain that the corporation's board of directors would not consider the cost of the vacation as either additional compensation or a gift to the president if the facts were known. What disclosure would you make in (a) the tax return and (b) the financial statements?

6. After accepting your unaudited September 30 financial statements, the bank notified the corporation that the December 31 financial statements must be accompanied by a CPA's opinion. You were asked to conduct the audit and told that your fee would be paid in cash. Discuss the ethical implications of accepting the engagement.

(AICPA Adapted)

4-24 *Quality Control*

In response to the AICPA's quality control program for individual public accounting firms, many firms have drafted quality control documents that describe policies and procedures designed to provide reasonable assurance that the firm is complying with *attestation standards* and *generally accepted auditing standards* on all engagements. Following is a selected list of policies and procedures taken from a public accounting firm's quality control document.

a. As a member of both practice divisions of the AICPA, the firm is subject to and cooperates in the Quality Control Peer Review Program. The firm's Audit Monitoring Committee is responsible for scheduling periodic working paper reviews for completed engagements and for ensuring that all professional personnel are made aware of the knowledge gained by the reviews.

b. The firm is not to express an opinion in an attestation or audit engagement if professional staff serve as executor, trustee, officer, or director of the organization. Other appointments to these positions in either client or nonclient organizations must be in agreement with the AICPA's *Code of Professional Conduct*.

c. Situations occur or questions arise that require certain technical accounting or auditing knowledge, or specialized industry knowledge that may not exist within the engagement team. In these cases, the engagement partner or others associated with the engagement shall consult with the Partner for Technical Services or other designated personnel to obtain the assistance needed or to otherwise resolve the issue.

d. The following factors are considered by the Scheduling Partner in achieving a balance of the personnel elements of the engagement: staffing requirements, personnel skills, individual development, and staff utilization during the job.

e. At the annual partners meeting, the Administrative Partner assures that no partner has any loan from a client other than those specifically permitted by professional ethics.

f. On each engagement, adequate review is to be performed at all organizational levels, as appropriate, considering the training, ability, and experience of the personnel assigned and the complexity of the engagement.

g. Each year, all professional staff are responsible to develop a personal plan that includes goals for participating in on-the-job training through challenging and diversified assignments, formal programs prepared and conducted by the firm and by professional organizations, individual development through self-study and other activities, and participation in and service to professional, community, and public and/or private organizations and activities.

h. The personal attributes sought in entry-level professional staff include but are not limited to the following: motivation, professional potential, language skills, demonstrated involvement, and leadership.

i. Personnel are periodically evaluated and are advised formally of their progress. Staff personnel files are maintained for each professional staff member and contain written evaluations of performance.

j. The reputation of a company's directors, officers, and principal shareholders or owners is of great importance. The firm seeks to minimize the likelihood of associating with a client whose management lacks integrity and a fair degree of stability over time. In addition, the nature of the business, its sources of financing and financial need, its internal controls, and the purpose for and nature of the audit or attestation engagement are all considerations in evaluating the relative risk of our professional liability in serving the company.

Required:

1. Explain the relationship between quality control and peer review for a public accounting firm.

2. For each of the policies and procedures listed above, indicate the element of quality control addressed by the firm.

RESEARCH PROJECTS

1. UNETHICAL BUSINESS PRACTICES

The financial press often reports business practices that raise ethical issues. For example, consider a single topical question confronting all major oil and gas exploration companies: although double hull oil tankers are less likely to spill crude oil in transit, single hull tankers are far less costly. Interestingly, this single issue affects several interested stakeholders (e.g., wildlife, shareholders), raises questions of alternative courses of action (e.g., accruals for environmental liabilities), and poses considerable practical constraints to the stakeholders (e.g., cost of double hulls v. benefits of preserving environment).

Required: Select an article or series of articles from the recent press (e.g., *Business Week, The Wall Street Journal, The New York Times*) about a business problem you think raises ethical issues and draft a report that addresses each of the seven questions developed in:

M. Velasquez. *Business Ethics,* 2nd. ed. Englewood Cliffs, NJ: Prentice Hall, 1988.

1. What are the relevant facts?
2. What are the ethical issues?
3. Who are the primary stakeholders?
4. What are the possible alternatives?
5. What are the ethics of the alternatives?
6. What are the practical constraints?
7. What actions should be taken?

2. SOMETHING'S WRONG, SOMETHING'S AMISS

Ethical issues are faced in all professions, including those for which there's a presumption that ethics drives the profession, such as the financial aid professionals in colleges and universities. For example, to attract students to less popular majors, the financial aid office of a prominent East Coast university, one long distinguished by their number of premed majors, awarded less aid to admitted premeds than to humanities majors in order to attract underrepresented majors to campus. Referring to an admitted premed, a piece in *The Wall Street Journal* (S. Stecklow, "Expensive Lesson: Colleges

Manipulate Financial Aid Offers, Shortchanging Many," April 1, 1996) reported, "And so in an experiment last spring, it quietly offered fatter financial-aid grants to incoming humanities majors than to most of their premed counterparts. While Peter is getting $14,000 a year, he might have snared about $3,000 more if he planned to major in, say, art history." An unethical practice? The article mentions "ethical concerns" and "ethical questions" and, for that matter, so does Peter's mother: "What you're telling the kid is, lie to get into college." No profession, no industry, is immune from the potential for unethical behavior.

Required: Select two articles from the recent press (e.g., *Business Week, The Wall Street Journal, The New York Times*) about problems you think raise ethical issues and draft a report that describes the issues. Discuss how you think the perpetrators could have satisfied their objective by a means you think ethical.

5

Legal Liability

Major topics discussed in this chapter are the:

- Issues underlying legal liability to clients and to third parties.
- Auditor's common law liability to clients, primary beneficiaries, and foreseen third parties.
- Scope of an auditor's involvement with the Securities Acts.
- Auditor's statutory liability to securities purchasers and sellers under the Securities Acts, and securities litigation reform.
- Auditor's liability for criminal offenses.
- Auditor's responsibility to detect and report fraud and illegal acts.
- Precautions to minimize the risk of legal liability.

More lawsuits have been filed against auditors in the last fifteen years than in the entire prior history of the profession, and two issues help explain why. First, under the doctrine of **joint-and-several liability**, a plaintiff in an action against an auditor could, until recently, potentially recover all damages from the auditor alone, even though the auditor's report may have contributed only partially to the plaintiff's loss, a bankrupt client for example having contributed the balance. Second, unlike a physician or lawyer, an auditor has little control over who uses his or her work product, and therefore may be liable to parties who are not in **privity** (parties in a contractual relationship with the auditor). Through the efforts of the Coalition to Eliminate Abusive Securities Suits (CEASS), the profession helped introduce and pass the *Private Securities Litigation Reform Act of 1995,* legislation that reduces joint-and-several liability to proportionate liability (defendants liable only for their share of responsibility), except for defendants who knowingly engage in fraud. And the courts in some jurisdictions have restored the privity doctrine, thereby restricting auditor liability to plaintiffs known to the auditor. Litigation reform and restoration of the privity doctrine offer welcome relief for the profession, although both were long in coming, partly because the public is reluctant to erase long-standing traditions of liability that evolved primarily to protect the public.

Practitioners have offered attestation services routinely since the 1980s, and assurance services somewhat more recently. However, case law for these services is quite limited compared to case law for auditing, a professional service with a rich tradition extending back to the Industrial Revolution. For example, this chapter cites precedent-setting *auditing* cases from six of the last seven decades, and two even from the nineteenth century. But generalizations about liability in attestation and assurance services are problematic, except for one: Although both services, like auditing, are generally three-party contracts (Chapter 1, Figure 1-1), the third-party plaintiff in attestation and assurance engagements is less likely to be a *class* of litigants (i.e., class action suits), and the plaintiff is more likely to prevail in suits brought for *breach of contract* than in suits demanding the wildly excessive punitive damages successfully brought against auditors in tort.

This chapter addresses the independent accountant's civil and criminal liability, beginning with a review of the basic questions that underscore most liability cases. Next, the chapter describes an auditor's common law liability to clients and third parties, introduces the *Securities Act of 1933* and the *Securities Exchange Act of 1934,* and summarizes an auditor's statutory liability to securities purchasers and sellers under the 1933 and 1934 Acts. In turn, the chapter discusses criminal liability and an auditor's responsibility to detect and report fraud and illegal acts. The chapter concludes by addressing an auditor's role in minimizing the risk of legal liability.

A word of caution: Be careful when transporting the contents of this chapter into practice. The generalizations drawn within the chapter are based on constantly evolving standards of liability, and in some instances represent majority rather than unanimous views. Generalizations are helpful in education, particularly in attempting to cope with the complex legal issues confronting practitioners today, but judgments in real world lawsuits against auditors are based on the facts and legal issues on trial and on legal precedent in the jurisdiction trying the case, not on generalizations.

AN OVERVIEW OF CIVIL LIABILITY
UNDER COMMON AND STATUTORY LAW

In civil liability cases against auditors, four questions underscore the issues at stake: Under what source of law is the plaintiff suing? Who is the plaintiff? What is the auditor's potential liability? And, which party—plaintiff or defendant—has the burden of proving what in court? The alternative answers to these questions are outlined in Figure 5-1 and explained in the following sections.

SOURCE OF LAW

A plaintiff may bring action against an auditor under common law or statutory law, two different sources of the law that the court may apply. The source of **common law** is the written opinions of prior courts within a state (called legal *precedent),* each state having its own common law. Common law is based in the doctrine of *stare decisis*—that is, handing down precedent-setting principles of law to succeeding cases. Lower courts in a state are bound by the precedent of the state's highest court, but the highest court is not bound by its own prior opinions and may borrow precedent from other states.

In contrast, **statutory law** refers to written statutes established by Congress at the federal level and by state legislatures at the state level. Federal (and state) courts are bound by federal (state) statutes, unless the statute violates the U.S. (state) constitution. At the federal level, the primary focus of this chapter, the *Securities Act of 1933* (usually Section 11) and the *Securities Exchange Act of 1934*

Figure 5-1:   Summary of Issues in Auditor Civil Liability Cases

Source of Law
- Common Law
- Statutory Law (federal):
  Securities Act of 1933
  Securities Exchange Act of 1934

Plaintiff
- Under Common Law:
  Client
  Third party primary beneficiaries
  Foreseen third parties
  Foreseeable third parties
- Under *Securities Act of 1933:*
  Initial purchasers of securities
- Under *Securities Exchange Act of 1934:*
  Subsequent purchasers or sellers of securities

Auditor's Potential Liability, Common and Statutory Law
- Ordinary negligence
- Gross negligence
- Fraud

Burden of Proof on Either Plaintiff or Defendant
- Damage or loss
- Misstated financial statements or erroneous advice
- Reliance on financial statements or advice
- Deficient auditor conduct

[usually Section 10(b), SEC Rule 10b-5, or Section 18], both administered by the SEC, are the two most prominent statutes affecting an auditor's legal liability.

IDENTITY OF PLAINTIFF

Plaintiffs in a civil proceeding against auditors vary depending on whether the action is brought under common law or statutory law.

Common Law

Under common law, an action may be initiated against an auditor by a client or by third parties. A client may bring action against an auditor for breach of contract or for tort. Clients may sue for **breach of contract** because clients are parties (they are *in privity)* to an express or implied contract for audit services. Suits for breach of contract usually allege that an auditor violated either *generally accepted auditing standards* or the auditor-client confidential relationship. A **tort** is a wrongful act, other than breach of contract, that results in injury to another person. Suits in tort usually allege negligence, gross negligence, or fraud.

Common law recognizes two major classes of third parties who may bring action against an auditor: third party primary beneficiaries and foreseen third parties. **Primary beneficiaries** are specifically identified to auditors as the beneficiaries of audit services—the auditor would not have been engaged were it not for the primary beneficiary. For example, many closely held, nonpublicly traded companies engage auditors primarily because a third party creditor, such as a specifically named commercial bank, requires audited financial statements as part of a credit application. In these cases, clients engage independent auditors to perform a financial statement audit for the third party creditor's primary benefit.

Foreseen third parties are not specifically identified as benefactors of audit services, although their general identity and specific purpose for relying on an audit report are known to the auditor. For example, if a client intended to use audited financial statements to secure a loan from an unnamed creditor, the party that extended credit to the client would be a foreseen third party. Whereas common law actions by clients may be brought for breach of contract or for torts, actions by primary and foreseen third parties are usually brought under tort law.

Closely related to foreseen third parties are other "foreseeable" third parties, parties who have a reasonable need to rely on an entity's financial statements but, because they're the furthest removed from a contractual agreement for audit services, generally enjoy the least favorable position in auditor liability cases. Examples of foreseeable third parties include bondholders, shareholders, and some creditors. Over the years, the rights of foreseeable third parties against auditors has depended largely on the affirmation, erosion, and later reaffirmation of the privity doctrine, discussed more fully later in the chapter.

Statutory Law

Under federal securities law, third parties may bring action against auditors for violating either of the *Securities Acts,* among other federal statutes. A plaintiff in an action under the *Securities Act of 1933* may be any person purchasing securities identified within a registration statement. A registration statement includes both: (1) a prospectus describing the entity and the securities offered, and (2) other detailed information such as balance sheets and earnings summaries. In contrast, a plaintiff in an action under the *Securities Exchange Act of 1934* may be any person purchasing or selling publicly traded securities.

POTENTIAL LIABILITY

Under either common or statutory law, an auditor may be liable for ordinary negligence, gross negligence, or fraud. **Ordinary negligence** means a lack of reasonable care when performing services, such as a departure from one of the ten *generally accepted auditing standards* introduced in Chapter 2. When used alone, the term "negligence" is generally understood to mean ordinary negligence. **Gross negligence**, in contrast, is a lack of even minimum care when performing services, such as a reckless departure from *generally accepted auditing standards.* **Fraud** is an intentional misstatement or omission of a material fact (or a theft) that results in another party being deceived and then injured, the operative word being "intentional." In a precedent-setting 1931 case, the New York Court of Appeals noted in *Ultramares Corp. v. Touche* that gross negligence could be so great as to constitute constructive (as opposed to actual) fraud. Constructive fraud lacks intent, an essential condition in actual fraud, but the result of both constructive and actual fraud is identical: Another party is deceived and then injured. The Court's use of constructive fraud has been confirmed many times over the years, including, more recently, in cases involving small firms (e.g., *Barger v. McCoy, Hillard and Parks*, North Carolina Court of Appeals, 1995).

Ordinary negligence imposes a higher degree of responsibility on an auditor than gross negligence, and gross negligence a higher degree than fraud. This is because a "departure" from *generally accepted auditing standards* (the operational definition of ordinary negligence) is less burdensome for a plaintiff to prove than a "reckless departure" (gross negligence), and reckless departure is less burdensome to prove than an "intent" to deceive and injure (fraud).

BURDEN OF PROOF

The extent of an independent auditor's liability under either common or statutory law rests on four essential points: The plaintiff or the independent auditor (defendant) may have the burden of proving or disproving that:

1. The plaintiff sustained a damage or loss,
2. The audited financial statements were materially misstated,
3. The plaintiff relied on the financial statements, and/or
4. The auditor's conduct was deficient.

The burden of proving the first point, *damage or loss*, always falls on the plaintiff. The amount of damage or loss may be represented by a decline in a security's market value or by the amount of an audit fee.

The second point, *misstated financial statements*, is the basis for a plaintiff to claim damage or loss—that is, what the plaintiff alleges to be the cause of their damage or loss. Like damage or loss, the plaintiff always has the burden of proving that audited financial statements are misstated materially.

Reliance on financial statements, the third point to be proven, entails two separate but related issues: Did the plaintiff actually rely on the statements to reach a decision? And, did reliance on the statements actually lead to the damage or loss? The burden of proving reliance falls on the plaintiff under both common law and the *Securities Exchange Act of 1934*. However, under the *Securities Act of 1933*, the plaintiff does not have to prove reliance. Rather, the defendant—the auditor—has the burden of proving that a plaintiff's damage or loss did not result from relying on the financial statements.

The fourth point, an *auditor's conduct*, represents the degree of due professional care exercised when performing audit or other attest services. The standard of conduct owed to a plaintiff depends on an auditor's knowledge of a plaintiff's existence and identity, and the plaintiff's reason for relying on the financial statements. For example, in comparison with some third parties, a client's existence, identity, and reason for relying on financial statements are more clearly known to an auditor. Thus, an auditor's expected level of conduct is higher for clients than for some third parties. Under the *Securities Act of 1933* and Section 18 of the *Securities Exchange Act of 1934*, an auditor has the burden of proving that a reasonable investigation was made and, therefore, that his or her level of conduct was adequate (referred to in practice as the "due diligence" defense). In contrast, the plaintiff suing the auditor has the burden of proving deficient auditor conduct under common law and Section 10(b) of the *Securities Exchange Act of 1934.*

SUMMARY OF LIABILITY UNDER COMMON AND STATUTORY LAW

Figures 5-2 and 5-3 summarize an auditor's minimum basis for potential liability (ordinary negligence, gross negligence, or fraud) to all classes of plaintiffs, and which party (the plaintiff or the defendant auditor) has the burden of proving which points under common law and statutory law, respectively. The following addresses more fully each entry in the figures, first for common law and then for statutory law, with the objective being to explain what drove the entries in Figures 5-2 and 5-3.

COMMON LAW LIABILITY

Under common law, an auditor may be liable to the party contracting for audit services (the client) and to third parties who, although not party to a contractual relationship, nevertheless are users of audited financial information. As explained above, third parties may be classified as primary beneficiaries, who are treated much like clients under common law, and foreseen third parties. A discussion of the auditor's potential liability to clients and third parties follows.

LIABILITY TO CLIENTS

An auditor's common law liability to clients is based on the contractual relationship between an auditor and a client and on the auditor's status as an independent contractor. A contractual relationship results because an auditor and a client enter into an express written agreement (introduced later in the chapter as an "engagement letter") for audit services. The auditor's status as an independent contractor, rather than an agent or employee, results because an auditor's tasks are not controlled by the client. A client may initiate a common law civil action when an auditor is alleged to have failed in carrying out the duties of an audit services contract. For example, a client may take

Figure 5-2: Liability Under Common Law

Plaintiff	Minimum Basis for Potential Auditor Liability	Burden of Proof upon Plaintiff
Client	Ordinary negligence	Damage or loss Misstated financial statements or erroneous advice
Third party: Primary beneficiary	Ordinary negligence	Reliance on financial statements or advice
Foreseen third party	Fraud (majority view) or gross negligence	Deficient auditor conduct

Figure 5-3: Liability Under Statutory Law

Plaintiff	Minimum Basis for Potential Auditor Liability	Burden of Proof Upon Plaintiff	Upon Defendant
Under 1933 Act, Section 11: Security purchaser	Ordinary negligence	Damage or loss Financial statements misstated or erroneous advice	Lack of reliance or Auditor conduct not deficient (due diligence)
Under 1934 Act, Section 10(b), Rule 10b-5: Security purchaser or Seller	Gross negligence or Fraud	Damage or loss Financial statements misstated or erroneous advice Reliance Auditor conduct not deficient (due diligence)	
Under 1934 Act, Section 18: Security purchaser or Seller	Gross negligence	Damage or loss Financial statements misstated or erroneous advice Reliance	Auditor conduct not deficient (due diligence)

action against an auditor when the client sustains a loss from relying on materially misstated financial statements or when the auditor fails to discover a fraud, such as a cash embezzlement.

The auditor's common law liability to clients is traceable to the first recorded legal action brought against an auditor, an 1887 case in England: *Leeds Estate, Building and Investment Co. v. Shepherd.* Leeds, a lending institution, sued the auditor for breach of duty, winning primarily on grounds that the auditor was wrongful in not inquiring into a balance sheet's "substantial accuracy." Similar to the Leeds case, an auditor's common law liability to clients today, summarized in Figure 5-2, is for ordinary negligence, although clients may bring action for gross negligence if they believe the auditor departed recklessly from *generally accepted auditing standards,* or for fraud if they believe the auditor intended to deceive and injure. To recover damages, a client has the burden of proving a damage or loss, misstated financial statements, reliance on the financial statements, and deficient auditor conduct. Damages are usually awarded in monetary terms.

An auditor's liability to clients also extends to parties who acquire a client's rights by subrogation (substitution). For instance, if a bonding company reimburses a client for an employee's embezzlement, the bonding company succeeds to the client's right to sue the auditor for failing to detect the embezzlement. A 1940 case, *Maryland Casualty Co. v. Jonathon Cook,* illustrates. Over a period of seven years, the Flint, Michigan, city treasurer embezzled monies from municipal funds. Jonathon Cook & Company accepted the 1932 audit engagement that was to be based on procedures included within an audit services contract. The procedures would have been sufficient to uncover the embezzlement, but Cook essentially ignored them. As a result, Maryland Casualty, which carried a surety bond on the treasurer, reimbursed the city of Flint and initiated action against Cook. The court ruled in favor of Maryland Casualty, arguing that the engagement should have been conducted in accordance with the terms of the contract.

The Maryland Casualty case also illustrates the importance of written contracts with clients for professional services, typically called **engagement letters**. Another case, though, *1136 Tenants' Corp. v. Max Rothenberg & Co.*, was a more prominent and precedent-setting case regarding engagement letters. 1136 Tenants' Corporation was an apartment cooperative that engaged Max Rothenberg & Co., without an engagement letter, to conduct nonaudit accounting services. Rothenberg provided services from 1963 to 1965 when it was discovered that a former manager had absconded with funds from the corporation. 1136 Tenants sued Max Rothenberg, arguing that an audit should have been performed. In defense, Rothenberg unsuccessfully argued that an audit was not agreed upon. The professional fees for this engagement amounted to only $600 per year, but Rothenberg was ordered to pay $230,000 in damages and, as a result, engagement letters have become quite common in practice.

Although *1136 Tenants* suggested that engagement letters could limit an accountant's liability to services included in the letter, *Congregation of the Passion, Holy Cross Province v. Touche Ross & Co.*, an Illinois Supreme Court case, suggests otherwise. The Congregation of the Passion, a Roman Catholic religious order, engaged Touche Ross to prepare unaudited financial statements in 1973. Beginning in 1976, the Congregation entrusted full responsibility for a $2 million investment portfolio to an investment advisor who entered into a leveraged arbitrage strategy that exposed the Congregation to losses far beyond the amount invested. The Congregation was fully informed by transaction confirmations from securities dealers, but sued Touche Ross in federal court for securities laws violations and then in Illinois state court for breach of contract and negligence. Federal charges were dismissed but the Illinois Supreme court ruled in favor of the Congregation, arguing that an accountant's duty to clients is defined both by the engagement letter and by *extracontractual* responsibilities, suggesting that an engagement letter is necessary but not always sufficient to define the limits of an accountant's responsibility to clients. The majority opinion did not define "extracontractual" responsibilities, prompting a dissenting justice to write, "What are these extracontractual duties? If these duties cannot be articulated in a contract, how is it that the client is able to articulate that they have been breached in a complaint?"[1] The boundary of an accountant's extracontractual responsibilities remains an open question. The role of engagement letters in the audit process is discussed more fully in Chapter 6.

LIABILITY TO PRIMARY BENEFICIARIES

English common law, the forebear of U.S. legal precedent, has traditionally held that only parties in privity to a contract may enforce the contract. However, in the mid-nineteenth century, U.S. courts began to equate primary beneficiaries with clients. For example, in an 1859 case, *Lawrence v. Fox*, the

1   D. Crawford, D. Franz, R. A. Zimmerman, and P. R. Fink, "Exposure to the Extracontractual," *Journal of Accountancy* (December 1995), pp. 90-91.

court effectively ruled that privity was not essential for primary beneficiaries to sue, assuming that contractual duties were limited to third parties rather than to clients. Some six decades later, however, in *Glanzer v. Shepard*, the court firmly established a primary beneficiary's right to sue for damages even though contractual duties extended only between the parties to the contract. Although *Glanzer v. Shepard* did not involve an auditor, it is generally recognized as an important influence on an auditor's legal liability to primary beneficiaries. Today, primary beneficiaries typically enjoy a status similar to that of clients.

Figure 5-2 summarizes an auditor's common law liability to primary beneficiaries. As is the case with clients, an auditor is liable to primary beneficiaries for lack of reasonable care (ordinary negligence), and primary beneficiaries have the burden of proving damage or loss, misstated financial statements, reliance on the financial statements, and deficient auditor conduct.

LIABILITY TO FORESEEN THIRD PARTIES

Some third parties are identified only tangentially to auditors (for example, commercial bank lenders or an unsolicited telephone call from a holding company) and others are not specifically identified at all (e.g., present or potential shareholders). Yet, their general identities and purposes for relying on audited financial statements (e.g., loans, takeovers, investments) can be reasonably foreseen. Are independent auditors liable to third parties who, although not parties to an audit services contract, nevertheless allege to have suffered losses from unpaid commercial loans, unprofitable takeovers, or poor investment decisions? An auditor's liability to foreseen beneficiaries derives from common law interpretations of the privity doctrine, a legal concept that evolved initially from British law, was established firmly in U.S. legal precedent in the 1930s, eroded in the early 1980s, and was reaffirmed in a series of cases decided in the 1980s and 1990s. As suggested below, few long-standing controversies have had more impact on an auditor's evolving culpability than the courts' inconsistent interpretations of the privity doctrine over time.

The Privity Doctrine: Ultramares
Ultramares Corp. v. Touche (1931), a landmark New York Court of Appeals case, established that auditors are liable to third parties for fraud—intentional misstatements, omissions, or theft—but they are not liable to unidentified third parties for negligence. Relying on financial statements audited by Touche, Ultramares Corporation made loans to Fred Stern & Co., a rubber importer that in reality was insolvent. Stern was unable to repay the loans and subsequently declared bankruptcy. The court ruled that accountants are liable for negligence only to those parties in privity—that is, to clients and to those third parties whom the accountant knows will rely on the financial statements, such as primary beneficiaries.

Erosion of the Privity Doctrine
In a New Jersey Supreme Court case, *H. Rosenblum, Inc. v. Adler* (1983), the court strayed from the privity concept established in *Ultramares*, ruling that accountants can be held liable not only to clients and primary beneficiaries, but also to foreseeable third parties who suffer a loss from relying on materially misstated financial statements. The *Rosenblum* decision was followed by several

similar decisions, such as *International Mortgage Co. v. John P. Butler Accounting Corp.* (California: 1986) and *Touche Ross v. Commercial Union Insurance Co.* (Mississippi: 1987). Together these cases served to erode the privity concept, creating a set of circumstances through which alert litigants could look to auditors as guarantors for ill-advised investment decisions.

Reaffirmation of the Privity Doctrine: Credit Alliance

But a 1985 New York Court of Appeals case, *Credit Alliance v. Arthur Andersen & Co.*, has been viewed by the profession as a strong reaffirmation of the privity concept in *Ultramares*. Credit Alliance, a finance company, loaned large sums of money to L. B. Smith, Inc., a heavy equipment lessor and audit client of Arthur Andersen. L. B. Smith subsequently went bankrupt and was unable to repay approximately $9 million. Credit Alliance prevailed, arguing it was in privity since L. B. Smith had used the audited financial statements to solicit financing. The court acknowledged that other courts throughout the nation had moved away from Ultramares, but reaffirmed preexisting New York law by ruling that negligence suits against auditors require privity or a relationship "so close as to approach that of privity." The court's opinion established a three-point test of the "linkage" between the auditor and third party, ruling that in the absence of a contract an accountant is liable to a third party only if:

1. The accountant knew the audited financial statements would be used for a specific purpose,
2. The accountant knew a specific third party would rely on the statements, and
3. Evidence linking the accountant with the plaintiff third party shows the accountant understood the statements would be relied on by the plaintiff.

Three years later, the New York Court of Appeals in *William Iselin and Co., Inc. v. Mann Judd Landau* (1988) extended the linkage test to review engagements (discussed in Chapter 18) as well.

The 1990s: Osborne, Security Pacific, and Cherry

Cases decided in the 1990s reaffirmed both the privity concept established in *Ultramares* and the linkage test in *Credit Alliance*. The most prominent, *Bily v. Arthur Young & Co.*, a 1993 California Supreme Court case, involved the extraordinary rise and fall of Osborne Computer Corporation, manufacturer of the first portable personal computer in 1981. The plaintiffs, venture capitalists who had invested heavily in a private offering of securities just months before Osbourne filed for bankruptcy in September 1993, sued Arthur Young, alleging errors in the 1992 audited financial statements on which they claimed to have relied. The court reversed a series of rulings by the state's appellate courts, among them *International Mortgage Co. v. John P. Butler Accounting Corp.* (above), holding that "an auditor owes no general duty of care regarding the conduct of an audit to persons other than the client." The court reasoned in part that, "If . . . third parties are simply permitted to recover from the auditor for mistakes in the client's financial statements, the auditor becomes, in effect, an insurer of not only the financial statements, but of bad loans and investments in general." All other plaintiffs, among them foreseen third parties, may recover only if they can demonstrate the auditor intended to deceive and injure—that is, fraud.

In *Security Pacific v. Peat Marwick* (1993), the New York Court of Appeals reasserted the three-point linkage test from *Credit Alliance,* holding that a single telephone call between a Security Pacific vice president and a Peat Marwick audit partner, was insufficient to establish a relationship sufficiently approaching privity. Consequently, the court ruled that Peat Marwick's work product benefited the client primarily and others only incidentally. Consistent with the *Security Pacific* case, the same New York Court of Appeals in *Cherry v. Joseph S. Herbert & Co.* (1995), a case about a solvency opinion, ruled that the linkage test in *Credit Alliance* was established by meetings among parties before a transaction occurs, a firm's knowledge of why a client required an opinion, and a firm's oral assurances of solvency. Figure 5-2 summarizes an auditor's common law liability to foreseen beneficiaries based on *Credit Alliance, Bily* (Osborne Computer), and *Security Pacific's* and *Cherry's* reaffirmation of the privity concept established originally in *Ultramares.* Note carefully, though, that the extent of an auditor's liability varies across the states. For example, auditors are protected under the privity doctrine by statute in Arkansas, Illinois, and Kansas, and by court decisions in Georgia, Indiana, and New York, but neither statutes nor court decisions protect auditors practicing in New Jersey or California. In all states, though, foreseen beneficiaries maintain the burden of proving damage or loss, that financial statements are misstated, reliance on financial statements, and deficient auditor conduct.

THE SECURITIES ACTS

This section explains the independent auditor's role in the two most prominent federal statutes affecting audit practice—the *Securities Act of 1933* and the *Securities Exchange Act of 1934*—and introduces the sections of each act that affect an auditor's liability. Thereafter, an auditor's statutory liability under the two acts is addressed in detail.

By 1933, most states had adopted so-called "blue-sky" laws to regulate the exchange of debt and equity securities. Although adequate for intrastate exchanges, the blue-sky laws were less effective in regulating interstate exchanges. As a result, the Securities Acts were enacted and the SEC created. An auditor's potential legal liability under the Securities Acts derives from an attempt by Congress to hold accountants and other professionals, such as lawyers and underwriters, more accountable to third parties than they would be under common law.

Created under the *Securities Exchange Act of 1934,* the **Securities and Exchange Commission (SEC)** was charged to administer both the 1934 Act and the *Securities Act of 1933,* which had been administered by the Federal Trade Commission. The SEC, headquartered in Washington, D.C., consists of five appointed Commissioners (one of whom is designated chair), a number of administrative divisions or offices (one of which is the Office of the Chief Accountant), and nine regional branches throughout the U.S. Today, in addition to the *Securities Acts,* the Commission also administers the *Public Utility Holding Company Act of 1935,* the *Trust Indenture Act of 1939,* the *Investment Company Act of 1940,* the *Investment Advisors Act of 1940,* the *Securities Investor Protection Act of 1970,* portions of the *Foreign Corrupt Practices Act of 1977,* the *Insider Trading Sanctions Act of 1984,* the *Securities Fraud Enforcement Act of 1988,* and *The Private Securities Litigation Act of 1995.*

THE SECURITIES ACT OF 1933

The **Securities Act of 1933**, sometimes referred to as the "truth in securities" law, regulates the initial public offering (IPO) and sale of securities. The Act prohibits fraudulent misrepresentations in IPOs and requires that an entity first file a registration statement, including a prospectus, with the Commission before offering securities for sale publicly.

The Registration Process

A **registration statement** is filed on a prescribed form, usually *Form S-1*, and reports required information, including:

- An entity's nature, history, and capital structure,
- Descriptions of the securities offered and the underwriting arrangements,
- Officers' and directors' salaries and security holdings,
- Estimated net proceeds from the offering and their intended use, and
- Detailed financial information.

Rather than "fill in the blank" questionnaires, registration forms require extensive narrative responses, and the completion process is both time-consuming and demanding. Once filed, a registration statement is examined by an SEC Division of Corporation Finance review team that consists of an accountant, an attorney, and a financial analyst. Following review, the SEC either accepts the registration statement or issues a letter of comment requesting corrections. If the statement is not corrected, the SEC can accept the original filing (rarely done), issue a refusal order that does not halt the registration process (sometimes done), or issue a stop order that halts the registration process. In practice, these alternatives are not often used, since most registrants respond promptly and properly to letters of comment.

The Independent Auditor

An auditor's liability under the *Securities Act of 1933* derives from his or her involvement in the registration process. In a typical registration, an auditor will ordinarily audit the registrant's financial statements, read the registration statement for material inconsistencies with the financial statements, review events from the date of the audited financial statements to the registration statement's effective date, and issue a letter for underwriters (called a "comfort letter"). The comfort letter addresses selected representations appearing in the registration statement and is prepared in accordance with *Statement on Auditing Standards No. 49*, "Letters for Underwriters" (AU Sec. 634), discussed in Chapter 18.

Most suits against auditors under the *Securities Act of 1933* are brought under Section 11. The statutory basis for an auditor's liability is contained in Section 11(a), which states in part:

> **Section 11(a)**
>
> In case any part of the registration statement, when such part became effective, contained an untrue statement of a material fact or omitted to state a material fact required to be stated therein or necessary to make the statements therein not misleading, any person acquiring such security . . . may sue . . . every accountant . . . who has with his consent been named as having prepared or certified any part of the registration statement . . .

In general, Section 11 is intended to protect potential investors by imposing liability on anyone who makes untrue statements or omits material facts in connection with a registration statement.

THE SECURITIES EXCHANGE ACT OF 1934

Whereas the 1933 Act regulates the initial public offering and sale of securities, the Securities Exchange Act of 1934 regulates the trading of previously issued securities. Under the 1934 Act, an entity must register securities with, and report to, the SEC if there are 500 or more shareholders and if assets exceed $10 million. In general, the Act's purpose is to promote adequate and accurate disclosure of material facts on a continuing basis.

The Registration and Periodic Reporting Process

Companies subject to the 1934 Act must register classes of traded securities and report selected information periodically. Of the registration forms available, *Form 10-K*, an annual financial statement, is used most commonly.

Form 10-K is filed by every company for which another form is not specified, and those that file *Form 10-K* also file *Form 10-Q*, a quarterly financial report. Companies that file registration forms other than *Form 10-K* are required to use specially designated forms for periodic reporting. However, all entities, regardless of the registration form filed, are required to file *Form 8-K*, a notice of significant current events affecting the company, which, in the case of a change in auditors, must be filed within three business days after the change. Through these various reports, the 1934 Act effectively provides continuous disclosure to interested parties.

The Independent Auditor

An auditor's liability under the *Securities Exchange Act of 1934* derives from the disclosure process, typically his or her involvement with *Forms 10-K* and *10-Q*. Most suits against auditors under the 1934 Act relate to either Section 10(b) or Section 18.

Section 10(b)

It shall be unlawful for any person, directly or indirectly, by the use of any means or instrumentality of interstate commerce or of the mails, or of any facility of any national securities exchange,

(b) To use or employ, in connection with the purchase or sale of any security registered on a national securities exchange or any security not so registered, any manipulative or deceptive device or contrivance in contravention of such rules and regulations as the Commission may prescribe as necessary or appropriate in the public interest or for the protection of investors.

Under Section 10(b) the SEC issued Rule 10b-5, "Employment of Manipulative and Deceptive Devices," which states:

Rule 10b-5

It shall be unlawful for any person, directly or indirectly, by the use of any means or instrumentality of interstate commerce, or of the mails, or of any facility of any national securities exchange,

(a) to employ any device, scheme, or artifice to defraud,

(b) to make any untrue statement of a material fact or to omit to state a material fact necessary in order to make the statements made, in the light of the circumstances under which they were made, not misleading, or

(c) to engage in any act, practice, or course of business which operates or would operate as a fraud or deceit upon any person, in connection with the purchase or sale of any security.

Section 10(b) and Rule 10b-5 are antifraud provisions that protect the purchasers and sellers of securities from manipulation and deception by an auditor or any other person.

Section 18 of the 1934 Act is a disclosure provision that states in part:

Section 18

Any person who shall make or cause to be made any statement in any application, report, or document filed . . . which . . . was . . . false or misleading with respect to any material fact, shall be liable to any person (not knowing that such statement was false or misleading) who, in reliance upon such statement, shall have purchased or sold a security at a price which was affected by such statement, for damages caused by such reliance, unless the person sued shall prove that he acted in good faith and had no knowledge that such statement was false or misleading.

Section 18 protects purchasers and sellers from false and misleading statements.

LIABILITY UNDER THE SECURITIES ACTS

An auditor may be liable to securities purchasers under the *Securities Act of 1933*, Section 11, for his or her involvement in the registration process, and to securities purchasers and sellers under the *Securities Exchange Act of 1934*, Sections 10(b) and 18, for involvement with a *Form 10-K or 10-Q*. An auditor's liability under each relevant section follows.

LIABILITY: 1933 ACT, SECTION 11

Under Section 11 of the 1933 Act, an auditor may be held liable to any party who purchases securities in an initial public offering and who alleges a material false or misleading statement within the registration statement.

Figure 5-3 summarizes an auditor's statutory liability to securities purchasers under Section 11 of the 1933 Act. An auditor is liable for lack of reasonable care (ordinary negligence) and, in contrast with common law, also sustains the burden for proving either: (1) the purchaser's damages or losses resulted from relying on information other than the registration statement, or (2) the auditor acted in good faith. The latter is referred to as the "due diligence" defense and is typically the defense chosen, since proving reliance on other information can be quite difficult. The plaintiff (purchaser), on the other hand, sustains the burden of proving damage or loss and that the financial statements are misstated.

Escott v. BarChris Construction Corp., illustrates an auditor's liability under Section 11. BarChris, which constructed recreational bowling centers, filed an S-1 registration statement on March 30, 1961. Peat Marwick had previously audited BarChris's December 31, 1960 financial statements, but a comfort letter (sometimes called an "S-1 review") was required, covering the period from the most recent balance sheet date to the registration statement's effective date. Most of the S-1 review was performed by a senior accountant who was not yet a CPA, was inexperienced in the construction industry, and was supervising his first engagement as a senior accountant. The senior and his assistants failed to discover material transactions and events occurring in the subsequent period. On October 29, 1962, after registered debentures (unsecured bonds) were offered and sold, BarChris filed for bankruptcy. Purchasers of the debentures subsequently filed suit against Peat Marwick, among others, alleging the registration statement contained false and misleading information. The court ruled for the purchasers, rejecting the auditors' due diligence defense:

There had been a material change for the worse in BarChris's financial position. That change was sufficiently serious so that the failure to disclose it made the 1960 figures misleading. (The senior) did not discover it. As far as results were concerned, his S-1 review was useless.

Accountants should not be held to a standard higher than that recognized in their profession. I do not do so here. (The senior's) review did not come up to that standard. He did not take some of the steps which Peat Marwick's written program prescribed. He did not spend an adequate amount of time on a task of this magnitude. Most important of all, he was too easily satisfied with glib answers to his inquiries.

. . . the burden of proof is on Peat Marwick. I find that the burden has not been satisfied. I conclude that Peat Marwick has not established its due diligence defense.

The court's opinion not only reaffirmed an auditor's potential liability for ordinary negligence under the 1933 Act, but also prompted *Statement on Auditing Procedure No. 47*, "Subsequent Events" (AU Sec. 560), discussed in Chapter 17.

LIABILITY: 1934 ACT, SECTION 10(B), RULE 10B-5

An auditor's liability under Section 10(b) is quite broad, since a plaintiff (purchaser or seller) may sue for any alleged false statement, whether the statement is filed with the SEC or not. Thus, even though, as explained in the following paragraphs, an auditor is not liable for ordinary negligence, there is significant exposure to liability under Section 10(b), since any form of statement may result in liability. Figure 5-3 summarizes an auditor's statutory liability to security purchasers and sellers under Section 10(b) and Rule 10b-5. In contrast with Section 11 of the 1933 Act, an auditor is liable under the 1934 Act for lack of minimum care (gross negligence), not lack of reasonable care (ordinary negligence). The plaintiff purchaser or seller has the burden of proving damage or loss, that financial statements are misstated, reliance on the statements, and deficient auditor conduct.

The courts have been inconsistent on the issue of negligent conduct under Section 10(b) and Rule 10b-5. Although *Ernst & Ernst v. Hochfelder* (1976), a landmark U.S. Supreme Court case, helped to resolve some issues, the court chose not to address all of the issues. Ernst & Ernst were auditors for the First

Securities Company of Chicago from 1946 through 1967. In 1968, Leston B. Nay, president and 92 percent stockholder of First Securities, left a suicide note stating that First Securities was bankrupt and describing his embezzlement from several escrow accounts. Nay perpetrated the embezzlement by inducing customers to invest in nonexistent high-yield accounts. Customers were instructed to make checks payable to Nay, who through his "mail rule" restricted employees from opening mail addressed to him, even during his absence. Nay diverted the proceeds to his own use, and the accounts were neither known nor available to Ernst & Ernst. Following Nay's suicide disclosure, investors sued Ernst & Ernst, claiming the firm was negligent in not discovering the mail rule. The investors reasoned that once discovered, the rule would have prevented a proper audit, prompting disclosure of the rule to the SEC and exposure of the embezzlement. Ernst & Ernst noted that the mail rule had no bearing on First Securities' internal controls, which were claimed to be adequate otherwise. On the other hand, the plaintiff produced three expert witnesses, all of whom agreed the mail rule reflected a significant inadequacy in internal control.

The U.S. Supreme Court ruled in favor of Ernst & Ernst, concluding that, for Ernst & Ernst to be held liable under Section 10(b) and Rule 10b-5, the plaintiff had to prove "scienter": the intent to deceive, manipulate, or defraud. As a result of the *Hochfelder* decision, accountants are not liable under Section 10(b) and Rule 10b-5 in the absence of scienter, thus eliminating ordinary negligence as a basis for liability. However, the court left open the question of whether gross negligence can satisfy the scienter requirement, stating:

In certain areas of the law recklessness is considered to be a form of intentional conduct for purposes of imposing liability for some act. We need not address here the question whether, in some circumstances, reckless behavior is sufficient for civil liability under 10(b) and 10b-5.

Since the *Hochfelder* decision, liability has been imposed on accountants in some cases under Section 10(b) and Rule 10b-5 for reckless or willful misconduct. For example, in *McLean v. Alexander,* the U.S. District court of Delaware held the accountant liable for recklessness, characterizing his conduct as "far more than mere negligence" but less than "a preconceived actual intent to defraud."

In both the *Hochfelder* and the *McLean* cases, the accountants were sued as "aiders and abettors" but not as "direct participants" with management in securities fraud, a far more aggressive allegation. A case decided in 1994 drew attention to the distinction. Heralded at first as a major victory for the profession, the U.S. Supreme Court swept aside decades of lower court precedents, ruling in *Central Bank of Denver v. First Interstate Bank of Denver* (1994) that accountants and other professionals could be sued in securities fraud cases as direct participants but not merely as aiders and abettors. However, the decision does not diminish the SEC's power, since ". . . the number of lawsuits that would be dismissed after the ruling was far less certain than the fact that aggressive plaintiffs' attorneys would redouble efforts to charge accountants not as mere abettors but as participating co-conspirators."[2] The issue of accountants' liability under Section 10(b) and Rule 10b-5 in the absence of intent remains unsettled. However, *McLean,* among other decisions subsequent to

2 R. Telberg, "Top Court's Ruling Rocks Profession," *Accounting Today* (May 2, 1994), p. 46.

Hochfelder, suggests that accountants are potentially liable for reckless misconduct (gross negligence).

LIABILITY: 1934 ACT, SECTION 18

An auditor's legal liability is narrower under Section 18 than under Section 10(b). A Section 18 action may be taken only for alleged false statements filed with the SEC, while a Section 10(b) action may be based on any alleged false statements, even those not filed. Figure 5-3 summarizes an auditor's statutory liability to securities purchasers and sellers under Section 18. As under Section 10(b), an auditor is liable under Section 18 for lack of minimum care (gross negligence). The plaintiff purchaser or seller has the burden of proving damage or loss, that financial statements are misstated, and reliance on the statements. In contrast with Section 10(b), an auditor must prove due diligence—that he or she acted in good faith and without knowledge that the statements were false or misleading.

SECURITIES LITIGATION REFORM

Although many lawsuits against accountants have merit, many more do not. For example, aggressive litigators commonly file or threaten lawsuits, hoping that accounting firms will settle out-of-court rather than risk the fate of an unsympathetic jury or an uninformed press. In legislation intended to reduce the number of frivolous class-action suits, Congress passed *The Private Securities Litigation Reform Act of 1995*. The Act imposes hefty sanctions against attorneys who rely on legally frivolous or factually impertinent arguments, but retains joint-and-several liability on parties who knowingly perpetrate a fraud. However, in an extraordinary departure from U.S. custom, the Act imposes **proportionate liability** on peripheral, less culpable defendants, although with some exceptions: All defendants are jointly-and-severally liable to investors who lose more than 10 percent of total net worths valued below $200,000, and proportionately liable defendants are further liable for up to 50 percent of proportionate liability to cover judgments against insolvent co-defendants. The Act was received as a welcome sign of relief to many practitioners. For example, referring to remarks by William Ezzell, a partner in Deloitte & Touche, the *Journal of Accountancy* said, ". . .under the new law, a defendant who is found only to have acted recklessly, but who did not knowingly commit fraud, would be responsible for only a proportionate amount of the damages."[3] However, a report released by the National Economic Research Association found both that the proportion of federal class action suits against accountants has not declined since enactment of the *Litigation Reform Act* and that more plaintiffs are suing accountants in state court, where tort reform has been slow in coming.[4]

CRIMINAL LIABILITY

An auditor can be held criminally liable under several federal statutes, including the *Securities Act of 1933* (Section 24), the *Securities Exchange Act of 1934*

---

3   "Securities Litigation Reform Bill is Now Law," *Journal of Accountancy* (February 1996), p. 14.
4   "Tort Reform, Short Reform," *The Public Accounting Report* (November 15, 1996), pp. 1, 5.

[Section 32(a)], the *Federal False Statements Statute,* the *Federal Mail Fraud Statute,* and the *Racketeer Influenced and Corrupt Organizations Act*. Section 24 of the 1933 Act holds an auditor criminally liable for willfully making a false statement or omitting a material fact in connection with a registration statement. Section 32(a) of the 1934 Act also holds an auditor criminally liable for willfully making a false or misleading statement in reports filed under the Act. Criminal penalties against individuals under either section may include fines or not more than five years imprisonment, or both. Under the *Federal False Statements Statute,* criminal liability can result from any issue within a federal department's or agency's jurisdiction; and under the *Federal Mail Fraud Statute,* from any mailing of or conspiracy to mail false financial statements. The *Racketeer Influenced and Corrupt Organizations Act,* discussed more fully later, is a federal criminal statute that includes a civil provision that can be imposed on independent auditors.

CONTINENTAL VENDING

Over the years there have been only a few criminal liability cases involving auditors, the overwhelming majority of cases having been for civil liability. A particularly prominent criminal liability case involving auditors was decided in 1969, *United States v. Simon,* popularly known as the "Continental Vending" case, and involved both Section 32(a) of the 1934 Act and the Federal Mail Fraud Statute.

Harold Roth was president of Continental Vending and owner of about 25 percent of both Continental and its affiliate, Valley Commercial Corporation. From 1958 to 1962, Continental loaned over $3 million to Roth through Valley Commercial, whose operations were supervised by Roth. Because Roth could not repay Valley, Valley could not repay Continental. Thus, Roth pledged collateral, about 80 percent of which was Continental stock. Although the receivable from Valley was recorded by Continental, it was not collectible because Roth was unable to pay Valley, and the market value of Roth's collateral was less than the amount owed. Bankruptcy followed, and the government sued the auditors, alleging that a footnote in Continental's September 30, 1962 financial statements did not adequately disclose that Roth ultimately received money loaned by Continental to Valley and that Roth's collateral consisted largely of Continental securities.

The auditors argued that they had followed generally accepted accounting principles and thus were free of criminal liability. However, the court ruled in the government's favor, stating that improper activities should be disclosed. In part the court stated:

But it simply cannot be true that an accountant is under no duty to disclose what he knows when he has reason to believe that, to a material extent, a corporation is being operated not to carry out its business in the interests of all the stockholders but for the private benefit of its president.

Further, regarding an auditor's obligations, the court stated:

Generally accepted accounting principles instruct an accountant what to do in the usual case when he has no reason to doubt that the affairs of the corporation are being honestly conducted. Once he has reason to believe that this basic assumption is false, an entirely different situation confronts him.

Thus, the court effectively ruled that compliance with accepted standards—due diligence—is not a wholly sufficient defense in criminal cases. The auditors were convicted of willfully making a false or misleading statement and for using the mails to distribute false and misleading financial statements, although they subsequently received a presidential pardon.

RACKETEER INFLUENCED AND CORRUPT ORGANIZATIONS ACT

Passed originally as part of the Organized Crime Control Act of 1970, the *Racketeer Influenced and Corrupt Organizations (RICO) Act* was intended to curtail the movement of organized crime into legitimate business. Although *RICO* is a federal criminal statute, a last-minute change by Congress added a civil provision that has been used widely against legitimate businesses and professionals, including independent accountants.

Rather than define the nebulous term "organized crime," Congress chose to list the acts typically associated with organized crimes, such as murder, arson, and extortion, and other acts such as mail fraud, wire fraud, and fraud in the sale of securities, all of which were growing in prominence in the late 1960s. Although targeted toward organized crime, RICO has greatly impacted the professions because the Act is broadly worded, defines a "pattern of racketeering activity" as two or more convictions (civil or criminal) within a 10-year period, and contains a provision that permits private parties, such as shareholders, to bring civil suits that include treble damages and attorneys' fees. As Congressman Frederick C. Boucher (D.-Va.) has stated, ". . . the result of combining this broadly worded statute with the unfettered use made of it by private parties has been an explosion of RICO treble-damage claims in cases against people Congress never intended to be victimized by this powerful weapon."[5] Among those individuals who may be victimized are professionals, such as certified public accountants, who are not even remotely connected with organized crime.

In 1985, the U.S. Supreme Court, in a 5-4 decision (*Sedima v. Imrex Company*), ruled that RICO's civil provisions could be applied to virtually any commercial dispute, which effectively increased the potential exposure of professional accountants, since suits against auditors typically involve a commercial dispute. However, the Court also noted that RICO has been legally applied to defendants not intended by Congress, and that any correction of the Act's defects must lie with Congress. For example, in an op-ed piece in *The Wall Street Journal*, U.S. Supreme Court Chief Justice William H. Renquist stated: "The legislative history of the RICO Act strongly suggests that Congress never intended it to be used in ordinary disputes divorced from the influences of organized crime . . . I think the time has arrived for Congress to enact amendments to civil RICO to limit its scope to the sort of wrongs that are connected to organized crime . . ."[6]

Consistent with Chief Justice Renquist's statement, the U.S. Supreme Court in 1993 upheld (7-2) an appeals court ruling in *Reves v. Arthur Young* that an independent audit does not meet *RICO's* criteria for involvement in the management of a corrupt organization and therefore that auditors cannot be sued

5   F. C. Boucher, "Why Civil RICO Must Be Reformed," *Journal of Accountancy* (December 1985), p. 103.
6   W. H. Renquist, "Get RICO Cases Out of My Courtroom," *The Wall Street Journal* (May 19, 1989).

under *RICO*. But the decision was narrow, providing no relief for auditors who participate directly with management to perpetrate a fraud. The Court's ruling is a significant victory for the profession, since the AICPA, among others in the financial community, had been working with Congress since 1985 to enact changes in RICO, among them proposed legislation that would reduce treble damages to single damages and would exclude securities cases from RICO's reach.

AN AUDITOR'S RESPONSIBILITY FOR FRAUD AND ILLEGAL ACTS

The scope paragraph of a standard audit report, introduced in Chapter 3, states that an auditor obtains ". . . reasonable assurance about whether the financial statements are free of material *misstatement*." Misstatements occur most often because of unintentional errors made by client personnel in recording, classifying, and summarizing transactions and events. But sometimes the misstatement is intentional, such as an undetected cash embezzlement perpetrated for example by an employee without management's knowledge, thereby prompting management to sue the auditor. Two prominent cases illustrate.

In *Cedars of Lebanon Hospital Corp. v. Touche Ross* (1982), the hospital and its board of directors brought suit against Touche Ross for failing to detect an embezzlement perpetrated by the hospital's administrator. A Circuit Court of Dade County, Florida, not only found Touche Ross not guilty, but also awarded the firm legal and accounting fees and punitive damages from Cedars of Lebanon. In *Cenco, Inc. v. Seidman & Seidman* (1982), new management at Cenco, a Chicago medical products firm, sued Seidman for failing to uncover a $25 million inventory fraud perpetrated by Cenco's former management. In a three-judge decision, the U.S. Court of Appeals for the Seventh Circuit in Chicago upheld a lower federal court, ruling that Seidman was not negligent for failing to uncover the fraud, since "auditors aren't detectives hired to ferret out fraud," and the fraud was quite difficult to detect because former management turned the company "into an engine of theft against outsiders."

In both cases, the auditors were not found legally liable for failing to detect fraud, as the courts concluded that an audit designed to obtain reasonable assurance about material misstatements does not impose a legal obligation to detect cleverly concealed fraud. Six years later, in response to recommendations by the *National Commission on Fraudulent Financial Reporting*, an auditor's responsibility to detect client errors and fraud would change markedly, as discussed next.

DETECTING FRAUD

Coincident with hearings conducted by the House Subcommittee on Oversight and Investigations, the AICPA, the American Accounting Association, the Institute of Internal Auditors, the Financial Executives Institute, and the National Association of Accountants reached agreement in 1985 to form an independent *National Commission on Fraudulent Financial Reporting*, chaired by James C. Treadway, Jr., a former SEC commissioner. Over its two-year existence, the

Treadway Commission considered the extent to which management fraud undermines the integrity of financial reporting, the extent to which fraud can be prevented, the role of independent auditors in detecting management fraud, and whether changes in auditing standards were necessary. Although the Commission appreciated that an auditor cannot be held responsible for detecting all frauds, particularly those involving a carefully concealed forgery or collusion, they recommended that auditors be held responsible to assess the likelihood of fraud in every audit and to design tests that would provide reasonable assurance of detection. Having noted that most frauds involve top management, the Commission also recommended that auditors be professionally skeptical of management, rather than assume unilaterally that management has integrity. *Statement on Auditing Standards No. 53*, "The Auditor's Responsibility To Detect and Report Errors and Irregularities," issued in 1988, responded to all three recommendations.

However, since *SAS No. 53* was issued, many in the financial community remained confused about an auditor's responsibility for fraud, partly because the pronouncement used the terms "errors" (unintentional misstatements in financial statements) and "irregularities" (intentional misstatements, one type of which is fraud), and mostly because the financial press continued to report highly material cases of undetected fraud, including some perpetrated in inventory at companies well known to the public, such as Leslie Fay and PharMor. More compelling, both the Public Oversight Board (the POB, introduced in Chapter 1) and Congress offered motivation for the Auditing Standards Board to reconsider *SAS No. 53*. The POB, in a 1993 report, *"In the Public Interest,"* recommended strongly that auditors exercise more professional skepticism in financial statement audits and that the profession develop better indicators of fraud. Congress, in the "Auditor Disclosure of Corporate Fraud" provision of *The Private Securities Litigation Reform Act of 1995*, required that auditors report fraud to management and the audit committee and, failing an immediate response, report in writing to the full board of directors and to the SEC within one business day. Clearly, the actions of the POB and Congress made plain the profession's need to again address fraud. In response, the Auditing Standards Board issued *SAS No. 82*, "Consideration of Fraud in a Financial Statement Audit," distinguishing between errors and fraud, and providing expanded guidance on a practitioner's responsibility for fraud in auditing.

Errors are unintentional misstatements or omissions in financial statements. Examples include mistakes in gathering or processing accounting data; mistakes in the application of accounting principles; and incorrect accounting estimates, such as the allowance for uncollectible receivables, that arise from oversight or misinterpretation of facts. Fraud, in contrast, arises from fraudulent financial reporting and from misappropriation of assets: *Fraudulent financial reporting* is an intentional misstatement or omission of an amount or disclosure in financial statements. Examples include the manipulation, falsification, or alteration of records or documents; the misrepresentation or omission of transactions or events; and the intentional misapplication of an accounting principle. *Misappropriation of assets* (sometimes called a "defalcation") is the theft of an entity's assets. Examples include embezzling cash, stealing inventory, or causing payment for services not received. Fraudulent financial reporting and misappropriation of assets differ in this way: The former is usually committed by management to deceive financial statement users, whereas the latter is usually committed by employees and deceives management.

As indicated by the definitions and examples, *intent* is the primary difference between an error and a fraud. In practice, however, intent is often difficult to measure. For example, an unreasonably low estimate of the allowance for uncollectible accounts receivable could result from an unintentional bias, which would constitute an error, or from an intentional attempt to misstate the financial statements, a fraud. As discussed in the following section, an auditor's responsibility for detecting errors and fraud is identical because both misstate the financial statements. However, distinguishing between the two in practice is important nevertheless, because fraud is intentional and, as a result, raises concerns about management's integrity.

Responsibility

In a financial statement audit, an auditor is responsible to obtain reasonable assurance about whether the financial statements are free of material misstatement, and whether any misstatement is caused by unintentional error or intentional fraud. However, fraud may occur on any audit, even those for which the unsuspecting auditor has no reason to believe it may. For example, Touche Ross did not suspect that an administrator had embezzled from Cedars of Lebanon Hospital, and Seidman & Seidman did not suspect inventory mismanagement at Cenco. As a result, *generally accepted auditing standards* require that:

The auditor should specifically assess the risk of material misstatement of the financial statements due to fraud and should consider that assessment in designing the audit procedures to be performed.

Despite the profession's heightened awareness of fraud, a properly planned and executed audit may still fail to detect a cleverly concealed fraud, particularly one involving forgery or collusion among employees or management. For example, auditors are neither trained nor expected under *generally accepted auditing standards* to judge the authenticity of forged documents. An auditor is not an insurer and an audit report is not a guarantee, because an audit opinion and audit procedures are based on the concept of reasonable, not absolute, assurance. Nevertheless, an auditor should exercise both due care and professional skepticism to provide reasonable assurance that material errors and fraud will be detected.

Considering the Risk of Errors and Fraud in Audit Planning

Audit risk, defined in Chapter 2, is the likelihood that an auditor may unknowingly fail to modify an opinion on materially misstated financial statements. For example, there is a risk that material error or fraud in accounts receivable may go undetected, leading the unknowing auditor to issue an unqualified opinion on the financial statements even though the statements are materially misstated because of the undetected error or fraud. To assess the risk that errors or fraud may cause material misstatements, an auditor, while planning an engagement, considers factors that influence audit risk both at the overall financial statement level and at the account balance level.

At the financial statement level, the auditor considers factors such as those listed in Figure 5-4 and judges whether the assessed level of audit risk may

Figure 5-4: Factors Affecting the Risk of Material Misstatement Arising from Fraud

Risk of Fraudulent Financial Reporting

Management Characteristics
- Management is unduly aggressive about maintaining stock prices or earnings trends.
- Management's incentive compensation is contingent on earnings performance or stock prices.
- Management is committed to achieving analysts' forecasts.
- Management turnover is high, particularly among senior financial personnel.
- Prior securities laws violations.

Industry Conditions
- Highly competitive industry, market saturation, or inadequate earnings relative to others in the industry.
- Operating results are highly sensitive to technological change, inflation, unemployment, etc.
- Significant declines in customer demand, rapid product obsolescence.
- Declining industry with increasing business failures.

Operating Characteristics and Financial Stability
- Pressure to obtain additional capital.
- Unusual or highly complex transactions close to year end.
- Vulnerability to interest rate changes.
- Aggressive sales incentive programs.
- Consequences of pending contract awards or business combinations.

Risk of Misappropriation of Assets

Susceptibility of Assets to Misappropriation
- Large amounts of cash processed or on hand.
- High-value, high-demand inventory.
- Easily convertible bearer bonds, diamonds, computer chips.
- Small, untraceable, marketable fixed assets.

Employee Relationships or Pressures
- Well-known future employee layoffs.
- Disgruntled employees who can access assets.
- Unusual behavior by employees who can access assets.
- Employees with known personal financial pressures.

Controls
- Inadequate segregation of duties or independent checks.
- Inadequate system of authorization and approval.
- Poor physical safeguards over cash, investments, inventory, or fixed assets.
- No mandatory vacation policy for employees who handle cash.

affect the overall strategy of the audit. Although the presence of one of the factors from Figure 5-4 would not necessarily indicate increased risk, the presence of several could affect the auditor's strategy. For example, if management is committed to achieving analysts' earnings forecasts and there are unusual or highly complex transactions close to year end, an auditor would likely assess inherent risk at the maximum level and assess allowable detection risk at a relatively low level. As a result, the auditor would alter his or her overall strategy by expanding the extent of planned audit procedures, engaging experienced staff, and encouraging assigned staff to exercise more than the usual level of professional skepticism.

At the account balance level, an auditor considers the effects of the financial statement level risk factors (Figure 5-4) on the specific financial statement accounts or classes of transactions affected. For example, if the rate of technological change in an industry is rapid, an auditor should consider whether any inventory is obsolete and therefore reported at inflated carrying values. In addition, the auditor should consider other factors that may influence the risk of material misstatements, such as complex calculations related to pension and warranty liabilities, imputed interest rates on receivables and payables, and loan loss reserves in the banking industry.

Professional Skepticism

An auditor should not presume without reason that management is dishonest, since a presumption of dishonesty in all cases would be contrary to the accumulated experience of practicing auditors. In fact, in considering the risk of material misstatements from errors and fraud, honesty is not necessarily the issue. Rather, the issue is that an audit should be planned and performed with professional skepticism, an attitude which recognizes that, honesty aside, management may have incentives to intentionally misstate amounts or disclosures in the financial statements—incentives, for example, that derive from the factors in Figure 5-4.

Professional skepticism should be exercised both at the planning stage of an engagement and while performing audit procedures and gathering evidence. For example, if an auditor concludes during the planning stage that there is significant risk of material misstatement, the audit strategy should be altered by assigning sufficiently experienced audit staff and by altering the nature, timing, and extent of audit procedures: The *nature* of procedures might be altered by obtaining more evidence from independent sources, *timing* might be altered by performing tests at or near the balance sheet date, and *extent* might be altered by increasing sample size or performing more extensive analytical procedures.

Evaluating Audit Test Results and Reporting

Material errors detected by applying audit procedures should be corrected through journal entries. Material fraud, in contrast, has additional implications because they are intentional. If an auditor detects fraud, but has also determined that the effect on the financial statements could not be material (for example, if there'd been misappropriations of small amounts of cash from a small imprest fund), the auditor should:

- Refer the matter to an appropriate level of management that is at least one level above those involved, and
- Be satisfied that, given the position of the likely perpetrator, the fraud has no implications for other aspects of the audit or that those implications have been adequately considered.

However, if the auditor detects a material fraud or has been unable to evaluate materiality, he or she should:

- Consider the implications for other aspects of the audit,

- Discuss the matter and the approach to further investigation with an appropriate level of management that is at least one level above those involved,
- Attempt to obtain evidence to determine whether in fact material frauds exist and, if so, their effect, and
- If appropriate, suggest that the client consult with legal counsel about questions of law.

If an auditor concludes that an entity's financial statements are affected materially by a fraud, he or she should insist that the statements be revised. If management agrees, the statements would be revised by management, and the auditor should issue an unqualified opinion. But if management refuses, the auditor should express a qualified or an adverse opinion because, as discussed in Chapter 3, the financial statements will have departed from generally accepted accounting principles. In turn, if the auditor is precluded from applying necessary audit procedures or is unable to reach a conclusion about materiality, he or she should issue a qualified opinion or disclaim an opinion on the basis of a scope limitation, explained in Chapter 3. Further, the auditor should report his or her findings to the board of directors or its audit committee. Disclosing fraud to parties other than senior management and the audit committee of the board of directors is not ordinarily part of an auditor's responsibility but may be necessary in some circumstances, such as disclosure in response to a court-ordered subpoena, an auditor change (SEC *Form 8-K*), an inquiry from a successor auditor, or a federal funding agency.

ILLEGAL ACTS BY CLIENTS

An auditor's responsibility for detecting client errors and fraud has long been a major preoccupation of regulatory agencies, the financial markets, the financial press, and professional accounting organizations such as the AICPA. In contrast, an auditor's responsibility for illegal acts by clients gained widespread prominence only within the last two decades. Prior to the 1970s, conventional wisdom held that material illegal corporate payments, such as bribes to influence political officials, were virtually nonexistent. But in a dramatic turn of events, a 1976 SEC-sponsored voluntary compliance program disclosed that over 250 U.S. corporations had made questionable or illegal payments both in the U.S. and abroad. Congress responded in 1977 by enacting the *Foreign Corrupt Practices Act,* discussed later in the chapter, and the AICPA issued a Statement on Auditing Standards (*SAS No. 17*). In 1988, the Auditing Standards Board issued *Statement on Auditing Standards No. 54,* "Illegal Acts by Clients" (AU Sec. 317), which defines **illegal acts** as violations of laws or governmental regulations, and provides guidance in three general areas:

- An auditor's responsibility for detecting and disclosing illegal acts,
- The audit procedures an auditor should consider both in the apparent absence of illegal acts and when illegal acts are possible, and
- How an auditor should respond to detected illegal acts.

Responsibility

Two important issues underscore an auditor's responsibility for illegal acts: dependence on legal judgment and the proximity of a questionable act to the financial statements. *Dependence on legal judgment* simply means that determining the illegality of specific acts is normally beyond the scope of an independent auditor's professional competence. Auditors are proficient in accounting and auditing, not the law. True, an auditor's experience and understanding of a client's industry may provide a basis for recognizing some illegal acts—for example, violations of federal tax or securities laws—but determining legality should generally be left to attorneys and, in the U.S., to due process of the law.

The likelihood of detecting an illegal act depends on the *proximity of the act* to recorded transactions and events. The further removed an illegal act is from the transactions and events normally reflected in financial statements, the less likely an auditor is to become aware of the act. For example, although violations of federal tax laws are likely to be detected during an audit, violations of other laws and regulations, such as the *Occupational Safety and Health Act*, are beyond the scope of an audit and therefore are far less likely to be detected. Even if they are detected, an auditor considers these laws from the perspective of their relation to audit objectives, not from the perspective of legality. Not surprisingly, many of the questionable or illegal payments disclosed through the SEC's voluntary compliance program were made through off-the-books accounts and therefore were not susceptible to reasonable audit investigation.

An auditor's responsibility to detect and report misstatements resulting from illegal acts that have a *direct and material* effect on financial statement amounts is identical to that for fraud: to assess the risk that they may cause materially misstated financial statements and to consider the assessment in designing audit procedures. Examples of illegal acts that have a direct and material effect include violations of federal tax laws or government grant contracts. Regarding illegal acts that have a material but *indirect* effect on the financial statements—i.e., those acts that are removed from the transactions and events reflected in financial statements—the auditor should be aware that they may have occurred, although an audit provides no assurance that they will be detected. Examples of material but indirect illegal acts include violations of antitrust and equal employment laws.

Auditing Procedures

A financial statement audit does not normally include procedures designed specifically to detect illegal acts. However, some audit procedures that are motivated by audit objectives unrelated to illegal acts could lend insight into violations of the law. For example, reading the minutes of the board of directors' meetings, a procedure not motivated by its potential to reveal illegal acts, may provide the auditor's first evidence of an impending investigation by the Environmental Protection Agency, which may require disclosure of fines and penalties as a contingent liability. When there is no reason to believe illegal acts exist, the auditor should make inquiries of management about the entity's compliance with laws and regulations and, where applicable, also inquire about management's policies for preventing illegal acts, such as the issuance of policy directives internally. No other audit procedures are necessary in the absence of evidence suggesting that illegal acts may possibly exist.

When an auditor becomes aware of information concerning a possible illegal act, he or she should obtain: (1) an understanding of the circumstances of the act—for example, by making inquiries of management above those involved, and (2) enough evidence to judge the effect of the act on the financial statements. If evidence provided by management does not convince the auditor that an illegal act has not occurred, the auditor should consult with the entity's legal counsel and consider other procedures. For example, the auditor might consider confirming significant information with intermediaries, such as bankers and lawyers, or with other parties to the transaction.

Responding to Detected Illegal Acts

When an illegal act has occurred or is likely to occur, an auditor should consider the effect of the act on the financial statements and on the audit report. This requires an evaluation of the materiality of the act. As discussed in Chapter 2, materiality is a somewhat elusive concept in accounting and auditing, and this is no less the case when applied to illegal acts. For example, in the past, several relatively high-ranking corporate officials dismissed their company's questionable payments as immaterial and therefore of little consequence to financial information users. Although specific acts alone may be immaterial in amount, two other factors, namely contingent monetary effects and loss contingencies, may render an act material.

Contingent monetary effects include fines, penalties, and damages that, in some circumstances, such as violations of the *Foreign Corrupt Practices Act* (discussed in the next section), may be quite substantial. **Loss contingencies**, such as the threat of expropriation of assets, enforced discontinuance of foreign operations, or possible litigation, are frequently more substantial than either contingent monetary effects or, for example, an illegal payment itself. Thus, when considering the materiality of an illegal act, an auditor should consider contingent monetary effects and loss contingencies, not just the dollar amount of the payment itself.

Illegal acts should be reported to the audit committee of the board of directors or to others with equivalent authority, such as the federal agencies that monitor direct federal grants to local governments and to nonprofit organizations like local community theaters. However, the "Auditor Disclosure of Corporate Fraud" provision of *The Private Securities Litigation Reform Act of 1995* (introduced earlier) requires that auditors report possible illegal acts to management and to the audit committee—if neither takes remedial action, the provision requires that the auditor notify the board of directors in writing, and that the entity forward the report to the SEC within one business day. Disclosure to other parties is not ordinarily the auditor's responsibility, although there is a duty to notify a successor auditor and there may be a duty to respond to a subpoena. If management does not disclose a direct and material illegal act properly in the financial statements, the auditor should express a qualified or an adverse opinion since, as explained in Chapter 3, failure to disclose is a departure from generally accepted accounting principles. If prevented by management from obtaining evidence, the auditor should disclaim an opinion on the financial statements.

THE FOREIGN CORRUPT PRACTICES ACT

The **Foreign Corrupt Practices Act (FCPA)** evolved primarily from investigations by the Office of the Watergate Special Prosecutor and an SEC voluntary disclosure program, both of which provided evidence of significant illegal acts perpetrated by U.S. multinational companies overseas. The intent of Congress in legislating the Act was to respond directly as critics of corporate governance and responsibility through legislation that would require corporations to implement internal controls sufficient to detect illegal payments and to enable accurate financial statements. The Act includes two provisions, one related to unlawful influence (bribes), and another to internal control and record keeping.

Unlawful Influence

The unlawful influence provision of the Act makes it illegal for any U.S. domestic company or foreign SEC-registrant company to influence foreign governments, officials, political parties, or political candidates through payments or gifts. For example, it would be unlawful for a U.S. company to protect their domestic market share in imported goods by bribing a foreign political official to influence legislation that would increase the foreign country's regulated export tariff. However, the Act does not prohibit so-called "grease" or "facilitating" payments made to ministerial or clerical government employees for the purpose, for example, of expediting the processing of shipments through customs. A company convicted of a bribe, whether willful or not, can be fined up to $1,000,000. An officer, director, or stockholder of a convicted company can be fined up to $10,000 and/or imprisoned for up to five years, although bribes by these parties must be willful. Fines imposed on individuals may not be paid by a company.

Record Keeping and Internal Control

The record keeping and internal control provision of the Act requires that the management of SEC-registrant companies implement internal controls sufficient to provide reasonable assurances that: (1) transactions are executed in accordance with management's authorization, (2) transactions are recorded as necessary, and (3) access to assets is permitted only in accordance with management's authorization. Because it amends Section 13(b) of the *Securities Exchange Act of 1934*, the provision is administered and enforced by the SEC. A company violating the internal control and record keeping provision of the Act can be fined up to $10,000. An officer, director, or stockholder of a violating company can be fined up to $10,000 and/or imprisoned for up to five years. Again, fines imposed on individuals may not be paid by the corporation.

COPING WITH POTENTIAL LIABILITY

How does an auditor cope with the inevitable risk of litigation, a risk sustained on virtually every audit engagement? The following describes several precautions an auditor could consider in attempting to minimize the risk of potential litigation.

ARBITRATION OR MEDIATION

In moves intended to minimize litigation costs, engagement letters used both by BDO Seidman and by Ernst & Young require that clients for all professional services waive the right to a jury trial, opting instead for mediation or arbitration to resolve disputes.[7] For example, Ernst & Young engagement letters call first for mediating discussions with an impartial mediator agreed to by each party or assigned by the American Arbitration Association (AAA), followed 90 days thereafter by binding arbitration using procedures in the AAA's *Arbitration Rules for Professional Accounting and Related Services Disputes.* Unlike jury trials, arbitration does not award punitive damages, does not incur court costs or excessive legal fees, and does not lack for timely resolutions.

PRACTICE DEVELOPMENT

If you think public accounting firms don't "fire" clients, think again. *Business Week* reports that one Big Six public accounting firm discontinued auditing a West Coast bank, another declined to audit about sixty companies considering initial public offerings, and that several major firms are refusing to audit small banks and thrift institutions at all.[8] Whereas firms once tripped over themselves to develop new business, practice development has taken a new twist in recent years. For example, all major firms now employ personnel whose primary job function is to investigate the backgrounds of new clients and their managements, and some use independent investigative firms like Pinkerton.

What's clear is that unlimited growth in client lists does not necessarily yield a successful audit practice and may lead to legal action, rendering increased audit fees trivial when compared to the damage settlements sometimes awarded to clients and other third parties. Practice development should not flourish at the expense of quality. Rather, new clients should be scrutinized carefully for integrity, and assigned audit staff should be alert to undue risk of fraudulent financial reporting. In short, the watchword today is professional skepticism.

ENGAGEMENT LETTERS

Both *Maryland Casualty Co. v. Jonathon Cook* and *1136 Tenants' Corp. v. Max Rothenberg & Co.*, discussed earlier, illustrate the importance of engagement letters. Among other things, engagement letters: (1) provide an explicit agreement of the professional services expected by a client and intended by the auditor, and (2) serve to eliminate, or at least minimize, misunderstandings between the auditor and client about the scope of the engagement, thereby eliminating potential legal liability for services neither contracted for nor performed. Engagement letters, discussed more fully and illustrated in Chapter 6, should be prepared for every professional engagement performed by an independent accountant, audit or otherwise. If a potential client refuses to sign an engagement letter, the practitioner should strongly consider refusing the engagement.

GENERALLY ACCEPTED AUDITING STANDARDS AND QUALITY CONTROL

Generally accepted auditing standards are the profession's guidelines for performing audit engagements, and measures of quality for evaluating completed engagements. Nevertheless, some courts have ruled that auditors should reach

---

7   B. Goodman, "E&Y Enacts Mediation Policy to Cut Courtroom Expenses," *Accounting Today* (May 6-19, 1996), pp. 5, 49.
8   K. Holland and L. Light, "Big Six are Firing Clients," *Business Week* (March 1, 1993), pp. 76-77.

for a higher standard of care, particularly in cases alleging criminal liability, as illustrated earlier for *United States v. Simon* (Continental Vending). Although it is not clear whether the courts will in the future require a higher standard of care than imposed by generally accepted auditing standards, it is clear the courts will never accept a lower standard.

The public accounting profession is self-regulated, with quality control and quality (peer) review providing the means for regulation. As explained in Chapter 4, quality control includes the internal policies and procedures that a firm establishes to regulate itself, and peer review is the process through which firms "audit" the quality control procedures of other firms. Of the two, quality control plays a more important role in minimizing potential legal liability, because it defines a standard of care that is applied to each of the firm's professional engagements, a "measuring stick" designed to minimize substandard performance on individual engagements. The stronger a system of quality control, the less likely a substandard engagement.

DEFENSIVE AUDITING

The purpose of a financial statement audit is to issue an opinion. That opinion, however, is dependent on the quality and quantity of audit evidence obtained. Defensive auditing implies that an auditor be mindful of potential litigation when conducting an engagement, clearly documenting the basis for all audit decisions. For example, it is one thing to obtain oral responses from management regarding questionable transactions, and quite another to document corroborative support for management's responses.

Closely related to defensive auditing is the awareness that some questions confronted in practice relate primarily to the law and not to accounting or auditing. An auditor should retain legal counsel for consultation when necessary. Auditors are generally neither trained nor experienced in the law, and therefore should reserve judgment until legal counsel is consulted.

PROFESSIONAL LIABILITY INSURANCE

In many instances over the years, independent accountants have been unsuccessful in coping with legal liability, resulting in highly publicized court cases and substantial settlements against public accounting firms. In fact, a study in the 1980s by the House Subcommittee on Oversight and Investigations indicated that since 1980, the Big Six public accounting firms had paid nearly $180 million in out-of-court settlements related to independent audits, and the amount has grown markedly since then. As a result of the large settlements involving the large national firms, malpractice insurance rates skyrocketed for all firms, and insurance companies became increasingly reluctant to underwrite professional liability insurance for independent accountants. For example, insurance premium increases of 200 to 400 percent in one year were not uncommon, and the number of insurance companies offering liability insurance to small- and medium-size firms dropped from almost a dozen in 1980 to a small handful a decade later. Even Lloyd's of London, the major insurer of the international firms, threatened to drop coverage unless awards against accountants were restrained. In short, the soaring malpractice suits once associated primarily with the medical profession had spread to public accounting.

In response to the high costs and diminishing sources of accountants' liability insurance, the AICPA established a special committee to consider the nature and extent of accountants' liability in general, and potential remedies to the explosion in liability suits in particular. In the 1990s, liability insurance rates became more reasonable, owing to the influence of the AICPA. But, among the profession's more far-reaching proposals has been a movement to seek Congressional legislation that would limit the liability of independent accountants in individual cases, a proposal that is not without precedent. For example, the Atomic Energy Act of 1954 limits liability for nuclear accidents to $650 million and, not unrelated, the liability of accountants in some foreign countries is limited by statute.

COUNTERSUITS

Although not yet a widespread practice, there is precedent for public accounting firms to countersue clients who, by perpetrating unscrupulous schemes to "cook the books," fraudulently induce unknowing auditors to issue unqualified opinions. In a 1992 precedent-setting development, Manor Care Inc., a Maryland company that acquired Cenco Inc. in 1981, agreed to settle a fourteen-year-old counterclaim filed by BDO Seidman in the case of *Cenco, Inc. v. Seidman & Seidman*, introduced earlier in the chapter. The settlement occurred just days before a jury trial was to begin in Illinois state court. Responding to the decision, Dan Goldwasser, an attorney and consultant to the New York State Society of CPAs, said, "It's likely that we're going to see more countersuits of this nature filed by accounting firms. The firms can no longer passively accept the risk of liability exposure when there has been clear evidence of fraud on the part of an audit client's management."[9]

LIMITED LIABILITY PARTNERSHIPS (LLPS)

Partnerships in some countries, among them the German GmbH (*Gesellschaft mit beschrankter Haftung*) and Latin American *limitada* companies, exempt partners from personal liability beyond their respective investments in the company. As discussed in Chapter 4, Rule 505 of the Code of Professional Conduct now allows a CPA firm to organize in any manner permitted by state law, and in all states, as in Germany and Latin America, a limited liability partnership (LLP) restricts the extent of a partner's liability to his or her investment in the partnership (or involvement in an obligation or illegal act). The first LLP legislation was enacted in Wyoming in 1977. Since then, all the states have responded and, as discussed in Chapter 1, so too have most of the major public accounting firms.

SUMMARY

In any civil liability case involving auditors, several issues are relevant, including the source of law (common or statutory); the identity of the plaintiff;

---

9   L. Berton, "BDO Seidman Wins Fraud Settlement in Countersuit Against an Audit Client," *The Wall Street Journal* (November 11, 1992), p. 7.

potential liability; and who sustains the burden of proving damage or loss, misstated financial statements, reliance on financial statements, and deficient auditor conduct. Under common law, an independent auditor may be liable to clients, primary beneficiaries, and foreseen third parties. Under Section 11 of the *Securities Act of 1933*, an auditor may be liable to purchasers of securities, and under Sections 10(b) and 18 of the *Securities Exchange Act of 1934*, an auditor may be liable to purchasers of securities, sellers, or both.

An independent auditor's criminal liability extends from several federal (and state) statutes, the most prominent being Section 24 of the 1933 Act, Section 32(a) of the 1934 Act, and the Federal False Statements and Mail Fraud Statutes. In addition, auditors may be held liable under the Racketeer Influenced and Corrupt Organizations Act. Few cases have been decided regarding an auditor's criminal liability; however, it is clear that criminal penalties have been and may continue to be levied.

Professional standards govern an auditor's responsibility for fraud and for illegal acts: An auditor is responsible to assess the risk that they may cause materially misstated financial statements and to consider the assessment in designing audit procedures. Even though determining illegality is beyond the scope of an auditor's expertise, he or she should have a reasonable basis for identifying potentially improper acts, although the likelihood of detection depends on the proximity of the act to the transactions and events underlying an entity's financial statements. The *Foreign Corrupt Practices Act* makes it unlawful for companies to influence foreign governments or officials through gifts or payments, and requires that SEC registrants comply with internal control and record keeping requirements.

Given today's legal environment, auditors should take precautions to minimize potential legal exposure, such as requiring mediation or arbitration, limiting practice development, preparing engagement letters for all professional engagements, adhering to *generally accepted auditing standards* and promoting quality control, documenting all audit decisions and conclusions, maintaining adequate professional liability insurance, filing countersuits, and consider forming as a limited liability company in those state where LLCs are allowed. Even with these precautions, though, the risk of litigation looms large.

KEY TERMS

Joint-and-several liability   130
Privity   130
Common law   131
Statutory law   131
Breach of contract   132
Tort   132
Primary beneficiaries   133
Foreseen third party   133
Ordinary negligence   133
Gross negligence   133
Fraud   133
Engagement letters   137
Securities and Exchange Commission (SEC)   140

Securities Act of 1933   141
Registration statement   141
Securities Exchange Act of 1934   142
Proportionate liability   146
Racketeer Influenced and Corrupt Organizations (RICO) Act   148
Errors   150
Illegal acts   154
Contingent monetary effects   156
Loss contingencies   156
Foreign Corrupt Practices Act (FCPA)   156

REFERENCES

LEGAL LIABILITY

Professional Report

Arthur Andersen & Co. *Lawsuit Reform*, Chicago: Arthur Andersen & Co., 1988.

Articles, Books

Baliga, W. "New York Clarifies Privity Requirements," and "Third Party Reliance on Audit Curtailed." *Journal of Accountancy* (January 1993), p. 17.

Batchelder, N. C. "Defensive Strategies for Accounting Firms," *The Practical Accountant* (July 1991), pp. 42-46.

Brodsky, R. E. "Osborne Decision Shows Sensitivity to Auditor's Task," *Accounting Today* (February 1, 1993), pp. 15, 17.

Causey, D. Y., Jr., and S. A. Causey. *Duties and Liabilities of Public Accountants*, 4th ed. Mississippi State: Accountant's Press, 1991.

Clolery, P. "Tips From a Litigator: Don't Pass the Buck on Liability," *The Practical Accountant* (January 1993), pp. 42-45.

Crawford, D., D. Franz, R. A. Zimmerman, and P. R. Fink, "Exposure to the Extracontractual," *Journal of Accountancy* (December 1995), pp. 89-91.

Foust, D. "They're Bean Counters, Not Gumshoes," *Business Week* (September 14, 1992), p. 92.

Geogham, P. "Punitive Damages: The Gathering Storm," *Journal of Accountancy* (July 1992), pp. 46-49.

Goldwasser, D. L. "Policy Considerations in Accountants' Liability to Third Parties for Negligence," *Journal of Accounting, Auditing & Finance* (Summer 1988), pp. 185-212.

Gormley, R. J. "Developments in Accountants' Liability to Nonclients for Negligence," *Journal of Accounting, Auditing & Finance* (Spring 1988), pp. 99-127.

Holland, K., L. Light, and M. Galen. "Big Six Firms are Firing Clients," *Business Week* (March 1, 1993), pp. 76-77.

Miller, S. H. "Avoiding Lawsuits," *Journal of Accountancy* (September 1988), pp. 57-65.

Murray, M. F. "When A Client is a Liability," *Journal of Accountancy* (September 1992), pp. 54-58.

Rubenstein, E. A., and C. J. Swastek. "The Nuts and Bolts of Malpractice Insurance," *The Practical Accountant* (July 1991), pp. 35-40.

Skousen, K. F. *An Introduction to the SEC*, 5th ed. Cincinnati: South-Western Publishing Co., 1991.

FRAUD

Professional Standards

AICPA. *Codification of Statements on Auditing Standards*. New York: AICPA (AU Sec. 316, 317).

SAS No. 54, "Illegal Acts by Clients" (AU Sec. 317).

SAS No. 82, "Consideration of Fraud in a Financial Statement Audit."

Professional Report

National Commission on Fraudulent Financial Reporting. *Report*, Chapter 3 (National Commission on Fraudulent Financial Reporting, 1987).

Articles

Berton, L. "Auditors Face Stiffer Rules for Finding, Reporting Fraud at Client Companies," *The Wall Street Journal* (February 5, 1996), p. A2.

Cheney, G. "Auditing Standards Board Pushes CPAs to Dig for Fraud," *Accounting Today* (April 8-21, 1996), pp. 14, 17.

Demry, P. "Increasing Auditors' Responsibility in Finding Fraud," *The Practical Accountant* (March 1996), p. 8

Editorial, "Competitive Bribing," *The Wall Street Journal* (April 19, 1996), p. A16.

Hall, J. J., "How to Spot Fraud," *Journal of Accountancy* (October 1996), pp. 85-88.

Heiman-Hoffman, V. B., K. P. Morgon, and J. P. Patton, "The Warning Signs of Fraudulent Financial Reporting," *Journal of Accountancy* (October 1996), pp. 75-78.

Loebbecke, J. L., M. M. Eining, and J. J. Willingham, "Auditor's Expertise with Material Irregularities: Frequency, Nature, and Detectability," *Auditing: A Journal of Practice & Theory* (Fall 1989), pp. 1-28.

Lowenstein, R. "Corporate Governance's Sorry History," *The Wall Street Journal* (April 18, 1996), p. C1.
Mancino, J. "The Auditing Standards Board Reconsiders Fraud in a Financial Statement Audit," *In Our Opinion: The Newsletter of the AICPA Auditing Standards Team* (January 1996), pp. 1, 2.
Wells, J. T. "Six Common Myths About Fraud," *Journal of Accountancy* (February 1990), pp. 82-88.

QUESTIONS

1. Discuss the two issues that help explain the litigation explosion against independent auditors.
2. Identify the major issues involved in a civil action against an independent auditor.
3. Distinguish between ordinary negligence, gross negligence, and fraud.
4. In general, what elements must be proved by various parties to a legal liability case involving auditors?
5. What is the auditor's common law liability to clients? What is the minimum basis for liability?
6. What lesson is learned from both *Maryland Casualty Co. v. Jonathon Cook* and *1136 Tenants' Corp. v. Max Rothenberg & Co.*?
7. Briefly describe the facts in *Ultramares Corp. v. Touche* and cite the significance of the case.
8. Explain how primary beneficiaries differ from foreseen beneficiaries. Give examples.
9. What is the significance to the profession of *Bily v. Arthur Young & Co.*, a 1993 California Supreme Court case?
10. Describe an auditor's alternative defenses under Section 11 of the *Securities Act of 1933*.
11. What lessons does *Escott v. BarChris Construction Corp.* offer about an inexperienced audit staff?
12. How does the burden of proof under Section 18 of the *Securities Exchange Act of 1934* differ from that under Section 10(b) and Rule 10b-5?
13. What is the significance of *United States v. Simon* to an independent auditor?
14. Identify several precautions an auditor might take to avoid litigation.
15. Distinguish between client errors and fraud.
16. In light of material undetected errors or fraud, what inherent risk does an auditor sustain by not auditing all of an entity's transactions and events during a financial statement audit? How do current auditing standards deal with that risk?
17. How should an independent auditor proceed if the effect of an illegal act on financial statements is not susceptible to reasonable investigation?
18. What is the purpose of the record keeping and internal control provisions of the Foreign Corrupt Practices Act?
19. What are "grease" or "facilitating" payments, and how are they treated in the Foreign Corrupt Practices Act?
20. What penalties may be imposed on an entity, officers, directors, or stockholders for violating the Foreign Corrupt Practices Act?

MULTIPLE CHOICE QUESTIONS

1. The arguments offered by third parties in litigation against a practitioner for an assurance service are likely to involve:

a. Joint-and-several liability.
b. Privity of contract.
c. Reliance on advice.
d. Due diligence.

2. A 1940 case, *Maryland Casualty Co. v. Jonathon Cook*, illustrates that:

a. Auditors are responsible to detect material embezzlements.
b. Auditors are culpable to clients who carry surety bonds on employees.
c. Auditors are liable to parties who acquire a client's rights by subrogation.
d. Auditors' liability under common law is dependent on the terms of the audit services contract.

3. Reaffirmed in the 1980s and 1990s, the privity doctrine, first established in *Ultramares Corp. v. Touche* (1931), now requires a three-point linkage test established in a New York Court of Appeals case, *Credit Alliance v. Arthur Andersen & Co.* Among other things, the linkage test requires that:

a. The accountant knew a specific third party would rely on the statements.
b. Evidence links the accountant with the client.
c. The accountant knew why the client required an opinion.
d. The accountant provided an oral assurance of the client's solvency.

Questions 4 and 5 each relate to the following:

Gilmore, Inc., a privately owned manufacturer of jewelry, was audited by Balch & Ferris, CPAs. Relying on Gilmore's financial statements, the Evergreen Commercial Credit Corp., a lending institution, granted Gilmore a long-term loan. Gilmore's statements were materially misstated, and Gilmore then went bankrupt. Evergreen Commercial Credit is suing Balch & Ferris for negligence in the audit.

4. Among other things, Evergreen must show:

a. Misstated financial statements.
b. Scienter.
c. Compliance with truth-in-lending laws.
d. Gross negligence.

5. In this case, Evergreen is most likely a:

a. Foreseeable third party.
b. Foreseen beneficiary.
c. Primary beneficiary.
d. Client.

6. Alsap Corporation's April 1999, $35 million initial public offering included Singer & Revine's unqualified opinion on Alsap's December 31, 1998 audited financial statements. Owing to material misstatements related to inventory and receivables, securities purchasers sued Singer & Revine, who likely can avoid liability if:

a. Singer & Revine can demonstrate due diligence.
b. Singer & Revine's engagement letter called for mediation and arbitration.
c. Alsap management caused the misstatements.
d. Some of the purchasers did not rely on the audited financial statements.

7. An auditor may be held liable under the *Securities Act of 1933* for materially false or misleading financial statements if the security purchaser:

a. Can establish reliance on the registration statement.
b. Can establish gross negligence.
c. Brings suit within four years after the security is offered to the public.
d. Can establish that the financial statements were misstated.

(AICPA Adapted)

8. Which of the following correctly portrays the scope of Section 10(b) of the *Securities Exchange Act of 1934?*

a. Section 10(b) protects shareholders of securities listed on a national stock exchange.
b. Section 10(b) applies exclusively to securities registered under the *Securities Exchange Act of 1934.*
c. Securities registered under the *Securities Act of 1933* are exempt from Section 10(b).
d. Section 10(b) applies to purchases as well as sales of registered securities.

9. A client sues Jane Corning, an independent accountant, for negligence, alleging that, because she failed to apply *generally accepted auditing standards,* she failed to discover large thefts of marketable securities. Under these circumstances:

a. Corning is not bound by *generally accepted auditing standards* unless she is a member of the AICPA.
b. Corning is negligent if she failed to apply *generally accepted auditing standards.*
c. *Generally accepted auditing standards* apply to financial statements taken as a whole, not to audits of individual accounts.
d. If Corning failed to apply *generally accepted auditing standards,* she would likely have committed a fraud.

10. Accountants' liability to third parties under common law:

a. Has not changed substantially over the years.
b. Is identical to accountants' liability under the *Securities Act of 1933.*
c. Is identical to accountants' liability under the *Securities Exchange Act of 1934.*
d. Is not uniform across all jurisdictions.

11. Columbus, Inc., a publicly traded corporation, is audited by Corrente & Corrente, CPAs. Because of inaccurate disclosures and serious losses from trading Columbus' securities, Columbus shareholders are suing Corrente & Corrente. In this case, the auditor's defense is:

a. The financial statements were not misleading despite the inaccurate disclosures.
b. Their conduct was not deficient under *generally accepted auditing standards.*
c. Lack of privity.
d. Lack of reliance.

12. Lincoln purchased Tally Corporation securities in a public offering subject to the *Securities Act of 1933.* Rosemere & Co., CPAs, issued an unqualified opinion on Tally Corporation's most recent financial statements (which were included in Tally's registration statement) and a comfort letter that revealed no material exceptions. Rosemere & Co. is being sued by Lincoln for alleged misstatements within in the registration statement. To prevail, Lincoln must prove:

a. Damages, reliance, and scienter.
b. Damages, material misstatements, and reliance.
c. Damages and material misstatements.
d. Material misstatements and reliance.

13. Which of the following, if material, would be a fraud?

a. Errors in the application of accounting principles.
b. Clerical errors in accounting data underlying the financial statements.
c. Misinterpretation of facts that existed when the financial statements were prepared.
d. Misappropriation of an asset or groups of assets.

(AICPA Adapted)

14. Which of the following is an inappropriate reaction to a material fraud detected in a publicly traded company?

a. Report the matter to the SEC.
b. Discuss the matter with at least one level of management above the perpetrator.
c. Obtain further evidence.
d. Suggest that the client consult with legal counsel about questions of law.

15. Which of the following statements best describes an auditor's responsibility to detect fraud?

a. The auditor is responsible for failing to detect fraud when the failure clearly results from not performing audit procedures described in the engagement letter.
b. The auditor must extend auditing procedures to search actively for fraud.
c. The auditor must assess the risk that material fraud may exist.
d. The auditor is responsible for failing to detect fraud only when an unqualified opinion is issued.

(AICPA Adapted)

16. If an auditor is certain a fraud has a material effect on financial statements and the client agrees to adjust the statements accordingly, the auditor should:

a. Withdraw from the engagement.
b. Disclaim an opinion on the financial statements taken as a whole.
c. Issue a qualified opinion.
d. Issue an unqualified opinion.

17. An auditor's responsibility for illegal acts by clients:

a. Depends on any contingent monetary effects and loss contingencies resulting from the act.
b. Requires that he or she assess the risk of material misstatement of the financial statements due to illegal acts.
c. Does not relate to direct, material illegal acts.
d. Is unrelated to the proximity of the act to the financial statements.

18. The *Foreign Corrupt Practices Act* requires that:

a. Auditors of publicly held companies report all illegal payments to the SEC.
b. Publicly held companies establish audit committees consisting only of outside directors.
c. U.S. firms doing business abroad report publicly all significant payments made to non-U.S. citizens.
d. Publicly held companies devise and maintain an adequate system of internal control.

PROBLEMS AND DISCUSSION CASES

5-1 *Common Law Liability and the Linkage Test*
Reno Poli, chief executive officer of Lincoln Avenue Bank, phoned Valerie Valentine, an audit partner in Tally & Rosemere LLP and the engagement partner for Bloomfield Plating Company, an electrolyte plating company serving the costume jewelry industry in southeastern New England. Poli told Valentine that he'd be forwarding a memorandum of understanding to Charles Bloomfield, the owner-manager of Bloomfield Plating, outlining the bank's understanding that a $300,000 working capital loan to Bloomfield

Plating was conditional on Tally & Rosemere's issuing an unqualified opinion on Bloomfield's financial statements. Valentine told Poli that, although she had taken over the engagement from a recently retired partner, she planned to offer the same quality service that Tally & Rosemere had for the past nine years. Tally & Rosemere issued an unqualified opinion, Lincoln granted the loan to Bloomfield and, owing to a cash embezzlement scheme perpetrated by Charles Bloomfield, the company defaulted on the loan. Lincoln Avenue Bank sued Tally & Rosemere. In a pretrial meeting, attorneys representing Lincoln Bank argued that Poli had satisfied the linkage test in *Credit Alliance v. Arthur Andersen & Co.* by having notified Valentine orally—and Bloomfield in writing—that the loan was conditional on the firm's audit.

Required:
1. Explain Lincoln's motive in arguing that the linkage test had been established.
2. Will Lincoln prevail? Discuss the merits of Lincoln's argument.

5-2 *Common Law Liability to a Third Party*
Milady's Fashions, Inc., a discount retailer of women's apparel, has an excessively large inventory on hand and is in urgent need of additional cash. The company is bordering on bankruptcy (especially if the inventory has to be liquidated by sale to other stores rather than to the public), and about 15 percent of the inventory is resalable only at a discount drastically below cost. Faced with this financial crisis, Milady's approached several suppliers, one of which, Brent Brothers Apparel, Inc., was willing to loan Milady's $300,000 under certain conditions: First, Milady's was to submit audited financial statements for the express purpose of revealing the company's financial condition. Milady's engagement letter with Penting & Dunn, LLP stated explicitly that the loan decision would be based on the financial statements. Second, Brent Brothers insisted on a secured position in all the unsecured inventory, accounts receivable, and other related personal property. In response, a security agreement was drawn and a financing statement was filed and recorded.

In preparing the financial statements, Milady's valued the inventory at cost, which was approximately $100,000 over current fair market value, and did not disclose two secured creditors to whom substantial amounts were owed and who took priority over Brent Brothers' security interests. Penting & Dunn issued an unqualified opinion, believing Milady's financial statements were presented fairly in all material respects. Six months later, Milady's filed for bankruptcy. Brent Brothers received $125,000 as its share in bankruptcy and is suing Penting & Dunn for the loss of $175,000. Penting & Dunn deny liability, claiming lack of privity and lack of negligence.

Required: Is Brent Brothers entitled to recover from Penting & Dunn? Why or why not?

5-3 *Initial Public Offerings and Securities Act of 1933*
Baldoni & Literick, LLP issued an unqualified opinion on the September 30, 1999 financial statements of Service Paper Company, a publicly owned paper products company. Owing both to an increasing market share and to limited capacity, Service Paper filed a registration statement for an initial public offering of class B common shares under the *Securities Act of 1933*, and engaged Baldoni & Literick to issue a comfort letter for the period between October 1, 1999 and December 15, 1999, the effective date of the registration statement. Following sale of the securities, Service Paper revealed that sales and receivables from transactions arising after October 1 were overstated materially, trading in the securities was suspended, and Baldoni & Literick was named as a defendant in a class action suit which alleged that the firm either intentionally disregarded, or failed to exercise reasonable care to discover, material facts that occurred subsequent to October 15, 1999, the date of the audit report.

Required: Discuss Baldoni & Literick's liability for events that occurred between the date of the auditor's report and the effective date of the public offering.

5-4 *Liability Under Section 10(b) and Rule 10b-5*

Gordon & Groton, CPAs, were the auditors of Jordan & Company, a brokerage firm and member of several national and international stock exchanges. Gordon & Groton audited and reported on the financial statements of Jordan, which were filed with the Securities and Exchange Commission.

Several of Jordan's customers were swindled by a fraudulent scheme perpetrated by Jordan's president, who owned 90 percent of the voting stock of the company. The facts established that Gordon & Groton were negligent, but not reckless nor grossly negligent, in conducting the audit, and neither participated in, nor knew of, the fraudulent scheme.

The customers are suing Gordon & Groton under the anti-fraud provisions of Section 10(b) and Rule 10b-5 of the *Securities Exchange Act of 1934* for aiding and abetting the president's fraudulent scheme. The customers' suit for fraud is grounded on the auditors' failure to conduct a proper audit under *generally accepted auditing standards* and, therefore, on failure to discover the fraudulent scheme.

Required: Discuss the issues and the probable outcome of the case.

(AICPA Adapted)

5-5 *Statutory Liability and the Private Securities Litigation Reform Act*

Andrew Christie, a recently hired entry level staff accountant in Fallon & Goff, LLP, was assigned to audit the receivables at the Edgemere Company, a publicly traded manufacturer of roofing materials. Owing to errors in entering credit sales in late June, the last month of the fiscal year, the reported earnings, credit sales and customer receivables balances were materially misstated, though unintentionally. A class action suit attributes significant stock price declines to public announcements of the errors. Fallon & Goff's audit program for receivables called for analytical procedures and for the confirmation of receivables balances with debtors, but neither Christie, nor the working paper review process, detected the need to follow up on unusual fluctuations in the receivables balance or in the number of days sales in receivables. Plaintiffs in a class action suit do not suggest fraud by Fallon & Goff, but do allege gross negligence. Fallon & Goff recognizes their culpability but argues that the firm should share responsibility under *The Private Securities Litigation Reform Act*. In a separate action, a small investor claims Fallon & Goff is jointly-and-severally liable under the same Act.

Required:

1. To recover, what must the plaintiffs show in the class action suit?
2. Discuss both Fallon & Goff's and the small investor's claims about *The Private Securities Litigation Reform Act*.

5-6 *Gross Negligence and Criminal Liability*

Cragsmore & Company, LLP was engaged to audit the financial statements of Marlowe Manufacturing, Inc., a publicly traded corporation. Prior to preparing the audit report, Susan Cragsmore, a partner, and Fred Willmore, a staff senior, reviewed the notes disclosed within the financial statements. One note reported the terms, costs, and obligations of a lease between Marlowe and Acme Leasing Company. Willmore suggested that the footnote read: "The Acme Leasing Company is owned by persons who have a 35 percent interest in the capital stock and who are officers of Marlowe Manufacturing, Inc.," although on Cragsmore's recommendation, the note was revised by substituting "minority shareholders" for "persons who have a 35 percent interest in the capital stock and who are officers."

The audit report and financial statements were forwarded to Marlowe Manufacturing for review. The officers-shareholders of Marlowe, who also owned Acme Leasing, objected to the revised wording and insisted that the footnote be changed to describe the relationship between Acme and Marlowe as an affiliation. Cragsmore agreed and issued an unqualified opinion that appears both within Marlowe's annual report to shareholders and within *Form 10-K* to the SEC. The audit working papers included drafts of the wording of the footnote. Thereafter, Marlowe suffered a substantial, uninsured fire loss and was forced into bankruptcy. The failure of Marlowe to carry any fire insurance coverage was not reported in the financial statements.

Attorneys representing Cragsmore & Company reveal in a private meeting with Susan Cragsmore that the plaintiffs may have grounds to allege fraud or gross negligence and, since the footnote was included within *Form 10-K*, the plaintiffs' attorneys may even have grounds to argue criminal liability.

Required: Discuss the grounds on which the plaintiffs could allege fraud, gross negligence, and criminal liability against Cragsmore & Company.

(AICPA Adapted)

5-7 *Legal Liability and Employee Fraud*

Jackson, an early career staff member in Harrison & Weeks, LLP, began but did not finish the audit of inventory in the Bosco Corporation, a manufacturer and marketer of expensive watches. During the audit, Jackson resigned from Harrison & Weeks and the firm assigned Davidson, an entry-level staff member, to complete Jackson's work. Due to the staff change and to busy season time pressure, the firm did not audit inventory adequately. Had appropriate procedures been used, Jackson and Davidson would likely have discovered that watches worth more than $20,000 were missing, all stolen by a sales clerk. The clerk stole $75,000 in watches before the thefts were discovered six months after Harrison & Weeks completed the audit.

Required: Discuss the legal problems that Harrison & Weeks will likely face.

(AICPA Adapted)

5-8 *Fraud Detection Responsibility and Audit Reports*

Several years ago, Dale Holden organized Holden Restaurants. Holden started with one small restaurant, but over time the restaurant became quite popular due largely to the quality of the food and service, an attractive yet modest atmosphere, and reasonable prices.

Success with his first restaurant encouraged Holden to open at least one new restaurant in each of the last five years, resulting today in eight successful restaurants located in metropolitan areas throughout the state. Owing to recent rapid expansion of the business, Holden has hired a controller and supporting staff to manage the individual restaurants, allowing Holden to focus attention on the aggregate operations and to plan future expansion.

Holden has applied to a bank for additional financing to open another restaurant this year. For the first time ever, the bank asked him to provide financial statements audited by an independent auditor. The bank assured Holden that the audited statements were not required because they doubted his integrity or thought him to be a poor credit risk. Rather, bank policy required all businesses over a certain size to supply audited statements with loan applications, and Holden's business had long since reached that size.

Holden was not surprised by the bank's requirement. He'd ruled out an audit previously because he trusts his controller's integrity and, besides, he wanted to avoid the fee associated with an initial audit as long as possible. However, his absence from everyday hands-on operations now make an audit advisable since, trust aside, he also believes an additional benefit of the audit will be the probable detection of any fraud that may have occurred at his restaurants.

To fulfill the bank's request for audited financial statements, Dale Holden has hired Hill & Associates, CPAs.

Required:

1. Discuss Hill & Associates' responsibilities to detect fraud in a financial statement audit.
2. What effect, if any, would the detection of fraud by Hill & Associates have on their opinion on the financial statements?

5-9 *A Client Resents a Search for Fraud*

Several months prior to beginning an audit engagement of the Taunton Manufacturing Company, you point out to Taunton's CFO, Marsha Wade, that as part of your responsibilities, you will design the audit to provide reasonable assurance of detecting any material errors or fraud that may exist. Wade, somewhat alarmed by your statement, responds that all of her employees are trustworthy and, therefore, refuses to pay any portion of the audit fee relating to a search for fraud. Further, she states her understanding that auditors are not responsible for detecting fraud, assuming *generally accepted auditing standards* are followed.

Required: Respond to each of the controller's statements.

5-10 *Reporting Fraud or Illegal Acts to Third Parties*

The partner in charge of your firm is concerned that staff members may not be aware of current professional standards about communicating material errors, fraud, and illegal acts to parties other than management and the board of directors, given particularly that the standards have changed in the 1970s, the 1980s, and again in the 1990s.

Required: Draft a memorandum for distribution to all staff members about procedures for reporting potential errors, fraud, and illegal acts. Be specific.

5-11 *A Controller Engaged in Fraud*

The CPA firm of Winston & Mall was engaged to audit the financial statements of the Fast Cargo Company, a retailer. The auditors tested a sample of 100 disbursement trasactions, all of which were to be supported by purchase orders, receiving reports, and invoices. However, tests revealed several instances where purchases had been recorded and paid, although a receiving report had not been filed. These exceptions were noted in working papers prepared by Martin, a staff auditor. Mall, the partner in charge of the engagement, called these exceptions to the attention of Harris, Fast Cargo's CFO, who promised to locate and file the receiving reports. Mall accepted this explanation, did nothing further to investigate, and issued an unqualified opinion on Fast Cargo's financial statements.

Unknown either to Mall or to Martin, Harris, the controller, was engaged in a fraud: Merchandise was diverted to a private warehouse where Harris leased space and the invoices were sent to Fast Cargo for payment. The scheme was discovered, and a preliminary estimate indicates that the loss to Fast Cargo will exceed $50,000.

Required:

1. Discuss Winston & Mall's liability, if any.
2. What additional steps, if any, should Mall have taken? Explain.

(AICPA Adapted)

5-12 *An Unpaid Bank Loan and Undetected Fraud*

Martinson, Brinks & Sutherland, LLP audited the financial statements of Masco Corporation, a medium-size wholesaler that leased warehouse facilities. Masco sought bank financing for the leases, assuring the bank that the leasehold improvements would result in efficiencies and therefore a more profitable operation. On the basis of these assurances, the bank granted Masco a line of credit.

The loan agreement required annual audited financial statements. Masco submitted 1998 audited financial statements to the bank which disclosed net income of $75,000, leasehold improvements of $250,000, and net worth of $350,000. Relying on the audited statements, the bank loaned Masco $200,000. The audit report accompanying the financial statements disclaimed an opinion because the cost of the leasehold improvements could not be determined from the company's records. The part of the audit report dealing with leasehold improvements reads as follows:

Additions to fixed assets in 1998 were found to include principally warehouse improvements. Practically all of this work was done by company employees and the cost of materials and overhead was paid by Masco. Unfortunately, fully completed, detailed cost records were not kept of these leasehold improvements, and no exact determination could be made as to the actual cost of said improvements. The total amount capitalized is set forth in Note 4.

In late 1999 Masco went out of business, and the claimed leasehold improvements were discovered to be totally fictitious. The labor expenses charged as leasehold improvements actually proved to be operating expenses, none of the materials costs had been recorded, and the auditors had not investigated whether the leasehold improvements existed. Had the $250,000 not been capitalized, the income statement would have reflected a substantial loss from operations and net worth would have decreased correspondingly.

The bank sustained a loss on the $200,000 loan to Masco and now seeks to recover damages from Martinson, Brinks & Sutherland, alleging the firm was negligent.

Required:
1. Will the disclaimer of opinion absolve Martinson, Brinks & Sutherland from responsibility for not detecting the fraud?
2. Are partners who did not take part in the audit liable?

(AICPA Adapted)

5-13 *Monitoring Compliance with the FCPA*
The *Foreign Corrupt Practices Act* can seriously impact the business operations of many corporations, especially Securities and Exchange Commission registrants who are subject both to the unlawful influence and to the internal control and record-keeping provisions of the Act. Assume you are the manager of internal auditing for a publicly traded multinational corporation that manufactures and distributes aluminum alloy products throughout the world. The corporation's chief executive officer requests that you draft a plan for complying with the Foreign Corrupt Practices Act.

Required: Draft a plan for complying with the FCPA. The plan should emphasize a strategy for encouraging and monitoring compliance with the Act, rather than detailed procedures for complying with specific provisions of the Act.

RESEARCH PROJECTS

1. LITIGATION AGAINST ACCOUNTING FIRMS AND CURRENT REFORM

The financial press has been, and continues to be, replete with references to legal liability cases—and to wildly excessive monetary judgments—against public accounting firms under both common law and federal securities law. Coincident with these cases, over 300 professional service firms, trade associations, accountants and corporations formed the Coalition to Eliminate Abusive Securities Suits (CEASS) that sought and won *The Private Securities Litigation Reform Act of 1995*, which adopted proportionate liability to replace joint-and-several liability, adopted a modified loser-pays-the-winner's-court-costs provision, and eliminated the payment of bounties to professional plaintiffs in class action suits.

Required: Using recent articles from the business and accounting press (e.g., *The Wall Street Journal*, *The New York Times*, *Accounting Today*), or an automated newspaper research service like NEXIS, INFOBANK, or ABI/INFORM:

1. Select an article (or, preferably, a series of articles) related to litigation against a public accounting firm and outline the case according to the summary of issues appearing in Figure 5-1 and discussed in the chapter:
   a. What is the source of law?
   b. Who is the plaintiff?
   c. What is the auditor's potential liability?
   d. Who has the burden of proving what?

2.   Would the outcome of the case likely have been any different had *The Private Securities Litigation Reform Act of 1995* applied to your case?

2. TORT REFORM

The Private Securities Litigation Reform Act of 1995 and the U.S. Supreme Court's decision in *Central Bank of Denver v. First Interstate Bank of Denver* represent major victories in the profession's deliberate stance against unmerited legal liability for public accounting firms. The Act imposes only proportionate liability on peripheral defendants and, although debatable, the Court's decision reduces the securities liability of aiders or abettors. However, one major effort has been less successful: tort reform. In legislation introduced at the state level, a number of stakeholders, including some state societies of CPAs, have introduced tort reform legislation. For example, Arizona Senate Bill 1383 attempted to conform Arizona securities laws to federal laws, and California Bill 1862 attempted to limit punitive awards to no more than three times compensatory damages. Other industries have sought tort reform as well, including liability limits in the automobile industry and contingency fee limits in the legal profession.

   Required: Identify tort reform legislation in the accounting profession or other industries for your state or others. Sources include a state representative or senator, and an article that briefly identifies state initiatives: "Accountants Resume Tort Reform Quest at State Level," *Public Accounting Report* (February 29, 1996), pp. 2, 7. Draft a report that:

1.   Identifies the stakeholders supporting and opposing the legislation, and discusses each stakeholder's interests.
2.   Describes the major provisions of the legislation.
3.   Lists the status of the legislation.

PART 2

TECHNOLOGY

6

Evidence

Major topics discussed in this chapter are the:

- Acquisition of evidence in assurance, attestation, and audit engagements.
- Cognitive biases in the evaluation of evidence.
- Purpose, content, and form of working papers in documenting evidence.
- Roles of financial statement assertions, audit objectives, audit procedures, tests of controls, substantive tests, and analytical procedures.
- Audit process, including the decision to accept an engagement, planning, and interim and year-end audit work.

The public accounting profession's comparative advantage in the marketplace for professional services is vested not so much in the rules of accounting as in the ways and means of acquiring and evaluating evidence. For that reason, above all reasons, certified public accountants are well positioned to transform their monopoly over the audit services market into a commanding presence in the attestation and assurance service markets. Only the most nimble among them will likely lead the profession's move into new markets. But, make no mistake about it: Those who do will do so because they are fluent in the acquisition and evaluation of evidence.

This chapter begins by introducing the means of acquiring—and the cognitive biases that can interfere with interpreting—evidence in assurance, attestation, and audit engagements. In turn, the chapter describes and illustrates audit working papers, the means by which an auditor documents the evidence acquired and the conclusions reached. Finally, the chapter answers the question, What is the sequence of steps an auditor takes to achieve the standards introduced in Chapter 2 and to issue the reports illustrated in Chapter 3?

EVIDENCE IN ASSURANCE, ATTESTATION, AND AUDIT ENGAGEMENTS

The purpose of acquiring evidence is not to seek data that confirms management's assertions but, rather, to afford a reasonable basis to conclude objectively *whether* management's assertions are confirmed. While subtle, this distinction is crucial to understanding the role served by *independent* certified public accountants. Acquiring and evaluating objective evidence is the common thread across all assurance, attestation, and audit services, and is the central theme in Chapters 8-17. Here, our interest turns to the intuition underlying the acquisition of evidence for all three services.

ACQUIRING EVIDENCE

W. P. Montague, in a classic work on the ways of acquiring evidence, offers an insightful scheme that includes five of what Montague calls "the ways of knowing": authoritarianism, mysticism, rationalism, empiricism, and pragmatism.[1] As summarized in Figure 6-1, all five apply to the assurance services offered by Underwriters Laboratories and Consumers Union (introduced in Chapters 1-3), and to the attestation and audit services offered by certified public accountants.

Authoritarianism means evidence obtained from written or oral testimony. For example, Underwriters Laboratories' *UL Listing Mark,* the company's most widely recognized safety certification program, begins with oral inquiries to, and written responses from, product manufacturers about components, design drawings, materials, and wiring. And Consumers Union's product quality services are based in part on customer satisfaction surveys of *Consumer Reports'* subscribers. Attestation and auditing examples include oral inquiries of management about potential contingent liabilities and written confirmations to third parties about contracts, such as warehousing arrangements, long-term purchase agreements, and the existence and carrying value of trade accounts receivable.

Figure 6-1: Acquiring Evidence: Assurance, Attestation, and Audit Services

Montague's Ways of Knowing	Examples	
	Assurance Services	Attestation and Audit Services
Authoritarianism Evidence from testimony	Inquiries of management. Customer satisfaction.	Inquiries of management. Confirm contracts.
Mysticism Evidence obtained intuitively	Product comparisons.	Ratio comparisons.
Rationalism Reasoning from accepted assumptions	Inverse relationship between product safety and risk of injury.	Inverse relationship between materiality and audit risk.
Empiricism Perceptual experience	Examine product quality. Compute quality ratings. Observe performance.	Examine documents. Compute earnings per share. Observe tangible assets.
Pragmatism Practical results	Review product recalls. Await warranty claims.	Review subsequent events. Await litigation.

1   W. P. Montague. *The Ways of Knowing, 4th ed.* New York: The Macmillan Company (1953).

Mysticism means evidence obtained intuitively. For example, interpretation of *Consumer Reports'* rankings of top freezer-refrigerators (like Amana, Kenmore, and General Electric) is based on the intuition that Consumers Union's product quality ratings are interval measures that distinguish relative quality. In attestation and auditing engagements, practitioners often rely on analytical procedures, such as ratio comparisons and regression analysis, to discern how account balances or streams of transactions relate to each other and to management's (and the auditor's) expectations. Authoritarianism and mysticism differ in this sense: The former is based on evidence obtained from others, and the latter is based on intuition or instinct about a pattern of relationships experienced or known.

Rationalism means reasoning from generally accepted assumptions. For example, Underwriters Laboratories' product safety certification program assumes that there is an inverse relationship between product safety and the risk of injury. Practitioners also assume inverse relationships in attestation and audit services—for example, between materiality and risk. That is, as the likelihood that management's assertions may contain material misstatements (risk) goes up, the attester's or auditor's judgment of the magnitude of the misstatements that would influence a third party relying on the assertions (materiality) would go down. As risk goes up, materiality goes down and, as illustrated in Chapter 2, the practitioner revises upward the amount of evidence needed to hold risk to a relatively low level.

Empiricism means perceptual experience or, stated another way, generalizing from direct observation. For example, Consumers Union and Underwriters Laboratories test product quality and product safety, respectively, by examining products directly, by computing ratings directly, and by observing performance directly. Practitioners use empiricism for the bulk of the attestation and audit conclusions they reach. For example, Price Waterhouse tested Stanley H. Kaplan's assertion about *Scholastic Assessment Test* (*SAT*) performance (Chapter 1) by examining self-reported *SAT* scores and by computing aggregate average improvement. Auditors commonly rely on empiricism, for example, when they examine documents like sales invoices and receiving reports, compute earnings per share, or observe the existence of tangible assets like inventory, property, plant, and equipment.

Finally, *pragmatism* means to rely on hindsight or practical results. For example, Consumers Union and Underwriters Laboratories monitor product recall data, press reports of unusual warranty claims, and public complaints by consumer activist groups, all of which lend hindsight useful in revising or updating product quality and safety ratings. In attestation and audit engagements, some of the same hindsight benchmarks are available, although practitioners attempt to predict them before they happen. For example, as discussed later in the chapter, auditors search for subsequent transactions and events that lend hindsight into financial statement disclosures, and hold audit risk to a relatively low level, in part to avoid subsequent litigation for audit failure.

Montague's ways of knowing are instructive about the acquisition of evidence, but overlook the potential to *misuse* the evidence acquired. Certified public accountants are limited in the same way that decision makers in all complex decision settings are limited: Our capacity to process information cognitively is limited, and our well-intentioned decision strategies are sometimes biased, as explained next.

COGNITIVE BIASES IN EVALUATING EVIDENCE

Practitioners who cast decisions into likelihood assessments—for example, the likelihood of fraud, misstatement, or financial distress—sometimes overlook the laws of probability, and rely instead on simplifying rules of thumb, called *heuristics*, that bias decision-making unnecessarily.[2] Three heuristics have troubled auditors: representativeness, availability, and anchoring-and-adjustment.

Representativeness occurs when decision makers evaluate the likelihood of, say, item *b* belonging to class *A* by judging how much item *b* resembles other items from class *A*, rather than by the laws of probability. The question is not, "How representative is item *b* of items in class *A*?" but rather, "What is the *probability* that item *b* came from class *A*?" For example, research has found that auditors overstate the likelihood that management perpetrated a fraud by overweighting the similarity between a manager's psychological profile and the profile of admitted perpetrators, and by underweighting the fact that not one of one hundred managers described in the study had been involved in fraud previously.[3]

Availability occurs when decision makers evaluate the likelihood of an outcome by the ease with which similar instances come to mind, particularly when the outcome is rare and sensational, like a plane crash, high-rise fire, or coal mine collapse. For example, an unsuspecting auditor may judge that infrequent, but highly publicized, illegal hazardous waste disposal occurs disproportionately more often than the profession's collected experience would predict.

Anchoring-and-adjustment occurs when decision makers assess the likelihood of an outcome by making initial, and sometimes biased, likelihood estimates (an anchor) and then adjusting the likelihood, though insufficiently, when presented with new information. For example, in practice, auditors often consult prior year working papers when planning the current engagement, but may fail to revise the current audit plan sufficiently for changed circumstances, such as management turnover, outsourced transaction processing, or newly implemented controls. Although mixed, the results of prior research suggest that auditor behavior is generally consistent with the anchoring-and-adjustment heuristic.[4]

Apart from heuristics, other biases can plague practitioners when evaluating evidence, among them over-trusting the source of written or oral evidence *(source credibility)*, seeking evidence that confirms a prior belief *(confirmatory bias)*, underestimating sampling error in small-sample tests *(insensitivity to sample size)*, and overlooking prior information *(base rate neglect)*. Because many decisions in practice are complex, time-constrained, and made under conditions of uncertainty, practitioners sometimes adopt decision rules that are fraught with the potential for bias. The task of the well-informed practitioner is to evaluate

---

2   For a review, see: J. F. Smith and T. Kida. "Heuristics and Biases: Expertise and Task Realism in Auditing," *Psychological Bulletin* (Vol. 109, No. 3, 1991), pp. 472-489.
3   See, for example, E. J. Joyce and G. C. Biddle. "Are Auditors' Judgments Sufficiently Regressive?" *Journal of Accounting Research* (Autumn 1981), pp. 323-349.
4   See, for example, E. J. Joyce and G. C. Biddle. "Anchoring and Adjustment in Probabilistic Inference in Auditing," *Journal of Accounting Research* (Autumn 1981), pp. 323-349; and W. R. Kinney and W. C. Uecker. "Mitigating the Consequences of Anchoring in Auditor Judgments," *The Accounting Review* (January 1982), pp. 55-69.

evidence with full respect for the pitfalls of bias, and with the unbreachable resolve to bear witness only to what the evidence reveals. Due care (Chapter 2) demands no less.

AUDIT EVIDENCE

Both the second *attestation standard* of field work and the third *GAAS* of field work (Chapter 2, Figure 2-1) address evidence, although the professional literature (e.g., *SAS No. 31*) is far more insightful about audit evidence. For example, the third *GAAS* of field work, reproduced below, is interpreted in *Statement on Auditing Standards No. 31*, "Evidential Matter" (AU Sec. 326):

Sufficient competent evidential matter *is to be obtained through inspection, observation, inquiries, and confirmations to afford a reasonable basis for an opinion regarding the financial statements under audit.*

Sufficient refers to the quantity of evidence an auditor acquires to test management's financial statement assertions, and *competent* refers to the relevance, validity, and reliability of the evidence acquired. For example, in a typical financial statement audit, an independent auditor must judge *how much* (sufficiency) and *what kinds* (competence) of evidence he or she need acquire to conclude whether the sales transactions management recorded actually occurred during the period ending on the balance sheet date.

Evidential matter consists of the accounting data that underlies management's financial statements and the corroborating information that supports the accounting data. *Underlying accounting data* includes records of original entry (e.g., journals), general and subsidiary ledgers, data files, and spreadsheets that capture the details summarized in financial statements. *Corroborating information* includes checks, records of electronic fund transfers, invoices, contracts, minutes of meetings, and other documents; written representations from vendors, attorneys, banks, and other third parties; and information obtained by questioning management or by observing a client's employees at work.

In some entities, some accounting data and corroborating information are available in electronic form only, such as electronic data interchange (EDI) or image processing systems. In *electronic data interchange systems*, paper source documents do not exist: Customers and suppliers are linked electronically to transact purchases, sales, shipping, billing, cash receipts, and cash disbursements. In *image processing systems*, paper source documents exist, but are scanned into electronic images and, in some systems, discarded thereafter. As noted in *SAS No. 80*, "Amendment to SAS No. 31, 'Evidential Matter'," information systems like EDI and image processing may produce electronic evidence that adds two extra hurdles for the auditor. First, the auditor should determine the time period that evidence is available, since evidence may not be retrievable after a period of time if files are changed and backup files are not maintained. Second, the auditor should be aware that unretrievable electronic evidence makes more problematic the practicality of using substantive tests (introduced in this chapter) *only* to reduce detection risk to an acceptably low level.

Because audits need to be completed within a reasonable time frame and at reasonable cost, auditors cannot examine evidence for every transaction or event relevant to management's assertions. Rather, auditors more often test samples of transactions and events, reach conclusions about the samples, and then generalize the results to the accounting populations from which the samples were drawn. For example, an auditor might examine purchase orders, receiving reports, and invoices supporting 100 randomly selected accounts payable and conclude from these results that assertions about the entire population of 5,000 payables are reliable. Because audit conclusions are drawn from testing some rather than all of the evidence underlying an accounting population, aggregate audit evidence is often *persuasive*, rather than wholly *convincing*, and an auditor's strategy is to gather the most persuasive evidence available.

RELATING ASSERTIONS AND OBJECTIVES

Much of an auditor's work consists of acquiring and evaluating evidence about the explicit and implicit assertions embodied in financial statements. That is, the auditor's role is to test the assertions underlying a financial statement disclosure, not merely to test the account balances disclosed. For example, in the disclosure "Inventory . . . $2,000,000," management makes no less than five **financial statement assertions**:

- Inventory physically exists,
- Inventory includes all products on hand,
- The entity has legal title or similar rights of ownership,
- Inventory is properly stated at the lower of cost or market, and
- Inventory is properly classified as a current asset.

Since the financial statements are management's responsibility, the assertions are management's representations and can be broadly categorized as in Figure 6-2. From the assertions contained within management's financial statements, an auditor develops *audit objectives*, which may vary from one engagement to another depending on an entity's business and on the accounting practices unique to its industry. The following explains each financial statement assertion and illustrates some related audit objectives.

Figure 6-2: Financial Statement Assertions

Existence or Occurrence
All recorded assets, liabilities, and equities exist, and all recorded transactions occurred.

Completeness
All transactions and accounts that should be presented in the financial statements are presented.

Rights and Obligations
Assets are the rights, and liabilities are the obligations, of the entity.

Valuation or Allocation
Assets, liabilities, equities, revenues, and expenses are included in the financial statements at appropriate amounts; revenues, costs, and expenses are allocated to the proper accounting periods.

Presentation and Disclosure
Financial statement components are properly classified, described, and disclosed.

Existence or Occurrence

In financial statements presented in conformity with generally accepted accounting principles (GAAP), management asserts that all assets, liabilities, and equities disclosed in the financial statements actually existed at the balance sheet date, and that all recorded transactions actually occurred during the period ending on the balance sheet date. The auditor's objective is to test whether the **existence or occurrence** assertion is appropriate. For example, in auditing inventory, an auditor's objective is to test whether inventory physically existed at the balance sheet date, whether recorded inventory purchases actually occurred, and whether sales transactions in the income statement represent the exchange of goods or services for cash or other consideration.

Completeness

In the occurrence assertion, management asserts that all *recorded* transactions actually *occurred*, but in **completeness** management asserts the opposite: All transactions that *occurred* during the period were *recorded.* In comparison with the other financial statement assertions, completeness is often the most challenging, since the auditor's task is to detect unrecorded transactions. In auditing inventory, for example, the auditor's objective is to test whether all purchases of goods and services are recorded, and in auditing payables the objective is to test whether all obligations are included as liabilities in the financial statements.

Rights and Obligations

Assertions about **rights and obligations** mean that the entity has property rights to all recorded assets, and that all liabilities represent obligations at the balance sheet date. In auditing plant assets, for example, an auditor's objective is to test whether the entity has title to land, equipment, and buildings, and in auditing long-term debt the objective is to test whether the entity has a bona fide obligation to debt holders. Note that the rights assertion does not necessarily mean the entity legally "owns" the asset, since not all assets on the balance sheet are owned by the entity, one example being capital leases in the hands of a lessee.

Valuation or Allocation

The valuation assertion means that the recorded value of all assets, liabilities, equities, revenues, and expenses are carried in the financial statements at appropriate amounts. Allocation, closely related to valuation, means that revenues, costs, and expenses are allocated to the proper accounting periods. An auditor's objective in testing **valuation or allocation** varies depending on the account audited. For example, in auditing inventory, the auditor's objective is to test whether inventories are valued at the *lower of cost or market* in accordance with the cost flow assumption adopted, (e.g., FIFO, LIFO) thereby affecting both the valuation of inventory at the end of the period and the allocation of costs to the appropriate periods.

Presentation and Disclosure

In the **presentation and disclosure** assertion, management represents that all financial statement components are properly classified (e.g., current versus noncurrent), adequately described (e.g., "Net income from operations," not

"Profit"), and disclosed in a manner that reflects GAAP for the entity's industry. For example, although depreciation is common in manufacturing companies, GAAP for state and local governmental entities preclude recording depreciation in any fund other than an enterprise fund. The auditor's objective is to assure that the financial statements and related notes reveal the substance, not just the form, of recorded transactions.

RELATING OBJECTIVES AND PROCEDURES

To achieve audit objectives, and thereby address each financial statement assertion for each material account, an auditor selects **audit procedures** to acquire sufficient, competent evidential matter. The selection of audit procedures is based on the objectives, the quantity and kinds of evidence available, materiality, and the assessed level of audit risk. Evidence acquired from a single audit procedure may address one or more objectives, or more than one procedure may be needed to acquire evidence for a single objective. For example, in the audit of accounts receivable, confirmations provide evidence about the existence, rights, and valuation assertions, but both confirmations and tests of bad debts are used to address the rights assertion (Chapter 11). Figure 6-3 lists the most common audit procedures used by auditors to gather evidence, and the following explains.

Observation

An auditor can acquire direct evidence about the existence of assets, such as inventory and plant assets, by physically observing the asset on the client's premises. Observation also provides information about the condition of tangible assets, an important determinant in addressing the valuation assertion. For example, an auditor may observe obsolete or damaged inventory during a physical inventory observation, and propose that management reduce the carrying value of inventory to its net realizable value. Observation, often a source of valuable impressions and insights, extends not only to tangible assets, but also to a client's accounting procedures. For example, observing client personnel perform tasks may be useful to an auditor's assessment of control

Figure 6-3:   Audit Procedures

Observation
Physically examine a tangible asset, or develop impressions.

Documentation
Examine documents and records.

Confirmation
Obtain written statements from third parties.

Mechanical Tests of Data
Recompute amounts, or trace transactions through an information system.

Comparisons
Develop and analyze trends and relationships among data.

Inquiries
Obtain oral or written statements from management.

risk, particularly in determining whether authorized employees actually perform their assigned duties.

Documentation

Documents used in auditing include internal evidence such as purchase orders, receiving reports, and sales invoices, and external evidence such as contracts, bank statements, and letters. The form of the documents may be paper or templates on computer screens. By inspecting documents and records, an auditor can determine whether recorded transactions are adequately supported and properly authorized. In applying this procedure, often called *vouching*, an auditor selects recorded transactions and then locates and examines the documents supporting the transactions selected. For example, an auditor could examine electronic transfers to vouch recorded cash disbursements, or contracts to support recorded liabilities.

Confirmation

The existence and valuation of some account balances can be substantiated by requesting confirmation in the form of letters or affidavits from independent third parties. In short, confirmations produce documents that represent evidence. For example, an auditor might confirm receivable and payable balances with debtors and creditors, respectively, confirm securities and other negotiable instruments held by independent custodians, confirm bank balances with banks and other depositories, or confirm the terms of a lease agreement with a lessor.

Mechanical Tests of Data

An auditor can verify the mathematical accuracy of underlying accounting data by *recomputing* calculations performed originally by management. For example, an auditor might total—some say "foot"—the columns in a receipts journal, or recalculate depreciation expense, prepaid insurance, or accrued vacation pay. *Tracing*, another type of mechanical test, means following a transaction through the accounting system—for instance from source document to journal, to subsidiary and general ledgers—and is used primarily to determine whether transactions are properly recorded and classified.

Comparisons

Auditors often compare current disclosures with similar disclosures from prior accounting periods to reveal trends, or with other disclosures in the current period to establish informative relationships. For example, a significant increase in current advertising expense (in the absence of either a new product launch or a major advertising campaign) may suggest that management has inadvertently misclassified expenses as advertising and therefore that the auditor may need to extend testing. Analyses of trends and relationships can be particularly useful in identifying areas requiring further audit work and are discussed later in the chapter as *analytical procedures*.

Inquiries

Evidence obtained from documentation, confirmation, and mechanical tests is often more persuasive than written and oral information obtained by the auditor from inquiries posed to management. Although management's responses can be quite insightful, particularly in generating "leads," the auditor should consider the respondent's incentives to misdirect the auditor—what was called *source credibility* earlier in the chapter. For example, a credit manager—an employee whose job depends on customers paying the debts he or she approved—has incentives to misdirect an auditor who believes the allowance for bad debts is understated. Oral responses should be corroborated through other procedures, among them documentation, confirmation, and mechanical tests.

TESTS OF CONTROLS, SUBSTANTIVE TESTS, AND AUDIT RISK

Depending on an auditor's objectives, the procedures in Figure 6-3—observation, documentation, confirmation, mechanical tests, comparisons, and inquiries—can be used to perform tests of controls or substantive tests. **Tests of controls** are audit procedures that assess the ability of management's internal controls to prevent or to detect material misstatements. In turn, **substantive tests** are audit procedures that detect material misstatements or that identify disclosures likely to contain material misstatements.

TESTS OF CONTROLS AND CONTROL RISK

Procedures used for tests of controls address questions like, "How are management's internal controls applied? Are controls applied consistently?" and, "By whom are the controls applied?" Evidence acquired from procedures used as tests of controls helps an auditor reach a conclusion about the *assessed level of control risk*, which is the auditor's assessment of the effectiveness of management's internal controls in preventing or detecting material misstatements in the financial statements. The assessed level of control risk is then used to determine an *acceptable level of detection risk*. As the assessed level of control risk increases, the acceptable level of detection risk decreases. Tests of controls are illustrated and discussed in detail in Chapters 10, 12, 14, 15, and 16.

Most of the control activities used by audit clients in practice can be classified into one of two categories: controls that create documentation—that is, "leave an audit trail"—and those that do not. The distinction between the two is essential to understanding which procedures from Figure 6-3 to apply as tests of controls. For example, consider two controls implemented by a company:

- *Credit approval. Sales orders are approved and initialed by the credit manager before goods are shipped, and*
- *Bank reconciliations. Monthly bank reconciliations are prepared by an employee not otherwise involved in the approval or recording of cash transactions.*

The first control, credit approval, is an example of a control that *creates documentation*: sales orders with the credit manager's approving initials. In contrast, the second control, bank reconciliations prepared by independent employees, creates a document (the reconciliation), but the documentation does not provide evidence about whether the preparer is independent of the cash function (who actually prepared the reconciliation?). As a result, for this control, as well as other procedures that rely on segregation of duties, an auditor would likely rely on the audit procedures of observation and/or inquiry as tests of controls. That is, the auditor could physically observe who prepares the reconciliation and/or make inquiries of other appropriate personnel.

SUBSTANTIVE TESTS AND DETECTION RISK

After considering inherent risk and control risk, an auditor performs substantive tests to hold detection risk to an acceptable level. Substantive tests provide evidence about monetary misstatements. However, the *extent* of substantive testing—that is, how much testing is done—depends on the acceptable level of detection risk, which depends on the assessed level of control risk, which depends on the results of tests of controls. For example, if tests of controls indicate that the two controls identified previously—credit approval and bank reconciliations—are operating as planned, then related substantive tests can be reduced, although not eliminated, because control risk is low.

Substantive tests can be classified either as *tests of details* of transactions and balances or as *analytical procedures*, each of which is discussed next.

Substantive Tests of Details

An auditor's substantive **tests of details** are intended to detect material misstatement in financial statement accounts. For example, to test whether recorded receivables exist at the balance sheet date, an auditor could confirm balances directly with customers and perform other tests to determine whether sales and receivables transactions are recorded in the proper accounting period.

Tests of details and tests of controls differ in one critical respect: Tests of controls provide evidence about whether misstatement is *likely* (a means to assess control risk), and substantive tests of details provide evidence about whether misstatement actually *exists* (a means to control detection risk). For example, if a test of controls indicates that a control procedure is not reliable and therefore that control risk is high, then the auditor concludes that material misstatement at the balance sheet date is likely. Therefore, substantive tests of details must be extended to control detection risk. But if tests of details reveal material monetary error, then the auditor concludes that misstatement actually exists and that further tests should be conducted or the financial statements adjusted. Examples of substantive tests of details are discussed and illustrated in Chapters 11, 13, 14, 15, and 16.

Analytical Procedures

The auditing procedures identified as "comparisons" are commonly referred to in practice as **analytical procedures** and are defined in *Statement on Auditing Standards No. 56*, "Analytical Procedures" (AU Sec. 329), as evaluations of financial information made by a study of plausible relationships among both financial and nonfinancial data. Auditors use three types of analytical procedures in practice: trend analysis, ratio analysis, and modeling. *Trend analysis* compares a current balance with either the prior year balance or with a series of prior year balances. *Ratio analysis* compares current year ratios—for example, number of days sales in receivables—with prior year ratios or with an industry average. *Modeling* applies statistical techniques, often regression analysis, to calculate expected values from financial and nonfinancial data. For example, a hospital's expected room revenue could be predicted from occupancy rates, capacity, and room rate charges, providing a benchmark against which to compare recorded room revenue. Trend and ratio analysis are easy to use and informative, but modeling has the advantage of correlating operating information (for example, occupancy rates) with related financial information (for example, recorded room revenue). Modeling signals to the auditor when recorded balances are inconsistent with operations.

Analytical procedures are based on the presumption that plausible relationships among data may reasonably be expected to exist since, in double entry accounting, two or more financial statement accounts are affected for each recorded transaction. For example, debits to Accounts Receivable require a corresponding credit to another account, often Sales, suggesting that Accounts Receivable and Sales are related to one another. That is, if gross sales for a company decrease from one period to the next by 50 percent, an auditor might reasonably expect a substantial decrease in accounts receivable as well. However, if accounts receivable did not decrease by a substantial amount, the auditor would probably make inquiries of management and/or perform additional tests of details to determine whether monetary misstatement exists in recorded gross sales, recorded receivables, or both. Thus, analytical procedures are not necessarily intended to isolate monetary misstatement, as for example a substantive test of details might, but rather to identify accounts that are *likely* to contain monetary misstatement.

In some cases, analytical procedures used as substantive tests can actually be more effective or efficient for achieving some audit objectives than a substantive test of details. Analytical procedures allow the auditor to reach conclusions about the details in an account by testing aggregated data within the account; tests of details, in contrast, allow an auditor to draw conclusions about aggregated data from testing details. Regardless of the auditor's intent in using an analytical procedure—whether for planning, overall review, or as a substantive test—all analytical procedures are intended to form expectations. The auditor's expectations are derived from plausible relationships and are based on his or her understanding of the client's business and industry. Examples of information an auditor uses in developing expectations include:

- Financial information for comparable prior periods.
- Anticipated results, such as projections or forecasts extrapolated from monthly, quarterly, or annual data.
- Relationships among elements of financial information within the period, such as the relationship between sales and accounts receivable.
- Information about the client's industry, such as market share, earnings, and gross margin.
- Relationships between financial and relevant nonfinancial information, such as the relationship between sales and a client's share of the market.

SAS No. 56 requires that analytical procedures be applied to some extent during an engagement's *planning stage* (as a predictor of accounts likely to be misstated materially) and *final review stage* (as an overall review of the financial statements), and recommends they be used as substantive tests during the engagement. Analytical procedures used in the planning stage of an engagement are discussed later in this chapter, and analytical procedures used in the final review stage are discussed in Chapter 17. Examples of analytical procedures used as substantive tests are discussed and illustrated in Chapters 11, 13, 14, 15, and 16.

DUAL-PURPOSE TESTS

In practice, auditors often perform **dual-purpose tests,** which are intended to provide evidence about both control risk and likely monetary error. For example, when recomputing the mathematical extensions on sales invoices (e.g., quantity unit price), an auditor is actually performing both a test of controls and a substantive test of details: a test of controls in the sense that the auditor is determining whether client personnel are properly extending sales invoices, and a substantive test in the sense that the auditor is determining whether monetary error exists.

DOCUMENTING EVIDENCE

Evidence compiled in assurance, attestation, and audit engagements is assembled in **working papers,** the practitioner's principal record of the work performed and the conclusions reached. The professional literature addresses audit working papers (i.e., *SAS No. 41*), but the guidance is limited. For example, Edmund Noonan, chair of the Auditing Standards Board, has said, "There are no auditing standards that prescribe a methodology and maintenance of work papers, only the fact that they need to exist."[5] In practice, an individual working paper page may take virtually any form, including, for example, a manual ("pencil and paper") or a computer-prepared schedule documenting ownership of an asset, a technical memorandum prepared by the tax staff about the accounting treatment of a complicated interperiod income tax allocation problem, or a schedule extracting significant matters from a client's board of directors meeting. In short, any documentary evidence bearing on management's assertions could potentially be presented as a working paper.

The specific quantity, form, and content of working papers varies from one engagement to another. For example, the working papers for the audit of a large, publicly traded client are likely to be far more voluminous than working papers for an attestation engagement. The practitioner's judgment about the quantity, form, and content of working papers for a particular engagement should be guided by factors such as:

- The nature of management's assertions (e.g., audit engagement v. attestation engagement; publicly traded v. privately owned company).
- The nature of the report (e.g., audit report v. review report).
- The nature and condition of the client's records.
- The extent of risk.
- Needs for supervision and review.

WORKING PAPER FILES

Working papers remain in the custody, and are the property, of the practitioner. In fact, in some states the auditor is designated by statute as owner of the

5   P. Demry. "Can Your Work Papers Come Back to Haunt You?" *The Practical Accountant* (January 1996), p. 6.

working papers, although the auditor's property rights are subject to the limitations of AICPA *Rule of Conduct 301*, "Confidential Client Information" (Chapter 4), which prohibits disclosure without management's consent. Completed working papers for an engagement are usually retained in the practitioner's office for at least two years following an engagement, after which the papers are moved to a remote location for storage, more often lately on computer diskettes or CD-ROM. For example, working papers compiled for a December 31, 1999 year end engagement might be retained in the firm's office files until completion of the December 31, 2001 engagement, after which they're optically scanned for storage. The retention period thereafter should be sufficient for the firm's needs and consistent with applicable federal and state statutes of limitation.

Certain information relating to an audit engagement is maintained separately from the working papers because the information is of continuing interest year after year or relates directly to the preparation of tax returns. Although groupings and classification of information may vary somewhat among public accounting firms, the following types of files are representative of the files maintained for each client apart from the current audit working paper file:

- Correspondence file.
- Permanent file.
- Tax file.

Correspondence File

The correspondence file, sometimes called the administrative file, contains all correspondence to, from, or on behalf of a client and is especially useful for planning an audit. For example, prior to the year end phase of an engagement, a client may have communicated with the auditor about accounting and reporting problems, such as a change in accounting for postretirement benefits other than pensions. Correspondence related to the problems should be included in the correspondence file, creating a "signal" to the audit staff that the current engagement should consider the problems.

Permanent File

The permanent file contains information of continuing interest and relevance to an engagement. For example, the file might include a client's background and history, organization charts, articles of incorporation, bylaws, charter, outstanding bond indenture agreements, contracts, articles from the financial press, and flowcharts of transaction cycles. Permanent files should be reviewed by all staff members unfamiliar with the client and should be updated during each engagement.

Tax File

The tax file contains information relevant to a client's past, current, and future income and property tax obligations, and serves as a basis for preparing current year returns or for performing other tax services, such as amending prior year returns or representing the client in an IRS audit. For example, the file might include prior year state and federal income tax returns, tax-related correspondence, research and rulings, and schedules of significant temporary differences between pretax accounting income ("book income") and taxable income. All relevant tax information arising during an engagement should be included in the tax file.

CONTENT AND ARRANGEMENT OF WORKING PAPERS

The sheer volume of working papers compiled during an engagement is inconsequential—quantity is no substitute for quality. But, the quality of working papers *is consequential*, because the papers provide the principal support for an auditor's opinion, demonstrate compliance with *GAAS*, aid an audit team in performing and reviewing work, and are well understood in the liability literature as the principal evidence for an auditor's due diligence defense under Section 11 of the Securities Act of 1933 and Section 18 of the Securities Exchange Act of 1934 (Chapter 5). In short, working papers represent a means—in most cases, the only means—for organizing and cataloging documented audit evidence.

Although content varies from engagement to engagement, working papers ordinarily include evidence that:

- Work was adequately planned, supervised, and reviewed (consistent with the first standard of field work),
- Internal control was considered as a basis for planning substantive tests (second standard of field work), and
- Sufficient competent evidential matter was obtained (third standard of field work).

Because there is no standard order for arranging working papers, order varies somewhat depending on custom within firms. Even the physical form of working papers varies. For example, some firms capture most working papers in automated files, some bind working papers, and others arrange loose, unbound papers within file folders. The physical form of completed working papers is inconsequential, although the arrangement should be logical and the working papers should be indexed, referenced, and accessible.

Figure 6-4 depicts a logical and typical arrangement for a set of working papers. In Figure 6-4, *a draft of financial statements* is presented first, followed by an *engagement letter* (introduced later) and a *preliminary audit planning memorandum*. The *working trial balance* is the source for preparing a draft of the audited financial statements. All dollar amounts within the working trial balance are referenced to detailed schedules within the working papers. Adjustments and reclassifications, an auditor's "correcting" journal entries, are presented next. **Adjusting entries (AJEs)** represent corrections to the client's books and therefore are given to the client to record. In contrast, **reclassification entries (RJEs)** are made within the auditor's working papers to reclassify accounts for presentation in the financial statements but are not recorded in the client's books.

Detailed audit working papers are subdivided and grouped by individual financial statement accounts, which, in turn, are often filed in balance sheet order—that is, the order of appearance in the financial statements. Hence, the Cash account working papers are typically first, followed by Marketable Securities, Accounts Receivable, and so on. However, research reveals that balance sheet order may actually increase the cognitive effort required to

Figure 6-4:   Arrangement of Audit Working Papers

```
Order of Working Papers
   Draft of financial statements
   Engagement letter
   Preliminary audit planning memo
   Working trial balance
   Adjusting entries (AJEs) and
       Reclassification entries (RJEs)
   Detailed working papers grouped
       by individual accounts
```

```
Order of Working Papers for Individual Accounts
   Lead schedule
   Audit programs
   Detailed working papers
```

complete audit tasks that rely on evidence compiled throughout the working papers, and that the increased effort interferes with decision tasks, such as the auditor's going concern decision (Chapter 3).[6] To avoid increased cognitive effort, some firms store going concern evidence in database management systems (introduced later) and then access the evidence with expert systems software that displays the evidence in an order that reduces cognitive effort (e.g., causal order) rather than in balance sheet order. In more traditional systems, working papers for each asset, liability, and equity account usually begin with a *lead schedule* summarizing the account's unaudited balance, adjusting and reclassification entries, and the final audited balance. The lead schedule also includes the auditor's conclusion about whether the account is fairly stated, and these conclusions are the basis for an auditor's opinion on the financial statements taken as a whole.

Audit programs are listings of detailed procedures applied to specific financial statement accounts or activities, and under *SAS No. 77* should be prepared in writing on every audit. Usually, a separate program is prepared for each significant account or activity audited. For example, there might be a separate program for marketable securities, a separate program for postretirement health care, and so on. As depicted in Figure 6-4, programs typically follow the related lead schedules, although programs for specific activities, such as a review for subsequent events, might be filed elsewhere (e.g., following adjusting and reclassification entries). A portion of a sample audit program appears in Figure 6-5. Three observations about the sample program:

- Listed program steps (audit procedures) are explicit and detailed.
- A reference is provided to other working paper schedules that contain detailed audit work.

6   D. N. Ricchiute. "Working-Paper Order Effects and Auditor's Going-Concern Decisions," *The Accounting Review* (January 1992), pp. 46-58.

Figure 6-5: Sample Audit Program (Partial)

Program Steps (Uncollectible Receivables)	Working Paper Reference	Performed By
•		
•		
7. Obtain prior year end balance from general ledger.	B6	KLR
8. Review accounts written off during the year.	B7	KLR
9. Calculate provision for uncollectible accounts.	B10	KLR
•		
•		

• The staff member initials the program step when completed, thereby taking responsibility for the work done.

Detailed audit working papers document completed audit program steps, are presented after the audit programs, and represent the bulk of working paper files. Figure 6-6 illustrates a typical detailed audit working paper in the form of a schedule. The significance of Figure 6-6 is not in the schedule itself, but in the following items, which are common to most working papers: The index, references, preparer and reviewer initials, dates of completion and review (plus the year end date), and tick marks and explanations.

The *index* serves the same purpose as the page number of a book. However, working papers are numbered sequentially within account groups with page numbers preceded by an account code. For example, the alphanumeric index *B6* in Figure 6-6 indicates the sixth page of the accounts receivable working papers. Account groups within the working papers could be identified as follows: Single letters (*A, B, C,* etc.) = asset accounts; double letters (*AA, BB, CC,* etc.) = liability and equity accounts; numerals (*10, 20, 30,* . . .) = revenue and expense accounts. For example, *10-1* might represent the schedule for sales revenue accounts.

References are a means for transferring information within the working papers. For example, in Figure 6-6, the $2,750 written off for Adams Company is referenced *from* working paper *B7*, and the $29,025, total uncollectible receivables, is referenced *to B1*, the accounts receivable lead schedule. The direction of transfer (*to* or *from*) determines the location of index references: A reference to the left of, or above, an item indicates "transferred *from*"; a circled reference to the right of, or below, an item indicates "transferred *to*." Some auditors write "From *B7*" and "To *B1*." Indexing and referencing provide a road map through working papers. A reviewer should be able to follow his or her way through an entire set of properly indexed and referenced working papers without difficulty.

Initials of preparers and reviewers of working papers are included to affix primary responsibility for work performed, allowing the manager or partner in charge of the engagement to direct specific inquiries about work performed to the individuals responsible. The preparer and reviewer should also indicate the *dates of completion and review*, respectively. The completion date for a

Figure 6-6: Sample Audit Working Paper

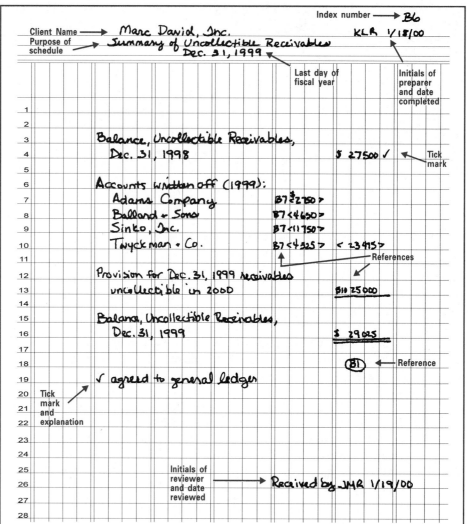

working paper indicates the last day on which related audit work was performed. Thus, transactions and events from this date to the audit report date should be reviewed before leaving the client's office on the last day of field work. Another date appearing on each working paper is the entity's fiscal year end. The *year end date* identifies the year under audit, distinguishing the working paper from similar papers prepared in other years.

Unless self-explanatory, all information or data contained in working papers should be referenced from another schedule or "tick marked" and explained. *Tick marks* are symbols (asterisks, etc.) used in working papers. An example of a tick mark and related explanation appears in Figure 6-6.

AUTOMATED WORKING PAPERS

For generations, audit working papers had been prepared manually, stored, and used as a single-copy record of audit evidence. However, with the advent of personal computers (PCs), particularly laptops, many practicing auditors now prepare and store some or virtually all of their working papers on computers. Unlike manually prepared working papers, automated working papers provide the distinct advantages of: (1) considerably easier data manipulation, since data entry, calculations, and postings can be accomplished instantaneously, and (2) significantly reduced storage costs, since a single diskette or CD-ROM, for example, can hold many pages of working papers.

When working papers are prepared on PCs, the auditor can either key in audit information, such as tick marks, index numbers, references, and explanations, or handwrite the information on the screen using a "wand." For example, Figure 6-7 illustrates an automated version of the working paper illustrated in Figure 6-6. (In fact, consistent with practice in many firms, Figure 6-6 is the only manual working paper in this text.) Note that the automated version (Figure 6-7) includes exactly the same information as the manual version (Figure 6-6)—only the format is different. However, whether an auditor prepares working papers manually or with a computer, the purposes and objectives are identical: to aid in the conduct and review of audit work and to provide the principal support for the auditor's report. The form of the working papers—manual or automated—is irrelevant.

Over the past several years, PCs have revolutionized both the working paper preparation process, discussed previously, and the mechanics of performing a financial statement audit, largely through the development of software for PCs, including *spreadsheet, database management,* and *text retrieval/ World Wide Web* capability.

Figure 6-7: Sample Automated Working Paper

B6
KLR
1/18/00

The Wilson Company
Summary of Uncollectible Receivables
December 31, 1999

Balance, Uncollectible Receivables 12/31/98			$ 27,500*
Accounts written off 1/01/99 to 12/31/99			
Adams Company	B7	$ (2,750)	
Ballard & Sons	B7	(4,650)	
Sinko, Inc.	B7	(11,750)	
Twyckman & Co.	B7	(4,325)	(23,475)
Provision for 12/31/99			
Receivables uncollectible in 2000	B10		25,000
Balance, Uncollectible Receivables 12/31/99			$ 29,025
			To B1

* Agreed to general ledger
Reviewed by JMR 1/19/00

Spreadsheet Software

Spreadsheet software—such as Microsoft's *Excel*, Lotus Development Corp.'s *Lotus 1-2-3*, and Borland International's *Quattro Pro*—is the most common PC application used in practice. Today, spreadsheets are easy to use, inexpensive, easily modified across engagements and are expected by clients, particularly those who know that spreadsheets save time and therefore can reduce audit fees. Auditors use spreadsheets for analytical procedures (such as ratio analysis and modeling), data import and export across files, graphing and sorting, financial statement automation, and all of the engagement applications listed in Figure 6-8.

Many public accounting firms have developed proprietary spreadsheet software that provides standard tabular formats for selected working paper schedules, thereby requiring that staff merely input data for the current engagement and manipulate the data as necessary. For example, a common but tedious year end audit activity often assigned to entry-level staff is the preparation of a *working trial balance* for all general ledger accounts and *lead schedules* for each individual balance sheet account. Preparing the trial balance and lead schedules manually is not only time-consuming, but can result in math errors, particularly when the auditor posts adjusting journal entries through the lead schedules to the working trial balance. However, when an auditor uses spreadsheets, each task is accomplished in significantly less time, and posting is accomplished simply by pressing function keys on the keyboard.

Database Management (DBM) Systems Software

DBM systems—such as Borland's *dBASE*, Microsoft's *FoxPro/Lan*, and DataEase Corporation's *DataEase*—are particularly powerful for what is called *relational structuring* across files—that is, combining two or more files to perform an application with a single query. For example, an auditor might relate data in an accounts receivable file and a cash receipts file to monitor collection of past due accounts. Auditors use DBM software for a variety of other applications, including advanced analytical procedures, receivables confirmation requests, sampling, engagement administration tasks (such as staff scheduling and staff time-and-expense control), and global data links (as illustrated next).

DBM software can be advantageous in either small or large engagements. However, for large multinational clients, there are additional advantages since the auditor acquires evidence from locations around the globe rather than from a single, centrally located accounting department. For example, the physical inventory observations (Chapter 15) for several international retail stores, including Sears and Wal-Mart, are now accomplished on linked spreadsheets which are prepared in various stores and warehouses around the world and then are transferred by password-protected e-mail to a centrally located office of the firm conducting the audit, usually the office in charge of the multinational engagement. Since the schedules are preformatted, all inventory data are in a common form, allowing easy manipulation and efficient reconciliation with the client's final priced inventory.

Text Retrieval Software

Auditors often research and retrieve accounting and auditing pronouncements. Text retrieval software (sometimes called *text database software*)—such as Folio's *Folio Views*, Lotus Development Corp.'s *Lotus Magellan*, and ZyLAB's *ZyIndex*—

Figure 6-8: PC Applications in Auditing

Cash
- Preparing cash lead sheets.
- Preparing bank reconciliations or proofs of cash.

Receivables
- Calculating estimated bad debt expense.
- Calculating turnover statistics.
- Preparing confirmation requests.
- Preparing aging summaries.

Inventory
- Calculating LIFO indexes, layers, and final balances.
- Calculating turnover statistics.
- Tracing inventory test counts to perpetual records.
- Analyzing variances.

Fixed Assets
- Calculating depreciation.
- Computing capitalized interest.
- Computing sale-leaseback gain deferral.

Investments
- Determining portfolio valuation at the lower of cost or market.
- Obtaining market prices at year end from public data sources.

Liabilities
- Calculating warranty reserves.
- Determining debt covenant compliance.
- Preparing loan amortization schedules.

Income Taxes
- Analyzing permanent and timing differences.
- Reconciling pretax accounting and taxable income.
- Computing deferred taxes.
- Calculating effective tax rates.

Equity
- Computing earnings per share.
- Computing stock splits, preferred stock dividends.
- Analyzing treasury stock.

Engagement Administration
- Controlling confirmations sent and responses received.
- Controlling correspondence.
- Monitoring time charged to engagements.
- Controlling and monitoring client-prepared schedules.
- Assigning staff to engagements.

can be used to access and retrieve any electronically stored text (sometimes called *infobases*), including FASB *Original Pronouncements* and AICPA *Professional Standards*, both of which are available on CD-ROM. Public databases, accessed by modem through telephone links, offer alternative text-search services, such as the National Automated Accounting Research System (NAARS), Dialog's *UMI/Data Courier Accounting and Tax Database,* and CompuServe's *SEC On-Line.*

Today, many practitioners use the Internet to link with accessible audit planning information useful to understanding a client's business and industry. For example, consider the case of a practitioner with a new client in the pharmaceutical industry. Using either of two browser services, Netscape's *Navigator* or Microsoft's *Explorer*, a practitioner could link from the search term "pharmaceutical industry" to a menu of directories including *Business*, to the business subdirectory *Companies*, to the *Health* industry, to the *Pharmaceuticals* subindustry, and finally to publication services such as *World Pharma Web* (an archived pharmaceutical news and company profile service) and to the home pages of major competitors such as Bristol-Myers Squibb, Eli Lilly, Merck, Pfizer, and Warner-Lambert, among others. Alternatively, the practitioner could access the home page of competitors directly, such as Merck *(http://www.merck.com)*, to access a company overview, an annual report, and product information, among other things.

ACCESS TO AUDIT WORKING PAPERS

Although working papers can be subpoenaed (Chapter 5), prior to the 1980s there had been no precedent for government agencies to access an auditor's papers. However, following nine years of judicial proceedings, the U.S. Supreme Court ruled in *United States v. Arthur Young & Co. et al.* that an auditor's tax accrual working papers—evidence used to determine a client's current and deferred tax liability—*are* relevant to an Internal Revenue Service (IRS) tax audit, and therefore *are not* protected from disclosure under the theory of accountant-client privileged communications provided by law in some states. Other cases have addressed the issue, but the Arthur Young case is particularly noteworthy because it caused considerable concern within the profession and is the first case to reach the U.S. Supreme Court.

The case first received attention in 1975 when the IRS, in an audit of Amerada Hess Corporation's 1972-1974 tax returns, detected questionable payments of $7,830. As a result of the questionable payments, what had been a routine tax audit became a criminal investigation. The IRS issued an administrative summons seeking the tax accrual working papers prepared by Arthur Young. Amerada Hess, however, instructed Young not to comply with the summons, prompting the IRS to seek enforcement in the U.S. District Court. The District Court ruled in favor of the IRS, arguing that the tax accrual working papers were relevant to the IRS audit and that the accountant-client privilege did not protect the papers. On appeal, the U.S. Court of Appeals agreed the tax accrual working papers were relevant to the IRS audit, but held that the public interest and the integrity of the securities markets were best served by protecting a client's confidential communications from public scrutiny.

The dispute ended on further appeal when the U.S. Supreme Court ruled that tax accrual working papers: (1) are relevant to an IRS audit within the meaning of *Internal Revenue Code (IRC) Section 7602*, and (2) are not protected from disclosure under *IRC Section 7602*. In general, the Court reasoned that an IRS summons should be judged by the *potential relevance* of tax accrual working papers to an IRS tax audit, and not by the relevance standards typically used in judging the admissibility of evidence in court. Interestingly, the financial community reacted to the Court's opinion with some alarm, since the ruling may discourage some audit clients from communicating openly with auditors about tax matters and, correspondingly, may alter how auditors prepare and maintain working papers, particularly working papers that may be subjected to public scrutiny through the courts.

THE AUDIT PROCESS

What is the sequence of steps an auditor pursues in a financial statement audit, and when during an engagement are tests of controls, substantive tests of details, and analytical procedures normally performed? Figure 6-9 lists the major steps in the audit process, including representative dates—assuming a December 31 fiscal year end, and either a continuing engagement or a new engagement accepted early in the year. In practice, the audit process may vary somewhat from engagement to engagement, depending on an entity's industry and size, among other things. However, generalizations can lend considerable insight since most financial statement audits are similar both in logic and in breadth—similar in logic because they are based on the scientific method of inquiry, and similar in breadth because they are all driven by the same set of guidelines: *GAAS*. Discussion of each step in the audit process follows.

COMMUNICATION WITH AUDIT COMMITTEE

An auditor's initial formal contact with a potential audit client is often through the **audit committee** of the entity's board of directors. An audit committee is typically composed of board members not otherwise employed by the entity, called *outside directors*. The audit committee serves as an intermediary between the independent auditor and the full board of directors in matters relating to the selection of an independent auditor, the scope and timing of the financial statement audit, and other financial and accounting matters, including the entity's internal controls and internal audit function. However, a research

Figure 6-9: The Audit Process

Approximate Dates	Activity
March	Communication with the audit committee. Decision to accept or continue the engagement. Engagement letter. General understanding of the business and industry.
April-May	First-level planning. (See Figure 6-12.)
July-August	Second-level planning. (See Figure 6-12.)
September-November	Interim audit work. (See Figure 6-13.)
December-February	Year end audit work. (See Figure 6-14.) Subsequent events.
Last day of field work	Management representation and legal letters. Reports.

study reports that, to be effective, audit committees require a strong organizational mandate, for example through a written charter and informal recognition by management and the independent auditor.[7]

Although not common until the 1970s, corporate audit committees were encouraged as early as 1940 in SEC *Accounting Series Release No. 19*, which recommended that registrants establish audit committees composed of nonofficer board members to nominate audit firms and to arrange and monitor the details of the engagement. In 1967, an AICPA Executive Committee's *Statement on Audit Committees of Boards of Directors* also encouraged audit committees composed of outside directors, emphasizing the advantages of promoting communications between auditors and the board of directors. In 1972, the SEC reiterated its support for audit committees in *Accounting Series Release No. 123*, "Standing Audit Committees Composed of Outside Directors." Thus, for a number of years audit committees were strongly encouraged, though not mandatory. However, in 1978, the New York Stock Exchange required all listed companies to appoint audit committees consisting of outside directors only. More recently, the National Commission on Fraudulent Financial Reporting (the Treadway Commission), a blue-ribbon commission charged with assessing the extent of fraudulent financial reporting in the U.S., recommended in a 1987 report that all public companies be required to have audit committees comprised entirely of outside directors.

To date, no definitive description of an audit committee's duties and responsibilities has appeared but, in practice, most audit committees have the following responsibilities:

- Nominate or terminate the independent auditors.
- Review the scope of an audit.
- Review audit results and discuss financial statements in depth with the independent auditors.
- Recommend to the board of directors changes in accounting policies.
- Monitor the entity's internal controls.
- Assure the existence of a framework for internal auditors to express their concerns, either directly to the audit committee or through the independent auditors.
- Assume responsibility for the quality of reported earnings.

Although not necessarily all-inclusive, this list of responsibilities indicates clearly the far-reaching issues an audit committee can address. Equally important, audit committees can improve the financial reporting process significantly. For example, a recent study reveals that audit committees reduce the frequency of shareholder lawsuits alleging management fraud, quarterly earnings restatements, SEC enforcement actions, illegal acts, and auditor turnover when management disagrees with an auditor about the application of accounting principles.[8] Not unrelated to the findings of this study, some public accounting firms are reluctant to be engaged by companies that lack an audit committee.

7   L. P. Kalbers and T. J. Fogarty. "Audit Committee Effectiveness: An Empirical Investigation of the Contribution of Power," *Auditing: A Journal of Practice & Theory* (Spring 1993), pp. 24-49.
8   D. A. McMullen. "Audit Committee Performance: An Investigation of the Consequences Associated with Audit Committees," *Auditing: A Journal of Practice & Theory* (Spring 1996), pp. 87-103.

DECISION TO ACCEPT OR CONTINUE AN ENGAGEMENT

Because an auditor cannot audit a client that lacks integrity, *Statement on Quality Control Standards No. 1*, "System of Quality Control for a CPA Firm," recommends that a public accounting firm establish policies and procedures for deciding whether to accept (or continue) an engagement, thereby minimizing the likelihood of associating with an untrustworthy or an unduly risky client. For example, the Big Six public accounting firms exercise considerable caution in deciding whether to accept or continue risky clients, although the responsibility for the decision varies across firms: In some firms, the decision is made by individual partners, in others by office managing or regional partners, and in others by national office partners.[9] However, as a result of investigating a client's integrity, a firm is in a position only to decide whether to accept or continue an engagement, not to vouch for a client's integrity.

A public accounting firm may use a variety of sources in deciding whether to accept or continue an engagement. For example, in considering a new engagement, an auditor could:

- Review the proposed client's financial statements,
- Inquire of third parties, such as bankers and lawyers, about a proposed client's reputation, and
- Evaluate the public accounting firm's ability to service the proposed client properly.

The firm should also consider whether the predecessor auditor's resignation or firing was linked to a disagreement between the predecessor and management about the application of accounting principles. Research reveals that auditor changes *after a disagreement* are associated with clients that have poorer earnings performance, more debt, fewer current assets, and poorer stock price performance than changes without a disagreement.[10] Given the potential for liability discussed in Chapter 5, a firm should continually monitor, and reevaluate when appropriate, a client's integrity. A firm should never accept or continue an engagement when there is a strong likelihood of material misstatement or management fraud, since the audit fee would not likely be worth the risk.

When a new engagement involves replacing a predecessor auditor, the successor auditor should communicate with the predecessor before accepting the engagement. *Statement on Auditing Standards No. 7*, "Communications Between Predecessor and Successor Auditors" (AU Sec. 315), places the initiative for communication on the successor auditor. However, research reveals that, despite the responsibility to communicate with predecessors, some successor auditors do not. For example, one study found that fully one-fourth of 550 successor auditors did not communicate with predecessors (and that the extent of noncommunication was higher in smaller firms),[11] and another found

9   H. F. Huss and F. A. Jacobs. "Risk Containment: Exploring Auditor Decisions in the Engagement Process," *Auditing: A Journal of Practice & Theory* (Fall 1991), pp. 16-32.
10   D. S. Dhaliwal, J. W. Schatzberg, and M. A. Trombley. "An Analysis of the Economic Factors Related to Auditor-Client Disagreements Preceding Auditor Changes," *Auditing: A Journal of Practice & Theory* (Fall 1993), pp. 22-38.
11   J. C. Lambert, S. J. Lambert III, and T. G. Calderon. "Communication Between Successor and Predecessor Auditors," *Auditing: A Journal of Practice & Theory* (Spring 1991), pp. 97-109.

that a startling three-fourths of 151 successors did not communicate.[12] Unless asked by the successor, the predecessor is under *no obligation* to communicate information to the successor auditor, even if the predecessor is aware of facts that would bear on the successor's decision to accept the new engagement, like repeated violations of authoritative accounting pronouncements.

The successor auditor explains to the prospective client the need to communicate with the predecessor, and requests permission to do so. Since Rule 301 of the *Code of Professional Conduct* precludes an auditor from disclosing confidential information without the client's permission (Chapter 4), the successor asks the prospective client to authorize the predecessor auditor to respond fully to the successor's inquiries. If the prospective client refuses to authorize communication with the predecessor auditor or limits the information that the predecessor may disclose, the successor determines the reasons for refusal and the impact upon the decision to accept the engagement.

Following authorization, the successor auditor asks the predecessor specific and reasonable questions about the proposed client, among them questions about management's integrity, disagreements with management about accounting principles or audit procedures, and the reasons for a change in auditors. The predecessor should respond promptly and fully to all reasonable and specific questions. However, if the predecessor decides not to respond fully due to unusual circumstances, such as pending litigation, he or she should inform the successor auditor that the responses are limited. The successor then considers the impact of the limitations on the decision to accept the engagement.

Engagement Letter

After a decision is made to accept (or continue) an engagement, an agreement is reached with management about the professional services desired, and an engagement letter is drafted by the auditor for the chief executive officer's signature. As illustrated in Figure 6-10, an engagement letter is a written agreement between an auditor and client that serves to minimize misunderstandings, alerts the client to the purpose of the engagement and role of the auditor, and helps minimize legal liability for services neither contracted for nor performed. Engagement letters are not required by professional standards but should be prepared for every professional engagement since the risk of misunderstanding can, and sometimes does, result in serious legal judgments against the independent auditor. See, for example, in Chapter 5, *Maryland Casualty Co. v. Jonathon Cook* and *1136 Tenant's Corp. v. Max Rothenberg & Co.*

UNDERSTAND CLIENT'S BUSINESS AND INDUSTRY

Audits cannot be conducted effectively without the cooperation of management and a considerable understanding of a client's business (e.g., products and services, capital structure, distribution system, incentive compensation schemes) and industry (e.g., pharamaceuticals, oil and gas, state and local government). An auditor needs also to consider risk factors such as supply source dependability and technological change, and the effect of uncontrollable

---

12   G. W. Glezen and M. B. Elser. "The Auditor Change Process," *Journal of Accountancy* (June 1996), pp. 73-77.

Figure 6-10: Engagement Letter

Cheever & Yates, CPAs
Suite 2600
650 Madison Avenue
New York, NY 10022

March 24, 2000

Mr. Raymond Carver, President
The Wilson Company
15 Artubus Drive
Stony Brook, NY 11790

Dear Mr. Carver:

This will confirm our understanding of the arrangements for our audit of the financial statements of The Wilson Company for the year ended December 31, 2000.

We will audit the company's balance sheet at December 31, 2000, and the related statements of income, retained earnings, and cash flows for the year then ended for the purpose of expressing an opinion on them. Our audit will be made in accordance with generally accepted auditing standards. Our procedures will include tests of documentary evidence supporting the transactions recorded in the accounts, tests of the physical existence of inventories, and direct confirmation of receivables and certain other assets and liabilities by correspondence with selected customers, creditors, legal counsel, and banks. At the conclusion of our audit, we will request certain written representations from management about the financial statements and related matters.

Management is responsible for the fair presentation of financial statements in conformity with generally accepted accounting principles and for the development, implementation, and maintenance of adequate internal controls. Although we may consult with you about accounting principles, management is responsible for their selection and application. Our engagement is subject to the risk that material errors, irregularities, or illegal acts, if they exist, will not be detected. However, we will inform you of any such matters that come to our attention.

We will review the company's federal and state income tax returns for the fiscal year ended December 31, 2000. These returns, we understand, will be prepared by the controller. Further, we will be available during the year to consult with you on the tax effects of any proposed transactions or contemplated change in business policies.

Our fee for these services will be at our regular per diem rates, plus travel and other out-of-pocket costs. Invoices will be rendered every two weeks and are payable on presentation.

We are pleased to have this opportunity to serve you.

If this letter expresses your understanding, please sign the enclosed copy where indicated and return it to us.

Sincerely,

_____

Cheever & Yates, CPAs

Arrangements accepted:

_____ _____
President   Date
The Wilson Company

constraints that impose regulatory requirements and reporting obligations. For example, *regulatory requirements* might include fair employment practices, employee retirement income security, occupational safety and health, air and water pollution prevention, and consumer product safety. *Reporting obligations* might include securities filings; federal, state, and local excise and income tax returns; and, in the case of governmental clients, reports on compliance with laws and regulations. For example, consider the case of Merck & Co., Inc., a multibillion-dollar pharmaceutical company that discovers, develops, manufactures, and markets a broad range of human and animal health products and services worldwide. Three issues about Merck and, for that matter, any pharmaceutical company, are important to an auditor:

First, the time span from research to market in the pharmaceutical industry can range roughly from ten to fifteen years, and is complicated by the need for U.S. Food and Drug Administration (FDA) approval. As illustrated in Figure 6-11, only about 100 of an estimated 5,000 experimental drugs (2 percent) reach FDA *Phase I-III* testing, and only about 20 of the 5,000 (0.4 percent) receive FDA approval. For example, Merck's *Pepcid AC*, a nonprescription stomach acid controller, received FDA approval for U.S. distribution in 1995. However, industry research had begun as early as 1963 on a competing drug, SmithKline Beecham's *Tagamet*, which became the first prescription drug ever to exceed $1 billion in sales. Second, owing to an extraordinary risk/return ratio—that is, the risk of success (0.4 percent) v. the revenue from success (>$1 billion)—competition in the industry is nothing less than ferocious. Third, to overcome the long lead time to market and the risk/return ratio, some pharmaceutical companies have entered into strategic alliances to bypass research and to share risk. For example, Merck entered into a strategic alliance with Astra AB, a German pharmaceutical company, to develop and market Astra products in the U.S., thereby allowing Merck to bypass developing the products and Astra to penetrate U.S. markets. And Merck entered into alliances with DuPont for radiopharmaceutical imaging agents and with Johnson & Johnson for nonprescription medicines, the intent of both alliances (for all three companies) being to share risk. An auditor could not serve Merck effectively

Figure 6-11:   Pharmaceuticals: From Research to Market

Phase	Years	Estimated Number
• **Discovery** Search for experimental drugs	2-10	5,000
• **Preclinical Tests** Lab and animal testing	1-3	250
• **Phase I** Is it safe?	< 1	100
• **Phase II** Does it work?	< 2	70
• **Phase III** Are there side effects?	1-4	33
• **FDA Review (Approval)**	≤ 7	20

without knowledge of these three among other issues the pharmaceutical industry faces.

Initially, an auditor should tour a client's facilities, becoming familiar with the production layout and arrangement of offices, and with key personnel, such as the chief operating and financial officers, production and sales managers, the controller, and department supervisors. Through interviews with client personnel, consultation with staff previously assigned to the engagement, available industry and accounting literature (e.g., AICPA *Industry Audit Guides*), and a review of significant transactions and events to date, an auditor develops an understanding of a client's business, industry, and environment sufficient to capture the unique business risks imposed on the client, enabling the auditor to impound those risks into the audit plan and to tailor the engagement to the conditions at hand.

FIRST-LEVEL PLANNING

Initial, first-level planning, usually performed soon after the first quarter of an audit client's fiscal year, is intended to identify early any important accounting, auditing, or reporting issues. An auditor's typical first-level planning activities, summarized in Figure 6-12, begin with reviews of the prior year's audit work (assuming a continuing engagement) and first quarter financial information for the current year.

The *review of prior year audit work* is designed to assess potentially risky audit areas, identify audit areas to be emphasized during the engagement, and consider improvements for the current year. For example, an unusually large number of adjusting journal entries and unexpectedly high actual hours in the audit of receivables last year may prompt the auditor this year to reallocate budgeted audit hours from a low risk account to receivables. The *review of first quarter financial results* is similarly motivated: The auditor attempts to isolate unexpected fluctuations or inconsistencies from prior year statements that may signal potentially risky audit areas this year. For example, an intensive January advertising campaign followed by poor first quarter sales may have implications for the valuation assertion in inventory. The review of first quarter results

Figure 6-12: Audit Planning

Approximate Dates	Activity
April–May	**First-Level Planning** Review prior year audit work. Review first quarter financial results. Prepare preliminary audit time budget.
July–August	**Second-Level Planning** Review second quarter financial results. Prepare final audit time budget. Perform analytical procedures. Prepare preliminary audit planning memo. Coordinate with assigned staff. Coordinate with client. Prepare interim audit programs.

also includes newspaper and magazine accounts that offer insights about product lines that support expected earnings. For example, *The Wall Street Journal* account about Merck's first quarter 1996 results reveals that "*Fosomax*, the company's new osteoporosis therapy, had sales of $44 million, surpassing [an analyst's] estimate," and that "*Zocor* and Merck's other cholesterol-lowering drug, *Mevacor*, together command about 40% of the worldwide market."[13] Both pieces of information are helpful to the auditor's understanding of Merck's business and to the company's competitive standing in the industry.

As part of first-level planning, an auditor also prepares a *preliminary audit time budget*, an estimate of total planned audit time by staff level and audit activity. To illustrate, a preliminary time budget for cash, marketable securities, and receivables might appear in part as follows:

Partial Preliminary Time Budget

Audit Area	Total Estimated Hours		Estimated Hours by Staff Level			
	Interim	Year End	Assistant	Senior	Manager	Partner
Cash	40	(35)	36 (31)	2 (2)	1 (1)	1 (1)
Marketable securities	20	(15)	17 (12)	1 (1)	1 (1)	1 (1)
Accounts receivable	40	(30)	34 (25)	4 (3)	1 (1)	1 (1)
•						
•						
•						

Audit time budgets should be realistic to the risks expected but respectful of the experience of assigned staff. A considerable research literature has addressed constraining time budgets and the propensity for audit staff to shirk. For example, one study in three offices of two firms revealed that time pressure drove over one-half of 152 responding staff auditors to sign off audit program steps prematurely, reduce audit effort below levels they considered appropriate, overlook researching an accounting principle, review client documents superficially, and accept weak oral explanations from management.[14] Although the study did not address the cause of shirking, the effect is clear: an inexcusable absence of due care that seriously undermines audit quality.

SECOND-LEVEL PLANNING

First-level planning focuses on preliminary evaluations—first pass, first thoughts—based on the auditor's general understanding of a client's business, industry, and other relevant factors. Second-level planning, also summarized in Figure 6-12, is usually performed after the second quarter, updates first-level planning, and begins with updating the results of first-level planning by *reviewing second quarter financial results* and *finalizing the audit time budget*.

13   E. Tanouye. "Merck Earnings Increased 14% in 1st Quarter," *The Wall Street Journal* (April 18, 1996), p. B4.
14   T. Kelly and L. Margheim. "The Impact of Time Budget Pressure, Personality, and Leadership Variables on Dysfunctional Auditor Behavior," *Auditing: A Journal of Practice & Theory* (Spring 1990), pp. 21-42.

During second-level planning, the auditor also *performs analytical procedures* that are used to assist in planning the nature, timing, and extent of anticipated auditing procedures and in drafting the preliminary audit planning memorandum. Under *Statement on Auditing Standards No. 56*, "Analytical Procedures," analytical procedures used in planning should focus on enhancing the auditor's understanding of the entity's transactions and identifying risky audit areas. The sophistication of the analytical procedures applied during planning will vary from firm to firm depending on the engagement. For example, some auditors use simple comparisons and ratios of account balances between the current and prior year(s), and investigate those accounts that deviate from expectations beyond a significant threshold, called an "investigation threshold." However, the economic significance of a threshold is difficult to interpret unaided (that is, how large need a threshold be to reveal a deviation worth testing?). As a result, some auditors use statistical decision aids designed to optimize audit effectiveness by predicting and overlooking unproductive thresholds.[15]

The auditor then prepares a *preliminary audit planning memorandum*, an overview of planned audit activity by staff level that includes the final audit time budget. Typically, the planning memorandum describes in general terms the audit approach intended for each audit area. For example, the memorandum might state the following for a client's income tax related transactions and accounts:

Income Taxes

A tax department representative will participate with the audit staff at interim, completing a tax planning checklist designed to isolate specific tax planning and disclosure problems. The tax department representative will prepare a memorandum of the findings for distribution to and discussion with the audit partner, manager, and if necessary, the client.

At year end, the audit staff will review the client's calculation of accumulated income tax prepayments, deferred income taxes, and income tax expense, consulting the tax department when necessary. A tax department representative will review year end audit working papers and prepare a memorandum on the adequacy of related tax accounts. The audit supervisor will reach a conclusion as to whether all tax accounts are fairly stated at the balance sheet date.

The planning memorandum includes similar paragraphs for each audit area and is distributed to each professional staff member assigned to the engagement.

Following completion and approval of the planning memorandum, an auditor schedules available staff members for the audit, and plans a meeting to *coordinate with professional staff assigned to the engagement*. The purpose of the meeting is to introduce each staff member to the engagement and discuss the planned audit approach. Since the meeting is ideally held in advance of interim and year end field work, the assigned staff should have sufficient time to prepare for the engagement, for example, by reviewing the planning memo-

---

15   For example, see R. M. Harper, Jr., J. R. Strawser, and K. Tang. "Establishing Investigation Thresholds for Preliminary Analytical Review," *Auditing: A Journal of Practice & Theory* (Fall 1990), pp. 115-133.

randum, the correspondence and permanent files, and prior year working papers. The auditor needs also to *coordinate with the client* about the scheduled audit dates and anticipated client assistance in preparing working paper schedules, retrieving documents, and providing administrative help.

The final second-level planning activity involves drafting *interim audit programs* for tests of controls. Illustrated (partially) in Figure 6-5, an **audit program** is a detailed list of procedures to be performed for a particular aspect of an engagement. Individually, each audit program assists an auditor in estimating the time required for a particular audit area, in determining staff requirements, and in scheduling audit work. Collectively, all of the programs prepared for an engagement assist in maintaining control as the audit progresses. In general, interim audit programs cannot be designed until the auditor reviews and documents the client's internal controls. However, in continuing engagements, interim audit programs can be drafted in advance of field work, since the auditor has prior knowledge of the client's control structure and prior information about the results of previous assessments of control risk. Of course, if necessary, the programs may be revised when actually used, although the reasons for revision should be justified (e.g., unreliable information during second-level planning, information system changes). For initial engagements, interim audit programs are not usually prepared until the client's internal controls have been reviewed and documented, since the auditor has no prior information about the controls.

Importantly, audit planning does not end with second-level planning. In fact, planning should continue throughout the engagement. A plan is an overall strategy, subject to revision as more current information becomes available.

INTERIM AUDIT WORK

Figure 6-13 summarizes an auditor's typical interim audit activities. The objective of interim work is to assess control risk (and inherent risk), thereby lending insight into the level of year end detection risk the auditor needs to assume to hold audit risk to a relatively low level. For example, assume an auditor's combined assessment of control and inherent risk (Chapter 2) is 30 percent and that he or she wishes to hold audit risk to 6 percent. The audit risk model, introduced in Chapter 2, is:

$$AR = IR \times CR \times DR$$

Where: $AR =$ Audit risk for an account
$IR =$ Inherent risk
$CR =$ Control risk
$DR =$ Detection risk

Rearranging the audit risk model reveals that the acceptable level of detection risk would be 20 percent, calculated as follows:

$$DR = \frac{AR}{IR \times CR}$$

$$= \frac{.06}{.30}$$

$$= .20$$

Figure 6-13:   Interim Audit Work

Approximate Dates	Activity
September-October	Obtain an understanding of internal control. Perform tests of controls. Assess control risk.
November	Prepare preliminary year end audit programs.

A thorough assessment of control risk usually requires that an auditor perform two tasks. First, the auditor *obtains an understanding of an entity's internal controls* by documenting the controls through questionnaires, flowcharts, and narrative memoranda. This understanding is used by the auditor to help predict the types of misstatements that may occur in an entity's financial statement assertions. For example, poor controls over the receipt and shipment of goods could result in purchase or sales transactions recorded in the wrong accounting period at year end, called a "cutoff" problem, affecting the occurrence or the completeness assertions. Second, after obtaining an understanding, the auditor *performs tests of controls*, often the most time-consuming part of interim work, focusing on the misstatements that could occur and the procedures used by management to control for misstatements. For example, tests of controls over purchase and sales transactions would give the auditor insight into the risk of misstatements related to the occurrence or completeness assertions. That is, tests of controls lend insight into whether poor controls identified when documenting the internal controls are likely to result in material misstatements. Next, the auditor *assesses control risk* from the auditor's understanding of internal control and from the results of tests of controls. The assessment may be quantitative (e.g., 30 percent) or qualitative (e.g., medium). The auditor's consideration of internal control is discussed in detail in Chapter 7.

The final interim audit activity involves drafting *preliminary year end audit programs*. The year end programs are heavily dependent upon the engagement's objectives, risky audit areas, audit areas to be emphasized, and, most importantly, results of the auditor's assessment of control risk. Thus, year end audit programs cannot be drafted during the first- and second-level planning stages, because a critical determinant of year end detection risk—control risk—is not yet known.

YEAR END AUDIT WORK

Figure 6-14 summarizes an auditor's typical year end audit activities. The objective of year end audit work, which derives from the third standard of field work, is to obtain sufficient competent evidential matter to afford a reasonable basis for an opinion on financial statements.

Because the fiscal year for many companies corresponds with the calendar year, December 31 year end audit engagements typically impose significant staff assignment and time pressure constraints for public accounting firms. As a result, firms carefully *coordinate with the client* before beginning audit work. For example, for publicly traded companies, when does management expect to announce earnings publicly? The auditor should meet with the client, usually well before year end, to confirm audit dates, finalize working paper schedules

Figure 6-14: Year End Audit Activities

Approximate Dates	Activity
December	Coordinate with client. Finalize year end audit programs.
January-February	Perform substantive tests and analytical procedures. Perform subsequent events review. Obtain representation letters. Review working papers. Draft and sign reports.

to be prepared by the client, and arrange for bank statements to be mailed directly to the auditor rather than to the client. Coordination is much more critical at year end than at interim, since year end work must be completed early enough to result in a timely audit report. For example, audit work for publicly traded corporations must be completed in sufficient time to allow timely filing of *Form 10-K* to the SEC by the fifteenth day of the third month following the balance sheet date—March 15 for calendar year companies. Interim audit work, in contrast, can be conducted at almost any time during the year under audit (although interim work is usually done during the second half of the client's fiscal year).

Prior to performing year end audit procedures, the auditor should *finalize year end audit programs* prepared initially at interim. The auditor reviews and evaluates any significant system changes or other circumstances occurring since interim and updates the audit programs. Finally, an auditor undertakes the most time-consuming year end audit activity: *performing year end substantive tests* that, as explained earlier in the chapter, include tests of details and analytical procedures. The purpose of all substantive tests is to detect material misstatements that had not been prevented or detected by the entity's internal controls. The nature, timing, and extent of substantive tests maps to the assessed level of detection risk and will vary depending on the client's industry. For example, a study of 368 adjusting journal entries for 171 engagements in six different industries reveals that, compared to companies in nonregulated industries (e.g., manufacturing, merchandising), companies in regulated industries (e.g., banks, insurance companies) have fewer total financial statement errors. However, the errors are more likely to be nonroutine (e.g., judgments about uncollectible accounts) than routine (e.g., miscalculations) and more likely to be detected using internal evidence (e.g., documentation) than external evidence (e.g., confirmations).[16]

Subsequent Events

An audit report is usually dated as of the last day of field work, e.g., February 14, 1999 for a December 31, 1998 fiscal year end. Although the audit report and audit work relate to the period January 1 through December 31, 1998, the auditor is also responsible for transactions and events occurring between January 1 and February 14, 1999, the *subsequent period*, that have an effect on the

---

16   M. Maletta and A. Wright. "Audit Evidence Planning: An Examination of Industry Error Characteristics," *Auditing: A Journal of Practice & Theory* (Spring 1996), pp. 71-86.

December 31, 1998 financial statements. For example, if an auditor learns on January 21, 1999, that a customer of an audit client is unable to pay a debt that arose in 1998, adjustment of the December 31, 1998 account receivable may be necessary depending on the circumstances. An auditor is responsible for, and must plan to search for, subsequent events, as discussed more fully in Chapter 17.

Representation Letters

During the course of an audit, management and other parties make many representations to an auditor, both oral and written. *Statement on Auditing Standards No. 19*, "Client Representations" (AU Sec. 333), requires that an auditor obtain certain written representations from management, in the form of a *management representation letter*. The specific representations to be obtained by an auditor depend on the circumstances of the engagement. Auditors also request written representations from other parties, such as *legal letters* from a client's lawyer, as required by *Statement on Auditing Standards No. 12*, "Inquiry of a Client's Lawyer Concerning Litigation, Claims, and Assessments" (AU Sec. 337). Management representation letters and legal letters are discussed more fully in Chapter 17.

WORKING PAPER REVIEW

Throughout an engagement, audit work is reviewed by staff levels above the staff member assigned—for example, an audit senior might review an audit staff member's accounts receivable working papers. Not surprisingly, research has found that the review process reduces the variance in judgments between supervisory and subordinate staff, and increases the accuracy of the working papers.[17] However, on or about the last day of field work, the engagement partner *reviews audit working papers* by reading carefully every working paper page, since the assigned supervisory staff may vary in their capability to detect errors made by subordinate staff. For example, research suggests that audit managers are more accurate than seniors in detecting conceptual errors (e.g., an undocumented audit procedure), and that audit seniors are more accurate than managers at detecting mechanical errors (e.g., disagreement between a working paper account balance and a financial statement balance).[18] The purpose of the partner's review is to judge compliance with *GAAS* and with the firm's quality control and performance standards.

REPORTS

Auditors conclude the audit process by preparing and issuing an audit report and a report on internal control related matters noted during the audit. The audit report, which expresses the auditor's opinion on the financial statements, results from evidence examined; the report on internal control results from significant deficiencies in the design or operation of an entity's internal controls—called "reportable conditions"—that are discovered during the audit engagement.

---

17   K. T. Trotman. "The Review Process and the Accuracy of Auditor Judgments," *Journal of Accounting Research* (Autumn 1985), pp. 740-752; K. T. Trotman and P. W. Yetton. "The Effect of the Review Process on Auditor Judgments," *Journal of Accounting Research* (Spring 1985), pp. 256-267.

18   R. J. Ramsey. "Senior/Manager Differences in Audit Workpaper Performance," *Journal of Accounting Research* (Spring 1994), pp. 127-135.

The auditor's opinion on financial statements and reported deficiencies in internal control should be documented clearly in the audit working papers and communicated on a timely basis. The audit report, required by the fourth standard of reporting, is dated as of the last day of field work. The report on internal control is required by *Statement on Auditing Standards No. 60,* "The Communication of Internal Control Structure Related Matters Noted in an Audit," although only if reportable conditions are detected. Audit reports are discussed in Chapter 3, and reports on internal control (and reportable conditions) are addressed in Chapter 7.

SUMMARY

No competent practitioner would dare issue any of the reports introduced in Chapter 3 without the evidence to back what they're reporting—not CPAs, and certainly not Consumers Union and Underwriters Laboratories, two prototypical suppliers of product quality and safety assurance services. The focus and intent of assurance, attestation, and audit engagements differ markedly, but Montague's ways of knowing suggest that evidence is acquired for all three in common ways: from testimony, intuition, assumption, perception, and practical results. Working papers are the practitioner's means for organizing and cataloging evidence obtained, and provide the principal support for an auditor's conclusions about management's assertions and for their opinion on the financial statements taken as a whole.

The audit process is logical and systematic and is designed to generate audit evidence. The process begins with communication between auditors and the audit committee, a decision to accept or continue an engagement, and preparation of an engagement letter. An auditor then proceeds to obtain an understanding of a client's business and industry, and conducts first- and second-level planning activities over the next few months. Interim audit work, designed to assess control risk, begins after the planning stages, though usually well before year end. Year end audit work, designed to control detection risk through substantive tests of account balances and disclosures, begins near the end of the fiscal year and includes a review for subsequent events. Obtaining representation letters and preparing reports is the final activity of the audit process.

KEY TERMS

Evidential matter   179
Financial statement assertions   180
Existence or occurrence   181
Completeness   181
Rights and obligations   181
Valuation or allocation   181
Presentation and disclosure   181
Audit procedures   182
Tests of controls   184
Substantive tests   184

Tests of details   185
Analytical procedures   185
Dual-purpose tests   187
Working papers   187
Adjusting entries (AJEs)   189
Reclassification entries (RJEs)   189
Audit committee   197
Engagement letter   200
Audit program   206

REFERENCES

Professional Standards

AICPA. *Codification of Statements on Auditing Standards.* New York: AICPA (AU Sec. 311, 313, 315, 325, 326, 329, 333, 334, 336, 337, 339).

SAS No. 7, "Communications Between Predecessor and Successor Auditors" (AU Sec. 315).

SAS No. 11, "Using the Work of a Specialist" (AU Sec. 336).

SAS No. 12, "Inquiry of a Client's Lawyer Concerning Litigation, Claims, and Assessments" (AU Sec. 337).

SAS No. 19, "Client Representations" (AU Sec. 333).

SAS No. 22, "Planning and Supervision" (AU Sec. 311).

SAS No. 31, "Evidential Matter" (AU Sec. 326).

SAS No. 41, "Working Papers" (AU Sec. 339).

SAS No. 45, "Substantive Tests Prior to the Balance Sheet Date" (AU Sec. 313).

SAS No. 45, "Related Parties" (AU Sec. 334).

SAS No. 56, "Analytical Procedures" (AU Sec. 329).

SAS No. 60, "The Communication of Internal Control Structure Related Matters Noted in an Audit" (AU Sec. 325).

SAS No. 77, "Amendments to SAS No. 22, Planning and Supervision, No. 59, The Auditor's Consideration of an Entity's Ability to Continue as a Going Concern, and No. 62, Special Reports."

SAS No. 81, "Amendment to SAS No. 31, Evidential Matter."

Professional Reports

AICPA. *Auditing with Computers.* Auditing Procedures Study, New York: AICPA (1994).

BDO Seidman. *Guide to Forming and Running an Effective Audit Committee.* New York: BDO Seidman.

National Commission on Fraudulent Financial Reporting (The Treadway Commission). *Report of the National Commission on Fraudulent Financial Reporting* (1987).

Articles, Books

Blocher, E., and G. F. Patterson, Jr. "The Use of Analytical Procedures," *Journal of Accountancy* (February 1996), pp. 53-55.

Carcello, J. V., R. H. Hermanson, and N. T. McGrath. "Audit Quality Attributes: The Perception of Audit Partners, Preparers, and Financial Statement Users," *Auditing: A Journal of Practice & Theory* (Spring 1992), pp. 1-15.

Deis, D. R., Jr., and G. A. Giroux. "Determinants of Audit Quality in the Public Sector," *The Accounting Review* (July 1992), pp. 462-479.

Glezen, W., and M. B. Elser. "The Auditor Change Process," *Journal of Accountancy* (June 1996), pp. 73-77.

Godwin, L. "Enhanced Engagement Letters," *Journal of Accountancy* (June 1993), pp. 53-58.

Maletta, M., and A. Wright. "Audit Evidence Planning: An Examination of Industry Error Characteristics," *Auditing: A Journal of Practice & Theory* (Spring 1996), pp. 71-86.

McMullen, D. A. "Audit Committee Performance: An Investigation of the Consequences Associated with Audit Committees," *Auditing: A Journal of Practice & Theory* (Spring 1996), pp. 87-103.

McMullen, D. A., and K. Raghunandan. "Enhancing Audit Committee Effectiveness," *Journal of Accountancy* (August 1996), pp. 79-81.

Schmidt, D. R., R. M. Spindle, and W. F. Yancey. "Tapping the World Wide Web," *Journal of Accountancy* (August 1996), pp. 73-78.

Smith, J. F., and T. Kida. "Heuristics and Biases: Expertise and Task Realism in Auditing," *Psychological Bulletin* (Vol. 109, No. 3, 1991), pp. 472-489.

Whittington, R. "Substantive Analytical Procedures," *Journal of Accountancy* (March 1990), pp. 79-81.

Wilson, A. C. "How Regression Analysis May Be Used as an Analytical Procedure," *The Practical Accountant* (April 1989), pp. 17-24.

QUESTIONS

1. What are *heuristics*, and why are they of concern to auditors?

2. Explain the terms *sufficient, competent*, and *evidential matter* as used in the third standard of field work.
3. An auditor attempts to obtain the most persuasive evidence available. What general criteria can an auditor apply to evaluate the competence of evidence?
4. Identify and briefly explain management's financial statement assertions, and explain the relationship among assertions, audit objectives, and audit procedures.
5. Identify and briefly describe the major files that are typically maintained separately from audit working papers.
6. Explain the major functions of audit working papers.
7. Describe a typical arrangement of working papers.
8. Explain the nature and purpose of an audit committee.
9. Briefly describe an auditor's decision process when deciding to accept or continue an engagement.
10. What are the purposes of an engagement letter?
11. Why does an auditor obtain an understanding of a client's business and industry before beginning an audit engagement?
12. What are the purpose and typical contents of a preliminary audit planning memorandum?
13. What is the objective of the interim phase of an audit engagement?
14. Why is coordination with the client prior to beginning year end audit work especially important?
15. *Subsequent events* occur after the last day of a client's fiscal year and on or before the report date. Why would an auditor be concerned about transactions and events subsequent to the period reported on?

MULTIPLE CHOICE QUESTIONS

1. In 1997 and 1998, an auditor found that approximately 4 percent of processed sales invoices were not mathematically accurate. In late 1998, the client implemented a control requiring that all sales invoices be extended by two independent employees. When planning the 1999 engagement, the auditor estimated a 4 percent error rate for processed sales orders. This is an example of which heuristic?

a. Availability.
b. Anchoring-and-adjustment.
c. Representativeness.
d. Base rate neglect.

2. Which of the following statements about the competence of evidence is always true?

a. Evidence gathered by an auditor from third parties is reliable.
b. Accounting data developed when control risk is low is more relevant than data developed when control risk is high.
c. Oral representations made by management are not valid evidence.
d. To be competent, evidence must be both valid and relevant.

3. Tests of controls:

a. Are intended to detect material misstatements in financial statement accounts.
b. Are concerned with how internal control policies or procedures are applied.
c. Are evaluations of financial information made by a study of plausible relationships among both financial and nonfinancial data.
d. Are procedures that lend hindsight to amounts and information disclosed in financial statements as of the balance sheet date.

4. Substantive tests of details:

a. Are intended to detect material misstatements in financial statement accounts.
b. Are concerned with how internal control policies or procedures are applied.
c. Are evaluations of financial information made by a study of plausible relationships among both financial and nonfinancial data.
d. Are procedures that lend hindsight to amounts and information disclosed in financial statements as of the balance sheet date.

5. Analytical procedures:

a. Are intended to detect material misstatements in financial statement accounts.
b. Are concerned with how internal control policies or procedures are applied.
c. Are evaluations of financial information made by a study of plausible relationships among both financial and nonfinancial data.
d. Are procedures that lend hindsight to amounts and information disclosed in financial statements as of the balance sheet date.

6. A public company's audit committee should consist of:

a. Representatives of management, shareholders, suppliers, and customers.
b. The audit partner, chief financial officer, legal counsel, and at least one outsider.
c. Representatives of the major equity interests (bonds, preferred stock, common stock).
d. Board members who are not officers or employees.

(AICPA Adapted)

7. An independent auditor has been approached to perform an audit. Research suggests that the auditor may fail to:

a. Distinguish between a regulated and nonregulated industry.
b. Coordinate audit dates with the client.
c. Initiate discussion with the predecessor auditor.
d. Establish investigation thresholds for analytical procedures.

8. To avoid misunderstandings between a practitioner and client, engagement arrangements are written in:

a. A legal letter.
b. An engagement letter.
c. A client representation letter.
d. A letter on reportable conditions.

9. Which of the following procedures would an auditor most likely perform when planning an audit?

a. Review prior year audit working papers.
b. Inquire about potential litigation, claims, and assessments.
c. Obtain a representation letter from management.
d. Determine whether internal controls are being applied as prescribed.

(AICPA Adapted)

10. A purpose of reviewing first quarter financial results during audit planning is to:

a. Identify unexpected fluctuations occurring in account balances since the prior year financial statements.
b. Become familiar with accounts likely to appear in the financial statements.
c. Plan evidence to be gathered in auditing accounts that are new to the first quarter financial statements.
d. Assess first quarter financial position, results of operations, and cash flows.

PROBLEMS AND DISCUSSION CASES

6-1 *Cognitive Heuristics*

Andrew Mills, an entry-level staff member with less than six months professional experience, is assigned to audit the cash accounts of Drexel Industries, a long-standing audit client of Rollins, Hunterfield, and Dodge, CPAs. Dodge, the engagement partner, tells Mills, "Drexel is a rather low-risk client. In fact, in all the years I've been associated with Drexel, I don't recall any serious problems, particularly in cash—controls are tight and management is trustworthy. Tell you what, I've got to be away for a few days. I haven't been out to Drexel or even talked with management in months, but why don't you look at last year's papers, and run with it." Following Dodge's advice, Mills copies last year's audit program and follows the procedures explicitly.

Upon returning, Dodge calls Mills and asks, "How did it go?" Mills says, "Fine—things seemed so clean, I only had to talk with management once, and that was just to locate the cash records."

Required: Which, if any, of the cognitive heuristics may apply here? Explain.

6-2 *Cognitive Heuristics*

Alpine Roofing Company, an audit client of Marques, CPA, manufactures two products: tar shingles and aluminum gutters. In examining Alpine's *Reserve for Warranty Guarantees* as of December 31, 1999—that is, the estimated liability for warranty repairs and allowances resulting from 1999 sales—Marques reviews internal quality control and engineering reports and learns the following:

* Alpine processes approximately 75 sales orders per business day for tar shingles and 25 orders for aluminum gutters.
* Warranty repairs and allowances are claimed on about 20 percent of the recorded sales orders for shingles and on 10 percent for gutters, both of which are of concern to management.

Because sales were unusually high in October and more than 25 percent warranty claims for either product could prove damaging to Alpine's reputation, management asks Marques which product, shingles or gutters, is more likely to have more than 25 percent warranty claims resulting from October sales. Marques concludes that tar shingles are more likely to have more than 25 percent claims because shingle sales outperformed gutter sales 3 to 1 in October, just as in the daily estimates.

Required:

1. Which one of the cognitive heuristics—representativeness, availability, or anchoring—may have caused bias in Marques' response? Explain.
2. Is Marques correct? Why, or why not?

6-3 *Cognitive Heuristics*

From data available in the public press, a public accounting firm estimates that undetected management fraud may occur in 20 out of every 1,000 large, publicly traded companies and in 80 out of every 1,000 small, privately owned companies. But because the data may not be wholly reliable, the firm's executive committee decides to poll its regular and small business audit partners at the annual partners' meeting. Regular partners will be surveyed about publicly traded companies, and small business partners will be surveyed about privately owned companies. The survey results will be used to redesign the firm's audit planning checklist, which, in the executive committee's view, does not adequately address the firm's responsibility to detect and report management fraud.

At the annual partners' meeting, all regular audit partners are given a questionnaire which asks the following two questions:

- From your experience, do you believe that the incidence of management fraud in large public companies is:
  a. *More* than 20 out of every 1,000 companies.
  b. *Less* than 20 out of every 1,000 companies.
- What is your estimate of the percentage of large public companies involved in management fraud?

Small business partners were asked the same questions for private companies:

- From your experience, do you believe that the incidence of management fraud in small private companies is:
  a. *More* than 80 out of every 1,000 companies.
  b. *Less* than 80 out of every 1,000 companies.
- What is your estimate of the percentage of small private companies involved in management fraud?

Compiled responses from each partner group indicated the incidence of management fraud was estimated to be 0.025 (2.5 percent) for large public companies and 0.18 (18 percent) for small private companies.

Required:
1. For the survey described, which one or more of the cognitive heuristics—representativeness, availability, or anchoring—could bias the responding partners? Discuss.
2. From the results indicated, have either or both of the partner groups apparently been biased by the heuristic(s) you identified in Question 1? Explain.
3. How could the firm have avoided any suspicion that heuristics might bias the survey results?

6-4 *Audit Evidence*

In a financial statement audit, an independent auditor must judge the validity of audit evidence obtained. Assume you have assessed a low level of control risk.

Required:
1. In the course of an audit, the auditor asks many questions of client officers and employees.
   a. Describe the factors an auditor should consider in evaluating oral evidence provided by officers and employees.
   b. Discuss the validity and limitations of oral evidence.
2. An auditor's tests may include recomputation of various balance sheet and operating ratios for comparison with prior years and industry averages. Discuss the validity and limitations of ratio analysis.
3. An auditor is observing the physical inventory of a manufacturing company's finished goods, which consists of expensive, highly complex equipment. Discuss the validity and limitations of the audit evidence provided by observation.

(AICPA Adapted)

6-5 *Financial Statement Assertions*

Much of an auditor's work during a financial statement audit consists of obtaining and evaluating evidence about the assertions embodied within an entity's financial statements. Following are several tasks or questions considered by an auditor:
1. Observe client personnel count inventory quantities.
2. Include the following statement within the management representation letter: "There are no material transactions that have not been properly recorded in the accounting records underlying the financial statements."
3. For a sample of product lines, trace prices used in the final priced inventory to recent invoice prices.

4. Do the financial statements include separate captions for raw materials, work in process, and finished goods inventory?

5. Confirm inventory held in public warehouses.

Required: For each of the tasks or questions indicate and discuss the dominant financial statement assertion addressed.

6-6 *Identifying Audit Procedures*

Auditors frequently refer to the terms "standards" and "procedures." Auditing standards relate to the measures of quality achieved in an engagement, and auditing procedures to the methods or techniques used by the auditor to gather evidence.

Required: Identify and discuss procedures an auditor typically uses in a financial statement audit.

6-7 *Underlying Accounting Data and Corroborating Information*

The third generally accepted auditing standard of field work requires that an auditor obtain sufficient competent evidential matter to afford a reasonable basis for an opinion regarding the financial statements audited. In considering what constitutes sufficient competent evidential matter, a distinction is often made between underlying accounting data and corroborating information available to the auditor.

Required: Discuss underlying accounting data, corroborating information available to the auditor, and the methods by which the auditor gathers competent evidential matter.

6-8 *Audit Procedures*

The purpose of all auditing procedures is to gather sufficient competent evidence for an auditor to form an opinion on an entity's financial statements taken as a whole.

Required: Using the format below, identify and describe the auditing procedures used most commonly in audit practice:

(AICPA Adapted)

Procedure	Description

6-9 *Analytical Procedures*

Analytical procedures consist of evaluations of financial information made by a study of plausible relationships among both financial and nonfinancial data. These procedures range from simple comparisons to complex models involving many relationships, and involve comparing recorded amounts, or ratios developed from recorded amounts, to expectations developed by the auditors.

Required:

1. Describe the broad purposes of analytical procedures.

2. Identify the sources of information from which an auditor develops expectations.

(AICPA Adapted)

6-10 *The Purpose of Audit Programs*

The first generally accepted standard of field work requires, in part, that "the work is to be adequately planned," and an audit program is one tool auditors use to plan audit work.

Required: What is an audit program, and what purposes does it serve?

6-11 *Working Paper Review*

Adam Fionte, an entry-level staff member in a public accounting firm, prepared the following working paper, the lead sheet, for J&K Sales Co., Inc., for December 31, 1998 trade accounts receivable:

Accounts Receivable

	Adjusted Balance 12/31/97	Balance Per Bks 12/31/98	Adjs./ Reclass Dr<Cr>	Adjusted Balance 12/31/98
Accounts Rec.: Trade Regular Customers	$450,000	$657,985		$ 657,985c
Special Discount Customers	105,000	135,760	(9,500)	126,260c
Allowance for Doubtful Accounts	(35,000)	(65,000)		(65,000)c
	$520,000	$728,745	$(9,500)	$ (719,245)c
	f	f	f	f

c Crosscast/AF
f Footed/AF

Required: Discuss the deficiencies in this working paper.

6-12 *Working Paper Review*

Following is an audit working paper that documents an auditor's test for *kiting*, an intentional irregularity that conceals cash shortages by transferring funds from one bank (or company) to another, recording the receipt on or before the balance sheet date, and recording the disbursement after the balance sheet date.

Elliot Enterprises   A9
December 31, 1999

Ck. No.	Transferred From	To	Amount	Disbursement Date Per Books	Disbursement Date Per Bank	Receipt Date Per Books	Receipt Date Per Bank
Interbank Transfers							
1021	Society Bank	St. Joe Bank *A5*	5,500	12/30#	01/02	12/30@	01/02&
1246	St. Joe Bank	Trust Corp. *A6*	15,000	12/31#	01/02	12/31@	01/02&
1524	Society Bank	Union Bank	7,500	12/31#	01/02	12/31@	01/02&
Intercompany Transfers							
4678	Westco (Subsidiary)	Elliot *A8*	25,000	01/01#	01/02	12/31@	01/02&

& Agreed to bank statement/RC
# Agreed to cash disbursement records/RC
@ Agreed to cash receipts records/RC

Required: Discuss the deficiencies in this working paper.

6-13 *The Purpose and Content of Working Papers*

Preparing working papers is an integral part of a financial statement audit.

Required:

1. a. What are the purposes or functions of audit working papers?
   b. What records may be included in audit working papers?

2. What factors affect the auditor's judgment about the type and content of working papers appropriate for a particular engagement?
3. Discuss the relationship between audit working papers and each of the standards of field work.
4. You are instructing an inexperienced staff member whose first auditing assignment is to audit an account. An analysis of the account has been prepared by the client for inclusion in the audit working papers. Prepare a list of the information and notations that the staff member should include in the account analysis to provide an adequate working paper as evidence of work accomplished. (Do not include a description of auditing procedures applicable to the account.)

(AICPA Adapted)

6-14 *Audit Planning*

In late spring of 1998, you are assigned as the in-charge auditor of your firm's recurring annual audit of a major client, the Lancer Company. You are given the engagement letter for the audit covering the calendar year ending December 31, 1998, and a list of personnel assigned to the engagement. Your responsibility is to plan and supervise field work for the engagement.

Required: Discuss the sources you should consult in preparing and planning the Lancer Company engagement, the type of information you should seek, the preliminary plans and preparations you should make for the field work, and the agenda you should plan for a preliminary meeting with staff assigned to the engagement.

(AICPA Adapted)

6-15 *Predecessor and Successor Auditors*

The audit committee of the board of directors of Unicorn Corp. asked Tish & Field, CPAs, to audit Unicorn's financial statements for the year ended December 31, 1998. Tish & Field explained the need to make an inquiry of the predecessor auditor and requested permission to do so. Unicorn's management agreed and authorized the predecessor auditor to respond fully to Tish & Field's inquiries.

After communicating with the predecessor auditor, Tish & Field drafted an engagement letter that was mailed to the audit committee of Unicorn's board of directors. The engagement letter set forth arrangements concerning the involvement of the predecessor auditor and other matters.

Required:
1. What information should Tish & Field have obtained during their inquiry of the predecessor auditor prior to accepting the engagement?
2. Describe what other matters Tish & Field would likely have included in the engagement letter.

(AICPA Adapted)

6-16 *Audit Committees*

For many years the financial and accounting community has recognized the importance of, and has endorsed forming, audit committees. Today, audit committees are quite common. Independent auditors have become increasingly involved with audit committees and consequently have become familiar with their nature and function.

Required:
1. What is an audit committee?
2. Identify the reasons why audit committees have been formed and are used currently.
3. What are the functions of an audit committee?

6-17 *The Decision to Accept an Engagement*

Jones is approached by a prospective client who wishes to engage him to perform an audit that in prior years was performed by another auditor.

Required: Discuss the procedures Jones should follow in accepting or declining the engagement.

(AICPA Adapted)

6-18 *Using Specialists*

Tom Majors, an entry-level staff auditor, has been assigned to observe the physical inventory of the Lewiston Chemical Company. Lewiston processes and distributes industrial chemicals.

Upon arriving at Lewiston's manufacturing plant, Majors learns that there are 15 above ground cylindrical-shaped storage tanks, each 50 feet tall, and there are three rectangular storage tanks located underground. The above ground tanks are connected in lots of five, and there are three different chemicals at the site; the underground pipes stretch over two miles in length. The underground pipes can be accessed at each of the tanks, and also at various access ports throughout the plant.

In addition to the tanks and pipes, there is a shipping/receiving depot. Three separate pipelines run to the depot so that each of the chemicals can be accessed for shipping and receiving. Tank trucks are used to deliver and ship chemicals to and from the depot.

Required:

1. Indicate the special audit problems Majors faces when observing Lewiston's chemical inventory.
2. Discuss what specialist(s) Majors should consider using to assist in the physical inventory observation. State specifically what problems the specialist(s) will be assigned to solve.

RESEARCH PROJECTS

1. USING THE INTERNET TO UNDERSTAND A CLIENT'S INDUSTRY

In the information age, an auditor has a wealth of readily accessible data available to help understand a client's business and industry, particularly for industries not served previously by the auditor. But what once had been done with newspapers, magazines, and hardbound volumes, can now be done instantaneously using a search engine, such as *Lycos, Magellan, or Yahoo!* that accesses links to and about a variety of industries such as aerospace, agriculture, apparel, entertainment, real estate, telecommunications, or transportation.

Required:

Select an industry that interests you. Prepare a report that:

1. Identifies and summarizes key news issues that would bear on an auditor engaged in the industry. For example, news that foreign crude oil exploration slowdowns had driven artificial price supports could affect an oil & gas refining client's oil supplies. Or, news of rising interest rates could affect a construction client's new housing starts.
2. For three companies in the industry:
   a. Summarize the companies' major products, and explain how the news you identify above could bear on the companies' results of operations.
   b. Summarize the companies' most recent reported financial results, and explain whether the news you identify above is good or bad for the companies' results of operations.

2. RESEARCH AND AUDIT PRACTICE

Throughout this chapter numerous references are made to audit research that lends insight into audit practice. For example, we learn from research that cognitive biases and working paper order affect audit decision-making, that successor auditors some-times fail to initiate communication with predecessor auditors, and that companies in regulated industries may have fewer financial statement errors than companies in nonregulated industries. Research in auditing appears in a variety of journals, including *Auditing: A Journal of Practice & Theory (A:AJP&T)*, *The Accounting Review (AR)*, and the *Journal of Accounting Research (JAR)*. Although the research methods described in articles appearing in these journals can be inaccessible to some nonresearchers, the abstracts, introductions, and conclusions are intended to be accessible to all interested readers.

Required: Select one of the steps in the audit process listed in Figures 6-9, 6-12, 6-13, and 6-14. For the step selected, locate at least two related articles from *A:AJP&T*, *AR*, and/or *JAR*, and prepare a report that summarizes how the articles add to your understanding of the audit process.

7

Internal Control and Computer Information Systems

Major topics discussed in this chapter are the:

- Types of computer information systems confronted in practice today, including microcomputers, local area networks, database management systems, end user computing, telecommunications, service bureaus, and Internet technology.
- Assurance services related to information systems, and attestation services related to internal control.
- Nature of internal control.
- *COSO Report's* components of internal control: the control environment, risk assessment, control activities, information and communication, and monitoring.
- Auditor's consideration of internal control.
- Computer assisted tests of controls.
- Communication of reportable conditions and material weaknesses in internal control.

Most all of the assurance, attestation, and audit services offered by public accounting firms today use evidence processed by computer information systems. This chapter identifies common computer systems, addresses assurance and attestation services related to information systems and internal control, and explains an auditor's approach to considering internal control in a financial statement audit. The chapter begins by introducing microcomputers, local area networks (LANs), database management systems, end user computing, telecommunications, service bureaus, and Internet technology, and by discussing related assurance and attestation services. In turn, the chapter introduces internal control and the five components of internal control identified by the *Committee of Sponsoring Organizations (COSO) of the Treadway Commission*. Next, the chapter describes an auditor's responsibility to consider internal control in a financial statement audit, focusing in particular on a question crucial to an auditor's planning for the year end phase of an audit engagement: What is the assessed level of control risk and, correspondingly, is the assessed level sufficiently low to allow a higher level of detection risk, thereby permitting the auditor to relax the nature, timing, and extent of substantive tests?

COMPUTER INFORMATION SYSTEMS

In practice today, businesses rely heavily on computer systems that differ both in technology and in processing capability. The following introduces several computer information systems that practitioners often confront and discusses developments in information software.

MICROCOMPUTERS

Sometimes referred to as personal computers (PCs), microcomputers today are powerful, affordable, and provide a cost-effective information processing alternative for entities that might otherwise be constrained by manual processing. Today, many small entities—among them retail pharmacies, town boards, and local real estate brokerage firms—handle all of their data processing needs with a single, stand-alone, desktop PC that may include 40 megabytes of RAM (random access memory), a one (or more) gigabyte hard drive, CD-ROM and diskette drives, and a letter quality laser printer.

LOCAL AREA NETWORKS (LANS)

To increase processing capability economically, microcomputers can be linked into **local area networks (LANs)** that access files and software from a central *file server* and direct print jobs from a central *print server*. LANs increase an entity's processing power-to-cost ratio because each linked microcomputer—called a *workstation*—shares application software, data files, and peripherals such as e-mail, facsimile boards, optical scanners, and printers. Today, LANs are common in entities where data files, software, and peripherals are accessed by a number of end users physically located within a single building or adjacent buildings. However, networks need not be restricted to local areas. For example, many large, multinational companies link local area networks into *wide area networks (WANs)* that allow access across LANs and to public databases.

DATABASE MANAGEMENT (DBM) SYSTEMS

Introduced in Chapter 6, **database management (DBM) systems** are an integrated collection of stored data—a database, which is organized by means of relationships among the data, not by the location of bits of stored data. Among the advantages of database systems is that they avoid unnecessary redundancy in data files. For example, in a college or university, data about a student—such as name, student identification number, address, and telephone number—could be included in several files, among them current semester registration files, tuition files, financial aid files, dormitory deposit files, automobile registration files, and library circulation files. A database management system eliminates data redundancy by storing relevant data in a single record, which authorized end users can then access with software.

END USER COMPUTING

In most microcomputer, LAN, or database management systems, end users access software that is purchased (or written and tested) by management. However, some entities also use **end user computing**, in which management empowers end users to develop task-specific application software. For example, in a mid-size bank served by a local access network, a commercial loan officer might write software to analyze loan-loss risk for the local recreational vehicle industry. End user computing demands that management implement controls over end user access to data files that lie beyond the end user's responsibility and authority.

TELECOMMUNICATIONS

Many entities use **telecommunications** to transmit alphanumeric, voice, video, facsimile and other data by wire, fiber optics, microwave stations, satellites, or laser. Telecommunications applications offer access to markets, information, and transactions not otherwise accessible by other information systems. Today, a variety of telecommunications links are used commonly, including *electronic data interchange (EDI)* systems that link trading partners (purchasers and sellers) without using paper and without incurring handling costs (Chapter 6); *point of sale (POS)* systems in the retail industry that link customers to price and order-entry information; *electronic funds transfer (EFT)* systems in the banking industry; and commercial on-line databases that offer access to financial news, market price quotations, and credit ratings.

SERVICE BUREAUS

Service bureaus provide computer services to entities wishing either to supplement limited internal computer capabilities or to outsource processing to outside vendors. For example, a construction contractor might outsource payroll and billing to a service bureau, but process accounts payable in house. In local area networks and end user computing, computers are owned or leased by the client and physically housed on site. However, the use of service bureaus creates an additional problem for auditors: because an audit client's accounting data are processed through the service bureau's computer, the service bureau's internal controls are part of the client's internal controls. To alleviate the logistical problem of many auditors descending on a single service bureau to consider internal control, large service bureaus commonly engage one independent auditor to report on the service bureau's internal controls, and the auditors of the bureau's customers rely on that report. *Statement on Auditing Standards No. 70,* "Reports on the Processing of Transactions by Service Organizations," provides guidance on preparing and using reports on service bureaus.

INTERNET TECHNOLOGY

Of the information systems discussed above, local area networks (LANs) have had the most impact on businesses and therefore on practitioners. However, there is ample reason to believe that LANs, among other information systems, may one day be as obsolete as the 80-column IBM cards of the 1960s. What's at work is the proliferation of technologies designed to service the Internet. For example, PCs and LANs rely on application software that is stored physically within the PC or on file servers. However, the Internet offers an alternative: import application software using an *integrated services digital network (ISDN)*, a high-speed phone line that can accommodate far more data than a traditional analog phone line. Some companies have leveraged the technology into *intranets*, linking coworkers in applications and communications around the globe. For example, Levi Strauss & Co. links approximately 10,000 employees worldwide, and intranets have been installed at Lockheed Martin, an aerospace company, and at Merrill Lynch & Co., a brokerage firm.[1] Although technological change is difficult to predict, that there *will be* change is not. The practitioner's task is to stay ahead of the technology curve.

SOFTWARE FOR INFORMATION SYSTEMS

Computer software, particularly operating software and application software, controls how computers are used. *Operating software* is a group of computer programs that monitors and controls all input, processing, and output operations. For example, many IBM compatible personal computers are operated by Microsoft Windows. In contrast, *application software* interacts with operating software to perform specific tasks, like processing customer orders, making airline reservations, scanning product codes at grocery checkout counters, or word processing.

Since the 1950s, computer software has matured through several generations of languages. The first generation, *machine languages,* consisted of simple strings of binary digits—*0s* and *1s* used to represent negative and positive electrical charges. Interestingly, the only language computers understand even today is machine language, although programmers now write software in higher generation languages that translate commands into machine language. The second generation, *assembly languages,* originated in the 1950s and consisted of symbolic codes translated by assemblers into machine-readable form. Although assembly languages are still used somewhat today, higher generation languages now dominate. Developed in the 1960s, third generation *procedural languages* were designed to meet application requirements in specific professions—for example, FORTRAN (for "formula translation") in the sciences, and COBOL (for "common business oriented language") in business. A number of computer applications used today were written using third generation languages.

Fourth generation languages (sometimes called *4GLs*) focus not on *how* a task ought to be performed (the role of first, second, and third generation languages), but on *what is to be done,* and they create at least one distinct advantage for the programmer: significantly fewer lines of code than third generation languages, often as few as one-tenth the number of lines. Today, 4GLs are user-friendly, easy to learn, easy to debug, and readily accessible by nonprofessionals. Developed more recently, a fifth generation of computer languages draws from stored knowledge bases (like tax laws or accounting rules) and accomplishes intelligent tasks (i.e., artificial intelligence). While it is not altogether necessary for an auditor to understand computer languages, it is appropriate to have a general understanding of developments that affect the processing of accounting information, since they have implications for an entity's internal controls.

ASSURANCE AND ATTESTATION SERVICES

Information systems have long been *the* single most important consulting market served by public accounting firms, although never more than in the past

---

S. Zarowin. "The New Computer," *Journal of Accountancy* (March 1996), pp. 51-52.

half decade as a result of developments in information technology, including networks, telecommunications, and fourth generation programming languages. Interestingly, developments in information technology have also led to new markets for assurance services, some of which some firms have entered already. New services offered independently by Bell Atlantic Corp., Deloitte & Touche, and Coopers & Lybrand help illustrate.

ASSURANCE SERVICES AND INFORMATION TECHNOLOGY

Bell Atlantic, among other of the regional Bell operating companies, markets a full suite of Internet services designed both for businesses and for consumers.[2] The business services include high-speed links to global markets, home page management on the Internet's World Wide Web, and one-button access to Netscape and Microsoft browser services. Coincident with Bell Atlantic's announcement, Deloitte & Touche and software developer Gradient Technologies partnered to offer *secure password access* by client network servers to the Internet,[3] and Coopers & Lybrand performed a *privacy audit* for Firefly Network, a Cambridge, MA, firm that uses intelligent-agent software to profile and shield the privacy of Internet users.[4]

Coopers & Lybrand's privacy audit is part of the firm's Internet Assurance Services practice, a line of business that includes data security assurances for companies that trade on the Internet. For example, Narrowline, a Web-based advertising brokerage, links Internet advertising-media suppliers with media buyers to facilitate low cost purchases of electronic advertising. Narrowline contracted with Coopers & Lybrand to perform quarterly assurance services about Narrowline's electronic architecture, thereby adding credibility to the company's control procedures over data security, confidentiality, and accountability to suppliers and buyers.[5] The services offered by Bell Atlantic, Deloitte & Touche, and Coopers & Lybrand point to a growing market for assurance services related to the *security* of information transmitted over the Internet through telecommunications channels that are exposed both to surveillance and to data piracy.

The profession's preemptive strike into new assurance markets will not likely be independent of developments in information technology. For example, the AICPA *Future Issues Committee* has observed that, "Given the technological developments and our increasing information-based society, CPAs will become more involved with information technology. In order to remain competitive in such an environment, firms will have to acquire access to technological developments . . . The demands for information management must be met to ensure the profession's continued relevance."[6] Interestingly, the profession's rich history with information systems in general and with internal control in particular offer ample reason to be optimistic about the profession's continued relevance. For example, in 1997 the AICPA *Special Committee on*

2   J. Sandberg, "Bell Atlantic Enters the Internet Arena, Planning Links for Business, Consumers," *The Wall Street Journal* (April 11, 1996), p. B5.
3   "D & T Pushes Internet/Intranet Security Services," *Public Accounting Report* (March 31, 1996), p. 3.
4   "Coopers & Lybrand Searches for Net Profit," *Public Accounting Report* (October 31, 1996), p. 2.
5   "C & L's Net Practice Snares Assurance Client," *The Public Accounting Report* (December 15, 1996), p. 3.
6   AICPA Future Issues Committee, *Strategic Thrusts for the Future*, 2nd edition (May 1991).

Assurance Services (the Elliott Committee) suggested several new services that the profession may have a comparative advantage in offering, among them electronic commerce assurance. Soon thereafter, the AICPA appointed Everett Johnson, Deloitte & Touche international director of computer assurance service, chair of an Electronic Commerce Task Force charged to design practice guidelines for CPAs.

ATTESTATION SERVICES AND INTERNAL CONTROL

In practice, certified public accountants have routinely issued two different types of reports on internal control, one an audit-related service and one an attestation service. The first, discussed and illustrated later in the chapter, is required in all financial statement audits by *SAS No. 60*: a report to the audit committee of the board of directors about significant deficiencies in internal control, called **reportable conditions**, discovered during an audit that could adversely affect the entity's ability to record, process, summarize, and report financial data. Rather than express an opinion on an audit client's internal control, an *SAS No. 60* report simply identifies reportable conditions that were noted during the financial statement audit.

In the second, an attestation engagement that addresses *all* of an entity's control activities (not just the subset of controls considered during an audit), a practitioner issues a report expressing an *opinion* on whether management's assertion about the effectiveness of internal control is fairly stated in all material respects. The following report illustrates standard introductory, scope, inherent limitation, and opinion paragraphs used by Ernst & Young, LLP for CoreStates Financial Corp.:

CoreStates Financial Corp.
Ernst & Young

The Board of Directors and Shareholders
CoreStates Financial Corp.

We have examined management's assertion that CoreStates Financial Corp. maintained an effective internal control structure over financial reporting as of December 31, 1994, included in the accompanying Management's Report on Internal Control over Financial Reporting, insofar as management's assertion relates to the internal control structure over the annual financial reporting in the 1994 consolidated financial statements of CoreStates Financial Corp.

Our examination was made in accordance with standards established by the American Institute of Certified Public Accountants and, accordingly, included obtaining an understanding of the internal control structure over financial reporting; testing, and evaluating the design and operating effectiveness of internal control; and such other procedures as we considered necessary in the circumstances. We believe that our examination provides a reasonable basis for our opinion.

Because of inherent limitations in any internal control structure, errors or frauds may occur and not be detected. Also, projections of any evaluation of internal control structure over financial reporting to future periods are subject to the risk that the internal control structure may become inadequate because of changes in conditions, or that the degree of compliance with the policies or procedures may deteriorate.

In our opinion, management's assertion that CoreStates Financial Corp. maintained effective internal control over financial reporting as of December 31, 1994,

> insofar as management's assertions relate to the internal control structure over the annual financial reporting in the 1994 consolidated financial statements of CoreStates Financial Corp., is fairly stated, in all material respects, based upon criteria established in "Internal Control: Integrated Framework" issued by the Committee of Sponsoring Organizations (COSO) of the Treadway Commission.

Notice that Ernst & Young's opinion (fourth paragraph) refers to criteria in *Internal Control: Integrated Framework* issued by the *Committee of Sponsoring Organizations (COSO) of the Treadway Commission*. Discussed in detail in the following sections, the *COSO Report* is the most comprehensive document issued on internal control to date.

For four decades, the profession has argued the advisability of *mandatory* public reporting on internal control, and the corresponding need for attestation reports similar to the one Ernst & Young issued for CoreStates Financial Corp. In the 1970s and 1980s, the main players in the debate were the *Commission on Auditors' Responsibilities* (the Cohen Commission), the AICPA, and the SEC, among others, and their arguments have been chronicled in the professional literature.[7]

Although the AICPA and the SEC remain as major influences in the debate, new players include the *Commission on Fraudulent Financial Reporting* (the Treadway Commission), the U.S. General Accounting Office, and the Federal Deposit Insurance Corporation (FDIC), all of whom have called for mandatory public reports.[8] To date, only one has succeeded: the FDIC, which, through the *FDIC Improvement Act,* a response to the savings and loan debacle of the 1980s, requires public reporting for federally insured banks and thrifts with assets exceeding $150 million. Today, about one in four public companies and three in five *Fortune 500* companies voluntarily report on internal control. However, except for the banking industry, there remains no requirement for mandatory public reporting.

INTERNAL CONTROL: THE COSO REPORT

In 1992, following three years of extensive study, the *Committee of Sponsoring Organizations (COSO)* of the *Commission on Fraudulent Financial Reporting* (the Treadway Commission, introduced in Chapter 5) issued a four-volume document, *Internal Control: Integrated Framework,* commonly referred to as the *COSO Report*. The *COSO Report* provides a framework against which entities can assess their internal controls and, for the first time ever, establishes a *common* definition of internal control that serves the needs of a variety of groups, including directors, management, internal auditors, independent accountants, legislators, and regulators, rather than fragmented definitions that serve the needs of only one group, as had been the case in the past. No document on

---

7   L. M. Savoie and D. N. Ricchiute, "Reports by Management: Voluntary or Mandatory?" *Journal of Accountancy* (May 1981), pp. 84-94.

8   "The COSO Report: Challenge and Counterchallenge," *Journal of Accountancy* (February 1993), pp. 10-18, reprints two pointed letters exchanged by the GAO, which favors public reporting, and COSO, which does not. The letters bear directly on the debate in the 1990s.

internal control issued before (and likely none that may appear hereafter) has been so far-reaching in scope, not even *Statement on Auditing Standards No. 55*, "Consideration of the Internal Control Structure in a Financial Statement Audit," since, although authoritative, *SAS No. 55* serves but one group: independent auditors.

DEFINITION

The *COSO Report* defines **internal control** as "a process, effected by an entity's board of directors, management and other personnel, designed to provide reasonable assurance regarding the achievement of objectives in the following categories:

- Effectiveness and efficiency of operations.
- Reliability of financial reporting.
- Compliance with applicable laws and regulations."[9]

The definition embodies four key concepts. First, internal control is a *process* (not a single event) integrated within (not added onto) another process: the process management uses to plan, to execute transactions and events, and to monitor results. An auditor considers internal control in every financial statement audit, but the responsibility to establish and maintain control is management's, not the independent auditor's. Second, internal control is accomplished by *people* at every level of the organization, including the board of directors, management, and staff employees. As a result, the effectiveness of internal control can be diminished by the inherent limitations of people. For example, even the most logically designed and carefully implemented internal controls may be undermined by employee errors, by management's intentional acts to circumvent the controls, by mistakes in judgment, and by misunderstandings. Third, rather than an end in itself, internal control is a means to achieving an entity's *objectives*, most of which generally fall within three categories: (1) operations objectives (e.g., market share, return on investment, product or service diversification), (2) financial reporting objectives (e.g., producing reliable financial statements), and (3) compliance objectives (e.g., compliance with laws and regulations). Fourth, internal controls can be expected to provide *reasonable, but not absolute, assurance* that objectives will be accomplished, since the benefits expected from some controls (for example, reduced risk of employee petty theft) may not be worth the cost of implementation.

COMPONENTS OF INTERNAL CONTROL

In addition to defining internal control, the *COSO Report* also identifies and describes five interrelated components of internal control that are—or should be—integrated within the management process.

- Control environment.
- Risk assessment.

9   Committee of Sponsoring Organizations (COSO) of the Treadway Commission. *Internal Control: Integrated Framework. Framework.* New York: COSO, 1992, p. 9.

- Control activities.
- Information and communication.
- Monitoring.

CONTROL ENVIRONMENT

An entity's **control environment** represents management's and the board of directors' attitude (i.e., what's the "tone at the top"?), awareness (e.g., do they know how cash is controlled?), and actions (e.g., does management implement internal auditors' recommendations?) about internal control. The control environment captures the importance of control in management's operating style. For example, an active audit committee, a competent internal audit department, and direct management control over the authority delegated to employees would all suggest that management is committed to effective internal control.

The auditor's objective in considering an entity's control environment is to obtain an understanding of management's and the board of directors' attitude, awareness, and actions concerning:

- Integrity and ethical values. For example, do codes of conduct describe acceptable business practice, conflicts of interest, and standards of ethical behavior?
- Commitment and competence. For example, are employees committed to quality?
- Board of directors or audit committee. For example, is the board independent of management?
- Management's philosophy and operating style. For example, what is management's attitude toward manipulated or falsified records?
- Organizational structure. For example, does information flow to the appropriate levels of management?
- Assignment of authority and responsibility. For example, are the responsibilities of key managers defined?
- Human resource policies and practices. For example, are there policies for hiring, training, promoting and compensating employees?

For some entities, an auditor may have additional concerns, such as the need for a nonprofit organization to comply with laws and regulations governing their direct federal grants. And for others, like a small owner-managed service company, there may be a strong sense of integrity and ethical values even though there is no written code of conduct.

RISK ASSESSMENT

Every entity faces risks, both external, such as technological developments and changing customer demands, and internal, such as employee pilferage and computer down time. Management's task is to identify the risks that bear on their operations, financial reporting, and compliance objectives and to take the action necessary to manage them. For example, following are risks management might confront solely as a result of managing change:

- Changed operating environment. For example, divestiture in the telecommunications industry.

- New personnel. For example, a new senior executive may not fully understand the entity's culture.
- New information systems. For example, unusually tight time constraints in redesigning systems software.
- Rapid growth. For example, capacity constraints may lead to excessive back orders.
- New technology. For example, just-in-time inventory may lead to production delays.
- New products or services. For example, unfamiliar services may impose unfamiliar risks.
- Corporate restructuring. For example, a leveraged buyout may be accompanied by staff reductions and inadequate supervision.
- Foreign operations. For example, the control environment in a foreign subsidiary may be driven by local customs and culture.

Although these risks are crucial to the entity, they're less problematic to an auditor, whose primary concern is audit risk (Chapter 2). However, an entity's response to managing change can influence the auditor's consideration of an entity's ability to continue as a going concern (Chapter 3).

CONTROL ACTIVITIES

Control activities (also called control procedures) are those policies and procedures in addition to the control environment and the information system that management establishes to provide reasonable assurance that their objectives are achieved. The independent auditor's objective is to understand an entity's control activities sufficiently to plan the audit.

In practice, control activities take various forms and have various objectives depending on the entity's business and industry. For example, daily "flash" reports, a control activity prepared by a parts distributor's regional managers and forwarded to the national sales manager, serve both to accrue sales commissions, an operations objective, and to record sales, a financial reporting objective. Generally, control activities are established over the: (1) authorization and execution of transactions, (2) segregation of duties, (3) design and use of documents and records, and (4) access to assets and records.

Transaction Authorization

All transactions should be authorized by responsible personnel acting within the scope of their prescribed authority and responsibility. Without a formal system of transaction authorization, any employee could commit resources without regard to the entity's objectives.

The type of authorization, specific or general, required for a transaction (or series of related transactions) depends on the nature, scope, and frequency of occurrence. *Specific authorization* means authorization is required each time the transaction is proposed and is typically used for unusual, material, or infrequent projects. For example, specific authorization might be required for plant expansion, purchases or sales of subsidiaries, or capital asset purchases in excess of a designated amount. In contrast, *general authorization* means the entity has policies and procedures that personnel should follow to determine if a proposed transaction or project is authorized in general. For example, an entity may have authorized pricing and credit-sale policies, and personnel may complete transactions meeting these prescribed policies without first obtaining specific authorization. General authorization avoids the inefficiencies of specifically reauthorizing routine transactions. No proposed transaction should be executed without first having general or specific authorization.

Authorization is not the same as approval—they're sequential though related events. Authorization means authority has been given to acquire or expend resources. *Approval*, in contrast, means the conditions for authorization have been met and resources may therefore be acquired or expended. For example, an employee might approve payment of a vendor's invoice for materials acquired to anchor a capital asset acquisition specifically authorized by the board of directors. Transaction authorization usually precedes approval, although they may occur simultaneously.

Segregation of Duties

No set of policies and procedures can prevent **collusion**, a fraud perpetrated by two or more employees, each of whom is necessary to complete the scheme. For example, even if different employees authorize, execute, and record cash payments, no information system could prevent them from conspiring to transact a fraudulent payment and sharing the misappropriated funds. As a result, preventing collusion is not usually an objective of an entity's system of internal control. The best alternative is the segregation of responsibilities to prevent any one employee, acting alone, from committing and concealing frauds. Optimum **segregation of duties** exists when collusion is necessary to circumvent controls.

To achieve optimum segregation of responsibilities, an entity's management, custodial, accounting, and monitoring functions should be performed by different employees. That is, the following responsibilities would be separated:

- Transaction authorization (a management function)
- Transaction execution (a custodial function)
- Transaction recording (an accounting function)
- Independent checks on performance (a monitoring function)

If any one employee were responsible for all four functions, his or her opportunities to misappropriate assets would be nearly limitless. If any one employee were responsible for three or for two functions, his or her opportunities would diminish progressively but would not vanish. Optimum segregation of duties would suggest that no employee be responsible for any more than one function, because:

- Restricting employee responsibility to one function means at least four different employees are required to authorize, execute, record, and check a transaction. Thus, a system of checks and balances reevaluates the validity of a transaction four separate times. If two, three, or four functions are performed by a single employee, the system of checks and balances becomes progressively weaker.
- The more employees required to complete a transaction, the more employees necessary to commit and conceal frauds, and it is reasonable to assume that employees are less apt to attempt collusion as the number of employees required to commit fraud increases. In cases of fraud, there is no safety in numbers, since, as the number of perpetrators increases, so too does the risk of exposure.

Design and Use of Documents and Records

To obtain accurate and reliable accounting data, transactions must be recorded promptly in the accounting periods and in dollar amounts actually executed, and classified properly in subsidiary and control accounts. Satisfying these requirements, however, depends on documents and accounting records that accurately reflect all executed transactions. Documents and records are evidence of executed transactions and collectively represent the **audit trail** that is so critical to an auditor when tracing transactions through an accounting system.

In computer systems, though, audit trails can be eliminated or otherwise distorted, since many hard copy documents and records common to manual systems are unnecessary. For example, many companies use employee time clocks that are on-line, allowing employees to punch in and out with magnetic identification cards; the system automatically accumulates and transfers hours worked to payroll. Because all payroll information is stored within the system's computer, employee time cards—source documents common to manual payroll systems—are not used, thereby eliminating a segment of the audit trail otherwise available to auditors in manual systems. With audit trails eliminated or distorted, auditors are often unable to trace the flow of transactions explicitly from source documents to journal entries and to general ledger postings. As a result, rather than focus on audit trails when auditing in computer systems, auditors focus on management's controls over the system, testing whether the controls are adequate and, therefore, whether the system is likely to be effective.

The design of documents and accounting records can have considerable impact on how efficiently an accounting system operates, and therefore on how efficiently an audit can be performed. For example, hard copy documents and records should be:

- Designed for multiple use if possible, thereby minimizing the number used,
- Prenumbered consecutively, thereby providing a control over those unused and missing, and
- Relatively easy to complete, thereby encouraging employees to complete them accurately.

The transaction recording process and the accounting records should be described clearly and unambiguously in a *procedures manual*. The purpose of a procedures manual is to encourage consistent use and completion of prescribed accounting records and documents and to provide a ready reference for newly hired personnel. A procedures manual can also represent an important reference for auditors attempting to determine how an entity's control activities are intended to operate.

Access to Assets and Records

Only authorized personnel should have access to assets and records. Several means can be used to limit access, including protection devices, on-line recording, and access codes. *Protection devices* restrict unauthorized personnel from gaining direct access to assets. For example, locked storerooms could restrict access to parts inventories, and fireproof vaults to petty cash vouchers. *On-line recording* limits access to assets and records by limiting the number of employees involved in recording and posting transactions. For example, optical-scan cash registers record cash sales both within the cash register and in off-site computer files, creating two records of a single transaction and yet requiring only one employee. *Access codes*, such as employee identification and personal identification (PIN) numbers, restrict access to data that could be used to alter records or to misappropriate assets.

INFORMATION AND COMMUNICATION

To operate efficiently, an entity needs to identify, capture, and communicate both external and internal information in a form and time frame that enables people to discharge their assigned responsibilities. External information includes market share, regulatory requirements, and customer complaints. Internal information, the source of most audit evidence, includes the **accounting system**, which consists of the methods and records established by management to record and report transactions and events and to maintain accountability for assets and liabilities. To be effective, an accounting system should: (1) include methods and records that will identify all valid transactions, (2) record them in the proper accounting period, and (3) describe them on a timely basis and in sufficient detail to permit proper classification, to measure the transaction properly, and to present summarized transactions and related disclosures accurately in the financial statements. The auditor's objective in considering an entity's accounting system is to obtain an understanding of:

- Major classes of transactions,
- How transactions are initiated,
- The records, documents, and accounts used in the processing and reporting of transactions,
- The processing of transactions, and
- Financial reporting procedures.

The central activity of most businesses typically involves a series of related functions, all of which must be captured within the accounting system. Although sometimes complex, these functions can be described in general as follows:

Capital funds are received from debt and equity security holders (creditors and owners) and either held for use in operations or invested; funds for operations are used to acquire resources (goods and services) from vendors and employees in exchange for obligations to pay; resources are used in operations, or held, or transformed and distributed to outsiders in exchange for promises of future payments; outsiders pay for resources distributed to them; and obligations to vendors and employees are paid.

Figure 7-1 categorizes these functions into four homogeneous and repetitive groups of transactions called **transaction cycles**, the vehicles through which transactions are processed by an entity's accounting system: (1) financing, (2) expenditure/disbursement, (3) conversion, and (4) revenue/receipt.[10] The

---

10   An external financial reporting cycle, also common to many entities, relates to preparing journal entries and posting transactions to the general ledger (to the extent such functions are not performed within other cycles), deciding the generally accepted accounting principles an entity should follow, gathering and summarizing information for preparing financial statements and other historical financial reports, and preparing and reviewing financial statements and other external reports. This cycle is not considered in this book, however, since it does not relate directly to the processing of transactions.

Figure 7-1: Relating Business Functions and Transaction Cycles

Business Functions	Cycles
• Capital funds are received from investors and creditors. • Capital funds are held for us in operations or invested.	Financing
• Resources (goods and services) are acquired from vendors and employees in exchange for obligations to pay. • Obligations to vendors and employees are paid.	Expenditure/ Disbursement
• Resources are used, held, or transformed.	Conversion
• Resources are distributed to outsiders in exchange for promises of future commitments. • Outsiders pay for resources distributed to them.	Revenue/ Receipt

number and nature of cycles will vary from industry to industry and from entity to entity, since business functions vary across industries and entities. Thus, these four cycles are representative, not definitive, although they include most of a manufacturing, merchandising, or service entity's business functions. In fact, if sufficiently significant to a particular entity, any one function could represent a separate transaction cycle.

Focusing on transaction cycles does not mean that individual financial statement accounts are ignored. Rather, it means an auditor focuses on processes (cycles) in order to understand end results (accounts). Financial statement accounts are location devices in which processed transactions are recorded, classified, and summarized. In fact, the dollar balances within some accounts actually result from transactions processed through more than one cycle. For example, debits to Cash result from cash received from customers, a function of the revenue/receipt cycle, and from creditors and investors, a function of the financing cycle. Credits to Cash result from cash disbursements, a function of the expenditure/disbursement cycle. Thus, the dollar balance in Cash reflects the net result of transactions processed through three cycles. Accounts are much more meaningful to an auditor if he or she understands the processes (cycles) relating to accounts and their dollar balances. Figure 7-2 illustrates the financial statement accounts that are generally contained within each cycle, and also indicates the chapters in this book devoted to each cycle.

MONITORING

To assure quality, internal controls should be monitored—through continuing evaluation, periodic evaluations, or both—and discrepancies resolved by management at least one level above those responsible. The reliability of an accounting system can be evaluated by comparing recorded assets with actual assets continually or periodically. For example, recorded quantities in perpetual inventory records can be compared with actual quantities in stock either

Figure 7-2:   Relating Transaction Cycles and Financial Statement Accounts

Cycles	Financial Statement Accounts	Text Chapters
Financing	Sales Receivables Cash Receipts Cash	10, 11
Expenditure/ Disbursement	Purchases Payables Personnel and Payroll Cash Disbursements	12, 13, 14
Conversion	Inventory Cost of Sales Fixed Assets	15
Revenue/ Receipt	Investments Long-Term Debt Capital Stock	16

continually in an on-line system (e.g., after every transaction) or periodically through a physical inventory count (e.g., annually). To maximize effectiveness, monitoring should take advantage of the element of surprise, be conducted by personnel independent of the functions tested, and result in appropriate corrective action. The element of surprise encourages employees to execute and record transactions accurately, since their work may be audited at any time. Of course, monitoring would be much less effective if conducted by employees responsible for the functions tested, since the results would lack objectivity. Thus, periodic monitoring should be conducted by personnel independent of the functions tested.

CONSIDERING INTERNAL CONTROL

Management's view of internal control is rather broad, its interest being to implement policies and procedures that channel resources toward meeting the entity's operations objectives, financial objectives, and compliance objectives. In a financial statement audit, the independent auditor's view of internal control, however, is narrower, since the auditor's interest is to issue an opinion on only one part of the entity's interests: management's financial statements. Thus, the auditor is concerned only with those policies and procedures that affect the assertions (introduced in Chapter 6) embodied within the entity's financial statements—the policies and procedures related to management's assertions about existence or occurrence, completeness, rights and obligations, valuation or allocation, and presentation and disclosure. However, in an attestation engagement about internal control, the practitioner's interest is to issue a report on yet another part of the entity's interests. For example, in the attestation report for CoreStates Financial Corp. (illustrated earlier), Ernst &

Young focused only on those policies and procedures affecting a much different assertion: that management maintained effective internal control over financial reporting.

Before designing substantive tests of account balances, an auditor first obtains an understanding of internal control sufficient to plan the audit. The auditor then assesses control risk for financial statement assertions related to the account balances and transaction classes that were processed by the internal controls. If control risk is low—that is, the controls can be expected to prevent or detect aggregate errors in excess of the auditor's planned materiality—then the auditor may restrict the extent of substantive tests of account balances, although not below a level sufficient to reduce audit risk to an amount the auditor judges appropriate for issuing an opinion on financial statements. The auditor's consideration of internal control is not a substitute for substantive tests of details; rather, tests of controls and substantive tests complement each other.

The second standard of field work, introduced in Chapter 2, provides the basis for an auditor's consideration of an entity's internal controls in a financial statement audit:

A sufficient understanding of internal control is to be obtained to plan the audit and to determine the nature, timing, and extent of tests to be performed.

An auditor's consideration of an entity's internal controls includes three phases:

1. *Obtain an understanding* of how management has designed policies and procedures for the control environment, risk assessment, the control activities, information and communication, and monitoring.
2. *Assess control risk* for the policies and procedures that have been placed in operation, and
3. *Determine the nature, timing, and extent of substantive tests.*

Figure 7-3 illustrates the three phases of the auditor's consideration of internal control, including the objective of each phase. The following discusses each phase separately, although some parts of each may actually be performed concurrently in practice.

OBTAINING AN UNDERSTANDING OF INTERNAL CONTROL

In every financial statement audit, an auditor should obtain an understanding of internal control sufficient to plan the audit, even for audits of small owner-managed businesses that employ only one or a few accounting personnel. An understanding of internal control allows an auditor to identify the types of material misstatements that could occur in the financial statements, to consider factors that affect the risk of material misstatements, and to design substantive tests of account balances and transaction classes that are processed by the internal controls. In practice, obtaining an understanding consists of: (1) performing a preliminary review, (2) documenting the internal controls and transaction cycles, (3) performing a transaction walk-through, and (4) identifying controls that reduce to a relatively low level the risk of material misstatements, each of which are discussed below. However, the level of understanding an auditor should obtain varies from engagement to engagement depending on the complexity and sophistication of an entity's operations and accounting

Figure 7-3: Considering Internal Control in a Financial Statement Audit

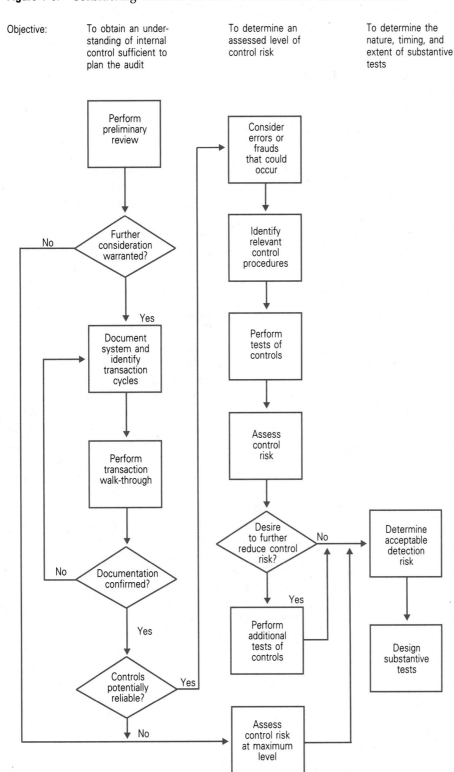

system (e.g., a publicly traded v. an owner-managed entity), the auditor's previous experience with the entity (e.g., an initial v. a continuing engagement), the assessed level of inherent risk, the auditor's understanding of the entity's industry, and the materiality of transactions processed through the internal controls.

Performing a Preliminary Review

Before expending time and effort to document an entity's internal controls, an auditor first reviews prior year audit working papers and client procedures manuals, makes inquiries of management, and observes client personnel to obtain a general understanding of the control environment, management's assessment of the risks they face, the control activities, the flow of information and communication throughout the accounting system, and how management monitors internal controls. An understanding of the control environment, risk assessment, and control activities provides the auditor with a general knowledge of the entity's organizational structure, of methods used to communicate responsibility and authority, and of methods used by management to supervise the system. In turn, an understanding of the flow of information and monitoring provides the auditor with a general knowledge of the various classes of transactions and the methods by which each significant class of transactions is authorized, executed, initially recorded, and subsequently processed.

In general, two audit approaches are available when an entity processes accounting information by computer: auditing around and auditing through the computer, and a purpose of the preliminary review is to decide which approach is more appropriate for a given client's computer system. When auditing *around* the computer, an auditor essentially ignores the computer and its controls, focusing solely on the source documents underlying computer input and the output resulting from computer applications; the auditor compares source documents with output (and vice versa), and data processing is ignored. Auditing around the computer is appropriate when only minor segments of an audit trail are eliminated or distorted—for example, when the computer is used primarily to perform computational tasks, as is typical in payroll. Advantages of auditing around the computer include lower direct audit costs and limited required technical expertise. But there are disadvantages: the data may be too voluminous to examine manually and no conclusions can be reached about data not examined specifically by the auditor.

In contrast, auditing *through* the computer focuses on all phases of the computer's applications, including the processing phase ignored when auditing around the computer. Of course, regardless of the audit approach adopted, segments of the audit trail are still missing, reduced to electrical impulses processed through the computer. Rather than focus on the flow of transactions or data, as was common in manual systems, an auditor focuses on an entity's computer controls when auditing through the computer. If the controls are effective, computer processed data are likely to be valid and reliable. Incorporated within auditing through the computer is the notion of auditing *with* the computer, the process of using a client's computer to aid in gathering evidence. An auditor is perfectly justified in using a client's computer to generate audit evidence about transactions and account balances if—and only if—he or she is satisfied that computer controls are effective.

Based on his or her understanding of an entity's internal controls, the auditor decides for each major class of transactions whether it is reasonable to continue considering internal control as shown in Figure 7-3. The decision is based on the auditor's answer to the following two questions:

1. Is further consideration of internal control likely to justify restricting substantive tests of details?
2. Is the audit effort needed to continue considering internal control likely to be less than the reduction in audit effort achieved by restricting substantive tests of details?

Answering "no" to either question would cause an auditor to discontinue further consideration of internal control and to assess control risk at the maximum, which translates roughly to planning an audit that relies heavily on substantive tests of account balances. If the auditor assumes a maximum level of control risk, he or she should document that conclusion, although not necessarily the reason for the conclusion, in the audit working papers. In contrast, answering "yes" to both questions would cause the auditor to continue considering internal control as follows.

Documenting the System

To document an entity's internal controls, an auditor relies on discussions with client personnel and reviews accounting records, documents, and employee procedures manuals. For example, an auditor might talk to the chief financial officer, to internal auditors, and to employees responsible for particular accounting functions (e.g., the manager of accounts receivable and his or her employees); review organization charts and transaction documentation (e.g., purchase orders, receiving reports, and vendor invoices); and consult the client's procedures manuals to confirm the procedures discussed or observed. The documentation need pertain only to those controls that are relevant to the financial statements audited, not all of the controls, since the auditor's interest is assessing control risk, not expressing a separate opinion on the entity's internal controls, an attestation service introduced earlier in this chapter.

In practice today, auditors use one or more of three means to document an entity's internal controls: narrative memoranda, flowcharts, and questionnaires. A **narrative memorandum** is a written description of a particular phase or phases of an accounting system. Figure 7-4 illustrates a narrative description for a company's cash collections on credit sales. Although useful for describing uncomplicated systems, narratives may be inappropriate when a system is complex or frequently revised.

A **flowchart**—or *data flow diagram* in database management systems—consists of interrelated symbols that diagram the flow of transactions and events through a system, or portions thereof. Flowcharts are powerful in the sense that they can capture the complexity of a system succinctly, allowing the auditor to focus sharply on key controls within the system. On the other hand, using flowcharts can be an overreaction when a system is routine, as for example in a small owner-managed company. Although different flowchart symbols can be used to depict the same operation, a public accounting firm should adopt standardized symbols in order to promote understanding and communication among auditors within the firm. Figure 7-5 illustrates several common flowcharting symbols, and in Figure 7-6 the symbols are used to flowchart the system described previously in narrative form in Figure 7-4. Note, though, that in practice an auditor would not use both a narrative

Figure 7-4:   Narrative Description of an Accounting System

The Wilson Company
Memorandum: Cash Collections on Credit Sales
December 31, 1999

Two departments are involved in the cash collection function: the Mail Room and Cash Receipts. In the Mail Room, envelopes containing remittance advices and the customers' checks are opened. Each check is restrictively endorsed, and a Mail Room employee prepares two copies of a list of the day's receipts. Copy 1 of the list of receipts and all remittance advices are forwarded to Accounts Receivable for posting; Copy 2 and all checks are forwarded to Cash Receipts.

In Cash Receipts, Copy 2 of the list of receipts and the checks are used to prepare a bank deposit slip and two copies of a cash summary sheet, and to update cash records. Checks and the deposit slip are hand carried to the First National Bank for deposit, and Copy 2 of the cash summary is forwarded to Accounts Receivable and General Accounting for recording. Copy 2 of the cash summary and Copy 2 of the list of receipts are filed in Cash Receipts.

BLK 9/30/99

description and a flowchart to document the same system or class of transactions; rather, one or the other would be used.

Unlike flowchart symbols, flowchart logic cannot be standardized. When preparing system flowcharts, an auditor should strive to be efficient, by displaying operations as concisely as practicable, and informative, by clearly indicating employee responsibilities and document flow. Flowcharting is a creative process, requiring keen imagination and thoughtful preparation.

An internal control **questionnaire** consists of a series of questions designed to detect control deficiencies. Questionnaires require *Yes, No,* or *Not Applicable* (*N/A*) responses: *Yes* responses suggest satisfactory control conditions, and *No* responses signal potentially significant deficiencies that could lead to errors, frauds, or illegal acts. Figure 7-7 illustrates an internal control questionnaire related to the cash collection procedures described in narrative form in Figure 7-4 and flowcharted in Figure 7-6. Note that the internal control questionnaire in Figure 7-7 indicates one *No* response and therefore suggests one potential deficiency: that "Cash collection employees are not bonded," which means that the company is not insured against losses from employees who misappropriate cash receipts.

Questionnaires can be adapted to almost any system, since they usually contain questions about many conceivable potential deficiencies, thereby increasing the likelihood of detection. On the other hand, questionnaires can result in unreliable documentation, since client employees may respond inaccurately to questions asked by the auditor. This may occur particularly when an employee attempts to provide the expected answer or responds to questions that should be directed to other employees. To avoid inaccurate responses, an auditor should attempt to verify responses with supervisory personnel and with the entity's procedures manual.

Figure 7-5:   Common Flowchart Symbols

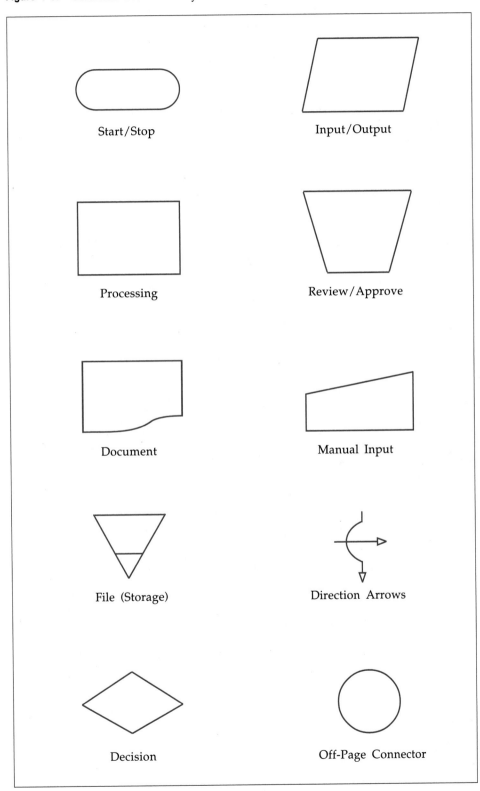

Figure 7-6: Flowchart of Accounting System

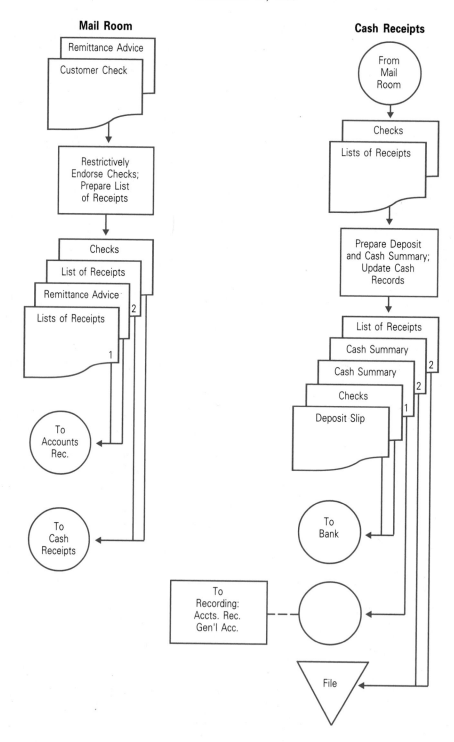

The Wilson Company
Cash Collection on Credit Sales Procedures
December 31, 1999

Figure 7-7: Questionnaire

The Wilson Company
Cash Collections on Credit Sales
December 31, 1999

Question	Answer: Yes, No, or N/A	Remarks	Performed By
1. Are mail receipts opened by personnel independent of shipping, billing, sales invoice processing, and recording?	yes		BLK
2. Are checks restrictively endorsed immediately upon opening the mail?	yes		
3. Are lists of receipts prepared when all mail receipts are opened?	yes		
4. Are checks forwarded promptly to personnel responsible for preparing bank deposits?	yes		
5. Are checks deposited daily?	yes		
6. Are cash summaries prepared and forwarded to recording?	yes		
7. Are all employees who handle cash adequately bonded?	no	cash collection employees are not bonded	

Of course, an auditor could use any combination of narratives, flowcharts, and/or questionnaires to document an entity's internal controls, thereby maximizing the advantages of each. For example, an auditor might decide to flowchart the major aspects of an entity's accounting system and use narratives to describe less important operations.

Identifying Transaction Cycles

Because the number and nature of transaction cycles varies from industry to industry and from company to company, an auditor must identify each client's major transaction cycles. Identifying cycles involves five steps:

1. Review account components for homogeneity.
2. Identify representative cycles.
3. Flowchart each cycle, supplementing with narratives and questionnaires as necessary.
4. Trace one or a few representative transactions through each cycle (a transaction walk-through).
5. Revise flowcharts if necessary.

Every financial statement account has two components: a debit side and a credit side. *Reviewing account components for homogeneity* involves examining the normal business function associated with each major account component. *Transaction cycles are then identified* by components with similar business functions. For example, Accounts Receivable is debited and Sales is credited when resources are distributed to outsiders in exchange for promises of future payments. Likewise, Cash is debited and Accounts Receivable is credited when outsiders pay for resources distributed to them. Because resource distribution and outsiders' payments are both functions of the revenue/receipt cycle, debits to Cash, credits to Sales, and debits and credits to Accounts Receivable are homogeneous account components related to the revenue/receipt cycle, as the following example illustrates:

	Revenue/Receipt Cycle Related Account Component	
Account	Dr.	Cr.
Cash	x	
Sales		x
Accounts Receivable	x	x

The process of reviewing account components is continued until all major cycles are identified. As noted earlier, a particular business function may be significant enough to represent a cycle by itself; others may justify grouping into one cycle, as in the preceding illustration.

After all major cycles are identified, each should be *flowcharted*, supplementing with narratives and questionnaires as necessary. The flowcharts are pictures of the cycles, and can be invaluable to an auditor in attempting to understand the logic and complexities of an entity's accounting system and control activities. Flowcharts are often far superior to narratives and questionnaires exclusively, since the information for an entire control system is compressed into so few cycles.

Performing a Transaction Walk-Through

Following documentation, a single transaction (or a small number of transactions) for each major segment of the internal controls is selected and followed, or "walked through," the accounting system. The purpose of the walk-through is to verify narrative, questionnaire, and/or flowchart documentation and to familiarize the auditor with the audit trail. Documentation is followed from beginning to end, tracing transactions from authorization, to execution, to recording. If the transaction walk-through isolates differences from narratives, questionnaires, or flowcharts, the reason for the differences should be resolved and the auditor's documentation revised if necessary.

Identifying Controls That Are Potentially Reliable

From information gathered by documenting the system, an auditor evaluates whether the entity's control activities can be relied on in assessing control risk below the maximum. If an entity's control activities are not suitably designed to justify reliance, the auditor would not perform tests of controls and therefore would discontinue considering the internal controls, assessing control risk at the maximum level and planning a primarily substantive audit approach. However, relying on substantive tests only can be problematic: In entities that process evidence electronically through *electronic data interchange (EDI)* or *image processing systems* (Chapter 6), the auditor may not be able to reduce detection risk to an acceptable level by substantive tests alone, since there is a risk that evidence may be altered. Rather, the auditor could perform tests of controls to support an assessed level of control risk, for example, for the completeness or occurrence assertions only. If control activities are suitably designed and potentially reliable in assessing control risk below the maximum, the auditor would continue to consider internal control as follows.

ASSESSING CONTROL RISK

Control risk, introduced in Chapter 2, is the risk that a material misstatement could occur in the financial statements and not be prevented or detected on a timely basis by the entity's internal controls. The auditor's role is to assess control risk for relevant assertions related to each significant account balance or transaction class, but the auditor need not assess every assertion for every account balance or transaction class, since some assertions may not be significant for a particular account. For example, the rights and obligations assertions may not be relevant for an entity's investment in an unconsolidated subsidiary.

To determine an assessed level of control risk, the auditor:

- Considers the *errors or frauds that could occur* and that could result in misstatements in the financial statements.
- Identifies relevant *control activities* designed to prevent or detect the errors or frauds.
- Performs *tests of controls* on the control activities that may prevent or detect the errors or frauds.

Errors, Frauds, and Control Activities

For each major transaction cycle, an auditor considers the errors or frauds that could occur and then identifies control activities that could serve either to prevent or to detect the errors or frauds. In view of the concept of reasonable assurance, introduced earlier, an auditor must have a general understanding of how employees could make errors or intentionally commit and conceal frauds. The risk of undetected errors or frauds could be affected by a number of situations that need exist only occasionally to result in material misstatements, such as:

- Transactions are not authorized.
- Transactions are approved but do not conform to what's authorized.
- Tangible assets, blank forms, or accounting records are exposed to unauthorized access.
- Tangible assets written off are exposed to unauthorized use or disposal.
- Accounting policies are not formally authorized and documented, or financial presentations do not conform to authorized policies.

Any of these situations could present opportunities for intentional frauds and therefore should be considered by an auditor when evaluating control effectiveness. But to commit and conceal a fraud, an employee would need access both to assets and to records: Access to assets is needed to commit a fraud, and access to records is needed for concealment.

After considering the types of errors or frauds that could occur, the auditor next considers control activities that management has implemented to detect or prevent the errors or frauds. For example, an auditor might identify the following potential error or fraud and related control activities for cash receipts transactions:

Example of an Error or Fraud That Could Occur	*Examples of Controls Designed to Prevent or Detect the Error or Fraud*
• Cash receipts on credit sales could be lost or diverted, potentially resulting in overstated receivables and unrecorded cash.	• Establish the cash receipts function in a centralized location. • Require daily reconciliation of cash receipts records with bank deposit slips. • Prepare list of cash receipts in the mail room. • Establish periodic procedures for reconciling cash records with bank statements.

The auditor would then apply tests of controls to each relevant control activity in order to assess control risk for the financial statement assertions related to account balances or transaction classes that may contain the identified errors or frauds.

Tests of Controls

In a financial statement audit, **tests of controls** consist of audit procedures directed toward testing the effectiveness of the design or the operation of an internal control policy or procedure. Tests of controls directed toward the *design* of a policy or procedure address one issue:

• Whether or not the policy or procedure is suitably designed to prevent or detect material misstatements in specific financial statement assertions.

Tests of controls over the design of a policy or procedure include inquiring of client personnel, inspecting documents and reports, and observing employees performing the policy or procedure. For example, to control cash admission receipts in a movie theater, a client may require that one employee receive cash and dispense tickets and another employee collect ticket stubs as patrons enter the theater. To assure that the control is operating as designed, the auditor might attend a movie unannounced, observing the cash and ticket collection functions firsthand.

In contrast, tests of controls directed toward the *operation* of a policy or procedure address three questions:

• Were the necessary control activities performed?
• How were they performed?
• By whom were they performed?

Like tests directed toward the design of a policy or procedure, tests directed toward their operation include inquiries, inspection of documents and reports, and observation, but they also include the auditor reperforming policies or procedures performed previously by the client. For example, to determine whether cash receipts are recorded and deposited promptly, an auditor might perform the tests of controls illustrated in Figure 7-8, which require both inspection of documentation and reperformance.

Ideally, tests of controls should be applied to transactions and detailed records that were executed and prepared throughout the entire fiscal year under audit. However, auditors often perform tests of controls at interim, such

Figure 7-8:   Tests of Controls

The Wilson Company
Cash Collection and Deposits
December 31, 1999

Program Step | *Performed by*

Collections

1. On a surprise basis, take control of the bank deposit (deposit slip and checks) just before delivery by client personnel to the bank.
2. Compare the total dollar amount of the checks to the total recorded on the deposit slip.
3. Compare the checks (in the deposit package) to details in the cash receipts records and the accounts receivable subsidiary records (e.g., customer names and amounts), and determine whether the lapse of time between cash receipt and deposit is reasonable.

Deposits

4. For sample Deposits:
   a. Compare the entries in the cash receipts journal with the deposits listed on the monthly statement to determine whether all cash receipts are deposited promptly.
   b. Determine whether cash receipts not listed on the bank statement are listed as deposits in transit in the bank reconciliation and are included with the deposits in the subsequent month's bank statement.
5. Trace the totals in the cash receipts journal to postings in the general ledger.
6. Document any weaknesses or discrepancies.

as during September or October for a December 31 year end engagement, thereby raising the question of whether additional tests are necessary for the remaining period. In deciding whether to perform tests of controls for the remaining period, an auditor should consider the following:

- The results of tests of controls that were performed at interim.
- Management's responses to inquiries concerning the remaining period.
- The length of the remaining period.
- The nature and amount of the transactions or balances involved.
- Evidence of the control activities within the remaining period that may be obtained from substantive tests performed by the auditor, by the internal auditors, or both.

When examining documentation, an auditor does not examine all of the transactions and detailed records related to the controls tested, but selects a sample from the population of all available transactions or records for the period. Audit sampling in tests of controls is discussed in detail in Chapter 8.

When performing tests of controls, an auditor may find differences between what was expected and what actually occurred. For example, a vendor's invoice may have been paid without the accounts payable manager's initials of approval. Such differences are appropriately called *exceptions, deviations*, or *occurrences*, rather than errors, because an exception does not necessarily mean that an error had been made in the accounting records. Thus, the fact that a vendor's invoice lacks approving initials does not necessarily mean that the invoice should not have been paid.

TESTS OF CONTROLS IN COMPUTER INFORMATION SYSTEMS

In fully automated computer systems, the nature of an auditor's tests of controls depends on whether audit evidence generated by the computer is:

- External to the computer, and therefore directly observable, or
- Internal to the computer, and therefore not directly observable.

Tests of controls involving *external, directly observable audit evidence* usually take the form of: (1) inquiries, (2) observation, and (3) inspection of documents. Figure 7-9 illustrates tests for computer controls when audit evidence can be observed directly by the auditor. For example, the first general control listed in Figure 7-9 is: "Segregate computer department and users," and the tests listed for this control include corroborative inquiries of computer personnel, management, and operating employees; observation of actual operations; and inspection of documentary evidence such as management reports and organization charts.

In contrast, tests of controls involving *internal, unobservable audit evidence* require that an auditor use the computer to obtain a reasonable degree of assurance that controls are operating as planned. Figure 7-10 lists several computer assisted tests of controls (called *computer assisted audit techniques: CAAT*), any one of which can be used alone or in conjunction with others. Each one approaches tests of controls from a different perspective, though all are designed to provide a basis for determining whether prescribed controls are complied with and operating as planned. Several computer assisted tests of controls are used commonly as *historical* audit techniques—that is, "cross-sectional" tests that audit computer controls at a point in time. Historical techniques include test data, base case system evaluation, integrated test data, and parallel simulation, each of which is introduced in turn in the following paragraphs.

An entity's computer system normally uses the client's software to process the client's data on the client's computer; client personnel control all phases of processing. However, **test data** shifts control over processing to the auditor by utilizing the client's software to process auditor-prepared test data that includes both valid transactions and invalid transactions. For example, invalid transactions may include unauthorized purchases or sales, transactions with missing data, or transactions for which control totals are wrong. If embedded controls are functioning properly, the client's software should detect all the exceptions planted in the auditor's test data; if not, errors or control overrides are possible, suggesting control risk is at the maximum. However, despite an auditor's proficiency and imagination in designing test data, the approach is totally ineffective if a client does not use the software tested! As a result, an auditor should run test data on a surprise basis, if possible, thereby increasing the likelihood of testing the software that is actually used by the client.

Figure 7-9:   Tests of Computer Controls

Controls	*Tests of Controls*

GENERAL CONTROLS

Organization and Operation Controls

- Segregate computer department and users.

  - Make inquiries of personnel and review organization charts and job descriptions for evidence of proper segregation of duties.
  - Observe actual operations and note the degree of management supervision being exercised.
  - Discuss with management and operating employees the extent and effectiveness of management supervision.
  - Review available management reports, studies, or evaluations concerning the operations of the data processing system.

- Provide general authorization over the execution of transactions.

  - Review the reconciliation of control totals maintained outside the computer department with the results of computer processing.
  - Examine available evidence indicating that reconciliations take place in the normal course of operations.
  - Review preprocessing, processing, and postprocessing controls to determine if they provide for processing in accordance with management's authorization.

- Segregate functions within the computer department.

  - Observe computer operations to determine that systems analysts and programmers do not have unrestricted access to hardware, files, or programs.
  - Review procedures for granting access to programs and data.
  - Observe the operation of the control group to determine whether it is independent of the systems and programming and processing groups.

Systems Development and Documentation Controls

- Participation by user department, accounting personnel, and internal auditors in system design.

  - Interview representatives of user departments for evidence of the level of their participation in systems design.

Figure 7-9: *(continued)*

Controls	Tests of Controls
	• Review appropriate documents and related approvals for evidence that user departments adequately understand input and processing requirements, control requirements, and system output.
	• Review the extent of internal auditors' involvement in system design and review their related work papers.
	• Interview users and computer department personnel about the extent of their involvement in systems design and implementation.
• Review and approval of system specifications.	• Review the computer department's guidelines for systems design.
	• Review design specifications, seeking written evidence of approval.
	• Interview management, users, and computer personnel to determine what approval procedures are used.
• Joint system testing by user department and computer personnel.	• Review testing and modification standards, test data, and resulting output for adequacy.
	• Interview user and computer department personnel to determine test procedures used during implementation.
	• Process independently prepared test data.
• Final approval over new applications.	• Review evidence of the approval of significant computer accounting applications.
	• Interview management and user and computer department personnel involved in the approval process, inquiring about their understanding of the system.
• Control over master file and transaction file conversion.	• Review the computer department's procedures for reconciling files.
	• Observe conversion procedures and controls.
	• Test conversions by tracing detailed records from original to updated files and vice versa.
• Approval of computer program changes.	• Interview systems, programming, and processing personnel to determine the procedures for controlling program changes.

Figure 7-9: *(continued)*

Controls	Tests of Controls
	• Review documentation in support of program changes to determine if changes are properly approved. • Review the results of tests made to verify system changes.
• Formal procedures to create and maintain documentation.	• Review documentation standards for adequacy. • Review selected documentation for compliance with prescribed documentation standards.
Hardware Controls • Controls built into computers by manufacturers.	• Review the computer manufacturer's literature or other sources to determine the available hardware control capabilities. • Review and evaluate available hardware controls. • Determine the potential misstatements that may result from ignored control features.
Access Controls • Limit access to computer hardware, software, data files, and software support documentation to authorized personnel.	• Review procedures for collecting and analyzing hardware utilization data. • Review selected available hardware utilization logs. • On a test basis, compare hardware utilization logs and processing schedules. • Review procedures for controlling access to programs, data files, and program support documentation. • Review the librarian's method of controlling unauthorized access to programs, data files, and support documentation.
Data and Procedural Controls • Written procedures and authorization manuals.	• Review procedures manuals, determining whether they provide operators with an understanding of processing requirements. • Observe operations on a test basis, determining whether prescribed procedures are followed.
• Control groups.	• Review the control group's organizational function.

Figure 7-9: *(continued)*

Controls	Tests of Controls
	• Interview users, computer department personnel, and control group personnel about control group activities.
	• Review procedures for distributing output to determine that only authorized users receive output.
	• Review control group working papers and reports to determine the extent and quality of the work.

APPLICATION CONTROLS

Input Controls

Controls	Tests of Controls
• Input authorization and approval.	• Obtain or prepare a list of input transaction sources along with required authorizations.
	• On a test basis, examine evidence that transactions were properly authorized.
	• Investigate significant authorization exceptions.
• Code verification.	• Review procedures for verifying identification codes.
	• On a test basis, trace identification codes to supporting source documents to assure that codes are accurate.
• Data conversion control.	• Review the procedures and techniques for controlling data conversion.
	• Observe the performance of verification procedures and the processing and disposition of exception listings.
	• Trace batch totals to control logs on a test basis.
	• Use a test deck (test data) to test the operations of specific controls.
• Data movement control.	• Review the adequacy of data movement controls.
	• On a test basis, trace a representative group of transactions through the system from initiation to completion.
	• Test the reconciliation of key department-to-department or run-to-run totals, reconciling any differences.

Figure 7-9: *(continued)*

Controls	Tests of Controls
• Occurrence correction.	• Review and/or observe the adequacy of procedures for resolving occurrences. • Determine if any occurrences remain unresolved for an unreasonable period of time. • Test representative occurrences for resolution.
Processing Controls • Control totals.	• Review the procedures for generating and reconciling control totals. • Observe the reconciliation process. • Trace control totals to related input totals.
• File labels.	• Review the adequacy of file controls. • Determine how selected occurrences were resolved.
• Limit (reasonableness) tests.	• Review program-support documentation for available limit tests. • Review representative output for evidence that limit tests are applied. • Use auditor-prepared test data to test the accuracy of limit tests.
Output Controls • Control totals comparisons.	• Review the procedures for comparison. • Observe personnel making comparisons.
• Output distribution.	• Review procedures for controlling output distribution. • Observe output distribution. • Test the distribution of selected output, determining whether recipients are properly authorized.

A special type of test data, **base case system evaluation (BCSE)** develops test data that purports to test *every* possible condition that an auditor expects a client's software will confront. BCSE can provide an auditor with much more assurance than test data alone, but is time-consuming (and expensive) to develop and therefore cost-effective only in rather large computer systems for which an auditor can rely on internal auditors to develop the base case. Yet another type of test data, **integrated test data** (sometimes called an *integrated test facility: ITF)* improves on test data by providing a vehicle for testing

Figure 7-10:   Computer Assisted Tests of Controls

Historical Audit Techniques
- Test data
- Base case system evaluation (BCSE)
- Integrated test data (integrated test facilities)
- Parallel simulation

Continuous Audit Techniques
- Audit modules
- Systems control audit review files (SCARFs)
- Audit hooks
- Transaction tagging

whether a client actually uses the software that the auditor tests. Unlike test data, which is run independent of client data, an ITF integrates fictitious data with actual client data without management's knowledge, allowing the auditor to compare the client's output with the results expected by the auditor. Because management is unaware of integrated test data, fictitious data must be removed from the client's records by journal entry or by program commands prior to compiling financial reports. When processed throughout the year, integrated test data provides assurance that the software tested is actually used to compile financial reports.

Parallel simulation is roughly the opposite of test data, shifting control over computer software—rather than over data—to the auditor. Thus, in parallel simulation, an auditor prepares software to process the client's data on the client's or the auditor's computer. If an entity's controls have been operating effectively, the client's software should generate the same exceptions as the auditor's software. The potential for control override is suggested when a client's software fails to detect exceptions detected by the auditor's software. Importantly, parallel simulation provides auditors with independence from client computer personnel in that software is prepared by the auditor rather than the client. However, much like test data, parallel simulation provides no assurance that the client's software is actually used throughout the entire year to process all data. Thus, parallel simulation should be performed on a surprise basis (or throughout the year) if possible.

Several other computer assisted tests of controls are used commonly as *continuous* audit techniques—that is, "time series" tests that audit computer controls throughout a period. Continuous techniques include audit modules, systems control audit review files, audit hooks, and transaction tagging, each of which is introduced in this and the following paragraphs. **Audit modules** differ from integrated test facilities (ITF) in that an ITF actually integrates fictitious data with the client's data, whereas audit modules are used to select client data for subsequent testing and analysis. For example, an auditor could place an accounts receivable confirmation module within an entity's monthly billing program. When desired, the audit module would be activated by the auditor, used to select customer accounts for confirmation, and commanded to print the confirmation wording directly on each selected customer's bill. Audit modules are sometimes used to create what are called **systems control audit review files (SCARFs)**, logs that collect transaction information for review subsequently by the auditor.

In general, **audit hooks** are "exits" in an entity's software that allow an auditor to insert commands for audit processing. That is, at appropriate points in the client's software, audit hooks allow an auditor to modify the software by inserting specific commands to accumulate totals or otherwise manipulate data for audit purposes. Of course, the use of audit hooks depends on whether an entity's software includes appropriate exit points, which are often built into software packages written by software vendors. Auditors sometimes use audit hooks to accomplish **transaction tagging** in which a transaction record is "tagged" and then traced through critical control points in the information system.

In practice, auditors apply both the manual tests of controls illustrated in Figure 7-8 and the computer assisted tests of controls listed in Figure 7-10. However, the objective of both manual and computer assisted tests of controls is to help the auditor assess control risk and, applied properly, both are equally powerful.

Assessing Control Risk: Further Considerations

The task of assessing control risk involves a judgment about whether to assess control risk at the maximum (in quantitative terms: 100 percent) or below the maximum for relevant financial statement assertions. An auditor assesses control risk from his or her understanding of the internal controls in general, and from evidence obtained by tests of controls in particular. Working paper documentation supporting assessed levels of control risk will vary, depending on whether the risk is assessed at the maximum or below. When control risk is assessed at the maximum, the auditor needs only to document the assessment—for example, "control risk for the rights and obligations assertion related to receivables is assessed at the maximum"—but not the basis for the assessment. However, when control risk is assessed below the maximum, the auditor does not need to document the specific level below maximum (for example, slightly below maximum, moderate, low), but he or she should document the basis for the assessment, such as the documented results of relevant tests of control. Generally, the lower the level of control risk an auditor desires, the more assurance he or she will require from evidence obtained in tests of controls.

On occasion, an auditor may desire a further reduction in the assessed level of control risk—that is, below the level indicated by completed tests of controls—in order to reduce even further the extent of substantive tests to be applied to year end account balances. In such cases, additional tests of controls would be necessary. However, the additional tests would be performed only if the auditor believes evidential matter is available to support a further reduction and if the expected effort to perform additional tests is likely to result in less audit effort for substantive tests.

DETERMINING THE NATURE, TIMING, AND EXTENT OF SUBSTANTIVE TESTS

After considering the assessed level of control risk (and inherent risk) for financial statement assertions, the auditor next determines the nature, timing, and extent of substantive tests necessary to restrict **detection risk** to an acceptable level. As explained in Chapter 2, control risk and detection risk are inversely related: As the assessed level of control risk *increases*, the acceptable level of detection risk *decreases*. Correspondingly, in planning substantive tests an auditor would perform *more persuasive* tests, perform tests at the *balance sheet date* rather than at interim dates, and would test *more* extensively. In contrast, as the assessed level of control risk *decreases*, the acceptable level of detection risk *increases*. Correspondingly, in planning substantive tests an auditor would perform *less persuasive* tests, perform tests at *interim dates* rather than at the balance sheet date, and would test *less* extensively. Figure 7-11 depicts the relationship between detection risk and the nature, timing, and extent of substantive tests. However, regardless of how low the assessed level of control risk, the acceptable level of detection risk could never be so high as to preclude the need for any substantive tests at all. The auditor always performs some substantive tests for all significant account balances and transactions.

COMMUNICATING REPORTABLE CONDITIONS AND MATERIAL WEAKNESSES IN INTERNAL CONTROL

Management is responsible for establishing, maintaining, and monitoring an entity's internal controls. Nevertheless, under *Statement on Auditing Standards No. 60*, "Communication of Internal Control Structure Related Matters Noted in an Audit," an auditor is required to communicate to the audit committee any "reportable conditions" identified while performing the financial statement audit. Reportable conditions are defined in *SAS No. 60* as:

. . . significant deficiencies in the design or operation of internal control, that could adversely affect the organization's ability to record, process, summarize, and report financial data consistent with the assertions of management in the financial statements.

Reportable conditions may involve deficiencies in any component of internal control, including the control environment (such as management's override of control activities) and the control activities (such as failure to prepare reconciliations on a timely basis). Sometimes, a deficiency may be of such a magnitude as to be considered a **material weakness**, defined in *SAS No. 60* as:

. . . a condition in which the design or operation of the specific internal control structure elements do not reduce to a relatively low level the risk that errors or frauds

Figure 7-11: Relationship of Detection Risk to the Nature, Timing, and Extent of Substantive Tests

Effect of Detection Risk	Acceptable Level of Detection Risk	
	Lower	Higher
Nature of Substantive Tests	Should use more persuasive tests (e.g., confirmations from independent parties)	Could use less persuasive tests (e.g., rely on documentation within the entity)
Timing of Substantive Tests	Perform tests at balance sheet date	Perform tests at interim dates
Extent of Substantive Tests	Test more extensively (e.g., increase sample size)	Test less extensively (e.g., decrease sample size)

in amounts that would be material in relation to the financial statements being audited may occur and not be detected within a timely period by employees in the normal course of performing their assigned functions.

Essentially, reportable conditions are significant deficiencies in internal control, and material weaknesses are those reportable conditions for which there's more than a relatively low risk that the deficiency may result in misstatements that are material to the financial statements. To illustrate the distinction between reportable conditions and material weaknesses, assume tests of controls reveal that, for a sample of 40 cash disbursements, 8 failed to have the approval initials of the accounts payable manager before payment, a control activity implemented by management to assure that only approved invoices are paid. Clearly, a reportable condition. But, a material weakness? In this case, assume management has implemented a compensating control which provides that all payments exceeding $1,000 require the manual signature of the chief operating officer beneath the facsimile signature of the chief executive officer that appears on all checks. If for all 8 deviations, the manual signature appears on the check and the auditor concludes all 8 are bona fide disbursements, then the reportable condition would not be a material weakness since, although a significant deficiency, the evidence suggests there's a relatively low risk of material misstatement.

Only an attestation engagement designed specifically to report on internal control, discussed earlier in the chapter, could be expected to give reasonable assurance that all potentially reportable conditions and, therefore, all significant deficiencies, are detected. Nevertheless, reportable conditions may come to an auditor's attention during an audit and, under *SAS No. 60*, should be communicated to the board of directors' audit committee or, lacking an audit committee, to individuals with equivalent authority and responsibility. The communication preferably should be written but, if done orally, should be documented by memoranda or notations in the working papers. An illustrative written report appears below, and identifies the one reportable condition (that, in this case, is also a material weakness) indicated by the questionnaire in Figure 7-7: *employees who handle cash are not bonded:*

Cheever & Yates, LLP
Suite 2600
650 Madison Avenue
New York, NY 10022

March 24, 2000

Audit Committee
Board of Directors
The Wilson Company
15 Artubus Drive
Stony Brook, NY 11790

In planning and performing our audit of the financial statements of The Wilson Company for the year ended December 31, 1999, we considered its internal controls. Our consideration was to determine our auditing procedures for the purpose of expressing our opinion on the financial statements and not to provide assurances on internal control. However, we noted certain matters involving internal control that we consider to be reportable conditions under standards established by the American Institute of Certified Public Accountants. Reportable conditions involve matters coming to our attention relating to significant deficiencies in the design or operation of internal control that, in our judgment, could adversely affect the organization's ability to record, process, summarize, and report financial data consistent with the assertions of management in the financial statements. These matters may involve aspects of the control environment, risk assessment, control activities, information and communication, or monitoring.

Our consideration of internal control disclosed the following conditions that we believe result in more than a relatively low risk that misstatements that would be material in relation to the financial statements of The Wilson Company may occur and not be detected within a timely period: Employees who handle cash are not bonded. This internal control weakness could result in material loss to the company if cash is diverted.

This report is intended solely for the information and use of the audit committee, management, and others in the company.

Cheever & Yates, LLP

Regardless of the form of communication, the reportable conditions communicated are those conditions detected as a result of considering internal control in accordance with the second standard of field work only. Additional conditions may exist and not be detected. An auditor's primary audit objective is to issue an opinion on financial statements. An audit engagement is designed and conducted with that objective in mind and cannot be relied on to detect all significant deficiencies in internal control.

SUMMARY

Developments in information technology—among them networks, telecommunications, and fourth generation computer languages—have opened new markets for consulting, assurance and attestation services, and have refocused an auditor's consideration of internal control in a financial statement audit. In turn, developments in our understanding of internal control, in particular COSO's four-volume document *Internal Control: Integrated Framework,* have altered the way that management and the independent auditor consider internal control.

The design, implementation, and monitoring of internal control—including the control environment, internal risk assessment, control activities, information and communication, and monitoring—are the responsibilities of management, not the independent auditor. The auditor's responsibility is to obtain an understanding of the internal controls sufficient to plan the audit and to determine the nature, timing, and extent of tests to be performed. However, any reportable conditions, including material weaknesses in internal control, should be communicated to the audit committee.

KEY TERMS

REFERENCES

Professional Standards

AICPA. *Codification of Statements on Auditing Standards.* New York: AICPA (AU Sec. 319, 325).

SAS No. 55, "Consideration of the Internal Control Structure in a Financial Statement Audit" (AU Sec. 319).

SAS No. 60, "Communication of Internal Control Structure Related Matters Noted in an Audit" (AU Sec. 325).

SAS No. 70, "Reports on the Processing of Transactions by Service Organizations."

SAS No. 78, "Consideration of the Internal Control in a Financial Statement Audit: An Amendment to SAS No. 55."

SSAE No. 2, "Reporting on an Entity's Internal Control Structure Over Financial Reporting."

SSAE No. 6, "Reporting on an Entity's Internal Control Over Financial Reporting: An Amendment to SSAE No. 2."

Professional Reports

AICPA. *Audit Guide: Consideration of the Internal Control Structure in a Financial Statement Audit.* New York: AICPA, 1990.

AICPA. *Auditing Procedure Study: Auditing in Common Computer Environments.* New York: AICPA, 1995.

AICPA. *Auditing Procedure Study: Auditing With Computers.* New York: AICPA, 1994.

AICPA. *Auditing Procedure Study: Consideration of the Internal Control Structure in a Computer Environment—A Case Study.* New York: AICPA, 1991.

Committee of Sponsoring Organizations of the Treadway Commission (COSO). *Internal Control: Integrated Framework. Executive Summary.* New York: COSO, 1992.

Committee of Sponsoring Organizations of the Treadway Commission (COSO). *Internal Control: Integrated Framework. Framework.* New York: COSO, 1992.

Committee of Sponsoring Organizations of the Treadway Commission (COSO). *Internal Control: Integrated Framework. Evaluation Tools.* New York: COSO, 1992.

Committee of Sponsoring Organizations of the Treadway Commission (COSO). *Internal Control: Integrated Framework. Reporting to External Parties.* New York: COSO, 1992.

Articles

Cashell, J. D. "The Effects of SAS No. 55 on Audits of Small Businesses," *Accounting Horizons* (September 1995), pp. 11-25.

Felix, W. L., Jr., and M. S. Niles. "Research in Internal Control Evaluation," *Auditing: A Journal of Practice & Theory* (Spring 1988), pp. 43-60.

Gallun, R. A., D. D. Heagy, and H. C. Lindsey. "How CPAs Use Computers," *Journal of Accountancy* (January 1993), pp. 38-41.

Gallun, R. A., D. D. Heagy, and H. C. Lindsey. "How CPAs Use Software," *Journal of Accountancy* (January 1993), pp. 41-43.

Luzi, A.D., and R. K. McCabe. "Harnessing the Power of Databases," *Journal of Accountancy* (January 1993), pp. 71-75.

Monk, H. L., Jr., and K. W. Tatum. "Applying SAS No. 55 in Audits of Small Businesses," *Journal of Accountancy* (November 1988), pp. 40-56.

Tempkin, R. H., and A. J. Winters. "SAS No. 55: The Auditor's New Responsibility for Internal Control," *Journal of Accountancy* (May 1988), pp. 86-98.

Zarowin, S. "Thinking Computers," *Journal of Accountancy* (November 1995), pp. 55-56.

Zarowin, S. "Staying in Touch," *Journal of Accountancy* (December 1995), pp. 55-59.

Zarowin, S. "The New Computer," *Journal of Accountancy* (March 1996), pp. 51-52.

QUESTIONS

1. What advantage do local area networks (LANs) offer over individual microcomputers?
2. What advantage does Internet technology offer over local area networks (LANs)?
3. What are the key concepts embodied within the *COSO Report's* definition of internal control?
4. Identify the components of internal control that are integrated within the management process.
5. Briefly explain the components of internal control.
6. Briefly explain management's responsibility for internal control.
7. Why is a formal system of transaction authorization necessary?
8. Which functions must be separated in order to achieve optimum segregation of duties? Why?
9. Briefly explain the concept of reasonable assurance.
10. What is an auditor's objective when obtaining an understanding of an entity's information system?
11. Identify and indicate the major components of each phase of an auditor's consideration of internal control.
12. What methods can an auditor use to document internal control?
13. What is the purpose of a transaction walk-through?
14. Briefly describe the process of identifying transaction cycles.
15. In your own words, briefly define what is meant by a "material weakness in internal control."

MULTIPLE CHOICE QUESTIONS

1. An integrated services digital network is a high-speed phone line that can be used to:
   a. Access software from a service bureau.
   b. Access software from the Internet.
   c. Enhance the processing capability of local area networks (LANs).
   d. Encourage end user computing.

2. Information systems that access software from file servers and direct print jobs from print servers are called:
   a. Local area networks (LANs).
   b. Telecommunications channels.
   c. Intranets.
   d. Service bureaus.

3. A public accounting firm has issued a report that refers to criteria established in *Internal Control: Integrated Framework* issued by the Committee of Sponsoring Organizations (COSO) of the Treadway Commission. The report likely relates to:

a. A consulting engagement.
b. An assurance engagement.
c. An attestation engagement.
d. An audit engagement.

4. As part of a periodic planning exercise, a company discovers that an eastern European political dispute may interfere with supply sources. This is an example of:

a. Control environment.
b. Risk assessment.
c. Control activities.
d. Monitoring.

5. Internal control should provide reasonable (but not necessarily absolute) assurance, which means that:

a. Internal control is management's, not the auditor's, responsibility.
b. An attestation engagement about management's internal control assertions may not necessarily detect all reportable conditions.
c. The cost of control activities should not exceed the benefits.
d. There is always a risk that reportable conditions may result in material misstatements.

6. Which of the following statements is an example of an inherent limitation of internal control?

a. The effectiveness of control procedures depends on segregation of duties.
b. Procedures are designed to assure that transactions are executed as management authorizes.
c. Errors may arise from mistakes in judgment.
d. Computers process large numbers of transactions.

7. An auditor considers internal control to:

a. Determine whether assets are safeguarded.
b. Suggest improvements in internal control.
c. Plan audit procedures.
d. Express an opinion.

8. After obtaining an understanding of an entity's internal controls, an auditor may assess control risk at the maximum for some assertions because the auditor:

a. Believes internal control activities are unlikely to be effective.
b. Determines that internal control is not well-documented.
c. Performs tests of controls to restrict detection risk to an acceptable level.
d. Identifies control activities that are likely to prevent material misstatements.

(AICPA Adapted)

9. After obtaining an understanding of an entity's internal controls and assessing control risk, an auditor may next:

a. Perform tests of controls to verify management's assertions that are embodied in the financial statements.
b. Consider whether to reduce the assessed level of control risk further.
c. Discontinue searching for reportable conditions.
d. Evaluate whether control activities can detect material misstatements.

10. The primary purpose of performing tests of controls is to provide reasonable assurance that:

a. Internal control is effective.
b. The accounting system is documented accurately.
c. Transactions are recorded at the amounts executed.
d. All control activities leave visible evidence.

(AICPA Adapted)

11. After obtaining an understanding of a client's controls, an auditor may decide to omit tests of the controls. Which of the following is not an appropriate reason to omit tests of controls?

a. The controls appear adequate.
b. The controls duplicate other controls.
c. Reportable conditions preclude assessing control risk below the maximum.
d. The effort to test controls exceeds the effort saved by not performing substantive tests.

(AICPA Adapted)

12. Which of the following statements is not true about test data?

a. Test data should consist only of conditions that interest the auditor.
b. Only one transaction of each type need be tested.
c. Test data must consist of all possible valid and invalid conditions.
d. Test data are processed by the client's software under the auditor's control.

13. Processing data through the use of simulated files provides an auditor with information about the effectiveness of control procedures. One of the computer assisted audit techniques that uses this approach is:

a. Test data.
b. Parallel simulation.
c. Base case system evaluation (BCSE).
d. Audit hooks.

14. General controls relate to all computer activities and application controls relate to specific tasks. General controls include:

a. Controls designed to assure that all data submitted for processing has been properly authorized.
b. Controls that relate to the correction and resubmission of data that were initially incorrect.
c. Controls for documenting and approving software and changes to software.
d. Controls designed to assure the accuracy of the processing results.

15. Which of the following computer assisted audit techniques allows fictitious and real transactions to be processed together without client personnel being aware of the testing process?

a. Parallel simulation.
b. Integrated test data.
c. Audit hooks.
d. Audit modules.

PROBLEMS AND DISCUSSION CASES

7-1   *Attestation Report on Internal Control*
Assume you have been requested by the Upton Corporation to prepare a report expressing an opinion on management's assertions about internal control. In each of the five years Upton has been an audit client, you have issued an unqualified opinion on management's financial statements, and in each year your consideration of internal control has not revealed any reportable conditions. Because no reportable conditions have been detected, Ken Pontarelli, Upton's CFO, asks that you issue a report on internal control without performing any additional procedures. Pontarelli says: "Simply issue the opinion, stating it's based on procedures performed during the audit. You know as well as I do that additional procedures won't disclose anything significant. So why make us pay for work that is a waste of time?"
   Required:
1. Respond to Pontarelli's request, indicating why you could or could not issue an opinion on Upton Corporation's internal controls.
2. What are the similarities and differences between your report on internal control issued in conjunction with the audit and a report expressing an opinion on Upton Corporation's internal control?

7-2   *Internal Control Objectives*
An entity's internal controls should be designed to achieve a variety of objectives. Assume that an entity wishes to accomplish the following four control objectives:
1. Transactions should be executed in accordance with management's authorization.
2. Transactions should be recorded as necessary: (1) to permit preparation of financial statements in conformity with generally accepted accounting principles and (2) to maintain accountability for assets.
3. Access to assets should be permitted only in accordance with management's authorization.
4. The recorded accountability for assets should be compared with the existing assets at reasonable intervals, and appropriate action taken for any differences.
To achieve these objectives, management could institute a number of control activities, including the following:
a. Unused, blank checks are stored in locked safes. *3*
b. A bank reconciliation is prepared monthly by personnel independent of the cash function. *4*
c. Credit approval is required for all new customers and for all credit purchases over $10,000. *1*
d. Accounts receivable postings are made from a listing of remittances prepared daily. *2*
e. Perpetual inventory records are updated daily from manufacturing reports. *2*
f. A physical inventory observation is performed monthly. *4*
g. All capital asset acquisitions are reviewed by the board of directors. *1*
h. Only authorized personnel are allowed to enter manufacturing sites. *3*
   Required: For each of the above control activities, *a* through *h*, indicate which objective, 1 through 4, is achieved.

7-3   *Controlling Against Concealed Fraud*
An auditor must have a general understanding of how employees could make errors or intentionally commit and conceal fraud. Otherwise, the auditor would be unable to

recognize potential deficiencies in internal control and, more important, less likely to detect misstatements that are material to the financial statements. Consider the following cases:

Case A

Checks from customers are received by the company's receptionist, who stamps each check received with a restrictive endorsement, and prepares a list of all funds received and the name of each corresponding customer.

Case B

A company has three accounts payable clerks, each of whom prepares vouchers for payment. Supporting documents, such as receiving reports and bills of lading, are attached to each voucher as backup for the payment request. The vouchers and support are then forwarded to the company's controller for approval and check signing.

Case C

A company maintains a petty cash fund to pay for small, miscellaneous items such as office supplies or postage. The fund is maintained at $500. Whenever funds are disbursed, a signed request form is filed with the remaining cash. One office clerk is designated as the fund's custodian, who makes all withdrawals and reimbursements.

Required: Evaluate each of the three cases independently. For each case discuss:
1. How an employee could attempt concealment.
2. What control(s) should be present to prevent concealment.

7-4 *Identifying Business Functions and Transactions Cycles*
You have been assigned to the audit of the F&S Savings and Loan Association. In preparing for the audit, you learn the following about F&S:

Total assets approximate $400 million. F&S has a main office downtown, and 13 branch offices throughout the city. Four hundred people are employed by F&S, with a total payroll of $6 million.

F&S derives revenue from two principle sources, the major source being interest and fee income from loans. According to its articles of incorporation, F&S is restricted to making loans only to consumers for purposes such as home mortgages, auto loans, and other personal loans; that is, it cannot make loans to commercial enterprises. The second revenue source is income from investments. F&S invests funds in short-term instruments, such as government securities and certificates of deposit, in order to have a ready source of available funds. Interest earned on investments may or may not be material to earnings, depending on the amount of funds invested during a period.

F&S has two major expenses: administrative costs, such as payroll, building maintenance, utilities, and taxes, and interest paid to depositors. The dollar magnitude of these interest payments varies considerably, depending on current market rates of interest.

Required: Using Figure 7-1 as a guide, identify the major business functions and related transaction cycles for the F&S Savings and Loan Association.

7-5 *Objectives and Limitations of Internal Control*
An auditor who has been engaged to audit the financial statements of Ajax Inc. is ready to begin considering Ajax's internal controls.

Required:
1. What are the objectives of internal control?
2. What are the reasonable assurances that internal control provides?
3. What are the inherent limitations of internal control?

(AICPA Adapted)

7-6 *Limitations of, and Communications About, Internal Control*
Apart from assessing control risk, an auditor's consideration of internal control lends insight into inherent limitations and significant deficiencies that ought to be communicated to management under *SAS No. 60*, "Internal Control Structure Related Matters Noted in an Audit."
    Required:
1. Describe the inherent limitations an auditor should recognize when considering the potential effectiveness of internal control.
2. Under generally accepted auditing standards, what is the auditor's obligation to communicate significant deficiencies detected while considering internal control?

7-7 *The Auditor's Consideration of Internal Control*
The Committee of Sponsoring Organizations' *COSO Report: Internal Control: Integrated Framework* defines internal control as a process, effected by an entity's board of directors, management and other personnel, designed to provide reasonable assurance regarding the achievement of objectives in the following categories: effectiveness and efficiency of operations, reliability of financial reporting, and compliance with applicable laws and regulations.
    Required:
1. What is the purpose of the auditor's consideration of an entity's internal controls?
2. What are the objectives of a preliminary evaluation of internal control?
3. How is the auditor's understanding of internal control documented? Discuss the advantages of each type of documentation.
4. What is the purpose of tests of controls?
5. If an auditor is satisfied after considering internal control that no significant deficiencies exist, is it necessary to perform substantive tests of details?

7-8 *The Auditor's Consideration of Internal Control*
Jim Harrison, CPA, is preparing a seminar on internal control for his entry-level professional staff. His predominant concern is to present the staff with an overview of critical issues confronted during an auditor's consideration of internal control under the second standard of field work.
    Required: To aid in developing the seminar's materials, Harrison asks you to respond to the following questions:
1. Why and how does an auditor consider internal control?
2. For each major class of transactions, how does an auditor decide whether to continue obtaining an understanding of internal control?
3. How does an auditor document internal control?
4. How does an auditor identify an entity's relevant transaction cycles?
5. What is the purpose of a transaction walk-through?
6. After obtaining an understanding, how would an auditor proceed if control activities were not suitably designed to justify reliance?
7. What is the purpose of tests of controls, and what general questions do tests of controls attempt to answer?
8. In tests of controls, what is the difference between an "exception" and an "error"?
9. How does an auditor evaluate internal control from having obtained an understanding of the system and performed tests of controls?

7-9 *Why Do Tests of Controls?*
An in-charge auditor is drafting interim tests of controls for the American Optical Company, a December 31 year end optics manufacturer located in Southbridge, Massachusetts. Tests will be performed in mid-September, engage three staff for two weeks each, and, assuming the audit team's tolerable rates of deviation exceed the estimated population rates of deviation, will likely drive the engagement partner to assess control risk below the maximum.

Required: Why bother? Why not simply perform substantive tests of financial statement account balances and disclosures at year end? After all, the firm's opinion will say everything about the financial statements, and nothing about control risk. Discuss.

7-10 *Identifying Weaknesses in Internal Control*
The town of Bullet Park operates a public parking lot near the railroad station for the benefit of town residents. The guard on duty issues annual prenumbered parking stickers to residents who submit an application form and show evidence of residency. The sticker is affixed to the auto and allows the resident to park anywhere in the lot for twelve hours if eight quarters are placed in the parking meter. Applications are maintained in the guard office at the lot. The guard checks to see that only residents are using the lot and that no resident has parked without paying the required meter fee.

Once a week the guard on duty, who has a master key for all meters, takes the coins from the meters and places them in a locked steel box. The guard delivers the box to the town storage building, where the box is opened and the coins are counted by a storage department clerk who records the total cash counted on a "Weekly Cash Report," which is sent to the town accounting department. The storage department clerk puts the cash in a safe, and on the following day the cash is picked up by the town's treasurer, who recounts the cash, prepares the bank deposit slip, and delivers the deposit to the bank. The deposit slip, authenticated by the bank teller, is sent to the accounting department where it is filed with the "Weekly Cash Report."

Required: Describe deficiencies in the existing system and recommend one or more improvements for each of the deficiencies to strengthen control activities over the parking lot cash receipts.

7-11 *Communicating Deficiencies in Internal Control*
As part of your annual audit of Call Camper Company, you are responsible for preparing a report communicating internal control related matters noted in the engagement. Your working papers include a completed internal control questionnaire and documentation of tests of controls. Your tests of controls and substantive tests identify a number of significant deficiencies in internal control; for some of these, corrective action by management is not practical.

Required: Discuss the form and content of the report on internal control related matters and the reasons for the report. Do not write a report.

7-12 *Defending a Material Weakness*
Several days prior to completing field work at Ansonia Wire & Cable Co., the engagement partner, Colleen Kelly, discusses with Ansonia's CFO, Alan Rothstein, reportable conditions that her audit staff detected while considering internal control and that she plans to include within the firm's letter communicating reportable conditions to the board of directors. Kelly reveals five reportable conditions and explains to Rothstein that one, *approval initials on the face of invoices prior to payment,* is—and will be communicated in the firm's letter as—a material weakness in internal control. Rothstein, visibly upset, argues that the reportable condition is not a material weakness.

Required: Discuss each of the following:
1. What is Kelly's argument?
2. Why would she care?
3. What is Rothstein's argument?
4. Why would he care?

7-13 *Reportable Conditions and Material Weaknesses in Internal Control*
During the course of a financial statement audit, an auditor may become aware of matters relating to the client's internal controls that may be of interest to the client's audit committee or to individuals with an equivalent level of authority and respon-

sibility, such as the board of directors, the board of trustees, or the owner of a middle market, owner-managed enterprise. Some of these matters may be reportable conditions; others may be material weaknesses.

Required:
1. What is meant by the terms "reportable conditions" and "material weaknesses"?
2. What are the auditor's responsibilities to identify and report these matters?

(AICPA Adapted)

7-14 *Internal Control and Computer Systems*

Shannon Bracken, CPA, is considering internal control for the Rumford Company, a December 31 year end company. Rumford's purchasing, billing, receivables, payables, and job-order cost accounting systems are fully computerized.

Required: Respond to each of the following:
1. Provide an overview of an auditor's consideration of internal control in a computerized system.
2. From the facts in the case, is Bracken more likely to audit *around* or *through* the Rumford Company's computer system? Why?
3. What is the purpose of an auditor's preliminary review of a computer system?
4. What is the purpose of tests of prescribed computer controls, and what specific questions are addressed by tests of controls?

7-15 *Conversion to Computer Information Systems*

When a company converts from a manual to a computer accounting system, many records and documents become unnecessary and therefore are not prepared. With the audit trail eliminated or distorted, the auditor must focus on controls over computer applications. Consider the following brief description of a manual cash disbursements system:

Purchase invoices are received in the accounting department from the various departments that have purchased goods and services. The accounts payable clerk matches the purchase invoices with supporting documents such as purchase orders, receiving reports, and inventory records. The clerk then prepares a voucher to record a liability for the amount of the purchase. Another clerk schedules the payments due to assure that all discounts for early payment are earned. Five days before the due date, the clerk prepares the documentation and the check, which are submitted to the controller for review and approval.

Required:
1. List and explain areas that could be automated.
2. What controls should be present in the proposed automated system?

7-16 *Tests of Controls in Computer Information Systems*

During your preliminary review of an entity's computer system, you note the following:
a. Purchase orders initiated by line personnel within the manufacturing plant may be authorized and executed by computer department personnel.
b. Software and data files are maintained in an unlocked filing cabinet in the information systems department. User department personnel are not denied access to the information systems department.
c. Transactions initiated by user departments are usually, but not always, processed, thereby requiring manual processing thereafter.
d. Line personnel sometimes receive weekly paychecks for amounts in excess of normal weekly pay. Overtime is not uncommon, particularly in peak production periods.
e. Transaction files may not be fully posted to updated master files.

Required: For each of the above observations, indicate the specific, general, or application control violated and the test(s) most likely to detect errors.

7-17 *Controls in Computer Information Systems*

When auditing a computer information system, the independent auditor should have a general familiarity with the effects of using a computer on the various characteristics of control and on the auditor's consideration of internal controls. The independent auditor must be aware of those control activities that are commonly referred to as general controls and those commonly referred to as application controls. General controls relate to all computer activities and application controls relate to specific accounting tasks.

Required:

1.   What are the general controls that should exist in computer information systems?
2.   What are the purposes of each of the following categories of application controls?
     a.   Input controls.
     b.   Processing controls.
     c.   Output controls.

(AICPA Adapted)

7-18 *Controls in Computer Information Systems*

Linder Company is completing the implementation of a new computerized inventory control and purchase order system. Linder's controller wants the controls that are incorporated into the software of the new system to be reviewed and evaluated, in order to ensure that all necessary controls are included and function properly. The controller respects and has confidence in the department's work and evaluation procedures, but would like a separate appraisal of the control activities by the internal audit department. Hopefully, a review would reveal any deficiencies in control activities and lead to immediate correction before the system is on-line. The internal audit department carefully reviews controls when evaluating a new system.

Required:

1.   Identify the types of controls that should be incorporated in the new software.
2.   Explain how the existence of the computer controls and their performance are verified by auditing through the computer.

(AICPA Adapted)

RESEARCH PROJECTS

1.   MANAGING CHANGE IN SELECTED INDUSTRIES

Of the four volumes in the *COSO Report*, one

Committee of Sponsoring Organizations of the Treadway Commission (COSO). *Internal Control: Integrated Framework. Evaluation Tools.* New York: COSO, 1992.

provides blank evaluation forms (called "evaluation tools") against which entities can assess each of their five components of internal control: control environment, risk assessment, control activities, information and communication, and monitoring. Pages 131-203 of the volume provide sample filled-in forms for a hypothetical medium-size aerospace parts manufacturer, including an overall internal control evaluation (pages 201-203) and an overall conclusion (page 203).

Unrelated to the *COSO Report*, the AICPA publishes AICPA *Audit & Accounting Guides*, reprinted as of May 1 each year, in a variety of industries, among them:

*   Airlines
*   Banks
*   Casinos
*   Colleges and universities

- Construction contractors
- Finance companies
- Investment companies
- Property and liability insurance companies
- Providers of health care services
- State and local governmental units

Required: Few risks are more crucial to an entity's long-term survival than its ability to adapt to change. For any industry you choose, use the blank and filled-in evaluation tools on pages 25-27 and 162-165 of the *COSO Report* (all of which relate to managing change within the risk assessment component of internal control), the related AICPA "Industry Audit & Accounting Guide" for the industry you choose, and articles in business periodicals (e.g., *Business Week, Forbes*) and newspapers (e.g., *The Wall Street Journal, Barrons*) to identify and briefly describe risks in the industry that relate specifically to managing change.

2. PUBLIC REPORTING ON INTERNAL CONTROL

The profession has argued for decades about the advisability of mandatory reporting on internal control by public companies and by governmental entities. In the 1970s and 1980s, the main players in the debate were the *Commission on Auditors' Responsibilities* (the Cohen Commission), the AICPA, and the SEC, among others; their arguments were chronicled in L. M. Savoie and D. N. Ricchiute, "Reports by Management: Voluntary or Mandatory?" *Journal of Accountancy* (May 1981), pp. 84-94. More recently, in addition to the AICPA and the SEC, new players, most supportive of mandatory reporting, have entered the debate, including the *Commission on Fraudulent Financial Reporting* (the Treadway Commission), the *Committee of Sponsoring Organizations (COSO) of the Treadway Commission,* the U.S. General Accounting Office, and the Federal Deposit Insurance Corporation (FDIC), which, through the FDIC Improvement Act, requires public reporting for large federally insured banks and thrifts. "The COSO Report: Challenge and Counterchallenge," *Journal of Accountancy* (February 1993), pp. 10-18, reprints two pointed letters exchanged by COSO and the GAO, some of which bears directly on the debate in the 1990s. Today, about one in four public companies and three in five Fortune 500 companies voluntarily report on internal control.

Required: Using the AICPA's National Automated Accounting Research System (NAARS) or copies of annual reports in a library, select an annual report that includes both management's report and the independent auditor's opinion on internal control, and draft a report that:

1. Explains the key issues addressed by management.
2. Compares the language used in the independent auditor's report to the language illustrated in the chapter from *SSAE No. 2,* "Reporting on an Entity's Internal Control Structure Over Financial Reporting."
3. Argues either for or against public reporting on internal control.

COMPREHENSIVE REVIEW CASE

CHAPTERS 1-7

"YOU'RE AHEAD"
A Long-Distance Cost Savings Initiative

Threatened by a declining share of the long-distance phone service market, Noy Holland, Vice President, Consumer Service, KLR Communications, suggests at a sales retreat that KLR bank on the reputation of Cheever & Yates, KLR's independent auditors, to vouch for claims made by KLR in their current advertising campaign. Holland says, "We say, *You save with KLR*. But who has reason to believe us? Particularly when Continental holds 70 percent of the market (even after the divestiture)! We need something, some hook, something that will give the market reason to believe us, something other than what we have now, when what we have now translates to nothing more than 'Trust us'."

Holland suggests a bold new advertising plan, what she coins "You're Ahead," a multimillion-dollar print, TV, and radio campaign that promises the unthinkable to preferred, corporate, long-distance customers: quarterly statements that: (1) compare the rates charged by KLR with the lowest rates published by Continental, and (2) extend a credit for the amount by which KLR charged more.

"What if we're not priced below Continental?" asks Sam Michel, KLR's chief financial officer.

"The question, Sam, is 'What if we *are*?'" Holland says.

The vice presidents for sales and for operations agree with Holland, and so in time does Michel. Gary Lutz, President and Board Chairman, asks Michel to contact Richard Yates, engagement partner for Cheever & Yates.

At a meeting among Richard Yates, Gary Lutz, Sam Michel, and Noy Holland, Michel proposes a methodology for comparing KLR's monthly bills with Continental Communication's published rates. Michel asks that Yates propose an attestation engagement to attest to the methodology.

"What, precisely, are you asking us to attest to?" asks Yates.

"Noy and our legal staff drafted what we need," says Lutz, "and what we apparently need is a statement from you that our methodology properly compares billing charges between KLR and Continental, and accurately reflects the price differences for the period July 1, 1999 through September 30, 1999, which is the first period we're offering the guarantee."

"For actual usage billed by KLR?" asks Yates.

"Yes," says Holland, "and—and Gary knows this—between alternative KLR services, since we'd like to offer a review not only against Continental, as Gary said, but also against our own alternative pricing plans, so the customer knows they're beating Continental *and* getting the best price we offer."

"This is risky," says Yates.

"To us?" asks Lutz.

"To us," says Yates. "What we're attesting to could be misrepresented in your written promotional materials or, for that matter, orally by your sales reps."

"What will you agree to?" asks Holland.

"This agreement," says Yates, referring to the contents of Exhibit 1.

Exhibit 1: Agreement Between KLR Communications and Cheever & Yates

What KLR May and May Not Do:
Summary of Rules
- *YOU'RE AHEAD* Statement:
  - May include excerpt of Cheever & Yates' attestation report only if full attestation report is enclosed with customer's statements.
  - May only refer to "independent accounting firm," not to Cheever & Yates.
  - May not use the words "certify," "guarantee," or "verify," but may use the words "examination," "opinion," and "report."
- Cheever & Yates' Attestation Report:
  - May be attached to a *YOU'RE AHEAD* Statement.
  - May not be included in advertising, either in whole or in part.
- Cheever & Yates Name:
  - May not be used in advertising, interviews, or press releases.

Lutz, Michel, and Holland read the agreement. Michel asks, "Why are we precluded from using an excerpt of your firm's attestation unless we include a full attestation report with a customer's statement?"

"We can't risk a customer taking the excerpt out of context," says Yates.

"But including a full report will increase our billing costs," says Michel.

"We can't take the risk," says Yates.

"And we can't use your firm's name?" asks Lutz.

"Only insofar as our name appears on the full attestation report," says Yates. "Nowhere else."

"Why?"

"Because all I can offer you is an attestation on your methodology, not on your services," answers Yates.

"And your report," says Michel. "What will your report look like?"

"I have a draft," says Yates, referring to Exhibit 2.

Exhibit 2: Attestation Report

DRAFT

Cheever & Yates, LLP
Suite 2600
650 Madison Avenue
New York, NY 10022

Report of Independent Attesters
on the *YOU'RE AHEAD* Methodology

November 1, 1999

To: KLR Communications Corporation

We have examined the *YOU'RE AHEAD* Methodology of KLR Telecommunications Corporation (KLR) for the period July 1, 1999 through September 30, 1999. Our examination was made in accordance with standards established by the American Institute of Certified Public Accountants and, accordingly, included such procedures as we considered necessary in the circumstances.

The *YOU'RE AHEAD* Methodology for comparing KLR Preferred billing charges with Continental Telephone charges is footnoted in the "What You Save with KLR" section of the enclosed customized *YOU'RE AHEAD* Statement (the Statement). The *YOU'RE AHEAD* Methodology for comparing billing charges between alternative KLR services is footnoted in the "We Guarantee KLR's Best Price" section of the enclosed statement. The methodology was designed by KLR to compute the lowest telephone service cost under the KLR program and the most widely used Continental programs (published tariff rates, excluding promotional discounts) indicated in the specified sections for each customer's actual usage billed by KLR during the specified period.

In our opinion, the *YOU'RE AHEAD* Methodology referred to above properly compares billing charges between KLR and Continental and between alternative KLR services and accurately reflects the price differences for the period July 1, 1999 through September 30, 1999, as applied to actual usage billed by KLR.

"This language," says Lutz. "We need stronger language."

"This language is the language required by our standards. We can offer no stronger statement."

Yates then explains that the attestation reporting standards (Chapter 2) are at the center of the language chosen by Cheever & Yates. Consistent with the first and second reporting standards, the draft:

1. Identifies the assertion attested to in the second paragraph (the accuracy of the "You're Ahead" Methodology for comparing KLR Preferred billing charges with Continental Telephone charges),
2. States the character of the engagement in the first paragraph (to examine the "You're Ahead" Methodology of KLR Telecommunications Corporation (KLR) for the period July 1, 1999 through September 30, 1999 in accordance with AICPA standards), and
3. States the firm's conclusion about whether the assertion is presented in conformity with the criteria against which it was measured in the third paragraph (the "You're Ahead" Methodology properly compares billing charges between KLR and Continental and between alternative KLR services and accurately reflects the price differences for the period July 1, 1999 through September 30, 1999).

Gary Lutz agrees both to the rules in Exhibit 1 and to the attestation report in Exhibit 2.

"And the 'You're Ahead' Statement," says Yates. "You have a draft?"

Noy Holland presents the statement in Exhibit 3, an exact duplicate for a customer, the Alpine Roofing Company.

Yates agrees to the "You're Ahead" statement, but asks what Holland proposes to excerpt from the attestation report. She types out the following:

Excerpt from independent attester's report:

"In our opinion, the 'You're Ahead' Methodology properly compares billing charges between KLR and Continental and between alternative KLR services and accurately reflects the price differences."

Turning the screen toward Yates, she says, "We'll use this below my facsimile signature on the statement."

Yates offers to deliver an engagement letter to Lutz after discussing the proposed engagement with the firm's managing partner. "But certainly by next week," Yates says. The attestation report would be dated November 1, 1999.

Required: As the profession ventures into new markets, the leadership in public accounting firms is confronted with questions they've not dealt with routinely in the past: For example, can we be profitable in the wake of uncertain risks and near certain liability? Why are companies like KLR *approaching us* if not in part to shift the risk of liability? Are we venturing into markets that we do not belong? In considering the following issues, assume that *you* are the managing partner of Cheever & Yates. Be mindful of the issues above as you consider the following questions. Be as critical of Richard Yates' proposed attestation service for KLR Communications as any managing partner would be of any engagement partner whose incentive compensation scheme is weighted in part on securing new business. The following questions correspond to Chapters 1-7 of the book:

Chapter 1:   Is this engagement advisable? If Cheever & Yates leverages off of the KLR engagement to market similar services in other industries, do you see problems related to market permissions and market sizing?

Chapter 2:   Discuss how you would comply with each of the AICPA's *Attestation Standards.*

Exhibit 3: You're Ahead Statement

Alpine Roofing Company
377 Elmwood Avenue
Providence, RI 02906

December 1, 1999

Dear Valued KLR Customer:

As a KLR Preferred[R] Customer, your company has been enrolled automatically in YOU'RE AHEAD free of charge. Every 90 days you will receive a statement like this one, which will prove to you how much you save —how much you are ahead!— by contracting long-distance service through KLR Telecommunications rather than through Continental Telephone.

What You Save with KLR

KLR has saved you **$67.23**

This is how much more you would have paid Continental for the exact same long-distance calls you placed through KLR. Here's a look at your savings for July, August, and September:

	KLR's Charges	Continental's Published Prices	KLR Saved You
Outbound calls	$212.67	$245.43	$32.76
800 calls to you	187.89	222.36	34.47
	$400.56	$467.79	**$67.23**

We Guarantee KLR's Best Price

You never need worry about whether you are enrolled in the lowest cost KLR business calling plan. Every 90 days, we automatically compare the amount you paid as a KLR Preferred[R] Customer with other KLR plans. If you paid more, we'll automatically credit the difference! Here's a look at your charges for July, August, and September:

	Your Charges	KLR's Best Price
July	$145.67	$145.67
August	133.89	133.89
September	121.00	121.00
	$400.56	$400.56

Congratulations! Your company is already receiving the lowest prices we offer. If you have any questions, please call me or your YOU'RE AHEAD Service Consultant. Otherwise, you'll receive your next YOU'RE AHEAD Statement in 90 days. Thank you for your business!

Noy Holland,
Vice President
Customer Service

Chapter 3:   Discuss the deficiencies in Yates' proposed attestation report. How would you improve the report?

Chapter 4:   Discuss the ethical issues you find important to the engagement.

Chapter 5:   Discuss the liability issues you find important to the engagement.

Chapter 6:   Discuss the risks you see accruing to Cheever & Yates from the wording of the agreement with KLR Communications and KLR's "You're Ahead" Statement. Discuss how Cheever & Yates will gather and evaluate evidence.

Chapter 7:   Discuss the information systems, technology, and internal control issues you find important to the engagement.

8

Sampling in Tests of Controls

Major topics discussed in this chapter are the:

- Nature of attributes sampling in audit, attestation, and assurance engagements.
- Role of audit risk, including sampling and nonsampling risk, and the risks of assessing control risk too high or too low.
- Distinction between statistical and nonstatistical sampling.
- Components of a general audit sampling plan appropriate for tests of controls.
- Alternative audit sampling techniques used in practice: attribute estimation sampling, sequential (stop-or-go) sampling, discovery sampling, and nonstatistical sampling for attributes.

There's neither sufficient time nor, given what we know about the laws of probability, sufficient reason to test all of the transactions underlying an entity's account balances or classes of transactions. As a result, many (if not most) of the conclusions auditors reach about account balances and classes of transactions are based on testing samples rather than entire populations. This chapter introduces audit sampling plans used by auditors when considering an entity's internal controls in general and when applying tests of controls to classes of transactions in particular. The chapter begins by introducing the nature of attributes sampling in audit, attestation, and assurance engagements; discussing audit risk in the context of audit sampling; and explaining the difference between statistical and nonstatistical sampling. Thereafter, the chapter introduces a general sampling plan for accomplishing tests of controls, and applies the plan to three important and frequently used audit sampling techniques: *attribute estimation sampling, sequential (stop-or-go) sampling,* and *discovery sampling.* Finally, the chapter discusses nonstatistical sampling for attributes.

ATTRIBUTES SAMPLING IN AUDIT, ATTESTATION, AND ASSURANCE SERVICES

Sampling has long been used in audit service engagements, largely as a means to draw conclusions about high-volume audit populations, such as recorded receivables and sales transactions. For example, attribute estimation, illustrated later in the chapter, was first applied routinely in audit tests of controls in the 1960s by public accounting firms such as Price Waterhouse, which used a sampling plan developed with Herbert Arkin, a statistician at the City College of New York. However, practitioners have also used attribute estimation (and sequential sampling, also illustrated later) in attestation and assurance service engagements. For example, engagements that attest to management's assertions about internal control—such as Ernst & Young's attestation for CoreStates Financial Corp., illustrated in Chapter 7—can use the same sampling plans that auditors use in audit service engagements, since the practitioner's interest in an attestation engagement and in an audit engagement is similar: Are management's assertions about control procedures reliable? The sampling plans introduced in this chapter are applicable to financial statement audits and to attestation and assurance service engagements about internal control, although the illustrations are drawn largely from auditing.

Sampling examines less than 100 percent of the items that constitute a population. In most cases, a sample can be sufficiently representative of a population to warrant reasonably reliable conclusions without testing the entire population. For example, a randomly selected sample of 100 sales invoices drawn from a population of 10,000 sales invoices can be audited in about 1 percent of the time it would take to audit the entire population (100/10,000) and, because of the laws of probability, can yield fairly reliable conclusions. A **population** consists of all the items within a class of transactions, such as all credit sales processed for the year ended December 31, or all the transactions constituting an account balance, such as Accounts Receivable. A **sampling plan**—the procedures used to test a sample—aids the practitioner in forming conclusions about one or more characteristics of either a particular class of transactions or a particular account balance. For example, the sample of 100 sales invoices could offer conclusions about credit approval controls and about recorded sales and receivables balances. In any sampling plan, however, the characteristic of interest depends on whether the practitioner is performing tests of controls or substantive tests. As introduced in Chapter 6, and discussed more fully in Chapter 7, tests of controls are designed to obtain evidence about whether an entity is complying with the controls that management prescribes, and the characteristic of interest is called an *attribute*.

An **attributes sampling plan** is most commonly used to test an entity's *rate of deviation* (also called *rate of occurrence*) from a prescribed control procedure. For example, an auditor might use an attributes sampling plan to test controls for disbursement processing, billing systems, payroll and personnel systems, inventory pricing, and depreciation, among other things. In contrast, substantive tests, also introduced in Chapter 6, are designed to obtain evidence about whether monetary error exists within a class of transactions or an account balance, and the auditor's characteristic of interest is called a *variable*. A **variables sampling plan** is most commonly used to test whether recorded account balances are fairly stated. For example, an auditor might use a variables sampling plan to test recorded dollar amounts for receivables, inventory, payroll expense, and fixed asset additions, among other things. In summary, attributes sampling is generally used to reach a conclusion about a population in terms of a rate of deviation, and variables sampling is generally used to reach conclusions about a population in terms of a dollar amount. This chapter is devoted to attributes sampling, and Chapter 9 is devoted to variables sampling.

SAMPLING AND AUDIT RISK

Sampling and audit risk are well-established in audit practice and implicitly recognized in the third standard of field work, which states in part that ". . . evidential matter is to be obtained . . . to afford a *reasonable basis* for an opinion" (emphasis provided). If an "absolute" basis were necessary to form an opinion, then auditors would have to examine entire populations rather than samples, thereby rendering financial statement audits far too costly. Furthermore, audit risk cannot be totally eliminated by 100 percent testing, because risks not related to sampling, such as human error, would still exist. But what risks are sustained by an auditor in a typical financial statement audit, and how does sampling add to those risks? The following discussion focuses on the components of audit risk, which are summarized in Figure 8-1.

COMPONENTS OF AUDIT RISK

In Chapter 2, **audit risk** was defined as the likelihood that an auditor may unknowingly fail to modify his or her opinion on materially misstated financial statements. Audit risk is a combination of two components:

1. The risk that material errors *will occur* in the process by which financial statements are developed.
2. The risk that any material errors that occur *will not be detected* by the auditor.

The first of these two components, the risk that errors will occur, can be classified further into control risk and inherent risk, both of which were introduced in Chapter 2. **Control risk** represents the risk that errors could occur, and would not be prevented or detected by the entity's internal controls. For example, control risk would be increased if an entity did not maintain effective physical controls over blank checks. **Inherent risk** represents the susceptibility of an account balance to errors that could be material and that are not monitored by related control procedures. For example, inherent risk is often higher

Figure 8-1:   Audit Risk in Tests of Controls

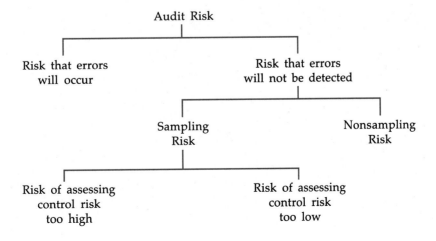

for liquid assets, such as cash, than for nonliquid assets, such as property, plant, and equipment. Because neither control risk nor inherent risk is directly controllable by an auditor, the risk that material errors will occur—the first component of audit risk—is not directly controllable by the auditor.

The second component of audit risk, the risk that material errors will not be detected, is referred to as **detection risk**, defined in Chapter 2 as the risk that errors could occur but would not be detected by the auditor's procedures. The risk that material errors will not be detected is directly controllable by the auditor through substantive tests of details and other substantive audit procedures. For example, if both control risk and inherent risk are high, an auditor could reduce allowable detection risk by increasing sample size.

SAMPLING RISK AND NONSAMPLING RISK

The risk that material errors may occur and remain undetected is influenced by two categories of uncertainties:

1. Sampling risk. Uncertainties related to sampling.
2. Nonsampling risk. Uncertainties arising from factors unrelated to sampling.

Sampling risk results from the fact that an audit sample may not be representative of the population tested. For example, a sample of sales invoices may contain disproportionately more or fewer control deviations than exist in the population of sales transactions, suggesting that the auditor's conclusions about recorded sales may be different if all of the sales invoices are tested. Since sampling risk can be reduced simply by increasing sample size, sampling risk varies inversely with sample size: The greater the sample size, the smaller the sampling risk. Why? Because, if sample size were increased to include all the items in a population, there would be no sampling and therefore no sampling risk.

Nonsampling risk includes all aspects of audit risk not due to sampling. For example, nonsampling risk could result from human errors, such as failing to detect pricing errors or overlooking shipments to fictitious customers. Several factors can serve to reduce nonsampling risk, including staff training and supervision, and encouraging effective working paper review.

RISKS OF ASSESSING CONTROL RISK TOO HIGH OR TOO LOW

Two aspects of sampling risk are critical in tests of controls:

1. Risk of assessing control risk too high.
2. Risk of assessing control risk too low.

The **risk of assessing control risk too high** is the risk that a sample deviation rate supports assessing control risk at the maximum when, unknown to the auditor, the true deviation rate in the population supports assessing control risk below the maximum. For example, assessing control risk too high would occur if an auditor estimated a 5 percent rate of deviation but was willing to tolerate only 3 percent, and the true but unknown population rate of deviation was really just 2 percent. In this example, the auditor would probably conclude that the control is not effective, since the sample deviation rate (5 percent) exceeded the tolerable deviation rate (3 percent). Therefore, he or she would assess a higher level of control risk in determining the nature, timing, and extent of substantive tests. But, unknown to the auditor, he or she would actually be *assessing control risk too high* because the true population deviation rate (2 percent) is less than the tolerable rate (3 percent).

The **risk of assessing control risk too low** is just the opposite of the risk of assessing control risk too high: It is the risk that a sample does support assessing control risk below the maximum when, unknown to the auditor, the true deviation rate in the population supports assessing control risk at the maximum. For example, assessing control risk too low would occur if an auditor estimated a 4 percent rate of deviation but was willing to tolerate as much as 6 percent, and the true but unknown population rate was really 7 percent. In this example, the auditor would conclude that the control is effective. Therefore, he or she would assess a lower level of control risk in determining the nature, timing, and extent of substantive tests, because the sample indicated fewer deviations (4 percent) than the auditor was willing to tolerate (6 percent). However, unknown to the auditor, he or she would actually be *assessing control risk too low* since the true population rate (7 percent) exceeds the tolerable rate (6 percent).

Assessing control risk too high is *inefficient*: When an auditor concludes that a control risk is high, he or she ordinarily sets a lower acceptable detection risk (introduced in Chapter 2) and expands the scope of substantive tests to compensate for the perceived control deficiency. If the expanded scope of substantive tests is unjustified, the audit will be less efficient since more substantive tests will be performed than necessary. Assessing control risk too low, in contrast, is *ineffective,* because the scope of substantive tests will be restricted under the erroneous assumption that the control is effective and control risk is low. Thus, the substantive tests may be ineffective in detecting material misstatements.

Sampling risk cannot be eliminated, but it can be controlled, as illustrated in the sampling plans introduced later in the chapter.

STATISTICAL AND NONSTATISTICAL SAMPLING

Statistical sampling plans apply the laws of probability to aid an auditor in designing an efficient sample, in measuring the sufficiency of evidence obtained, and in evaluating the sample results. In contrast, **nonstatistical sampling plans** rely exclusively on subjective judgment to determine sample size and to evaluate sample results. A properly designed nonstatistical sampling application can provide results as effective as those from a properly designed statistical sampling application. However, there is one crucial difference between a statistical and a nonstatistical sampling application: Statistical sampling plans allow an auditor to *measure sampling risk* quantitatively; nonstatistical sampling plans do not.

The choice between a statistical and a nonstatistical sampling plan is based primarily on the auditor's assessment of the relative costs and benefits. For example, an auditor might use nonstatistical sampling if the cost of selecting a statistical random sample were too high. However, an auditor might consider the cost justifiable if the related controls were critical, and a measure of sampling risk was therefore essential. Note that the choice between a statistical and a nonstatistical sampling plan is made independently of the selection of audit procedures, since audit sampling, whether statistical or nonstatistical, is merely a means for accomplishing audit procedures.

In some instances, audit sampling is inappropriate, and the auditor must therefore test the entire population. For example, an auditor may not be willing to accept any sampling risk for contingent liabilities. Sampling is also inappropriate in tests of control procedures that depend primarily on segregation of duties, or that otherwise provide no audit trail. Audit evidence for these types of controls is gathered through observation and inquiry.

TESTS OF CONTROLS: AN ATTRIBUTES SAMPLING PLAN

A general sampling plan appropriate for tests of controls is presented in Figure 8-2 and discussed in the following sections. Thereafter, three specific methods of attributes sampling are explained and illustrated: attribute estimation sampling, sequential (stop-or-go) sampling, and discovery sampling.

STEP 1:   DETERMINE THE OBJECTIVES OF THE TEST

As discussed earlier, tests of controls are designed to assess the effectiveness of control procedures in preventing or detecting material misstatements in the financial statements. Thus, in general terms, an auditor's objectives are stated in the context of determining whether the controls for a particular transaction cycle are sufficiently effective to conclude that control risk is below the maximum tolerable level.

In practice, sampling is generally used when an entity's controls leave a trail of observable evidence (such as approval initials on the face of a vendor's invoice) and when the controls do not depend primarily on adequate segregation of duties, which is observable but not documented. Sampling can still be used when evidence is observable but not documented. However, the sampling plan requires that observations be planned early in the engagement. For example, if an auditor wishes to observe cash collection procedures at a theater, he or she would have to select the days for observation early in the engagement in order to allow each day in the period audited an equal chance of being selected for observation.

Figure 8-2: Audit Sampling Plan: Tests of Controls

1. Determine the objectives of the test.
2. Define the attribute and deviation conditions.
3. Define the population.
4. Determine the method of sample selection.
5. Determine sample size.
6. Perform the sampling plan.
7. Evaluate the sample results.

STEP 2: DEFINE THE ATTRIBUTE AND DEVIATION CONDITIONS

Not all of a client's existing controls are tested in a financial statement audit, only those relevant to assertions embodied within the financial statements audited. For each control that is tested, the auditor identifies what are called *attributes* and *deviations*.

An **attribute** is a characteristic of a control, and a **deviation** is the absence of an attribute. To illustrate, assume an auditor's objective is to determine whether controls over sales returns are effective. The client prepares a credit memorandum for each return. In this case, one attribute—that is, one characteristic of the control system—is that quantity and other data on the credit memorandum agrees with the receiving report, a document prepared when the client receives returned goods. For this attribute, a deviation would occur each time an auditor found that the quantities or other data indicated on a credit memorandum disagreed with the related receiving report.

STEP 3: DEFINE THE POPULATION

In attributes sampling, a *population* consists of all the items constituting a class of transactions. Because sample results can be projected only onto the population from which the sample is selected, the defined population must be appropriate for the auditor's objectives. For example, if an auditor's objective is to test controls designed to assure that all shipped goods are billed, the population would be all shipping documents issued during the period, not all sales invoices. Erroneously defining the population as all invoices issued during the period would ignore shipped goods that were not billed, which the test is intended to detect.

Define the Period Covered

As discussed in Chapter 6, tests of controls are typically accomplished during the interim period of an engagement, which for a December 31 year end client might be as early as the summer months or during the fall. Performing tests of controls prior to year end, however, creates an audit problem because, in order to design substantive tests, the auditor needs to reach a conclusion about the entire population of transactions covered by the year end financial statements—for example, January 1 to December 31—not just the months subjected to interim tests. Thus, when tests are conducted at interim, the auditor might define the population to include transactions through December 31, perform initial tests through the interim date, and complete the tests at year end.

Alternatively, the auditor might decide to define the population to include transactions through the interim date, and then consider the following factors in judging whether additional tests are necessary for the remaining period: the results of interim tests, responses to inquiries of management about the remaining period, the length of the remaining period, the nature and amount of the transactions completed during the remaining period, and evidence of effective controls within the remaining period obtained through year end substantive tests. The important point to recognize is that sample results can be generalized only to the population from which the sample items are selected. As a result, if interim tests are performed on transactions completed through October 31 for a December 31 year end client, then the auditor's conclusions relate only to the ten-month period ended October 31.

Define the Sampling Unit

A **sampling unit** is any of the individual elements constituting a population, and should be defined in the context of the control to be tested and in light of audit efficiency. For example, if the audit objective is to test whether disbursements contain signatures authorizing payment, the sampling unit might be defined as a voucher, which is a summary form attached to a purchase document, such as a vendor's invoice. Alternatively, if one voucher pays several invoices from the same vendor, the sampling unit might be defined as a line item on a voucher, with each line item representing an individual vendor invoice. Thus, a sampling unit might be a document, a line item on a document, or even a journal entry, among other things, depending on the auditor's objective.

STEP 4:   DETERMINE THE METHOD OF SAMPLE SELECTION

The objective of audit sampling is to draw conclusions about one or more population characteristics without testing the entire population. But even with the most carefully designed sampling plan, there is still a degree of uncertainty about whether sample results represent the population. Examining every item in the population is the only way to eliminate uncertainty arising from sampling risk. However, if a sample is selected at *random*—i.e., if each sampling unit is given an equal chance of being selected—the laws of probability can be applied to determine the likelihood that the sample is representative of the population from which it was drawn. A sample can be evaluated in terms of probability only if the sample is randomly selected and thus free from sampling bias. If each item in a population is not given an equal chance of selection, the sample would be biased toward the population items with the greater chance of selection.

Some commonly used methods of selecting a sample are:

- Random-number sampling.
- Systematic sampling.
- Block sampling.
- Haphazard sampling.

Each method is discussed below. In practice, populations may be subdivided in some cases, and samples chosen separately for each subgroup. This technique, known as stratified sampling, is also discussed.

Random-Number Sampling

Random-number sampling uses random-number tables or computer-generated random numbers to select sampling units from a population. Random-number tables contain columns and rows of randomly generated digits. An auditor begins at any digit in the table—a random start—and proceeds along a column or row or diagonal, selecting digits corresponding to identification numbers on the sampling units (e.g., invoice numbers or check numbers). If the sampling units do not have identifying numbers, the auditor could establish correspondence between population items and random digits by assigning numbers to each population item. To minimize potential bias in starting point selection, an auditor could periodically proceed to a new starting (or continuing) point while selecting the sample. Random-number sampling is appropriate both for statistical sampling and for nonstatistical sampling.

Systematic Sampling

Systematic sampling involves selecting every n^{th} item from a population of sequentially ordered items. Systematic sampling eliminates the need to establish correspondence between population items and random numbers, and therefore is useful when population items lack identification numbers. The number of sequential items to skip when selecting a sample systematically is determined by dividing population size by sample size. For example, assuming population and sample sizes of 5,000 and 200, respectively, an auditor would select a random starting point and proceed to select every 25th sampling unit (5,000/200). Continuing points may be changed periodically to minimize any potential starting point bias. Systematic sampling is useful for nonstatistical sampling, and if the starting point is selected at random, it can be useful for statistical sampling.

Block Sampling

A block sample is a group of items arranged contiguously within a larger grouping of sampling units. For example, a block sample could consist of all vendor invoices processed on January 21, May 24, September 28, and November 13. In this case, if 75 invoices had been processed on these four days, then the sample would consist of 4 items, not 75, since the sampling unit is expressed in blocks of time—that is, in days—not transactions. Generally, so few blocks of sample items are insufficient to justify generalizing sample results to the population, suggesting that block sampling often results in excessively high sampling risk. Although a block sample could be designed with enough blocks to minimize sampling risk, testing large numbers of blocks is likely to be inefficient. Thus, an auditor should not use block sampling for either statistical or nonstatistical sampling, unless he or she exercises considerable care in controlling sampling risk.

Haphazard Sampling

A haphazard sample consists of sampling units selected without special reason, but also without conscious bias. For example, a haphazard sample could consist of 80 items selected simply by pulling vendor invoices from a file cabinet drawer. Like block sampling, haphazard sampling may fail to select samples that are wholly representative of the population tested. Although it may be useful for nonstatistical sampling, haphazard sampling is inappropriate for statistical sampling.

Stratified Sampling

Stratified sampling involves subdividing populations into homogenous subgroups or strata, and selecting (and evaluating) separate samples for each subgroup. The samples may be selected by random numbers, systematically, in blocks, or haphazardly. Stratified sampling is based on the assumption that items in some population strata are more similar to each other than to any other items in the population. For example, individual vendor invoices of less than $100 are apt to be more similar to each other than to invoices over $100,000.

When compared, the subgroups are apt to have strikingly dissimilar characteristics, such as different credit terms and different potential for material errors or fraud. Thus, each group represents a stratum, and the variability of sampling units in each stratum is apt to be less than the variability of all population items.

STEP 5: DETERMINE SAMPLE SIZE

In order to determine sample size for an attributes sampling plan, an auditor must first consider:

- Acceptable risk of assessing control risk too low.
- Tolerable rate of deviation.
- Expected population deviation rate.

Each is discussed below.

Acceptable Risk of Assessing Control Risk Too Low

As discussed earlier, an auditor is concerned with the risks of assessing control risk too high and too low. However, attributes sampling plans usually quantify the risk of assessing control risk too low only, since assessing risk too low relates to an audit's effectiveness—that is, to the likelihood of issuing an inappropriate audit report. The risk of assessing control risk too high, on the other hand, relates to efficiency only.

Auditors sometimes refer to their reliability or confidence levels when applying attributes sampling. *Reliability level* or *confidence level* is actually the complement of the risk of assessing control risk too low (i.e., one minus the risk). For example, for a 5 percent risk of assessing control risk too low, the reliability level would be 95 percent (i.e., 1.00 − .05). Therefore, specifying an acceptable risk of assessing control risk too low depends largely on the degree of confidence an auditor desires. Because there is an inverse relationship between sample size and the risk of assessing control risk too low (as the acceptable risk decreases, sample size increases), sample sizes are larger when an auditor specifies a lower acceptable risk of assessing control risk too low and smaller for higher acceptable risks. In some engagements, an auditor might accept the same risk of assessing control risk too low for all tests of controls. In other engagements, the auditor might vary the risk for individual controls, assigning a lower acceptable risk to controls deemed critical by the auditor.

Tolerable Rate of Deviation

A tolerable rate of deviation (sometimes called a tolerable rate of occurrence) is the maximum population rate of deviation from a control procedure that an auditor will tolerate without modifying the assessed level of control risk. Specifying a tolerable rate of deviation is a matter of professional judgment and depends primarily on the auditor's assessment of control risk when planning the nature, timing, and extent of substantive tests. In general, a lower tolerable rate is appropriate when an auditor assesses a lower control risk.

After completing tests of controls, an auditor may find that the rate of deviation in the sample is close to or exceeds the tolerable rate. Under these conditions, an auditor could decide to increase the assessed level of control risk, since there is an unacceptably high sampling risk that the population deviation rate exceeds the tolerable rate. Increasing control risk would decrease detection risk correspondingly, likely resulting in the need to increase the extent of substantive tests at year end.

Expected Population Deviation Rate

The expected population deviation rate can be estimated from either the prior year's results of testing the identical control or from a pilot sample. The prior year's sample deviation rate can be used only if the related control and client personnel have not changed since the prior year's sampling plan was applied. If there have been changes, the prior year's results would not be applicable, since the rate of deviation would not reflect current conditions. When prior year results are either nonexistent or inapplicable, an auditor can estimate the expected population deviation rate from a *pilot sample* drawn from the population of interest. Pilot sample items can be used as part of the audit sample, and typically are. For example, if 40 items are examined in a pilot sample and the audit sample size is 100, only 60 additional sample items need to be selected and examined.

If an auditor judges that the expected population deviation rate equals or exceeds the tolerable rate, then the auditor expects to find more deviations than he or she is willing to tolerate, leading to the conclusion that the control is not effective. Under these conditions, the auditor would assess a higher control risk and, correspondingly, require extensive substantive tests to restrict detection risk to a relatively low level.

Determine Sample Size

Once the auditor has specified an acceptable risk of assessing control risk too low and tolerable and expected population rates of deviation, audit sample size can be determined from standard tables, as illustrated later in the chapter. In a nonstatistical sampling plan, sample size can also be determined from tables or may be based solely on the auditor's professional judgment.

Importantly, increasing or decreasing any of the sample size parameters (i.e., acceptable risk of assessing control risk too low, tolerable rate of deviation, and expected population deviation rate) will have an impact on the required sample size. Figure 8-3 illustrates the effect on sample size of changes in any

Figure 8-3: The Effect on Sample Size of Increasing or Decreasing Parameters: Attributes Sampling

Parameter	Direction of Change	Effect on Sample Size Increase	Decrease
Acceptable risk of assessing control risk too low	Increase		X
	Decrease	X	
Tolerable rate of deviation	Increase		X
	Decrease	X	
Expected population deviation rate	Increase	X	
	Decrease		X

one parameter; the effect of changes in more than one would depend on the magnitude and direction (increase or decrease) of each change.

In general, population size has very little effect on sample size, particularly for populations over 5,000 items. The following table illustrates the limited effect of population size on sample size, assuming a 5 percent acceptable risk of assessing control risk too low, a 5 percent tolerable deviation rate, and a 1 percent expected population deviation rate.[1]

Population Size	Required Sample Size
50	45
100	64
500	87
1,000	90
2,000	92
5,000	93
100,000	93

Illustrations throughout this chapter assume a large population size.

STEP 6:   PERFORM THE SAMPLING PLAN

Once selected, the sampling units should be examined for the attributes of interest, and deviations should be documented in the working papers. (Examples of working paper documentation for attributes sampling appear later in the chapter.)

In practice, auditors usually select more sampling units than required, thereby providing replacements for voided items and for documents that cannot be located. For example, an auditor might select 75 sampling units even though required sample size is 65, and then use the remaining ten in the order selected if needed. Voided items generally should not be considered deviations. However, missing items would ordinarily be considered deviations, since the auditor would have no basis to conclude that the tested controls were operating as prescribed by management.

Occasionally, an auditor might find a large number of deviations before completing tests of the entire sample. If the large number of deviations suggested that the sample deviation rate were likely to exceed the tolerable rate, the auditor would probably discontinue the sampling plan and conclude that the control is ineffective. In this case, the benefits of continuing the sampling plan are not likely to exceed the cost.

STEP 7:   EVALUATE THE SAMPLE RESULTS

After performing the sampling plan, an auditor summarizes and evaluates the results by:

- Determining the sample deviation rate.
- Determining the maximum population deviation rate, and the allowance for sampling risk.

---

1   AICPA. *Audit and Accounting Guide*, "Audit Sampling." New York: AICPA (1983), p. 35.

- Considering qualitative information.
- Reaching an overall conclusion.

Each is discussed next.

Determine the Sample Deviation Rate

The **sample deviation rate** is the auditor's estimate of the true but unknown population deviation rate and is determined as follows:

$$\text{Sample Deviation Rate} = \frac{\text{Number of Deviations Observed}}{\text{Sample Size}}$$

For example, if an auditor observed two deviations in a sample of 100, the sample deviation rate would be 2 percent (2/100).

Determine the Maximum Population Deviation Rate and Allowance for Sampling Risk

An estimate of the maximum population deviation rate is represented by the following:

$$\begin{matrix}\text{Maximum Population} \\ \text{Deviation Rate}\end{matrix} = \begin{matrix}\text{Sample Deviation} \\ \text{Rate}\end{matrix} + \begin{matrix}\text{Allowance for} \\ \text{Sampling Risk}\end{matrix}$$

In practice, the allowance for sampling risk is not calculated directly, but can be determined deductively from standard tables that yield maximum population deviation rates at specified risks of assessing control risk too low. For example, assuming a 10 percent acceptable risk of assessing control risk too low, sample size of 100, and two observed deviations, the maximum population deviation rate would be 5.3 percent, determined from tables that are illustrated later in the chapter. In this case, the sample deviation rate is 2 percent (2/100), the maximum population deviation rate is 5.3 percent, and the allowance for sampling risk is therefore 3.3 percent (5.3 percent – 2 percent). Summarizing, these results indicate that there is a 10 percent chance (the risk of assessing control risk too low) that the true but unknown population deviation rate exceeds 5.3 percent. Stated another way, the auditor is 90 percent confident (recall that the level of confidence, or reliability, is the complement of the risk of assessing control risk too low) that the true population deviation rate is less than or equal to 5.3 percent.

In a statistical sampling application, an auditor compares the maximum population deviation rate and the tolerable rate of deviation and evaluates the effectiveness of a control accordingly. The results suggest a control is effective when the tolerable rate equals or exceeds the maximum population deviation rate. That is, the results would support assessing a low level of control risk only if the population is estimated to contain no more deviations than the auditor is willing to tolerate.

However, in a nonstatistical sampling application, sampling risk cannot be measured directly, as discussed earlier. Only the sample deviation rate can be determined. The results of a sampling plan would certainly not support assessing control risk below the maximum if the sample deviation rate exceeds the auditor's tolerable rate. The results would also not support assessing control risk below the maximum if the sample deviation rate exceeds the expected population deviation rate used initially to design the sampling plan. This is true because there is likely to be an unacceptably high risk that the true population rate exceeds the tolerable rate.

Consider Qualitative Information

When judging the results of a sampling plan, an auditor considers not only the frequency of deviations, but also the qualitative characteristics of the deviations, such as the nature and cause of the deviations and the possible relationship of the deviations to other phases of the audit. For example, if the observed deviations in a sample resulted from intentional acts (fraud) rather than carelessness, an auditor would assess a higher control risk, even if the tolerable rate of deviation exceeded the maximum population deviation rate.

Reach an Overall Conclusion

An auditor considers all available quantitative and qualitative information in assessing control risk. If the results support assessing control risk below the maximum—for example, if the maximum population deviation rate does not exceed the tolerable rate, and all deviations result from unintended random errors—an auditor would judge the controls effective and therefore would restrict the extent of substantive tests. However, if the results do not support assessing control risk below the maximum, the controls would not be judged effective, and substantive tests would be extended accordingly.

The following three sections of this chapter discuss and illustrate three commonly used attributes sampling techniques:

1.   Attribute estimation sampling.
2.   Sequential (stop-or-go) sampling.
3.   Discovery sampling.

The discussion and illustrations apply the steps identified in the general audit sampling plan in Figure 8-2. Nonstatistical sampling for attributes is also discussed.

ATTRIBUTE ESTIMATION SAMPLING: A CASE ILLUSTRATION

Attribute estimation sampling, a statistical sampling plan for tests of controls, is appropriate when an auditor wishes to estimate a true but unknown population rate of deviation. To illustrate attribute estimation sampling and to apply the general attributes sampling plan in Figure 8-2, assume a first-year audit engagement is being planned for the Chandler Wire & Cable Company, a large supplier of synthetic conductor cable for U.S. and foreign electronics manufacturers.

DETERMINE THE OBJECTIVES, ATTRIBUTES, AND DEVIATION CONDITIONS

Although Chandler has long been respected for high-quality products, discussions with Chandler personnel reveal that quality control may have deteriorated recently, a contention supported by an excessively large number of returns. The auditor's objective in this case is to determine whether control procedures for sales returns can be relied on during substantive tests of details.

Discussion with the predecessor auditor revealed that tests of sales returns in prior years had indicated relatively high deviation rates. Based on this information and on interviews with client personnel, the auditor designs the following tests of controls for sales returns, all of which are explained more fully in Chapter 10:

Step	Tests of Controls
1.	Obtain a random sample of credit memoranda from files in the customer order department.
2.	Test unit pricing and extensions on sampled credit memoranda.
3.	Trace details of sampled credit memoranda to:
	a. Receiving reports,
	b. Perpetual inventory records,
	c. Entries in Inventory and Cost of Goods Sold, and
	d. Entries in Sales Returns and in the accounts receivable subsidiary ledger and general ledger.
4.	Review the credit register (a listing of credit memoranda) for unusual items such as credits for very large amounts, or an unusually large number of credits for the same customer, and investigate.
5.	Document test results.

The auditor is now confronted with a very real and recurring question in auditing: Can any of these procedures be accomplished with statistical or nonstatistical sampling, thereby potentially saving audit time and cost? In this case, nonstatistical sampling is likely inappropriate, because the auditor has prior knowledge of potential problems and therefore needs an estimate of sampling risk. Statistical sampling, though, can be useful, particularly since the population of credit memoranda is assumed to be too large to justify testing the entire population. But which of the tests of controls can be accomplished statistically?

Steps 4 and 5 of the tests of controls cannot be accomplished by statistical sampling: Step 4 requires reviewing the entire population of credit register entries for attributes not clearly defined as either existing or not existing (a requirement of attribute estimation), and Step 5 does not involve testing. Steps 1, 2, and 3, however, involve attributes that can be defined clearly as either existing or not existing. For example, the credit memoranda are either recorded properly in perpetual inventory records [Step 3(b)] or they are not; there are no uncertainties about outcome. Thus, Steps 1, 2, and 3 can be accomplished with attribute estimation.

Steps 1, 2, and 3 require one sampling unit and five attributes, as follows:

Sampling unit:
Credit memorandum

Attributes of interest:
1. Unit pricing and extensions on the credit memorandum are accurate.
2. Quantity and other data on the credit memorandum agrees with the receiving report.
3. Quantity and other data on the credit memorandum agrees with perpetual inventory records.
4. The journal entry is properly recorded as a debit to Inventory and a credit to Cost of Goods Sold.
5. The journal entry is properly recorded as a debit to Sales Returns and a credit to Accounts Receivable.

For each attribute, the deviation condition would be defined as the absence of the attribute. For example, for the first attribute, the deviation condition would be defined as: "Unit pricing and extensions on the credit memorandum are *not* accurate."

DEFINE THE POPULATION

In this case, the population would be defined as all credit memoranda issued from the first day of the fiscal year, January 1, through the date that tests are performed. Assume that Chandler's balance sheet date is December 31, that interim testing of sales returns is planned for October 19, and that the first sequentially numbered credit memorandum issued on January 1 was No. 4329 and the last issued on October 19 was No. 5948. From this information, the population would be represented by all credit memoranda numbered 4329 to 5948. The sampling unit in this case would be individual credit memoranda.

DETERMINE SAMPLE SIZE

The auditor's acceptable risk of assessing control risk too low, tolerable rate of deviation, and expected population deviation rate are indicated in Figure 8-4 for each of the five attributes of interest. (Note that the sample size, number of deviations, sample results, and audit conclusion are also indicated on the completed Figure 8-4, but are discussed later.) For example, for the first attribute, accurate unit pricing and extensions on credit memoranda, the auditor is willing to accept a 5 percent risk of assessing control risk too low, which, as discussed earlier, corresponds to 95 percent reliability, the auditor's planned level of confidence. The tolerable and expected rates of deviation for Attribute 1 are .04 and .0075, respectively, indicating that the auditor expects a .0075 deviation rate but is willing to tolerate 4 percent, more than four times the rate of deviation expected.

Sample size for each attribute is determined from Figures 8-5 or 8-6. Figure 8-5, used when the acceptable risk of assessing control risk too low is 5 percent, is appropriate for Attributes 1, 2, 4, and 5. Figure 8-6, used when the acceptable risk is 10 percent, is appropriate for Attribute 3. Required sample size for each attribute is indicated in Figure 8-4. For example, for Attribute 1, required sample size per Figure 8-5 is 117, the intersection of the column associated with a 4 percent tolerable rate of deviation and the row associated with a .75 percent expected population deviation rate. Note that in Figure 8-4, the auditor has rounded sample size up to 125 items (to accommodate the sample evaluation tables in Figure 8-9).

PERFORM THE SAMPLING PLAN

Selecting and testing sampling units is typically the most time-consuming phase of any sampling plan, since documents or other evidence must be gathered and then evaluated. As discussed earlier, either random-number sampling or systematic sampling is most appropriate for statistical sampling.

The auditor for Chandler selects random-number sampling, because the sequential four-digit credit memorandum numbers correspond readily to random-number tables. However, because sample size varies for the attributes tested—i.e., 50 for Attribute 3, 100 for Attributes 4 and 5, and 125 for Attributes

Figure 8-4:   Audit Working Paper: Documentation of Sample Results

B12
DM
10/21/1999

Chandler Wire & Cable Co.
Attribute Estimation Worksheet—Sales Returns
December 31, 1999

Attribute	1 Acceptable Risk of Assessing Control Risk Too Low	2 Tolerable Rate of Deviation	3 Expected Population Deviation Rate	4 Sample Size Table	4 Sample Size Used	5 Number of Deviations	Sample Deviation Rate	6 Maximum Population Deviation Rate
1. Unit pricing and extensions on the credit memo are accurate.	.05	.04	.0075	117	125	1*	.008	.038
2. Quantity and other data on the credit memo agrees with the receiving report.	.05	.05	.015	124	125	2*	.016	.05
3. Quantity and description on the credit memo agrees with perpetual inventory.	.10	.08	.02	48	50	1*	.02	.076
4. The entry is properly recorded as a debit to Inventory and a credit to Cost of Goods Sold.	.05	.05	.01	93	100	0	0	.03
5. The entry is properly recorded as a debit to Sales Returns and a credit to Accounts Receivable.	.05	.05	.01	93	100	0	0	.03

*See analysis of deviations at B13.

Audit Conclusion

Based on procedures performed, the tolerable rate of deviation equals or exceeds the maximum population deviation rate for all five attributes tested; therefore, controls over sales returns are considered effective in preventing or detecting misstatements. Control risk for assertions related to sales returns is set below the maximum.

Figure 8-5: Statistical Sample Sizes for Tests of Controls, Five Percent Risk of Assessing Control Risk Too Low

Expected Population Deviation Rate	Tolerable Rate										
	2%	3%	4%	5%	6%	7%	8%	9%	10%	15%	20%
0.00%	149	99	74	59	49	42	36	32	29	19	14
.25	236	157	117	93	78	66	58	51	46	30	22
.50	*	157	117	93	78	66	58	51	46	30	22
.75	*	208	117	93	78	66	58	51	46	30	22
1.00	*	*	156	93	78	66	58	51	46	30	22
1.25	*	*	156	124	78	66	58	51	46	30	22
1.50	*	*	192	124	103	66	58	51	46	30	22
1.75	*	*	227	153	103	88	77	51	46	30	22
2.00	*	*	*	181	127	88	77	68	46	30	22
2.25	*	*	*	208	127	109	77	68	61	30	22
2.50	*	*	*	*	150	109	77	68	61	30	22
2.75	*	*	*	*	173	129	95	68	61	30	22
3.00	*	*	*	*	195	148	95	84	61	30	22
3.25	*	*	*	*	*	167	112	84	61	30	22
3.50	*	*	*	*	*	185	112	84	76	40	22
3.75	*	*	*	*	*	*	129	100	76	40	22
4.00	*	*	*	*	*	*	146	100	89	40	22
5.00	*	*	*	*	*	*	*	158	116	40	30
6.00	*	*	*	*	*	*	*	*	179	50	30
7.00	*	*	*	*	*	*	*	*	*	68	37

*Sample size is too large to be cost-effective for most audit applications.

1 and 2—an initial sample of 50 can be selected for all attributes, an additional 50 for Attributes 1, 2, 4, and 5, and another 25 for Attributes 1 and 2. Figure 8-7 illustrates how the auditor for Chandler selected the first 25 credit memoranda.

After selecting the necessary sampling units, the auditor examines them and documents any observed deviations for each attribute. Figure 8-4 indicates that one deviation was observed for Attribute 1, two were observed for Attribute 2, and one for Attribute 3; none were observed for Attributes 4 and 5. Figure 8-8 is the auditor's analysis of each individual deviation. Note particularly the auditor's judgment expressed in Figure 8-8 about the effect of each

Figure 8-6: Statistical Sample Sizes for Tests of Controls, Ten Percent Risk of Assessing Control Risk Too Low

Expected Population Deviation Rate	Tolerable Rate										
	2%	3%	4%	5%	6%	7%	8%	9%	10%	15%	20%
0.00%	114	76	57	45	38	32	28	25	22	15	11
.25	194	129	96	77	64	55	48	42	38	25	18
.50	194	129	96	77	64	55	48	42	38	25	18
.75	265	129	96	77	64	55	48	42	38	25	18
1.00	*	176	96	77	64	55	48	42	38	25	18
1.25	*	221	132	77	64	55	48	42	38	25	18
1.50	*	*	132	105	64	55	48	42	38	25	18
1.75	*	*	166	105	88	55	48	42	38	25	18
2.00	*	*	198	132	88	75	48	42	38	25	18
2.25	*	*	*	132	88	75	65	58	38	25	18
2.50	*	*	*	158	110	75	65	58	38	25	18
2.75	*	*	*	209	132	94	65	58	52	25	18
3.00	*	*	*	*	132	94	65	58	52	25	18
3.25	*	*	*	*	153	113	82	58	52	25	18
3.50	*	*	*	*	194	113	82	73	52	25	18
3.75	*	*	*	*	*	131	98	73	52	25	18
4.00	*	*	*	*	*	149	98	73	65	25	18
5.00	*	*	*	*	*	*	160	115	78	34	18
6.00	*	*	*	*	*	*	*	182	116	43	25
7.00	*	*	*	*	*	*	*	*	199	52	25

*Sample size is too large to be cost-effective for most audit applications.

deviation on substantive tests of details: In each case, no additional audit work—none beyond the substantive tests necessary to control detection risk to the level planned—was considered necessary, for the reasons cited.

EVALUATE THE SAMPLE RESULTS

The results of the attribute estimation sampling plan are tabulated in the last two columns of Figure 8-4. The sample deviation rate for each attribute is calculated by dividing the number of deviations by the sample size used. For example, for Attribute 1, the sample deviation rate is .008 (1 deviation divided by 125 sampling units).

Figure 8-7: Audit Working Paper: Documentation of Sample Selection

B14
DM
10/19/1999

Chandler Wire and Cable Co.
Random Number Sample Selection Sales Returns
December 31, 1999

7248	2987	⑥ 5392	7504	㉑ 4639	4302
8536	③ 4507	9502	7510	2094	㉓ 5646
4589	9076	⑦ 5647	9706	1039	8970
3905	0125	⑧ 4710	9626	2049	9574
9087	8965	8526	7524	2049	6589
2908	4075	7921	⑭ 4650	㉒ 5647	9706
start (0012)	1283	⑨ 4628	⑮ 4909	5960	㉔ 4657
↓ 1490	6904	6103	4310	3429	6720
4326	3209	3029	⑯ 5610	9706	㉕ 4382
① 5902	6520	2049	9706	6794	6857
3246	2840	⑩ 4900	⑰ 5820	8796	0978
7869	7512	⑪ 5930	7906	2538	0098
6793	④ 4629	⑫ 5291	⑱ 5647	6059	4039
7302	⑤ 5402	7946	8694	6721	8593
6739	8734	7501	⑲ 4910	8796	6758
② 4521	8053	⑬ 5342	⑳ 5768	6970	8079

Population: 4329-5948
Route: Select random start and proceed vertically down column; continue with next
column at right.

The maximum population deviation rate for each attribute is determined from
Figures 8-9 and 8-10. Figure 8-9, used when the risk of assessing control risk
too low is 5 percent, is appropriate for Attributes 1, 2, 4, and 5. Figure 8-10,
used when the risk is 10 percent, is appropriate for Attribute 3. The maximum
population deviation rate for each attribute is indicated in Figure 8-4. For
example, for Attribute 1, the maximum population deviation rate from Figure
8-9 is .038, the intersection of the column associated with one deviation and
the row associated with a sample size of 125. In statistical terms, the auditor's
conclusion for Attribute 1 could be expressed as follows:

*Based on procedures applied, the estimated population deviation rate is .008, and there
is a 95 percent probability (i.e., 5 percent risk of assessing control risk too low) that
the true but unknown population rate of deviation is less than or equal to .038.*

Figure 8-8: Audit Working Paper: Analysis of Deviations Observed in Sample

B13
DM
10/21/1999

Chandler Wire & Cable Co.
Analysis of Deviations: Sales Returns and Allowances
December 31, 1999

Attribute	Number of Deviations	Nature of Deviations	Effect on Substantive Detailed Testing
1	1	Cr. memo #4823: $1,269. Although unit prices were correct, the extensions were incorrect, resulting in a $59 understatement.	No additional audit work is considered necessary at year end because: (1) the resulting error is immaterial and (2) the maximum population deviation rate (.038) is less than the tolerable rate (.04).
2	2	Cr. memo #4934: $2,528. Cr. memo #4687: $1,729. In both cases, the description of returned inventory was inaccurate.	No additional audit work is considered necessary at year end because: (1) both cr. memos were recorded properly, despite the inaccurate descriptions, and (2) the maximum population deviation rate (.05) is equal to the tolerable rate (.05).
3	1	Cr. memo #4731: $5,421. The quantity recorded within perpetual records was inaccurate.	No additional audit work is considered necessary at year end because: (1) journal entries were properly recorded for this credit memo (Attributes 4 and 5) and (2) the maximum population deviation rate (.076) is less than the tolerable rate (.08).

A similar conclusion is reached for each of the other attributes tested.

Based on the statistical conclusions, the auditor formulates an audit conclusion for the entire set of attributes tested (or for individual attributes, in the case of mixed results). Because the tolerable rate is greater than or equal to the maximum population deviation rate for all five attributes (see Figure 8-4), and no other qualitative evidence exists to the contrary, the audit conclusion would be that the controls are effective in preventing or detecting material misstatements. The auditor's conclusion for Chandler Wire & Cable Company appears in Figure 8-4.

Figure 8-9: Statistical Sample Results Evaluation Table for Tests of Controls, Maximum Population Deviation Rates at Five Percent Risk of Assessing Control Risk Too Low

Sample Size	Actual Number of Deviations Found										
	0	1	2	3	4	5	6	7	8	9	10
25	11.3	17.6	*	*	*	*	*	*	*	*	*
30	9.5	14.9	19.6	*	*	*	*	*	*	*	*
35	8.3	12.9	17.0	*	*	*	*	*	*	*	*
40	7.3	11.4	15.0	18.3	*	*	*	*	*	*	*
45	6.5	10.2	13.4	16.4	19.2	*	*	*	*	*	*
50	5.9	9.2	12.1	14.8	17.4	19.9	*	*	*	*	*
55	5.4	8.4	11.1	13.5	15.9	18.2	*	*	*	*	*
60	4.9	7.7	10.2	12.5	14.7	16.8	18.8	*	*	*	*
65	4.6	7.1	9.4	11.5	13.6	15.5	17.4	19.3	*	*	*
70	4.2	6.6	8.8	10.8	12.6	14.5	16.3	18.0	19.7	*	*
75	4.0	6.2	8.2	10.1	11.8	13.6	15.2	16.9	18.5	20.0	*
80	3.7	5.8	7.7	9.5	11.1	12.7	14.3	15.9	17.4	18.9	*
90	3.3	5.2	6.9	8.4	9.9	11.4	12.8	14.2	15.5	16.8	18.2
100	3.0	4.7	6.2	7.6	9.0	10.3	11.5	12.8	14.0	15.2	16.4
125	2.4	3.8	5.0	6.1	7.2	8.3	9.3	10.3	11.3	12.3	13.2
150	2.0	3.2	4.2	5.1	6.0	6.9	7.8	8.6	9.5	10.3	11.1
200	1.5	2.4	3.2	3.9	4.6	5.2	5.9	6.5	7.2	7.8	8.4

*Over 20 percent.
Note: This table presents maximum population deviation rates as percentages. This table assumes a large population.

OTHER CONSIDERATIONS

Three observations about the results achieved and documented in Figure 8-4: First, the auditor's conclusions relate only to the period for which credit memoranda were available for testing—January 1 through October 19. Thus, the conclusions do not apply to the period October 20 through December 31, in the absence of additional sampling procedures. Second, recall that the prior auditor experienced relatively high deviation rates for tests of sales returns. However, the results in Figure 8-4 indicate otherwise for the current year, illustrating the very real phenomenon of changing audit conditions from year to year.

Third, note that for Attribute 2 in Figure 8-4 the maximum population deviation rate, .05, is equal to the tolerable rate. Because the maximum popu-

Figure 8-10: Statistical Sample Results Evaluation Table for Tests of Controls, Maximum Population Deviation Rates at Ten Percent Risk of Assessing Control Risk Too Low

Sample Size	Actual Number of Deviations Found										
	0	1	2	3	4	5	6	7	8	9	10
20	10.9	18.1	*	*	*	*	*	*	*	*	*
25	8.8	14.7	19.9	*	*	*	*	*	*	*	*
30	7.4	12.4	16.8	*	*	*	*	*	*	*	*
35	6.4	10.7	14.5	18.1	*	*	*	*	*	*	*
40	5.6	9.4	12.8	16.0	19.0	*	*	*	*	*	*
45	5.0	8.4	11.4	14.3	17.0	19.7	*	*	*	*	*
50	4.6	7.6	10.3	12.9	15.4	17.8	*	*	*	*	*
55	4.1	6.9	9.4	11.8	14.1	16.3	18.4	*	*	*	*
60	3.8	6.4	8.7	10.8	12.9	15.0	16.9	18.9	*	*	*
70	3.3	5.5	7.5	9.3	11.1	12.9	14.6	16.3	17.9	19.6	*
80	2.9	4.8	6.6	8.2	9.8	11.3	12.8	14.3	15.8	17.2	18.6
90	2.6	4.3	5.9	7.3	8.7	10.1	11.5	12.8	14.1	15.4	16.6
100	2.3	3.9	5.3	6.6	7.9	9.1	10.3	11.5	12.7	13.9	15.0
120	2.0	3.3	4.4	5.5	6.6	7.6	8.7	9.7	10.7	11.6	12.6
160	1.5	2.5	3.3	4.2	5.0	5.8	6.5	7.3	8.0	8.8	9.5
200	1.2	2.0	2.7	3.4	4.0	4.6	5.3	5.9	6.5	7.1	7.6

*Over 20 percent.
Note: This table presents maximum population deviation rates as percentages. This table assumes a large population.

lation rate and tolerable rate are equal, the auditor might consider the control questionable. On the other hand, the control attribute itself—credit memo quantity and other data agree with the receiving report—may not be sufficiently critical to warrant assessing control risk at the maximum, since there may be compensating controls and existing evidence that credit memoranda are recorded properly in the accounts. The auditor's decision, the assessed level of control risk, would be based on weighing these two points of view and is an example of the types of trade-offs considered by auditors in practice. In this case, it's likely the auditor would assess control risk for sales returns below the maximum.

In Chapter 10, attribute estimation is illustrated for tests of controls applied to the billing function of a medium-sized supplier of handheld power tools.

SEQUENTIAL (STOP-OR-GO) SAMPLING

Audit sampling can be accomplished with either a fixed or a sequential sampling plan. In a *fixed sampling plan*, such as attribute estimation, the auditor tests a single sample. However, in **sequential (stop-or-go) sampling**, the sampling plan is performed in several steps. Following each step, an auditor decides whether to stop testing or to go on to the next step, thus accounting for why the plan is sometimes called *stop-or-go sampling*.

Sequential sampling can be used as an alternative to attribute estimation when an auditor expects zero or very few deviations within an audit population. For example, for a continuing audit engagement, an auditor might decide to use sequential sampling if the prior year's attribute estimation sampling plans yielded very low maximum population deviation rates, the prior year's observed deviations did not result in material misstatements, and there was no reason to expect that deviations in the current year would result in material misstatements. For this set of circumstances, an auditor could possibly minimize sample size by using sequential sampling, thereby minimizing audit time and improving audit efficiency.

Assuming that the objectives, attributes, deviation conditions, and population are defined properly and that the sample selection method is chosen, an auditor would proceed through Steps 5 through 7 of the general sampling plan in Figure 8-2 as discussed below.

DETERMINE SAMPLE SIZE

Determining sample size in sequential sampling requires that an auditor first specify the desired reliability and the tolerable rate of deviation. As noted earlier, *desired reliability* is the complement of the risk of assessing control risk too low, which was needed to determine sample size in attribute estimation sampling. As a result, desired reliability is also a matter of professional judgment and may be deduced from an auditor's acceptable risk of assessing control risk too low. That is, if an auditor intended to assess control risk below the maximum and therefore decided on a rather low risk of assessing control risk too low, such as 2 percent, then desired reliability would be 98 percent (i.e., 1.00 − .02). Note that because there is an inverse relationship between sample size and the risk of assessing control risk too low, there is a direct relationship between desired reliability and sample size: Sample size must be larger when an auditor specifies a higher desired reliability. In general, a higher desired reliability is appropriate when an auditor believes the internal controls may be effective, resulting in a lower control risk; a lower reliability level is appropriate otherwise.

As in attribute estimation, the *tolerable rate of deviation* is the maximum rate an auditor is willing to accept in the sample without deciding a control is ineffective. A lower tolerable rate of deviation is appropriate when an auditor plans to assess a lower control risk. Unlike attribute estimation sampling, sequential sampling does not require an estimate of the expected population deviation rate, because sequential sampling is applied only when an auditor expects zero or very few deviations.

In sequential sampling, sample size can be determined from standard tables such as the one shown in Figure 8-11 which is also used to evaluate

Figure 8-11: Sequential Sampling: Table for Determining Sample Size and Evaluating Sample Results

Size Sample Examined	No. of Deviations Found	Probability That Deviation is Less Than:														
		1%	2%	3%	4%	5%	6%	7%	8%	9%	10%	12%	14%	16%	18%	20%
50	0	39.50	63.58	78.19	87.01	92.31	95.47	97.34	98.45	99.10	99.49	99.83	99.95	99.98	100.00	100.00
	1	8.94	26.42	44.47	59.95	72.06	81.00	87.35	91.73	94.68	96.62	98.69	99.52	99.83	99.94	99.98
	2	1.38	7.84	18.92	32.33	45.95	58.38	68.92	77.40	83.95	88.83	94.87	97.79	99.10	99.65	99.87
	3	0.16	1.78	6.28	13.91	23.96	35.27	46.73	57.47	66.97	74.97	86.55	93.30	96.88	98.64	99.43
	4	0.02	0.32	1.68	4.90	10.36	17.94	27.10	37.11	47.23	56.88	73.21	84.72	91.92	96.01	98.15
	5		0.05	0.37	1.44	3.78	7.76	13.51	20.81	29.28	38.39	56.47	71.86	83.23	90.71	95.20
	6		0.01	0.07	0.36	1.18	2.89	5.83	10.19	15.96	22.98	39.35	56.16	70.81	81.99	89.66
70	0	50.52	75.69	88.14	94.26	97.24	98.69	99.38	99.71	99.86	99.94	99.99	100.00	100.00	100.00	100.00
	1	15.53	40.96	62.47	77.51	87.03	92.81	96.10	97.93	98.92	99.45	99.86	99.97	99.99	100.00	100.00
	2	3.34	16.50	35.08	53.44	68.63	79.87	87.59	92.60	95.72	97.58	99.28	99.80	99.95	99.99	100.00
	3	0.54	5.19	15.87	30.71	46.61	61.15	73.07	82.10	88.53	92.88	97.48	99.19	99.76	99.93	99.98
	4	0.07	1.32	5.93	14.85	27.21	41.13	54.77	66.80	76.61	84.12	93.36	97.51	99.16	99.74	99.92
	5		0.28	1.86	6.12	13.72	24.27	36.58	49.24	61.06	71.28	85.94	93.92	97.64	99.17	99.73
	6		0.05	0.50	2.18	6.04	12.61	21.75	32.70	44.40	55.82	74.98	87.57	94.50	97.81	99.20
	7			0.12	0.68	2.34	5.80	11.54	19.54	29.33	40.12	61.33	78.13	89.04	95.08	98.00
	8			0.02	0.19	0.80	2.38	5.49	10.54	17.59	26.37	46.66	66.03	80.85	90.36	95.63
	9				0.05	0.25	0.88	2.36	5.14	9.60	15.86	32.88	52.46	70.10	83.23	91.55
100	0	63.40	86.74	95.25	98.31	99.41	99.80	99.93	99.98	99.99	100.00	100.00	100.00	100.00	100.00	100.00
	1	26.42	59.67	80.54	91.28	96.29	98.48	99.40	99.77	99.91	99.97	100.00	100.00	100.00	100.00	100.00
	2	7.94	32.33	58.02	76.79	88.17	94.34	97.42	98.87	99.52	99.81	99.97	100.00	100.00	100.00	100.00
	3	1.84	14.10	35.28	57.05	74.22	85.70	92.56	96.33	98.27	99.22	99.86	99.98	100.00	100.00	100.00
	4	0.34	5.08	18.22	37.11	56.40	72.32	83.68	90.97	95.26	97.63	99.47	99.90	99.98	100.00	100.00
	5	0.05	1.55	8.08	21.16	38.40	55.93	70.86	82.01	89.55	94.24	98.48	99.66	99.93	99.99	100.00
	6	0.01	0.41	3.12	10.64	23.40	39.37	55.57	69.68	80.60	88.28	96.33	99.03	99.78	99.96	99.99
	7		0.09	1.06	4.75	12.80	25.17	40.12	55.29	68.72	79.40	92.39	97.67	99.39	99.86	99.97

Figure 8-11: *(continued)*

Sample Size Examined	No. of Deviations Found	Probability That Deviation is Less Than:														
		1%	2%	3%	4%	5%	6%	7%	8%	9%	10%	12%	14%	16%	18%	20%
	8		0.02	0.32	1.90	6.31	14.63	26.60	40.74	55.06	67.91	86.14	95.08	98.53	99.62	99.91
	9			0.09	0.68	2.82	7.75	16.20	27.80	41.25	54.87	77.44	90.78	96.84	99.08	99.77
	10			0.02	0.22	1.15	3.76	9.08	17.57	20.82	46.68	66.63	84.40	93.93	98.00	94.43
	11				0.07	0.43	1.68	4.69	10.29	18.76	29.70	54.58	75.91	89.39	96.05	98.74
	12				0.02	0.15	0.69	2.24	5.59	11.38	19.82	42.39	65.66	82.97	92.89	97.47
	13					0.05	0.26	0.99	2.82	6.45	12.39	31.14	54.36	74.69	88.19	95.31
	14					0.01	0.09	0.41	1.33	3.41	7.26	21.60	42.94	64.90	81.77	91.96
	15						0.03	0.16	0.59	1.69	3.99	14.15	32.27	54.20	73.70	87.15
120	0	70.06	91.15	97.41	99.25	99.79	99.94	99.98	100.00	100.00	100.00	100.00	100.00	100.00	100.00	100.00
	1	33.77	69.46	87.82	95.53	98.45	99.48	99.83	99.95	99.98	100.00	100.00	100.00	100.00	100.00	100.00
	2	11.96	43.13	70.16	86.28	94.25	97.75	99.17	99.71	99.90	99.97	100.00	100.00	100.00	100.00	100.00
	3	3.30	22.00	48.67	71.13	85.56	93.40	97.19	98.87	99.60	99.84	99.98	100.00	100.00	100.00	100.00
	4	0.74	9.38	29.24	52.67	72.18	85.27	92.83	96.75	98.61	99.44	99.92	99.99	100.00	100.00	100.00
	5	0.14	3.41	15.29	34.83	55.85	73.23	85.23	92.47	96.42	98.40	99.72	99.96	99.99	100.00	100.00
	6	0.02	1.07	7.03	20.57	39.37	58.50	74.26	85.35	92.26	96.18	99.21	99.87	99.98	100.00	100.00
	7		0.30	2.86	10.90	25.24	43.20	60.81	75.25	85.57	92.16	98.08	99.62	99.94	99.99	100.00
	8		0.07	1.04	5.21	14.74	29.39	46.15	62.85	76.21	85.86	95.89	99.05	99.82	99.97	100.00
	9		0.02	0.34	2.26	7.86	18.43	33.12	49.44	64.70	77.14	92.18	97.89	99.53	99.91	99.99
	10			0.10	0.89	3.85	10.66	21.93	36.49	52.06	66.39	86.56	95.79	98.94	99.78	99.96
	11			0.03	0.32	1.73	5.70	13.50	25.23	39.56	54.45	78.90	92.39	97.80	99.48	99.90
	12			0.01	0.11	0.72	2.83	7.75	16.33	28.33	42.39	69.41	87.35	95.83	98.88	99.75
	13				0.03	0.28	1.31	4.15	9.91	19.11	31.27	58.66	80.53	92.71	97.78	99.44
	14				0.01	0.10	0.56	2.07	5.64	12.13	21.82	47.45	72.05	88.17	95.95	98.86
	15					0.03	0.23	0.97	3.01	7.26	14.40	36.66	62.30	82.06	93.10	97.82
	16					0.01	0.09	0.43	1.51	4.10	8.99	26.99	51.88	74.42	89.00	96.12
	17						0.03	0.18	0.72	2.18	5.31	18.93	41.50	65.52	83.49	93.53
	18						0.01	0.07	0.32	1.10	2.97	12.64	31.84	55.82	76.57	89.81

Figure 8-11: (continued)

Size Sample Examined	No. of Deviations Found	Probability That Deviation is Less Than:														
		1%	2%	3%	4%	5%	6%	7%	8%	9%	10%	12%	14%	16%	18%	20%
150	0	77.86	95.17	98.96	99.78	99.95	99.99	100.00	100.00	100.00	100.00	100.00	100.00	100.00	100.00	100.00
	1	44.30	80.39	94.15	98.41	99.60	99.90	99.98	100.00	100.00	100.00	100.00	100.00	100.00	100.00	100.00
	2	19.05	57.91	83.07	94.16	98.19	99.48	99.86	99.96	99.99	100.00	100.00	100.00	100.00	100.00	100.00
	3	6.47	35.28	66.16	85.42	94.52	98.14	99.42	99.83	99.95	99.99	100.00	100.00	100.00	100.00	100.00
	4	1.80	18.30	46.93	72.04	87.44	95.01	98.20	99.40	99.81	99.95	100.00	100.00	100.00	100.00	100.00
	5	0.42	8.19	29.57	55.76	76.56	89.17	95.52	98.31	99.41	99.81	99.98	100.00	100.00	100.00	100.00
	6	0.08	3.20	16.60	39.37	62.71	80.16	90.66	96.03	98.45	99.44	99.94	99.99	100.00	100.00	100.00
	7	0.02	1.11	8.34	25.32	47.72	68.34	83.12	91.94	96.50	98.60	99.82	99.98	100.00	100.00	100.00
	8		0.34	3.78	14.85	33.62	54.84	72.98	85.58	93.04	96.93	99.52	99.94	99.99	100.00	100.00
	9		0.10	1.55	7.97	21.91	41.26	60.93	76.85	87.65	94.00	98.89	99.84	99.98	100.00	100.00
	10		0.02	0.58	3.93	13.22	29.03	48.15	66.16	80.13	89.40	97.66	99.61	99.95	99.99	100.00
	11		0.01	0.20	1.79	7.40	19.09	35.90	54.32	70.66	82.91	95.54	99.14	99.87	99.98	100.00
	12			0.06	0.75	3.85	11.74	25.23	42.40	59.82	74.55	92.19	98.25	99.70	99.96	100.00
	13			0.02	0.29	1.87	6.77	16.70	31.39	48.43	64.70	87.34	96.70	99.35	99.90	99.99
	14				0.11	0.85	3.66	10.42	22.03	37.41	53.98	80.86	94.25	98.70	99.77	99.97
	15				0.04	0.36	1.86	6.13	14.64	27.53	43.18	72.85	90.62	97.58	99.52	99.92
	16				0.01	0.14	0.89	3.40	9.22	19.28	33.06	63.64	85.63	95.78	99.05	99.83
	17					0.05	0.40	1.79	5.51	12.86	24.19	53.74	79.24	93.07	98.24	99.65
	18					0.02	0.17	0.89	3.13	8.16	16.92	43.76	71.54	89.26	96.92	99.31
	19					0.01	0.07	0.42	1.68	4.93	11.30	34.31	62.84	84.21	94.90	98.72
	20						0.03	0.19	0.86	2.84	7.21	25.87	53.56	77.92	92.01	97.76
	21						0.01	0.08	0.42	1.56	4.40	18.74	44.22	70.50	88.08	96.28
	22							0.03	0.20	0.82	2.56	13.04	35.29	62.22	83.02	94.10
	23							0.01	0.09	0.41	1.43	8.72	27.20	53.43	76.84	91.07
	24								0.04	0.20	0.76	5.60	20.24	44.58	68.66	87.06

results. Figure 8-11 is appropriate for populations over 2,000 items and is used as follows:

- Locate the column associated with the tolerable rate of deviation (the percentages in the table) and row associated with zero errors.
- Beginning with the smallest sample size (i.e., 50 at the extreme top left column of the table) and continuing for increasingly higher sample sizes, review the column and row (zero deviations) intersections until you locate the sample size that achieves at least the desired level of reliability.

For example, assume:

Desired reliability   = .95
Tolerable rate of deviation = .05

Per Figure 8-11, the smallest sample size that achieves at least 95 percent reliability for zero expected deviations is 70.

Note that a smaller sample size of 50 (which is at the intersection of a 5 percent tolerable rate of deviation and zero expected deviations) results in a reliability level of 92.31 percent, which is clearly below the desired reliability level of 95 percent. However, for a sample size of 70, the intersection of a 5 percent tolerable rate and zero expected deviations results in a reliability level of 97.24 percent, a level that is acceptable—i.e., at least 95 percent for this example.

PERFORM THE SAMPLING PLAN AND EVALUATE THE RESULTS

Sampling units are selected using, for example, random-number sampling or systematic sampling, as in attribute estimation. After examining the sampling units included within the initial sample selection, an auditor then decides from the sample results whether to stop or to go on with the sampling plan. The decision to stop or go depends primarily on how many deviations are observed. If no deviations are observed, the auditor can conclude that the actual population deviation rate is within the predetermined tolerable rate, and therefore may stop the sampling plan. For the preceding example, no observed deviations would yield a conclusion as follows:

Based on procedures applied, there is a 97.24 percent probability that the actual population deviation rate is less than .05.

However, if one or more deviations are observed within the original sample, the auditor could decide to increase sample size in an attempt to seek additional deviation-free sampling units and reevaluate the sample accordingly. In this situation, Figure 8-11 would be used in essentially the same way as in determining initial sample size.

In Chapter 12, sequential sampling is illustrated for tests of controls applied to the cash disbursements function of a medium-sized manufacturer of paper products.

DISCOVERY SAMPLING

Discovery sampling for attributes is appropriate when the expected rate of deviation is near zero and when the auditor's objective is to find at least one deviation in a sample if the actual population deviation rate exceeds or equals a predetermined critical rate of deviation. In discovery sampling, a single deviation in a sample is sufficient to conclude that the population deviation rate exceeds the critical rate. The critical rate in discovery sampling is comparable to the tolerable rate in attribute estimation and sequential sampling.

Discovery sampling is used most often when no deviations would be expected and therefore even one would cause concern, such as suspected fraudulent cash payments. Thus, a discovery sampling plan may be appropriate when the audit objective is to observe at least one deviation at a specified critical rate, the expected population deviation rate is near zero, and an auditor desires a specified probability of observing at least one deviation if the actual population rate exceeds the critical rate. Although discovery sampling is concerned with population rates of deviation, it does not specifically yield an estimated rate of deviation; rather, it generates sample sizes appropriate for finding at least one deviation for various size populations, various critical rates of deviation, and various probabilities of success.

Assuming that the objectives, attributes, deviation conditions, and population are defined properly, an auditor would proceed through the remaining phases of the plan as follows:

DETERMINE SAMPLE SIZE

Determining sample size in discovery sampling plans requires that an auditor first specify a critical rate of deviation and the desired probability of observing at least one deviation. The *critical rate of deviation* is the minimum population deviation rate that must exist if one deviation is to be observed at a specified probability. Much like a tolerable rate in attribute estimation, the critical rate is a matter of professional judgment and depends partly on control risk and partly on materiality. The *desired probability* of observing at least one deviation is comparable to desired reliability in sequential sampling and is also a matter of professional judgment.

Increasing or decreasing the critical rate or desired probability will influence sample size. Increasing either will increase sample size; decreasing either will decrease sample size. The impact on sample size of increasing one and decreasing the other would depend on the magnitude of both the increase and the decrease.

Required sample sizes for discovery sampling plans can be determined from standard tables designed to yield the minimum sample size required to find at least one deviation with a specified probability. Figure 8-12 can be used to determine sample size for populations between 2,000 and 5,000, and Figure 8-13 for populations between 5,000 and 10,000; other tables are required for populations over 10,000. To determine sample size from the tables, identify the column associated with the critical rate of deviation, reading down the column to the desired probability. Required sample size is the number to the far left on the row containing the desired probability. For example, assume the following:

Population size   = 6,500 items
Critical rate of deviation = .0075 (.75%)
Desired probability   = .95   (95%)

Figure 8-12: Probability in Percent of Including at Least One Deviation in a Sample for Populations Between 2,000 and 5,000

Sample Size	Upper Precision Limit: Critical Rate of Deviation							
	.3%	.4%	.5%	.6%	.8%	1%	1.5%	2%
50	14%	18%	22%	26%	33%	40%	53%	64%
60	17	21	26	30	38	45	60	70
70	19	25	30	35	43	51	66	76
80	22	28	33	38	48	56	70	80
90	24	31	37	42	52	60	75	84
100	26	33	40	46	56	64	78	87
120	31	39	46	52	62	70	84	91
140	35	43	51	57	68	76	88	94
160	39	48	56	62	73	80	91	96
200	46	56	64	71	81	87	95	98
240	52	63	71	77	86	92	98	99
300	61	71	79	84	92	96	99	99+
340	65	76	83	88	94	97	99+	99+
400	71	81	88	92	96	98	99+	99+
460	77	86	91	95	98	99	99+	99+
500	79	88	93	96	99	99	99+	99+
600	85	92	96	98	99	99+	99+	99+
700	90	95	98	99	99+	99+	99+	99+
800	93	97	99	99	99+	99+	99+	99+
900	95	98	99	99+	99+	99+	99+	99+
1,000	97	99	99+	99+	99+	99+	99+	99+

From Figure 8-13, used since population size is between 5,000 and 10,000, sample size would be obtained by reading down the column at .75 percent critical rate to 95 percent probability and left to required sample size of 400.

PERFORM THE SAMPLING PLAN AND EVALUATE THE SAMPLE RESULTS

Sampling units should be selected at random and examined for the attribute of interest. If no deviations are observed, an auditor's conclusion would be stated in terms of the critical rate of deviation and desired probability. Continuing the preceding example, assume no deviations are found. An auditor's statistical conclusion would be:

Figure 8-13: Probability in Percent of Including at Least One Deviation in a Sample for Populations Between 5,000 and 10,000

Sample Size	Upper Precision Limit: Critical Rate of Deviation							
	.1%	.2%	.3%	.4%	.5%	.75%	1%	2%
50	5%	10%	14%	18%	22%	31%	40%	64%
60	6	11	17	21	26	36	45	70
70	7	13	19	25	30	41	51	76
80	8	15	21	28	33	45	55	80
90	9	17	24	30	36	49	60	84
100	10	18	26	33	40	53	64	87
120	11	21	30	38	45	60	70	91
140	13	25	35	43	51	65	76	94
160	15	28	38	48	55	70	80	96
200	18	33	45	56	64	78	87	98
240	22	39	52	62	70	84	91	99
300	26	46	60	70	78	90	95	99+
340	29	50	65	75	82	93	97	99+
400	34	56	71	81	87	95	98	99+
460	38	61	76	85	91	97	99	99+
500	40	64	79	87	92	98	99	99+
600	46	71	84	92	96	99	99+	99+
700	52	77	89	95	97	99+	99+	99+
800	57	81	92	96	98	99+	99+	99+
900	61	85	94	98	99	99+	99+	99+
1,000	65	88	96	99	99	99+	99+	99+
1,500	80	96	99	99+	99+	99+	99+	99+
2,000	89	99	99+	99+	99+	99+	99+	99+

Based on procedures performed, there is a 95 percent probability that the population rate of deviation is less than or equal to the critical rate of deviation (.0075).

If an occurrence is observed, an auditor could use an attribute estimation evaluation table (e.g., Figure 8-9) to estimate a maximum population deviation rate.

NONSTATISTICAL SAMPLING IN TESTS OF CONTROLS

Even though nonstatistical sampling plans do not measure sampling risk, they can provide results as effective as statistical plans, and are often chosen by auditors when the costs of generating statistical samples exceed the benefits. Generally, the steps in a nonstatistical sampling plan are the same as those in a statistical plan, although the auditor's judgment is guided less by statistical theory and more by experience and by prior knowledge and current information about the client. The following discussion addresses some considerations in nonstatistical sampling not specifically covered earlier in the chapter.

DETERMINE SAMPLE SIZE

An auditor considers precisely the same parameters when determining nonstatistical sample size as when calculating statistical sample size: the risk of assessing control risk too low, the tolerable rate of deviation, and the expected population deviation rate. However, in nonstatistical sampling, the parameters may be expressed in relative terms, such as low, medium, high, etc., rather than in quantitative terms. When determining sample size in nonstatistical sampling, the auditor should consider the impact of increasing or decreasing the acceptable risk of assessing control risk too low and of increasing or decreasing the tolerable and expected rates of deviation, as illustrated earlier in Figure 8-3. For example, an auditor could justifiably consider decreasing sample size if his or her tolerable rate of deviation increased.

Alternatively, in a nonstatistical sampling plan the auditor could subjectively quantify each population parameter and then use standard tables (e.g., Figure 8-5 or 8-6) to determine sample size. Calculated sample size could then either be used or altered according to the auditor's judgment to reflect any reconsideration of the parameters in Figure 8-3 and sampling risk.

As in statistical sampling, sampling units can be selected using random-number sampling or systematic sampling, either of which could achieve randomness, thereby improving the likelihood of selecting representative sample items. Two other selection methods are available: block sampling and haphazard sampling, both of which require extreme care by the auditor, as discussed earlier.

EVALUATE SAMPLE RESULTS

Because nonstatistical sampling plans do not yield an estimate of sampling risk, the auditor must use professional judgment to determine whether the difference between his or her tolerable rate of deviation and the estimated population deviation rate is an adequate allowance for sampling risk. For example, assume that an auditor will tolerate 8 percent deviations and observes 3 deviations in a sample of 50. In this case, the estimated population rate of deviation is the sample deviation rate of 6 percent (3/50). Since the tolerable rate of deviation is 8 percent, the auditor would be faced with the decision of whether 2 percent (8 percent tolerable rate minus 6 percent estimated population rate) is an adequate allowance for sampling risk.

SUMMARY

Audit sampling, whether statistical or nonstatistical, involves testing less than 100 percent of the items that compose an audit population and is intended to aid an auditor in reaching cost-effective conclusions about audit populations. This chapter discusses audit sampling in tests of controls and Chapter 9 addresses audit sampling in substantive testing.

Attributes sampling plans focus on rates of deviation from prescribed internal controls and are used to accomplish tests of controls during an auditor's consideration of internal control. However, attributes sampling does entail some risk, partly because the auditor is not certain that a sample is wholly representative of the population from which the sampling units were drawn. Therefore, the auditor is not certain whether he or she is likely to assess control risk too high, which would affect the efficiency of the audit, or too low, which would affect the effectiveness of the audit.

Attributes sampling plans may be either statistical or nonstatistical, and either approach can provide reliable results if designed properly. A properly designed statistical or nonstatistical sampling plan should consider the following: the auditor's objectives; properly defined attributes, deviation conditions, and population; a defendable method of sample selection; a rational means of determining sample size; and justifiable procedures for performing the sampling plan and evaluating the results. Three generally accepted statistical sampling plans commonly used in practice today are attribute estimation sampling, sequential (stop-or-go) sampling, and discovery sampling, all of which are illustrated in detail in the chapter.

KEY TERMS

Sampling 276
Population 276
Sampling plan 276
Attributes sampling plan 276
Variables sampling plan 276
Audit risk 277
Control risk 277
Inherent risk 277
Detection risk 278
Sampling risk 278
Nonsampling risk 278
Risk of assessing control risk too high 278

Risk of assessing control risk too low 279
Statistical sampling plans 279
Nonstatistical sampling plans 279
Attribute 281
Deviation 281
Sampling unit 282
Tolerable rate of deviation 284
Sample deviation rate 287
Attribute estimation sampling 288
Sequential (stop-or-go) sampling 298
Discovery sampling 302

REFERENCES

Professional Standards

AICPA. *Codification of Statements on Auditing Standards.* New York: AICPA (AU Sec. 312, 319, 350).
AICPA. *Audit and Accounting Guide,* "Audit Sampling." New York: AICPA (1983).
SAS No. 39, "Audit Sampling" (AU Sec. 350).

SAS No. 47, "Audit Risk and Materiality in Conducting an Audit" (AU Sec. 312).

SAS No. 55, "Consideration of the Internal Control Structure in a Financial Statement Audit" (AU Sec. 319).

SAS No. 78, "Consideration of Internal Control in a Financial Statement Audit: An Amendment to SAS No. 55."

QUESTIONS

1. What is meant by the term *audit sampling*?
2. Distinguish between sampling for attributes and sampling for variables.
3. What is the purpose of attributes sampling in tests of controls?
4. Describe the nature and components of audit risk.
5. What is nonsampling risk and how can it be controlled?
6. Identify the sampling risks inherent in sampling for attributes.
7. Compare and contrast nonstatistical and statistical audit sampling plans.
8. Why is it important that audit populations be defined properly?
9. How can an auditor achieve randomness when selecting a statistical sample?
10. What is the purpose of stratifying an audit population?
11. Identify the three parameters necessary to determine sample size in attribute estimation sampling plans.
12. Describe the alternative available to an auditor when an attributes sampling plan suggests that a control is not effective.
13. When is attribute estimation appropriate?
14. When is sequential sampling appropriate?
15. Under what conditions may discovery sampling be appropriate?

MULTIPLE CHOICE QUESTIONS

1. When using statistical sampling for tests of controls, an auditor's evaluation would include a statistical conclusion about whether:

a. Deviations in the population are within an acceptable range.
b. Monetary precision exceeds a predetermined amount.
c. The population's total monetary value is not in error by more than a predetermined amount.
d. Population characteristics occur at least once in the population.

2. Tests of controls provide reasonable assurance that controls are applied as prescribed. A sampling method that is useful when testing controls is:

a. Nonstatistical sampling.
b. Attribute estimation sampling.
c. Discovery sampling.
d. Stratified random sampling.

3. Statistical sampling:

a. Measures quantitatively the risk from testing only part of an audit population.
b. Allows the same degree of confidence as nonstatistical sampling but with substantially less work.
c. Allows the auditor to replace some judgments with quantitative measures.
d. Measures the reliability of misstatements.

4. Assessing control risk too high is the risk that the sample:

a. Does not support tolerable error for some or all of management's assertions.
b. Contains proportionately more deviations from prescribed control procedures than actually exist in the population as a whole.
c. Contains monetary misstatements that could be material to the financial statements when aggregated with misstatements in other account balances or classes of transactions.
d. Contains proportionately fewer deviations from prescribed control procedures than actually exist in the population as a whole.

5. Assessing control risk too low relates to:

a. The efficiency of the audit.
b. The effectiveness of the audit.
c. The preliminary estimate of materiality.
d. Tolerable error.

6. Statistical sampling may be applied to test controls when a client's control procedures:

a. Depend primarily on segregation of duties.
b. Are carefully reduced to writing and are included in client accounting manuals.
c. Leave an audit trail as evidence of compliance.
d. Enable the detection of fraud.

(AICPA Adapted)

7. Which of the following statements is correct?

a. The expected population deviation rate has little or no effect on sample size.
b. As the population size doubles, the sample size also should double.
c. For a given tolerable rate, a larger sample size should be selected as the expected population deviation rate decreases.
d. The population size has little or no effect on sample size except for very small populations.

(AICPA Adapted)

8. When sampling for attributes, which of the following would decrease sample size?

	Risk of Assessing Control Risk Too Low	Tolerable Rate of Deviation	Expected Population Deviation Rate
a.	Increase	Decrease	Increase
b.	Decrease	Increase	Decrease
c.	Increase	Increase	Decrease
d.	Increase	Increase	Increase

9. An auditor is performing an attribute estimation sampling plan. Assuming a .05 acceptable risk of assessing control risk too low, a .04 tolerable rate of deviation, and a .01 expected population deviation rate, what is the required sample size?

a. 156.
b. 96.
c. 93.
d. Not determinable from the facts given.

10. An auditor is performing an attribute estimation sampling plan. The risk of assessing control risk too low is .05 and sample size is 80. Assuming one deviation is detected, what is the auditor's estimate of the maximum population deviation rate?

a. .037.
b. .048.
c. .058.
d. Not determinable from the facts given.

11. An auditor is performing a sequential (stop-or-go) sampling plan. Assuming 95 percent desired reliability, and a .04 tolerable rate of deviation, what is the auditor's initial sample size?

a. 50.
b. 70.
c. 100.
d. Not determinable from the facts given.

12. An auditor is performing a discovery sampling plan. Assuming population size is 6,759, the critical rate of deviation is .4 percent, and the desired probability of observing at least one deviation is 90 percent, what is the auditor's sample size?

a. 460.
b. 600.
c. 700.
d. Not determinable from the facts given.

13. Which of the following sampling plans varies sample size?

a. Attribute estimation sampling.
b. Sequential sampling.
c. Discovery sampling.
d. Stratified sampling.

14. When using statistical sampling for attributes, an auditor should assess control risk at the maximum assuming:

a. The sample rate of deviation plus the allowance for sampling risk is less than the tolerable rate.
b. The sample rate of deviation plus the allowance for sampling risk is equal to the tolerable rate.
c. The sample rate of deviation plus the allowance for sampling risk exceeds the tolerable rate.
d. The sample rate of deviation is roughly proportional to the sample rate from the prior year.

15. Which of the following statements is true about nonstatistical sampling in tests of controls?

a. Nonstatistical sampling plans provide a quantitative measure of sampling risk.
b. The auditor's judgment in nonstatistical sampling is guided by classical statistical sampling concepts.
c. The calculated nonstatistical sample should never be altered by the auditor.
d. The auditor considers the same parameters when determining a nonstatistical sample size as when determining a statistical sample size.

PROBLEMS AND DISCUSSION CASES

8-1 *Sampling and Audit Risk*
Auditors do not often have the luxury of testing 100 percent of the transactions and events underlying account balances or classes of transactions. More often, they rely on samples, thereby reducing audit costs, but also creating a risk that the samples selected will not be representative of the population.
Required:
1. What risks does an auditor sustain solely as a result of sampling?
2. Explain how an inefficient audit can increase audit risk.

8-2 *Sampling and Audit Judgment*
The use of statistical sampling in a financial statement audit does not eliminate the need for professional judgment.
Required: Identify and explain four areas where judgment may be exercised by an auditor in planning a statistical sample.

(AICPA Adapted)

8-3 *Methods of Sample Selection*
A sample of 80 accounts payable vouchers is to be selected from a population of 3,200. The vouchers are numbered consecutively from 1 to 3,200 and are listed in a computer spreadsheet file.
Required: Describe the techniques for selecting a random sample of vouchers for review.

(AICPA Adapted)

8-4 *Selecting Sampling Plans*
Within the chapter, three alternative statistical sampling plans are introduced and illustrated for use when conducting tests of controls under the second standard of field work: attribute estimation sampling, sequential sampling, and discovery sampling. Importantly, no one of the three statistical sampling plans is necessarily appropriate for all tests. Rather, each is appropriate for particular audit circumstances, and blindly applying a sampling plan to inappropriate populations can lead to audit inefficiencies and, in some cases, ineffectiveness.
Required:
1. Explain the circumstances under which attribute estimation, sequential sampling, and discovery sampling are appropriate.
2. Explain the circumstances under which an auditor might justifiably decide to switch to attribute estimation after sequential sampling has already begun.

8-5 *Attributes Sampling*
Sampling for attributes is often used to allow an auditor to reach a conclusion concerning the rate of occurrence in a population. A common use in auditing is to test the rate of deviation from a prescribed control procedure in order to assess control risk.
Required:
1. When an auditor samples for attributes, identify the factors that should influence the auditor's judgment about the: (a) acceptable risk of assessing control risk too low, (b) tolerable deviation rate, and (c) expected population deviation rate.
2. State the effect on sample size of an increase in each of the following factors, assuming all other factors are held constant: (a) acceptable risk of assessing control risk too low, (b) tolerable deviation rate, and (c) expected population deviation rate.
3. Evaluate the sample results of a test for attributes if authorizations are found to be missing on seven check requests out of a sample of 100 tested. The population consists of 2,500 check requests, the tolerable deviation rate is 8 percent, and the acceptable risk of assessing control risk too low is, itself, low.

4. How may the use of statistical sampling assist the auditor in evaluating the sample results in #3?

8-6   *Attribute Estimation*

Assume that your audit objective is to estimate a true but unknown population rate of deviation. The risk of assessing control risk too low is .05, the maximum tolerable rate of deviation is .07, and the expected population deviation rate is .0325.

Required:

1. Determine sample size.
2. What would be your statistical conclusion if four deviations were observed?
3. How would the sample results be interpreted in forming an audit conclusion?

8-7   *Attribute Estimation*

Walter Cole has decided to use statistical, rather than nonstatistical, sampling to test a client's control over purchase transactions. Specifically, Cole is testing whether vendor invoices are properly approved for payment as evidenced by the initials of authorized personnel on the face of the invoice. Cole estimates that a sample size of more than 80 could prove uneconomical, since he simply does not have sufficient budgeted audit hours to examine more than 80 documents. In addition, Cole believes that the expected population rate of deviation lies between 2 and 5 percent, and his tolerable rate of deviation cannot exceed 8 percent.

Required:

1. Given the parameters established by Cole, indicate the combination of tolerable and expected population rates of deviation that will achieve a sample size of 80 or less, assuming a 10 percent risk of assessing control risk too low.
2. Can Cole justifiably alter the tolerable rate of deviation for the express purpose of limiting sample size? Why or why not?

8-8   *Using Statistical Sampling to Achieve Audit Program Steps*

Robin Hamilton, a first-year staff accountant, is reviewing the following selected audit procedures scheduled for use during the consideration of Windham Incorporated's internal controls.

Step	*Tests of Controls*
1.	Review evidence of internal controls for:
	a. Reconciliation of daily sales summaries with sales journal totals by General Accounting personnel.
	b. Periodic reconciliation of accounts receivable trial balances with general ledger control balances.
2.	Scan the sales journal for unusual transactions or unusually large amounts and follow up on any such items identified.
3.	Examine shipping documents to determine whether each document:
	a. Is accompanied by a sales order bearing Credit and Inventory Control authorization.
	b. Agrees with the sales order as to description of goods, quantity, and destination.
4.	Trace details of sales invoices to entries in the sales journal and accounts receivable subsidiary ledger.

Required:

1. Indicate which of the above procedures could be accomplished with statistical sampling. Assume attribute estimation is to be used.
2. Identify the sampling unit you would use for each test of controls accomplished with statistical sampling.

8-9 *Attribute Estimation*

Assume you are considering controls over a client's purchasing activities, and estimate the following for acceptable risk of assessing control risk too low, tolerable rate of deviation, and expected population deviation rate:

Attribute	Risk of Assessing Control Risk Too Low	Tolerable Rate of Deviation	Expected Population Deviation Rate
1. Voucher package (e.g., purchase requisition, purchase order, receiving report, and invoice) is canceled after payment is made.	.05	.07	.01
2. Purchase is properly authorized.	.05	.05	.015
3. Details on purchase requisition, purchase order, receiving report, and invoice agree.	.05	.06	.0125
4. Purchase order in voucher package agrees with copy filed in the purchasing department.	.10	.07	.035
5. Canceled checks contain appropriate signatures and endorsements.	.05	.08	.02
6. Details on voucher package agree with canceled check (e.g., check number, date, payee, and amount).	.05	.08	.03

The sampling results for each attribute follow:

Attribute	Number of Deviations
1	2
2	2
3	1
4	4
5	2
6	2

Required:

1. Using Figure 8-4 as a guide, prepare a worksheet documenting the attribute estimation sampling results for the attributes above. Your worksheet should indicate required sample size determined (and sample size used, if different), estimated population deviation rate, and maximum population deviation rate.
2. Write a statistical conclusion and an audit conclusion for each attribute.

8-10 *Sequential (Stop-or-Go) Sampling*

From prior audits of Bristol, Inc. and recent discussions with management, an auditor believes that sales invoices agree in detail with related shipping documents, with very few exceptions. Therefore, zero or very few deviations are expected, and sequential sampling is selected as the statistical sampling plan. The auditor defines each relevant line item on the sales invoice as a separate sampling unit. Following are the auditor's desired reliability and tolerable rates of deviation for each attribute:

Attribute	Desired Reliability	Tolerable Rate of Deviation
1. Customer name	.90	.04
2. Description	.90	.05
3. Quantity	.95	.06
4. Unit price	.95	.05
5. Extensions	.95	.05

No deviations were observed for Attributes 1 and 2, and one deviation each was observed for Attributes 3, 4, and 5, though not on the same sales invoices.

Required:
1.   Determine initial sample size for each attribute.
2.   How can the sales invoices be selected if sample size varies from attribute to attribute?
3.   For each attribute, indicate whether to stop or go, and why.

8-11 *Discovery Sampling*

Assume your audit plan requires observing at least one deviation at a specified critical rate of deviation, and the expected rate of occurrence is zero. Population size is 7,750, the critical rate of deviation is .01, and the desired probability of observing one deviation is 98 percent.

Required:
1.   Determine sample size.
2.   What would be your statistical conclusion if no deviations are observed?

8-12 *Nonstatistical Sampling*

Statistical sampling is not a panacea and is not necessarily appropriate for all tests of controls; nonstatistical sampling is often applied by practicing auditors, and for good reason.

Required:
1.   Describe three conditions under which nonstatistical sampling would probably be inappropriate.
2.   What sample selection techniques are available in nonstatistical sampling? Do they differ from those used in statistical sampling? Why?

8-13 *Sample Selection and Evaluation*

You are auditing the financial statements of Elite Corporation, a continuing audit client, for the year ended December 31, 1998. Unlike prior years, you decide to use a statistical sampling plan to test the effectiveness of the company's controls over sales invoices, all of which are sequentially numbered. In prior years, you selected one representative two-week period during the year and tested all of the invoices issued during that period.

Required:
1.   Explain the procedures you would use to determine sample size.
2.   Once sample size has been determined, how would you select the individual invoices to be included in the sample? Explain.
3.   Compared with the selection procedure used in prior years, would the use of statistical sampling improve the audit of sales invoices? Discuss.
4.   Assume that the company issued 50,000 sales invoices during the year and that you specified an acceptable risk of assessing control risk too low of 5 percent and a tolerable rate of 5 percent. Does this mean that you would be willing to conclude a control is effective if errors are found on no more than 4 sales invoices out of every 95 invoices examined (i.e., a sample deviation rate of .0421)? Discuss.

(AICPA Adapted)

RESEARCH PROJECTS

1. ATTRIBUTES SAMPLING AND THE PROFESSIONAL LITERATURE

Although the attributes sampling plans introduced in this chapter are accurate portrayals of plans applied in practice, they are by necessity generic. Over the years, professional journals such as the *Journal of Accountancy* (a monthly journal published by the American Institute of CPAs) have published articles offering advice about potential practical problems (e.g., A. D. Akresh and K. W. Tatum. "Audit Sampling: Dealing with the Problems," *Journal of Accountancy*, December 1988) and about the experiences of practitioners (e.g., B. J. Epstein. "Attributes Sampling: A Local Firm's Experience," *Journal of Accountancy*, January 1986), among other things. These articles not only provide timely cautions about audit sampling applications but also lend insight into the practical problems faced by auditors in practice.

Required: Select an article about attributes sampling from one of the following (or from another) professional accounting journals: *The CPA Journal, Journal of Accountancy,* or *The Practical Accountant*. For the article selected, draft a report that addresses each of the following questions:

1. Summarize the article in your own words.
2. What recommendations does the article offer to practitioners?
3. Do you believe that the article addresses the efficiency or the effectiveness (or both) of audit sampling?

2. SAMPLING RISK, REASONABLE ASSURANCE, AND AUDIT RISK: WHO BUT US UNDERSTANDS?

Translating *sampling risk* and *audit risk* into layman's terms is rather straightforward: Sampling risk translates loosely to "the risk that what you're looking for is not where you're looking," and audit risk to "the risk of issuing an inappropriate opinion." But reconciling those risks with the concept of *reasonable* (rather than absolute) *assurance* is somewhat more of a trick when the audience is an aggrieved financial statement user. How do you explain to a commercial lender swindled in a high-profile embezzlement scheme that you were looking somewhere else, that your opinion was wrong, but that, because no audit guarantees absolute assurance, you're not culpable. Remember, this lender was swindled.

Required: Select an article that reports fraud in a corporate or governmental entity from the business or accounting press (e.g., *The Wall Street Journal, Accounting Today, Public Accounting Report, Business Week, The New York Times*) or from an automated newspaper research service like NEXIS, and draft a report about:

1. How attribute estimation or sequential sampling might have signaled the fraud, or how discovery sampling might have detected the fraud.
2. Arguments that might explain the relationship among sampling risk, audit risk, and reasonable assurance to the defrauded parties.

9

Sampling in Substantive Tests

Major topics discussed in this chapter are the:

- Nature of variables sampling in audit, attestation, and assurance engagements.
- Risks of incorrect rejection and incorrect acceptance in variables sampling.
- Steps in a general variables sampling plan appropriate for substantive testing.
- Alternative audit sampling plans used in practice: difference estimation, ratio estimation, mean-per-unit (MPU) estimation, probability-proportional-to-size (PPS) sampling, and nonstatistical sampling for variables.

Chapter 8 introduces several attributes sampling plans applicable to tests of controls—that is, plans used to test an entity's rate of deviation from prescribed internal controls. This chapter, in contrast, introduces variables sampling plans used to accomplish substantive tests of details, and therefore to test whether an entity's recorded account balances are fairly stated in all material respects. The chapter begins by introducing the nature of variables sampling in audit, attestation, and assurance engagements; discussing audit risk in the context of substantive testing; and introducing a general plan for accomplishing variables sampling. In turn, two classical variables sampling plans—*ratio estimation* and *difference estimation*—are presented, and *mean-per-unit estimation*, a variables sampling plan with narrow applicability, is introduced. Next, *probability-proportional-to-size* (dollar-unit) *sampling*, a highly popular plan for sampling both attributes and variables, is explained and illustrated. Finally, *stratified sampling* is discussed, and a *nonstatistical sampling plan* is presented as an alternative to traditional variables and probability-proportional-to-size sampling.

VARIABLES SAMPLING IN AUDIT, ATTESTATION, AND ASSURANCE SERVICES

The attributes sampling plans introduced in Chapter 8 are equally applicable to audit engagements and to attestation or assurance engagements that attest to management's assertions about internal control. In contrast, the variables sampling plans introduced in this chapter are generally more useful in audit service engagements, since the plans were designed to reach conclusions about whether recorded financial statement account balances contain material misstatements. However, the plans can be used to varying degrees in some attestation service engagements. For example, practitioners have used ratio estimation, difference estimation, and mean-per-unit estimation in agreed-upon procedures engagements (introduced in Chapter 1 but discussed more fully in Chapter 18) that offer limited assurance on health management facilities' assertions about cost reimbursement claims and on mall lessees' assertions about gross receipts.

Other variables sampling plans are also used in attestation or assurance service engagements. For example, Crowe Chizek uses regression analysis to help insurance carriers settle loss-of-profit business interruption claims on property and casualty insurance policies. Insurance carriers engage Crowe Chizek because loss-of-profit claims are often based on limited information (e.g., pre-claim sales for newer businesses may not be a good predictor of loss-period sales) and fraught with the potential for moral hazard (i.e., insured companies have incentives to overstate losses). The analysis uses prior financial information (e.g., assets, revenues) and nonfinancial information (e.g., market share, orders) to calculate an estimated loss range at confidence levels specified by the insurance carrier. The sampling plans introduced in this chapter are applicable to financial statement audits and to some attestation and assurance service engagements, although the illustrations are drawn largely from auditing.

AUDIT RISK IN SUBSTANTIVE TESTING

As explained in Chapter 2, **audit risk**, the risk that an auditor may unknowingly fail to modify his or her opinion on materially misstated financial statements, consists of two components: (1) the uncontrollable risk that material *errors will occur* in financial statements (a combination of control risk and inherent risk, as discussed in Chapter 2), and (2) the controllable risk that material *errors will not be detected* (detection risk, as discussed in Chapter 2). In turn, the risk that material errors will occur and remain undetected is influenced by two categories of uncertainties: (1) **sampling risk**, the risk that a sample may contain disproportionately more or less monetary error than exists within the population, and (2) **nonsampling risk**, those aspects of audit risk not attributable to sampling, such as human error.

As illustrated in Figure 9-1, two additional aspects of audit risk are critical in substantive tests of account balances:

1. Risk of incorrect rejection.
2. Risk of incorrect acceptance.

The **risk of incorrect rejection** is the risk that a sample supports the conclusion that a recorded account balance is materially misstated when, unknown to the auditor, the account is not materially misstated. For example, owing to sampling risk, an auditor could select a sample that contains disproportionately *more* error than is contained in the population. Like the risk of assessing control risk too high in attributes sampling, the risk of incorrect rejection relates to the *efficiency* of an audit, because an initially erroneous conclusion that an

Figure 9-1: Audit Risk in Substantive Tests of Account Balances

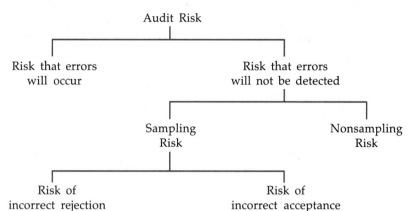

account balance is misstated would ordinarily be revised after the auditor considered other evidence or performed additional audit procedures. For example, an auditor would ordinarily revise an initial conclusion that Cost of Goods Sold is misstated if a physical inventory observation and inventory price testing revealed that Inventory was not misstated, and other procedures also revealed that Accounts Receivable and Sales were not misstated.

The **risk of incorrect acceptance**, in contrast, is the risk that a sample supports the conclusion that a recorded account balance is not materially misstated when, unknown to the auditor, the account is materially misstated. For example, owing to sampling risk, an auditor could select a sample that contains disproportionately *less* error than is contained in the population. Like the risk of assessing control risk too low in attributes sampling, the risk of incorrect acceptance relates to audit *effectiveness* and is particularly critical to an auditor: Incorrectly accepting a misstated account balance could result in financial statements that are materially misstated and therefore misleading.

When planning difference, ratio, and mean-per-unit (MPU) estimation sampling plans, an auditor considers explicitly, and attempts to control, both the risk of incorrect rejection and the risk of incorrect acceptance. The following presents a general variables sampling plan applicable to substantive testing, and expands further on the risks of incorrect rejection and incorrect acceptance.

SUBSTANTIVE TESTING: A VARIABLES SAMPLING PLAN

A **variables sampling plan** generally includes the steps outlined in Figure 9-2. This section discusses the sampling plan and, thereafter, explains and illustrates four statistical sampling techniques: difference estimation, ratio estimation, mean-per-unit (MPU) estimation, and probability-proportional-to-size (PPS) sampling.

STEP 1: DETERMINE THE OBJECTIVES OF THE TEST

A sampling plan applied to substantive tests of details is designed either: (1) to estimate an account balance that is not recorded within an entity's accounts, called dollar-value estimation, or (2) to test the reasonableness of a

Figure 9-2:   Audit Sampling Plan: Substantive Tests

1. Determine the objectives of the test.
2. Define the population.
3. Choose an audit sampling technique.
4. Determine sample size.
5. Determine the method of sample selection.
6. Perform the sampling plan.
7. Evaluate the sample results.

recorded account balance, called hypothesis testing. Although a substantive test, *dollar-value estimation* is not actually an auditing procedure, since its purpose is to create an account balance rather than to audit a recorded balance. For example, an auditor might be requested by management to convert a FIFO-basis inventory to LIFO for purposes of external reporting. *Hypothesis testing*, however, is an auditing procedure, since its purpose is to evaluate, not create, an account balance. For example, as part of a financial statement audit, an auditor might use sampling to test whether recorded accounts receivable are fairly stated at the balance sheet date. The variables sampling plan introduced in this section is used for hypothesis testing, not dollar-value estimation.

In general, an auditor's objective in hypothesis testing is to determine whether a recorded account balance is fairly stated. Once an objective is stated, the auditor must then identify the *characteristic of interest*. For example, if an auditor's objective is to determine whether an account is fairly stated, the characteristic might be defined as monetary error—that is, monetary differences between recorded and audited dollar amounts.

STEP 2:   DEFINE THE POPULATION

As explained in Chapter 8, an **audit population** consists of all the items constituting an account balance or class of transactions, and should be defined by the auditor's characteristic of interest, since sample results can be generalized only to the population from which a sample is selected. For example, defining the population as "all recorded payables" would be inappropriate if an auditor's objective is to detect unrecorded liabilities, since the population would not include unrecorded accounts.

As in attributes sampling, the **sampling unit** is any of the individual elements constituting a population. For example, a sampling unit in variables sampling might be a customer account balance, an individual transaction, or an individual entry within a transaction, among other things.

STEP 3:   CHOOSE AN AUDIT SAMPLING TECHNIQUE

Audit sampling is not used to accomplish all substantive tests of details, but only those for which the auditor believes sampling is appropriate. For example, an auditor would not use sampling to accomplish the audit procedures of inquiry and observation, such as interviewing management and observing cash handling procedures, or to accomplish analytical procedures, such as comparing current period financial statement accounts with prior period balances. However, when sampling is considered appropriate, auditors generally choose from among three types of techniques: (1) classical variables sampling techniques (e.g., difference, ratio, or mean-per-unit estimation), which use normal distribution theory to evaluate sample results; (2) probability-proportional-to-size (PPS) sampling, which uses attributes sampling theory to evaluate results; and (3) nonstatistical sampling. Thus, assuming variables sampling is appropriate to an audit objective, an auditor first decides between statistical and nonstatistical sampling; if statistical sampling is chosen, the auditor then decides between classical variables sampling and probability-proportional-to-size sampling.

The choice between a statistical and a nonstatistical sampling plan is generally based on whether the auditor requires a quantitative estimate of sampling risk (which, as explained in Chapter 8, can only be accomplished with a statistical sampling plan) and the relative costs and effectiveness of each plan in the circumstances. In turn, the choice between classical variables sampling and probability-proportional-to-size sampling is based on the relative advantages and disadvantages of each plan—several of which are listed in Figure 9-3.

STEP 4:   DETERMINE SAMPLE SIZE

To determine sample size in a variables sampling plan, an auditor must generally consider:

- Variation within the population.
- Acceptable risk of incorrect rejection.
- Acceptable risk of incorrect acceptance.
- Tolerable error.

Each is discussed next.

Variation Within the Population

The dollar amounts included within audit populations tend to vary widely. In general, audit populations tend to include very few large dollar items, some moderately large items, and many small items. Because sample size varies in the same direction as the variation in population amounts (for example, as population variation increases, so does sample size), auditors require an estimate of the population variation.

In nonstatistical sampling, auditors consider population variation in general terms (e.g., high or low), and in probability-proportional-to-size sampling, variation is considered indirectly. However, classical variables sampling requires an explicit estimate of population variation, which, in practice, is usually approximated by a *population standard deviation*. The standard deviation can be calculated by computer for an audit population or approximated from a *pilot sample*, an initial sample of 30 to 50 sampling units drawn from the population. (Pilot sample items can be, and typically are, used as part of the audit sample.) In some cases, auditors using classical variables sampling do not calculate a population standard deviation directly, but rely instead on the results of prior year tests updated to reflect any changes in the current year that would affect population variation.

Acceptable Risk of Incorrect Rejection

As discussed earlier in the chapter, the risk of incorrect rejection is the risk of concluding that a recorded account balance is misstated when, in fact,

Figure 9-3: Relative Advantages and Disadvantages of Classical Variables Sampling and Probability-Proportional-to-Size (PPS) Sampling

Classical Variables Sampling

Advantages:

- If there are many individual differences between recorded and audited amounts in the population, classical variables sampling may result in a smaller sample size.
- Selection of zero or negative balances within a sample generally does not require special sample design considerations.
- If necessary, expanding classical variables samples may be easier than expanding probability-proportional-to-size samples.

Disadvantages:

- Classical variables sampling is more complex than probability-proportional-to-size sampling.
- To determine sample size, the auditor must have an estimate of the population standard deviation.
- Normal distribution theory, the basis underlying classical variables sampling, may not be appropriate when the sample size is not large and there are either very large items or very large differences between recorded and audited amounts in the population.

Probability-Proportional-to-Size (PPS) Sampling

Advantages:

- PPS sampling automatically results in a stratified sample because items are selected in proportion to their dollar amounts.
- If no errors are expected, PPS sampling usually results in a smaller sample size than classical variables sampling.
- A PPS sample can be designed more easily and sample selection can begin before the complete population is available.

Disadvantages:

- If a PPS sample includes understatement errors, evaluation of the sample will require special design considerations.
- When errors are found, PPS evaluation may overstate the allowance for sampling risk.
- PPS sampling generally includes an assumption that the audited amount of a sampling unit should not be less than zero or greater than the recorded amount.

material monetary error does not exist. Two alternative and undesirable outcomes can occur when an auditor incorrectly rejects a fairly stated account balance. First, the auditor might propose an unnecessary audit adjustment, thereby materially misstating an otherwise fairly stated account. Second, and more likely, the auditor could increase sample size or perform other audit procedures, both of which require additional work and therefore additional cost, thereby producing additional evidence from which to conclude that an account is *not* materially misstated.

Generally, the risk of incorrect rejection in variables sampling is of greater concern to the auditor than the risk of assessing control risk too high in attributes sampling: Incorrectly rejecting an account balance could result in an incorrect audit adjustment that, when recorded, would render the account misstated. The risk of incorrect rejection is also more problematic because incorrect rejection is likely to be more costly than assessing control risk too high. For example, if an auditor increases sample size, the results could reverse an initially erroneous conclusion to reject an account balance. However, additional testing is costly, particularly when the sole purpose is to gather additional evidence about a previously rejected balance. The risk of assessing control risk too high, in contrast, is usually not quite as costly. If control risk is assessed too high, rather than perform additional unplanned procedures at the end of the engagement, an auditor could simply plan ahead to modify year end substantive tests—a less costly change of plans.

Acceptable Risk of Incorrect Acceptance

As discussed earlier, the risk of incorrect acceptance is the auditor's risk of concluding that an account balance is not materially misstated when, in fact, material monetary error exists. One predominant and undesirable outcome typically occurs when an auditor incorrectly accepts an account balance: A materially misstated account is believed by the auditor to be fairly stated, the account is not adjusted, and therefore the audited financial statements are misleading.

In determining the acceptable risk of incorrect acceptance, an auditor considers the level of audit risk (AR) he or she is willing to sustain and the level of assurance provided by internal controls (IC) and by analytical procedures and other tests (AP). The general relationship among these three factors and the auditor's risk of incorrect acceptance (TD) can be stated as follows:

$$TD = \frac{AR}{IC \times AP}$$

Where:

TD = The acceptable risk of incorrect acceptance for the substantive tests of details.

AR = The acceptable risk that an auditor may unknowingly fail to modify his or her opinion on materially misstated financial statements.

IC = The risk that the internal controls fail to detect material errors that occur.

AP = The risk that analytical procedures and other tests fail to detect material errors that occur and that are not detected by the internal controls.

Acceptable audit risk (AR) is often, but not always, set at 5 percent or 10 percent by those auditors who use the preceding model. IC, in contrast, the auditor's assessment of the effectiveness of the internal controls, and AP, the auditor's assessment of the effectiveness of analytical procedures and other tests, might be guided as follows:

Effectiveness of Internal Controls, Analytical Procedures, and Other Tests	IC and AP Risks
Very effective	10-40 percent
Moderately effective	30-70 percent
Marginal or ineffective	60-100 percent

To illustrate, assume that an auditor is willing to accept 5 percent audit risk (*AR*) and judges *IC* to be 25 percent and *AP* to be 70 percent. The acceptable risk of incorrect acceptance would be:

$$TD = \frac{.05}{.25 \times .70}$$
$$= .29$$

Although seemingly precise, note carefully that the preceding risk model is neither authoritative nor intended as a mathematical formula. Rather, the model provides insight into how the risk of incorrect acceptance relates to other aspects of an audit. In short, the model is a decision aid, not a decision.

Tolerable Error

When planning a variables sampling plan, an auditor considers **tolerable error** for the population—that is, the maximum monetary error that may exist in an account balance without causing the financial statements to be materially misstated. Tolerable error is closely related to an auditor's planned level of materiality in that the combined tolerable error for an entire audit should not exceed the auditor's preliminary estimate of materiality for the complete set of financial statements taken as a whole.

Effect on Sample Size of Changing Parameters

Increasing or decreasing any one of the three sample size parameters—acceptable risk of incorrect rejection, acceptable risk of incorrect acceptance, and tolerable error—has the opposite effect on sample size: Increasing any one decreases sample size, and vice versa. In some circumstances, other aspects of the audit may be affected as well. For example, when an auditor decides to accept a higher risk of incorrect rejection, required sample size declines. But by decreasing sample size, the auditor simultaneously increases the risk of incurring additional costs to investigate differences between the sample results and the recorded account balance.

STEP 5:   DETERMINE THE METHOD OF SAMPLE SELECTION

The four sample selection methods discussed for attributes sampling in Chapter 8—random-number sampling, systematic sampling, block sampling, and haphazard sampling—are equally applicable to variables sampling. As in attributes sampling, an auditor should attempt to achieve randomness—that is, to assure that each sampling unit in a population is given an equal chance of selection, thereby not biasing either the sample selection or the sample results. In general, random-number sampling and systematic sampling are likely to achieve randomness if applied properly, whereas both block and haphazard sampling require extreme care by the auditor to avoid bias.

STEP 6:   PERFORM THE SAMPLING PLAN

After a sample is selected, an auditor applies audit procedures to each sampling unit selected. However, in some instances, selected sampling units may be missing or lack supporting documentation, thereby creating uncertainty about whether the related transactions are recorded properly.

The treatment of missing or unsupported sampling units depends on how the related transactions would affect the auditor's overall evaluation of the sample. In general, if the auditor believes the overall sample evaluation would not change, even if the related transactions were misstated, he or she would not seek alternative evidence. However, if the auditor believes that misstated sampling units would cause the account balance to be misstated, alternative procedures should be performed. For example, as discussed in Chapter 11, an auditor would review the cash receipts records after the balance sheet date to determine whether payment was received from a customer that did not return a receivables confirmation.

STEP 7:   EVALUATE THE SAMPLE RESULTS

Upon completing audit procedures for the sampling units, an auditor summarizes and evaluates the results by:

- Projecting the sample error to the population.
- Considering sampling risk.
- Considering qualitative information.
- Reaching an overall conclusion.

Each is discussed next.

Project Sample Error and Consider Sampling Risk

In a properly designed and executed sampling plan, an auditor draws conclusions about an audit population by examining randomly selected samples. The intent is to reach defendable conclusions about a population without testing the entire population. As a result, auditors use the sample results to project detected monetary error to the population—that is, to generalize the sample results to the population from which the sample was selected. However, the projected error may not be a fair representation of true monetary error within the population. As a result, the auditor must also consider sampling risk, the risk that the auditor's conclusion about a population might be different if the entire population were examined.

All variables sampling techniques evaluate projected error and sampling risk, although the method of evaluation varies from one technique to another. Later in the chapter, the evaluation process is discussed for each specific sampling technique.

Consider Qualitative Information and Reach an Overall Conclusion

In variables sampling, an auditor considers not only the amount of misstatements, but also the qualitative characteristics of the misstatements, such as their nature and cause and the possible relationship of the misstatements to other phases of the audit. For example, in considering the nature and cause of misstatements, the auditor should consider whether the misstatements resulted from intentional acts (fraud), which would require special procedures (discussed in Chapter 5), or from carelessness and misunderstanding.

To reach an overall conclusion from a sampling plan, an auditor considers both quantitative and qualitative information. In some instances, however, the sample results may suggest that the auditor's assumptions in planning the variables sampling application were inappropriate, thereby requiring additional action. For example, if the number of misstatements observed in substantive testing exceeded the number expected given the presumed effectiveness of internal controls, the auditor should reconsider control risk and also judge whether to modify the substantive testing of related accounts.

The following sections of this chapter discuss and illustrate four commonly used variables sampling techniques:

1. Difference estimation.
2. Ratio estimation.
3. Mean-per-unit (MPU) estimation.
4. Probability-proportional-to-size (PPS) sampling.

The discussion and illustrations apply the steps introduced in the general sampling plan outlined in Figure 9-2. Nonstatistical sampling for variables is also discussed.

DIFFERENCE AND RATIO ESTIMATION

Difference estimation and ratio estimation are two similar classical variables sampling techniques that may be appropriate when the audit objective is to estimate a population's true but unknown monetary balance. Some general considerations in applying difference and ratio estimation are discussed below.

CONDITIONS FOR USING DIFFERENCE AND RATIO ESTIMATION

Three conditions must exist before either difference or ratio estimation can be applied:

1. Each population item must have a recorded book value (e.g., perpetual, rather than periodic, inventory).
2. Total population book value must be known (e.g., a recorded general ledger book value) and must correspond to the sum of all individual population items.
3. Expected differences between audited and recorded book values must not be too rare.

The first and second conditions are related, and necessary because recorded book values are required in order to calculate either differences or ratios between audited and recorded book values.

The third condition, that differences must not be too rare, is necessary because sample size would be too large otherwise. If differences are rare, a relatively large number of sampling units would be required in order to observe representative population differences. Ordinarily, about 30 sample differences are sufficient to assure a reasonable estimate of the true but unknown population monetary balance.

CHOOSING BETWEEN DIFFERENCE AND RATIO ESTIMATION

When the three necessary conditions exist, an auditor may choose either difference or ratio estimation, although one method may be more efficient than the other depending on the relationship between differences and recorded book values. In general, ratio estimation is more appropriate when the differences are nearly proportional to book values—that is, when the amounts of the differences tend to increase as book values increase. Difference estimation, on the other hand, is more appropriate when there is little or no relationship between the amounts of the differences and the book values. When differences are somewhat proportional but there is no strong tendency toward either proportionality or nonproportionality, ratio and difference estimation will yield similar results.

THE FOCUS OF EACH TECHNIQUE

Difference estimation focuses on the monetary difference between a sampling unit's audited and recorded book values. In contrast, ratio estimation focuses on the ratio between a sampling unit's audited and book values. Except for their focus on differences and ratios, respectively, the two sampling plans are identical in approach.

Applying either technique involves following each of the steps outlined in the general variables sampling plan in Figure 9-2. The statistical aspects of the sampling plan—determining sample size, selecting the sample, and evaluating the results—are discussed in the following sections. Difference estimation is considered first, followed by ratio estimation.

DIFFERENCE ESTIMATION

In **difference estimation**, the strategy is to estimate the amount of monetary misstatement in the population, called the difference estimate, from misstatement observed in the sample, and then to calculate an estimated audited value for the population by netting the difference estimate with the recorded account balance. To determine a difference estimate, the auditor sums all sample differences between recorded and audited values to yield a net sample difference, divides the net sample difference by sample size, and then multiplies the result by population size. The difference estimate is then added to the recorded account balance if there is a net understatement (or subtracted if there is a net overstatement) to yield the estimated audited value. In turn, the auditor estimates an allowance for sampling risk.

The following example illustrates difference estimation, focusing on how an auditor defines the population (and sampling unit), determines sample size, chooses the method of sample selection, and evaluates the sample results.

DEFINE THE POPULATION

In this illustration, assume that an auditor is applying difference estimation to The Wilson Company's trade accounts payable, and that the conditions for applying either difference or ratio estimation are met: Each payable has a recorded book value, the sum of all recorded payables agrees with the general ledger balance, and expected differences between audited and recorded book values are not rare. The auditor has selected difference rather than ratio estimation because past experience indicates that differences are not proportional to recorded book values, and therefore there is no discernible relationship between the amounts of differences and the recorded book values.

The audit population consists of 4,100 individual payable accounts, each one of which represents a sampling unit. Recorded book value for all payables is $3,350,000.

DETERMINE SAMPLE SIZE

As discussed previously in the chapter, sample size requires estimates of:

- Variation within the population: the estimated population standard deviation.
- Acceptable risk of incorrect rejection.
- Acceptable risk of incorrect acceptance.
- Tolerable error.

In difference estimation, each can be determined as follows.

Estimated Population Standard Deviation

A pilot sample can be used to estimate a population standard deviation from the following formula:

$$S = \sqrt{\sum_{i=1}^{n} \frac{d_i^2 - n(\bar{d})^2}{n - 1}}$$

Where:

S = Estimated population standard deviation.
d = Difference between audited value (a_i) and book value (b_i) of the ith item.
n = Sample size.
$\bar{d}$ = Average difference between audited and book value for all pilot sample items.

In this case, assume that the sum of all squared differences in the pilot sample, d_i^2, is $765,000; the pilot sample size, n, is 50; and the average difference in the pilot sample, $\bar{d}$, is $10. From these facts, the estimated population standard deviation would be:

$$S = \sqrt{\frac{\$765,000 - 50\ (10)^2}{50 - 1}}$$

= $125 (rounded)

Risk and Tolerable Error

Sample size calculations also require that the auditor specify the acceptable risk of incorrect rejection, the acceptable risk of incorrect acceptance, and tolerable error. Once these parameters have been established, the auditor then calculates the *desired allowance for sampling risk* (sometimes called desired precision), which is the auditor's allowance for the risk that the sample selected may contain disproportionately more or less monetary misstatement than exists within the population as a whole. The allowance for sampling risk is calculated as follows:

$A = R \times TE$

Where:

A = Desired allowance for sampling risk.
R = Ratio of desired allowance for sampling risk to tolerable error.
TE = Tolerable error.

The ratio of desired allowance for sampling risk to tolerable error (R) is determined from Figure 9-4. For example, assume the auditor specifies the following parameters for the Wilson case:

Acceptable risk of incorrect rejection   = .10
Acceptable risk of incorrect acceptance = .05
Tolerable error   = $170,000

From Figure 9-4, the ratio of desired allowance for sampling risk to tolerable error is .500, the intersection of the column associated with a 10 percent risk of incorrect rejection and the row associated with a 5 percent risk of incorrect acceptance. Desired allowance for sampling risk is then calculated as follows:

A = .500 × $170,000
   = $85,000

Sample Size

Audit sample size can be determined with the following formula, designed to generate the minimum number of observations required given population size and estimated variability, the acceptable risk of incorrect rejection, and the desired allowance for sampling risk:

$$n' = \left(\frac{S \times U \times N}{A} \right)^2$$

and

$$n = \frac{n'}{1 + \dfrac{n'}{N}}$$

Figure 9-4: Ratio of Desired Allowance for Sampling Risk to Tolerable Error

Risk of Incorrect Acceptance	Risk of Incorrect Rejection			
	.20	.10	.05	.01
.01	.355	.413	.457	.525
.025	.395	.456	.500	.568
.05	.437	.500	.543	.609
.075	.471	.532	.576	.641
.10	.500	.561	.605	.668
.15	.511	.612	.653	.712
.20	.603	.661	.700	.753
.25	.653	.708	.742	.791
.30	.707	.756	.787	.829
.35	.766	.808	.834	.868
.40	.831	.863	.883	.908
.45	.907	.926	.937	.952
.50	1.000	1.000	1.000	1.000

Where:

S = Estimated population standard deviation.
U = Standard normal deviate for the acceptable risk of incorrect rejection.
N = Population size.
A = Desired allowance for sampling risk.
n' = Uncorrected sample size.
n = Sample size.

U, the standard normal deviate for the desired risk of incorrect rejection, is determined from Figure 9-5, a table of commonly used risk levels. In this case, the risk of incorrect rejection is .10, and from Figure 9-5, the standard normal deviate is 1.65. The risk levels in Figure 9-5 vary from .01 to .30, the typical range of risk levels accepted by most practicing auditors. Note from the table that as the risk of incorrect rejection increases—for example, from .01 to .05—the standard normal deviate decreases (from 2.58 to 1.96) and, because U is in the numerator of the sample size formula, sample size decreases as well.

The expression:

$$1 - \frac{n'}{N}$$

is called a *finite population correction factor*, and is often used because auditors sample "without replacement"—that is, sampling units selected for testing are not returned to the population for possible reselection. A finite population correction factor is less important when n is less than 5 percent of population size, because the amount of correction is trivial, although it may still be used.

Based on the information given for The Wilson Company, sample size would be:

$$n' = \left(\frac{\$125 \times 1.65 \times 4{,}100}{\$85{,}000}\right)^2$$

= 99 (rounded)

Since the uncorrected sample size (99) is less than 5 percent of population size (4,100), the finite population correction factor is not used in this illustration. Thus, $n = 99$.

DETERMINE THE METHOD OF SAMPLE SELECTION

As noted in Chapter 8, in a statistical sampling plan, sampling units must be selected at random. Otherwise, sampling risk could not be measured, and the

Figure 9-5: Standard Normal Deviate for Selected Risks of Incorrect Rejection

Risk of Incorrect Rejection	U: Standard Normal Deviate
.01	2.58
.05	1.96
.10	1.65
.15	1.44
.20	1.28
.25	1.15
.30	1.04

sampling plan would be nonstatistical. For this reason, random-number sampling and systematic sampling are commonly used in difference estimation.

PERFORM THE SAMPLING PLAN AND EVALUATE THE SAMPLE RESULTS

Continuing the illustration, the auditor examines evidence supporting each of the 99 sampled payable accounts. An audited value is determined for each account, differences between audited and recorded book values are documented, and the following summary calculations are made:

$\hat{D}$ = The total projected monetary difference between the actual population value and the recorded account balance.

$\hat{X}$ = The estimated population value.

A' = The achieved allowance for sampling risk.

In difference estimation, the total projected monetary difference between the population value and the recorded account balance ($\hat{D}$) is calculated as follows:

$$\hat{D} = N \, \bar{d}$$

Where:

N = Population size.

$\bar{d}$ = Average difference, calculated by dividing the sum of the differences by sample size.

To illustrate the evaluation of sample results for a difference estimation sampling plan, partial sample data for The Wilson Company are presented in Figure 9-6. Book and audited values are shown for the first through the tenth sample items and for the 99th item, with totals presented for all sample items. As shown in Figure 9-6, total book value for the 99 accounts examined is $74,416, and total audited value for these accounts is $76,000, yielding a net understatement difference of $1,584.

Figure 9-6: The Wilson Company: Sample Data—Trade Accounts Payable

Sample Item	Book Value (b_i)	Audited Value (a_i)	Difference ($d_i = a_i - b_i$)
1	$ 1,550	$ 1,550	$ 0
2	1,700	1,740	40
3	930	930	0
4	520	907	387
5	841	841	0
6	1,335	1,225	(110)
7	655	655	0
8	185	185	0
9	420	420	0
10	310	320	10
•	•	•	•
•	•	•	•
•	•	•	•
99	489	312	(177)
	$74,416	$76,000	$1,584

The average difference ($\bar{d}$) is \$16 (\$1,584 ÷ 99), and the population size (N) is 4,100. Thus, the total projected monetary difference is:

$$\hat{D} = 4{,}100 \times \$16$$
$$= \$65{,}600$$

The estimated population value ($\hat{X}$), sometimes referred to as the point estimate, is calculated by adding the total projected difference ($\hat{D}$) to the recorded account balance (B):

$$\hat{X} = \hat{D} + B$$
$$= \$65{,}600 + \$3{,}350{,}000$$
$$= \$3{,}415{,}600$$

In order to determine the achieved allowance for sampling risk (A'), the auditor must first calculate the sample standard deviation from the formula used earlier to calculate the pilot sample standard deviation. Assume that for the 99 sampling units examined, the sample standard deviation is \$120. The achieved allowance for sampling risk is calculated as follows:

$$A' = \frac{S \times U \times N}{\sqrt{n}} \sqrt{1 - \frac{n}{N}}$$

$$= \frac{\$120 \times 1.65 \times 4{,}100}{\sqrt{99}} \sqrt{1 - \frac{99}{4{,}100}}$$

$$= \$80{,}602 \text{ (rounded)}$$

Note that the finite population correction factor is used in the above calculation even though it was not used in calculating sample size earlier. Although inconsistent, this is done in practice sometimes to achieve more conservative sample sizes and allowances for sampling risk. That is, ignoring the correction factor earlier resulted in a larger (more conservative) sample size, thereby reducing sampling risk, and using the correction factor now results in a smaller (more conservative) allowance for sampling risk, thereby reducing the risk of incorrect acceptance.

A *precision interval*, determined from the estimated population value and achieved allowance for sampling risk, is calculated as follows:

$$\text{Precision interval} = \hat{X} \pm A'$$
$$= \$3{,}415{,}600 \pm \$80{,}602$$
$$= \$3{,}334{,}998 \text{ to } \$3{,}496{,}202$$

From the sample results, the auditor would conclude:

Based on procedures applied, the estimated population value is \$3,415,600, and there is a 95 percent probability (1 – risk of incorrect acceptance) that the true but unknown population value is included in the precision interval, \$3,334,998 to \$3,496,202. Conversely, there is a 5 percent risk that the true but unknown population value falls outside the precision interval.

In this case, the sample results support the conclusion that trade accounts payable for The Wilson Company are not materially misstated, since the precision interval (\$3,334,998 to \$3,496,202) includes the recorded account balance (\$3,350,000), illustrated as follows, and the achieved allowance for sampling risk ($80,602) does not exceed the desired allowance ($85,000). Therefore, the auditor would accept the recorded account balance. However, what if the recorded account balance fell outside the precision interval and/or the achieved allowance for sampling risk exceeded the desired allowance for sampling risk? These conditions are discussed in the appendix to this chapter.

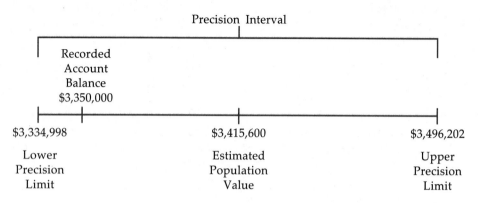

RATIO ESTIMATION

In **ratio estimation**, the strategy is to estimate the ratio between the population value and the recorded account balance—called the ratio estimate—from the ratio calculated for the sample, and then to calculate the estimated population value by multiplying the ratio estimate times the recorded account balance. To determine a ratio estimate, the auditor divides the sum of all audited values for the sample items by the sum of all recorded values for the sample items. The ratio is then multiplied by the recorded account balance, yielding an estimated audited value, and the achieved allowance for sampling risk is calculated.

Sample size is determined using exactly the same formula as in difference estimation, although the estimated population standard deviation, one of the variables in the sample size formula, is computed somewhat differently. Once the sampling units are selected and examined, an estimated audited value ($\hat{X}$) is calculated by multiplying the ratio between audited and recorded values in the sample ($\hat{R}$) times the recorded account balance (B). For example, using the data in Figure 9-6, the total audited value of the sampling units in The Wilson Company accounts payable test is $76,000 and the total recorded (book) value is $74,416. The ratio estimate would thus be 102 percent ($76,000/$74,416), and the estimated population value would be:

$$\hat{X} = \hat{R} \times B$$
$$= 1.02 \times \$3,350,000$$
$$= \$3,417,000$$

The auditor would next calculate the achieved allowance for sampling risk from the same formula used in difference estimation, except that the estimated population standard deviation, one of the variables in the sampling risk formula, is calculated differently. The standard deviation formula is quite cumbersome and, as a result, is usually calculated by computer in practice. Once the estimated audited value and achieved allowance for sampling risk are calculated, a precision interval is determined and the results evaluated as they are in difference estimation. If the recorded account balance falls outside the precision interval and/or the achieved allowance for sampling risk exceeds the desired allowance for sampling risk, the auditor evaluates the sample results using the approach illustrated at the end of this chapter. In Chapter 11, ratio estimation is illustrated more fully for substantive tests applied to a health care supplier's recorded accounts receivable.

MEAN-PER-UNIT ESTIMATION

Mean-per-unit (MPU) estimation (sometimes called simple extension) is similar to difference estimation but is often less efficient than either difference or ratio estimation, both of which can usually achieve the same results with a smaller sample size. In general, MPU estimation is used only if the necessary conditions for difference and ratio estimation are not present, and particularly when: (1) recorded amounts are not available for individual sampling units (e.g., a periodic, rather than a perpetual inventory) or (2) there are few expected differences between audited and recorded values.

In MPU estimation, the strategy is to estimate the average audited value for each population item from the average in the sample, and then to calculate estimated audited value for the account by multiplying the average audited value times population size. In turn, the auditor calculates an achieved allowance for sampling risk. The following section illustrates MPU estimation, focusing on how an auditor defines the population (and sampling unit), determines sample size, chooses the method of sample selection, and evaluates the sample results.

DEFINE THE POPULATION

In this illustration, assume an auditor is applying statistical sampling to The Wilson Company's inventory. Wilson does not maintain perpetual inventory records. Thus, there are no recorded amounts for individual sampling units in the population, and MPU estimation is chosen as the sampling technique. The audit population consists of 2,500 inventory items, each of which represents a sampling unit, and recorded book value is $850,000.

DETERMINE SAMPLE SIZE

As indicated in the variables sampling plan introduced earlier in the chapter, sample size calculations require estimates of variation in the population (estimated population standard deviation), acceptable risks of incorrect rejection and incorrect acceptance, and tolerable error.

The population standard deviation can be estimated from a pilot sample using a formula similar to the standard deviation formula for difference estimation. The auditor draws a randomly selected pilot sample, examines each sampling unit, and calculates the estimated population standard deviation. In this case, assume the estimated population standard deviation is $185.

As in difference and ratio estimation, the auditor calculates a desired allowance for sampling risk after first specifying the acceptable risk of incorrect rejection, the acceptable risk of incorrect acceptance, and tolerable error. For example, assume the following:

Acceptable risk of incorrect rejection	=	.10
Acceptable risk of incorrect acceptance	=	.05
Tolerable error	=	$150,000

From Figure 9-4, the ratio of desired sampling risk to tolerable error is .500, and the desired allowance for sampling risk is:

$$A = R \times TE$$
$$= .500 \times \$150,000$$
$$= \$75,000$$

Once the population standard deviation is estimated and the allowance for sampling risk is determined, sample size can be calculated from the formula below, which assumes sampling without replacement, thereby accounting for the finite population correction factor.

$$n' = \left(\frac{S \times U \times N}{A} \right)^2$$

and

$$n = \frac{n'}{1 + \dfrac{n'}{N}}$$

Where:

S = Estimated population standard deviation.
U = Standard normal deviate for the acceptable risk of incorrect rejection.
N = Population size.
A = Desired allowance for sampling risk.
n' = Uncorrected sample size.
n = Sample size.

U, the standard normal deviate for the desired risk of incorrect rejection, is determined from Figure 9-5. In this case, the risk of incorrect rejection is .10, and from Figure 9-5, the standard normal deviate is 1.65. Thus, for the audit of The Wilson Company's inventory, sample size would be:

$$n' = \left(\frac{\$185 \times 1.65 \times 2,500}{\$75,000} \right)^2$$
$$= 104 \text{ (rounded)}$$

Since the uncorrected sample size is less than 5 percent of population size, the finite population correction factor is not necessary. However, assume the auditor chooses to use the correction factor nevertheless, which is not uncommon in practice.

$$n = \frac{104}{1 + \dfrac{104}{2,500}}$$
$$= 100 \text{ (rounded)}$$

DETERMINE THE METHOD OF SAMPLE SELECTION

As in other statistical sampling techniques, sampling units for MPU estimation must be selected at random, and random-number sampling and systematic sampling are used most often. After the sampling units are examined and audited amounts determined for each sampling unit, the results are evaluated and conclusions reached.

PERFORM THE SAMPLING PLAN AND EVALUATE THE SAMPLE RESULTS

Evaluating results in MPU estimation requires calculations of:

$\hat{X}$ = The estimated total audited value.

A' = The achieved allowance for sampling risk.

The estimated total audited value ($\hat{X}$) is calculated by multiplying the average audited value for all sampling units ($\bar{x}$) times population size (N). In the inventory illustration for The Wilson Company, population size was 2,500. Assume that the total audited value for all 100 sampling units is $32,500, and therefore that the average audited value is $325 ($32,500/100). Thus, the estimated total audited value is:

$$\hat{X} = N\bar{x}$$
$$= 2{,}500 \times \$325$$
$$= \$812{,}500$$

Assuming the sample standard deviation is $159 (which is less than the $185 calculated from the pilot sample), the achieved allowance for sampling risk is calculated from the following formula, the same formula used previously for difference estimation:

$$A' = \frac{S \times U \times N}{\sqrt{n}} \sqrt{1 - \frac{n}{N}}$$

$$= \frac{\$159 \times 1.65 \times 2{,}500}{\sqrt{100}} \sqrt{1 - \frac{100}{2{,}500}}$$

$$= \$64{,}262 \text{ (rounded)}$$

Finally, the precision interval, determined from the estimated total audited value and the achieved allowance for sampling risk, is:

Precision interval = $\hat{X} \pm A'$
$$= \$812{,}500 \pm \$64{,}262$$
$$= \$748{,}238 \text{ to } \$876{,}762$$

From these results, the auditor would conclude as follows:

Based on procedures applied, the estimated population value is $812,500, and there is a 95 percent probability (1 − risk of incorrect acceptance) that the true but unknown population value is included in the precision interval, $748,238 to $876,762. Conversely, there is a 5 percent risk that the true but unknown population value falls outside the precision interval.

In this case, the sample results support the conclusion that inventory for The Wilson Company is not materially misstated, because the precision interval

($748,238 to $876,762) includes the recorded account balance ($850,000), and the achieved allowance for sampling risk ($64,262) does not exceed the desired allowance ($75,000). An appendix to this chapter discusses the auditor's judgment process if the recorded account balance falls outside the precision interval and/or the achieved allowance for sampling risk exceeds the desired allowance.

PROBABILITY-PROPORTIONAL-TO-SIZE SAMPLING

Difference, ratio, and MPU estimation use classical variables sampling theory to compile and express sampling results in dollars. In contrast, **probability-proportional-to-size (PPS) sampling**[1] also expresses results in dollars but, like the sampling techniques introduced in Chapter 8, is derived from attributes sampling theory. Although appropriate when one or a few population errors are expected, PPS sampling is best applied when no errors are expected. When errors are expected, required sample size may be much higher for PPS sampling than for difference, ratio, or MPU estimation.

In PPS sampling, the strategy is to randomly select individual dollars from a population and then to audit the balances, transactions, or documents—called *logical units*—that include the individual dollars selected. Each dollar in the population has an equal chance of being selected, but the likelihood of selecting any one logical unit for testing is directly proportional to its size, thereby accounting for the name "probability-proportional-to-size." For example, if an entity's trade accounts receivable balance is $1,750,000, then the population size is 1,750,000 and an individual customer account with a balance of $87,500 has a 5 percent chance ($87,500/$1,750,000) of being selected for testing. For this reason, PPS sampling has two unique properties. First, PPS sampling automatically stratifies audit populations by monetary value, since larger-dollar-value balances or transactions have a higher probability of being selected. Second, because larger-dollar-value accounts have a higher probability of being selected, overstatements are more likely to be detected than understatements. As a result, PPS sampling is most appropriate when an auditor desires to test for material overstatements, since understated accounts have less chance of being selected for testing.

The following illustrates PPS sampling, focusing on how an auditor defines the population, determines sample size, chooses the method of sample selection, and evaluates the sample results.

DEFINE THE POPULATION

In PPS sampling, the population represents the class of transactions or the account balance that an auditor intends to test, and may vary depending on the circumstances. For example, in testing trade accounts receivable, the audit population could consist of debit balances only or all customer balances, including debit balances, credit balances, and zero balances.

---

[1]   Variations of PPS sampling include *dollar-unit sampling, cumulative monetary amount sampling,* and *combined attributes variables sampling.*

Negative balances in a population, such as credit balances in accounts receivable, usually require special consideration because they may contain properties not present in positive balances. For example, credit balances in accounts receivable may indicate overpayments or progress payments on revolving accounts. In practice, negative balances are often excluded from the sample selection process and tested separately. In addition, zero balances may be treated separately, since they have no chance of being selected otherwise.

In this illustration, assume that an auditor's objective is to determine whether the trade accounts receivable of The Wilson Company are materially overstated. The population is defined as all customer accounts with debit balances, and the recorded book value of these accounts is $1,750,000.

DETERMINE SAMPLE SIZE

Sample size calculations in PPS sampling require that an auditor determine:

- A reliability factor for overstatement errors.
- Tolerable error.
- Anticipated error and an expansion factor.

Each is discussed below.

Reliability Factor for Overstatement Errors

The reliability factor for overstatement errors can be determined from tables after first specifying the expected number of overstatement errors and the risk of incorrect acceptance. In PPS sampling, the risk of incorrect acceptance is specifically incorporated into the sampling plan through the reliability factor for overstatement errors. However, the risk of incorrect rejection is not incorporated explicitly.

Since PPS sampling is most appropriate when no errors are expected, zero is the appropriate estimate for the *expected number of overstatement errors* (even when errors are expected). As was the case in classical variables sampling, the *risk of incorrect acceptance* is a matter of professional judgment and, in PPS sampling, represents an auditor's risk that book value is not materially overstated when, in fact, material monetary overstatement exists.

Figure 9-7 can be used to determine a reliability factor at various risks of incorrect acceptance and for various numbers of overstatement errors. The reliability factor appears where the identified column and row intersect. For example, if the auditor's risk of incorrect acceptance is 15 percent for The Wilson Company's trade accounts receivable balance, the reliability factor would be 1.90, the intersection of the column associated with a 15 percent risk of incorrect acceptance and the row associated with zero expected overstatement errors.

Tolerable Error

As in classical variables sampling, tolerable error in PPS sampling is closely related to an auditor's planned level of materiality, since it represents the maximum monetary error that may exist in an account balance without causing the financial statements to be materially misstated. In the trade accounts receivable illustration for The Wilson Company, assume the auditor judges tolerable error to be $43,750.

Figure 9-7: PPS Sampling: Reliability Factors for Overstatement Errors

Number of Over-statement Errors	Risk of Incorrect Acceptance								
	1%	5%	10%	15%	20%	25%	30%	37%	50%
0	4.61	3.00	2.31	1.90	1.61	1.39	1.21	1.00	.70
1	6.64	4.75	3.89	3.38	3.00	2.70	2.44	2.14	1.68
2	8.41	6.30	5.33	4.72	4.28	3.93	3.62	3.25	2.68
3	10.05	7.76	6.69	6.02	5.52	5.11	4.77	4.34	3.68
4	11.61	9.16	8.00	7.27	6.73	6.28	5.90	5.43	4.68
5	13.11	10.52	9.28	8.50	7.91	7.43	7.01	6.49	5.68
6	14.57	11.85	10.54	9.71	9.08	8.56	8.12	7.56	6.67
7	16.00	13.15	11.78	10.90	10.24	9.69	9.21	8.63	7.67
8	17.41	14.44	13.00	12.08	11.38	10.81	10.31	9.68	8.67
9	18.79	15.71	14.21	13.25	12.52	11.92	11.39	10.74	9.67
10	20.15	16.97	15.41	14.42	13.66	13.02	12.47	11.79	10.67
11	21.49	18.21	16.60	15.57	14.78	14.13	13.55	12.84	11.67
12	22.83	19.45	17.79	16.72	15.90	15.22	14.63	13.89	12.67
13	24.14	20.67	18.96	17.86	17.02	16.32	15.70	14.93	13.67
14	25.45	21.89	20.13	19.00	18.13	17.40	16.77	15.97	14.67
15	26.75	23.10	21.30	20.13	19.24	18.49	17.84	17.02	15.67
16	28.03	24.31	22.46	21.26	20.34	19.58	18.90	18.06	16.67
17	29.31	25.50	23.61	22.39	21.44	20.66	19.97	19.10	17.67
18	30.59	26.70	24.76	23.51	22.54	21.74	21.03	20.14	18.67
19	31.85	27.88	25.91	24.63	23.64	22.81	22.09	21.18	19.67
20	33.11	29.07	27.05	25.74	24.73	23.89	23.15	22.22	20.67

Anticipated Error and Expansion Factor

As noted earlier, PPS sampling is best applied when no errors are expected, since sample size may be too high otherwise. However, if some errors are expected, the dollar value of anticipated error is explicitly incorporated into the sample size formula. For the Wilson case, assume anticipated error is $9,000, determined from the auditor's prior experience with the client.

An expansion factor for expected errors is based on the auditor's risk of incorrect acceptance and is determined from Figure 9-8. For the Wilson illustration, the risk of incorrect acceptance is 15 percent, and the expansion factor from Figure 9-8 is 1.4. The expansion factor is multiplied by anticipated error, and the result is subtracted from the denominator in the sample size formula below, thereby serving to increase sample size. If no errors are anticipated in the sample, anticipated error and the expansion factor are not used.

Sample Size Calculation

Sample size for a PPS sampling plan can be calculated as follows:

$$n = \frac{RF \times B}{TE - (AE \times EF)}$$

Where:

RF = Reliability factor for overstatement errors.
B = Recorded book value.

Figure 9-8: PPS Sampling: Expansion Factors for Expected Errors

| | Risk of Incorrect Acceptance | | | | | | | | |
	1%	5%	10%	15%	20%	25%	30%	37%	50%
Factor	1.9	1.6	1.5	1.4	1.3	1.25	1.2	1.15	1.0

TE = Tolerable error.
AE = Anticipated error.
EF = Expansion factor.

To illustrate, sample size in the accounts receivable application for The Wilson Company would be:

$$n = \frac{1.90 \times \$1,750,000}{\$43,750 - (\$9,000 \times 1.4)}$$

$$= 107 \text{ (rounded)}$$

DETERMINE THE METHOD OF SAMPLE SELECTION

In PPS sampling, logical units—the documents, transactions, or accounts tested—may be selected using random-number sampling or systematic sampling. Assume that the auditor in The Wilson Company example has elected to use systematic sampling.

To facilitate sample selection, all population items are arrayed, a cumulative listing of logical units is formed, and logical units are then selected from the cumulative listing. For example, in the Wilson accounts receivable illustration, sample size is 107 and population size is 1,750,000. As a result, the *sampling interval* is 16,355 (1,750,000/107) and, following a randomly selected start, every 16,355th dollar from the cumulative balance would be selected and the related customer account tested. Assuming a random start at the 5,000th cumulative dollar, the following customer accounts would be selected:

Customer No.	Book Value	Cumulative Dollars	Dollar Selected
1001	$ 6,500	1–6,500	5,000
1002	18,945	6,501–25,445	21,355
1003	2,210	25,446–27,655	
1004	12,500	27,656–40,155	37,710
1005	3,200	40,156–43,355	
•	•	•	•
•	•	•	•
•	•	•	•
	$ 1,750,000		

In this illustration, Customer Number 1001 would be selected for testing because 5,000, the random start, falls within the cumulative dollars range 1 through 6,500; Customer 1002 is selected because 21,355 (5,000 + 16,355, the sampling interval) falls within the cumulative dollars range 6,501 through

25,445; and Customer 1004 is selected because 37,710 [5,000 + (16,355 × 2)] falls within the cumulative range 27,656 through 40,155. The selection process would continue until all logical units, in this case customer accounts, have been identified.

PERFORM THE SAMPLING PLAN AND EVALUATE THE SAMPLE RESULTS

To evaluate the results of a PPS sample, an auditor estimates the *upper error limit*, which is the sum of the projected risk in the sample and the allowance for sampling risk. However, the procedure for evaluating results depends on whether overstatement errors are found in the sample.

No Errors in the Sample

If no errors are found in the sample, then the projected population error is zero, and the allowance for sampling risk is no more than tolerable error. As a result, when no errors are found in the sample, the upper error limit is less than or equal to tolerable error. The auditor can therefore conclude that the recorded book value in the population is not overstated by more than tolerable error at the specified risk of incorrect acceptance. For example, if no errors are found in the trade accounts receivable illustration for The Wilson Company, then the auditor could conclude that the recorded book value of the population, $1,750,000, is not overstated by more than $43,750 (tolerable error) with a 15 percent risk of incorrect acceptance.

Errors Found in the Sample

If overstatement errors are found (that is, if the recorded book value exceeds the audited value), the auditor calculates the projected population error (or basic precision) and the incremental allowance for sampling risk and sums the two to arrive at an estimate of the upper error limit. Understatement errors, in contrast, require special consideration, in part because PPS sampling is designed primarily for overstatements.[2]

The *projected population error* is calculated differently depending on whether logical units containing errors are recorded at: (1) amounts less than the sampling interval or (2) greater than or equal to the sampling interval. The calculation is done separately for each logical unit containing error. For each logical unit recorded at less than the sampling interval, the error in the logical unit is projected to the population in the same proportion that the overstatement percentage, called a *tainting percentage*, bears to the sampling interval. For each logical unit recorded at an amount greater than or equal to the sampling interval, the projected error equals the overstatement error found. To illustrate, assume that overstatement errors are found in three account receivable balances, the logical unit in The Wilson Company illustration. The projected error is calculated as follows:

---

2   Further discussion of understatement errors appears in the AICPA's *Audit and Accounting Guide,* "Audit Sampling" New York: AICPA, p. 77. The guide suggests that where understatement errors may be significant, the auditor should consider whether a separate test specifically designed to detect understatements is appropriate. One appropriate test appears in D. M. Roberts. *Statistical Auditing,* New York: AICPA (1978), p. 124.

Error Number	(a) Book Value	(b) Audited Value	(c) Difference (a) − (b)	(d) Tainting Percentage (c) ÷ (a)	(e) Sample Interval	(f) Projected Error (d) × (e)
Logical units recorded at less than sampling interval:						
1	$12,000	$ 9,000	$3,000	.25	$16,355	$4,089
2	10,000	9,500	500	.05	16,355	818
						$4,907
Logical unit greater than or equal to sampling interval:						
3	29,000	25,500	3,500	—	—	3,500
	$51,000	$44,000	$7,000			$8,407

The *allowance for sampling risk* requires two separate calculations: basic precision and an incremental allowance for sampling risk. *Basic precision* is determined by multiplying the sampling interval by the reliability factor in Figure 9-7 associated with the auditor's risk of incorrect acceptance for zero errors. For example, in the Wilson illustration, basic precision is:

Sampling interval	$16,355
RF: reliability factor for .15 risk of incorrect acceptance	× 1.90
Basic precision	$31,075 (rounded)

The *incremental allowance* is determined from the projected error for each logical unit recorded at less than the sampling interval—for example, Error Numbers 1 and 2 in the Wilson illustration—and the actual error for each logical unit greater than (or equal to) the sampling interval.

One approach to calculating the incremental allowance for logical units less than the sampling interval is to: (1) rank the logical units containing errors in order of tainting percentage, and (2) multiply the projected error for each logical unit by the incremental change in reliability factor at a specified risk of incorrect acceptance. This approach is illustrated for The Wilson Company accounts receivable example as follows (note that for Error Number 3, recorded in an amount greater than the sampling interval, the projected error is the actual error detected):

Error No.	Projected Error	Incremental Change in Reliability Factor No. of Errors	Reliability Factor	Increment	Projected Error × Increment
Logical units recorded at less than sampling interval:					
		0	1.90		
1	$ 4,089	1	3.38	1.48	$ 6,052
2	818	2	4.72	1.34	1,096
	$ 4,907				$ 7,148
Logical unit greater than or equal to sampling interval:					
3	$35,500	—	—	—	3,500
					$10,648

Thus, in the Wilson illustration, the allowance for sampling risk is:

Basic precision	$31,075
Incremental allowance	10,648
Allowance for sampling risk	$41,723

From these results, the auditor could conclude that there is a 15 percent risk (i.e., the risk of incorrect acceptance) that the recorded book value, $1,750,000, is overstated by $41,723 or more. If the upper error limit is less than tolerable error, the results support the conclusion that the recorded book value in the population is not overstated by more than tolerable error at the specified risk of incorrect acceptance. For example, in the Wilson case, the upper error limit, $41,723, is less than tolerable error, $43,750. Therefore, the auditor can conclude that recorded book value, $1,750,000, is not overstated by more than $43,750 with a 15 percent risk of incorrect acceptance.

However, if the upper error limit exceeds tolerable error, recorded book value may be overstated. If this occurs, an auditor could: (1) examine additional logical units from the population, (2) perform additional substantive tests directed toward the same audit objective and, following these two steps, (3) have the client correct the errors found, reduce the upper error limit accordingly, and compare the revised upper error limit with tolerable error.

STRATIFIED SAMPLING

In any audit sampling plan, sample size is tied closely to the variability of population items: As the population variability increases, so too will sample size. In an effort to control sample size without sacrificing reliability, an auditor can *stratify* a highly variable audit population into segments or strata, thereby minimizing variability within strata and eliminating variability between strata. As a result, total sample size for all strata combined will be less, since total variability will decrease.

Audit populations can be stratified on the basis of several different criteria, including the following for trade accounts receivable:

Criteria	Strata
Monetary values	• Accounts over $20,000 • Accounts between $10,000 and $20,000 • Accounts under $10,000
Time	• Accounts outstanding more than 90 days • Accounts outstanding from 60 to 90 days • Accounts outstanding from 30 to 59 days • Accounts outstanding less than 30 days

The emphasis in this chapter has been on understanding the nature of variables sampling applications in auditing. As a result, except for PPS sampling—which automatically stratifies the population—the statistical plans discussed in the chapter have focused on unstratified rather than stratified sampling. Stratified sampling is based on the same logic as unstratified sampling, though the calculations are somewhat more involved.

NONSTATISTICAL SAMPLING IN SUBSTANTIVE TESTS OF DETAILS

There are two general approaches to audit sampling, statistical and nonstatistical, and either approach can provide competent evidential matter when applied properly. In short, a properly designed nonstatistical sampling plan can be just as effective as a properly designed statistical sampling plan, although, as discussed in Chapter 8, there is one critical difference: Statistical plans provide a quantitative measure of sampling risk and nonstatistical plans do not. Generally, auditors select a nonstatistical sampling plan when:

- There is no apparent need to quantify sampling risk,
- The cost of designing individual samples to meet statistical sampling requirements exceeds the benefits, and/or
- The cost to select sampling units randomly exceeds the expected benefits.

Following is an example of a nonstatistical sampling plan. The discussion focuses on how an auditor might determine sample size and evaluate the sample results. Note carefully that the discussion addresses only one example of a nonstatistical sampling plan; others are also applied in practice.

DETERMINE SAMPLE SIZE

In a nonstatistical sampling plan, an auditor must first determine the following:

- The degree of audit assurance desired.
- An appropriate assurance factor.
- An estimated tolerable error.

Each is explained below.

The Degree of Audit Assurance Desired and the Assurance Factor
The degree of audit assurance desired is based on the auditor's judgment, including an assessment of the effectiveness of internal controls (i.e., control risk) and on other procedures. For example, the degree of audit assurance could be assessed as follows:

Degree of Audit Assurance	Effectiveness of Internal Control and Other Procedures
Substantial	Little or none
Moderate	Some
Little	Considerable

In general, the degree of audit assurance is determined after the auditor obtains an understanding of internal control.

From the desired degree of audit assurance, the auditor next chooses a numerical factor based on the frequency and amount of errors expected in the population. For example, the assurance factor could be chosen as follows:

Audit Assurance Desired	Assurance Factor	
	Little Error Expected	Some Error Expected
Substantial	6	12
Moderate	4	8
Little	2	2

These numerical assurance factors are illustrative only.

Estimate of Tolerable Error and Key-Dollar Items

As in statistical sampling, tolerable error is the auditor's assessment of the maximum monetary error that may exist without causing the financial statements to be materially misstated. *Key-dollar items*, in contrast, are the items an auditor plans to test 100 percent. For example, assuming tolerable error of $8,000, the key-dollar items would at a minimum include all population items of $8,000 or more, because a misstated item of at least $8,000 would alone consume the auditor's tolerable error for the entire account balance. As a result, the key-dollar items would be items of at least $8,000, and probably items of lesser value.

Once an appropriate assurance factor is chosen and tolerable error and key-dollar items are estimated, preliminary sample size could be calculated as follows:

$$n = \left(\frac{B - KD}{TE} \right) \times AF$$

Where:

B = Recorded account balance.
KD = Sum of key-dollar items.
TE = Tolerable error.
AF = Assurance factor.

To illustrate, assume the recorded account balance is $150,000, 12 key-dollar items sum to $70,000, tolerable error is $8,000, and the auditor desires moderate assurance and expects little error (i.e., assurance factor = 4). From this data, preliminary sample size would be 52, represented by the 12 key-dollar items and 40 sampling units calculated from the formula above:

$$n = \left(\frac{\$150,000 - 70,000}{\$8,000} \right) \times 4$$

$$= 40$$

Alternatively, the auditor could use tables rather than a formula to determine sample size.

Unlike statistical sample sizes, preliminary nonstatistical sample sizes do not represent the minimum number of items necessary to achieve an auditor's acceptable risks of incorrect rejection and incorrect acceptance. Rather, the above nonstatistical sample size is preliminary and may be lowered according to the auditor's judgment—for example, if the auditor decides to increase reliance on other substantive tests or expects smaller and less frequent errors—and may be raised if the auditor judges otherwise.

As in nonstatistical sampling for attributes (Chapter 8), an auditor can select the 40 sampling units with random-number sampling or systematic sampling, or select (carefully) with block or haphazard sampling.

EVALUATE THE SAMPLE RESULTS

An auditor completes the nonstatistical sampling plan by determining *known error* (the misstatement observed within the sampling units tested) and by projecting *likely error* (the auditor's estimate of total population misstatement). An example follows.

For the preceding illustrative data, assume that for the 12 key-dollar items, two overstatement errors are observed totaling $6,000, and for the remaining 40 sampling units, five overstatement errors are observed totaling $1,000. Thus, known error is $7,000. Assume population size is 500 items.

Likely error can be estimated by adding the $6,000 overstatement error for the key-dollar items to the error projected from the 40 sampling units:

Key-dollar error   = $ 6,000
Sampling units:

$$\frac{\$1,000}{\left(\frac{40}{(500-12)}\right)} = \underline{12,195}$$

Total projected error $\underline{\underline{\$18,195}}$

Projected error for the 40 sampling units is estimated by dividing known error, $1,000, by the ratio of the number of sampling units to population size less the number of key-dollar items. In this case, likely error is $18,195, and the auditor has three alternative courses of action: (1) propose an audit adjustment, (2) perform additional substantive tests, or (3) request that the client revalue the entire population. In Chapter 13, nonstatistical sampling is applied to the accounts payable of a wholesaler of college and high school supplies.

SUMMARY

Variables sampling plans focus on population monetary balances rather than rates of deviation, the focus of the attributes sampling plans introduced in Chapter 8. Difference and ratio estimation, two long-established statistical sampling plans for variables, can be applied when each population item has a recorded value, total recorded value is known and corresponds to the sum of all population items, and differences between audited and recorded values are not too rare. When the preconditions underlying difference and ratio estimation are not present, an auditor can apply mean-per-unit estimation.

Probability-proportional-to-size (PPS) sampling applies concepts from attributes sampling to reach conclusions about dollar amounts. The name "probability-proportional-to-size" derives from the fact that each sampling unit's likelihood of being selected for testing is directly proportional to its size. For this reason, PPS sampling automatically stratifies an audit population.

As an alternative to classical variables sampling and PPS sampling, an auditor could choose a nonstatistical sampling plan and probably would if there were no apparent need to quantify sampling risk, or if the cost of designing and selecting statistical samples exceeded the benefits of quantifying sampling risk.

APPENDIX: ADJUSTING RECORDED ACCOUNT BALANCES IN CLASSICAL VARIABLES SAMPLING

In the chapter illustrations of difference and mean-per-unit estimation, re-corded account balances were accepted as fairly stated because: (1) the precision interval included the recorded account balance and (2) the desired allowance for sampling risk exceeded the achieved allowance for sampling risk. But what if these two conditions were not met? Each situation is discussed separately next.

RECORDED ACCOUNT BALANCE FALLS OUTSIDE PRECISION INTERVAL

A recorded account balance falling outside the precision interval could still be accepted as fairly stated if tolerable error exceeds the difference between: (1) the recorded account balance and (2) the farthest end of the precision interval. For example, assume that the recorded account balance is $1,020,000, tolerable error is $125,000, estimated population value is $950,000, and the achieved allowance for sampling risk is $50,000, yielding a precision interval from $900,000 to $1,000,000, as illustrated in Figure 9-9.

From Figure 9-9, the difference between the recorded account balance ($1,020,000) and the farthest end of the precision interval (in this case, the lower precision limit, $900,000) is $120,000, which is less than the auditor's tolerable error ($125,000). As a result, the recorded account balance is accepted as fairly stated, since the amount of error the auditor is willing to tolerate (tolerable error) exceeds the maximum likely error in the population. Incidentally, this situation typically occurs when the auditor's tolerable error greatly exceeds the achieved allowance for sampling risk, as in the illustration (i.e., tolerable error = $125,000; achieved allowance for sampling risk = $50,000).

Figure 9-9:   Recorded Account Balance Falls Outside Precision Interval

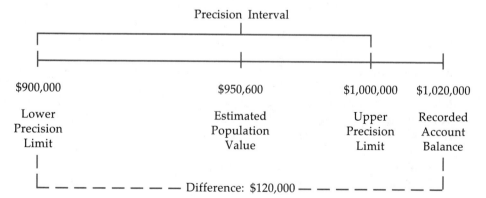

In contrast, if tolerable error does not exceed the maximum likely error, an auditor could: (1) increase sample size and reevaluate for all sampling units, (2) request that the client revalue the population, or (3) propose an audit adjustment, as illustrated below.

ACHIEVED ALLOWANCE FOR SAMPLING RISK EXCEEDS DESIRED ALLOWANCE

If the achieved allowance for sampling risk (A') exceeds the desired allowance for sampling risk (A), the risk of incorrect acceptance becomes greater, because the precision interval, $\hat{X} \pm A'$, is larger than $\hat{X} \pm A$. Thus, for the larger $\hat{X} \pm A'$, there is a greater probability of accepting a materially misstated account balance—i.e., the risk of incorrect acceptance. The alternatives available to the auditor are the same as those identified in the preceding illustration (increase sample size, request that the client revalue the population, or propose an audit adjustment).

Altering the facts from the previous illustration, assume tolerable error is $60,000, and the desired allowance for sampling risk is $40,000. In this case, the recorded account balance could not be accepted as fairly stated, absent additional substantive tests, because: (1) the recorded account balance ($1,020,000) falls outside the precision interval ($900,000 to $1,000,000), (2) the achieved allowance for sampling risk ($50,000) exceeds the desired allowance for sampling risk ($40,000), and (3) tolerable error ($60,000) does not exceed the difference between the recorded account balance ($1,020,000) and the lower precision limit ($900,000). As a result, an audit adjustment could be proposed. The adjusted book value would be $960,000, the lower precision limit ($900,000) plus tolerable error ($60,000), and the proposed audit adjustment would be $60,000, computed by subtracting the adjusted book balance from the recorded balance.

KEY TERMS

Audit risk 317	Sampling unit 319
Sampling risk 317	Tolerable error 323
Nonsampling risk 317	Difference estimation 326
Risk of incorrect rejection 317	Ratio estimation 332
Risk of incorrect acceptance 318	Mean-per-unit (MPU) estimation 333
Variables sampling plan 318	Probability-proportional-to-size (PPS)
Audit population 319	sampling 336

REFERENCES

Professional Standards

AICPA. *Codification of Statements on Auditing Standards.* New York: AICPA (AU Sec. 312, 350).
AICPA. *Audit and Accounting Guide,* "Audit Sampling." New York: AICPA.
SAS No. 39, "Audit Sampling" (AU Sec. 350).
SAS No. 47, "Audit Risk and Materiality in Conducting an Audit" (AU Sec. 312).

Articles, Books

Guy, D., D. Carmichael, and O. R. Wittington. *Audit Sampling: An Introduction.* New York: Wiley (1994).
Peek, L., J. Neter, and C. Warren. "AICPA Nonstatistical Audit Sampling Guidelines: A Simulation," *Auditing: A Journal of Practice & Theory* (Fall 1991), pp. 33-48.

Ponemon, L. A., and J. P. Wendell. "Judgmental Versus Random Sampling in Auditing: An Experimental Investigation," *Auditing: A Journal of Practice & Theory* (Fall 1995), pp. 17-34.

QUESTIONS

1. Identify and briefly describe two aspects of audit risk that are critical in an auditor's substantive tests of account balances.
2. Explain the difference between *dollar-value estimation* and *hypothesis testing* in audit sampling. Which of the two is more common in auditing?
3. Define what is meant by an *audit population*. What is the importance of an auditor's *characteristic of interest* when defining an audit population?
4. What is a *sampling unit*?
5. Identify the relative advantages and disadvantages of classical variables sampling.
6. Identify the relative advantages and disadvantages of probability-proportional-to-size sampling.
7. Define *tolerable error*.
8. Identify three conditions that must exist before either difference or ratio estimation can be applied.
9. Under what condition is difference estimation more appropriate than ratio estimation?
10. Assume an auditor sets acceptable risks of incorrect rejection and incorrect acceptance at .10 and .05, respectively, applies ratio estimation, and obtains the following results: estimated population value, $250,000; achieved allowance for sampling risk, $32,500. Draft the auditor's conclusion.
11. Briefly describe the auditor's strategy when applying mean-per-unit (MPU) estimation.
12. Difference and ratio estimation, mean-per-unit estimation, and probability-proportional-to-size (PPS) sampling all express sampling results in dollars. How, though, does PPS sampling differ from the other three sampling techniques?
13. Briefly describe the auditor's strategy when applying probability-proportional-to-size sampling.
14. Why is probability-proportional-to-size sampling most appropriate when an auditor desires testing for material overstatements?
15. Under what conditions would an auditor choose a nonstatistical sampling plan in substantive tests of details?

MULTIPLE CHOICE QUESTIONS

1. Tolerable error, a measure of the maximum monetary error that may exist in an account balance without causing materially misstated financial statements, is directly related to:

   a. Precision.
   b. Audit risk.
   c. Materiality.
   d. Confidence level.

2. Which of the following is necessary to determine sample size?

   a. Population size.
   b. Expected population deviation rate.
   c. Estimated population monetary error.
   d. Risk.

3. Which of the following statements is an advantage of classical variables sampling?

a. If no errors are expected, classical variables sampling will result in a smaller sample size than probability-proportional-to-size sampling.
b. A classical variables sampling plan can begin before the completed population is available.
c. Classical variables sampling may result in a smaller sample size than probability-proportional-to-size sampling if there are many differences between recorded and audited amounts.
d. Classical variables sampling does not require recorded values for individual sampling units.

4. Which of the following situations would increase sample size? A decrease in:

a. Risk of incorrect rejection.
b. Estimated population standard deviation.
c. Expected frequency of errors.
d. Tolerable error.

5. The risk of incorrect acceptance relates to the:

a. Effectiveness of the audit.
b. Efficiency of the audit.
c. Preliminary estimate of materiality.
d. Allowable risk of tolerable error.

(AICPA Adapted)

6. Sample results support the conclusion that a recorded account balance is materially misstated but, unknown to the auditor, the account is not misstated, suggesting the risk of:

a. Incorrect rejection.
b. Incorrect acceptance.
c. Assessing control risk too high.
d. Assessing control risk too low.

7. Calculate an acceptable risk of incorrect acceptance assuming: (1) audit risk is 5 percent, (2) the risk that the internal controls fail to detect material errors is 40 percent, and (3) the risk that analytical procedures fail to detect material errors not detected by the internal controls is 50 percent.

a. .04.
b. .16.
c. .25.
d. Indeterminate.

8. Assume the acceptable risk of incorrect rejection is .10, the acceptable risk of incorrect acceptance is .075, and tolerable error is $100,000. What is the desired allowance for sampling risk?

a. $50,000.
b. $47,800.
c. $53,200.
d. Indeterminate.

9. In a difference estimation sampling plan for a population of 1,500 items, an auditor found total recorded and audited values for a sample of 100 items to be $120,000 and $126,000, respectively. What is the total projected monetary difference for the population?

a. $6,000.
b. $90,000.
c. $126,000.
d. Indeterminate.

10. Ratio estimation is inappropriate when:

a. The total population book value is known and corresponds to the sum of all population items.
b. There are some observed differences between audited and recorded book values.
c. Differences between recorded and audited values are nearly proportional to the recorded values.
d. There are no recorded values for some items in the population.

11. Probability-proportional-to-size sampling will likely result in selecting a sample with characteristics roughly equivalent to:

a. A classical variables sampling plan stratified by dollar amount.
b. Difference estimation.
c. Ratio estimation.
d. Nonstatistical sampling.

12. In probability-proportional-to-size sampling, each invoice:

a. Has an equal probability of being selected.
b. Can be represented by no more than one dollar unit.
c. Has an unknown probability of being selected.
d. Has a probability proportional to its dollar value of being selected.

(IIA Adapted)

13. Which of the following is improper when using probability-proportional-to-size sampling?

a. Combining negative and positive dollar error items.
b. Using a sample selection technique in which the same account balance could be selected more than once.
c. Selecting a random starting point and then sampling every n^{th} dollar unit.
d. Defining the sampling unit as an individual dollar and not as an individual account balance.

14. In a probability-proportional-to-size sampling plan with a $10,000 sampling interval, an auditor discovered that a selected account receivable with a recorded amount of $5,000 had an audited amount of $2,000. The projected error for the sample is:

a. $3,000.
b. $4,000.
c. $6,000.
d. $8,000.

15. A nonstatistical sampling plan can:

a. Overstate the estimate of sampling risk.
b. Misdirect an auditor to unreliable sampling units.
c. Replicate the results of a statistical sampling plan.
d. Understate the degree of audit assurance desired.

PROBLEMS AND DISCUSSION CASES

9-1 *Audit Risk in Substantive Testing*
Assume you are the newly assigned senior on a continuing audit engagement for the Ranson Corporation, and are meeting with Tom Porter, partner in charge of the engagement. Interim field work is already complete but was accomplished under another senior's supervision, before you were assigned to the engagement. You have reviewed the interim working papers and are discussing year end audit risk with Porter.

Porter observes that in prior years few material audit adjustments were proposed and that, in his judgment, management has integrity and Ranson is economically stable. Interim field work revealed no significant deficiencies in internal control, except that controls over recorded credit sales transactions were deficient in one respect: Credit approval documentation was missing for several material sales to new customers. In addition, Porter reminds you that in the prior year, the most significant audit adjustment was related to Accounts Receivable, an account which usually represents about 25 percent of reported total assets, although the adjustment was prompted by an unusual fluctuation in receivables turnover and the number-of-days-sales-in-accounts-receivable, rather than by substantive tests of details.

Required:
1. From the information available, determine an acceptable risk that monetary errors greater than tolerable error might remain undetected after the audit team has completed all audit procedures deemed necessary. Justify the risk you accept.
2. Determine a risk that, should errors greater than tolerable error occur, the internal controls fail to detect them. Justify the risk level determined.
3. Determine a risk that analytical and other procedures fail to detect errors greater than tolerable error. Justify the risk level determined.
4. Determine an acceptable risk of incorrect acceptance for this engagement. How should the quantified risk of incorrect acceptance be interpreted?

9-2 *The Risks of Incorrect Rejection and Incorrect Acceptance*
The risks of incorrect rejection and incorrect acceptance are related but involve two entirely different outcomes: Incorrect rejection means the risk of concluding that recorded book value is materially misstated when material monetary error does not exist, and incorrect acceptance means the risk of concluding that recorded book value is not materially misstated when in fact material monetary error does exist. Importantly, all three classical variables sampling plans—ratio estimation, difference estimation, and mean-per-unit estimation—require estimates of the risks of incorrect rejection and incorrect acceptance, and probability-proportional-to-size sampling requires an estimate of the risk of incorrect acceptance.

Required:
1. Explain why the risks of incorrect rejection and incorrect acceptance are competing risks. Why, for example, does increasing the risk of incorrect acceptance necessarily decrease the risk of incorrect rejection?
2. How can an auditor systematically reduce both the risk of incorrect rejection and the risk of incorrect acceptance simultaneously?

9-3 *Relating the Risks of Incorrect Rejection and Incorrect Acceptance to Sampling Risk*
When applying a classical variables sampling plan, such as ratio or difference estimation or MPU estimation, an auditor must estimate the risk of incorrect rejection, the risk of incorrect acceptance, and tolerable error, each of which is determined separately, but integrated before calculating sample size.

Required:
1. How are the risks of incorrect rejection and incorrect acceptance and tolerable error integrated in variables sampling plans?
2. Determine a desired allowance for sampling risk assuming:

Acceptable risk of incorrect rejection   = .20
Acceptable risk of incorrect acceptance = .10
Tolerable error   = $40,000

9-4   *Difference Estimation*
Because there is no discernible relationship between the absolute amount of differences
(i.e., audited value v. recorded book value) and recorded book value for 50 preliminary
sample items, an auditor decides to use difference estimation in the audit of accounts
receivable. The following data are known:

Population size   = 2,500
Estimated population standard deviation   = $20
Acceptable risk of incorrect rejection   = .05
Desired allowance for sampling risk   = $10,000

After sample size is calculated and the sampling units are selected and examined, the
following summary data are available:

Total recorded value for all sampling units   = $65,220
Total audited value for all sampling units   = $64,970
Net difference (i.e., between recorded and
    audited amounts) for all sampling units   = $250
Squared differences for all sampling units   = $215,000
Estimated population standard deviation   = $48.53

Required: Assume difference estimation is applied and total recorded book value
is $500,000. Determine:
1.   Sample size.
2.   Total projected monetary difference.
3.   Estimated population value.
4.   Achieved allowance for sampling risk.
5.   Precision interval.

9-5   *Difference Estimation*
The following information is available for 50 sample items:

	Sample Item	Book Value	Audited Value
Subtotals, nondifference items	—	$55,265	$55,265
Difference items	5	670	720
	11	1,265	1,165
	18	1,980	1,800
	24	895	1,030
	29	725	912
	34	230	215
	38	415	490
		$61,445	$61,597

Population size is 2,100 items, recorded book value is $1,235,000, the risk of incorrect
rejection is .10, the risk of incorrect acceptance is .05, and the sample standard deviation
is $46.
   Required: Formulate a conclusion for the above data assuming difference estimation is used. Show all work supporting your conclusion.

9-6   *Ratio Estimation*
Following are data for four different audit populations to which variables sampling
will be applied:

	Population			
	1	2	3	4
Acceptable risk of incorrect rejection	.10	.05	.05	.01
Acceptable risk of incorrect acceptance	.20	.10	.25	.05
Population size	2,500	3,000	2,750	2,100
Estimated population standard deviation	$20	$12	$10	$15
Tolerable error	$8,750	$6,200	$7,000	$9,000

Required: Calculate sample size for each population. Assume sampling without replacement and do not ignore the finite population correction factor.

9-7 *Mean-per-Unit Estimation*

Following are data for four different audit populations. Mean-per-unit estimation will be applied to each population.

	Population			
	1	2	3	4
1. Allowable risk that monetary error greater than tolerable error might remain undetected after the auditor has completed all audit procedures.	.05	.10	.07	.05
2. The risk that, should errors greater than tolerable error occur, the internal controls fail to detect them.	.20	.30	1.00	.50
3. The risk that analytical procedures and other tests fail to detect errors greater than tolerable error that occur and are not detected by internal control.	.50	.80	.70	.70

Required:

1. Calculate an acceptable risk of incorrect acceptance for each population.
2. For Populations 1 and 3, calculate a desired allowance for sampling risk, assuming tolerable error is $100,000 and the risk of incorrect rejection is .10.

9-8 *Mean-per-Unit Estimation*

Because a client does not maintain perpetual records, an auditor elects to use mean-per-unit estimation to determine whether ending inventory is fairly stated. The following data are available:

Acceptable risk of incorrect rejection	= .05
Acceptable risk of incorrect acceptance	= .20
Estimated population standard deviation	= $70
Tolerable error	= $25,000
Population size	= 1,800

After sample size is determined and sampling units are selected and examined, the auditor compiles the following results:

Total audited value for all sampling units	= $25,060
Sample standard deviation	= $67

Required:

1. From the information available, what is the auditor's desired allowance for sampling risk?
2. Calculate sample size.
3. Determine the estimated population value.
4. Calculate the achieved allowance for sampling risk.

5. Determine the precision interval.
6. State a statistical conclusion.

9-9 *Probability-Proportional-to-Size Sampling*
An auditor expects no errors in an audit population but is concerned about potential monetary overstatement and, therefore, elects to use probability-proportional-to-size sampling. Recorded book value is $1,200,000, maximum tolerable overstatement is $67,500, and the risk of incorrect acceptance is preset at 15 percent.

After sample size is determined and sampling units are selected and examined, the following differences are noted:

Invoice No.	Recorded Value	Audited Value
1826	$15,000	$12,000
2041	$16,000	$15,050

Required:
1. Calculate sample size.
2. Calculate the allowance for sampling risk.
3. Reach a conclusion.

9-10 *Probability-Proportional-to-Size Sampling*
Assume your audit objective is to estimate the upper error limit for an audit population and, therefore, you select probability-proportional-to-size (PPS) sampling. From prior year working papers and evidence accumulated during the consideration of internal control, you conclude that errors are expected and that the risk of incorrect acceptance is .10.

The following information is also known:

Recorded book value   = $1,000,000
Maximum tolerable overstatement   = $1,100,000
Anticipated error   = $15,000

After testing logical units, three differences are observed as follows:

Recorded Value	Audited Value	Difference
$20,000	$18,000	$2,000
$15,000	$14,250	$750
$40,000	$38,000	$2,000

Required: From this information, determine the following:
1. The reliability factor for overstatement errors.
2. The expansion factor.
3. Sample size.
4. The sampling interval.
5. Basic precision.
6. The incremental allowance.
7. The allowance for sampling risk (the upper error limit).
8. The audit conclusion.

9-11 *Nonstatistical Sampling*
An auditor has no apparent need to quantify sampling risk and, therefore, uses a nonstatistical sampling plan for inventory price testing. From prior experience with the client and current information about internal control, the auditor expects some pricing errors but also desires moderate assurance that the pricing of physical goods is fairly accurate. The auditor presets tolerable error at $12,000 and decides to test the 15 highest

dollar items, totaling $50,000, which represents 40 percent of total recorded book value, $125,000.

After determining sample size and selecting and examining the sampling units, the auditor compiles the following results:

	Number of Errors	Total Error
Key-dollar items	3	$5,000 overstatement
Sampled items	5	$1,500 overstatement

Population size is 600.

Required:
1. Determine an appropriate assurance factor.
2. Determine sample size.
3. Calculate likely error from the results indicated above.
4. Is recorded book value acceptable to the auditor? Why or why not?

9-12 *Nonstatistical v. Statistical Sampling*
An auditor is selecting from among alternative variables sampling plans for accounts receivable and gathers the following information. The client, a Midwestern manufacturer of high-technology electrical components, had been audited previously by a crosstown public accounting firm. In five prior engagements, the predecessor auditors had issued unqualified opinions, except for last year when they issued a qualified opinion because of departures from generally accepted accounting principles. The client maintains subsidiary records for each individual customer account, and supporting documents are filed within Accounts Receivable. A review of selected sections of the predecessor auditor's working papers indicates that differences between recorded and audited values for individual customer accounts tended to increase as recorded book value increased.

Required:
1. Is nonstatistical sampling appropriate in this case? Explain.
2. Explain why each of the following statistical sampling plans may be appropriate or inappropriate in this case:
   a. Ratio estimation.
   b. Difference estimation.
   c. Mean-per-unit estimation.
   d. Probability-proportional-to-size sampling.

9-13 *Adjusting Recorded Account Balances*
When completing a variables sampling plan, an auditor's evaluation is based on the relationship between and among a number of factors, including recorded account balance, estimated total population value, tolerable error, the desired allowance for sampling risk, and the achieved allowance for sampling risk. The following table contains data for the above factors.

	Case			
	1	2	3	4
Recorded account balance	$260,000	$255,000	$217,000	$238,000
Estimated population value	$235,000	$235,000	$223,000	$220,000
Tolerable error	$20,000	$37,500	$18,000	$32,000
Desired allowance for sampling risk	$12,000	$18,000	$10,000	$22,000
Achieved allowance for sampling risk	$15,000	$15,000	$12,000	$20,000

Required: For each case, indicate whether the recorded account balance can be accepted as fairly stated, or not accepted, and why. If an account balance is not accepted as fairly stated, determine the proper adjusted book value.

RESEARCH PROJECTS

1.   CLASSICAL VARIABLES SAMPLING AND PPS SAMPLING

Applied widely first in the 1960s and 1970s, the use of statistical sampling was initially motivated largely by questions raised in legal liability cases involving public accounting firms, among them: Why did the public accounting firm not become aware of embezzlement schemes that, when made public thereafter (often by the perpetrators themselves, e.g., *Ernst & Ernst v. Hochfelder*: Chapter 5), led to an audit client's financial collapse? In response, several major public accounting firms consulted with statisticians to develop sampling plans that would document not only the strategy used to examine the account balance or class of transactions audited, but that would also provide a defense for why specific transactions were selected for testing and others were not (e.g., random sampling).

However, in recent years some auditors have become more cautious about applying classical variables sampling and probability-proportional-to-size sampling in practice, partly because some sampling plans may result in excessive sample sizes in some circumstances, and partly because research suggests caution before blindly over-relying on the sampling results obtained from some sampling applications. For example, D. W. Wright, "Augmenting a Sample Selected with Probabilities Proportional to Size" (*Auditing: A Journal of Practice and Theory*, Spring 1991), raises a timely caution to audit practice given the popularity of PPS sampling today: Augmented (i.e., supplemental) samples obtained with systematic monetary-unit skip-intervals will tend to include sampling units that over- (or under-) represent the smaller (or larger) population items.

Required: Select an article about classical variables sampling or probability-proportional-to-size sampling from one of the following journals: *Auditing: A Journal of Practice and Theory, The Accounting Review*, or *Journal of Accounting Research*. For the article selected, draft a report that addresses each of the following questions:

1.   What is the researcher's motivation for the study—that is, why is the study important? (Note: The motivation for a study is typically communicated in the opening sections of a journal article.)
2.   Summarize the article in your own words.
3.   What, if any, are the implications of the article for audit practice—that is, should auditors think differently about audit sampling as a result of the article?

2.   APPLYING PROBABILITY-PROPORTIONAL-TO-SIZE SAMPLING IN PRACTICE

Owing to economical sample sizes and ease of application, probability-proportional-to-size (PPS) sampling has become the most widely used statistical sampling plan in practice today, even by local practitioners, some of whom had been reluctant to apply the more cumbersome classical variables sampling plans. Applications in practice range from inventory valuation in single site retail stores to elaborate receivables confirmation plans for user fees, property taxes, and gaming receipts in state government.

Required: Select an *AICPA Audit & Accounting Guide* for an industry (e.g., airlines, banks, casinos, colleges and universities, construction contractors, finance companies, investment companies, property and liability insurance companies, providers of health care services, or state and local governmental units). Draft a PPS sampling plan that could be applied to a financial statement account the guide leads you to believe is *characteristic* of the industry, such as third-party reimbursements in the health care industry or frequent-flier liabilities in the airline industry.

PART 3

METHOD

10

Tests of Controls in the Revenue/Receipt Cycle: Sales and Cash Receipts Transactions

Major topics discussed in this chapter are:

- The nature of the revenue/receipt cycle, including the flow of information through customer order, credit, inventory control, shipping, billing, recording, and cash collection.
- Assurance and consulting service opportunities related to revenue recognition.
- An auditor's consideration of internal control in the revenue/receipt cycle.
- The integration of computer auditing, sampling, and tests of controls within the revenue/receipt cycle.

Designing an assurance, attestation, or audit services engagement is a creative process in which a practitioner captures professional responsibilities (Chapters 1-5) and available technology (Chapters 6-9) into his or her judgments about the nature, timing, and extent of the procedures to be applied. This chapter—and the next six—introduce the procedures typically applied in a financial statement audit, focusing sharply on how an auditor performs tests of controls and substantive tests within the four transaction cycles introduced in Chapter 7: the revenue/receipt, expenditure/disbursement, conversion, and financing cycles. Each chapter is one in a series of interrelated segments in a financial statement audit, and each of four chapters (10, 12, 15, and 16) also introduces assurance and consulting service opportunities for one of the four cycles.

This chapter and Chapter 11 focus on auditing the revenue/receipt cycle: Tests of controls are introduced here, and substantive tests are introduced in Chapter 11. The chapter begins by introducing the nature of the revenue/receipt cycle and representative internal controls over customer order, credit, inventory control, shipping, billing, recording, and cash collection functions. In turn, the chapter offers examples of assurance and consulting service opportunities related to revenue recognition, some of which are being offered today. Next, an auditor's consideration of internal control within the revenue/receipt cycle is discussed. Finally, the chapter presents a case illustration that integrates material introduced in Chapter 7 (computer information systems), Chapter 8 (audit sampling), and this chapter.

THE REVENUE/RECEIPT CYCLE

The revenue/receipt cycle encompasses both the sale of goods or services to customers ("revenue" in the cycle's title) and the collection of cash ("receipt"). The cycle is related to each of the other three transaction cycles, since it:

- Receives resources and information provided by the financing and conversion cycles, and
- Provides resources and information to the expenditure/disbursement cycle.

For example, the revenue/receipt cycle might receive cash from the proceeds of a public offering of securities through the financing cycle, receive inventory produced by the conversion cycle to sell to customers, and provide cash to pay for raw materials purchased through the expenditure/disbursement cycle.

Figure 10-1 summarizes the scope of the revenue/receipt cycle, listing the primary business functions and activities, journal entries, and forms common to the cycle. Two major business functions are associated with the cycle:

- Resources (goods or services) are sold to customers in exchange for promises of future payment.
- Cash is collected from customers.

The cycle begins when a customer order is received by fax, mail, e-mail, telephone, or *electronic data integration (EDI)*, and a decision is made to grant or deny credit. If credit is granted, the ordered goods are shipped, the sale is recorded, and the customer is billed, usually by the same medium in which the order is placed. In turn, the customer remits either cash (e.g., a check) or digital cash in accordance with the terms of sale.

Throughout the revenue/receipt cycle, journal entries are made for sales, including discounts and returns and allowances, cash receipts, allowances for potentially uncollectible accounts, and writeoffs of accounts that won't be collected. Paper or computer image documents affecting the revenue/receipt cycle include the:

- **Customer order.** A request from a customer to purchase goods.

Figure 10-1: The Scope of the Revenue/Receipt Cycle

Business Functions	Common Activities	Common Entries	Common Forms
• Resources are sold to customers in exchange for promises for future payments • Cash is collected from customers for resources sold to them	• Customer orders (order entry) • Credit approval • Inventory control • Shipping • Billing • Recording • Cash collection (and deposits) • Sales returns	• Sales • Sales discounts • Sales returns and allowances • Cash receipts • Allowance for uncollectible accounts • Write off of specific uncollectible accounts	• Customer order • Sales order • Shipping document • Sales invoice • Customer remittance advice

- **Sales order.** Identifies goods ordered by a customer, including relevant information about price, quantity, payment terms, etc.
- **Shipping document.** Identifies goods shipped, and represents a contract between the seller and carrier (e.g., trucking company); a shipping document is often in the form of a **bill of lading**, a *Uniform Commercial Code* document used by common carriers.
- **Sales invoice.** Identifies goods sold and represents formal notice to a customer about the amount and terms of payment (often called the *bill*).
- **Customer remittance advice.** Accompanies a sales invoice but is intended to be returned with a customer's payment (remittance); a returned remittance advice indicates the purpose of a cash payment, facilitating handling and recording.

Paper and/or computer image documents used throughout the revenue/receipt cycle are necessary to authorize, execute, and record a transaction. The documents form an audit trail and are an important source of audit evidence, although the form of the trail varies depending on whether the documents take the form of paper or computer images. For example, in systems that process paper, the audit trail consists of paper documents filed within departments, and access to the documents is restricted by restricting access to the department. In systems that process computer images only, rather than paper, the audit trail consists of computer images, and access to the screens is restricted by access codes.

Revenue/receipt cycle activities and controls vary from one entity to another and are influenced by several factors, including the nature of an entity's industry (e.g., manufacturing, service, financial, government), the entity's size and organizational structure, and the extent to which accounting information is processed by computer. However, the activities of most businesses that sell goods are similar to those identified in Figure 10-1, although the activities would be modified somewhat for service companies. Credit sales activities and controls are explained next for each of the following functions (cash collection is discussed separately later):

- Customer order,
- Credit,
- Inventory control,
- Shipping,
- Billing, and
- Recording.

CREDIT SALES

Figure 10-2 flowcharts representative credit sales activities and common documents. In turn, Figure 10-3 summarizes the credit sales activities flowcharted in Figure 10-2. The following explains each major activity and related documents.

When a customer order is received by phone, fax, electronic transmission or mail, a *sales order* is prepared by an employee of the customer order department. A *sales order* describes the goods ordered, including catalog or stock numbers, prices, quantities, and payment terms. Copies of *sales orders* are transmitted to customers, and to the credit, shipping, and billing departments,

Figure 10-2: Revenue/Receipt Cycle: Credit Sales

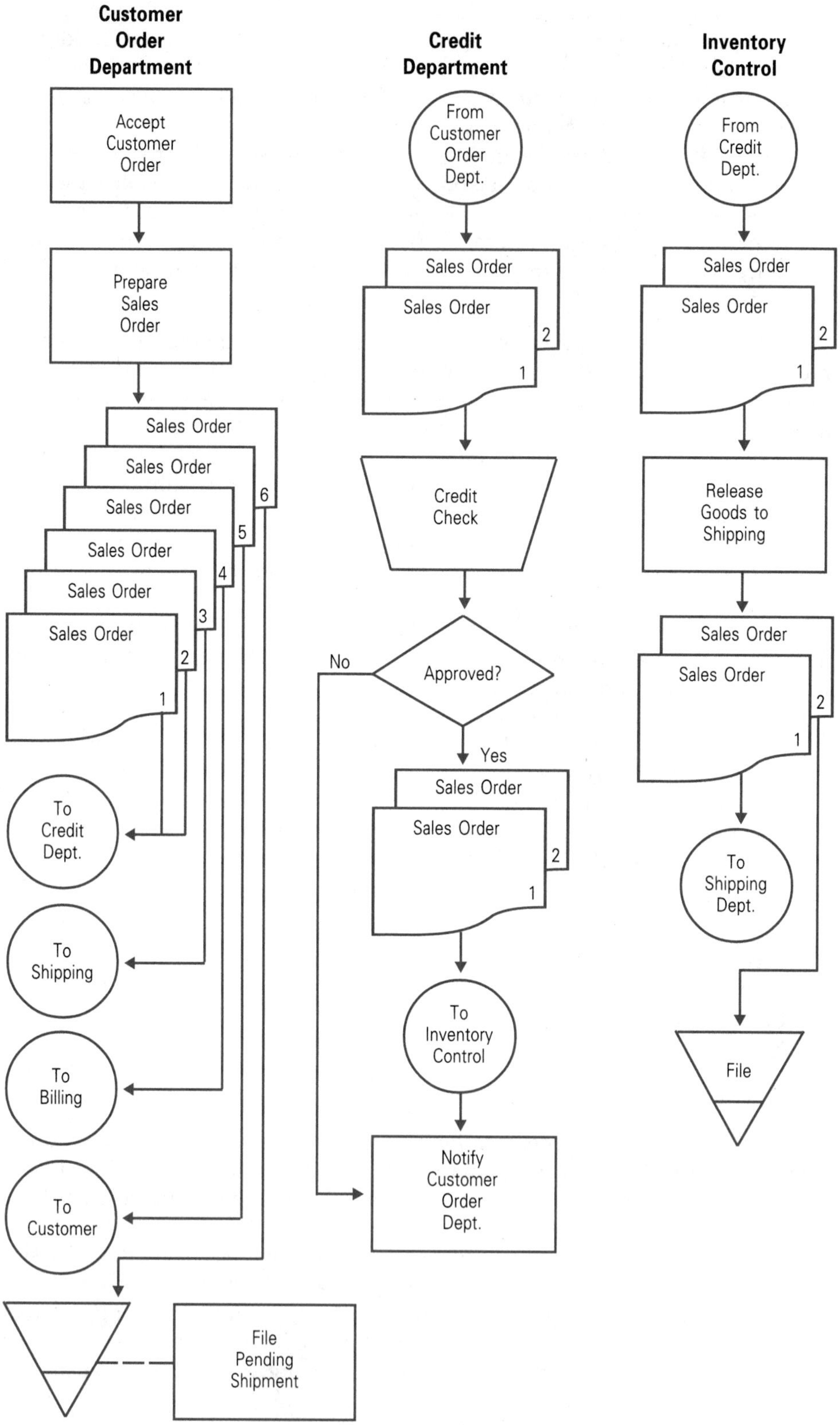

Figure 10-2: *(continued)*

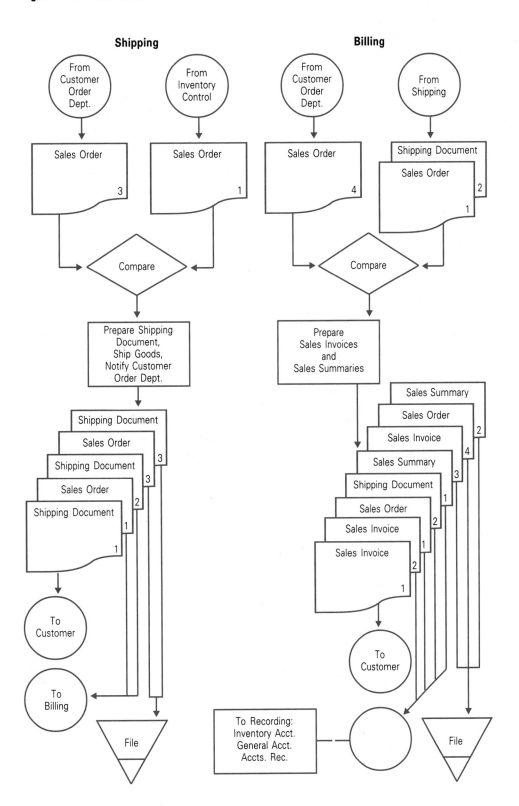

Figure 10-3: Summary of Credit Sales Activities

Customer Order Department
- Accept customer order.
- Prepare sales order, distribute copies, and retain copy in unfilled order file.

Credit Department
- Review sales order and investigate customer credit information.
- Initial copy of sales order if credit is approved and forward the order to Inventory Control. If credit is denied, notify the customer order department.

Inventory Control
- Review sales order.
- Initial copy of sales order to authorize the release of goods from the warehouse.
- Forward goods and a copy of the sales order to Shipping, and retain a file copy of the sales order.

Shipping
- Compare sales order from Inventory Control with sales order from Customer Order Department.
- Examine goods from warehouse and compare with sales orders.
- Prepare goods for shipment and complete shipping documents.
- Release goods to carrier and obtain receipt.
- Notify Customer Order Department that goods have been shipped.
- Forward copy of sales order and shipping documents to Billing; retain file copy of sales order and shipping documents.

Billing
- Compare documents from Shipping with sales order from Customer Order.
- Prepare sales invoice, send copy to customer and to Inventory Accounting along with copy of sales order and shipping documents, and retain file copy.
- Prepare daily sales summary, send copy to General Accounting, and retain file copy.

Recording
- Inventory Accounting: Enter cost information on sales invoice, update inventory records, and forward sales invoice and related documents to General Accounting.
- General Accounting: Record sale and forward sales invoice and related documents to Accounts Receivable.
- Accounts Receivable: Post sale to customer's account and file sales invoice and related documents.

as indicated in Figure 10-2. A copy of the *sales order* is retained by the customer order department—either in the form of paper filed in an *unfilled order file,* or in the form of a computer image—until notice is received from Shipping that ordered goods have been shipped.

Before a credit sale is executed, a customer's credit is first reviewed and approved by Credit Department personnel to minimize the likelihood of shipping goods to high-risk customers. Approved *sales orders* are forwarded to Inventory Control (whose role is addressed more fully in Chapter 15), where the goods are released for shipment. Goods transferred from Inventory Control to Shipping are accompanied by a copy of the *sales order* bearing the approval of an inventory control employee authorized to release goods from inventory.

Shipping personnel compare the goods received from Inventory with what's listed on the *sales order*, and prepare *shipping documents*. When goods are shipped, Shipping personnel obtain a receipt for the goods from the common carrier (e.g., a trucking company). Receipts often take the form of a *Uniform Commercial Code (UCC) bill of lading*, which describes the goods shipped and represents a contract between the seller and the carrier. Shipping notifies Customer Order that the goods have been shipped, and Customer Order updates the unfilled order file.

After shipment, a copy of the *shipping documents* and a copy of the *sales order* approved by Credit and Inventory Control are sent to Billing. Billing personnel compare *shipping documents* and *sales orders* and prepare *sales invoices*, which are faxed, mailed, e-mailed, or transferred by EDI to customers, and distributed to Inventory Accounting, General Accounting, and Accounts Receivable for recording. A *sales invoice* describes the goods sold, and the customer's copy (their "bill") notifies the customer of the amount due and the terms of payment. Some companies prepare a *remittance advice* to accompany each customer *sales invoice*. A *remittance advice* is intended to be returned with a customer's payment (their remittance) and facilitates the company's handling and recording of cash receipts.

Copies of *sales invoices* prepared by Billing personnel, as well as *sales orders* and *shipping documents*, are sent to Inventory Accounting. Billing employees also prepare *daily sales summaries*, which are sent to General Accounting. Inventory Accounting personnel determine the cost of the goods described in each *sales invoice* and update inventory records accordingly. The cost information is also recorded on the *sales invoice*, which is then sent to General Accounting where sales are recorded in the sales journal and posted to the general ledger. Daily totals of sales journal entries are compared with daily sales summaries prepared by Billing. Finally, the sales invoices are routed from General Accounting to Accounts Receivable, where sales are posted to individual customer accounts in the accounts receivable subsidiary records.

The paper or computer image documents processed through the revenue/receipt cycle provide evidence that transactions are properly authorized, executed, and recorded. Note that a document is prepared by each execution function: *sales orders* by Customer Order, *shipping documents* by Shipping, and *sales invoices* by Billing. Authorization functions do not generate documents; rather, they approve documents initiated elsewhere. Recording functions neither prepare nor approve documents; instead, they transfer information from documents to accounting records.

All documents should be prenumbered consecutively and any missing forms accounted for. Copies of documents should be distributed to appropriate functional areas. Multiple documentation provides important cross-checks that minimize the potential for errors or fraud.

CASH COLLECTION

The revenue/receipt cycle is completed for a transaction when cash is collected for the goods or services sold. Collection from customers and activities related to uncollected accounts are illustrated in Figure 10-4 and discussed in the following sections.

Figure 10-4:   Revenue/Receipt Cycle: Cash Collection on Credit Sales

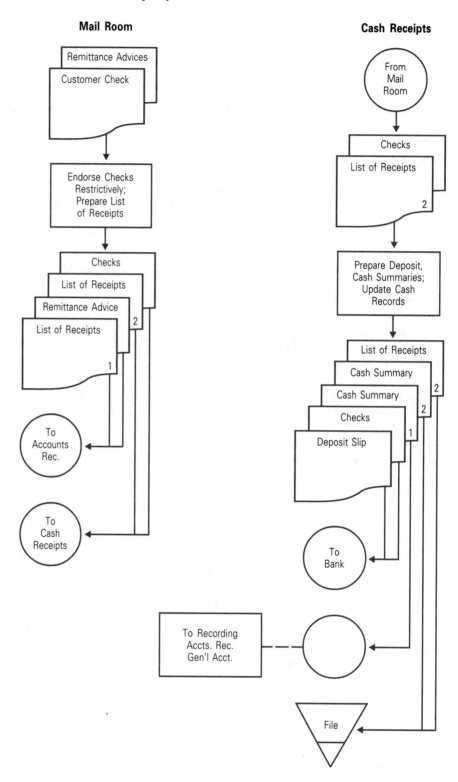

The Cash Collection Process

Assuming cash remittances are mailed, incoming *checks* are listed immediately and endorsed restrictively (e.g., "for deposit to First National Bank account number . . .") by Mail Room personnel. One copy of the list of incoming *checks* (and returned *remittance advices*, if applicable) is forwarded to Accounts Receivable for posting to individual customer accounts. All incoming, customer *checks* and another copy of the list of *checks* are forwarded to the cash receipts department, where a daily bank deposit is assembled, cash summaries are prepared, and cash records are updated. Separate lists of totals are forwarded to General Accounting for recording in the cash receipts journal and posting to the general ledger.

In all but rather small entities, personnel involved in cash collection are segregated from Accounts Receivable, General Accounting, and Billing, since combining cash collection with any of these other three functions provides opportunities to misappropriate cash.

Sales Returns and Allowances

Customer requests for adjustments on returned goods should be reviewed by personnel independent of cash collection and recording—for example, by Customer Order personnel and, if appropriate, by the salesperson or regional sales manager who services the account. An approved request is documented as a **credit memorandum**, copies of which are forwarded to Accounts Receivable for posting and to Inventory Control. Control totals are forwarded to General Accounting for recording and posting. Returned goods are handled through the Receiving Department and returned to the warehouse along with a **receiving report**. Inventory Control personnel match the *receiving report* with a copy of the *credit memorandum*.

Uncollected Accounts

Accounts Receivable should review individual customer accounts periodically as a check against unauthorized credit limits and prepare monthly accounts receivable trial balances (i.e., summaries of unpaid balances) for reconciliation with general ledger control accounts. In addition, accounts receivable balances are aged periodically and reviewed by personnel independent of the credit department.

Delinquent accounts should be reviewed periodically by personnel who report to the Treasurer and are independent of recording functions. When an individual customer account is judged to be uncollectible, written authorization to write off the account is sent to Accounts Receivable and to General Accounting.

INTERNAL CONTROL OBJECTIVES
AND POTENTIAL ERRORS OR FRAUDS

The following discussion, summarized in Figure 10-5, identifies control objectives, describes examples of errors or frauds that may arise if an objective is not achieved, and offers examples of control procedures designed to prevent or detect the errors or frauds in the revenue/receipt cycle. The control objectives relate generally to transaction authorization, execution, and recording and access to assets.

Figure 10-5: Revenue/Receipt Cycle: Control Objectives, Potential Errors or Frauds, and Control Procedures

Control Objectives	Types of Errors or Frauds That Could Occur if Objective Is Not Met	Control Procedures Designed to Prevent or Detect Errors or Frauds
Transaction Authorization		
• Customers' credit should be approved prior to shipping goods.	Shipments could be made to unauthorized parties, potentially resulting in uncollectible accounts receivable.	Perform a credit check for all new customers. Prepare and periodically update lists of authorized customers, indicating a maximum credit limit for each customer.
• Unit prices and sales terms should be established for all products or services.	Orders could be accepted at unauthorized prices or unfavorable sales terms, potentially resulting in reduced revenues or inadequate cash flows.	Maintain updated lists of authorized prices and sales terms. Establish procedures for reviewing and approving prices and sales terms before shipment.
• Sales-related deductions and adjustments should be made in accordance with management's authorization.	Unauthorized deductions or adjustments could be granted to undeserving customers, potentially resulting in uncollectible receivables. Otherwise collectible accounts receivable could be written off, potentially resulting in failure to realize the service potential of an asset.	Establish written criteria and policies for granting sales deductions and adjustments. Prenumber and control credit memoranda or other related forms.
Transaction Execution		
• Approved orders should be shipped in accordance with customer specifications and on a timely basis.	Shipments could be delivered to the wrong party, potentially resulting in uncollectible accounts receivable. Shipments could be delivered too late, potentially resulting in returned goods and canceled sales. Incorrect shipments could be delivered, potentially resulting in returned goods and canceled sales.	Verify that ordered products are in stock, and therefore can be shipped on a timely basis. Limit access to shipping documents to authorized personnel. Document policies and procedures for scheduling shipments.

Figure 10-5: (continued)

Control Objectives	Types of Errors or Frauds That Could Occur if Objective Is Not Met	Control Procedures Designed to Prevent or Detect Errors or Frauds
• All shipments should be followed by prompt billing.	Shipments could go unbilled, potentially resulting in loss of revenue. Shipments could be billed late, resulting in delayed cash payments from customers.	Prenumber bills of lading and assure that related billings are made on a periodic (e.g., daily) basis. Establish procedures for prompt reporting and investigation of shipments not billed (and billings not shipped). Require prompt delivery of bills of lading (and related sales orders) to the billing department.
Recording		
• Sales, cash receipts, and related transactions should be recorded at the correct amounts, in the proper period, and should be properly classified.	General ledger account balances may be inaccurate, potentially resulting in misstated financial statements.	Total input documents (e.g., number of documents, dollar amounts) and reconcile appropriate journals and ledgers. Establish processing and recording procedures. Compare actual and planned (e.g., forecasted, budgeted) results, and analyze variances.
• Billings, collections, and related adjustment transactions (e.g., returns and allowances) should be posted accurately to individual customer accounts.	Summaries of detailed records may not agree with control accounts, potentially resulting in adjusting journal entries prompted by inaccurate information. Transactions may be posted to improper customer accounts, potentially resulting in improper billings.	Reconcile totals of individual customer accounts with control totals. Promptly investigate correspondence from customers. Reconcile input totals with processed and output totals. Review customer statements for accuracy and follow up on discrepancies.

Figure 10-5: (*continued*)

Control Objectives	Types of Errors or Frauds That Could Occur if Objective Is Not Met	Control Procedures Designed to Prevent or Detect Errors or Frauds
• Recorded accounts receivable balances (and related transactions) should fairly reflect underlying transactions and events.	Accounts may include errors or frauds, potentially resulting in materially misstated financial statements. Management decisions may be based on erroneous data, potentially resulting in improper decisions.	Periodically substantiate and evaluate recorded account balances. Reconcile subsidiary ledgers with general ledger control accounts. Establish policy and procedures manuals, organization charts, and supporting documentation (e.g., compare selected customer balances with underlying documents). Follow up promptly on customer complaints.
Access to Assets • Access to cash and cash-related records should be restricted to personnel authorized by management.	Cash receipts on credit sales could be lost or diverted, potentially resulting in overstated accounts receivable and unrecorded cash. Cash receipts on noncredit sales could be unreported, potentially resulting in unrecorded cash. Cash shortages could go undetected, potentially resulting in lost cash and overstated cash balances.	Establish the cash receipts function in a centralized location. Require daily reconciliation of cash receipts records with bank deposit slips. Prenumber and control cash remittance advices. Prepare separate lists of incoming cash receipts. Separate responsibility for handling and recording cash. Establish periodic procedures for reconciling cash records with bank statements. Establish physical barriers over cash and unused checks. Maintain insurance and fidelity bonds for personnel handling cash. Maintain listings—and signature samples—of authorized signatories.

Figure 10-5: (*continued*)

Control Objectives	Types of Errors or Frauds That Could Occur if Objective Is Not Met	Control Procedures Designed to Prevent or Detect Errors or Frauds
		Inform the bank that no checks payable to the company are to be cashed (i.e., deposited only). Restrictively endorse checks received from customers.
• Access to shipping, billing, inventory control, and accounting records should be restricted to personnel authorized by management.	Records or assets may be misused, potentially resulting in misappropriated assets.	Segregate responsibilities for authorization, execution, and recording functions. Prenumber and control custody of forms and documents.

Transaction Authorization

Before accepting a customer's *sales order*, the customer's credit should be approved. Otherwise, shipments could be made to poor credit risk customers, potentially resulting in uncollectible receivables. Most companies perform a credit check for all new customers and prepare (and periodically update) authorized customer lists, indicating maximum credit limits for each customer.

In addition to authorizing credit limits, management should establish unit prices and sales terms that are consistent with the company's revenue objectives and cash flow needs. Prices should also be set so that no customers are treated unfairly, since differential pricing could result in dissatisfaction among customers not offered favorable terms and could even lead to violations of federal antitrust laws. Management can remove the risk of differential pricing by updating price and sales terms lists periodically and by establishing procedures for reviewing and approving sales transactions before shipment.

Following shipment and delivery, customers may request allowances or adjustments for damaged, defective, or unwanted goods. All sales-related allowances and adjustments should be made only in accordance with policies and practices authorized by management. Management should establish written policies for sales-related deductions and adjustments. Forms, such as *credit memoranda*, should be numbered and controlled.

Transaction Execution

Once customer orders are approved, goods should be shipped on a timely basis. Delayed or incorrect shipments would not only tie up resources (e.g., delay cash collection) but could result in returned goods, canceled orders, or uncollectible receivables. To encourage timely and accurate shipments, management should establish policies for scheduling prompt shipment and for verifying that ordered products are in stock.

Following shipment, customers should be billed promptly, thereby avoiding either losses arising from unbilled shipments or from delayed cash collections. To avoid unbilled shipments, management should require prenumbered shipping documents, periodically assuring that all sequentially numbered documents result in timely billing. Management should also establish procedures to investigate unbilled shipments promptly.

Recording

All sales, cash receipts, and related transactions should be recorded at the correct amounts, in the proper period, and be classified properly within the accounts. Obviously, inaccurate recording can result in inaccurate account balances and misstated financial statements. Management can control the recording function by establishing written procedures, reconciling control totals (e.g., tracing the number and dollar amounts of input documents to summarized output) and periodically comparing actual results with budgets, if available.

Proper recording within general ledger control accounts, though, does not necessarily mean that billing, collection, and returns and allowances will be posted accurately to individual customer accounts. As a result, even if general ledger control accounts are accurate, summaries of detailed records may not agree to the control accounts, potentially resulting in improper billings or adjusting journal entries prompted by insufficient or inaccurate information.

Several procedures are available to control inaccurate postings, among them: promptly investigating customer complaints and reconciling customer account balances to control accounts.

Related to the accurate recording and posting of sales, billings, and receipts, management should also establish procedures to assure that recorded receivables balances fairly reflect the underlying transactions and events they represent. Otherwise, billings and management decisions may be based on improper data, or, equally distressing, recorded receivables may reflect material errors or frauds. To control the recording of receivables, management could periodically substantiate and evaluate individual customer balances and reconcile supporting detailed ledgers to the general ledger.

Access to Assets

Within the revenue/receipt cycle, management attempts to safeguard assets by restricting access to cash, cash receipts, and cash-related records, thereby controlling against loss or diversion and, correspondingly, against misstated cash balances. Restricting access is critical throughout a business organization, but particularly for cash because, unlike most types of inventory and plant assets, cash is liquid and therefore highly susceptible to theft or diversion. Normally, the cash receipts function is maintained in a centralized location that is off-limits to unauthorized personnel. As further controls over authorized personnel, however, management could establish procedures to prenumber and control remittance advices, prepare separate lists of incoming mail receipts, and periodically reconcile cash receipts records to deposit slips and bank statements.

Management should also limit physical access within Shipping, Billing, and Inventory Control, primarily to avoid the misappropriation of assets between or among related departments. For example, Shipping personnel could be restricted from Inventory Control, thereby minimizing opportunities for unauthorized shipments. In many companies, however, access is not restricted, although employees are restricted from performing job functions outside of their own departments.

ASSURANCE AND CONSULTING SERVICES

Compared to other professionals, certified public accountants have a comparative advantage in marketing value-added assurance services, since practitioners have long been considering internal control and designing accounting information systems, particularly in transaction cycles which, like the revenue/receipt cycle, leverage heavily in information system technology to process large volumes of transactions. In practice, information system assurance services could include both *system assurance* (e.g., does the system provide reliable, relevant output information?) and *data assurance* (e.g., is input data reliable, relevant?). For example, consider information system assurance services for retailers who, like industry leaders Wal-Mart and Kmart, use proprietary *point-of-sale* (POS) systems rather than generic *electronic data integration* systems to transact electronic commerce. Practitioners could offer system and data assurances both to the retailer and to their customers about, for example, the POS system's price, order entry, customer identification, document protection, and digital cash remittance security features. In fact, the retailers' incumbent independent auditors may be particularly well-suited for these engagements, since knowledge acquired on the financial statement audit could spill over to the assurance engagement, and vice versa.

Knowledge spillovers, technological savvy, and, in particular, an existing client base have proven particularly fortuitous for the Big Six firms in partnering with worldwide technology leaders. For example, over the past three decades, the consulting practices of the Big Six public accounting firms have designed and installed customized information systems for their firms' audit and nonaudit clients. More recently, however, all six firms have partnered with German-based SAP AG to install a full suite of SAP prepackaged, client-server application software to clients seeking company-wide technological reengineering. The relationship is arguably the most productive in the profession's history, worldwide SAP consulting fees and worldwide Big Six SAP consulting personnel having been estimated at $3 billion and 8,900, respectively.[1] Clearly, the public accounting profession's training and existing client base forecast well for information system services. In fact, a 1996 study by Dataquest revealed that fully two-thirds of the surveyed companies preferred to purchase business reengineering and information system services from their independent auditors.

The profession has routinely offered consulting services in the revenue/receipt cycle, most notably the design of automated billing and collection systems. However, some firms have offered revenue-related consulting services that are neither routine nor associated typically with the public accounting profession. For example, Joseph Decosimo & Co. in Chattanooga, Tennessee, consults with professional athletic teams—among them, the Baltimore Orioles, Texas Rangers, San Diego Padres, and St. Louis Cardinals—to determine whether stadiums are located optimally and operated economically to maximize home game revenue.[2] Location, real estate, demographic, and marketing services account for about 5 percent of the firm's gross annual billings, up five times from five years prior. The profession also offers consulting services that benefit both the providers and users of information processed through the revenue/receipt cycle. For example, Moss Adams, a West Coast regional firm, consults with record companies and musicians about royalty revenues earned for the use of music written and recorded under contract. Although these services are becoming more prominent, none have been more prominent than financial statement audits, discussed next.

CONSIDERING INTERNAL CONTROL IN A FINANCIAL STATEMENT AUDIT

As explained in Chapter 7, an auditor's consideration of an entity's internal controls involves obtaining an understanding of the controls, performing tests of controls, and assessing control risk. The following discussion focuses on an auditor's consideration of revenue/receipt cycle controls.

---

1   "Big Six IT Practices Tap SAP Success," *Public Accounting Report* (April 30, 1996), pp. 1, 4.
2   L. Berton, "Accountants Expand Scope of Audit Work," *The Wall Street Journal* (June 17, 1996), pp. B1, B8.

OBTAIN AN UNDERSTANDING

An auditor's objective when considering internal control is to obtain an understanding of a client's prescribed policies and procedures sufficient to plan the audit. As discussed in Chapter 7, obtaining an understanding of the system includes:

1. Performing a *preliminary review*,
2. *Documenting* the system,
3. Performing a *transaction walk-through*, and
4. Determining whether existing control procedures are potentially reliable in assessing *control risk* below the maximum.

Preliminary Review

An auditor begins considering a client's internal control by developing a general understanding of the *control environment*; the *control procedures*; and how the entity *identifies, captures, communicates, and monitors external and internal information* in a form and time frame that enables employees to discharge their assigned responsibilities. To illustrate, an auditor could obtain an understanding by reviewing the client's procedures manuals and by interviewing employees in the customer order department, credit department, inventory control, shipping, billing, and cash receipts. The purpose of the preliminary review is to determine whether further consideration of internal control is likely to justify assessing control risk below the maximum, thereby allowing the auditor to relax detection risk and therefore to reduce the extent of substantive tests on Sales, Accounts Receivable, and Cash, three financial statement accounts processed by the revenue/receipt cycle. If the preliminary review reveals that management's control procedures are inadequate to justify assessing control risk below the maximum, then the auditor's documentation of the system would be limited to a memorandum in the working papers describing the reasons for deciding not to consider internal control further. However, if the control procedures appear potentially adequate, the auditor would continue by documenting the system.

System Documentation

Auditors typically document an entity's internal controls with flowcharts, questionnaires, and/or written narratives. Flowcharts generally provide concise, informative, and unambiguous descriptions of internal controls and are used when an entity's system is complex and processes large volumes of transactions. Although *flowcharts* vary in physical layout, the format used in Figures 10-2 and 10-4 is particularly useful to an auditor, since the activities are grouped by department, thereby clearly indicating responsibilities and providing the auditor with a basis for judging whether segregation of duties is adequate.

Questionnaires, in contrast, are designed to detect control deficiencies and, as explained in Chapter 7, typically require one of three responses for each question: *yes, no,* or *N/A* (not applicable). *No* responses indicate potential deficiencies. Figure 10-6 illustrates a questionnaire for the customer order, credit, shipping, billing and recording, and cash receipts functions within the revenue/receipt cycle.

Figure 10-6:   Questionnaire: Credit Sales and Cash Collection

	Prepared by_____	
	Date_____	
Question	*Answer: Yes, No, or N/A*	*Remarks*

Customer Order

1. Are policies and procedures for accepting and approving customer orders clearly defined?
2. Are prenumbered sales orders prepared for all approved customer orders?
3. Is current information regarding prices, policies on discounts, sales taxes, freight, warranties, and returned goods available and communicated to Customer Order personnel?
4. Are copies of sales orders forwarded to Credit, Shipping, and Billing?

Credit

1. Are policies for approving credit established and clearly communicated to Credit personnel?
2. Is credit investigated before approval?
3. Are Credit personnel independent of Billing, Cash Collection, and Accounting personnel?
4. Is information about past due accounts communicated to Credit personnel?

Shipping

1. Are goods shipped only in accordance with approved sales orders?
2. Are shipping documents prepared for all shipments?
3. Is access to Inventory Control restricted so that goods are released only in accordance with approved sales orders?
4. Are quantities of shipped goods verified either by double-counting or by independent counts (e.g., by the shipping company)?
5. Are shipping documents reviewed and compared with billings to assure that all shipped goods are billed?
6. Are Shipping personnel independent of billing, cash collection, and recording?

Billing and Recording

1. Are prenumbered sales invoices prepared for all shipped goods?
2. Are sales invoices matched with approved sales orders and shipping documents, and are they checked for clerical accuracy?
3. Are prenumbered credit memos matched with receiving reports, and are they recorded promptly?
4. Is the accounts receivable subsidiary ledger reconciled periodically with the general ledger?

Figure 10-6: *(continued)*

Question	Answer: Yes, No, or N/A	Remarks

5. Are monthly statements reviewed and mailed by personnel independent of Accounts Receivable and Cash Receipts?
6. Is an aged schedule of accounts receivable prepared monthly by personnel independent of Billing and Cash Receipts?
7. Does the credit manager review receivables balances and the aged analysis, and does he or she investigate past-due accounts?
8. Is billing performed by personnel independent of Credit and Cash Receipts?

Cash Collection

1. Are mail receipts opened by personnel independent of Shipping, Billing, and Accounting?
2. Are checks endorsed restrictively immediately upon opening the mail?
3. Are lists of receipts prepared when mail is opened?
4. Are checks forwarded promptly to personnel responsible for preparing bank deposits?
5. Are checks deposited daily?
6. Are cash summaries prepared and forwarded to Accounting?
7. Are all employees who handle cash bonded adequately?

Written *narratives* describe in prose one or more phases of management's controls. Because narratives are more difficult to comprehend than flowcharts, they are used most often for phases that are not complex or do not process material transactions, such as petty cash. In practice, auditors use all three means of documentation. For example, in considering revenue/receipt cycle controls, an auditor might document the system as follows:

- *Flowchart* selling activities from customer order acceptance through recording of the sale and related receivable.
- Document cash collection activities with a *questionnaire*.
- Prepare a *narrative* description of activities related to sales returns and allowances and writeoffs of uncollectible accounts.

Regardless of the form of documentation, employee responsibilities and document flow should be identified clearly.

An auditor obtains information about a system through inquiries of management and employees, by observing employees perform tasks, and by reviewing written policies and procedures in the entity's procedures manuals, if any. In the case of a continuing engagement, an auditor should review the prior year's documentation and determine whether it accurately reflects current conditions. Prior documentation can be relied on only if there have been no changes in assigned responsibilities and prescribed procedures.

Transaction Walk-Through

An auditor tests his or her understanding of a system by performing a transaction walk-through. For example, an auditor could select a sales transaction and trace it through the system from customer order acceptance through cash collection. If the tracing of one or a few transactions reveals deviations from the system as documented by the auditor, the reasons for the differences should be determined and the documentation revised if necessary.

Identification of Control Procedures

Once an auditor understands an entity's internal controls and determines the controls are potentially reliable in assessing control risk below the maximum, he or she continues as follows:

- Identify the system's *control objectives*. The first column of Figure 10-5 identifies control objectives for credit sales and cash receipts transactions.
- Consider the *potential errors or frauds* that might result if specific control objectives are not achieved. The second column of Figure 10-5 identifies examples of potential errors or frauds.
- Determine what *control procedures* management uses to prevent or detect potentially material errors or frauds. The third column of Figure 10-5 identifies examples of control procedures.
- Design *tests of controls*.

Only those control procedures relevant to management's financial statement assertions are subjected to tests of controls, which are discussed next.

TESTS OF CONTROLS: CREDIT SALES AND CASH COLLECTIONS

Sales, receivables, and cash receipts usually represent a rather large volume of transactions for most entities, suggesting that if control risk is at the maximum and acceptable detection risk at the minimum, then the extent of substantive tests of details at year end is likely to be quite extensive. As a result, auditors frequently expend considerable effort at interim when considering internal controls in the revenue/receipt cycle, because evidence from tests of controls that suggests control risk is below the maximum would justify assessing acceptable detection risk above the minimum and, therefore, reduce the extent of substantive tests of account balances at year end. But first, tests of controls are necessary in order to provide a reasonable degree of assurance that employees comply with management's control procedures and that the procedures operate as management planned. Tests of an entity's sales activities usually focus on whether sales are properly authorized, executed, and recorded. In turn, tests of cash collection activities focus on whether cash receipts are recorded and deposited promptly. And tests of controls over returns, allowances, and uncollectible accounts focus on proper authorization and recording.

Some representative tests of controls follow for the shipping, billing, recording, and cash collection (and deposit) functions illustrated in Figures 10-2 and 10-4, and for sales returns and allowances and uncollectible accounts. For each function, the discussion briefly introduces an auditor's major risks, lists a series of representative tests of controls, and then describes the purpose of each test listed. The tests of controls are derived from the second column of Figure 10-5—that is, the auditor first considers what errors or frauds are possible and then designs tests to determine whether the related control procedures are effective. At this point, the discussion introduces the purpose and role of a variety of tests used in testing controls of the revenue/receipt cycle. Later, the chapter describes further how an auditor documents some of the tests.

Shipping

Weaknesses in Shipping Department controls present two major risks for errors or frauds: Goods may be shipped without authorization (for example, to fictitious or related parties), or shipped goods may not be billed and recorded at all. Thus, tests of controls for Shipping are intended to determine whether shipments are made only in accordance with approved sales orders and whether shipments have been billed and recorded properly. Following are some illustrative tests for shipping.

Tests of Controls: Shipping

1. Randomly select a sample of *shipping documents* from Shipping Department files.
2. Examine each *shipping document* to determine whether the document:
   a. Is accompanied by a *sales order* bearing Credit and Inventory Control authorization, and
   b. Agrees with the *sales order* as to description of goods, quantity, destination, etc.
3. Trace details of sampled *shipping documents* to copies of *shipping documents* and their related *sales invoices* in Billing Department files.
4. Trace details of the related *sales invoices* (e.g., customer name, extended dollar amount) to entries in the sales journal and accounts receivable subsidiary ledger.
5. Trace *sales invoices* to inventory records in Inventory Accounting.

As suggested by Step 1 of the tests of controls, *shipping documents* are the primary source from which the remaining tests of shipping are performed. That is, all further tests of shipping are derived from information contained on the *shipping documents*. The tests are intended to determine whether shipped goods are for bona fide sales and whether shipments are recorded and billed properly.

In Step 2(a), the auditor tests two issues. First, by comparing *shipping documents* with their related *sales orders*, the auditor is testing whether shipments are properly authorized and, therefore, whether goods may have been shipped without authorization for an employee's or management's benefit. Second, by comparing *shipping documents* with Inventory Control authorization on the *sales order*, the auditor is testing whether goods were actually transferred from the warehouse to Shipping. In Step 2(b), the auditor tests whether clerical, mathematical, or other errors have been made in transcribing information from sales orders to shipping documents. Step 3 is designed to determine that shipments are billed, and that the bills reflect the quantities shipped.

While Steps 2 and 3 address transaction authorization and execution, Steps 4 and 5 focus on the recording of transactions. Step 4 tests whether the *sales invoices* related to sampled shipments are accurate and recorded properly in the sales journal and receivables ledger. Step 5 is intended to determine whether Inventory records reflect the transfer of goods to Shipping.

Billing

The preceding tests of controls address an entity's billing function from the standpoint of whether shipments are billed properly. The following tests, in contrast, focus on whether billed goods have been shipped and whether bills (that is, *sales invoices*) are accurate and have been prepared properly and recorded.

> **Tests of Controls: Billing**
> 1. Randomly select a sample of *sales invoices* from Billing Department files.
> 2. For each sampled *invoice*, verify unit prices and clerical accuracy.
> 3. Trace details of sampled *sales invoices* to *shipping documents*.
> 4. Trace details of sampled *sales invoices* to entries in the sales journal and accounts receivable subsidiary ledger.
> 5. Trace *sales invoices* to inventory records in Inventory Accounting.

Just as *shipping documents* are the primary source document for tests of shipping, *sales invoices* are the primary source for tests of billing. Step 2 requires that an auditor compare unit prices and sales terms on *sales invoices* with lists of authorized prices and sales terms. Thus, Step 2 tests whether goods are billed at appropriate prices and terms.

In Step 3, the auditor traces *sales invoices* to *shipping documents* and, therefore, focuses on whether the goods listed on *sales invoices* were actually shipped. Step 3 is analogous to Step 3 of the shipping tests: The shipping test addressed whether all shipments were billed, and the billing test addresses whether recorded sales are shipped.

Step 4 turns attention to the recording function, testing whether *sales invoices* are properly recorded in the sales journal and the accounts receivable subsidiary ledger. Step 5, also a test of recording, tests whether inventory records accurately reflect transfers of goods—that is, for every sales entry, there should be a corresponding cost-of-sales entry.

Recording

The tests described for shipping and billing included tracing the details of *shipping documents* to *sales invoices* and *sales invoices* to accounting records, the purpose being to verify that the sampled transactions were recorded. Following are additional tests related specifically to the recording function.

> **Tests of Controls: Recording**
> 1. Review evidence of internal procedures for:
>   a. Reconciliation of daily sales summaries with sales journal totals by General Accounting personnel, and
>   b. Periodic reconciliation of accounts receivable trial balances with general ledger control balances.
> 2. Scan the sales journal for unusual transactions or unusually large amounts.
> 3. Verify the clerical accuracy of the sales journal for selected periods and trace totals to postings in the general ledger.

The objective of all three tests for recording is to determine whether details are summarized, periodically reconciled, and, most important, accurately posted to sales journals, to the accounts receivable ledger, and finally to the general ledger. Steps 1(a) and 1(b) are not tests per se, but rather are intended to determine whether management has implemented procedures to reconcile sales summaries with sales journals [Step 1(a)] and accounts receivable subsidiary records with the general ledger [Step 1(b)]. In short, sales summaries should agree with sales journals, and accounts receivable subsidiary records should agree with the general ledger. If all sales are made on credit, the sales journal should also agree with accounts receivable records.

In Step 2, the auditor scans the sales journal for unusual transactions. For example, large sales to related parties, such as sales to, or for the indirect benefit of, officers, directors, or shareholders, may require special disclosure as discussed in Chapter 17. Step 3 tests the mathematical accuracy of the sales journal and traces totals to postings in the general ledger—that is, from details to the control accounts.

Cash Collection

An entity's cash collection activities are particularly susceptible to fraud, since receipts in the form of checks are easily convertible into cash or easily deposited into improper accounts—only a forged endorsement is necessary. Representative tests of controls over cash collections and deposits follow.

Tests of Controls: Cash Collection and Deposits

Cash Collection:
1. On a surprise basis, take control of bank deposits (*deposit slip* and *checks*) just prior to delivery by client personnel to the bank.
2. Compare the total dollar amount of *checks* to the total recorded on the *deposit slip*.
3. Compare *checks* to details in cash receipts records and the accounts receivable subsidiary ledger (e.g., customer names, amounts) and determine that the lapse of time between cash receipt and deposit is reasonable.

Deposits:
4. For an interim month (or months):
   a. Compare entries in the cash receipts journal with deposits listed on the monthly bank statement.
   b. Determine that cash receipts not listed on the bank statement are listed as deposits in transit in the bank reconciliation and are included with deposits in the subsequent month's bank statement.
5. Trace totals in the cash receipts journal to postings in the general ledger.

Steps 1 through 3 are designed to detect misappropriation of cash receipts, and, in particular, **lapping,** a fraud that conceals cash shortages resulting from delays in recording cash collections. Lapping simultaneously involves both execution (cash collection) and recording (accounts receivable) functions and, therefore, is most likely to occur when one employee is responsible both for cash collections and for receivables.

To accomplish lapping, an employee responsible for cash collections and accounts receivable simply retains a customer's payment for his or her personal use, and covers the shortage with a payment from a second customer; the first customer's receivable balance is credited when the second customer's check is received. In turn, the second customer's receivable balance is credited when a third customer's check is received, and so on. The lapping procedure may cease when the perpetrating employee replaces the cash shortage, may continue indefinitely, or may multiply in scope as a result of additional cash misappropriations.

Absent *lock box* systems (customers remit checks directly to a bank) or *digital cash* (customers remit electronically), segregation of cash collection and accounts receivable is the best control against lapping. Mandatory vacations for all employees is a second, though less effective, control. However, even if collections and accounts receivable are segregated, an auditor should still test for lapping, in the event that two or more employees are in collusion. Steps 1, 2, and 3 address lapping by determining whether a customer's check is both deposited and recorded promptly. Of course, the tests should be performed on a surprise basis to minimize the likelihood of an employee (or employees) temporarily correcting a cash shortage in anticipation of an audit.

Steps 4 and 5 address whether recorded cash collections are deposited in total and promptly. Step 4(a) traces entries from the cash receipts journal to deposits listed on bank statements, thereby testing whether recorded receipts are deposited. Step 4(b) relates to cash received and deposited too late to appear on the next bank statement; the receipts are traced to a bank reconciliation (deposits in transit) and to subsequent bank statements when available. Step 5 traces cash receipts totals to the general ledger in order to assure that detailed records agree in total with the control accounts.

Sales Returns and Allowances

An auditor's tests of controls for sales returns and allowances focus on whether *credit memoranda* are approved and recorded properly. Selected tests follow.

> **Tests of Controls: Sales Returns and Allowances**
> 1. Obtain a random sample of *credit memoranda* from the files of the issuing department (e.g., Customer Order).
> 2. Trace details of sampled *credit memoranda* to:
>   a. *Receiving reports,*
>   b. Perpetual inventory records, and
>   c. Entries in the accounts receivable subsidiary ledger and general ledger.
> 3. Review the credit register (or other listing of approved *credit memoranda*) for unusual items, such as credits for very large amounts or an unusually large number of credits for the same customer, and investigate.

In Step 1, *credit memoranda*, the primary source document for tests of sales returns and allowances, are obtained from the issuing department, often the customer order department. Step 2 addresses whether goods were actually returned by tracing *credit memoranda* details to *receiving reports* and to entries in perpetual inventory and accounts receivable records; this step also traces totals from accounts receivable to the general ledger, thereby testing the accuracy of postings. Step 3 is designed to detect unusual credits. For example, credits for very large amounts could signal excessive returns in the future as well, suggesting that material receivables may not be collectible.

Uncollectible Accounts

An auditor's tests of controls over uncollectible accounts focus on whether writeoffs are properly authorized and recorded. Some representative tests follow.

Tests of Controls: Uncollectible Accounts

1. Select a sample of writeoff entries (100 percent testing may be elected if writeoffs are infrequent).
2. Trace each entry to the related *writeoff authorization memo*; examine the memo for appropriate authorization and compare the authorized amount with the recorded amount.
3. Trace each entry to a posting in the general ledger.
4. Review all writeoff entries for unusual items, such as very large amounts or multiple writeoffs for the same customer, and investigate.

Tests of controls over uncollectible accounts start from recorded writeoff entries, rather than from a source document as in the tests of controls discussed previously. In Step 2, the auditor tests whether writeoffs are authorized, usually by examining *writeoff authorization memoranda* and related correspondence between the company and a customer. Step 3 traces writeoff entries to the general ledger, thereby testing controls over posting. Assuming writeoffs are sampled rather than tested 100 percent, Step 4 reviews writeoff entries for unusual items, such as multiple writeoffs for one customer, which could suggest an error or fraud, because orders generally should not be accepted for previously uncollectible accounts.

ASSESS CONTROL RISK

To complete the consideration of internal control within the revenue/receipt cycle, an auditor reviews system documentation and the results of tests of controls, and he or she determines whether existing controls are effective and can be relied on to:

1. Assess control risk below the maximum,
2. Assess detection risk above the minimum, and therefore
3. Restrict substantive tests of sales, receivables, and cash.

If existing controls are not effective, control risk is set at the maximum, detection risk at the minimum, and the auditor plans expanded substantive tests.

In practice, auditors assess control risk for the financial statement *assertions* embodied in a transaction cycle's related account balances, transaction classes, and financial statement disclosures—that is, the five assertions introduced in Chapter 6: existence or occurrence, completeness, rights and obligations, valuation or allocation, and presentation and disclosure. To illustrate, consider in Figure 10-5 (first column) the first objective for transaction authorization:

Objective:
"Customers' credit should be approved prior to shipping goods,"

and the first corresponding control procedure (third column) for that objective:

Control procedure:
"Perform a credit check for all new customers."

Step 2(a) of the tests of controls for shipping tests whether the control procedure from Figure 10-5 is operating effectively:

Test of control:
"Examine each shipping document to determine whether the document is
accompanied by a sales order bearing Credit and Inventory Control authorization."

Assume the auditor performs the test and discovers that most of the accompanying sales orders *do not* bear Credit Department authorization. In this case,
the auditor would conclude that control risk for the assertion *valuation* is at
the maximum. Why? Because failure to check and approve credit before the
sale may serve to overstate the net realizable value—i.e., the balance sheet
valuation—of trade accounts receivable, because the entity may be granting
credit to poor credit risk customers. Thus, in assessing control risk, the auditor
must link the results of a test of controls to its related financial statement
assertion. Substantive tests applicable to revenue/receipt cycle accounts are
introduced in Chapter 11.

COMPUTER AUDITING AND SAMPLING APPLIED TO
TESTS OF CONTROLS IN THE REVENUE/RECEIPT CYCLE

To illustrate the material introduced in this chapter and, equally important,
to integrate with material presented on computer information systems (Chapter 7) and audit sampling (Chapter 8), assume a continuing audit engagement
for a December 31 year end client, the Letts Corporation, a medium-sized
supplier of handheld power tools. The specific objective in this case is to
determine whether Letts' controls over billing are effective.

COMPUTER SYSTEM: BILLING, DATA ENTRY, AND COMPUTER PROCESSING

Early this year, Letts automated the billing function, resulting in the billing,
data entry, and computer processing system partially flowcharted in Figure
10-7. As shown in Figure 10-7, the billing department's activities are similar
to those illustrated in Figure 10-2. Here, though, sales invoices and sales
summaries, which were prepared manually in Figure 10-2, are prepared by
computer, as illustrated in Figure 10-7. Orders are entered and the data is
sorted, compared with the price and sales terms master file, and merged with
the accounts receivable master file to yield: (1) an updated accounts receivable
master file, (2) *sales invoices*, (3) *sales summaries*, and (4) an *exception report*. Even
though the system shown in Figure 10-7 is processed by computer, the auditor's
objectives in considering Letts' internal controls are no different than when
documents are prepared manually.

CONSIDERATION OF INTERNAL CONTROL

The auditor's understanding of the system, tests of controls, and evaluation
of Letts Corporation's billing function follow.

Understanding the System

Because Letts' billing system has not been reviewed previously, the auditor
decides to document the system by flowcharting and by using a questionnaire. The flowchart appears in Figure 10-7, and a transaction walk-through

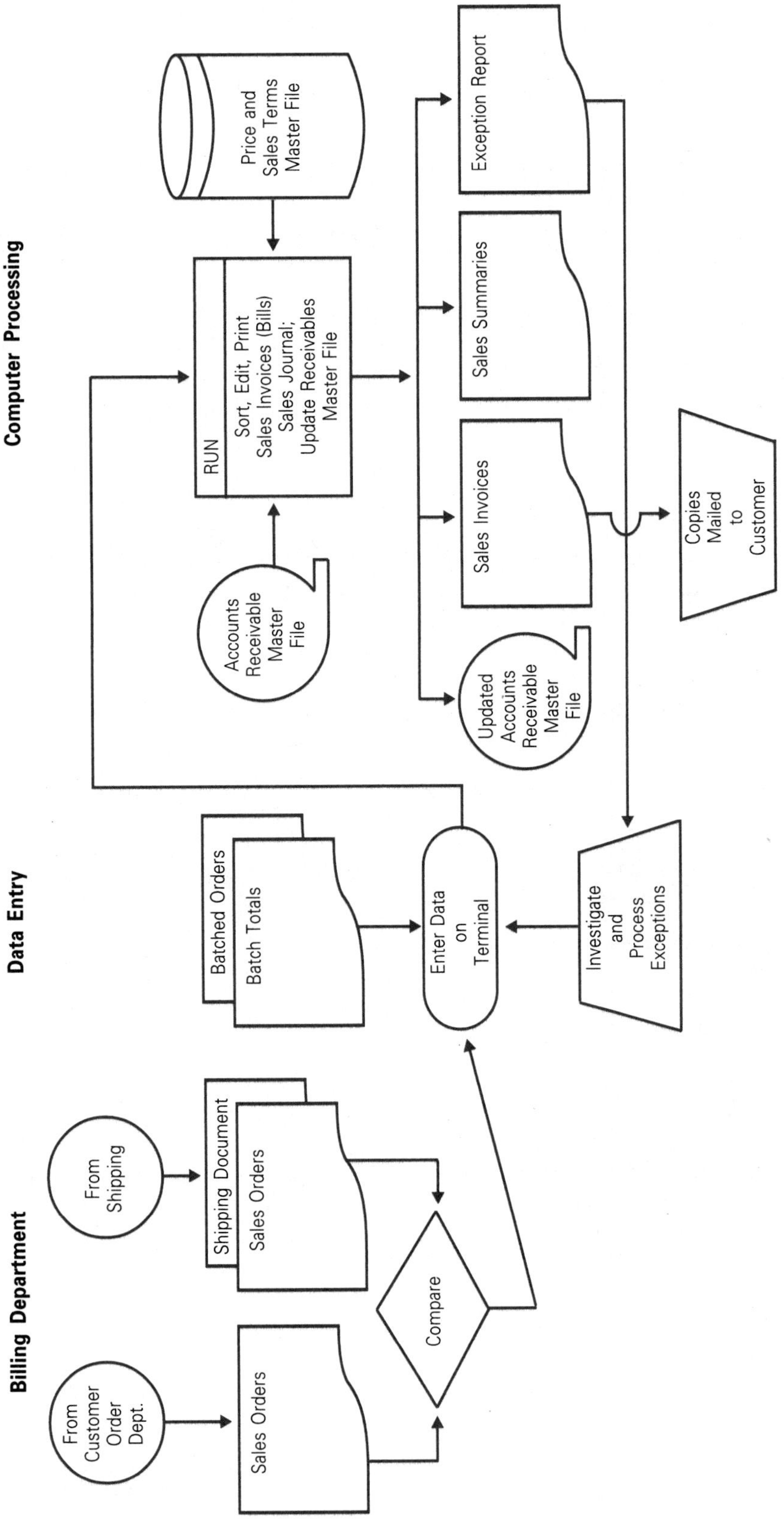

Figure 10-7: Letts Corporation: Flowchart of Billing, Data Entry, and Computer Processing

indicates that the flowchart is accurate. The questionnaire consists of the eight billing and recording questions from the questionnaire shown in Figure 10-6. Questions 4 and 5 received *no* responses, indicating the following deficiencies:

- The accounts receivable subsidiary ledger is not reconciled periodically with the general ledger.
- Monthly statements and bills are not reviewed by personnel independent of Accounts Receivable.

Despite these weaknesses, the auditor decides to continue considering internal control because Billing processes large volumes of transactions and the deficiencies relate to manual output controls only, not to computer processing controls.

Tests of Controls

Because of the deficiencies, the auditor elects a twofold strategy for testing controls. First, test data (explained in Chapter 7) will be used to test the effectiveness of computer controls over data entry and computer processing. Second, sampling will be used to test transactions processed during the year. Thus, the test data will focus on the effectiveness of controls when the system processes error-packed auditor-prepared test data, and the sampling plan will focus on live data previously processed by the system.

The auditor prepares a file of test data that is planted with errors intended to test the following input and processing controls:

Controls	*Planted Errors*
Input Controls:	
• Code verification	• False user identification codes
• Data entry controls	• Inaccurate control totals
Processing Controls:	
• Control totals	• Processed records do not agree with record counts
• Limit test	• Transactions exceed the authorized maximum dollar amount

The test data are processed on Letts' computer under the auditor's supervision, and no exceptions are found.

Given the deficiencies noted per the questionnaire, two types of errors or frauds could occur. The first appears at the sixth objective of Figure 10-5 (middle column) and the second appears at the seventh objective:

Potential errors or frauds:

- "General ledger account balances may be inaccurate, potentially resulting in misstated financial statements."
- "Transactions may be posted to improper customer accounts, potentially resulting in improper billings."

After considering these potential errors or frauds and other evidence, the auditor decides to focus tests of controls on the posting of sales information from detailed records to control accounts and, therefore, drafts the following tests, all of which are explained earlier in the chapter:

Steps	Tests of Billing Controls
1.	Randomly select a sample of *sales invoices* from Billing Department files.
2.	For each sampled *sales invoice*, verify unit prices and clerical accuracy.
3.	Trace details of sampled *sales invoices* to *shipping documents* (*bills of lading*).
4.	Trace details of sampled *sales invoices* to entries in the sales journal and accounts receivable subsidiary ledger.
5.	Trace *sales invoices* to inventory records in Inventory Accounting.

As discussed in Chapter 8, the auditor next determines whether the above steps can be accomplished by sampling and, in turn, whether to use statistical or nonstatistical sampling. In this case, Steps 2 through 5 can be accomplished with sampling. In addition, the auditor decides to sample statistically, because the computer billing system has not previously been tested (a newly implemented system) and, therefore, the auditor desires a quantified estimate of sampling risk. Because the auditor has no reason to expect low deviation rates, attributes estimation rather than sequential (stop-or-go) sampling is chosen as the statistical sampling plan. The results of the attributes estimation sampling plan are summarized in Figure 10-8, an attributes estimation worksheet, and Figure 10-9, an analysis of deviations.

Assessing Control Risk

The auditor's assessment of control risk for Letts Corporation's controls over billing would be based on the following quantitative and qualitative factors:

- No exceptions were noted when test data were run with client-prepared programs.
- The tolerable rate of deviation exceeded the maximum population deviation rate for all four billing-related attributes tested (Figure 10-8).
- The internal control questionnaire revealed two deficiencies in internal control.

In this case, the auditor's decision would probably be to assess control risk below the maximum for assertions related to controls over billing, since test data and audit sampling indicate that the two deficiencies are not likely to produce aggregate error in excess of tolerable error.

SUMMARY

The revenue/receipt cycle encompasses an entity's selling and collection activities and involves two major business functions: distribution of resources to outsiders and subsequent collection for resources distributed. Internal activities typically associated with the selling or distribution function include customer order, credit, inventory control, shipping, billing, and recording. Basic documentation associated with selling activities, including sales orders, shipping documents, and sales invoices, provides both a basis for recording

Figure 10-8:   Attributes Estimation Spreadsheet

Letts Corporation
Attributes Estimation Spreadsheet—Billing
December 31, 1999

B15
KR
11/20/99

Attribute	1 Risk of Assessing CR Too Low	2 Tolerable Rate	3 Expected Rate	4 Sample Size Table*	4 Sample Size Used	5 Number of Deviations	6 Sample Rate	6 Maximum Population Deviation Rate
1. Unit pricing and extensions on the sales invoice are accurate.	.05	.05	.01	93	100	1**	.01	.047
2. Details on the sales invoice agree with bill of lading.	.05	.04	.005	117	125	1**	.008	.038
3. Details on the sales invoice tie to sales journal and accounts receivable postings.	.05	.05	.0125	124	125	0	0	.024
4. Details on the sales invoice tie to inventory records.	.05	.07	.01	66	70	0	0	.042

*See Figures 8-5, 8-6.
**See analysis of deviation at B16.

Conclusion

Based on procedures performed, the tolerable rate of deviation exceeds the maximum population deviation rate for all four attributes tested.

Figure 10-9: Analysis of Deviations

	Letts Corporation	B16
	Analysis of Deviations—Billing	KR
	December 31, 1999	11/20/99

Attribute	Number of Deviations	Nature of Deviations	Effect on Substantive Tests of Details
1	1	Sales Invoice #12267, August 23, $10,657; unit prices did not reflect August 22 price increase.	No additional audit work is necessary because: (1) the price and sales terms master file disk was updated on August 23, and (2) the maximum population deviation rate (.047) is less than the tolerable rate (.05).
2	1	Sales Invoice #17631, November 15, $7,650; shipping documents indicate 170 units were shipped, but the sales invoice bills for only 165 units.	No additional audit work is necessary because: (1) the client's November 15 exception report noted the difference and customer was rebilled, and (2) the maximum population deviation rate (.038) is less than the tolerable rate (.04).

sales transactions and an audit trail. Effective control over selling activities requires proper transaction authorization, execution, and recording, and appropriate segregation of duties.

An auditor tests controls within the revenue/receipt cycle after documenting the system and identifying control procedures to be relied on. The results of tests of controls are used to assess control risk which is crucial in assessing allowable detection risk, the basis for judging the extent of year end substantive tests of details. Substantive tests of accounts receivable, sales, and cash balances are performed to satisfy the audit objectives of existence or occurrence, rights, valuation, completeness, and presentation or disclosure, and are discussed next, in Chapter 11.

KEY TERMS

Revenue/receipt cycle   360
Customer order   360
Sales order   361
Shipping document   361
Bill of lading   361

Sales invoice   361
Customer remittance advice   361
Credit memorandum   367
Receiving report   367
Lapping   381

REFERENCES

Professional Standards

AICPA. *Codification of Statements on Auditing Standards*. New York: AICPA.

Books

Committee of Sponsoring Organizations of the Treadway Commission (COSO). *Internal Control: Integrated Framework*. Executive Summary. New York: COSO (1992).
Committee of Sponsoring Organizations of the Treadway Commission (COSO). *Internal Control: Integrated Framework*. Framework. New York: COSO (1992).
Committee of Sponsoring Organizations of the Treadway Commission (COSO). *Internal Control: Integrated Framework*. Evaluation Tools. New York: COSO (1992).
Committee of Sponsoring Organizations of the Treadway Commission (COSO). *Internal Control: Integrated Framework*. Reporting to External Parties. New York: COSO (1992).

QUESTIONS

1. What are the major business functions and activities common to the revenue/receipt cycle?
2. How does a transaction cycle create an audit trail?
3. Explain why the billing function should be segregated from credit granting, cash collection, and accounting.
4. What potential errors or frauds could occur if customer credit were not approved by authorized personnel? Identify controls that management could implement to assure that a customer is creditworthy.
5. How can management assure that all shipped goods are billed?
6. Accurate recording within general ledger control accounts does not necessarily mean that billing, collection, and adjustment transactions will be posted accurately to individual customer accounts. What controls can management implement to mitigate the likelihood of inaccurate postings to individual customer accounts?
7. In most circumstances, management is more concerned with restricting employee access to cash than restricting access to inventory. But shouldn't management be more concerned with inventory, since inventory is usually more material to the financial statements than cash? Explain.
8. What is the primary focus of the tests of controls performed on an entity's selling and cash receipts activities?
9. Identify the two major errors or frauds that could result from weaknesses in shipping controls.
10. What is the primary source document from which most shipping-related tests of controls evolve?
11. In performing tests of controls, why would an auditor compare shipping documents with approved sales orders?
12. What is the focus of an auditor's tests of billing, and how do the tests complement tests of shipping controls?
13. What is the primary source document for an auditor's tests of billing?
14. If a credit memorandum were issued for returned goods, how might an auditor determine whether the goods were actually returned?
15. How does an auditor evaluate the effectiveness and reliability of a client's control procedures over revenue/receipt cycle activities?

MULTIPLE CHOICE QUESTIONS

1. Which of the following business functions is associated with the revenue/receipt cycle?

a. Obligations are paid to vendors and employees.
b. Resources are distributed to outsiders in exchange for promises of future payments.
c. Resources are used, held, or transformed.
d. Capital funds are received from investors and creditors.

2. To test whether sales have been recorded, a sample should be drawn from a file of:

a. Purchase orders.
b. Sales orders.
c. Sales invoices.
d. Bills of lading.

3. Tracing copies of sales invoices to shipping documents provides evidence that:

a. Shipments were recorded as receivables.
b. Billed sales were shipped.
c. Debits to the accounts receivable were for sales shipped.
d. Shipments were billed.

4. Tracing shipping documents to sales invoices provides evidence that:

a. Shipments were billed.
b. Shipments were recorded as sales.
c. Recorded sales were shipped.
d. Invoiced sales were shipped.

5. Which of the following control procedures could prevent or detect errors or frauds arising from shipments made to unauthorized parties?

a. Document policies and procedures for scheduling shipments.
b. Establish procedures for reviewing and approving prices and sales terms before sale.
c. Prenumber bills of lading and assure that related billings are made on a periodic basis.
d. Prepare and periodically update lists of authorized customers.

6. Which of the following control procedures would most likely assure that access to shipping, billing, inventory control, and accounting records is restricted to personnel authorized by management?

a. Segregate responsibilities for authorization, execution, and recording, and prenumber and control custody of documents.
b. Establish the cash receipts function in a centralized location and require daily reconciliation of cash receipts records with deposit slips.
c. Establish policy and procedures manuals, organization charts, and supporting documentation.
d. Periodically substantiate and evaluate recorded account balances.

7. An entity has implemented a control procedure which requires that authorized personnel reconcile the total of individual customer accounts receivable with control totals. This control relates to which of the following control objectives?

a. Sales, cash receipts, and related transactions should be recorded at the correct amounts, in the proper period, and should be properly classified.

b. Recorded accounts receivable balances should reflect underlying transactions and events.

c. Billings, collections, and related adjustments transactions should be posted accurately to individual customer accounts.

d. Access to cash and cash-related records should be restricted to personnel authorized by management.

8. A purpose of tests of controls over shipping is to determine whether:

a. Billed goods are shipped.

b. Shipments are made in accordance with approved sales and orders.

c. Sales orders are properly recorded.

d. Shipping personnel route goods to related parties.

9. A purpose of tests of controls over billing is to determine whether:

a. Billed goods have been shipped.

b. Sales orders agree to shipping documents.

c. Sales orders have been approved by Credit Department personnel.

d. Billing personnel process returned goods properly.

10. What sequence of steps does an auditor undertake when identifying control procedures that are potentially reliable in assessing control risk below the maximum?

a. Consider the errors or frauds that might occur, determine control procedures, identify control objectives, and design tests of controls.

b. Determine control procedures, design tests of controls, consider the errors or frauds that might occur, and identify control objectives.

c. Identify control objectives, consider the errors or frauds that might occur, determine control procedures, and design tests of controls.

d. Design tests of controls, determine control procedures, consider the errors or frauds that might occur, and identify control objectives.

PROBLEMS AND DISCUSSION CASES

10-1 *Tests of Controls and Credit Sales*
Within the revenue/receipt cycle, several paper and computer image documents are typically used to create an accounting system and, correspondingly, an audit trail for credit sales and cash collections. Among these documents are:
* Sales orders,
* Shipping documents, and
* Sales invoices.
  Required:
1. Explain how approved sales orders can be used to test credit sales for understatements.
2. Explain how shipping documents can be used to test whether all sales transactions that should be recorded are actually recorded.
3. Explain how an auditor can use sales invoices to test whether billed sales were actually shipped.

10-2 *Controls Over Credit Sales and Cash Collections*
Assume you are considering an entity's internal controls over credit sales and cash collection. System documentation was accomplished through a questionnaire and written

narratives and, in conjunction with a transaction walk-through, revealed the following potential weaknesses in internal control, some of which, depending on their severity, could prompt you to set control risk at the maximum:

a. New customers are not approved before ordered goods are shipped.
b. Sales prices vary from customer to customer.
c. No approval is required for returned goods from customers.
d. Subsidiary accounts receivable records do not always agree with the general ledger control account.
e. Blank checks are left unprotected in an unlocked safe.

Required: For each potential weakness, indicate a control or controls that management could implement to reduce the likelihood of errors or frauds.

10-3 *Errors, Fraud, and Control Procedures*

During your audit of Lish and Company's December 31, 1998 financial statements, you become aware of the following controls or procedures Lish has implemented over credit sales and cash collections:

a. Sales terms are approved by supervisory personnel before shipment.
b. All credit memoranda are prenumbered sequentially and controlled.
c. Shipping documents are prenumbered sequentially and controlled.
d. Copies of shipping documents are hand-carried to the billing department within one hour after shipment.
e. Sales invoices are compared with sales journals and with customers' individual subsidiary records.
f. In contrast to prior years, noncredit (cash) sales are handled in one centralized location, rather than throughout all departments.
g. Unused checks are prenumbered and locked in a fireproof vault accessible only to the treasurer, who is one of two endorsers on customers' checks.

Required: For each control or procedure, indicate: (1) a potential error or fraud that might circumvent the control or procedure, and (2) the internal control objective that is served by the control or procedure. Organize your answer as follows.

Control or Procedure	*Potential Error or Fraud That Might Circumvent the Control or Procedure*	*Control Objective*
1.		

10-4 *Interpreting a Systems Flowchart*

A partially completed flowchart for the Bottom Manufacturing Corporation's credit sales is presented on the following page. When a customer's order is received, a six-part sales order is prepared and copies are distributed as follows:

Copy No. 1:	Billing copy	to	Billing Department
Copy No. 2:	Shipping copy	to	Shipping Department
Copy No. 3:	Credit copy	to	Credit Department
Copy No. 4:	Stock request copy	to	Credit Department
Copy No. 5:	Customer copy	to	Customer
Copy No. 6:	Sales order copy	filed	Customer Order Department

When a sales order copy reaches a department, control procedures and documents are required. Some of the procedures and documents are identified on the flowchart. Others are labeled with letters *a* to *r*.

Required: List the unidentified procedures or documents that are labeled *c* to *r* in the flowchart. Organize your answer as follows (procedures for the letters *a* and *b* are listed):

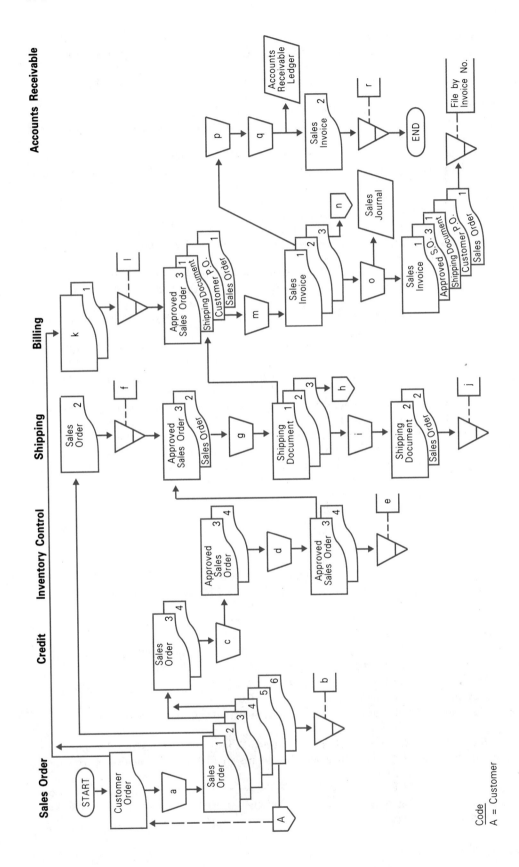

Flowchart Letter	Procedure or Document
a.	Prepare six-part sales order
b.	File by order number.

(AICPA Adapted)

10-5 *Designing Software to Extract Receivables Data*
You are auditing trade accounts receivable for the Winston-McCabe Company, a farm equipment retailer doing business in three Midwestern cities. All accounting, shipping, billing, and receivables records are maintained on a local area network (LAN). You are particularly interested in the validity, accuracy, and age of the receivables. Winston-McCabe has a programmer available to develop software for extracting data from the receivables files.

    Required: Discuss procedures you'd want the software to perform, including any reports, schedules, and lists you'd expect.

10-6 *Identifying Weaknesses and Recommending Improvements*
The Art Appreciation Society operates a museum for the benefit of the community. During hours when the museum is open to the public, two clerks are positioned at the entrance and collect a $5 admission fee from each nonmember patron. Members of the Art Appreciation Society are permitted to enter free of charge on presentation of their membership cards.

    At the end of each day, one of the clerks delivers the proceeds to the treasurer. The treasurer counts the cash in the presence of the clerk and places the cash in a safe. Each Friday afternoon the treasurer and one of the clerks deliver all cash held in the safe to the bank and receive a deposit slip that drives a weekly entry in the cash receipts records.

    The board of directors of the Art Appreciation Society has identified a need to improve the system of internal control over cash admission fees. The board has determined that the cost of installing turnstiles or sales booths or otherwise altering the physical layout of the museum, will greatly exceed the potential benefits. However, the board agrees that controls over the sale of admission tickets needs improvement.

    Smith has been asked by the board of directors to review internal control over cash admission fees and provide suggestions for improvement.

    Required: Indicate weaknesses in the existing system of internal control over cash admission fees and recommend one improvement for each weakness. Organize your answer as follows:

Weakness	Recommendation
1. There is no basis for establishing the number of paying patrons.	Prenumbered admission tickets should be issued upon payment of the admission fee.

10-7 *Identifying Potential Frauds and Recommending Procedures to Improve Control*
You are auditing the Alaska branch of Far Distributing Co., a branch that has substantial annual sales, all of which are billed and collected locally. During your preliminary review of internal controls, you discover the following procedures for handling cash receipts:

    Cash collections on over-the-counter and COD sales are received by the cashier from the customer or from the delivery service. Upon receiving cash, the cashier stamps the sales ticket "paid" and files a copy. The only record of COD sales is a copy of the sales ticket, which is given to the cashier to hold until cash is received from the delivery service.

    Mail is opened by the credit manager's secretary, and remittances are given to the credit manager for review. The credit manager then places the remittances in a tray on the cashier's desk. At the time of the daily deposit—called "deposit cutoff time"—the cashier delivers the checks and currency to the assistant credit manager, who prepares remittance lists and the bank deposit, and carries the deposit to the bank. The assistant credit manager also posts remittances to customer accounts receivable files and verifies allowable cash discounts.

You also learn that the credit manager obtains approval to write off uncollectible accounts from the executive office of Far Distributing Co., located in Chicago, and that as of the end of the fiscal year some remittances that were received on various days during the last month are retained in the credit manager's custody.

Required:
1. Describe the frauds that might occur under the procedures now in effect for handling cash collections and remittances.
2. What procedures would you recommend to improve control over cash collections and remittances?

(AICPA Adapted)

10-8 *Recommending Improvements to Internal Control*
You are auditing the financial statements of Fashionation, Inc., a retail clothing store, and have prepared the following narrative description for cash sales procedures:

All sales are for cash; no credit cards are accepted. Each individual sale is rung up by the sales clerk on a cash register that ejects a sales slip. The sales slip is given to the customer, and a copy of the sales slip is made by the cash register on a continuous tape locked inside the machine. At the end of the day, the sales clerk presses a total key and the machine prints the total sales for the day on the continuous tape. The clerk then unlocks the cash register, removes the day's tape, makes an entry in the cash receipts book, counts the cash in the drawer, retains a change fund of $100, and turns the rest of the cash over to the cashier. The sales clerk then files the cash register tape and is ready for the next day.

Required: From the narrative description of Fashionation's cash sales procedures, indicate specific recommendations to improve controls over cash.

10-9 *Designing Controls Over Cash Receipts and Warehousing*
Trapan Retailing, Inc. has decided to diversify operations by selling through vending machines. Trapan plans on purchasing 312 vending machines to be placed in 78 different locations within one city, and renting a warehouse to store merchandise. Trapan plans to vend canned beverages only.

Management has hired an inventory control clerk to oversee the warehousing functions and two truck drivers who will periodically fill the machines with merchandise and deposit cash collected at a designated bank. Drivers will be required to report to the warehouse daily.

Required: What procedures will control the cash receipts and warehousing functions?

(AICPA Adapted)

10-10 *Drafting Tests of Controls From an Internal Control Questionnaire*
Following are selected questions from internal control questionnaires about a company's customer order, credit, shipping, billing, and cash receipts functions. A *yes* response to any question would indicate a potential strength, and a *no* response a potential weakness of the system.
a. Are sales orders prepared for all approved customer orders?
b. Are copies of sales orders forwarded to the credit, shipping, and billing departments?
c. Is credit investigated before the customer is approved?
d. Are goods shipped only in accordance with approved sales orders?

e. Are shipping documents reviewed and compared with billings to assure that all shipped goods are billed?

f. Are all credit memos prenumbered, matched with approved sales orders and shipping documents, and checked for clerical accuracy?

g. Is the accounts receivable subsidiary ledger reconciled periodically with the general ledger?

h. Are mail receipts opened by personnel independent of shipping, billing, sales invoice processing, and recording?

Required: Assume that inquiries indicate the answer is *yes* to each question. For each question, draft a test you believe would provide persuasive evidence that controls are reliable.

10-11 *Cash Receipts Controls and Designing Audit Procedures*

You are the in-charge accountant auditing the financial statements of the Gutzler Company for the year ending December 31, 1999. During late October, 1999, you, with the help of Gutzler's controller, complete an internal control questionnaire and prepare a memorandum describing Gutzler's accounting procedures. Your comments about cash receipts follow.

All cash receipts are sent directly to the accounts receivable clerk with no processing by the mail department. The accounts receivable clerk keeps the cash receipts journal, prepares the bank deposit slip in duplicate, posts from the deposit slip to the subsidiary accounts receivable records, and mails the deposit to the bank.

The controller receives the validated deposit slips directly (unopened) from the bank and also receives the monthly bank statement directly (unopened) from the bank and prepares a reconciliation.

At the end of each month, the accounts receivable clerk sends the monthly totals of the cash receipts journal to the accounting clerk for posting to the general ledger.

Each month, the accounting clerk makes an entry to record the total debits to Cash from the cash receipts journal. In addition, the general ledger clerk on occasion makes debit entries in the general ledger cash account from sources other than the cash receipts journal—e.g., funds borrowed from the bank.

You also performed the following procedures on cash receipts:

a. Totaled and cross-totaled all columns in the cash receipts journal.

b. Traced postings from the cash receipts journal to the general ledger.

c. Examined remittance advices and related correspondence to support entries in the cash receipts journal.

Required: Considering Gutzler's control over cash receipts and the audit procedures performed already, list and give reasons for all other auditing procedures that should be performed to obtain audit evidence for cash receipts. (Do not discuss cash disbursements and cash balances.) Assume adequate controls exist to assure that all sales transactions are recorded. Organize your answer as follows:

Other Audit Procedures	*Reason for Other Audit Procedures*

(AICPA Adapted)

10-12 *Detecting Delays in the Posting of Receivables: Lapping*

During the year, Strang Corporation began to encounter cash flow difficulties, and a cursory review by management revealed collection problems. Strang's management engaged Stanley, CPA to perform a special review. Stanley studied the billing and collection functions of the revenue/receipt cycle and noted the following:

The accounting department employs one bookkeeper who receives and opens all incoming mail. The bookkeeper is also responsible for depositing receipts, filing remittance advices daily, recording receipts in the cash receipts journal, and posting receipts in the individual customer accounts and the general ledger accounts. There are no cash sales. The bookkeeper prepares and controls the mailing of monthly statements to customers.

The concentration of duties entrusted to the bookkeeper and the collection problems cause Stanley to suspect a systematic delay in the posting of customers' remittances (lapping of accounts receivable). Stanley was surprised to find that no customers complained about receiving erroneous monthly statements.

Required: Identify procedures Stanley could perform to determine whether lapping exists. Do not discuss deficiencies in internal control.

(AICPA Adapted)

10-13 *Sales Returns and Fraud*
Within the revenue/receipt cycle, controls must be implemented not only for sales and shipments, but also for sales returns and allowances. Otherwise, sales could be overstated and the financial statements significantly misstated.
   Required:
1. Draft and explain the journal entry an employee could make to commit a fraud with sales returns and allowances.
2. In tests of controls over credit memoranda, how can an auditor test whether goods related to sales returns and allowances were actually returned?

10-14 *Control Objectives in Data Entry*
The president of I&M Electric, a large regional utility, has asked that you perform a special engagement unrelated to the financial statement audit: Audit the customer payment system but with emphasis on data entry and data transmission at local branch offices. Customers may send their payments to the central office or may pay in person at any of the company's 25 branch locations. When a customer pays a utility bill at a branch office, an employee enters the payment immediately into the branch payment system via a workstation that is connected on-line to the company's main office. I&M divides the branch office collection procedures into three categories: data entry, data transmission, and data processing.
   Required: List data entry control objectives and, for each, briefly describe control techniques to accomplish each objective.

10-15 *Steps in an Audit Sampling Plan*
Barry Hannah, CPA, plans to use attributes estimation to help assess control risk for the Oxford Company's control procedures over credit sales transactions. Hannah has begun to outline main steps in the sampling plan:
a. State the objectives of the test (e.g., to test the reliability of controls over sales).
b. Define the population (and the period covered by the test).
c. Define the sampling unit (e.g., sales invoices).
   Required:
1. What are the remaining steps Hannah should include in the statistical test of sales invoices?
2. How does statistical sampling help the auditor?

10-16 *Attributes Estimation and Tests of Shipping Controls*
Galway Kinnell plans to apply an attributes estimation sampling plan to the shipping controls used by the Raffel & Olds Corporation, a December 31, 1999 year end printing company in New York. Based on a planning meeting with Jack Gilbert, engagement partner, Kinnell assesses the following risks of assessing control risk too low and expected population deviation rates for each of five tests of controls:

Test of Control	Risk of Assessing Control Risk Too Low	Expected Population Deviation Rate
1. Examine each *shipping document* to determine whether the document:		
a. Is accompanied by a *sales order* bearing Credit and Inventory Control authorization, and	.06	.0125
b. Agrees with the *sales order* as to description of goods, quantity, destination, etc.	.04	.0075
2. Trace details of sampled *shipping documents* to copies of *shipping documents* and their related *sales invoices* in Billing Department files.	.05	.0125
3. Trace details of the related *sales invoices* to entries in the sales journal and accounts receivable subsidiary ledger.	.07	.015
4. Trace *sales invoices* to inventory records in Inventory Accounting.	.07	.015

The tolerable rate of deviation is .05 for all five tests. Kinnell performs the sampling plan on September 15 and finds one deviation each for tests No. 1(b) (although shipping document #0167, May 21, $21,450 reads 1,200 units, the sales order reads 1,050 units) and No. 4 (although sales invoice #21261, July 12, reads 1,725 units, the inventory records reflect 1,275 units).

Required: Prepare audit working papers to document the attributes estimation sampling plan and the analysis of deviations.

RESEARCH PROJECT

INTERNAL CONTROL AND TRANSACTION CYCLES IN SELECTED INDUSTRIES

Auditors facing engagements within a given industry, say airline companies or commercial banks, face clients with largely similar control environments, risk assessment profiles, control activities, information and communication needs, and monitoring requirements. In short, in all but the very smallest owner-managed companies, systems of internal control are likely to be similar among clients competing within the same industry and quite different for clients operating in dissimilar industries.

Required:

- Select an AICPA *Audit & Accounting Guide* for the industry of your choice (for example, the AICPA publishes guides for airlines, banks, casinos, colleges and universities, construction contractors, finance companies, investment companies, property and liability insurance companies, and providers of health care services, among others), and

- Select an annual report for an entity in the same industry (use the annual report file in the National Automated Accounting Research System [NAARS] or copies of annual reports in a library).

Draft a report that:

1. Describes the major control considerations identified in the *Audit & Accounting Guide*.

2. Identifies the financial statement accounts likely processed by the entity's revenue/ receipt, expenditure/disbursement, financing, and (if a manufacturer) conversion cycles. (Use the selected entity's financial statements, including footnotes, and other disclosures in the annual report to address this question.)

11

Substantive Tests in the Revenue/ Receipt Cycle: Sales, Receivables, Cash, and Management Discretion in Revenue Recognition

Major topics discussed in this chapter are the:

- Relationship between financial statement assertions and audit procedures within the revenue/receipt cycle.
- Relationship between audit risk and the nature, timing, and extent of substantive tests.
- Substantive tests applicable to assertions about sales, accounts receivable, and cash balances.
- Application of audit judgment to questions of earnings manipulation and revenue recognition.
- Application of audit sampling in substantive tests of accounts receivable.
- Computer assisted substantive tests of accounts receivable.

Based on the assessed levels of control and inherent risk for assertions within the **revenue/receipt cycle**, an auditor determines acceptable levels of detection risk and then designs substantive tests for the major financial statement accounts processed by the cycle: Sales, Accounts Receivable, and Cash. This chapter focuses on substantive tests of details for these accounts. The chapter begins by discussing how each of the financial statement assertions introduced in Chapter 6—existence or occurrence, completeness, rights and obligations, valuation or allocation, and presentation and disclosure—is tested for audits of Sales, Accounts Receivable, and Cash, and how audit risk bears on the nature, timing, and extent of an auditor's substantive tests. In turn, the chapter relates the assertions to substantive tests for these accounts and then describes and illustrates each test. Thereafter, the chapter addresses audit, legal, and ethical questions that arise when the timing of revenue recognition is subject to management's discretion. The chapter concludes by illustrating how audit sampling, introduced in Chapter 9, can be used in substantive tests of receivables balances, and by discussing computer assisted audit procedures (Chapter 7) applicable to the revenue/receipt cycle.

FINANCIAL STATEMENT ASSERTIONS,
OBJECTIVES, AND AUDIT PROCEDURES

As explained in Chapter 6, much of an auditor's work during a financial statement audit consists of obtaining and evaluating evidence about the assertions embodied within an entity's financial statements. For example, management asserts that recorded receivables and cash balances:

- Exist
- Include all transactions that should be presented
- Represent rights of the entity
- Are valued appropriately
- Are presented and disclosed properly within the financial statements

Each financial statement assertion translates to an audit objective for which auditors design procedures to obtain evidence. For example, management's assertion that cash and receivables exist creates a corresponding audit objective to determine whether each asset actually does exist, and auditors generally use confirmation procedures to test their existence. Hence, financial statement assertions are synonymous with audit objectives. But, specifically, what procedures do practicing auditors commonly use to address which financial statement assertions? The following relates each financial statement assertion to the audit procedures that practitioners commonly use to audit revenue/receipt cycle accounts. The assertions and procedures are summarized in Figure 11-1.

EXISTENCE OR OCCURRENCE

Within the revenue/receipt cycle, the existence or occurrence assertion addresses whether all recorded sales, receivables, and cash balances actually exist and whether all recorded transactions actually occurred. Existence is normally tested by physical observation or confirmation with outside parties. In practice, the existence of receivables is often tested by confirming balances with debtors (customers). The existence of cash on deposit is tested by confirming bank balances with banks, and the existence of cash on hand can be observed physically and counted. In addition, auditors use cutoff testing to determine whether recorded sales transactions and related receivables and cash transactions are recorded in the proper period.

COMPLETENESS

The completeness assertion addresses whether all receivables, sales, and cash transactions and accounts that should be presented in the financial statements are actually presented. Generally, completeness is tested by examining documentation and by applying analytical procedures, such as making comparisons among related accounts. For sales and receivables, completeness is tested by performing analytical procedures, which helps determine whether recorded receivables and sales balances are reasonable at the balance sheet date, and by testing cutoff, which determines whether transactions are recorded in the proper accounting period. Auditors typically test completeness for cash balances by examining cutoff bank statements to assure that all receipts and

Figure 11-1: Relating Financial Statement Assertions and Audit Procedures: Sales, Receivables, and Cash Balances

Assertions	Audit Procedures		
	Sales	Receivables	Cash Balances
Existence or occurrence	Test cutoff.	Confirm with debtors. Test cutoff.	Confirm with banks. Test cutoff.
Completeness	Perform analytical procedures. Test cutoff.	Perform analytical procedures. Test cutoff.	Test cutoff. Examine bank reconciliations or proofs of cash. Examine intercompany and interbank transfers.
Rights and obligations		Confirm with debtors. Review collectibility.	Confirm with banks.
Valuation or allocation	Perform analytical procedures.	Confirm with debtors. Review collectibility. Verify accuracy of aged trial balance.	Confirm with banks. Verify mathematical accuracy of recorded cash balances. Test cutoff.
Presentation and disclosure	Compare statement presentation and disclosures with those required by GAAP.	Compare statement presentation and disclosures with those required by GAAP.	Compare statement presentation and disclosures with those required by GAAP.

disbursements are recorded in the proper period, and by examining bank reconciliations (or proofs of cash) and records of intercompany and interbank transfers.

RIGHTS AND OBLIGATIONS

Within the revenue/receipt cycle, the rights and obligations assertion addresses whether an entity has property rights—e.g., claims against third parties—for recorded receivables and cash balances. That is, does the company have legally binding claims against customers for receivables balances and against commercial banks and other depositories for recorded cash balances? Generally, an auditor tests rights by examining documentation and through confirmations and inquiries. Rights to receivables are typically tested by confirming balances with debtors and by reviewing the collectibility of confirmed and unconfirmed customer balances. In turn, rights to cash are tested primarily by confirming balances and deposit terms (e.g., demand deposits and compensating balances) with banks.

VALUATION OR ALLOCATION

The valuation assertion addresses whether receivables, sales, and cash balances are reported in the financial statements at appropriate amounts. That is, are they valued in accordance with generally accepted accounting principles? In general, auditors test valuation by examining documentation, confirming, observing, performing mechanical tests, and making inquiries. More specifically, the carrying value of receivables is tested by confirming balances with debtors and reviewing collectibility—both of which also address rights and obligations—and by verifying the accuracy of management's aged trial balance. Recorded values for cash are tested by confirming balances with banks, by verifying the mathematical accuracy of recorded cash balances, and by examining the details within cutoff bank statements.

PRESENTATION AND DISCLOSURE

The presentation and disclosure assertion addresses whether recorded transactions and balances are properly classified, described, and disclosed in the financial statements. Generally, auditors address this assertion by comparing an entity's financial statement presentation and disclosures with those required by generally accepted accounting principles. Presentation and disclosure guidelines, such as the AICPA's annually updated *Accounting and Audit Manual*, are often used by practicing auditors to address this assertion.

AUDIT RISK AND THE NATURE, TIMING, AND EXTENT
OF SUBSTANTIVE TESTS IN THE REVENUE/RECEIPT CYCLE

As explained in Chapter 6 (Figure 6-13), an auditor completes interim audit work by drafting preliminary year end audit programs—that is, detailed descriptions of planned substantive procedures, the *nature, timing,* and *extent* of which are based on

- *Detection risk (DR),* the likelihood that error could occur and not be detected by audit procedures

which is based in turn on the auditor's interim assessments of

- *Control risk (CR),* the likelihood that material error could occur and not be detected by internal control, and
- *Inherent risk (IR),* the susceptibility of an account balance to material error for which there is no related internal control.

The audit programs illustrated in this chapter assume that an auditor has assessed control risk and inherent risk for the assertions of *existence, completeness, rights,* and *valuation* at the *maximum* because tests of controls over shipping, billing, and cash deposits (Chapter 10) reveal that internal control deficiencies are *likely* to produce aggregate error in excess of tolerable error for the following control procedures:

- *Shipping.* Shipping documents are accompanied by a sales order bearing credit and inventory control authorization.
- *Billing.* Sales invoices are agreed to shipping documents.
- *Deposits.* Deposits are compared with entries in the cash receipts journal.

As a result, to hold down audit risk to a *minimum,* the auditor assesses the acceptable level of detection risk at the *minimum.* That is, from Chapter 2:

$$DR = \frac{AR}{IR \times CR}$$

$$Minimum = \frac{Minimum}{Maximum \times Maximum}$$

Assessing the acceptable detection risk at the minimum bears directly on the nature, timing, and extent of planned substantive tests as follows:

- *Nature.* Use more persuasive procedures (e.g., receivables confirmations).
- *Timing.* Perform procedures at the balance sheet date.
- *Extent.* Test more extensively (e.g., increase sample sizes).

Prior to performing substantive tests at year end, auditors review and evaluate any significant changes that might have occurred since assessing control and inherent risk at interim and revise the year end audit programs as necessary. For example, if internal controls over shipping, billing, and cash deposits have changed since interim, an auditor could perform additional tests of controls, reevaluate control and inherent risk, reassess detection risk, and rethink the nature, timing, and extent of substantive tests.

   In substantive tests of revenue/receipt cycle accounts, an auditor obtains and evaluates evidence about transactions and events that bear on an entity's sales and collection activities. However, an auditor does not blindly apply the same audit procedures on every engagement, largely because both audit risk and materiality vary from engagement to engagement. In an effort to make clear the intuition underlying an auditor's role in substantive tests of revenue/receipt cycle accounts, the discussion below proceeds through two categories of audit problems. First, tests for receivables, sales, and cash balances are introduced in representative audit programs that assume control and inherent risk are at the maximum, and that are keyed to and discussed in the context of the financial statement assertions presented earlier: existence or occurrence, completeness, rights and obligations, valuation or allocation, and presentation and disclosure. Second, the discussion then focuses on problems an auditor confronts when, unlike typical sales transactions for which revenue is recognized at the point of sale, the recognition of revenue is less certain, such as accounting for area franchise fees.

ACCOUNTS RECEIVABLE AND SALES

Figure 11-2 illustrates a program of representative year end substantive tests for accounts receivable and sales. The tests are explained in the context of the financial statement assertions the tests address and, as discussed above, assume maximum levels of control and inherent risks and a minimum level of

Figure 11-2: Substantive Tests: Accounts Receivable and Sales

Assertions	Procedures

Valuation	1. Verify mathematical accuracy of accounts receivable.
	   a. Obtain an accounts receivable aged trial balance from Accounts Receivable Department personnel.
	   b. Foot (add columns) and cross-foot (add column totals across) the trial balance.
	   c. Compare total accounts receivable per the trial balance to accounts receivable in the general ledger.

Existence Rights Valuation	2. Confirm year end accounts and notes receivable balances with debtors.
Existence or occurrence Completeness	3. Test cutoff to determine whether sales and receivables are recorded in the proper accounting period.
Valuation Rights	4. Review the collectibility of receivables, and determine the adequacy of the allowance for doubtful accounts.
Existence or occurrence Completeness Valuation	5. Perform analytical procedures to determine whether recorded sales and receivables balances appear reasonable.

Presentation and disclosure	6. Review financial statements to determine whether:
	   a. Accounts and notes receivable and sales are properly classified and described.
	   b. Disclosures are adequate.

acceptable detection risk. Again, not all of these procedures would necessarily be performed in every audit, since risk varies from engagement to engagement. For example, if control risk is assessed below the maximum, detection risk would be assessed above the minimum and, therefore, the auditor would plan less extensive substantive tests.

VERIFY MATHEMATICAL ACCURACY

The financial statement assertion of valuation is addressed in part by recomputing the mathematical accuracy of amounts recorded in the client's general ledger. For example, to accomplish tests of mathematical accuracy, an auditor could import a client's electronic, aged trial balance into a spreadsheet file, such as the Microsoft *Excel* screen illustrated in Figure 11-3, and write commands to foot [e.g., =SUM(H010:H598)] and cross-foot [e.g., =SUM(C598:H598)] the trial balance and to compare and reconcile the trial balance total with the client's recorded general ledger balance.

The mathematical accuracy of a client's aged trial balance is crucial, since the trial balance is also used as the basic source for other receivables tests included in Figure 11-2. For example, the aged trial balance is typically used to select individual customer balances for confirmation, discussed next, and

Figure 11-3: Accounts Receivable Aged Trial Balance

(Schedule prepared by client)

The Wilson Company
Accounts Receivable Aged Trial Balance
December 31, 1999

Account Number	Customer Name	Balance Dec. 31, 2000	0-30 Days	31-60 Days	61-90 Days	Over 90 Days
0103	Alpine Roofing	$ 1,754.00	$ 1,754.00			
0107	Andrie Supplies	6,319.07	6,319.07			
0108	Atwells, Inc.	5,629.83	5,629.83			
0110	Bennington & Co.	10,743.76		$10,243.76	$ 500.00	
0112	Blakely & Schuster	8,250.00	7,250.00	1,000.00		
0115	Burns & Alec	1,805.00				$1,805.00
...	...	...	...	...	...	...
0960	Van Allen Sales	2,500.00	1,500.00		1,000.00	
0961	Victor Company, Inc.	16,000.00	16,000.00			
0967	Webster Corporation	1,724.30	1,724.30			
0968	Wellington & Shine	6,225.40	6,225.40			
0971	Yellowstone Stores	5,280.50	5,280.50			
0974	Zelanie & Aveno	17,250.00	17,250.00			
		$232,228.57	$190,922.50	$21,222.42	$ 14,462.15	$5,621.50

to identify credit balances that should be reclassified to accounts payable under generally accepted accounting principles.

CONFIRM RECEIVABLES BALANCES

Confirming receivables balances with debtors—that is, asking a customer in writing whether a recorded receivable is the responding entity's account payable—is a powerful audit procedure because confirmations address simultaneously no fewer than three financial statement assertions:[1]

- *Existence.* Do recorded receivables exist at the balance sheet date?
- *Rights.* Do recorded receivables represent rights the audited entity holds over debtors (e.g., have the receivables been assigned or sold?)?
- *Valuation.* Are receivables reported at appropriate amounts?

As a result, there is a presumption in the profession that an auditor bears the burden of justifying his or her opinion on an entity's financial statements when receivables are not confirmed. Given the information content of confirmations, under what circumstances might an auditor judge that confirmations are unnecessary? *Statement on Auditing Standards No. 67,* "The Confirmation Process," lists three cases in which failing to confirm receivables is justifiable: (1) when receivables are immaterial to the financial statements, (2) when confirmations would likely be ineffective (e.g., the federal government does not respond to receivables confirmations), or (3) when audit risk is acceptably low. Receivables balances are usually confirmed as of the balance sheet date, although it's appropriate to confirm receivables at interim when an auditor is satisfied that internal control is effective (and, therefore, that control risk is below the maximum) and when the balances in receivables and sales accounts can be reconciled from the interim confirmation date (say, October 31) to the balance sheet date (say, December 31).

Confirming receivables balances requires direct communication in writing with customers through what are called positive or negative confirmation requests. **Positive confirmations** request that a customer review the account balance listed on the confirmation and respond to the auditor directly about whether the balance is correct or incorrect, as illustrated in Figure 11-4. (A variation on positive confirmations, called *blank form* confirmations, request that the respondent supply the balance.) In contrast, **negative confirmations** request that a debtor respond to the auditor only if the balance in an attached statement is *in*correct, as illustrated in Figure 11-5. For positive or negative confirmations inadvertently returned by fax rather than by mail, the auditor should call the respondent, confirm what the faxed confirmation reveals, and, for a sample of the faxed confirmations, request that the customer mail the original confirmation, thereby allowing the auditor to compare the return postmark to the customer's address. If the customer has discarded the original confirmation, the auditor could mail a new one.

In general, positive confirmations are appropriate when individual account balances are relatively large or when substantial numbers of inaccuracies or frauds are expected. Negative confirmations are generally appropriate when

---

1   Apart from these assertions, confirmations of accounts receivable are also used to test for lapping, a fraud introduced in Chapter 10.

Figure 11-4:   Positive Accounts Receivable Confirmation

THE WILSON COMPANY
15 Artubus Drive
Stony Brook, NY 11970

January 4, 2000

Wellington Products, Inc.
6540 Lincolnway Road
Los Angeles, CA 90041

   Please confirm the correctness of your December 31, 1999 account balance of
$15,652 directly to our auditors:

Cheever & Yates, LLP

who are auditing our financial statements.   This is not a request for payment.

   An envelope addressed to our auditors is enclosed.

_____

Maxine Kuman
Controller

☐   The above balance is correct.

☐   The above balance is incorrect as noted below.

_____

_____

By: _____

Date: _____

internal control is adequate, balances are small, and the auditor has no reason
to believe that debtors will not return the confirmation request. In practice,
auditors often use both types of confirmations for a particular engagement—
for example, positive requests could be used for larger account balances, and
negative requests for smaller balances. Regardless of the type of confirmation
used, the request should be mailed in the auditor's, not the client's, envelope—
that is, an envelope that includes the auditor's return address—to assure that
envelopes "returned to sender" by the postal service are mailed to the auditor,
not the client, thereby precluding the client from tampering with the confirmation and allowing the auditor to test whether the customer actually exists.
Likewise, the return self-addressed envelope included with the confirmation

Figure 11-5: Negative Accounts Receivable Confirmation

> Please examine the attached statement. If the statement disagrees with your records, respond directly to our auditors:
>
> Cheever & Yates, LLP
>
> who are auditing our financial statements. An envelope addressed to our auditors is enclosed.
>
> THIS IS NOT A REQUEST FOR PAYMENT

mailing (and referred to on the confirmation form: see Figures 11-4 and 11-5) should also be addressed to the auditor, not the client.

When positive confirmations are used, an auditor should mail second (and perhaps even third) requests to nonrespondents, attempting to maximize the number of responses. If a statistical sampling plan is used to select and evaluate the confirmations, a poor response rate could affect sampling risk, requiring that an auditor alter or abandon the sampling plan. However, despite the efforts expended to maximize response rates, a number of customers invariably will fail to respond, thereby requiring alternative audit procedures for those accounts. In the absence of a returned confirmation, an auditor could examine other evidence, such as:

- Reviewing subsequent cash collections to determine whether the customer has paid,
- Examining shipping documents to determine whether goods were shipped to the customer, and
- Examining sales invoices to determine whether the customer was billed.

Notes receivable confirmation requests are similar in substance to positive accounts receivable requests, although notes receivable confirmations are not commonly used in practice.

Leveraging off of *SAS No. 67*, one Big Six public accounting firm has significantly reduced the extent of receivables confirmations for *low risk* clients that agree to allow the firm off-site, on-line access to automated collections records. The firm uses software to monitor customer collection data, to compile collection profiles (e.g., days sales in receivables, the percentage of receivables per aging category), and to confirm only those accounts, if any, that appear unusual, such as erratic payment trends on past due accounts. The firm's strategy is based on this logic: Although confirmations address no less than three assertions (existence, rights, and valuation), they're also relatively expensive, since preparing and following up on confirmations is rather labor intensive. What it comes to is balancing audit evidence with audit effort in the face of audit risk.

TEST CUTOFF

Auditors acquire additional evidence of existence, and initial evidence of completeness, through *cutoff* tests that address whether sales transactions are recorded in the same period that title to the goods passed to the customer. Cutoff could be inaccurate if, for example, a December 31, 1998 year end client inadvertently or intentionally recorded a $100,000 January 2, 1999 sales transaction as a 1998 sale: 1998 sales and receivables would be overstated by $100,000. To test cutoff, auditors examine a sample of sales entries recorded at or near the balance sheet date. For example, assuming a December 31, 1998 year end, an auditor might examine a sample of sales transactions recorded for a reasonable period around December 31, say, from December 20 through January 10. For each sampled sale, the auditor obtains the related shipping documents and notes the shipping terms—*FOB* (free-on-board) *shipping point* v. *FOB destination*—to determine when title passed and therefore whether the sampled sales entry was recorded in the proper period. Sales should be reflected in the current year, 1998, if shipping terms were:

- *FOB shipping point,* and the goods were shipped on or before December 31, 1998, or
- *FOB destination,* and the goods were received by the customer on or before December 31.

REVIEW COLLECTIBILITY OF RECEIVABLES

Despite management's policies and procedures for reviewing and approving customer requests for credit, the entity cannot eliminate completely the risk that some accounts will not be paid. As a result, the valuation or carrying value of receivables is usually less than the sum of all outstanding balances. An auditor evaluates the carrying value of receivables by reviewing their collectibility, and by determining the adequacy of an entity's allowance for uncollectible accounts. For example, an auditor might obtain evidence of collectibility by examining an accounts receivable aged trial balance, by discussions with Credit Department personnel, by review of post-balance-sheet-date collections, by review of any available correspondence with delinquent debtors, and by examining credit ratings with recognized bureaus such as Dun & Bradstreet, Inc.

PERFORM ANALYTICAL PROCEDURES

In general, the role of analytical procedures is to direct an auditor's attention to accounts or balances that appear unusual or unreasonable, and therefore that may require additional substantive tests of details in order to reduce audit risk to an acceptably low level. Thus, within the revenue/receipt cycle, analytical procedures can be used to identify accounts that appear to be either:

- *Reasonable.* That is, accounts appear to be behaving as expected, and therefore do not require additional testing, or
- *Unreasonable* (or *unusual*). That is, accounts do *not* appear to be behaving as expected, and therefore require additional testing beyond the extent of procedures planned.

For example, if the number-of-days-sales in receivables was at or around 30 days for four successive years, this would suggest that sales, receivables, and collection activity were behaving similarly for the four-year period and would not signal the need for additional substantive tests of details. However, if the number-of-days-sales were at or around 30 days for the three preceding years and 45 days for the current year, then this unexpected variation would indicate the need for additional tests of collectibility. For sales and receivables, an auditor might use, among others, any or all of the following analytical procedures, in addition to the number-of-days-sales procedure above:

- Compare the ratio of credit sales to average net receivables—called receivables turnover—to identify trends in the entity's credit policies.
- Compare product-line sales and gross margin percentages by month and by year to identify potential overstatements or understatements of sales.
- Compare receivables aging categories (e.g., 0-30 days, 31-60 days, 61-90 days, etc.) and uncollectible accounts as percentages of accounts receivable for a series of years to test the reasonableness of the allowance for uncollectible accounts.
- Compare actual bad debt writeoffs with recorded bad debt expense for prior years to test the reasonableness of the provision for bad debts in the current year.
- Compare the ratio of the provision for bad debts to total receivables to the ratio for prior years to address the reasonableness of the provision for bad debts in the current year.
- Compare both the average balance and the largest individual balances to prior years to test the reasonableness of the allowance for uncollectible accounts.
- To estimate the reasonableness of the year end balance in receivables, compare the recorded year end balance to the following analytical estimate: last year's audited year end balance, plus credit sales during the year, less cash receipts during the year.

No one of the preceding analytical procedures will necessarily detect material misstatements. Rather, the procedures will direct an auditor's attention to accounts or balances requiring additional inquiries or substantive tests of details.

REVIEW FINANCIAL STATEMENT PRESENTATION AND DISCLOSURE

The audit program in Figure 11-2 concludes with the auditor's review of financial statement presentation and disclosure of revenue/receipt cycle accounts. An auditor should determine whether the accounts, notes, and other receivables and related sales accounts are classified, described, and disclosed in accordance with generally accepted accounting principles.

Accounts and notes receivable are usually classified as current or noncurrent assets, depending on the terms of payment, and carried at net realizable value—i.e., net of an allowance for uncollectible accounts, unearned discounts, interest, and finance charges. Trade notes and accounts receivable should be segregated from nontrade receivables, such as employee or officer receivables. All material information should be disclosed in the financial statements or in the notes to the financial statements. Disclosures should include, for example, information about pledged or assigned receivables.

CASH BALANCES

Figure 11-6 presents a program of representative year end substantive tests for cash balances. Each procedure is tied to related financial statement assertions and discussed in the following sections.

Figure 11-6:   Substantive Tests: Cash Balances

Assertions	Procedures
Existence Rights Valuation	1. Confirm year end cash balances with all banks and other depositories.

Valuation	2. Verify mathematical accuracy of recorded cash balances.
	   a. Foot cash journals.
	   b. Trace totals to the general ledger and to year end bank reconciliations prepared by the client.
	   c. Test cash on hand as necessary.

Existence
Completeness
Valuation
	3. Test cutoff.
	   a. Obtain cutoff bank statements directly from banks.
	     (1) Verify accuracy of cutoff bank statements.
	     (2) Examine information (e.g., dates and amounts) on cutoff bank statement and trace to reconciling items in year end bank reconciliation and to entries in cash journals.
	     (3) Consider necessity of preparing a proof of cash.
	   b. Reconcile recorded cash balances with returned bank confirmations.
	   c. Examine intercompany and interbank transfers near year end.

Presentation and disclosure	4. Review financial statements to determine whether:
	   a. Cash balances are properly classified and described.
	   b. Disclosures are adequate.

CONFIRM CASH BALANCES

Cash deposited in banks (e.g., checking accounts and certificates of deposit) and in other depositories (e.g., money market funds) is confirmed by auditors in much the same manner as accounts receivable. However, unlike receivables, an auditor confirms all, rather than a sample, of the cash accounts using a standard form approved in 1990 by the AICPA, the American Bankers Association, and the Bank Administration Institute. All cash accounts are confirmed with banks because, as illustrated in Figure 11-7, the standard confirmation also requests information about whether the client was directly liable to the financial institution for loans (Question 2). For example, note in Figure 11-7 that the First National Bank discloses not only a $175,517.10 cash balance (Question 1), but also a long-term loan of $150,000 (Question 2), a disclosure that is crucial to the audit of the entity's liabilities, as discussed in Chapter 13.

VERIFY MATHEMATICAL ACCURACY

To test the mathematical accuracy of recorded cash balances, and therefore to address in part the valuation of cash balances, an auditor recomputes totals in the cash journals and in client-prepared bank reconciliations, such as the reconciliation illustrated in Figure 11-8. The auditor then traces the cash journal

Figure 11-7: Bank Confirmation

	STANDARD FORM TO CONFIRM ACCOUNT
	BALANCE INFORMATION WITH FINANCIAL INSTITUTIONS A6

<u>**The Wilson Company**</u>

CUSTOMER NAME

Financial
Institution's   **First National Bank**
Name and
Address

We have provided to our accountants the following information as of the close of business on <u>**Dec. 31, 1999**</u>, regarding our deposit and loan balances. Please confirm the accuracy of the information noting any exceptions to the information provided. If the balances have been left blank, please complete this form by furnishing the balances in the appropriate space below.* Although we do not request nor expect you to conduct a comprehensive, detailed search of your records, if during the process of completing this confirmation, additional information about other deposit and loan accounts we may have with you comes to your attention, please include such information below. Please use the enclosed envelope to return the form directly to our accountants.

1. At the close of business on the date listed above, our records indicated the following deposit balance(s):

ACCOUNT NAME	ACCOUNT NO.	INTEREST RATE	BALANCE*
General Account	158-6798-321	None	$175,517.10 (A5)

2. We were directly liable to the financial institution for loans at the close of business on the date listed above as follows:

ACCOUNT NO./ DESCRIPTION	BALANCE*	DATE DUE	INTEREST RATE	DATE THROUGH WHICH INTEREST IS PAID	DESCRIPTION OF COLLATERAL
158-6799 -322	$150,000 (BB10)	6/10/01	9.5	12/1/99	Warehouse

Maxine Kuman   Controller   December 31, 1999
(Customer's Authorized Signature)   (Date)

The information presented above by the customer is in agreement with our records. Although we have not conducted a comprehensive, detailed search of our records, no other deposit or loan accounts have come to our attention except as noted below.

Anne Sexton   January 7, 2000
(Financial Institution Authorized Signature)   (Date)

Manager
(Title)

EXCEPTIONS AND/OR COMMENTS
None

Please return this form directly to our accountants: | **Cheever & Yates, LLP** |
                                                        | **Certified Public Accountants** |

*Ordinarily, balances are intentionally left blank if they are not available at the time the form is prepared.

D451 5061

Approved 1990 by American Bankers Association, American Institute of Certified Public Accountants, and Bank Administration Institute. Additional forms available from: AICPA–Order Department, P.O. Box 1003, NY, NY 10106-1003

Figure 11-8: Bank Reconciliation

(Schedule prepared by client)   A5
                                                                      SC 1/18/00

The Wilson Company
Bank Reconciliation: Peoples Bank—Acct. 1001
December 31, 1999

Balance per bank, 12/31/99		$17,551,710[b]
Add: Deposits in transit, 12/31/99	$1,578,143[c]	
Check drawn by Martin Davis Co. charged to Marc David, Inc., by bank in error	275,000[d]	1,853,143
Deduct outstanding checks:		
No. 5775 12/24	$1,431,000[e]	
No. 5776 12/26	156,050[e]	
No. 5779 12/26	181,021[e]	
No. 5780 12/27	2,169,540[e]	
No. 5781 12/29	1,589,176[e]	
No. 5785 12/30	1,191,240[e]	
Adjusted bank balance, 12/31/99		(6,718,027)
		$12,686,826
		a
Balance per books, 12/31/99		$13,241,386[f]
Deduct: December bank service charge	$ 28,500[b]	
Check from Apex Services, Inc., deposited 12/15, returned for insufficient funds, 12/18	526,060[b]	(554,560)
Adjusted book balance, 12/31/99		$12,686,826
		a

a Footed.
b Agreed to 12/31/99 bank statement.
c Agreed to cutoff bank statement and to cash receipts journal.
d Agreed to cutoff bank statement.
e Agreed to cutoff bank statement and to cash disbursements journal.
f Agreed to general ledger.

totals to postings in the general ledger and to the bank reconciliation caption "balance per books" (Figure 11-8, Note f).

Even though often immaterial in relation to the financial statements taken as a whole, cash funds on hand, sometimes called "petty cash," is tested on some audit engagements, primarily because cash is highly susceptible to misappropriation. To test cash on hand, an auditor counts the cash fund in the presence of the fund custodian and examines undeposited cash receipts and paid vouchers that reconcile cash on hand to the imprest balance. For example, if cash on hand is imprest at $500 and $175 is on hand, undeposited receipts and paid vouchers should total $325.

TEST CUTOFF

Like tests of sales cutoff, tests of cash cutoff address the existence and completeness assertions, and question whether recorded transactions, in this case receipts and disbursements, are recorded in the proper accounting period. The tests reconcile internal documents created by the client, such as:

- cash journals,
- the general ledger, and
- bank reconciliations

with external documents created by banks, such as

- year end bank statements,
- cutoff bank statements, and
- returned bank confirmations.

Item 3a of the audit program in Figure 11-6 requires that the auditor obtain cutoff statements directly from the bank (or banks) for each bank account. Unlike typical month end bank statements, **cutoff bank statements** do not represent a full month's transactions. Rather, they represent transactions (cleared checks, deposits, and miscellaneous debits and credits) for a short period after year end (e.g., seven to ten days) and are used by auditors to verify reconciling items appearing on year end bank reconciliations prepared by the client. For example, December 31 year end bank reconciliations usually include deposits in transit and outstanding checks that could not otherwise be verified until January bank statements are received in early February. Cutoff bank statements are requested in a cover letter attached to the standard bank confirmation request and, like receivables confirmations, are sent directly to the auditor by the bank, thereby providing the auditor with persuasive external evidence received directly from third parties rather than external evidence received, held, and potentially altered by a client. (When the auditor is finished testing the cutoff bank statement, it is given to the client and a statement for the remaining days in the month is forwarded by the bank directly to the client at month's end.)

If returned by the bank, individual canceled checks, deposit slips, and debit/credit memoranda accompanying each cutoff bank statement should be compared with listings printed on the statement. Each item on the cutoff statement should then be traced to the client-prepared year end bank reconciliation and to cash journals. Dates of entries in cash journals and clearings on bank statements should be examined to verify that receipts and disbursements near year end are recorded in the proper period, thereby providing insights into two prominent irregularities:

- Delays in recording cash disbursements to present a more favorable cash position on the balance sheet, and
- Checks written and recorded as disbursements prior to year end, but not mailed until after the balance sheet date to understate liabilities.

Copies of client-prepared bank reconciliations are typically included in the audit working papers as evidence of tests of cutoff. Figure 11-8 presents an illustrative year end bank reconciliation with appropriate working paper indexes, tick marks, and explanations. Note that the reconciliation adjusts both the bank and the book balances, yielding a true cash balance as of a particular date.

Internal auditors typically prepare a form of reconciliation called a *proof of cash* at one or more times during the year to verify the reliability of monthly bank reconciliations. However, if the client lacks an internal audit department or if discrepancies are observed in client-prepared year end bank reconciliations, the independent auditor may decide to prepare a proof of cash for one or more periods. Routine monthly bank reconciliations, audited in item 3b (illustrated in Figure 11-8), focus on cash balances, while a proof of cash focuses both on balances and on transactions. Figure 11-9 depicts a four-column proof of cash for two successive months, November and December, 1999. Like the bank reconciliation in Figure 11-8, the proof of cash adjusts both the bank and book balances, although for two successive months rather than one particular date.

Item 3c, cutoff tests applicable when an entity engages in intercompany transactions or maintains more than one bank account, are illustrated in Figure 11-10. *Intercompany cash transfers* at or near year end should be tested to determine whether they are recorded properly as both a receipt by one entity and a disbursement by another in the same accounting period; if not, cash balances for the consolidated group of entities could be misstated. For example, if a subsidiary records a $10,000 cash receipt from a parent on December 31, but the parent defers recording the disbursement until January 1, consolidated December 31 financial statements would overstate cash by $10,000, because the related receipt and disbursement are recorded in different accounting periods. Intercompany transfers can be tested by reviewing all transfers between related entities for a period, e.g., five days before and after year end; corresponding receipt and disbursement entries should accompany each transfer and should be recorded in the same accounting period.

Interbank transfers, similar in nature to intercompany transfers, can also be tested by examining transactions near the year end date. For each transfer of funds between banks, a receipt and corresponding disbursement should be recorded in the same period; otherwise, cash will be misstated on the balance sheet. While tests of interbank transfers may reveal understatements of cash (i.e., a disbursement recorded on or before year end and corresponding receipt recorded after year end), such tests are primarily designed to detect overstatements of cash. For example, concealment of a cash shortage could be attempted by transferring funds from one bank account to another and recording the receipt on or before year end and the disbursement after year end. Overstating cash through interbank transfers is called **kiting**.

REVIEW FINANCIAL STATEMENT PRESENTATION AND DISCLOSURE

The audit program in Figure 11-6 concludes with the auditor's review of financial statement presentation and disclosure of cash balances. An auditor should determine whether cash balances are classified, described, and disclosed in accordance with generally accepted accounting principles.

Amounts presented as Cash in the current assets section of a balance sheet should represent cash on hand and unrestricted deposits. Special-purpose funds, such as cash set aside for plant expansion, should be reported separately from Cash. Balances subject to withdrawal restrictions, such as compensating

Figure 11-9: Proof of Cash

(Schedule prepared by client)

A10
FM 1/15/00

The Wilson Company
Proof of Cash: Old Stone Bank—Acct. 101
December 31, 1999

	11/30/99	December Receipts	December Disbursements	12/31/99
Balance per bank	$ 8,576,110[b]	$41,954,430[b]	$(41,694,175)[b]	$ 8,836,365[b]
Deposits in transit: 11/30	2,462,590[c]	(2,462,590)		
12/31		2,170,050		2,170,050
Outstanding checks: 11/30	(3,156,129)[e]		2,876,582	(279,547)
12/31			(1,933,212)[f]	(1,933,212)
Adjusted bank balance	$ 7,882,571	$41,661,890	$(40,750,805)	$ 8,793,656
	a	a	a	a
Balance per books	$ 7,905,571[g]	$41,661,890[h]	$(40,748,805)[i]	$ 8,818,656[g]
Bank service charge: 11/30	(23,000)[j]		23,000	
12/31			(25,000)[b]	(25,000)
Adjusted book balance	$ 7,882,571	$41,661,890	$(40,750,805)	$ 8,793,656
	a	a	a	a

a   Footed.
b   Agreed to December bank statement.
c   Agreed to December bank statement and cash receipts journal.
d   Agreed to cutoff bank statement and to cash receipts journal.
e   Agreed to December bank statement and to cash receipts journal.
f   Agreed to cutoff bank statement and to cash disbursements journal.
g   Agreed to general ledger.
h   Agreed to cash receipts journal.
i   Agreed to cash disbursements journal.
j   Agreed to November bank statement.

Figure 11-10: Interbank and Intercompany Transfers

A9
KC 1/21/00

The Wilson Company
Schedule of Interbank and Intercompany Transfers
December 31, 1999

Check No.	Transferred From	Transferred To	Amount	Disbursement Date Per Books	Disbursement Date Per Bank	Receipt Date Per Books	Receipt Date Per Bank
Interbank Transfers							
6721	First Nat'l Bk	Union Trust	$25,000[a]	12/30[b]	1/2[c]	12/30[d]	1/2[c]
6741	First Nat'l Bk	People's Bk	35,500[a]	12/31[b]	1/3[c]	12/31[d]	1/2[c]
6743	First Nat'l Bk General Account	First Nat'l Bk Payroll Account	75,000[a]	12/31[b]	1/2[c]	12/31[d]	1/2[c]
Intercompany Transfers							
6742	Wilson (Union Trust)	Westco (subsidiary)	25,000[a]	12/31[b]	1/2[c]	12/31[d]	1/2[e]

a Agreed check number, payee, payor, and amount to cash disbursements journal.
b Per cash disbursements journal.
c Agreed to Wilson cutoff bank statement.
d Per cash receipts journal.
e Agreed to Westco cutoff bank statement.

balances and certificates of deposit, should be reported as separate components of Cash or described and disclosed in the balance sheet or in notes to the financial statements.

MANAGEMENT DISCRETION, EARNINGS MANIPULATION, AND REVENUE RECOGNITION

The discussion thus far has addressed the audit of revenue/receipt cycle accounts when the point of sale is known and therefore when, fraud aside, there's little opportunity for management to manipulate the recognition of revenue. That is, the discussion assumed that two critical revenue-recognition criteria in *FASB Concepts Statement No. 5*, "Recognition and Measurement in Financial Statements of Business Enterprises," had been met:

1. The amount and timing of revenue is reasonably determinable, and
2. The earnings process is complete or virtually complete.

But, if the timing of revenue is not reasonably determinable or if the earnings process is not complete, management has some discretion in timing the recognition of revenue. For example, consider *The Wall Street Journal's* account of some savings & loan institutions' accounting for fees from mortgage sales in the 1980s:

When an S&L sells a mortgage to another company, it often continues to service the mortgage by accepting delivery of the monthly payments. After deducting a service fee, it passes on the money to the new owner of the mortgage. Many thrifts immediately book all their expected fee income as profit when they sell a mortgage.[2]

In short, should revenue from mortgage fee sales be recognized at the point of sale or, since the earnings process is not complete, over some reasonable period, such as the life of the mortgage? Interestingly, the accounting for mortgage-sale fees is only one among many revenue recognition problems that provides management with some, though not complete, discretion in accelerating earnings and therefore that impose upon the auditor an obligation to consider **earnings manipulation**. Others include the accounting for area franchise fees, long-term construction contracts, deposits on health club memberships, and one-time membership fees in recreational camping facilities.

MANAGEMENT AND AUDITOR INCENTIVES

Accelerating the timing of revenue recognition is crucially important to auditors for two related reasons. First, management has incentives to manipulate reported earnings since, as research reveals, earnings is the most important determinant in management compensation contracts[3] and poor earnings increases both the likelihood of replacing a chief executive officer[4] and the threat of a hostile takeover.[5] Second, auditors have incentives to detect earnings manipulation, since shareholders entrust independent auditors to act as monitors over management's stewardship function and, under the *Securities Act of 1934* (Chapter 5), may bring action against an auditor for negligently overlooking inflated earnings. To demonstrate the audit implications of competing incentives and earnings manipulation, the following illustrates issues auditors confront when auditing a franchisor's accounting for area franchise fees.

AREA DEVELOPMENT FRANCHISES

Franchise operations such as Taco Bell, Burger King, Century 21, and Radisson Inns grant local franchisees the exclusive right to market trade-name products or services within a clearly defined geographical area. In the typical franchise arrangement, both the franchisor and franchisee can accrue benefits otherwise not available to either party: The franchisor establishes control over a sales outlet without a capital investment, and the franchisee markets an established product or service without incurring the cost of development. To illustrate, consider the case of a fast food franchisor's accounting for **area franchise fees**—that is, the up-front, lump sum fee a franchisee must pay Grinder Shoppe

2   "Accounting at Thrifts Provokes Controversy as Gimmickry Mounts," *The Wall Street Journal* (March 21, 1985), p. 23.
3   E.g., Jensen, M., and K. Murphy, "CEO Incentives: It's Not How Much You Pay, It's How," *Journal of Applied Corporate Finance*, Vol. 3, No. 3 (1990), pp. 36-49.
4   E.g., Warner, J., R. Watts, and K. Wruck, "Stock Prices and Top Management Changes," *Journal of Financial Economics*, Vol. 20 (1988), pp. 461-492.
5   Palepu, K., "Predicting Takeover Targets: A Methodological and Empirical Analysis," *Journal of Accounting and Economics*, Vol. 8 (1986), pp. 3-35.

Restaurants, Inc., to operate counter-service sandwich stores within a greater metropolitan area.

Grinder Shoppe, a publicly traded national chain, offers area development franchises which, under the company's Uniform Franchise Offering Circular (a disclosure document required by the *Federal Trade Commission*), grants franchisees exclusive rights to open and operate at least two but no more than three Grinder Shoppe restaurants within five years from the inception of the agreement. The development schedule calls for Grinder Shoppe's approval of store locations, construction, and interior design. Prior to opening the first store, the franchisee attends a two-week training program. The first two weeks of all first, second, and third store operations are supervised by an on-site manager assigned by Grinder Shoppe's national office. The on-site manager returns for two-day visits after each store's first two six-month periods of operation. The area development fee is:

- Fully refundable if the franchisee cannot obtain construction and working capital financing within 90 days of signing the development agreement,
- Fifty percent refundable after the first store is opened, and
- Nonrefundable after the second store is opened.

Although Grinder Shoppe had been highly successful in the first decade of operations, the company's earnings have flattened and the stock price has declined. To rescue both earnings and stock prices, Grinder Shoppe management proposes that area franchise fees be recognized as revenue when an area franchisee obtains financing to construct the first store in an area. Management argues that, once financing is obtained, few if any area franchisees renege on the area franchise agreement.

AUDIT JUDGMENT: ACCOUNTING, LIABILITY, AND ETHICS

As noted in Chapter 1, *"auditors are accountants first,"* and they are because accounting and auditing are inextricably related. This suggests that, in the case of Grinder Shoppes, the auditor need first search the professional literature to identify generally accepted accounting principles that bear on accounting for area franchise fees. Grinder Shoppe apparently proposes that revenue be recognized when area franchisees have obtained financing—that is, the point at which area development fees are no longer fully refundable. Does GAAP concur? And if it doesn't, are there legal liability and ethical issues the auditor need address?

A search of the NAARS library, an accounting research subdirectory within Mead Data Central's NEXIS data retrieval network, discloses for the key word search "Area Franchise Fee" that an FASB Statement bears on Grinder Shoppe's proposed accounting: *FASB Statement No. 45,* "Accounting for Franchise Fee Revenue." Paragraph 8 reveals that for area franchise fees:

. . . *revenue ordinarily shall be recognized when all material services or conditions relating to the sale(s) have been substantially performed or satisfied by the franchisor. If the franchisor's substantial obligations under the franchise agreement relate to the area franchise and do not depend significantly on the number of individual franchises to be established, substantial performance shall be determined using the same criteria applicable to individual franchises (paragraph 5). However, if the franchisor's substantial obligations depend on the number of individual franchises established within the area, area franchise fees shall be recognized in proportion to the initial mandatory services provided. Revenue that may have to be refunded because future services are not performed shall not be recognized by the franchisor until the franchisee has no right to receive a refund.*

Every sentence in Paragraph 8 bears on the auditor's judgment that, in the Grinder Shoppe case, revenue should be recognized in proportion to the services management provides to area franchisees, not fully when a franchisee obtains financing. That is, in the Grinder Shoppe franchise agreement:

- *Material services are not substantially performed by the franchisor until well beyond the point that a franchisee obtains financing:* Two two-day on-site visits occur during and after each store's first year of operations.
- *The franchisor's obligations depend on the number of individual franchises established within the area:* The franchisee must open at least two stores, and the fee is partially refundable after the first store is opened and nonrefundable only after the second store is opened.

Clearly, management's proposal violates GAAP, specifically *FASB Statement No. 45*, leaving the client no discretion in manipulating the timing of area franchise fee revenue. If the client insists on accelerating earnings, the auditor has no alternative but to alert the client that:

- Accelerating the recognition of revenue is a departure from GAAP,
- A departure from GAAP will cause the auditor to issue a qualified or adverse opinion, depending on materiality, and an explanatory paragraph that discloses the effect of the departure on reported earnings (Chapter 3, Figure 3-9),
- The change in accounting for area franchise fees is also an inconsistency in the application of accounting principles which management cannot justify, since the change is from a generally accepted principle to a practice that is not generally accepted, and
- Research reveals that qualified opinions are associated with declines in stock prices,[6] a risk that runs contrary to management's apparent objectives.

Make no mistake about it: What the auditor must conclude is not what the client wants to hear. As a result, there's some likelihood that the client may exert influence on the auditor, for example by threatening to put next year's engagement out to bid. If the auditor considers concurring with the client to violate *FASB Statement No. 45*, the legal and ethical implications are enormous. Since Grinder Shoppes is publicly traded, statutory law applies and Sections 10(b) and 18 of the *Securities Exchange Act of 1934* (Chapter 5) provide shareholders with a means to recover losses resulting from false or misleading statements. In this case, shareholders could likely recover under Section 10(b) because the auditor knew that revenue had been accelerated and that *FASB Statement No. 45* had been violated, although the plaintiff's basis for action, Section 10(b) or Section 18, would be arranged in consultation with an attorney. Further, recall from Chapter 5 that the auditor could be liable for treble

---

6   E.g., Chow, C. W. and S. J. Rice, "Qualified Audit Opinion and Share Prices: An Investigation," *Auditing: A Journal of Practice & Theory, Vol. 1, No. 2* (Winter 1982), pp. 35-53.

damages under the Racketeer Influenced and Corrupt Organizations (RICO) Act, since *Reves v. Arthur Young*, a 1993 U.S. Supreme Court case, does not provide relief from RICO when, as is the case in Grinder Shoppe, he or she participated directly with management to perpetrate the fraud.

Interestingly, the case raises at least two ethical issues. First, the auditor violates the *Code of Professional Conduct*, Rule 203—Accounting Principles (Chapter 4), which provides that an AICPA member cannot issue an unqualified opinion if the financial statements contain a departure from an "accounting principle promulgated by bodies designated by Council." In the Grinder Shoppe case, the accounting principle violated is that "area franchise fees shall be recognized in proportion to the initial mandatory services provided" *(FASB Statement No. 45)* and the body issuing the principle is the Financial Accounting Standards Board. Violating Rule 203 can result in an administrative reprimand, such as suspension to practice before the SEC, or, worse still, revocation of a CPA's license to practice public accountancy. Second, unethical business practices impose upon an offending auditor the risk of losing the set of characteristics on which his or her reputation capital rests: integrity, objectivity, and credibility. What, after all, does the public rely on us for if not for our claims to credibility?

APPLYING AUDIT SAMPLING IN SUBSTANTIVE TESTS OF ACCOUNTS RECEIVABLE

To integrate material presented in this chapter with the statistical sampling plans introduced in Chapter 9 and with the tests of revenue/receipt cycle controls introduced in Chapter 10, assume a continuing audit engagement for the Madison Corporation, a relatively large manufacturer and supplier of health care equipment, whose fiscal year ends December 31. Madison is a publicly held corporation and has been an industry leader for over two decades. The objective in this case is to accomplish program step 2, Figure 11-2: confirm accounts receivable balances with debtors.

UPDATING THE INTERIM ASSESSMENT OF CONTROL RISK

Assume the interim tests of controls were accomplished during September and revealed that controls over customer order, credit, shipping, billing, recording, and cash collection—Madison's major revenue/receipt cycle activities—were effective and that undetected control deficiencies were not likely to produce aggregate error in excess of tolerable error. The auditor assesses control risk below the maximum. However, because of employee turnover since September and to assure that controls remained effective during the remaining period (i.e., from September to year end), the auditor:

- Updated tests of controls through December 31 by applying nonstatistical sampling to transactions recorded in October, November, and December.
- Made inquiries of management about any significant changes to revenue/ receipt cycle controls.

In contrast to the interim tests of controls, the auditor's updated tests for October through December reveal a significant number of inaccuracies in recorded receivables. Inquiries indicate that two key employees were replaced on October 1, thereby explaining the markedly higher rate of data entry errors in October, November, and December. No other personnel or procedures had changed since September 30.

PLANNING THE RECEIVABLES CONFIRMATION AND SELECTING A SAMPLING PLAN

In this case, the auditor elects to use positive confirmations to control detection risk, because the updated tests of controls suggest that inaccurate balances are likely. The likelihood of inaccurate balances also suggests that differences between audited and recorded amounts are not apt to be rare, indicating that ratio or difference estimation may be the most effective statistical sampling plan, particularly since Madison maintains subsidiary records for each customer account. Ratio estimation (Chapter 10) is selected by the auditor because in prior years—and for October through December of this year—differences between audited and book values tended to increase as book values increased, indicating differences were highly proportional to book values.

Population, Sampling Unit, and Estimated Standard Deviation

The audit population consists of 1,550 customer accounts, each represented by detailed subsidiary records totaling $1,250,000 at December 31. An aged trial balance is obtained from accounts receivable personnel, footed, cross-footed, traced in part to detailed subsidiary records, and agreed in total with the general ledger. The sampling unit is represented by individual customer accounts, not invoices, because account balances, not invoice terms, will be confirmed.

In this case, the auditor would not use a preliminary sample to estimate the population standard deviation, because audited amounts could only be obtained by confirmation, which is time-consuming and inefficient to pretest. As a result, the auditor estimates the standard deviation to be $175, because in three successive years the population standard deviation was approximately $150, and changes in conditions since September 30 suggest greater variation is likely.

Risk and Tolerable Error

To continue the sampling plan, the auditor requires estimates of the risk of incorrect rejection, the risk of incorrect acceptance, and tolerable error, all three of which are used to determine the allowance for sampling risk, the remaining variable needed to calculate sample size.

The risks of incorrect rejection and incorrect acceptance are both set at .05, a relatively low level, because (1) updated tests of controls revealed clerical inaccuracies and mispostings and (2) no other procedures within the audit program in Figure 11-2 address directly whether trade receivables exist at December 31. Tolerable error, the maximum monetary error that may exist without causing the financial statements to be misstated materially, is judged to be $90,000 by the auditor.

From Figure 9-4, R (the ratio of desired sampling risk to tolerable error) is .543, the intersect of the column associated with a .05 risk of incorrect rejection and the row associated with a .05 risk of incorrect acceptance. Because TE, tolerable error, is $90,000, then A, the desired allowance for sampling risk, is:

$$A = R \times TE$$
$$= .543 \times \$90,000$$
$$= \$48,870$$

SAMPLE SIZE

Recapping, the following variables are known or have been estimated:

- Population size (N) = 1,550
- Estimated standard deviation (S) = \$175
- Risk of incorrect rejection (U) = .05 (1.96 standard deviations)
- Desired allowance for sampling risk (A) = \$48,870

From this information, sample size (n) is calculated as follows:

$$n' = \left(\frac{S \times U \times N}{A}\right)^2$$
$$= \left(\frac{\$175 \times 1.96 \times 1,550}{\$48,870}\right)^2$$
$$= 118$$

and

$$n = \frac{n'}{1 + \frac{n'}{N}}$$
$$= \frac{118}{1 + \frac{118}{1,550}}$$
$$= 110$$

Thus, given the auditor's acceptable risks and tolerable error, 110 randomly selected account balances must be confirmed in order to acquire evidence bearing on whether the 1,550 customer accounts are fairly stated at December 31.

Method of Sample Selection

To select the 110 sample accounts, the auditor assigns sequential numbers from 0001 through 1550 to the client's alphabetically arrayed aged trial balance. A computer generated random number list is used to select individual customer accounts for confirmation.

All confirmations are mailed in early January, and second requests are sent to nonrespondents within ten days. For disputed balances and for nonrespondents, the auditor applies alternative procedures, which include: (1) determining whether the account was paid subsequent to year end and, therefore, was collectible at December 31, (2) examining copies of sales invoices to determine if and when billing occurred, and (3) examining shipping documents to determine if and when goods were shipped.

EVALUATE SAMPLE RESULTS

Assume that from compiled confirmation responses and alternative procedures for disputed accounts and nonrespondents, the sampling plan indicates that the audited value for all 110 sampled accounts is $89,000 and the book value is $92,710, yielding $\hat{R}$, the ratio of audited value to book value—.96 (i.e., $89,000/$92,710). The estimated total population value, $\hat{X}$, is determined by multiplying total book value, B, times $\hat{R}$:

$$\hat{X} = \hat{R} \times B$$

$$= .96 \times \$1,250,000$$

$$= \$1,200,000$$

Assume the population standard deviation, calculated from sample data, is $167. The achieved allowance for sampling risk, A', is calculated next as follows:

$$A' = \frac{S \times U \times N}{\sqrt{n}} \sqrt{1 - \frac{n}{N}}$$

$$= \frac{\$167 \times 1.96 \times 1,550}{\sqrt{110}} \sqrt{1 - \frac{110}{1,550}}$$

$$= \$46,580$$

Finally, the auditor determines a precision interval from the estimated population audited value, $\hat{X}$, and the achieved allowance for sampling risk, A':

$$\text{Precision interval} = \hat{X} \pm A'$$

$$= \$1,200,000 \pm \$46,580$$

$$= \$1,153,420 \text{ to } \$1,246,580$$

The precision interval leads to the following statistical conclusion:

Based on procedures applied, the estimated population value is $1,200,000, and there is a 95 percent probability (1.0 minus the risk of incorrect acceptance, .05) that the true but unknown population value is included in the precision interval, $1,153,420 to $1,246,580.

In this case, even though the desired allowance for sampling risk, $48,870, exceeds the achieved allowance for sampling risk, $46,580, an audit adjustment could be proposed because:

- Recorded book value, $1,250,000, falls outside the precision interval, $1,153,420 to $1,246,580, and
- Tolerable error, $90,000, does not exceed the difference between recorded book value, $1,250,000, and the furthest end of the precision interval away from book value, $1,153,420; that is, $90,000 is less than $96,580 ($1,250,000 − $1,153,420).

As a result, using the methodology introduced in Chapter 9, the auditor could propose an adjustment of $6,580, calculated as follows:

$$\text{Adjustment} = \frac{\text{Recorded}}{\text{book value}} - \left(\frac{\text{Lower precision}}{\text{limit}} + \frac{\text{Tolerable}}{\text{error}} \right)$$

$$= \$1,250,000 - (\$1,153,420 + \$90,000)$$

$$= \$6,580$$

As indicated in Chapter 9, the auditor need not necessarily propose an audit adjustment. Rather, he or she could increase sample size and reevaluate for all sampling units, or request that the client revalue the entire population. In this case, the auditor would likely propose an audit adjustment, reducing recorded book value, $1,250,000, to the adjusted value, $1,243,420 (i.e., the lower precision limit, $1,153,420, plus tolerable error, $90,000). Assuming no other evidence surfaces to the contrary, the auditor's conclusion would be as follows:

Based on audit procedures applied, I am satisfied that Accounts Receivable—Trade, excluding the allowance for uncollectibles, is fairly stated at December 31.

COMPUTER ASSISTED SUBSTANTIVE TESTS OF ACCOUNTS RECEIVABLE

When a client's revenue/receipt cycle activities are recorded, classified, and summarized wholly or in part by computer, an auditor's substantive tests of details can be accomplished in part by computer assisted audit techniques. Figure 11-11 lists several audit procedures and related computer assisted techniques common to audits of accounts receivable.

To illustrate the application of computer assisted audit techniques, assume an auditor wishes to accomplish portions of the following three substantive tests (included in Figure 11-11) with the aid of a computer:

1. Verify mathematical accuracy of the accounts receivable subsidiary records.
2. Age receivables according to computer stored invoice dates.
3. List credit balances in accounts receivable for reclassification to accounts payable.

The auditor may either design software to accomplish these procedures or use generalized audit software. Generalized software is available from outside

Figure 11-11: Computer Assisted Substantive Tests: Accounts Receivable

Audit Procedure	Computer Assisted Substantive Test
Test mathematical accuracy.	Verify footings, cross-footings, and extensions of the accounts receivable aged trial balance and/or the subsidiary records.
Summarize data for further testing or analysis.	Age receivables according to invoice dates. List credit balances in accounts receivable for reclassification to accounts payable. Print accounts receivable confirmations.
Test accuracy of recorded data.	Trace details in subsidiary records with source documents.
Select samples.	Select samples from random number generators and aged trial balances (or subsidiary records).
Compare similar data files.	Compare aged trial balance with accounts receivable subsidiary records.

vendors, including some of the larger public accounting firms. Auditor prepared software, in contrast, is designed for each client application and requires that the auditor accomplish all of the tasks normally associated with software preparation, including developing systems flowcharts and software specifications, coding, testing, and debugging, before the software is applied in a specific audit engagement.

Figure 11-12 flowcharts the tasks necessary to accomplish the three preceding substantive tests and would be identical whether the auditor used a generalized software package or prepared tailored software. As illustrated in Figure 11-12, the computer assisted tests require three separate files: the client's accounts receivable master file, the client's sales journal, and the auditor's software. The software would be designed to perform the following tasks for each substantive test:

Substantive Test	Computer Software Task
Verify mathematical accuracy.	Foot and cross-foot the amounts recorded in each customer account within the accounts receivable master file.
	Total the balances of all customer accounts, leading to a total for all receivables.
	Display/print exceptions.
Age receivables.	Trace individual customer balances in the accounts receivable master file to related sales entries in the sales journal.
	For each customer, print balances by invoice dates, i.e., 0-30 days, 31-60 days, 61-90 days, 91-120 days, and over 120 days.
	Display/print aged trial balances.
List credit balances in receivables.	Scan the accounts receivable master file for net credit balances.
	Display/print listing of credit balance accounts.

The software would be run on the client's computer, either directly by the auditor or by client personnel under the auditor's supervision. The exception report, aged trial balances, and credit balance listing—the output depicted in Figure 11-12—would be obtained by the auditor directly, either in the form of a diskette or as printed hard copy (or both). The output and computer assisted tests are then documented in the auditor's working papers and used in conjunction with other audit evidence to help form conclusions about whether receivables are fairly stated at the balance sheet date.

SUMMARY

As discussed in Chapter 10, the revenue/receipt cycle encompasses two major business functions—selling resources to customers and, subsequently, collecting cash for resources sold. In turn, these functions are reflected in three major

Figure 11-12: Flowchart of Computer Assisted Tests of Accounts Receivable

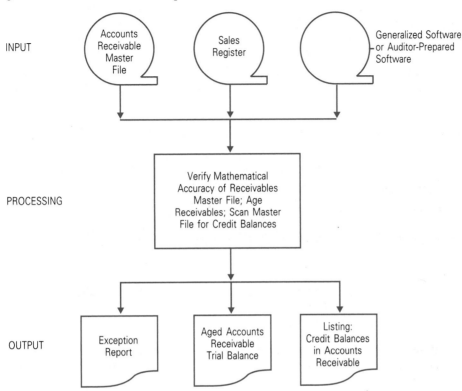

financial statement accounts: Sales, Accounts Receivable, and Cash, each of which is discussed in this chapter in the context of substantive tests. When performing substantive tests of sales, receivables, and cash balances, an auditor's objectives are to determine that each account balance exists, represents all transactions that should be presented, represents rights of the entity, is valued appropriately, and is presented and disclosed properly in the financial statements. Importantly, the material presented in Chapter 7 on computer auditing and in Chapter 9 on audit sampling is directly applicable to substantive tests of sales, receivables, and cash, since most U.S. companies now process most all of their revenue/receipt cycle transactions by computer and the typically large volume of revenue/receipt cycle transactions lends nicely to the efficiencies provided by audit sampling.

When the timing of revenue is not reasonably determinable or if the earnings process is not complete, management has some discretion in timing the amount of revenue recognized, creating opportunities for earnings manipulation. Auditors should be aware that management may have incentives to overstate earnings, since reported earnings is typically the most important variable in management compensation contracts and poor earnings performance increases both the likelihood of replacing a chief executive officer and the threat of a hostile takeover. Undetected earnings manipulation can result both in legal liability and ethical implications for the auditor.

KEY TERMS

Revenue/receipt cycle 401
Positive confirmations 408
Negative confirmations 408
Cutoff bank statements 416

Kiting 417
Earnings manipulation 420
Area franchise fees 420

REFERENCES

Auditing Standards

SAS No. 47, "Audit Risk and Materiality in Conducting an Audit."
SAS No. 67, "The Confirmation Process."

Accounting Standards

FASB Concepts Statement No. 5, "Recognition and Measurement in Financial Statements of Business
   Enterprises."
FASB Statement No. 45, "Accounting for Franchise Fee Revenue."

QUESTIONS

1. What are financial statement assertions, audit objectives, and audit procedures?
   How are they related?
2. How does an auditor test whether recorded accounts receivable exist?
3. Why does an auditor perform analytical procedures on receivables?
4. How does an auditor test whether recorded receivables represent bona fide rights
   of the client?
5. How does an auditor test the valuation of accounts receivable and sales?
6. Describe and distinguish between positive and negative confirmation requests.
7. Explain the purpose and nature of sales cutoff tests.
8. How does an auditor test whether cash balances actually exist?
9. Aside from cash balances, what other information is requested by an AICPA
   standard form to confirm account balance information with financial institutions
   (Figure 11-7)?
10. Identify the internal and external documentation available to an auditor to test
    cutoff.
11. Explain the purpose and nature of cutoff tests of cash balances.
12. How and why does an auditor test intercompany and interbank transfers?
13. Describe some computer assisted substantive tests an auditor might apply to
    accounts receivable.
14. What conditions must an entity meet before recognizing revenue for financial
    statement reporting purposes?
15. What advantages do both franchisors and franchisees enjoy by entering into a
    franchise agreement, rather than conducting the entire scope of operations indi-
    vidually?

MULTIPLE CHOICE QUESTIONS

1. Which of the following might be detected by sales cutoff tests?

a. Overstated receivables.
b. Overstated sales.
c. Kiting.
d. Misappropriated inventory.

2. To test whether all sales transactions have been recorded, an auditor should test a sample drawn from an entity's file of:

a. Receiving reports.
b. Bills of lading.
c. Sales orders.
d. Sales invoices.

3. Positive accounts receivable confirmations are appropriate when:

a. There is reason to believe that a substantial number of accounts may be in dispute.
b. Control risk is low.
c. Accounts receivable consists of many small balances.
d. Confirmations are mailed during an interim period.

4. An auditor requests a cutoff bank statement primarily to:

a. Verify the cash balance reported on the bank confirmation.
b. Verify reconciling items on the client's bank reconciliation.
c. Detect lapping.
d. Detect kiting.

5. Which of the following procedures could reveal unrecorded sales at the balance sheet date?

a. Comparing shipping documents with sales records.
b. Applying gross profit percentages to inventory shipped during the period.
c. Tracing payments received after the balance sheet date to accounts receivable records.
d. Sending accounts receivable confirmations.

6. Assuming cash receipts from credit sales have been misappropriated, which of the following is likely to conceal the misappropriation and unlikely to be detected?

a. Understating the sales journal.
b. Overstating the accounts receivable control account.
c. Overstating the accounts receivable subsidiary ledger.
d. Overstating the cash receipts journal.

7. Which of the following cash transfers misstates cash at December 31, 1999?

Interbank Transfers

| | Disbursement | | Receipt | |
	Recorded in books	Paid by bank	Recorded in books	Received by bank
a.	12/31/99	01/04/00	12/31/99	12/31/99
b.	01/04/00	01/05/00	12/31/99	01/04/00
c.	12/31/99	01/05/00	12/31/99	01/04/00
d.	01/04/00	01/11/00	01/04/00	01/04/00

8. Which of the following accounting issues is most likely to raise an auditor's professional skepticism about earnings manipulation?

a. Progress payments.
b. Allowance for doubtful accounts.
c. Sales returns.
d. Cash receipts.

9. Which of the following is most likely to provide management with incentives to overstate earnings?

a. Projected quarterly dividends.
b. Issuance of preferred stock.
c. Unbudgeted increases in materials prices.
d. A projected stock split.

10. Under which of the following circumstances does management have some discretion in timing the recognition of revenue?

a. The timing of revenue is not reasonably determinable and the earnings process is not complete.
b. The amount and timing of revenue is reasonably determinable.
c. The earnings process is complete or reasonably complete.
d. The transaction is at arm's length.

PROBLEMS AND DISCUSSION CASES

11-1 *Relating Errors, Frauds, Audit Procedures, and Assertions in Substantive Tests of Accounts Receivable*

Following are errors, frauds, or other circumstances that an auditor might encounter as a result of applying year end substantive tests to accounts receivable as of December 31, 1999:

a.   Sales totaling $12,500 were shipped on January 2, 2000 and recorded on December 31, 1999.
b.   Balances in selected individual customer accounts do not reconcile with supporting documentation (e.g., sales invoices, cash receipts).
c.   Not all sales transactions are recorded.
d.   The aged trial balance prepared by the client includes a customer account within the 30- to 60-day category that is actually 120 days old.
e.   Positive confirmations were not returned by 27 of 100 mailed receivables confirmations.
f.   Actual writeoffs during 1999 of receivables arising from 1998 sales were greater than the December 31, 1999 allowance for doubtful accounts.

Required: For each of the preceding items indicate: (1) procedures that might address the error, fraud, or circumstance and (2) the financial statement assertion addressed by each procedure.

11-2 *Receivables Confirmations*

An independent auditor is engaged to audit the financial statements of a manufacturing company that, consistent with prior years, maintains a significant balance in trade accounts receivable. The auditor is satisfied that the accounts are properly summarized and classified, and that reclassifications and valuations are made in accordance with generally accepted accounting principles. The auditor is planning to use accounts receivable confirmation requests to satisfy the third standard of fieldwork.

Required:

1.   Identify and describe the two forms of accounts receivable confirmation requests commonly used in practice and indicate what factors the auditor will consider to determine which form to use.
2.   What alternative procedures could the auditor use to address no replies?

11-3 *Drafting a Tailored Audit Program for Credit Sales Transactions*

You have audited the financial statements of the Heft Company, a December 31 year end client, for several years. The interim phase of the engagement, completed on

August 31, included confirming accounts receivable and indicated that internal controls over receivables are effective and therefore that control risk is below the maximum.

Credit sales are made principally to manufacturers. Of 1,500 active trade accounts receivable, about 35 percent represent 65 percent of the total dollar balance. Receivables are maintained alphabetically in five subsidiary files, and the files are controlled by one general ledger account.

Sales are posted by an operation that simultaneously updates the customer's balance (and monthly statement) and records the transaction in the sales journal. All cash receipts are in the form of customers' checks that, when posted, simultaneously update the customer's ledger balance, monthly statement, and the cash receipts journal. Information for posting cash receipts is obtained from remittance advices that are returned in envelopes with the customers' checks. The bookkeeper compares the remittance advices with the list of checks that was prepared by another person when the mail was received.

Summary totals are produced monthly by the bookkeeper for posting to general ledger accounts such as Cash, Sales, and Accounts Receivable. An aged trial balance for each subsidiary is prepared monthly.

Sales returns and allowances and bad debt writeoffs are summarized periodically and recorded in the general journal. Supporting documents for these journal entries are available. The usual documents arising from billing and shipping are also available.

Required: Prepare an audit program to test Heft Company's year end trade accounts receivable. Use the substantive tests introduced within the chapter as a guide, but not as a final and complete answer.

(AICPA Adapted)

11-4 *Analytical Procedures and Accounts Receivable*
Martin Kline, engagement partner for RCT Manufacturing Company, a February 28, 1999, year end client, is performing analytical procedures to better understand RCT's business and to determine where audit effort ought to be concentrated. The condensed balance sheet and income statements for 1998 and 1999 follow.

RCT Manufacturing Company
Condensed Balance Sheets
February 28, 1999 and 1998

Assets	1999	1998
Cash	$ 12,000	$ 15,000
Accounts receivable, net	93,000	50,000
Inventory	72,000	67,000
Other current assets	5,000	6,000
Plant and equipment, net of Depreciation	60,000	80,000
Total assets	$242,000	$218,000
Liabilities and Equities		
Accounts payable	$ 38,000	$ 41,000
Federal income tax payable	30,000	14,400
Long-term liabilities	20,000	40,000
Common stock	70,000	70,000
Retained earnings	84,000	52,600
Total liabilities and equities	$242,000	$218,000

RCT Manufacturing Company
Condensed Income Statements
Years Ended February 28, 1999 and 1998

	1999	1998
Net sales	$ 1,684,000	$ 1,250,000
Cost of goods sold	927,000	710,000
Gross margin on sales	$ 757,000	$ 540,000
Selling and administrative expenses	682,000	504,000
Income before federal income taxes	$ 75,000	$ 36,000
Income tax expense	30,000	14,400
Net income	$ 45,000	$ 21,600

Additional information:
1. Cash sales are insignificant.
2. Year end figures are comparable to the average for each respective year.

Required: For each year, compute accounts receivable turnover and, based on turnover, identify and discuss procedures Kline should include in the audit of accounts receivable.

(AICPA Adapted)

11-5 *Sales Cutoff Tests*
During an audit of the financial statements of Houston Wholesalers, Inc., for the year ended June 30, 1999, an auditor performs several cutoff tests.
   Required:
1. What are cutoff tests and why are they performed?
2. The auditor wishes to test Houston's sales cutoff at June 30, 1999. Discuss procedures that should be included in the test.

11-6 *Relating Errors, Frauds, Audit Procedures, and Assertions in Substantive Tests of Cash*
Following are errors, frauds, or other circumstances that an auditor might encounter as a result of applying substantive tests to cash balances as of December 31.
a. The petty cash fund is short $75.
b. Cash in banks is overstated by $1,500.
c. Several checks were issued on December 31, but were postdated January 2.
d. Outstanding checks per the bank reconciliation do not agree with the cash disbursements journal.
e. On December 31, the sum of $15,000 was transferred from an account in the First National Bank to an account in Tower Savings Bank.
f. The December 31 bank reconciliation contains several discrepancies.
g. On December 31, the client transferred $25,000 to a wholly owned subsidiary.
   Required: Indicate a specific procedure (or procedures) that might detect each error, fraud, or circumstance and identify the assertion(s) addressed by each procedure.

11-7 *Cash Cutoff Tests*
During year end substantive procedures for cash balances as of June 30, 1999, an auditor obtains a July 10, 1999 bank statement directly from a bank.
   Required: Explain how the auditor will use the cutoff bank statement:
1. When auditing the June 30, 1999, bank reconciliation.
2. To obtain other audit information.

11-8 *Auditing a Client Prepared Bank Reconciliation*
The following client prepared bank reconciliation is presented to Kautz during an audit of the financial statements of Cynthia Company:

Cynthia Company
Bank Reconciliation
Village Bank Account 2
December 31, 2000

Balance per bank (a)		$ 18,375.91
Deposits in transit: (b)		
12/30	$ 1,471.10	
12/31	2,840.69	4,311.79
Subtotal		$ 22,687.70
Outstanding checks: (c)		
No. 837	$ 6,000.00	
No. 1941	671.80	
No. 1966	320.00	
No. 1984	1,855.42	
No. 1985	3,621.22	
No. 1987	2,576.89	
No. 1991	4,420.88	(19,466.21)
Subtotal		$ 3,221.49
NSF check returned,		
12/29 (d)		200.00
Bank charges		5.50
Error: Check No. 1932		148.10
Customer note collected by the bank		
($2,750 plus $275 interest) (e)		(3,025.00)
Balance per books (f)		$ 550.09

Required: Indicate one or more audit procedures Kautz should perform to gather evidence to support each of the items (a) through (f).

(AICPA Adapted)

11-9 *Computer Assisted Audit Tests*

After determining that computer controls are valid, Hastings is reviewing the sales system of Rosco Corporation to determine how computer assisted audit techniques may be used to assist in performing tests of Rosco's sales records. Rosco sells corn from one central location. All orders are received by mail or fax and indicate the preassigned customer identification number, desired quantity, proposed delivery date, method of payment, and shipping terms. Since price fluctuates daily, orders do not indicate a price. Price sheets are printed daily, and details are stored on computer. The details of orders are also maintained on computer.

Each morning the shipping clerk receives a computer printout that indicates details of customers' orders to be shipped that day. After the orders have been shipped, the shipping details are entered in the computer, which simultaneously updates the sales journal, perpetual inventory records, accounts receivable, and sales accounts. The details of all transactions, as well as daily updates, are maintained on computer and are accessible by Hastings.

Required:

1. How may Hastings use computer assisted audit techniques to perform substantive tests of Rosco's sales records?
2. What other auditing procedures should Hastings perform in order to complete the audit of Rosco's sales records?

(AICPA Adapted)

11-10 *Identifying and Criticizing a Receivables Confirmation*
An entry level staff member in the Providence, RI office of DeMarinis & Harrison, LLP,
has drafted the following receivable confirmation for the Newman Crosby Company,
a December 31, 1998 year end client:

January 2, 1999

Newman Crosby Company
305 Columbus Avenue
Pawtucket, RI 02861

Carter, Rice, Storrs & Bement
Industrial Highway
Providence, RI 02906

Please confirm the correctness of your December 31, 1998 account balance, $45,897,
directly to us. Our auditors are DeMarinis & Harrison, CPAs. This is not a request for
payment.

_____
Tess Gallagher, Controller

_____   The above balance is correct.

_____   The above balance is incorrect, as noted below:

Required:
1.   What type of confirmation is illustrated?
2.   What is wrong with the confirmation?

11-11 *Interpreting Working Paper Evidence*
Following is partial evidence from an audit working paper:

Disbursement Date		Receipt Date	
Per Books	Per Bank	Per Books	Per Bank
12/31	01/01	01/02	12/31
12/31	01/01	12/31	12/31
01/01	01/01	12/31	12/31
12/31	01/01	12/30	12/30

Required:
1.   What is the evidence attempting to detect?
2.   Did it? Why or why not?

11-12 *Interpreting Working Paper Evidence*
Following is partial evidence from an audit working paper:

	Shipped	Recorded
FOB: Destination	December 31	January 02
FOB: Shipping Point	December 30	December 31
FOB: Destination	January 01	January 01
FOB: Shipping Point	December 31	January 01

Required:
1. What is the evidence attempting to detect?
2. Did it? Why or why not?

11-13 *Working Paper Review: Bank Reconciliation*
Following is an audit working paper that documents an auditor's tests of a client's bank reconciliation.

<table>
<tr><td colspan="2" align="center">Ansonia Wire & Cable Co., Inc.
Bank Reconciliation
December 31, 1999</td><td align="right">A5
ARE</td></tr>
<tr><td>Balance per bank, 12/31/99</td><td></td><td align="right">$17,551,710@</td></tr>
<tr><td>Add: DIT, 12/31/99</td><td></td><td align="right">1,578,143*</td></tr>
<tr><td>Less: O/S checks:</td><td></td><td></td></tr>
<tr><td>No. 5775 12/24</td><td align="right">$1,431,897&</td><td></td></tr>
<tr><td>No. 5776 12/26</td><td align="right">156,050&</td><td></td></tr>
<tr><td>No. 5777 12/27</td><td align="right">234,875&</td><td></td></tr>
<tr><td>No. 5779 12/29</td><td align="right">2,169,549&</td><td></td></tr>
<tr><td>No. 5780 12/31</td><td align="right">1,191,240&</td><td align="right">(5,183,611)</td></tr>
<tr><td>Adjusted bank balance</td><td></td><td align="right">$13,946,242</td></tr>
<tr><td>Balance per books, 12/31/99</td><td></td><td align="right">$14,473,098#</td></tr>
<tr><td>Less: Check from Apex, Inc.,
    deposited 12/15,
    returned NSF on 12/18</td><td></td><td align="right">(526,856)@</td></tr>
<tr><td>Adjusted book balance</td><td></td><td align="right">$13,946,242</td></tr>
</table>

@ Agreed to 12/31/99 bank statement obtained from client/*ARE*
* Agreed to cash receipts records/*ARE*
& Agreed to cash disbursements records/*ARE*
# Agreed to client bank reconciliation/*ARE*

Required: List the deficiencies in this working paper.

11-14 *Earnings Manipulation and Area Franchise Fees*
Burger Buddy Restaurants grants area franchises to operate up to two restaurants within a 100 square mile area. The Uniform Franchise Offering Circular reveals that, following payment of the lump sum fee, Burger Buddy agrees to assist in selecting franchise locations and obtaining financing, negotiate lease terms for existing structures or construction costs for a new building, and provide both initial management training and periodic on-site consultation. The area franchise fee can be refunded. To date, no area franchisees have either reneged on the franchise agreements or gone out of business. In most markets, Burger Buddy ranks at least fourth in market-wide fast food revenue. The product line consists of beef, fish, and poultry-based sandwiches and a full service salad bar.
    Required: Identify, and explain the motive for, the key questions an auditor would address to judge when area franchise fees may be recognized as revenue.

RESEARCH PROJECT

MANAGEMENT DISCRETION AND EARNINGS MANIPULATION

Earnings manipulation has been the subject of considerable attention both in the financial press and in academic research. For example, *The Wall Street Journal*, *Forbes Magazine*, and *Business Week* have all carried pieces on suspicious income and the 1988 *Supplement* to the University of Chicago's *Journal of Accounting Research* is devoted exclusively to studies addressing earnings management. Interestingly, many of the earnings manipulation issues disclosed by the press have resulted in professional pronouncements intended to improve the quality of reported earnings, among them *FASB Statement No. 45*, "Accounting for Franchise Fee Revenue."

Required: Using the annual report file in the National Automated Accounting Research System (NAARS) or copies of annual reports in a library, select the annual reports of three national franchisors (e.g., Burger King, Century 21, Holiday Inn, McDonald's, Radisson Inns, Taco Bell, U-Haul) and draft a report that accomplishes both of the following:

1. Compare the footnote and line-item disclosures for area development and individual site franchises.
2. Using *FASB Statement No. 45*, paragraphs 5 through 11, as a guide, list and explain the questions an auditor would ask the management of any one of the three franchisors to monitor whether the franchisor complied with generally accepted accounting principles.

12

Tests of Controls in the Expenditure/ Disbursement Cycle: Purchases and Cash Disbursements Transactions

Major topics discussed in this chapter are:

- The nature of the expenditure/disbursement cycle, including the flow of information through purchasing, receiving, accounts payable, and cash disbursements.
- Internal control objectives and potential errors or frauds.
- Assurance and consulting services related to purchases.
- An auditor's consideration of internal control in the expenditure/ disbursement cycle.
- Computer auditing and sampling applied to tests of controls in the expenditure/disbursement cycle.

Like Chapters 10 and 11 for the revenue/receipt cycle, this chapter and Chapter 13 focus on auditing the expenditure/disbursement cycle: Tests of controls are introduced here and substantive tests are introduced in Chapter 13. This chapter begins by describing the nature of the expenditure/disbursement cycle and representative internal controls over an entity's purchasing, receiving, and cash disbursements functions. Next, an auditor's consideration of internal control within the expenditure/disbursement cycle is discussed. Finally, the chapter presents a case illustration that integrates material introduced in Chapter 7 (computer information systems), Chapter 8 (audit sampling), and this chapter.

THE EXPENDITURE/DISBURSEMENT CYCLE

The **expenditure/disbursement cycle** encompasses both the acquisition of goods and services ("expenditure" in the cycle's title) and the payment of cash ("disbursement") for the goods and services acquired. The cycle is related to each of the other three cycles, since it:

- Uses resources and information provided by the revenue/receipt cycle, and
- Provides resources and information for the financing and conversion cycles.

For example, the expenditure/disbursement cycle might use cash provided from the sale of inventory (revenue/receipt cycle), disburse cash to meet principal and interest payments on funds borrowed from investors in exchange for bonds (financing cycle), and disburse cash to employees who assemble inventory (conversion cycle).

Figure 12-1 summarizes the scope of the expenditure/disbursement cycle, listing the primary business functions and representative activities, journal entries, and forms. Two major business functions are associated with the cycle:

- Resources (goods and services) are acquired from vendors and employees in exchange for obligations to pay.
- Obligations to vendors and employees are paid.

Each of these business functions relates both to vendors and to employees (although, employees, personnel, and payroll are discussed separately in Chapter 14).

An entity purchases inventory or supplies (among other things) from vendors, who are selected by purchasing department personnel from specifications on an approved purchase requisition. A purchase order is sent to the vendor selected and, when the goods are received (and a receiving report prepared), a liability (an account payable) is recorded. The expenditure/disbursement cycle continues when the vendor's invoice arrives by fax, mail, e-mail, or *electronic data integration* (EDI) and is matched with the receiving report, the purchase requisition, and the purchase order. From these paper or computer image documents, a voucher is prepared and the documents are physically attached or linked by computer, forming a voucher package, which is the basis for making a cash payment to a vendor. When payment is made, the voucher package is canceled, for example by perforation on a paper voucher package or by notation on a computer screen.

Throughout the expenditure/disbursement cycle, journal entries are made for purchases, prepaid and accrued expenses, cash disbursements, adjustments, and account distributions. Paper or computer image documents affecting the expenditure/disbursement cycle include:

Figure 12-1: Scope of the Expenditure/Disbursement Cycle

Related Business Functions	Common Activities	Common Entries	Common Forms
• Resources (goods and services) are acquired from vendors (and employees) in exchange for obligations to pay. • Obligations to vendors (and employees) are paid.	• Purchasing • Receiving • Recording • Payment (including authorizing and preparing checks)	• Purchases • Account distribution • Prepaid and accrued expenses • Adjustments • Cash disbursements	• Purchase requisitions • Purchase orders • Receiving reports • Vendors' invoices • Vouchers

- **Purchase requisition.** A request from an employee or department supervisor requesting that goods be purchased.
- **Purchase order.** A request issued by the purchasing department to a vendor to purchase goods.
- **Receiving report.** Identifies information about goods received from a vendor.
- **Vendor's invoice.** Identifies goods purchased and represents formal notice of the amount and terms of payment (often called the *bill*).
- **Voucher package.** The purchase requisition, purchase order, receiving report, and vendor's invoice. (Includes a summarizing document, the *voucher*.)

As indicated in Chapter 10, organizational structure and control procedures vary from one entity to another, although the expenditure/disbursement cycle activities identified in Figure 12-1 are relatively common. Controls within the expenditure/disbursement cycle are explained below in the context of two functions common to the cycle:

- Purchasing (including ordering, receiving, and recording accounts payable), and
- Cash disbursements.

Personnel and payroll, also related to the expenditure/disbursement cycle, are discussed in Chapter 14.

Figure 12-2 flowcharts representative purchasing and cash disbursement activities. In turn, Figure 12-3, derived from Figure 12-2, lists purchasing and cash disbursement activities common to the expenditure/disbursement cycle. The following explains each major activity.

PURCHASING

Purchasing involves the acquisition of goods and services from vendors. *Goods* include tangible resources, such as inventory, supplies, and equipment, and *services* include nontangible resources, like advertising, repairs and maintenance, utilities, and insurance. Goods and services may be acquired for use by, or for the benefit of, any department within an entity. Regardless of what department acquires the goods or services, though, the purchase and subsequent payment are processed through the expenditure/disbursement cycle, since the cycle serves all departments, even those for example like shipping and billing which, as discussed in Chapter 10, serve the revenue/receipt cycle.

An employee of the department that requests the purchase prepares a *purchase requisition,* which is submitted to a supervisor for approval. Approved purchase requisitions are forwarded to Purchasing, where the request is reviewed, a vendor selected, and a *purchase order* prepared. A *purchase order* describes the goods or services requested, specifying price, quantity, shipping terms, and catalog numbers. Copies of *purchase orders* are sent by Purchasing to the vendor, to the requisitioning department, to Receiving, and to Accounts Payable, as depicted in Figure 12-2.

Goods ordered from vendors are delivered to the receiving department, where the goods are compared with the *purchase order* and a *receiving report* is prepared. Receiving Department personnel also maintain a *receiving log* cross-referenced to related *receiving reports.* A copy of the *receiving report* is forwarded to Purchasing and to Accounts Payable. Similar procedures are required for

Figure 12-2:   Expenditure/Disbursement Cycle: Purchases and Cash Disbursements

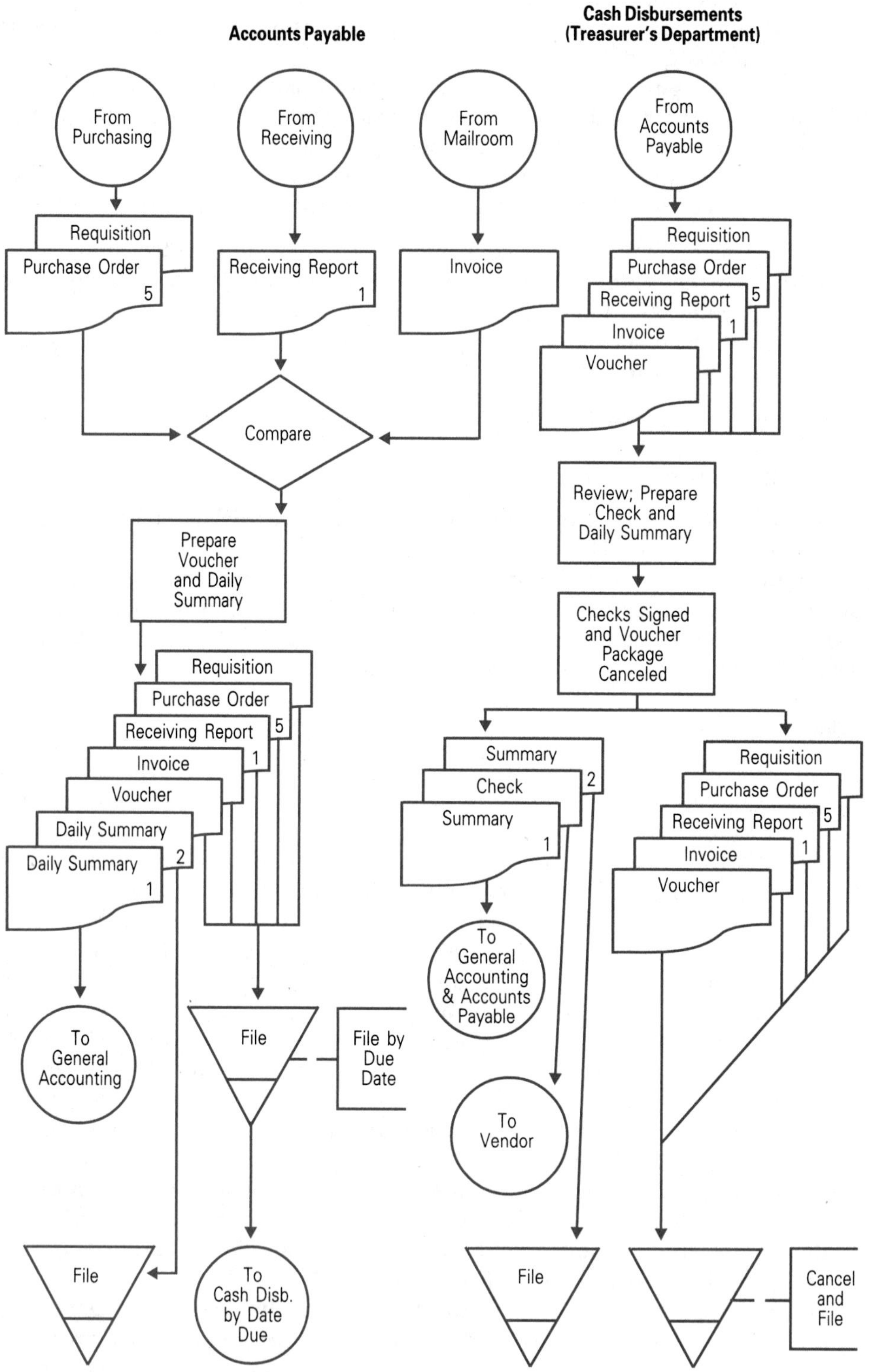

Figure 12-2:   *(continued)*

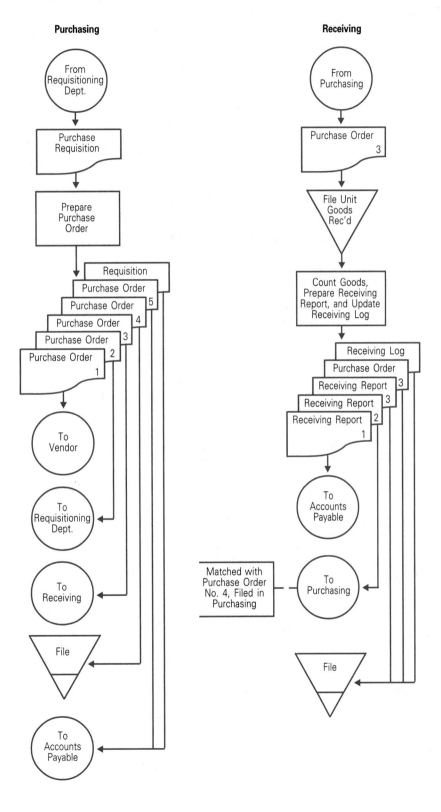

Figure 12-3: Summary of Purchasing and Cash Disbursement Activities

Purchasing
- Accept approved purchase requisitions from user departments.
- Prepare a purchase order, distribute copies, and retain a file copy.

Receiving
- File purchase orders until goods are received.
- Upon receipt of goods, count quantities and compare with the purchase order.
- Prepare a receiving report.
- Forward goods to Inventory Control.
- Forward copies of the receiving report to Accounts Payable and to Purchasing; retain a file copy of the receiving report, purchase order, and updated receiving log.

Accounts Payable
- Compare the purchase requisition, purchase order, receiving report, and vendor's invoice.
- Prepare a voucher and daily summary; assemble a voucher package.
- File the voucher packages by due date; forward each to Cash Disbursements (Treasurer's Department) on the date due.
- Forward the daily summary to General Accounting for recording; retain a file copy.

Cash Disbursements (Treasurer's Department)
- Review the voucher packages received from Accounts Payable on due dates.
- Prepare checks and a daily summary.
- Have checks signed by authorized signatories.
- Forward checks to vendors.
- Forward the daily summary to General Accounting and Accounts Payable for recording; retain a file copy of the summary.
- Cancel and file voucher packages.

the purchase of services—that is, memoranda are completed indicating that the services have been rendered.

Accounts Payable personnel file *receiving reports* with related *purchase requisitions* and *purchase orders* pending receipt of a vendor's *invoice*, the bill. Some companies use a voucher system for recording and controlling payables. Typically, a *voucher* is prepared by Accounts Payable (or Vouchers Payable) upon receipt of a vendor's *invoice*. A *voucher package* consisting of the *voucher*, vendor's *invoice, receiving report, purchase order,* and *purchase requisition* is filed in an unpaid voucher file by due date, and a copy of the daily summary of vouchers, prepared in Accounts Payable, is forwarded to General Accounting for recording in a voucher register. Column totals in the voucher register are posted (often instantaneously by computer) to general ledger accounts.

CASH DISBURSEMENTS

Cash disbursements should be authorized and executed by personnel who report to the Treasurer and are independent of purchasing and recording, as illustrated in Figure 12-2. *Voucher packages* in the unpaid voucher file are forwarded to the Treasurer's department, usually prior to the date payment is due. Personnel in the Treasurer's department review voucher packages for accuracy and authenticity before approving vouchers for payment and submitting vouchers for *check* printing. For vouchers involving new or unfamiliar vendors, special precautions should be taken to assure that the transaction is bona fide, since employees are more apt to perpetrate disbursement frauds with fictitious company names than with established vendors.

To minimize opportunities for unauthorized use, blank checks should be prenumbered, and all voided checks should be retained and accounted for. Unused checks should be controlled physically (preferably under lock and key), thereby limiting access to authorized personnel only. Once printed by computer, drawn checks (i.e., checks completed as to payee, date, amount, and facsimile signature) and approved supporting vouchers should be reviewed by an individual not otherwise involved in either processing or recording payables. Checks drawn in amounts above specified limits may require a second, manual signature. For example, it's common to have a facsimile signature printed on all checks processed by computer, but to require a second manual signature for checks drawn for an amount above, say, $25,000. In no circumstances should checks be signed "blank" (without payee, date, and amount) or drawn to "Cash" (bearer paper that can be cashed by anyone).

Signed checks should be mailed directly to the payee without intervention by employees responsible for approving, recording, or processing the transaction. Paid voucher packages should be canceled immediately—for example, some small entities cancel voucher packages in the presence of check signers. Cancellation prevents duplicate payments and is often accomplished by perforating the voucher package or by notation on a computer screen. Canceled voucher packages, with check numbers entered on the vouchers, should be filed. A daily summary of all remittances should be prepared and forwarded to Accounts Payable for posting to the subsidiary payables ledger and to General Accounting for recording in the voucher register. In a voucher system, the voucher register replaces the cash disbursements journal.

Payments are sometimes made in advance of actually receiving the goods or services. Examples include deposits with vendors for goods ordered and prepayments for insurance, rent, and advertising. Advance payments should be made only when authorized and only with supporting documents. Prepayments should be carefully reviewed by accounting personnel to determine the appropriate account classification. At the end of an accounting period, all advance payments should be reviewed by designated personnel and adjusting journal entries made to reflect expenses in the proper period.

INTERNAL CONTROL OBJECTIVES AND POTENTIAL ERRORS OR FRAUDS

The following discussion, summarized in Figure 12-4, identifies control objectives, describes examples of errors or frauds that may arise if an objective is not achieved, and offers examples of control procedures that management may implement to prevent or detect the errors or frauds in the expenditure/disbursement cycle. The control objectives relate generally to transaction authorization, execution, and recording and restricting employee access to assets.

Transaction Authorization

Effective control over an entity's purchasing activities requires that purchases be made only in accordance with general or specific authorization. All purchases should be initiated by user departments and approved by authorized

Figure 12-4: Purchasing and Cash Disbursements: Control Objectives, Potential Errors or Frauds, and Control Procedures

Control Objective	Types of Errors or Frauds That Could Occur if Objective Is Not Met	Control Procedures Designed to Prevent or Detect Errors or Frauds
Transaction Authorization		
• Vendors should be approved prior to purchasing goods.	Purchase could be made from unauthorized vendors, potentially resulting in purchasing from related parties without senior management's knowledge or from foreign vendors in violation of import quotas.	Prepare lists of authorized vendors. Establish criteria for adding to, changing, or deleting from the vendor list.
• Types, quantities, terms, and prices should be approved for all products and services.	Unnecessary goods may be ordered, potentially resulting in write-downs of unusable or unsalable inventory. Goods could be purchased at noncompetitive prices or unfavorable terms, resulting in reduced earnings.	Maintain updated guidelines for purchase transactions (e.g., competitive bids, specific authorization for all purchases exceeding minimum dollar amounts). Establish procedures for reviewing and approving purchase prices and terms prior to purchase.
Transaction Execution		
• Received goods should be counted and inspected for quality.	Damaged or unordered goods could be accepted, potentially creating delays in receiving the goods desired.	Establish procedures for inspecting and counting goods received before releasing the carrier.
• All cash disbursements for goods and services should be based on a bona fide liability.	Cash could be disbursed to unauthorized parties, for goods or services not received, or as a duplicate payment.	Prenumber and control vouchers and checks. Cancel voucher packages immediately upon payment. Require a manual signature for all checks over a prespecified amount.

Figure 12-4: *(continued)*

Control Objective	Types of Errors or Frauds That Could Occur if Objective Is Not Met	Control Procedures Designed to Prevent or Detect Errors or Frauds
Recording		
• All goods and services received should be accurately and promptly reported.	Goods may be received but not recorded, potentially resulting in understated inventory and liabilities.	Prenumber receiving reports, and subsequently review for prompt recording.
• Purchases and cash disbursement transactions should be recorded properly and in the proper accounting period.	Account balances may be inaccurate, potentially resulting in misstated financial statements.	Total input documents (e.g., number of documents, dollar amounts) and reconcile journals and ledgers. Establish processing and recording procedures.
• Purchase and cash disbursement transactions should be posted accurately to individual vendor accounts.	Summaries of detailed records may not agree with control accounts. Transactions may be posted to improper vendor accounts, potentially resulting in improper payments.	Establish validation procedures to verify postings (e.g., check digits). Batch and reconcile input totals to processed and output totals. Promptly investigate correspondence from vendors (e.g., collection notices).
Restricting Access to Assets		
• Access to purchasing and cash disbursement records and to forms and documents should be restricted to personnel authorized by management.	Records, forms, or documents may be misused by unauthorized personnel, potentially resulting in misstated payables or diversion of assets for personal use.	Prenumber and establish physical controls over unused forms and documents. Segregate responsibility for authorization, execution, and recording functions. Maintain listings and samples of authorized signatories.

supervisors. Goods or services should not be ordered in the absence of authorized purchase requisitions. Required authorization procedures vary with the cost or nature of the goods or services requested, but should be specified in writing.

Vendors should be approved by management before Purchasing executes an order. For example, many companies prepare lists of authorized vendors and establish criteria for adding to, changing, or deleting from the list. Otherwise, purchases could be made from vendors whose product quality is repeatedly inferior, from related parties without management's knowledge, or from foreign vendors in violation of regulated import quotas.

In addition to authorizing vendor lists, management should also establish policies for the types, quantities, payment terms, and prices of goods and services purchased. Failure to establish the types of goods and services authorized for purchase could result in reduced earnings caused by write-downs of unusable or unsalable inventory, or unnecessary purchases made for the benefit of employees or related parties. In turn, authorizing quantities, payment terms, and prices protects against excessive warehousing costs for unnecessary inventory, unfavorable payment terms, and noncompetitive prices. As a result, management should maintain current price lists and actively seek suppliers whose goods and services optimize price and quality. Where applicable, competitive bids or formal price quotations should be obtained from suppliers, particularly for purchases involving high-priced items, large quantities, or infrequently ordered items.

Transaction Execution

Goods should be inspected for quality when received, and quantities should be verified by physical count and compared with *purchase orders*. If not inspected, counted, and compared, a company could experience significant production delays while returning damaged or unordered goods and awaiting delivery of the goods ordered. To avoid delays, management should require that receiving personnel inspect and count all received goods before releasing the carrier.

After goods or services are received, a liability is incurred and, in turn, cash is disbursed. Management should institute policies to assure that cash is disbursed only for bona fide liabilities, thereby protecting against disbursements for goods not received, payment to unauthorized parties, and duplicate payments. To control against improper disbursements, management could prenumber and control vouchers and checks, require a second manual signature for checks exceeding prespecified amounts, and cancel paid *voucher packages* immediately upon payment.

Recording

After purchase transactions are executed, all goods and services received should be reported promptly to Accounts Payable, indicating title has passed, and to Purchasing, indicating ordered goods have been received. Otherwise, goods and services may be received and used, but not recorded, thereby understating inventory and liabilities. Many companies control the receipt of goods and services by prenumbering receiving reports, reviewing for prompt recording, and maintaining a *receiving log* that lists sequentially each *receiving report* processed.

To protect against inaccurate account balances and therefore against misstated financial statements, management should institute policies to assure that all purchases and cash disbursements are recorded properly and in the proper period. Management could control the recording function by preparing input totals, by reconciling journals and subsidiary ledgers, and by establishing procedures for processing and recording.

However, proper recording within general ledger control accounts does not necessarily mean that transactions are posted properly to individual vendor subsidiary accounts, since summaries of detailed records may not agree with control accounts. To control against inaccurate vendor accounts and improper payments, management could establish validation procedures to verify postings, and reconcile input totals to processed and output totals. In addition, authorized personnel should investigate correspondence from vendors, particularly collection notices.

Access to Assets

Management should establish procedures to safeguard assets by restricting access to purchasing and to cash disbursement records and forms. Otherwise, records or forms may be misused by unauthorized personnel, potentially resulting in misstated payables or diversion of cash or other assets for personal use. Many companies control access to purchasing and cash disbursements by prenumbering and controlling forms and documents, maintaining lists and samples of authorized signatories, and segregating responsibility for authorizing, executing, and recording.

ASSURANCE AND CONSULTING SERVICES

Private companies purchase goods and services within the boundaries of criteria set by management, and are under no obligation to reveal purchasing patterns publicly. In contrast, state and local governmental units purchase goods and services under the constraint of public scrutiny. Governmental units such as cities, housing authorities, port authorities, and school boards are bound by procurement laws imposed, for example, by local laws, by taxpayer referendum, or by oversight authorities such as a city council. For example, many governmental units require that purchases over a minimum dollar amount, say $10,000, be opened to competitive bids (if not public hearings) and that the sealed bids be opened at a preannounced public forum. Over the years, governmental units have often engaged public accounting firms to provide either assurance or attestation services that report on management's compliance with local procurement laws. For example, following alleged extortion charges against a New England mayor in the awarding of city contracts, the city council engaged the Boston office of a Big Six public accounting firm to report on management's compliance with city procurement laws for publicly funded construction contracts. As discussed and illustrated in Chapter 18, compliance with contractual agreements, among them government regulations, is a common attestation service guided in practice by *SAS No. 62,* "Special Reports."

In practice, purchase and payables consulting services are rather common. Two examples: First, Coopers & Lybrand entered into an alliance with Bank of

America to promote the bank's corporate MasterCard and to provide purchase consulting services to the bank's corporate card users.[1] Targeted to Bank of America corporate users that have revenues exceeding $75 million and small purchases (typically under $350) exceeding $10 million annually, Coopers & Lybrand evaluates the small purchase practices of the bank's corporate card users to identify potential consulting clients in need of substantially more cost-effective purchasing systems. Second, Andersen Worldwide reached an agreement with the national headquarters of Camp Fire Boys & Girls to surrender the financial statement audit in order instead to provide the company with full-time, on-site accounting and information systems services, including payables processing, network and personal computer support, and financial reporting.[2] Camp Fire's national executive director reported that although Arthur Andersen's audit fee had been less that $50,000 annually, fees for the outsourcing arrangement would total $300,000 to $400,000 annually.

Similar to Camp Fire's arrangement with Arthur Andersen, many companies have outsourced work previously done internally. Outsourcing is not at all new. For example, companies first outsourced payroll to Automated Data Processing, Inc. in the 1950s and colleges began to outsource cafeteria management to Aramark Corporation in the 1960s. However, outsourcing services are far more common today. For example, a poll in the mid-1990s reported that 86 percent of some well-recognized companies like American Airlines, DuPont, Exxon, Honda, and IBM outsource, and that the most frequently outsourced activities were manufacturing, transportation/distribution/warehousing, temporary services, travel, and forms management.[3] In fact, among the Big Three U.S. auto makers, General Motors outsources 30 percent of vehicle production, Ford outsources 50 percent, and Chrysler, 70 percent. The outsourcing of technology and information processing has been a boom industry, particularly for niche consultants and public accounting firms, although the benefits accruing to the purchasers of outsourced services can be clouded by some costly downsides over time, among them long-term information services contracts that, owing to cheaper technology prices, are no longer competitive.

CONSIDERING INTERNAL CONTROL IN A FINANCIAL STATEMENT AUDIT

As introduced in Chapter 7 and illustrated for the revenue/receipt cycle in Chapter 10, considering internal control involves obtaining an understanding of the system, performing tests of controls, and assessing control risk. The following addresses an auditor's consideration of internal control within the expenditure/disbursement cycle, focusing on purchasing, receiving, cash disbursements, and recording.

OBTAIN AN UNDERSTANDING

Obtaining an understanding of internal control is a means to an end—the end being an audit plan—that addresses the questions: how is the system supposed

1   "C&L, Bank of America Ally," *Public Accounting Report* (February 29, 1996), p. 3.
2   "In with Outsourcing, Out with Audit: AA/KC Chooses Bigger Payoff, Deeper Client Relationship," *Public Accounting Report* (April 15, 1996), p. 2.
3   "Has Outsourcing Gone Too Far?" *Business Week* (April 1, 1996), pp. 26-28.

to work, and what control procedures has management implemented to assure that the system does indeed work? An auditor obtains an understanding of internal control in four steps:

1. Performing a *preliminary review,*
2. *Documenting* the system,
3. Performing a *transaction walk-through,* and
4. Determining whether existing control procedures are potentially reliable in assessing *control risk* below the maximum.

Preliminary Review

During preliminary review, an auditor interviews client personnel—for example, the purchasing manager, the receiving clerk, and the accounts payable department manager—and reviews accounting procedures manuals to develop a general understanding of the client's control environment, accounting system (for example, the flow of purchase and payment transactions), and how the entity identifies, captures, communicates, and monitors external and internal information in a form and time frame that enables employees to discharge their assigned responsibilities. The preliminary review determines whether investing additional audit effort—for example, documenting and performing tests of controls—is likely to support a decision to assess control risk below the maximum, thereby allowing the auditor to assess detection risk above the minimum and therefore to restrict the extent of substantive tests of the very account balances that are processed through the expenditure/disbursement cycle: accounts payable, prepaid expenses, and accrued liabilities. If the preliminary review reveals that existing controls are inadequate to justify assessing control risk below the maximum, then the auditor's documentation of the system is limited simply to a memorandum in the working papers that describes the reasons for not continuing to consider internal control.

System Documentation

A company's expenditure/disbursement cycle can be documented with flowcharts, questionnaires, and/or narratives. For example, Figure 12-2, discussed earlier, illustrates a flowchart for purchases and cash disbursements. In turn, Figure 12-5 illustrates a questionnaire for purchasing, receiving, cash disbursements, and recording. As in Chapter 10, the questionnaire is designed to elicit a *No* response when a potential deficiency is apparent. That is, a *No* response would indicate a commonly used control is not used and therefore that, lacking compensating controls, a significant deficiency might exist. Alternatively, or in conjunction with a flowchart and/or questionnaire, an auditor could describe the system—or segments of the system—in a written narrative. For example, a narrative could be used to describe the distribution of documents and reports outside of the dominant areas of concern—that is, outside of purchasing, receiving, accounts payable, and cash disbursements.

Transaction Walk-Through

To confirm his or her understanding of the system flowcharted in Figure 12-2, the auditor could select a canceled voucher package, and compare the *purchase requisition, purchase order, receiving report,* and *invoice* for compliance with company policies and with documents filed in Purchasing, Receiving, and Accounts Payable. System documentation—for example, the

Figure 12-5: Questionnaire: Purchases and Cash Disbursements

Question	Answer: Yes, No, or N/A	Remarks

PURCHASING:

1. Are policies and procedures for reviewing and processing purchase requisitions clearly defined?
2. Are prenumbered purchase orders prepared for all approved purchase requisitions?
3. Are competitive bids or price quotations obtained for purchased goods and services?
4. Are price lists maintained for repetitive transactions that do not require competitive bids or price quotations?
5. Are purchase transactions reviewed periodically by personnel independent of Purchasing?
6. Are copies of purchase orders forwarded to the requisitioning department and to Receiving and Accounts Payable?
7. Are lists of previously authorized vendors maintained by Purchasing?

RECEIVING:

1. Are prenumbered receiving reports prepared for all goods received?
2. Is a receiving log maintained for all receiving reports processed?
3. Are all received goods inspected, counted, and compared with copies of purchase orders?
4. Are receiving personnel independent of purchasing, accounts payable, and cash disbursement?

CASH DISBURSEMENTS AND RECORDING:

1. Are voucher packages reviewed before being approved for payment?
2. Are steps taken to assure that unfamiliar payees (vendors) are bona fide?

Figure 12-5: *(continued)*

Question	Answer: Yes, No, or N/A	Remarks
3. Are voucher packages and checks reviewed by signatories before they sign checks (or before submitting vouchers for check preparation)?		
4. Are voucher packages canceled when, or immediately after, checks are signed?		
5. Are signed checks delivered directly to the mail room without intervention by other personnel?		
6. Are cash disbursements personnel (e.g., Treasurer's Department) independent of Purchasing, Receiving, and Accounts Payable?		
7. Is account distribution indicated on the purchase requisition by the requisitioning department?		
8. Are voucher packages prepared from requisitions and purchase orders received from Purchasing, from receiving reports received from Receiving, and from invoices received from the mail room?		
9. Are daily summaries of processed vouchers forwarded by Accounts Payable to General Accounting for summary entries?		

flowchart—would be revised if the transaction walk-through reveals that the auditor's understanding of internal control is inaccurate.

Identification of Control Procedures

Following system documentation, and assuming that controls are potentially reliable in assessing control risk below the maximum, an auditor continues as follows:

- Identify the system's *control objectives*. The first column of Figure 12-4 identifies control objectives for purchases and cash disbursements transactions.
- Consider the *potential errors or frauds* that might result if specific control objectives are not met. The second column of Figure 12-4 identifies examples of potential errors or frauds.
- Determine what *control procedures* management uses to prevent or detect potentially material errors or frauds. The third column of Figure 12-4 identifies examples of potential controls.
- Design *tests of controls*.

Those control procedures relevant to management's financial statement assertions about Accounts Payable, Prepaid Expenses, and Accrued Liabilities are subjected to tests of controls, described next.

TESTS OF CONTROLS: PURCHASING AND CASH DISBURSEMENTS

In tests of controls over high-volume transactions like purchases and cash disbursements, an auditor's strategy is to expend significant audit effort performing tests of controls, since evidence supporting the assessment of control risk below the maximum would justify restricting substantive tests of account balances at year end. Tests for the purchasing, receiving, and cash disbursement system flowcharted in Figure 12-2 are presented in the following sections. Later in the chapter, a case illustrates how an auditor can use sampling to accomplish tests of controls in the expenditure/disbursement cycle.

Purchasing

Given the significant resources often spent on goods and services, purchases made at anything other than competitive and authorized prices can spell the difference between successful and unsuccessful enterprises. Tests of controls of an entity's purchasing activities focus on whether all purchases are properly authorized. Representative tests follow.

Tests of Controls: Purchasing

1. Randomly select a sample of paid voucher packages.
   a. Review each voucher package for cancellation (e.g., perforation).
   b. Review documents in each sampled voucher package for authorization.
   c. Compare details on *purchase requisitions, purchase orders, receiving reports, vendors' invoices* and *vouchers;* and verify mathematical accuracy.
2. For each sampled voucher package, obtain a copy of the related *purchase order* and *requisition* from Purchasing Department files.
   a. Compare *purchase orders* in voucher packages with copies of *purchase orders* in Purchasing Department files.
   b. Trace prices on *purchase orders* to competitive bids, formal price quotations, or other pricing sources.
   c. Examine periodic reports by personnel independent of the purchasing department about prices and vendor selection practices.

A paid voucher package is the primary source from which the tests of purchasing are performed. In Step 1a, the auditor tests whether paid voucher packages are canceled, thereby addressing whether duplicate payments could occur. However, the test does not assure that cancellation occurred simultaneously with (or immediately after) payment—only direct observation by the auditor could assess whether the time span between payment and cancellation is reasonable.

Step 1b addresses transaction authorization and requires that the auditor examine signatures or initials on the: (1) *purchase order*, indicating an authorized transaction, (2) *receiving report*, indicating responsibility for incoming goods, and (3) *voucher*, indicating a cash payment was authorized. In Step 1c, the auditor tests whether all documents agree and, therefore, that goods were received and paid for at the price quoted and in the quantity ordered.

In Step 2a, the auditor compares sampled voucher packages with copies of *purchase orders* and *requisitions* filed in the purchasing department, as shown in Figure 12-2. Here, the intent is to determine if all paid *vouchers* resulted from authorized purchases. Steps 2b and 2c, in contrast, address whether the prices paid are competitive. That is, evidence of competitive bids or price quotations would suggest management is conscientiously attempting to safeguard assets—in particular, cash—by seeking the best prices available.

Receiving

The receipt of goods is the first step in readying inventory for conversion and in recognizing a liability. Since little can be done after the fact to determine if receiving procedures are applied appropriately, an auditor could consider visiting the receiving department on a surprise basis to determine whether received goods are conscientiously counted and compared with *purchase orders*. Some additional tests follow.

Tests of Controls: Receiving

For each sampled voucher package, obtain the related copy of the *receiving report* from Receiving Department files.

1. Compare *receiving reports* in voucher packages with copies of *receiving reports* in Receiving Department files.
2. Review *receiving reports* for evidence that received goods have been inspected, counted, and compared with *packing slips* and *purchase orders*.
3. Trace *receiving reports* to entries in the *receiving log*.

In addition to observing the receiving department on a surprise basis, an auditor can design tests that address whether goods received per the voucher packages used to test purchasing controls (above) agree with Receiving Department files, such as the copy of the *receiving report* filed in Receiving and the *receiving log* (a chronological listing of goods received). In Step 1, the auditor compares the *receiving report* in Accounts Payable with the copy filed in Receiving and tests whether the copy used by Accounts Payable to prepare a *voucher* is in error. Step 2 addresses the accuracy of quantities received by examining evidence that received goods are inspected, counted, and agreed with a *packing slip*, the vendor's list of goods shipped, which is normally found on or within a shipped carton. In Step 3, the auditor tests further for discrepancies in reported quantities by comparing *receiving reports* to entries in the company's *receiving log*.

Cash Disbursement and Recording

Cash payment activities are particularly susceptible to frauds, because cash is liquid and only an unauthorized payee and forged endorsement are necessary to misappropriate funds. An auditor's tests of controls over payments to vendors focus on approvals for payment, proper journal entries and, to the extent possible, the authenticity of signatures.

The recording function for purchases and cash disbursements encompasses entries to Accounts Payable, requiring that an auditor determine whether details recorded within a voucher register are recorded in the proper vendor accounts and agree in total with the general ledger. Representative tests follow.

Tests of Controls: Cash Disbursement and Recording

For each sampled voucher package, obtain the canceled check.

1. Examine canceled checks for signatures and endorsements.
2. Compare details of the voucher package with the canceled check: check number, date, payee, and amount.
3. Trace voucher packages and canceled checks to postings in the accounts payable subsidiary ledger and to entries in the voucher register.
   a. Review entries in the voucher register for appropriate account distribution (classification).
   b. Verify the mathematical accuracy of the voucher register for selected periods and trace totals to entries in the general ledger.
   c. Scan the voucher register for unusual items (e.g., unfamiliar vendor names) and unusually large amounts, and investigate any items identified.

The tests discussed thus far addressed whether purchases are authorized, executed, and recorded properly. But they ignore the possibility that authorized transactions might be executed with unauthorized or fictitious vendors. Thus, the tests for cash disbursement and recording focus on canceled checks, the primary evidence that vendors were paid and bona fide.

In Step 1, the auditor examines the signatures and endorsements on canceled checks, looking specifically for unusual items. For example, a manually signed check would be unusual for a company that normally processes disbursements by computer. On the one hand, the check might have been for an amount exceeding limits authorized, thereby legitimately requiring manual signatures. On the other hand, the manual signature might indicate a fraud.

Step 2 compares details of the canceled check with the related voucher package, thereby assuring that the amount paid was the amount owed. In Step 3, the auditor traces the voucher package to entries in Accounts Payable and in the voucher register. The entries are tested for appropriate account distribution, such as expense classification for financial reporting and tax purposes, and the voucher register is tested for mathematical accuracy and unusual items.

ASSESS CONTROL RISK

To complete the consideration of internal control within the expenditure/ disbursement cycle, an auditor reviews system documentation and the results of tests of controls and determines whether existing controls can be relied on to:

1. Assess control risk below the maximum,
2. Assess detection risk above the minimum, and, therefore
3. Restrict substantive tests.

The assessment of control risk is made for the financial statement assertions (Chapter 6) embodied within the expenditure/disbursement cycle's related account balances (Accounts Payable, Prepaid Expenses, and Accrued Liabilities), transaction classes (purchases and cash disbursements), and financial statement disclosures. In general, the assessment is based on the types of errors or frauds that could occur, necessary control procedures that should prevent the errors or frauds, whether the necessary procedures exist and are followed, and any deficiencies in internal control.

To illustrate, consider in Figure 12-4 (first column) the first objective for transaction authorization:

Objective:
Vendors should be approved prior to purchasing goods,

and the first corresponding control procedure (third column) for that objective:

Control procedure:
Prepare lists of authorized vendors.

Step 3c of the tests of controls for Cash Disbursement and Recording tests whether the control procedure for approving vendors in Figure 12-4 is operating effectively:

Test of control:
Scan the voucher register for unusual items (e.g., unfamiliar vendor names) and unusually large amounts, and investigate any items identified.

Assume the auditor examines the voucher register for unfamiliar vendors and large amounts and discovers that an intolerable number of purchase transactions are made with unauthorized vendors. In this case, the auditor would conclude that control risk for the assertion *obligations* is at the maximum, because accounts payable may include liabilities for purchases not rightfully owed by the entity. For example, an employee who commits an employer's resources to purchase goods for his or her personal benefit is a liability of the employee, not the entity. Substantive tests applicable to the expenditure/disbursement cycle in general and to Accounts Payable in particular are introduced in Chapter 13.

COMPUTER AUDITING AND SAMPLING APPLIED TO TESTS OF CONTROLS IN THE EXPENDITURE/DISBURSEMENT CYCLE

To illustrate the material introduced in this chapter and to integrate with material presented on computer information systems (Chapter 7) and audit sampling (Chapter 8), assume a continuing audit engagement for the Gorham Corporation, a medium-size manufacturer of paper products, whose fiscal year ends June 30. The specific objective in this case is to determine whether Gorham's controls over cash disbursements are effective.

COMPUTER SYSTEM: ACCOUNTS PAYABLE, DATA ENTRY, AND COMPUTER PROCESSING

For the past two years, Gorham has used the accounts payable, data entry, and computer processing system flowcharted in Figure 12-6. Data entry and processing are accomplished by computer. The vouchers and batched totals are entered at workstations connected by a local area network (LAN). Consistent with the cash disbursements functions depicted in Figure 12-2, input data are sorted and edited, checks and the voucher register are printed, and all processed files are updated.

The following sections discuss the review of the system, tests of controls, and control risk for Gorham Corporation's payables and disbursements.

Figure 12-6: Gorham Corporation: Flowchart of Accounts Payable, Data Entry, and Computer Processing

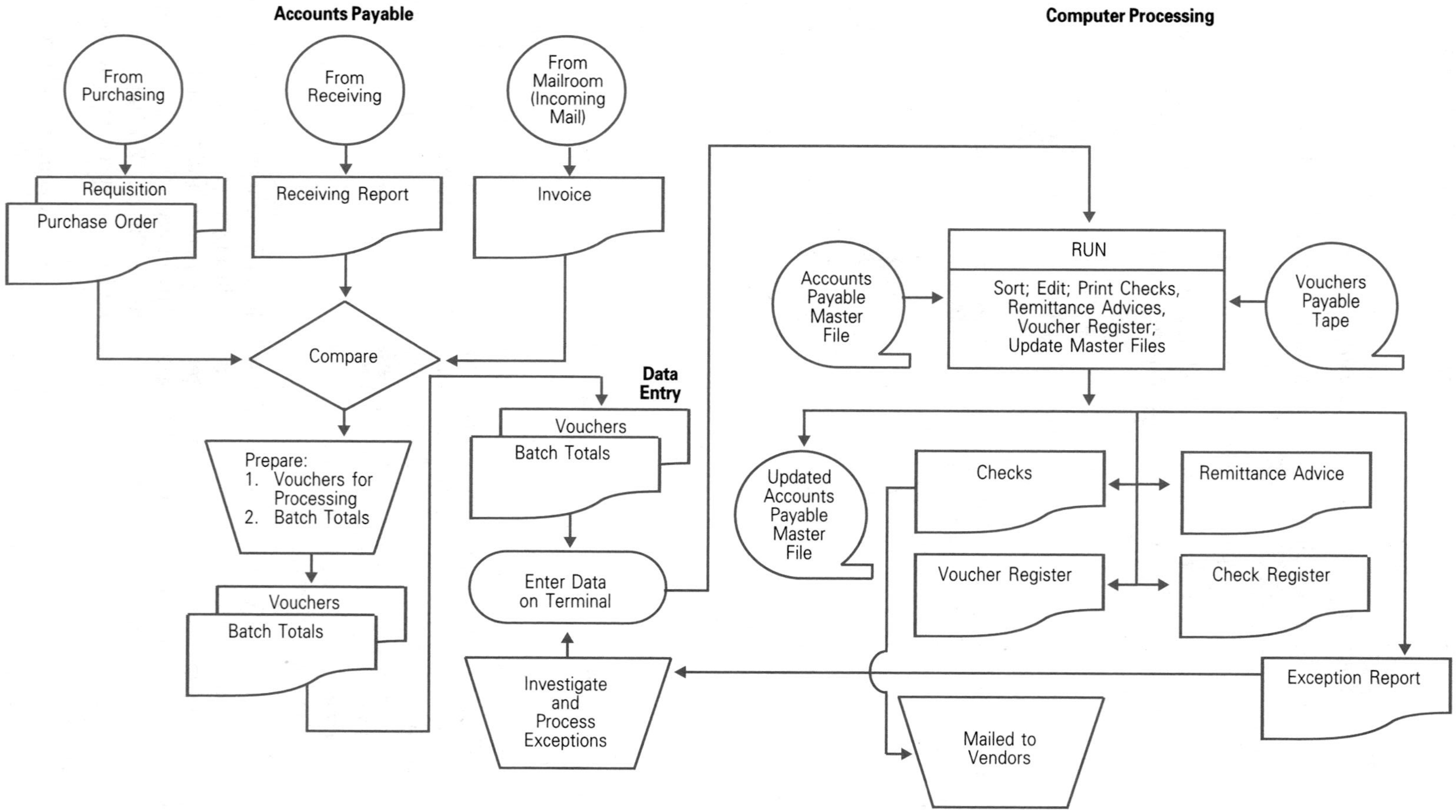

UNDERSTANDING THE SYSTEM

The auditor decides to document the system with both a flowchart and a questionnaire. The flowchart appears in Figure 12-6, and a transaction walk-through indicates that the flowchart is accurate. The questionnaire consists of the nine disbursement and recording questions listed in Figure 12-5. Questions 1, 3, 5, 6, 8, and 9 result in *Yes* responses, but Questions 2, 4, and 7 receive *No* responses, indicating the following deficiencies:

- No procedures exist to assure that unfamiliar payees are bona fide.
- Voucher packages are not canceled when, or immediately after, checks are signed.
- Account distribution is not indicated on the *purchase requisition* by the requisitioning department.

Although significant, the auditor believes no one or combination of these deficiencies is sufficient to render the system wholly ineffective. In this case, the auditor reaches this conclusion for three reasons. First, even though no steps are taken to assure that unfamiliar payees are bona fide, inspection of the check register indicates that vendors unfamiliar to the auditor accounted for less than one percent of the cash payments during the year. Thus, payments to unfamiliar vendors are immaterial and therefore of little audit consequence. Second, although voucher packages are not canceled simultaneously when (or immediately after) checks are signed, inquiries indicate they are canceled by Accounts Payable personnel at the end of the day that the checks are prepared. To assure that cancellation does in fact occur at day's end, the auditor visits Accounts Payable unannounced at the end of two successive business days, observes the cancellation process, and notes no discrepancies or deficiencies. Because checks are prepared only once per day and cancellation occurs on the same day, the auditor concludes that the likelihood of duplicate payment is remote. Third, account distribution is not indicated by the requisitioning department, but it is indicated by the accounts payable department in consultation with the requisitioning department, which the auditor believes is a sufficient compensating control.

TESTS OF CONTROLS

Because all checks are prepared by computer and payables are processed manually, the auditor elects the following strategy for testing controls. Parallel simulation, which requires that the auditor prepare software to process client-prepared input under controlled conditions (Chapter 7), will be used to test the effectiveness of controls over data entry and computer processing. To accomplish parallel simulation, the auditor prepares software that focuses on code verification and selected data conversion controls: batch totals, character validity, limit tests, and sequence tests. All of these tests relate to input controls, which are of particular concern in this case because data entry is accomplished on remote workstations (see Figure 12-6), which are susceptible to frauds if unauthorized personnel gain access to user identification numbers. Assume that parallel simulation is accomplished on Gorham's computer and that no significant exceptions are found.

Given the deficiencies noted per the questionnaire, three types of errors or frauds could occur. The first two appear at the fourth objective of Figure 12-4 (middle column), and the third appears at the sixth objective:

Potential Errors or Frauds:
- *Cash may be disbursed to unauthorized parties, potentially resulting in fraudulent payments.*
- *Duplicate payments could be made, potentially resulting in misspent cash.*
- *General ledger account balances could be inaccurate, potentially resulting in misstated financial statements.*

After considering the above potential errors or frauds and other evidence gathered during interim tests, the auditor drafts the following tests for cash disbursements and recording, all of which were explained earlier in the chapter.

Step	Tests of Controls
	For each sampled voucher package, obtain the canceled check.
1.	Examine canceled checks for appropriate signatures and endorsements.
2.	Compare details of the voucher package with the canceled check: check number, date, payee, and amount.
3.	Trace voucher packages and canceled checks to postings in the accounts payable subsidiary ledger and to entries in the voucher register.
	a. Review entries in the voucher register for appropriate distribution (classification).
	b. Verify the accuracy of the voucher register (foot and cross-foot) for selected periods, and trace totals to entries in the general ledger.
	c. Scan the voucher register for unusual items (e.g., unfamiliar vendor names) and unusually large amounts, and investigate any items identified.

As discussed in Chapter 8, the auditor next determines which, if any, of the tests can be accomplished by sampling and whether to use statistical or nonstatistical sampling. For Gorham Corporation's cash disbursements system, Steps 1, 2, and 3a can be accomplished using sampling. Further, the auditor decides to use statistical sampling, because the system processes very large numbers of checks (i.e., large population sizes). Because interim tests of controls in prior years revealed very few errors, the auditor selects sequential (stop-or-go) sampling as the statistical sampling plan. The results of the sequential sampling plan are summarized in Figure 12-7, a sequential sampling worksheet, and Figure 12-8, an analysis of deviations.

Two observations about Figure 12-7 are noteworthy. First, note that for Attribute 2 the achieved probability, 80.54 percent, is *less* than desired reliability, 95.0 percent, suggesting the auditor should increase sample size—that is, the auditor should go on with the sequential sampling plan for Attribute 2. However, note that in the explanation in Figure 12-7 and the analysis of deviations in Figure 12-8, the deviation resulted from an oversight by the payee's employees. As a result, the auditor does not believe that Gorham's failure to investigate the matter is sufficiently compelling to warrant increasing sample size. Second, even though Attribute 5 resulted in one deviation, the achieved probability from Figure 8-11 (Chapter 8), 91.73 percent, exceeds desired reliability, 90.0 percent. As a result, the auditor does not need to increase sample size. Steps 3b and 3c are performed by the auditor, and no exceptions are noted.

CONTROL RISK

The auditor's assessment of control risk for Gorham Corporation's controls over cash disbursements would be based on the following quantitative and qualitative factors:

Figure 12-7: Sampling Worksheet—Cash Disbursements

A10
RJW 5/12/99

Gorham Corporation
Sampling Worksheet—Cash Disbursements
June 30, 1999

Attribute	Desired Reliability	Tolerable Rate	Sample Size*	Number of Deviations	Achieved Probability*
1. Signatures on checks are appropriate	.98	.04	100	0	98.31
2. Endorsements on checks are appropriate	.95	.03	100	1†	80.54
3. Details of voucher pkg. agree with canceled check	.95	.05	70	0	97.24
4. Details of voucher tie to entries	.95	.05	70	0	97.24
5. Account distribution is appropriate	.90	.08	50	1††	91.73

* Table 8-5
† As noted at A11, failure to endorse was an oversight by Elston employees. Therefore, there is no need to increase sample size.
†† See analysis of occurrence at A11.

Conclusion

Based upon procedures performed, the achieved probability exceeds desired reliability for 4 of 5 attributes, and the one deviation for Attribute no. 2 resulted from a vendor's oversight.

Figure 12-8:   Analysis of Deviations—Cash Disbursements

A11
RJW 5/12/99

Gorham Corporation
Analysis of Deviations—Cash Disbursements
June 30, 1999

Attribute	Number of Deviations	Nature of Deviations	Effect on Substantive Detailed Testing
2	1	Ck. no. 3267, $5,320, Elston Corp. Check was accepted for deposit by Elston's bank, but not endorsed.	No add'l audit work is necessary because of alternate procedures (i.e., review of Dun & Bradstreet reports; telephone conversation with Elston Corp. officials indicate failure to endorse was an oversight by Elston employees).
5	1	Ck. no. 9861, $2,319, Davis Co. Purchase was charged to Travel & Entertainment Expense rather than Advertising Expense.	No add'l audit work is necessary because: (1) achieved probability (91.73) exceeds desired reliability (.90) and (2) the error does not affect income, and neither expense affects overhead in inventory. (The client corrected the error.)

- No exceptions were noted when parallel simulation was run with actual client data.
- Achieved reliability exceeded desired reliability for four of five attributes tested, and for one attribute, the deviation observed was: (1) the result of a vendor's oversight and (2) not deemed sufficiently compelling to warrant additional testing.
- The questionnaire revealed three control deficiencies.

In this case, the auditor's decision would probably be to assess control risk below the maximum for assertions related to controls over cash disbursements and recording, because parallel simulation and audit sampling indicate that the three deficiencies are not likely to produce aggregate error in excess of tolerable error.

SUMMARY

The expenditure/disbursement cycle encompasses the acquisition of resources from vendors (and employees: Chapter 14) and subsequent payments for resources acquired. Common vendor-related activities include purchasing, receiving, recording, and cash payment. Documents evidencing appropriate transaction authorization and execution typically include *purchase requisitions, purchase orders, receiving reports, vendors' invoices,* and *vouchers.* Together these documents form a voucher package that serves as a basis for making payments to vendors.

Cash disbursements should be authorized and executed by personnel independent of the recording function, and access to unused checks and check preparation should be limited to authorized personnel. Tests of controls of an entity's purchasing activities focus on whether purchases and related disbursements are properly authorized, executed, and recorded. Substantive tests of Accounts Payable, Prepaid Expenses, and Accrued Liabilities, three accounts that bear on the expenditure/disbursement cycle, are introduced next, in Chapter 13.

KEY TERMS

Expenditure/disbursement cycle 439	Receiving report 441
Purchase requisition 441	Vendor's invoice 441
Purchase order 441	Voucher package 441

REFERENCES

Professional Standards

AICPA. *Codification of Statements on Auditing Standards.* New York: AICPA.

Books

Committee of Sponsoring Organizations of the Treadway Commission (COSO). *Internal Control-Integrated Framework* Executive Summary. New York: COSO, 1992.

Committee of Sponsoring Organizations of the Treadway Commission (COSO). *Internal Control-Integrated Framework* Framework. New York: COSO, 1992.

Committee of Sponsoring Organizations of the Treadway Commission (COSO). *Internal Control-Integrated Framework* Evaluation Tools. New York: COSO, 1992.

Committee of Sponsoring Organizations of the Treadway Commission (COSO). *Internal Control-Integrated Framework* Reporting to External Parties. New York: COSO, 1992.

QUESTIONS

1. Identify the major business functions and activities common to the expenditure/disbursement cycle.
2. Why should policies assure that goods and services be purchased only from approved vendors?
3. How can management control against unauthorized or duplicate cash payments?
4. Proper recording within general ledger control accounts does not necessarily mean that transactions are posted accurately to individual vendor accounts. What controls can management institute to assure that detailed records agree with control accounts?
5. Why should the receiving department be segregated from inventory control and, if possible, from shipping?

6. Explain how an auditor could perform a transaction walk-through for purchases and cash disbursements.

7. Why do auditors not usually rely on substantive tests alone when auditing accounts payable that result from credit purchase transactions?

8. What is the primary focus of an auditor's tests of controls over purchasing?

9. How does an auditor test whether purchase transactions are authorized in accordance with management's prespecified criteria?

10. Explain the primary focus of an auditor's tests of cash disbursements to vendors.

11. As a normal part of tests of controls for cash disbursements, an auditor examines signatures and endorsements on canceled checks, if they're available, looking specifically for unusual items. Give two examples of unusual items an auditor might confront.

MULTIPLE CHOICE QUESTIONS

1. Which of the following functions is not common to the expenditure/disbursement cycle?

a. Resources are acquired from vendors in exchange for obligations to pay.
b. Obligations to vendors are paid.
c. Resources are held, used, or transformed.
d. Resources are acquired from employees in exchange for obligations to pay.

2. The expenditure/disbursement cycle begins with requisitions from user departments and ends with the receipt of materials and the recognition of a liability. An auditor's primary objective in reviewing the cycle is to:

a. Obtain an understanding of the client's prescribed policies and procedures sufficient to plan the audit.
b. Investigate the handling and recording of unusual acquisitions.
c. Consider the need to increase substantive tests of purchases and accounts payable.
d. Assure that materials ordered, received, and paid for are actually on hand.

3. When considering internal controls over purchases and disbursements, the auditor will be influenced least by:

a. Procedures manuals.
b. Audit work done by an entity's internal auditors.
c. Compensating controls that offset deficiencies.
d. Controls in other cycles.

4. Which of the following is most crucial to a purchasing department?

a. Authorizing the acquisition of goods.
b. Assuring the quality of goods acquired.
c. Verifying the propriety of goods acquired.
d. Reducing the cost of goods acquired.

5. Which of the following control procedures would most likely prevent or detect purchases from unauthorized vendors?

a. Maintain updated guidelines for purchase transactions.
b. Establish procedures for reviewing and approving purchase prices and terms prior to purchase.
c. Require a second manual signature on all checks over a prespecified amount.
d. Establish criteria for adding to, changing, or deleting from the approved vendor list.

6. An auditor's primary concern when performing tests of controls over purchasing is to determine whether:

a. Purchases are properly authorized.
b. Purchases are properly recorded.
c. Purchase orders agree to purchase requisitions.
d. Purchasing personnel are performing their assigned functions properly.

7. How can an auditor test to determine whether Receiving Department procedures are applied properly?

a. Test a sample of receiving documents.
b. Observe receiving procedures on a surprise basis.
c. Review procedures manuals.
d. Interview Receiving personnel.

8. Which of the following control procedures could prevent or detect payment of goods not received?

a. Counting goods when received.
b. Matching the purchase order, receiving report, and vendor's invoice.
c. Comparing goods received with goods requisitioned.
d. Verifying vouchers for accuracy and approval.

9. An internal control questionnaire indicates that an approved receiving report accompanies every check request. To test this control, an auditor could select and examine:

a. Receiving reports, to determine that the related canceled checks are dated no earlier than the receiving reports.
b. Receiving reports, to determine that the related canceled checks are dated no later than the receiving reports.
c. Canceled checks, to determine that the related receiving reports are dated no earlier than the checks.
d. Canceled checks, to determine that the related receiving reports are dated no later than the checks.

10. Which of the following would prevent a paid disbursement from being paid a second time?

a. Individuals responsible for signing checks should prepare vouchers.
b. Disbursements should be approved by at least two responsible officials.
c. The disbursement date should be within a few days of the date the voucher is presented for payment.
d. The official signing the check should cancel the supporting documents.

PROBLEMS AND DISCUSSION CASES

12-1 *Controls Over Purchases and Cash Disbursements*
Assume you are considering a client's controls over purchases and cash disbursements. System documentation was accomplished through flowcharts and narratives and, in conjunction with a transaction walk-through, revealed the following potential deficiencies:
a. Carrying costs of inventory have increased significantly since the prior year.
b. Prices for purchases are sometimes unusually high or fluctuate significantly from month to month.

c. Purchase discounts are not taken frequently.
d. During lunch, the controller commented to you that on two occasions during the
    year duplicate payments had been made for a single transaction.
e. Cash disbursements records do not always reconcile with general ledger control
    accounts.
    Required: For each potential deficiency, indicate a control or controls that man-
    agement could implement to reduce the likelihood of errors or frauds.

12-2   *Errors, Fraud, and Control Procedures*
During an audit of Dundee Corporation's financial statements, you become aware of
the following control procedures over purchasing and cash disbursement activities:
1. Purchases are made only from companies that warrant products for workmanship
    and related damages.
2. Competitive bids are required for all purchases in excess of $12,000.
3. A written memorandum is required for each purchase discount not taken.
4. Receiving reports are prenumbered sequentially and access is controlled.
5. Voucher packages are canceled immediately after payment.
6. A procedures manual is maintained for all job functions related to processing
    purchases and cash disbursements transactions.
7. Postings are verified by check digits.
    Required: For each control procedure, indicate: (a) a potential error or fraud that
might be prevented or detected by the control procedure, and (b) the objective served
by the control procedure. Organize your answer as follows:

Control Procedure	Potential Error or Fraud That Might Be Prevented or Detected	Related Objective
1.	(a)	(b)

12-3   *Identifying Weaknesses and Inefficiencies in a Purchasing System*
Madeline Jones, the Lecimore Company's purchasing department manager, has established new policies and procedures to guide the day-to-day operations of purchasing
agents and clerical staff. She's satisfied that the policies and procedures conform with
management's objectives and that there are no major deficiencies either in the
department's policies or in the procedures that control the department's operations.
Some of the policies and procedures follow:
* All significant purchases are put out to competitive bid, although the likelihood
  of timely delivery and vendor reliability are considered in awarding contracts.
* Purchasing provides vendors with memoranda detailing minimum acceptable
  product quality specifications.
* The materials department manager, rather than Purchasing personnel, is responsible to assure that vendors adhere to quality specifications.
* The materials department manager prepares purchase requests based on a four-
  month production schedule.
* Ninety percent of a critical raw material is supplied by a single vendor. The vendor,
  low bidder in each of the past few years, has a good delivery record and is quite
  reliable.
* As production plans change, rush and expedite orders are made directly to Purchasing by production managers. Materials ordered for canceled production runs
  are stored for future use. Although the costs for rush and expedite orders are borne
  exclusively by the purchasing department, Jones considers the costs essential to the
  department's reputation as a contributing team player.
* Materials needed to accomplish engineering changes are ordered by Purchasing
  immediately after Engineering approves changes. Jones is proud of the purchasing
  department's quick response. Materials on hand are not reviewed before any orders
  are placed.

- Partial shipments and advance shipments (i.e., those received before the requested date of delivery) are accepted by the materials department manager, who notifies the purchasing department of the receipt. The purchasing department is responsible to follow up on partial shipments. No action is taken to discourage advance shipments.

Required: Identify weaknesses and inefficiencies in Lecimore Company's purchasing policies and procedures, and make recommendations to improve each.

12-4   *Interpreting a Systems Flowchart*
The flowchart on the following two pages illustrates a system for executing purchases and cash disbursement transactions.

Required: Indicate what each of the letters *A* through *L* represents in the flowchart. (Do not discuss inadequacies in internal control.)

12-5   *Judging the Adequacy of Control Procedures*
Dunbar Camera, Inc., manufactures high-priced motion picture cameras for the movie industry. The component parts specifications are vital to the filmmaking process. Dunbar buys valuable camera lenses and large quantities of sheet metal and screws. Vendors bill screws and lenses on a unit basis, and sheet metal on the basis of weight. The receiving clerk is responsible for documenting the quality and quantity of all merchandise received. A preliminary review of internal control indicates the following procedures:

- *Receiving report.* Approved purchase orders are prenumbered and filed numerically. The copy sent to the receiving clerk is an exact duplicate of the copy sent to the vendor. The receiving clerk records the receipt of merchandise on the purchase order copy.
- *Sheet metal.* The company receives sheet metal by rail. The rail company weighs the sheet metal independently, and reports both the weight and receipt date on the bill of lading that accompanies deliveries. The receiving clerk agrees the weight on the bill of lading to the purchase order.
- *Screws.* The receiving clerk opens cartons containing screws, and inspects and weighs the contents. The weight is converted to number of units by conversion charts. The receiving clerk then agrees the computed quantity to the purchase order.
- *Camera lenses.* Each camera lens is delivered in a separate corrugated carton. Cartons are counted as they are received by the receiving clerk, who agrees the number of cartons to the purchase order.

Required:
1. Explain why the control procedures for receiving reports and the receipt of sheet metal, screws, and camera lenses, respectively, are adequate or inadequate.
2. For each inadequate procedure you identify, describe misstatements that might appear in the financial statements.

(AICPA Adapted)

12-6   *Identifying Procedures for Purchase Requisitions and Purchase Orders*
Long has been engaged to audit the financial statements of Maylou Corporation. To help consider controls over purchases, Long obtained the purchases flowchart (on page 470):

Required: Identify the procedures for purchase requisitions and purchase orders that Long would expect to find if Maylou's controls over purchases are effective. For example, purchase orders should be prepared only after first considering the quantity to order.

(AICPA Adapted)

12-7   *Recommending Improvements to a Purchase Requisition*
Properly designed documents and forms improve the likelihood that employees will adhere to prescribed policies and procedures. For example, consider a multicopy purchase

Problem 12-4: Flowchart

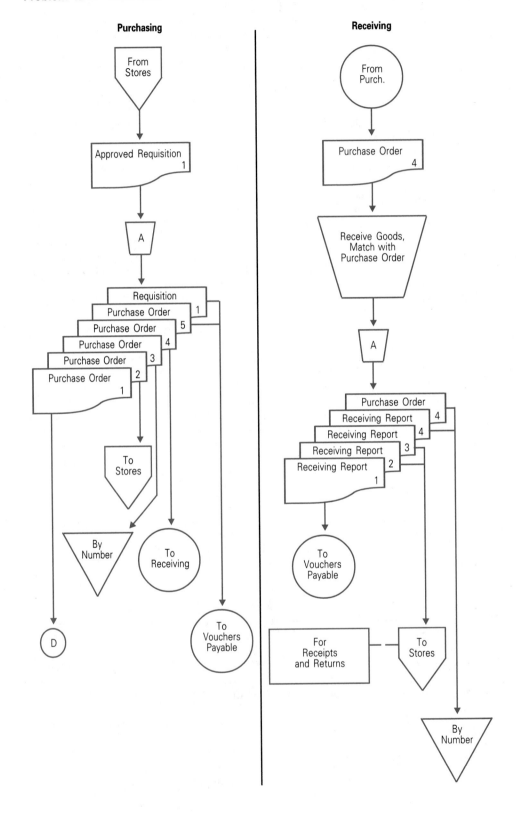

Problem 12-4: *(continued)*

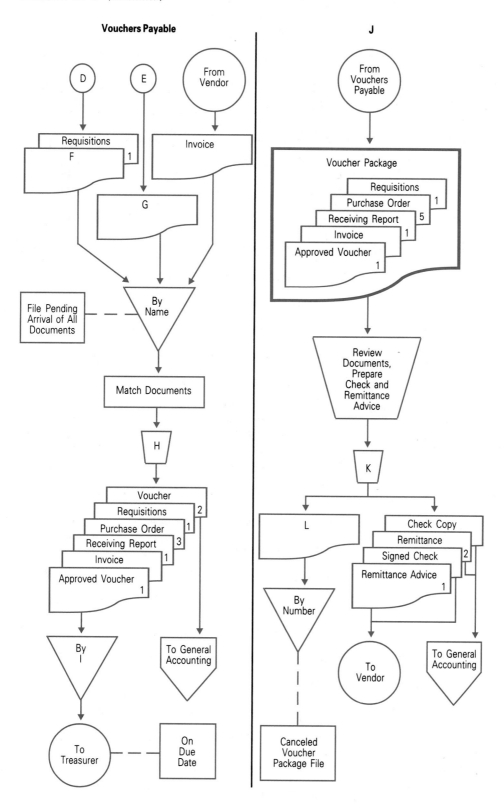

Problem 12-6:   Flowchart

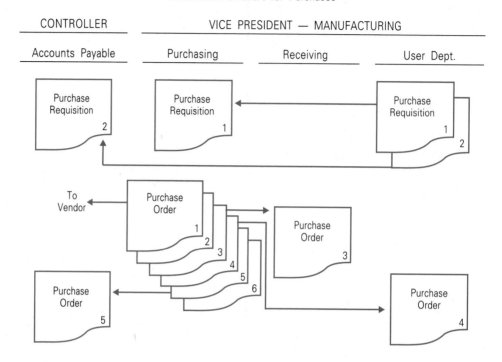

MAYLOU CORPORATION
Document Flowchart for Purchases

order, with one copy intended for mailing to the vendor and the remaining copies distributed to individual stores and to the purchasing, receiving, and accounting departments. The purchase order currently used by the National Industrial Corporation appears on the following page.

Required:
1.   In addition to the name of the company, what other information would an auditor recommend be included in the purchase order illustrated?
2.   What control objectives are served by distributing copies of the purchase order to the stores and to the purchasing, receiving, and accounting departments?

12-8   *Drafting an Internal Control Questionnaire*
Taylor has been engaged to audit the financial statements of University Books, Inc., a full-service college bookstore serving the university community and the general public. University Books maintains a large imprest cash fund exclusively for the purpose of buying used books from students. The cash fund is active year round because the university offers a variety of courses throughout the year, many with varying starting and completion dates. Receipts are prepared for each purchase, and reimbursement vouchers are submitted periodically.

Required: Draft a questionnaire to use in documenting University Book's controls over the imprest cash fund. The questionnaire should elicit *Yes* or *No* responses.

(AICPA Adapted)

12-9   *Drafting Tests of Controls From an Internal Control Questionnaire*
Following are selected questions from internal control questionnaires relating to a company's purchasing, receiving, cash disbursement, and recording functions. A *Yes*

Problem 12-7:   Purchase Order

```
                                                    PURCHASE ORDER

                        SEND INVOICE ONLY TO:
                        297 HARDINGTEN DR., BX., NY 10461


        TO  _____          SHIP TO _____

            _____                  _____

            _____                  _____
```

DATE TO BE SHIPPED	SHIP VIA	DISC. TERMS	FREIGHT TERMS	ADV. ALLOWANCE	SPECIAL ALLOWANCE
QUANTITY		DESCRIPTION			

PURCHASE CONDITIONS

1. Supplier will be responsible for extra freight cost on partial shipment, unless prior permission is obtained.

2. Please acknowledge this order.

3. Please notify us immediately if you are unable to complete order.

4. All items must be individually packed.

response to a question would indicate a potential strength of the system, and a *No*, a potential deficiency.

a. Are prenumbered purchase orders prepared for all approved purchase requisitions?

b. Are competitive bids or price quotations obtained for purchased goods and services?

c. Are price lists maintained for repetitive transactions that do not require competitive bids or price quotations?

d. Are copies of purchase orders forwarded to the requisitioning department and to Receiving?

e. Are all goods received, inspected, counted, and compared with copies of purchase orders?

f. Are voucher packages reviewed before being approved for payment?

g. Are voucher packages and checks reviewed by signatories before signing checks?

Required: Assume that inquiries indicate the answer is *yes* to each question. For each question, draft a test of controls that you believe would provide persuasive evidence that the answer is correct.

12-10 *Identifying the Purpose of Tests of Controls*

Following are several tests of controls introduced in the chapter:

- Examine periodic reports by non-Purchasing Department personnel regarding purchase prices and practices.
- Observe Receiving Department procedures, determining whether received goods are counted and compared with quantities and descriptions on purchase orders.
- Foot the voucher register for a selected period and compare with posting in the general ledger.
- Observe voucher cancellation procedures, determining whether vouchers are canceled by or in the presence of check signers.

Required: For each test, indicate the expenditure/disbursement cycle activity tested and the purpose of the test.

12-11 *Sequential Sampling and Tests of Receiving Controls*

Harold Brodkey plans to apply sequential sampling to the receiving controls used by the Ozyck Corporation, a December 31, 1999 year end manufacturer and supplier of home lighting fixtures. Based on a review of prior year working papers, Brodkey assesses the following risks and expected deviation rates for each of three tests of controls:

Test of Control	Risk of Assessing Control Risk Too Low	Expected Population Deviation Rate
1. Compare *receiving reports* in voucher packages with copies of *receiving reports* in Receiving Department files.	.95	.06
2. Review *receiving reports* for evidence that received goods have been inspected, counted, and compared with *packing slips* and *purchase orders*.	.90	.05
3. Trace *receiving reports* to entries in the *receiving log*.	.85	.07

Brodkey performs the sampling plan on September 10 and finds one deviation each for tests numbered 2 (although receiving report no. 1429 includes a receiving clerk's approval initials indicating the receiving report agrees with the packing slip and P.O., the received goods were apparently not counted) and 5 (although receiving report no. 2137, Winston-Raleigh Co., reads 12,500 units, the receiving log reads 12,250 units).

Required: Prepare audit working papers to document the sequential sampling plan and the analysis of deviations.

RESEARCH PROJECT

THE PURCHASING FUNCTION IN A REAL ENTITY

Few departments within a corporation, not-for-profit institution, or governmental entity can have quite as significant an influence on cost containment as Purchasing, since the purchasing function directly affects so many financial statement accounts, among them Cash, Advertising, Insurance, Inventory, Supplies, and Accounts Payables. As a result, in many entities, the policies and procedures for purchasing are typically centralized, meaning that all purchases for all departments are processed by the purchasing department, and quite formal, meaning the documentation supporting each purchase is standardized, explicit, and controlled. In short, much is at stake.

Required: Although access to the purchasing department of a real world entity can be problematic, there's much to be learned from how individual entities process purchase transactions. Contact and interview the purchasing manager for a corporation, not-for-profit institution, or governmental entity in your area and:

1. Document the purchasing procedures in a flowchart or a narrative memorandum.
2. Obtain blank copies of forms used in the purchasing function (e.g., purchase requisitions, purchase orders, receiving reports) and explain each form's purpose and distribution throughout the entity.
3. What recommendations would you make to improve the entity's purchasing procedures?

13

Substantive Tests in the Expenditure/Disbursement Cycle: Payables, Prepaids, Accrued Liabilities, and Management Discretion in Accounting for Environmental Liabilities

Major topics discussed in this chapter are the:

- Relationship between financial statement assertions and audit procedures within the expenditure/disbursement cycle.
- Relationship between audit risk and the nature, timing, and extent of substantive tests.
- Substantive tests applicable to assertions about accounts payable.
- Substantive tests applicable to prepaid expenses and accrued liabilities.
- Application of audit judgment to environmental liabilities.
- Application of nonstatistical sampling in substantive tests of accounts payable.
- Computer assisted substantive tests of accounts payable.

This chapter begins by discussing how each of the financial statement assertions introduced in Chapter 6—existence or occurrence, completeness, rights and obligations, valuation or allocation, and presentation and disclosure—is tested for audits of Accounts Payable, a major financial statement account within the expenditure/disbursement cycle, and how audit risk bears on the nature, timing, and extent of substantive tests. The chapter then relates the assertions to substantive tests of Accounts Payable, Prepaid Expenses, and Accrued Liabilities. In turn, the chapter addresses audit, legal, and ethical questions auditors face when a client is confronted with liabilities for which management has some discretion in avoiding otherwise sensitive disclosures: environmental liabilities. The chapter concludes by illustrating how auditors apply nonstatistical sampling (Chapter 9) and computer assisted audit techniques (Chapter 7) in substantive tests of accounts payable.

474

FINANCIAL STATEMENT ASSERTIONS, OBJECTIVES, AND AUDIT PROCEDURES

Within the expenditure/disbursement cycle, Purchases and Accounts Payable are usually the highest transaction volume, and the largest dollar balance, accounts processed by the cycle. The expenditure/disbursement cycle affects other financial statement accounts—for example, Prepaid Expenses and Accrued Liabilities, both of which are discussed in this chapter—but the volume of prepaid and accrual transactions is not often large. The audit of purchases and payables is emphasized in this chapter and discussed later in the context of specific financial statement assertions. Figure 13-1 relates each assertion to specific audit procedures and summarizes the discussion that follows.

EXISTENCE OR OCCURRENCE

Within the expenditure/disbursement cycle, the existence or occurrence assertion addresses whether all recorded payables exist at the balance sheet date and whether all recorded purchase transactions occurred during the period. The existence of accounts payable balances may be tested by confirming balances with creditors, although payables confirmations are used less frequently than receivables confirmations and generally are not used when the auditor suspects understatements. When confirmations are not used, the auditor can test existence by examining the documents—for example, purchase orders, receiving reports, and invoices—that support recorded payables. The occurrence assertion is addressed by testing cutoff to determine whether purchases are recorded in the proper accounting period.

COMPLETENESS

The completeness assertion addresses whether all purchase transactions and payables balances that should be presented in the financial statements are actually presented. That is, were all transactions recorded? Completeness is

Figure 13-1:   Relating Financial Statement Assertions and Audit Procedures: Purchases and Accounts Payable

Assertions	Audit Procedures
Existence or occurrence	Confirm with creditors. Test cutoff.
Completeness	Test for unrecorded liabilities. Perform analytical procedures. Test cutoff.
Rights and obligations	Confirm with creditors Test for unrecorded liabilities.
Valuation or allocation	Verify accounts payable aged trial balance. Confirm with creditors. Test for unrecorded liabilities.
Presentation and disclosure	Compare statement presentation and disclosures with those required by GAAP.

tested by reviewing post-balance sheet date cash disbursements for payments made on previously unrecorded payables, and by examining unmatched receiving reports (those filed in an unpaid vouchers file) to assure that liabilities have been recorded at the balance sheet date. In addition, analytical procedures are used to detect any unusual relationships that might suggest unrecorded liabilities, like a significant increase in the average number of days purchases in accounts payable. Testing cutoff also addresses completeness.

RIGHTS AND OBLIGATIONS

Within the expenditure/disbursement cycle, the rights and obligations assertion addresses whether payables and other recorded liabilities are bona fide obligations of the entity. Payables obligations may be tested by confirming recorded balances with creditors and by searching for unrecorded liabilities—that is, by examining cash disbursements for the period subsequent to the balance sheet date, as explained above.

VALUATION OR ALLOCATION

The valuation assertion addresses whether existing payables are reported in the financial statements at appropriate dollar amounts. The value of payables is tested by verifying the mathematical accuracy of the accounts payable aged trial balance, by confirming payables with creditors, and by testing for unrecorded liabilities.

PRESENTATION AND DISCLOSURE

The presentation and disclosure assertion addresses whether recorded payables are properly classified, described, and disclosed in the financial statements. To test presentation and disclosure, an auditor compares a client's financial statement disclosures with those required by generally accepted accounting principles. Disclosure guidelines, such as the AICPA's *Accounting and Audit Manual*, are frequently used by practicing auditors.

AUDIT RISK AND THE NATURE, TIMING, AND EXTENT OF SUBSTANTIVE TESTS IN THE EXPENDITURE/DISBURSEMENT CYCLE

Substantive testing of expenditure/disbursement cycle accounts involves obtaining and evaluating evidence about an entity's acquisition of resources and the obligations that often result from resource acquisitions, like accounts payable. Although cash disbursements are encompassed by the expenditure/disbursement cycle, they're not addressed in this chapter since substantive tests of cash balances were discussed and illustrated in Chapter 11.

Like the revenue/receipt cycle, the expenditure/disbursement cycle varies in scope from one entity to another and, therefore, so do the audit procedures applied to the cycle. Thus, the substantive tests discussed in this chapter are representative, not definitive. The nature, timing, and extent of the procedures applied in an engagement depend on the assessed levels of *control risk* (the likelihood that material error could occur and not be detected by internal control) and *inherent risk* (the susceptibility of an account balance to material error for which there is no related internal control) and the resulting level of *detection risk* (the likelihood that error could occur and not be detected by audit procedures) that an auditor is willing to accept for each assertion. When control and inherent risks are assessed below the maximum and detection risk above the minimum, auditors are less apt to confirm payables balances, more apt to perform substantive tests at interim dates, and more apt to restrict the extent of substantive tests applied to purchases and payables. However, the audit programs illustrated in this chapter assume that an auditor has assessed control risk and inherent risk for the assertions of *occurrence, completeness, obligations,* and *valuation* at the *maximum,* because tests of controls over purchasing, receiving, and cash disbursements (Chapter 12) reveal that internal control deficiencies are likely to produce aggregate error in excess of tolerable error for the following control procedures:

- *Purchasing.* Purchase orders are authorized by a department manager's signature or initials.
- *Receiving.* Receiving reports are agreed to purchase orders.
- *Disbursements.* Disbursements are compared with entries in the accounts payable subsidiary ledger.

As a result, to hold down audit risk to a *minimum,* the auditor assesses the acceptable level of detection risk at the *minimum.* That is, from Chapter 2:

$$DR = \frac{AR}{IR \times CR}$$

$$Minimum = \frac{Minimum}{Maximum \times Maximum}$$

That is, the auditor holds down audit risk to a minimum by assessing the acceptable level of detection risk at the minimum, which bears directly on the nature, timing, and extent of planned substantive tests as follows:

- *Nature.* Use more persuasive procedures (e.g., test for unrecorded payables).
- *Timing.* Perform procedures at the balance sheet date.
- *Extent.* Test more extensively (e.g., increase sample sizes).

ACCOUNTS PAYABLE

A program of substantive tests for purchases and accounts payable is presented in Figure 13-2, and is keyed to—and discussed in the context of—the financial statement assertions presented in Chapter 6: existence or occurrence, completeness, rights and obligations, valuation or allocation, and presentation and disclosure. If an entity's system of internal control has changed since the auditor assessed control risk at interim, he or she should either reassess the level of control risk through additional tests of controls or, in contrast, unilaterally increase the assessed level of control risk without additional tests of controls and increase the extent of substantive testing at the balance sheet date.

Figure 13-2: Substantive Tests: Purchases and Accounts Payable

Assertions	Procedures

Valuation	1. Verify mathematical accuracy of accounts payable.
	   a. Obtain an accounts payable aged trial balance from Accounts Payable Department personnel.
	   b. Foot and cross-foot the trial balance.
	   c. Compare total accounts payable per the trial balance with accounts payable in the general ledger.
	   d. Trace sampled vendor accounts to voucher packages and examine supporting documents.

Existence Obligations Valuation	2. Consider the need to confirm year end accounts payable directly with creditors.
Existence or occurrence Completeness	3. Test cutoff to determine whether purchases and payables are recorded in the proper accounting period.
Completeness Valuation Obligations	4. Test for unrecorded liabilities.
Existence or occurrence Completeness Valuation	5. Perform analytical procedures.

Presentation
  and disclosure
	6. Review financial statements to determine whether:
	   a. Accounts and notes payable and other liabilities are properly classified and described.
	   b. Disclosures are adequate.

VERIFY MATHEMATICAL ACCURACY

The first step in addressing the valuation assertion is to verify the mathematical or clerical accuracy of recorded accounts payable. For example, to accomplish tests of mathematical accuracy, an auditor could import an aged trial balance into a spreadsheet file similar to Figure 13-3, and write commands to foot and cross-foot the trial balance and to compare and reconcile the client's trial balance total with the general ledger balance. If discrepancies are observed, or if deficiencies were detected in tests of controls, the auditor may conduct additional tests of mathematical accuracy. For example, the auditor may select a sample of accounts from the trial balance and trace each account to a voucher package in the unpaid vouchers file and to the voucher register and accounts payable subsidiary records.

CONFIRM PAYABLES

Unlike the confirmation of receivables (Chapter 11), there's no presumption in the profession that an auditor is required to justify his or her opinion on financial statements when payables are not confirmed. In fact, payables are not commonly confirmed in practice, unless internal control is inadequate (and

Figure 13-3: Accounts Payable Aged Trial Balance

(Schedule prepared by client)

The Wilson Company
Accounts Payable Aged Trial Balance
December 31, 1999

Acct. No.	Vendor Name	Balance Dec. 31, 1999	0-30 Days	31-60 Days	Over 60 Days
0001	Adams Supply	$ 7,859.76	$ 7,859.76		
0002	Alpine Roofing Co.	17,621.40	17,621.40		
0003	Art Design Inc.	784.50	784.50		
0004	Ashton Mfg.	10,005.00	9,000.00	$ 1,005.00	
0005	Attleboro Bindings	1,147.61	1,147.61		
0006	Bates Motel	123.49	123.49		
0007	Christie & Co.	1,456.90			$1,456.90
•	•	•	•	•	•
•	•	•	•	•	•
•	•	•	•	•	•
0162	Van Nuys & Co.	6,724.82	6,724.82		
0163	Wallace's	12,654.09	12,654.09		
0164	Western Electric	1,164.21	1,164.21		
0165	Yantze Inc.	550.00		550.00	
		$238,858.89	$225,282.64	$10,125.50	$3,450.75

other forms of evidence, such as detailed vendors' invoices, are unavailable) or the auditor is concerned that liabilities may be overstated.

A dominant concern in auditing *receivables* is the detection of overstatements, and confirmation is an effective procedure for verifying the existence, rights, and valuation of recorded accounts receivable, since any overstated receivables would be listed on the entity's accounts receivable trial balance. In auditing *payables*, however, the risks are quite different: An auditor is usually concerned with the risk of understatement, since an understated liability (e.g., an account payable) results typically in an understated expense (e.g., advertising expense) and, correspondingly, in overstated income. Confirming recorded payables with vendors is not an effective means for detecting unrecorded liabilities because the *unrecorded* payable obligation would not be listed on an accounts payable trial balance and, therefore, a confirmation request would not be sent.

This does not mean that auditors are never concerned with the risk of overstated liabilities, only that understatement is more common. An auditor may suspect overstatement, for example, if he or she has reason to believe that an entity motivated by tax avoidance has overstated liabilities and thus understated taxable income. Also, if an entity's income is significantly lower than in preceding years and liabilities are significantly higher, an auditor may suspect that liabilities are overstated if there is no other apparent cause for the reduction in income.

When the confirmation of payables is considered necessary by an auditor, balances are usually confirmed as of the balance sheet date rather than at interim. Confirming payables balances requires direct communication with vendors, requesting that an itemized statement of account be sent directly to the auditor. Unlike positive and negative receivables confirmations, payables confirmation requests usually do not reveal the audited entity's recorded balance; rather, they request a statement reflecting the vendor's records. A sample payables confirmation request appears in Figure 13-4.

As in the case of receivables confirmations, an auditor should mail second (and perhaps even third) requests to vendors who fail to respond. For accounts that are not confirmed, an auditor could examine subsequent cash payments, vendors' invoices, and receiving documents.

TEST CUTOFF

Purchases cutoff tests are quite similar in nature and logic to sales cutoff tests, discussed in Chapter 11. An auditor tests purchases cutoff to determine whether purchases and the corresponding payables are recorded in the appropriate period—i.e., whether purchases of goods are recorded in the period that title to the goods passed to the purchasing entity, and whether services are recorded in the period rendered. Cutoff tests relate most directly to the existence and completeness assertions.

Cutoff tests of purchase transactions involve selecting and examining a sample of purchase entries on or near year end—for example, ten days before

Figure 13-4:   Accounts Payable Confirmation Request

THE WILSON COMPANY
15 Artubus Drive
Stony Brook, NY 11790

January 7, 2000

Alpine Roofing Company
305 Columbus Avenue
Pawtucket, RI 02861

Our auditors, Cheever & Yates, LLP, are auditing our financial statements for 1999. Will you please furnish them with the following information as of December 31, 1999:

- An itemized statement of amounts that we owe you.
- An itemized statement of any merchandise that you have consigned to us.
- An itemized list of any notes, acceptances, or other obligations that we owe you.

Please reply directly to our auditors. An envelope addressed to our auditors is enclosed.

Maxine Kuman
Controller
The Wilson Company

to ten days after year end. Receiving reports are examined for each sampled purchase entry. A purchase of goods and a related payable should have been recorded in the year under audit if shipping terms were:

1. *FOB shipping point* (origin), and goods were shipped by the seller on or before year end, or
2. *FOB destination,* and goods were received on or before the year end date. Transactions relating to services should be reflected in the year under audit if the services were received by the entity on or before the year end date.

Another aspect of cutoff relates to prepayments and accruals. An auditor should review the entity's year end entries relating to prepaid and accrued expenses to determine whether expenses are recognized in the appropriate accounting period. Prepayments and accruals are discussed more fully later in the chapter.

TEST FOR UNRECORDED LIABILITIES

Auditors are often concerned that liabilities may be understated as a result of unrecorded payables. However, as noted previously, this does not mean that an auditor is never concerned with overstated liabilities, only that understatement is more common, since understating liabilities can result in overstated income. Figure 13-5 depicts the sources for testing accounts payable balances for both understatements and overstatements. Testing for understatements, or unrecorded liabilities, is discussed first.

A **search for unrecorded liabilities** is closely related to tests of cutoff and, in fact, may result in the detection of items recorded in the wrong accounting period. Similarly, cutoff tests may reveal unrecorded liabilities. However, auditors usually conduct an investigation specifically designed to detect unrecorded liabilities, and thus specifically related to the assertions of completeness, valuation, and obligations.

Four basic sources are used to search for unrecorded payables:

- A year end accounts payable trial balance.
- The cash disbursements journal.
- Canceled (paid) voucher packages.
- The file of unmatched receiving reports (filed in an unpaid vouchers file).

Assuming a December 31 year end, an auditor would trace a sample of disbursements for January to receiving reports contained in canceled voucher packages; if goods were received or title to the goods passed on or before December 31, the accounts payable trial balance should reflect a liability. Likewise, because many accounting systems require a completed **voucher package**—purchase requisition, purchase order, receiving report, and vendor's invoice—before a payable is recorded, an auditor would examine unmatched (unprocessed) receiving reports; again, if goods were received or title passed on or before December 31, the accounts payable trial balance should reflect the liability. The search for unrecorded liabilities is completed by asking management whether they are aware of any significant payables not recorded and not detected by the above tests.

Even though payables understatement is often an overriding concern, an auditor cannot ignore the potential for overstatement, since some clients may

Figure 13-5:   Auditing Accounts Payable Balances

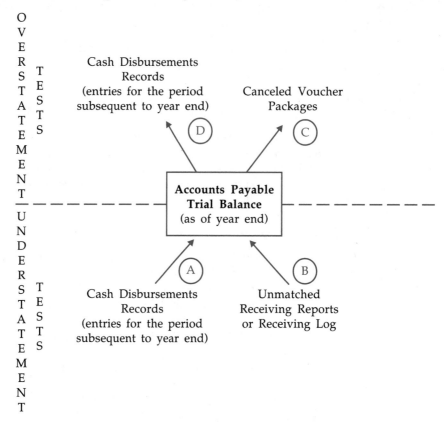

Direction of arrows indicates the "from – to" of each test:

(A) To determine that all payments made subsequent to the balance sheet
date for items originating before the balance sheet date were recorded.

(B) To determine that all items for which a liability existed were recorded.

(C) To determine that recorded amounts are accurate and supported by
documents.

(D) To determine that subsequent payments support/confirm recorded
balances.

have incentives to overstate expenses (e.g., to avoid income taxes). Three basic
sources are used to test for overstated payables:

- A year end accounts payable trial balance.
- The cash disbursements journal.
- Canceled (paid) voucher packages.

Assuming a December 31 year end, an auditor would trace sample items from
the accounts payable trial balance to receiving reports and shipping terms
contained in canceled voucher packages; title should have passed on or before
December 31. In addition, sampled items would be traced to subsequent

payments in the cash disbursements book, assuring that the liability was paid and, therefore, that documentation for returned goods was not concealed. For example, a payable recorded on or before December 31 with payment terms of 2/10, net 30, should have been paid no later than January 10 to take advantage of the two percent discount and no later than January 30 if the discount were not taken. If not paid, an auditor would obtain an explanation from management; nonpayment could suggest the liability did not exist as of December 31, despite documentation to the contrary.

PERFORM ANALYTICAL PROCEDURES

As in tests of receivables balances (Chapter 11), the role of year end analytical procedures for payables is to direct attention to unusual, unreasonable, or otherwise unexplainable relationships among accounts or account components. That is, analytical procedures can be used to identify accounts that appear reasonable in relation to other accounts and therefore do *not* require additional substantive testing, or accounts that appear unusual or unreasonable and therefore *do* require additional substantive testing. For accounts payable, an auditor might use any of the following analytical procedures, among others, to assess the reasonableness of recorded balances:

- Compare the current listing of accounts payable with the prior year, noting significant fluctuations in either the total balance or in individual vendor balances.
- Compare the average number-of-days-purchases-in-accounts payable at the end of the current year with prior years.
- Compare purchases divided by payables for the current and prior years.
- Compare payables divided by total current liabilities for the current and prior years.
- Compare both purchases and payables with budgeted or forecasted amounts.

An auditor should investigate any unusual relationships between or among accounts and design additional substantive tests of details if warranted. For example, if payables divided by total current liabilities appears low in comparison with prior years, the auditor might increase the scope of testing for unrecorded liabilities, as discussed earlier in the chapter.

REVIEW FINANCIAL STATEMENT PRESENTATION AND DISCLOSURE

Item 6 of the program for substantive testing of purchases and payables requires that an auditor assess whether expenditure/disbursement cycle accounts such as Accounts Payable, Accrued Liabilities, and related purchase and expense accounts are classified and disclosed in accordance with generally accepted accounting principles. Payables and accrued liabilities are usually classified as current if due within one year, or are expected to be paid either with existing current assets or by incurring additional current liabilities. Depending on materiality, liabilities such as trade accounts payable, advances (for example, from officers), customer credit balances, dividends payable, interest payable, and liabilities for product warranties should all be disclosed separately.

PREPAID EXPENSES AND ACCRUED LIABILITIES

For most entities, the balance in Accounts Payable summarizes a rather large volume of recurring transactions, is material and, therefore, is often the most time-consuming audit area within the expenditure/disbursement cycle. However, two other expenditure/disbursement cycle accounts are also important to an audit: Prepaid Expenses and Accrued Liabilities. But they're important because they result from timing differences between when cash is expended and when an asset or liability is recorded, not because of volume or even materiality necessarily. In fact, the volume of transactions underlying the prepaid expenses and accrued liabilities is often small. As a result, auditors usually either test all of the transactions and events underlying individual prepaid expense and accrued liability accounts or rely on analytical procedures.

PREPAID EXPENSES

Prepaid expenses normally result because the future service potential of assets may extend beyond the period in which payment is made. Common examples include prepaid insurance, prepaid rent, prepaid advertising, and supplies. To illustrate, the following discussion focuses on prepaid insurance, although the audit issues discussed apply equally to other prepaid expenses as well.

Controls

In general, an auditor is concerned with three predominant controls in the audit of prepaid insurance—control procedures over:

- The acquisition of new insurance policies,
- The disbursement of cash for premiums, and
- The recording of expense and premium disbursements.

The acquisition of new insurance coverage should be authorized by the board of directors, and the insurance company and policy selected should be approved by personnel authorized by management. As in other types of cash payments within the expenditure/disbursement cycle, the authority to disburse cash for premiums should be segregated from the responsibility to record both the disbursement and the charge to Insurance Expense, thereby separating the execution and recording functions. As a further control over recording, an *insurance register* should be maintained with detailed information about coverage, terms, and payment due dates.

Substantive Tests

Figure 13-6 illustrates an audit working paper for prepaid insurance and indicates how an auditor addresses each of the financial statement assertions. To test existence, the auditor examines current insurance policies and, as documented on the working paper, may confirm the coverage, terms, due dates, and unexpired premiums directly with insurance carriers.

Completeness is tested two ways, though neither is apt to reveal errors or frauds because the transactions in Figure 13-6 have been tested 100 percent. First, the auditor assures that total insurance coverage exceeds the replacement cost of all tangible assets. Second, cutoff testing is performed, but not directly

Figure 13-6: Analysis of Prepaid Insurance

The Wilson Company
Prepaid Insurance
December 31, 1999

D4
SEB 1/15/00

Insurer Policy Number	Coverage	Period	Premium	Year Paid	Unexpired Premium 12-31-98	Additions	Expense	Unexpired Premium 12-31-99
Provident Casualty AE-1067-48139[d]	Automobiles-collision, comprehensive, uninsured motorist; covers all autos operated	Jan 1, 98- Dec 31, 2000	$9,000[e]	98	$6,000[f]	—	$3,000[g]	$3,000[a,h]
Washington Ins. Co. PBL-462-1986-63[d]	Casualty-buildings, covers all buildings and equipment	July 1, 99- June 30, 2004	$7,000	99	—	$7,000[i]	1,750[g]	5,250[a,h]
New York Equitable NY 743-96218[d]	Business interruption	Oct 1, 98- Sept 30, 2000	$3,000[e]	98	2,625[f]	—	1,500[g]	1,125[a,h]
					$8,625	$7,000	$6,250	$9,375[h]
					c	c	b,c,j	b,c,j

Note: Total coverage exceeds the replacement cost of all insured assets.

a Cross-footed.
b Agreed to general ledger.
c Footed.
d Examined insurance policy, agreeing policy number, terms, period covered, and premium.
e Examined premium notice in company files, and traced to prior year's working papers which indicated payment was agreed to cash disbursement records in the year paid (1998).
f Agreed to 12-31-98 general ledger and last year's working papers.
g Calculated.
h Confirmed with insurance company. See insurance confirmation file.
i Examined premium notice and traced to cash disbursements; policy is for five years, but premiums are paid two years in advance during the first four years, and the fifth year is paid one year in advance.
j Agreed to trial balance.

on the prepaid insurance working paper. Rather, cutoff testing is addressed during substantive tests of accounts payable and the auditor's search for unrecorded liabilities, both of which were discussed earlier in the chapter.

Rights and obligations are tested by examining the insurance policies and, as in Figure 13-6, confirming each policy with the insurance carrier. In turn, an auditor tests valuation by recalculating unexpired premiums through evidence obtained from the prior year's unexpired insurance and from current premiums. In addition, to address clerical accuracy, the auditor reconciles premium payments with cash disbursements records, and the total expense and unexpired premiums with the general ledger.

Finally, the presentation and disclosure assertion is not particularly problematic except in one area: the adequacy of insurance coverage. An auditor should determine whether total insurance coverage exceeds his or her best estimate of the replacement cost for all tangible assets, insured or otherwise. If replacement cost exceeds insurance coverage, the client is partially self-insured. In this case, the excess of replacement cost over insurance should be disclosed in a note to the financial statements, though not accrued as a liability, since the conditions for accruing loss contingencies in FASB *Statement of Financial Accounting Standards No. 5*, "Accounting for Contingencies,"—that is, (1) the loss is probable, and (2) the amount of the loss can be estimated reasonably—would not have been met.

ACCRUED LIABILITIES

Accrued liabilities result because some unpaid obligations for services may have been incurred before the balance sheet date. Common examples include accrued property taxes, accrued payroll taxes, accrued product warranty costs, accrued rent, accrued interest, and accrued income taxes. The discussion below focuses on accrued property taxes, although the issues are common to other accrued liabilities.

Controls
In the audit of property taxes, an auditor is concerned with an entity's controls over three activities:

- Recognition of accrued taxes,
- Recording of expense for taxes owed, and
- Disbursement of cash for taxes.

When an entity conducts business in several locations, particularly across the country or overseas, management should institute policies to assure that liabilities for property taxes in all relevant municipalities, states, or countries are accrued at the balance sheet date. The recording of property tax expense should be based on bills actually received or estimated from prior years (adjusted for tax rate changes), if any. As with other cash payments processed through the expenditure/disbursement cycle, responsibility for disbursing cash and for recording disbursements should be separated. If property taxes are paid in several localities, separate property tax records should be maintained to compile and control both accruals and payments.

Substantive Tests

Figure 13-7 illustrates an audit working paper for accrued property taxes and indicates how each relevant financial statement assertion is addressed. To test occurrence, obligations, and valuation, an auditor examines receipted property tax bills for the current year, if available, or, as in Figure 13-7, compares the current provision for property tax expense with prior year payments for reasonableness. In testing reasonableness, though, the auditor should consider plant asset additions/disposals and tax rate changes, because either or both could alter the amount owed for the current year. In turn, reasonableness tests also address completeness, since unusual fluctuations in accrued property taxes from one year to the next could signal underaccruals or overaccruals.

Figure 13-7:   Analysis of Accrued Property Taxes

D7
SEB 1/16/00

The Wilson Company
Accrued Property Taxes
December 31, 1999

Balance, Dec. 31, 1998		$34,230[a]
Provision for property tax expense		35,000[d]
Payments:		
State of Missouri	$15,473[b]	
State of Illinois	12,696[b]	
City of St. Louis	3,210[b]	
City of Chicago	2,842[b]	(34,221)
Balance, Dec. 31, 1999		$35,009
		c,e

a Agreed to general ledger and to financial statements.
b Traced to receipted tax bill and cash disbursements records.
c Footed.
d Provision for property tax expense appears reasonable, since the provision reasonably approximates 1998 actual payments adjusted for plant asset additions less retirements (See E1).
e Agreed to trial balance.

MANAGEMENT DISCRETION AND ENVIRONMENTAL LIABILITIES

The discussion thus far has centered on issues that are challenging but, given the state of the art in accounting and auditing, fairly predictable for experienced practitioners: challenging because timing the incurrence of an expense (prepaids, accruals) or the recognition of a liability (payables) presents opportunities for management to manipulate earnings, but predictable because, although not the subject of an authoritative pronouncement, GAAP for payables, prepaids, and accruals is fairly well understood. But what about expenses and liabilities that are at once both challenging and *unpredictable*? This section addresses environmental liabilities, an issue that imposes upon the auditor considerable responsibilities that are made more daunting by the thousands of pages of environmental regulations accompanying a variety of federal statutes, among them the *Congressional Comprehensive Environmental Response, Compensation, and Liability Act of 1980* (CERCLA or, more popularly, the "Superfund" legislation); the *Superfund Amendment and Reauthorization Act of 1986*; and the *Clean Air Act of 1990*.

The figure to ground relationship between industry and the environment has reversed since the Industrial Revolution. Rather than a natural setting on which industry selectively intrudes, the environment has become a commodity within an artificial setting of high stakes economic and societal constraints. At the extreme, the economic interests are represented by industrial polluters to whom the commodity exists for little more than unrelenting exploitation and the promise of short-term gain. In contrast, society's interests are represented by environmental law, and what's at stake is nothing less than a legal system's triumph over chaos. In the short term, the economy may prosper, in the long term society pays, and at the intersect lies the independent auditor, mindful both of management's incentives and of the compelling environmental liabilities management may leave in its wake.

LEGAL LIABILITY FOR INDUSTRIAL POLLUTION

Industrial polluters may be held liable for noncompliance with existing laws and regulations, for personal injury or property damage, and for the contingent liability potentially most significant to audited financial statements: the remedial cleanup responsibilities imposed by the Superfund legislation. Parties responsible for hazardous waste-site cleanup costs may include not only current site owners and operators, but also hazardous waste transporters and the owners and operators of the site at the time waste was disposed. As illustrated in the Eleventh Circuit Court of Appeals precedent-setting decision in *U.S. v. Fleet Factors Corp.* (1990), liability can also extend to secured creditors, even those that did not participate directly in dumping hazardous waste:

. . . a secured creditor will be liable if its involvement with the management of the facility is sufficiently broad *to support the inference that it could affect hazardous waste disposal discussions if it so chose. (emphasis supplied)*

For example, involvement may be ruled sufficiently broad when a credit agreement requires that the borrower obtain the secured creditor's approval to ship products.

The liability of industrial polluters is joint and several (Chapter 6), since the federal government may recover from any one party identified by the Environmental Protection Agency (EPA) as a potentially responsible party (PRP). But the question of who dumped what and when, and therefore who exactly is a PRP, is not without controversy. For example, *The Wall Street Journal* reported that Westinghouse had disputed an EPA order to pay an estimated

$14.9 million to clean an upstate New York contamination site, in part because Westinghouse disputed responsibility for the contamination.[1]

CLEANUP COSTS: EXPENSE V. CAPITALIZATION AND CONTINGENT LIABILITIES

Once identified as a PRP for a Superfund site, an entity is then responsible to estimate the costs of cleanup. For example, in an extensive and rather forthcoming footnote accompanying their audited financial statements, Columbia Gas System, Inc., reported in part the following about Columbia Transmission, a subsidiary:

As a consequence of its self-assessment program, Columbia Transmission in recent years recorded projected compliance costs relating to the remediation of low levels of contamination by PCB-based lubricating oils in certain air compressors and other pollutants, including mercury. Further progress by Columbia Transmission in its self-assessment activities resulted in additional pre-tax charges of $65 million . . .

Although it's clear from the note that Columbia Gas expensed the costs of cleanup, could the costs have been capitalized? The FASB has not issued a Statement of Financial Accounting Standards about whether to expense or capitalize current cleanup costs, but the Board's Emerging Issues Task Force has issued a consensus opinion in *Issue 90-8, Capitalization of Costs to Treat Environmental Contamination*. The consensus was that costs incurred to treat environmental contamination—such as engaging consulting engineers, and removing and neutralizing toxic waste—generally should be expensed, but may be capitalized, if for example the costs extend the life of the property, prevent future contamination, or further ready property currently held for sale.

    Contingent liabilities for future cleanup costs present at least two problems, one related to measurement and a second to recognition. The measurement problem is management's role in casting into discrete dollars a liability based on preliminary estimates and on interpreting the EPA's definition of acceptable cleanup. Under AICPA *Statement of Position 96-1*, "Environmental Remediation Liabilities," the recognition problem—should a liability be recognized on the balance sheet?—is judged by criteria established in *FASB Statement of Financial Accounting Standards No. 5*, "Accounting for Contingencies," introduced earlier in the chapter: Recognize a loss contingency if: (1) the loss is probable, and (2) the amount of the loss can be estimated reasonably. In many cases, because cleanup cost estimates are not sufficiently reliable to justify recording a liability, the entity will disclose the liability in a footnote rather than on the balance sheet. For example, the Columbia Gas footnote referred to above lends insight into the difficulty of estimating costs and also discloses a reserve for future cleanup costs:

The eventual total cost of full future environmental compliance for the Columbia Gas System is impossible to estimate due to, among other things: (1) the possibility of as

1   "Westinghouse Told to Pay $14.9 Million in Superfund Cleanup," *The Wall Street Journal* (July 30, 1991), p. C11.

yet unknown contamination, (2) the possible effect of future legislation and new environmental agency rules, (3) the possibility of future litigation, (4) the possibility of future designations as a potential responsible party by the EPA and difficulty of determining liability, if any, in proportion to other responsible parties, (5) possible insurance and rate recoveries, and (6) the effect of possible technological changes relating to future remediation. However, reserves have been established based on information currently available which resulted in a total recorded net liability of $110.9 million for the Columbia Gas System . . . As new issues are identified, appropriate additional liabilities will be recorded.

MANAGEMENT AND AUDITOR INCENTIVES

Clearly, the management of a potentially responsible party has incentives to understate the costs of cleanup and therefore to overlook or to underestimate the magnitude of the potential liability, largely because the reported estimated costs and liabilities can affect stock prices when disclosed. For example, Arco, Exxon, and Phillips all experienced significant declines in stock prices as a result of environmental disasters.[2] Likewise, auditors have incentives to provide themselves with a reasonable degree of assurance that material environmental liabilities are disclosed, since shareholders may bring action against an auditor for negligently overlooking unreported environmental liabilities. To demonstrate the audit implications of competing incentives, the following illustrates issues auditors confront when auditing environmental liabilities.

GROUND WATER CONTAMINATION

Owing mostly to a major fresh water aquifer, several square miles in the town of Grainert, Illinois, had undergone significant residential development over a fifteen year period. Utilities were drawn from a regional power affiliate, and water from pumps located on each homeowner's property. Coexisting with the residential subdivisions was a preexisting regional storage facility built originally by an ethanol plant but operated now by the Humbolt Oil Co., Inc., a publicly traded Louisiana-based distributor of refined oil and gas products.

Following complaints from residents whose property abutted the storage facility, *The Grainert Daily Herald*, a local newspaper, published a front-page article citing speculation by local engineers that a floating oil pool may have formed atop the aquifer. A photo accompanying the article showed surface contamination one hundred yards from a chain link fence, a sign on the fence reading, "Humbolt Oil." Although the piece did not otherwise implicate Humbolt, the article's closing line read: "A spokesperson for Humbolt Oil's Grainert storage facility refused comment." After the news story broke, Humbolt's chief executive officer revealed in a private conversation with the auditor that the *Daily Herald's* account was patently false, that the EPA had recently completed an unreported investigation, that management planned to fight vigorously if the EPA issued a Superfund notice letter, and that disclosure of environmental liabilities in the financial statements was out of the question.

2   L. B. Cahill, "Issues in Environmental Auditing," *Petroleum Independent* (November 1992), p. A2.

AUDIT JUDGMENT: ACCOUNTING, LIABILITY, AND ETHICS

The newspaper article and the conversation that followed have more than trivial implications for Humbolt's auditors, since they raise no less than four related audit issues:

- Illegal acts,
- Audit risk,
- Current cleanup costs (if any), and
- The potential for material contingent liabilities.

Under *Statement on Auditing Standards No. 54*, "Illegal Acts by Clients," an auditor is not responsible to design audit procedures to detect *in*direct illegal acts (Chapter 5), among them violations of environmental laws, unless specific information, such as *The Grainert Daily Herald* article and the impending EPA report, directs his or her attention to a potential violation. Here, the auditor should make inquiries of Humbolt Oil's management about policies they've implemented to prevent ground water contamination, to assure compliance with environmental laws and regulations, and to estimate cleanup costs.

Given the considerable attention drawn to environmental disasters, including oil spills on both U.S. coasts and in the Gulf of Mexico, the AICPA issued a *Risk Alert* that suggests auditors inquire of management whether a company has been named a potentially responsible party and whether the company has a high risk of exposure to environmental liabilities. Although the auditor's conversation lent insight into both questions, both should be asked again when the EPA letter arrives, and, given the newspaper account, the auditor should, under *Statement on Auditing Standards No. 47*, "Audit Risk and Materiality in Conducting an Audit," consider assessing the inherent risk (Chapter 2) of environmental liabilities at the maximum when planning audit risk.

Consistent with the FASB's *EITF Issue 90-8, Capitalization of Costs to Treat Environmental Contamination*, discussed previously, the auditor should consider whether management has incurred current cleanup costs and whether the costs have been charged to expense in the current period. More problematic is the difficult judgment about whether disclosure is required by FASB *Statement of Financial Accounting Standards No. 5*, "Accounting for Contingencies." In this case, the EPA has neither named Humbolt a potentially responsible party nor claimed violation of federal laws or regulations, although the threat looms large. Thus, although it's unclear whether a loss is probable and, if so, whether the amount of the loss can be estimated reasonably, it is clear that no disclosure at all may be inappropriate. In addressing the issue of environmental liabilities with Humbolt Oil's management, the auditor should point out that:

- Once named a potentially responsible party, the company will be jointly and severally liable for all cleanup costs, even if the prior storage facility operator was responsible for only some of the ground water contamination,
- Although disclosure of a contingent liability under *FASB Statement No. 5* requires disclosure in the financial statements only if a loss is "probable," *SEC Financial Reporting Release No. 36* requires disclosure in Form 10-K's Management Discussion and Analysis unless management determines that the loss is *not* "reasonably likely,"—a lower level of probability,

- Although disclosure of environmental liabilities has been associated with stock price declines (see footnote 2), failure to comply with *FASB Statement No. 5* is a departure from GAAP, and
- A departure from GAAP will cause the auditor to issue a qualified or adverse opinion, depending on materiality, and an explanatory paragraph that discloses the effect of the departure on reported earnings (Chapter 3, Figure 3-9).

If the auditor considers concurring with the client to overlook environmental liabilities, he or she risks serious legal and ethical implications. Since Humbolt Oil is publicly traded, statutory law applies and Sections 10(b) and 18 of the *Securities Exchange Act of 1934* (Chapter 5) provide shareholders with a means to recover losses resulting from false or misleading statements. In this case, if disclosure was not made, shareholders could likely recover under Section 10(b) since publication of a newspaper account makes plain that the auditor knew, or should have known, that exposure to environmental liabilities was likely. The plaintiff's basis for action, though (Section 10(b) or Section 18), would be judged by the plaintiff in consultation with an attorney. Further, as discussed in Chapter 5, the auditor could be liable for treble damages under the *Racketeer Influenced and Corrupt Organizations Act* (RICO), since *Reves v. Arthur Young*, a 1993 U.S. Supreme Court case, does not provide relief from RICO when, as would be the case in Humbolt, he or she participates directly with management to perpetrate the fraud.

The case raises at least two ethical issues. First, the auditor violates the *Code of Professional Conduct*, Rule 203—Accounting Principles (Chapter 4), which provides that an AICPA member cannot issue an unqualified opinion if the financial statements contain a departure from an "accounting principle promulgated by bodies designated by Council." In the Humbolt Oil case, the accounting principle violated is failure to disclose a contingent liability for cleanup costs, and the body issuing the principle is the FASB. Violating Rule 203 can result in an administrative reprimand, such as suspension to practice before the SEC, or revocation of a CPA's license to practice public accountancy. Second, overlooking disclosure of environmental liabilities raises serious questions about the auditor's ethical character, since siding with the client injures at least two major stakeholders: Humbolt Oil shareholders and all those who rely on Humbolt management to preserve the land they're entrusted with.

APPLYING NONSTATISTICAL SAMPLING IN SUBSTANTIVE TESTS OF ACCOUNTS PAYABLE

To integrate material presented in this chapter with the nonstatistical sampling applications introduced in Chapter 9, assume a continuing audit engagement for the Skynob Corporation, a wholesaler of college and high school supplies whose fiscal year ends December 31. The objective in this case is to determine whether recorded accounts payable are fairly stated at December 31.

ASSESSMENT OF CONTROL RISK

Assume the consideration of internal control was accomplished as of October 31 and revealed that controls over payables were effective and, therefore, not likely to produce aggregate error in excess of tolerable error. The auditor assessed control risk below the maximum. However, these tests did reveal delays of 36 to 48 hours in recording disbursements, thereby suggesting potential year end cutoff problems that could result in overstated payables and overstated cash at December 31, the balance sheet date. At year end, the auditor made inquiries of management which indicated that neither the control procedures nor responsible personnel had changed since interim. Thus, the auditor had no reason to perform additional tests of controls for the period November 1 to December 31, although the delay in recording disbursements would affect planned audit procedures.

SELECTING A SAMPLING PLAN

Although Skynob's cash disbursements volume is high, payables represent only 5 percent of total liabilities, an amount the auditor judges material but not highly material. Rather, long-term debt, leaseholds, and equity are far more material to the Skynob audit and, further, tests of controls suggest debt and leaseholds may entail more audit risk than payables.

For the Skynob engagement, the auditor now has three important pieces of information:

- Controls over payables are effective.
- Disbursement recording is sometimes delayed, suggesting the possibility of overstated payables and overstated cash at the balance sheet date.
- Payables are material, but neither as material nor as risky as long-term debt and leaseholds.

From this information, the auditor decides to confirm a sample of the accounts payable balances, since year end balances could be overstated and, in this case, the auditor believes confirmations would be less costly than extensive cutoff tests. The auditor elects to use a nonstatistical sampling plan because there is no apparent reason to quantify audit risk.

The auditor's confirmation of Skynob Corporation's payables balances is accomplished by the nonstatistical sampling-for-variables plan introduced in Chapter 9.

Population, Sampling Unit, and Determination of Sample Size

At December 31, the audit population consists of 253 vendor accounts, totaling $475,000. The accounts payable trial balance, the source for selecting accounts for confirmation, is clerically accurate and agrees in total with the general ledger. Each vendor account represents a sampling unit. To choose an appropriate sample size, the auditor must next classify the degree of audit assurance desired, choose an appropriate assurance factor, and estimate tolerable error and key-dollar items, all of which appear in the nonstatistical sampling plan in Chapter 9, pages 343-345.

Because the auditor plans some reliance on internal control in assessing control risk below the maximum, and some reliance on cutoff tests, the auditor requires a moderate degree of audit assurance (see the decision aid on page 322, Chapter 9). Because some error is anticipated, the auditor's assurance factor is 8.

The auditor decides to set tolerable error, the maximum monetary error that may exist without causing the financial statements to be misleading, at

$25,000, which is a little over 5 percent of Skynob's recorded book value. The amount of key-dollar items is set at $8,000, and 28 of the 253 account balances in the population are $8,000 or more, and in total sum to $275,000.

Recapping, the following information is known:

B = Recorded book value = $475,000

KD = Key-dollar items   = $275,000

TE = Tolerable error   = $25,000

AF = Assurance factor   = 8

From these data, sample size can be calculated using the method introduced in Chapter 9, page 344:

$$n = \frac{(B - KD)}{TE} \times AF$$

$$n = \frac{(\$475,000 - \$275,000)}{\$25,000} \times 8$$

$$= 64$$

Ninety-two confirmations are mailed on January 3: 28 to vendors with balances of $8,000 or more (the key-dollar items) and 64 to vendors whose accounts were selected randomly from the 225 remaining accounts (i.e., 253 accounts less 28 key items).

Evaluating Results

Assume confirmations are received from 24 of the key-dollar accounts and from 61 of the 64 randomly selected accounts. For nonresponding vendors, the auditor examines subsequent payments and voucher packages. The confirmations and other procedures reveal $5,975 of known error:

Known error:

Key-dollar items....................................	$3,625	overstatement
Randomly selected items...........................	2,350	overstatement
	$5,975	overstatement

From this information, likely error, the auditor's estimate of total population error, is a $11,887 overstatement, calculated as follows:

Likely error:

Key-dollar error   = $3,625

Other error:

$$\frac{\$2,350}{\left(\dfrac{64}{253 - 28}\right)} = \frac{\$8,262}{\$11,887 \text{ overstatement}}$$

In this case, because tolerable error ($25,000) exceeds likely error ($11,887), the auditor could propose adjusting known error only; that is, propose an audit adjustment reducing payables by $5,975.

COMPUTER ASSISTED SUBSTANTIVE TESTS OF ACCOUNTS PAYABLE

When an entity's accounting information system processes data by computer, some of an auditor's substantive tests of details can be accomplished by computer. Figure 13-8 lists several computer assisted techniques for a series of audit procedures common to accounts payable. These procedures can be accomplished through software prepared by the auditor or through generalized audit software available from outside vendors.

Figure 13-8: Computer Assisted Substantive Tests: Accounts Payable

Audit Procedures	Computer Assisted Substantive Tests
Test mathematical accuracy	Verify footings, cross-footings, and extensions of the accounts payable aged trial balance and/or detailed subsidiary records.
Summarize data for further testing or analysis	Age payables according to due dates. List debit balances in accounts payable for reclassification to accounts receivable. Print accounts payable confirmations.
Test accuracy of recorded data	Compare details in accounts payable trial balance with detailed subsidiary records. Compare details in subsidiary records with source documents (e.g., voucher packages).
Sample selection	Select accounts for testing from a random number generator and the aged accounts payable trial balance.
Compare similar data files	Compare charges/credits in detailed subsidiary records with the purchases/cash disbursements master files.

SUMMARY

The expenditure/disbursement cycle encompasses two major business functions: (1) acquiring resources from vendors and employees, and (2) paying obligations to vendors and employees. These business functions lead to one major balance sheet account: Accounts Payable. The functions also result in prepaid expenses and accrued liabilities. When performing substantive tests of payables, an auditor's major objectives are to determine that each account exists, represents all transactions that should be presented, represents rights or obligations of the entity, is valued properly, and is presented and disclosed properly within the financial statements.

Environmental liabilities result not from transactions incurred during the period but from events like hazardous waste disposal and ground water contamination perpetrated currently or over a period of years. Federal statutes, like the Superfund legislation and the Clean Air Act, impose considerable penalties on potentially responsible parties, penalties that management has incentives to avoid, since disastrous environmental liabilities can affect both stock prices and financial position. Auditors need be aware of the risk of illegal acts from environmental contamination and the potential for material contingent liabilities.

KEY TERMS

Expenditure/disbursement cycle 474 Environmental liabilities 488
Search for unrecorded liabilities 481 Potentially responsible party 488
Voucher package 481

REFERENCES

Auditing Standards

SAS No. 47, "Audit Risk and Materiality in Conducting an Audit."
SAS No. 54, "Illegal Acts by Clients."

Accounting Standards

AICPA Statement of Position (SOP) 96-1, "Environmental Remediation Liabilities."
FASB Emerging Issues Task Force (EITF), Issue 90-8, "Capitalization of Costs to Treat Environmental Contamination."
FASB Emerging Issues Task Force (EITF), Issue 93-5, "Accounting for Environmental Liabilities."
FASB Statement No. 5, "Accounting for Contingencies."

Articles

Cahill, L. B. "Issues in Environmental Auditing," Petroleum Independent (November 1992), p. A2.
Roussey, R. S., Jr. "Auditing Environmental Liabilities," Auditing: A Journal of Practice & Theory (Spring 1992), pp. 47-57.
Stevens, M. G. "New Accounting for Environmental Liabilities," The Practical Accountant (December 1996), pp. 47-51.

QUESTIONS

1. How can an auditor test whether all payables transactions that should be recorded are actually recorded?
2. Explain how an auditor determines whether all recorded payables actually represent bona fide obligations of the entity.
3. What procedures might an auditor use in testing the valuation assertion for purchases and payables?
4. Under what conditions is an auditor most likely to confirm payables?
5. Why is confirmation ineffective in detecting understatement of liabilities?
6. How and why does an auditor test purchases cutoff?
7. Describe how an auditor searches for unrecorded liabilities.
8. What sources does an auditor use to test for overstated accounts payable, and how are those sources used?
9. In testing prepaid insurance, how does an auditor address rights and obligations?
10. What are the major internal controls an auditor considers when designing substantive tests of accrued property taxes?
11. What is meant by a "potentially responsible party"?

12. Under what conditions might an entity not responsible for dumping toxic waste be held responsible by the U.S. Environmental Protection Agency?

MULTIPLE CHOICE QUESTIONS

1. Which of the following procedures is most telling in addressing the existence assertion for accounts payable?

   a. Test for unrecorded liabilities.
   b. Confirm balances with creditors.
   c. Verify the accounts payable trial balance.
   d. Perform analytical procedures.

2. Assume an auditor's interim consideration of internal control in the expenditure/disbursement cycle reveals that control risk can be assessed below the maximum and detection risk above the minimum for some assertions. Which of the following is true about substantive tests applied to accounts payable?

   a. The auditor is more apt to confirm payables balances.
   b. The auditor is less apt to perform substantive tests at the balance sheet date only.
   c. The auditor is more apt to increase the extent of substantive tests.
   d. The auditor is more apt to ignore the risk of incorrect acceptance when sampling accounts payable.

3. Which of the following procedures would help an auditor test for overstatements of accounts payable at the balance sheet date?

   a. Trace entries in the cash disbursements records to items in the accounts payable trial balance.
   b. Agree items in the file of unmatched receiving reports to the accounts payable trial balance.
   c. Trace items in the accounts payable trial balance to documentation contained in canceled voucher packages.
   d. Coordinate cutoff tests performed for receiving and for shipping.

4. In testing cutoff for purchases and payables at December 31, an auditor is confronted with the following four scenarios. Which of the four most likely represents a cutoff error, requiring that the auditor propose an adjusting journal entry?

   a. Shipping terms are FOB shipping point. Goods were shipped on December 31. The purchase was recorded on December 31.
   b. Shipping terms are FOB destination. Goods were shipped on December 31. The purchase was recorded on December 31.
   c. Shipping terms are FOB shipping point. Goods were shipped on January 2. The purchase was recorded on January 4.
   d. Shipping terms are FOB destination. Goods were shipped on December 31. The purchase was recorded on January 2.

5. In performing analytical procedures in the expenditure/disbursement cycle, an auditor detects that payables divided by current liabilities appears low in comparison with prior years. Which of the following courses of action might this unusual relationship suggest?

   a. Increase the scope of testing for unrecorded liabilities.
   b. Confirm payables balances with creditors.

c. Decrease the scope of cutoff testing at the balance sheet date.
d. Decrease the scope of testing for unrecorded liabilities.

6. In addressing control procedures for prepaid insurance, which of the following controls would not be relevant to the auditor?

a. Controls over purchase cutoff.
b. Controls over the acquisition of new insurance policies.
c. Controls over the disbursement of cash for insurance premiums.
d. Controls over the recording of expenses and premium disbursements.

7. Which of the following procedures is most relevant to testing the completeness assertion for prepaid insurance?

a. Testing whether insurance coverage exceeds the replacement value of insured tangible property.
b. Confirming insurance policies with carriers.
c. Reconciling premium payments with cash disbursement records.
d. Agreeing total expense and unexpired premiums with the general ledger.

8. In addressing control procedures for accrued property taxes, which of the following controls would not be relevant to the auditor?

a. Controls over the recognition of accrued taxes.
b. Controls over recording expense for taxes owed.
c. Controls over the disbursement of cash for taxes.
d. Controls over fixed asset additions.

9. Which of the following are likely legitimate reasons why a potentially responsible party would have difficulty estimating environmental cleanup costs?

a. Possible as yet unknown contamination.
b. Possible future legislation.
c. Possible insurance recoveries.
d. Possible preexisting contamination.

10. Under which of the following conditions would it be inappropriate for a potentially responsible party to capitalize toxic waste cleanup costs?

a. The costs relate to a long existing disposal site.
b. The costs extend the life of the property.
c. The costs prevent future contamination.
d. The costs further ready property currently held for sale.

PROBLEMS AND DISCUSSION CASES

13-1 *Relating Errors, Frauds, Audit Procedures, and Assertions in Substantive Tests of Accounts Payable*
Following are errors, frauds, or other circumstances an auditor might encounter as a result of applying year end substantive tests of details to accounts payable as of December 31, 1999:

a. The aged trial balance does not agree with individual accounts payable ledger records.
b. The auditor suspects that accounts payable may be overstated.
c. Several shipments were received from an overseas FOB shipping point on January 2, 2000.

d. The December 31, 1999, accounts payable balance appears low in comparison with the prior two years.

e. The accounts payable department maintains a file of unmatched receiving reports, i.e., receiving reports for which an invoice has not yet been received.

f. Payables are not usually recorded until two days following the date that goods are received.

Required: For each of the above, indicate (1) a specific detailed test or tests that might address the error, fraud, or circumstance and (2) the financial statement assertion addressed by each test.

13-2 *Confirming Accounts Payable*

Stanford Seeles, engagement partner for the audit of the Torgesen-Tate Corporation, is planning the nature, timing, and extent of audit procedures for accounts payable. Prior year working papers reveal that confirmation requests were mailed to 100 of Torgesen-Tate's 1,000 suppliers, the sample consisting mostly of large dollar balances. Management and Seeles spent a substantial number of hours resolving rather minor differences between the confirmation replies and Torgesen-Tate's accounting records. Alternative audit procedures were used for those suppliers who did not respond to the confirmation requests.

Required:

1. What are the audit objectives Seeles ought to consider when planning audit procedures?

2. Discuss circumstances that would compel Seeles to confirm payables. Is Seeles required to confirm payables?

3. Discuss why large dollar balances might not be an efficient basis for selecting accounts to confirm. Suggest a more efficient basis.

13-3 *Designing Substantive Procedures for Accounts Payable*

Taylor is engaged to audit Rex Wholesaling for the year ended December 31, 1999. Taylor considered internal controls over purchasing, receiving, trade accounts payable, and cash disbursement and has decided not to proceed with tests of controls. Based on analytical procedures, Taylor believes that trade accounts payable may be understated at December 31. Taylor requested and obtained from management a client prepared trade accounts payable spreadsheet listing the amount owed each vendor.

Required: Discuss additional substantive audit procedures that Taylor should apply to trade accounts payable.

13-4 *Comparing Receivables and Payables Confirmations*

There is a presumption in the profession that an auditor is required to justify his or her opinion on financial statements when *accounts receivable* are not confirmed (Chapter 11), but not when *accounts payable* are not confirmed. In fact, as noted in Chapter 13, payables are not commonly confirmed in practice.

Required: Compare the confirmation of accounts receivable with the confirmation of accounts payable on two issues: generally accepted procedures of auditing, and the form of confirmation requests.

13-5 *Purchase Cutoff*

Partly to address the existence and completeness assertions, auditors typically test purchase cutoff at the balance sheet date, thereby addressing whether purchase transactions are recorded in the proper accounting period. Your audit supervisor has asked that you perform a purchase cutoff test for the Ridgeview Corporation, a December 31, 1999, year end client. The supervisor suggests that you test all purchase transactions over $5,000 for the period December 25, 1999 through January 5, 2000. Audit working papers compiled during the December 31 physical inventory observation indicate that the last receiving report used on December 31 was No. 13402. The following data is available for eight purchase transactions:

Receiving Report Number	Amount	Date Shipped	Date Received	Shipping Terms
13398	$13,500 **	Dec. 26	Dec. 28	FOB: Origin
13399	7,560 *	Dec. 27	Dec. 27	FOB: Dest.
13400	24,000 *	Dec. 29	Dec. 29	FOB: Origin
13401	5,000 **	Dec. 31	Dec. 31	FOB: Origin
13402	15,980 *	Dec. 29	Dec. 31	FOB: Dest.
13403	9,765 *	Dec. 30	Jan. 02	FOB: Dest.
13404	45,000 **	Jan. 01	Jan. 03	FOB: Dest.
13405	10,855 **	Dec. 31	Jan. 02	FOB: Origin

*Indicates the purchase was included in December 31 payables.
**Indicates the purchase was *not* included in December 31 payables.

Required: For the purchase data above, indicate whether (and why) each purchase is treated properly or improperly in December 31 accounts payable. Prepare an adjusting journal entry for the purchases treated improperly.

13-6 *The Motivation to Understate or Overstate Payables*
Auditors are often concerned that liabilities may be understated as a result of unrecorded payables. On the other hand, auditors may be concerned that liabilities are overstated as a result of payables recorded in the wrong accounting period, among other things.
Required:
1. Give several reasons why an entity may want to understate payables.
2. Give several reasons why an entity may want to overstate payables.

13-7 *Tests for Unrecorded Payables*
Unrecorded payables result in two potentially material misstatements in an entity's financial statements: *understated liabilities*, because the credit to Payables is not recorded, and *overstated net income*, because a corresponding expense is not recorded. As a result, auditors typically perform a search for unrecorded payables during year end substantive testing.
Required: Prepare an audit program to search for unrecorded payables.

13-8 *Unrecorded Payables*
You are in the final stages of your audit of the Ozine Corporation's financial statements for the year ended December 31, 1999, when the corporation's chief executive officer, Gordon Sumner, approaches you. Sumner believes there is no point in your examining purchases transacted on or after January 1, 2000, since: (1) bills pertaining to 1999 that were received too late to be included in the December voucher register were recorded as of year end by journal entry, (2) the internal auditor made tests after year end, and (3) he (Sumner) would furnish you with a letter certifying that there were no unrecorded liabilities.
Required:
1. Should an auditor's test for unrecorded liabilities be affected by the fact that the client made a journal entry to record 1999 bills that were received late? Discuss.
2. Should an auditor's test for unrecorded liabilities be affected by the fact that a letter is obtained in which a responsible management official certifies that to the best of his or her knowledge all liabilities have been recorded? Discuss.
3. Should an auditor's test for unrecorded liabilities be eliminated or reduced because of the internal audit tests? Discuss.

4. Assume that the corporation had no internal auditor but, owing to some government contracts, an auditor for a federal agency had spent three weeks auditing the records. How would the auditor's unrecorded liability test be affected by the work of the federal auditor?
5. What sources, in addition to the 2000 voucher register, should the auditor consider to locate possible unrecorded liabilities?

(AICPA Adapted)

13-9 *Liability for Loss Contingencies*
Harper has completed tests of accounts payable and other liabilities for the Hawthorne Corporation, and now plans to determine whether there are any loss contingencies arising from litigation, claims, or assessments.

Required: Discuss the procedures Harper should follow to audit the existence of loss contingencies arising from litigation, claims, and assessments.

(AICPA Adapted)

13-10 *Testing an Automated Payables System*
During your audit of the financial statements of the John Delaney Manufacturing Company for the year ended December 31, 1999, you find that at January 1, 1999, the company had installed the following computer system for recording raw material purchases and accounts payable:

a. Vendors' invoices are sent directly to Accounts Payable by the mail department.
b. All supporting documents are attached to the invoices and accumulated in the accounts payable department. Cash discounts are computed, and the invoices are totaled, tied to supporting documents, and entered in a local area network by an employee at a workstation.
c. At the workstation, the employee enters the payable on a template which requires data entry for the related debit distribution to departmental inventories.
d. An invoice register is compiled automatically by payable and by debit distribution from the accumulated templates. In this operation, totals are compared with the amounts recorded for the related account payable.
e. The general ledger control account is posted monthly from the totals shown in the invoice register and all other journals.
f. Accounts payable are sorted by due dates.
g. On the due dates, the payables are processed to prepare checks.
h. At the end of the month, the accounts payable in the unpaid file are compared with the general ledger control account.

Required: What audit procedures would you use to test the accounts payable balance at December 31, 1999?

13-11 *Auditing Property and Casualty Insurance*
During an audit of the financial statements of Custer-McClurg, Inc., Timothy Barnes, the engagement manager, requested and received a client prepared property and casualty insurance spreadsheet that included information about premiums.

Required:
1. Identify the type of information, in addition to premium information, that would ordinarily be included in a property and casualty insurance schedule.
2. What audit procedures should Barnes perform to test the client prepared property and casualty insurance schedule?

13-12 *Working Paper Review: Accounts Payable*
Following is an audit working paper that documents an auditor's work for Feldman Services, Inc.'s accounts payable aged trial balance for the year ended December 31, 1999.

Feldman Services, Inc.
Accounts Payable Aged Trial Balance

Account Number	Vendor Name	Balance 12/31/99	0-30 Days	31-60 Days	Over 60 Days
00001	Acorn Shops	$ 31,890	$ 31,890		
00002	Aftran Inc.	17,869	15,432		$ 2,437
00003	Astrid & Strugg	6,670	6,670		
00005	Baldoni Corp.	500	500		
00006	Balfour	12,980	11,980		
00007	Benton Inc.	23,930	23,930		
00008	Boylston & Way	12,403	12,403		
00009	Britton Company	10,944		10,944	
00010	Cristwich Inc.	4,530		4,530	
•	•	•	•	•	•
•	•	•	•	•	•
00452	Youngstown Co.	23,907	23,907		
		$2,569,340	$2,158,320	$301,020	$110,000
		a			

a Footed.

Required: List the deficiencies in this working paper.

13-13 *Working Paper Review: Accrued Property Taxes*
Following is an audit working paper that documents an auditor's work for Sempier & Fiske, Inc.'s accrued property taxes payable for the year ended December 31, 1999. Sempier & Fiske is a first year audit client.

Sempier & Fiske, Inc.
December 31, 1999

Balance, 12/31/98		$75,984[a]
Provision for property tax expense		75,000
Payments:		
State of Indiana	$34,930[b]	
City of Indianapolis	17,340[b]	
City of Ft. Wayne	8,450[b]	
City of So. Bend	10,346[b]	(71,066)
Balance, 12/31/99		$79,918
		c

a Agreed to prior auditor's working papers.
b Traced to cash disbursements records.
c Footed.

Required: List the deficiencies in this working paper.

13-14 *Earnings Manipulation and Environmental Liabilities*

During the planning stage of an audit, the engagement partner and manager tour the assembly facilities of York Chemicals, a manufacturer and supplier of chemical solvents to auto body shops nationwide. Solvent is stored in forty gallon drums stacked by stock number in a warehouse awaiting shipment. Fifty yards from the assembly plant, but within a chain link fence that surrounds the property, is a ditch containing damaged barrels. Seepage is apparent beneath the barrels and on the unpaved roadway leading to the ditch.

Required: Identify, and explain the motive for, the key questions an auditor must ask management about the ditch, damaged barrels, and seepage.

RESEARCH PROJECT

MANAGEMENT DISCRETION AND ENVIRONMENTAL LIABILITIES

Since the Exxon Valdez incident brought surface contamination to the evening news, the press has been replete with references to environmental disasters, making most everyone conscious of the devastating effects of industrial pollution, toxic waste disposal, and manufacturing and transport accidents. Underscoring many of these articles and newscasts is the unmistakable implication that industry is mortgaging the future of the planet and, in particular, that audited financial statements may not adequately portray the effects of environmental liabilities. For example, the March 9, 1993, late edition of the *New York Times* in a piece by John Holusha entitled, "Stocks May Not Reflect Cleanup Liabilities That May Come Soon," began, "The earnings of Smokestack America seem likely to face new setbacks because of future liabilities for cleaning up the environment, according to a Price Waterhouse survey. The survey, which covered manufacturing companies, public utilities and extractive industries, found that 62 percent have known environmental liabilities that are both material and undisclosed."

Required: Using the newspaper and magazines file in NEXIS, Mead Data Central's automated data retrieval system, or newspapers and magazines in a library, select an article or series of articles about environmental matters involving a particular company in, for example, the manufacturing, utilities, or extractive industries. Using the annual report file in the National Automated Accounting Research System (NAARS) or copies of annual reports in a library, select the annual report of the same company issued for the fiscal year that includes the date of the article. Draft a report that accomplishes the following:

1. Summarize the article(s), indicating key issues that would suggest the need for disclosing environmental liability in the financial statements.

2. From the key issues in (1) list and explain questions an auditor would likely pose to the management of the company you've selected.

3. Determine whether the company's financial statements include disclosures you think are related to the article and, either if so or if not, explain why you believe the company is or is not among those implicated in the *New York Times* article referred to above.

14

Tests of Controls and Substantive Tests of Personnel and Payroll, and Management Discretion in Accounting for Postretirement Health Care

Major topics discussed in this chapter are the:

- Nature of the personnel management and payroll functions of the expenditure/disbursement cycle.
- Control objectives, control procedures, and potential errors or fraud that relate to personnel and payroll activities.
- Auditor's consideration of controls over personnel and payroll.
- Substantive tests applicable to payroll accounts.
- Application of audit judgment to questions about management discretion and postretirement health care benefits.

The previous two chapters focused on tests of controls and substantive tests of purchases and accounts payable, both of which are processed through the expenditure/disbursement cycle. This chapter continues the discussion of the expenditure/disbursement cycle, focusing on tests of controls and substantive tests related to personnel and payroll. The chapter begins by reviewing the nature of the cycle, introducing activities and controls common to personnel and payroll, and explaining an auditor's consideration of controls over personnel, payroll preparation, and payroll-related cash disbursements. In turn, substantive tests of payroll account balances are introduced. Finally, the chapter addresses audit, legal, and ethical questions auditors face when auditing postretirement benefits other than pensions, in particular postretirement heath care obligations.

THE EXPENDITURE/DISBURSEMENT CYCLE: PERSONNEL MANAGEMENT AND PAYROLL

As discussed in Chapter 12, the expenditure/disbursement cycle encompasses the acquisition of, and payment for, resources acquired from vendors and from employees. Figure 14-1 summarizes the scope of the cycle as it relates to

504

Figure 14-1: The Scope of the Expenditure/Disbursement Cycle: Personnel and Payroll

Related Business Functions	Common Activities	Common Entries	Common Forms
• Resources (services) are acquired from employees in exchange for obligations to pay • Obligations to employees are paid	• Prepare and update personnel records • Prepare and record payroll • Distribute paychecks to employees	• Payments to employees (cash disbursements) • Account distribution • Accrued payroll	• Personnel records • Time records • Payroll register • Employee earnings records

personnel and payroll, and indicates the two major business functions encompassed by personnel and payroll:

- Resources (services) are acquired from employees in exchange for obligations to pay, and
- Obligations to employees are paid.

Personnel and payroll are critical to most entities for at least three reasons. First, salaries and wages are a major expenditure for most service, manufacturing, and nonprofit entities. Second, in manufacturing companies, labor is an important component in valuing inventory and, if misclassified, both inventory and cost of goods sold could be misstated materially. Third, payroll typically includes several categories of employee compensation, including salaries, hourly wages, incentive compensation and bonuses, overtime, vacation pay, and employee benefits such as pensions, health care, and profit sharing.

Personnel and payroll activities include hirings and terminations, payroll preparation and recording, and the distribution of payroll checks to employees. Journal entries are made for wage and salary payments, for account distribution, and for end-of-period accruals. Paper and computer image documents include:

- **Personnel records.** Information for each employee, including date of hire, job classification, salary or hourly pay rate, promotions, payroll deductions, termination date, etc.
- **Time records.** Hours worked by each employee during a pay period.
- **Payroll register.** A record of gross pay, withholdings, deductions, and net pay for each employee for a pay period; the basis for preparing paychecks, for recording payroll, and for updating employee earnings records.
- **Employee earnings records.** A cumulative, year-to-date summary of total earnings, withholdings, and deductions for each employee.

Figure 14-2 flowcharts representative personnel and payroll activities within the expenditure/disbursement cycle. Figure 14-3, derived from Figure 14-2, briefly summarizes the flow of documents and activities common to personnel and payroll. The following explains.

Figure 14-2:   Flowchart of Expenditure/Disbursement Cycle: Personnel and Payroll

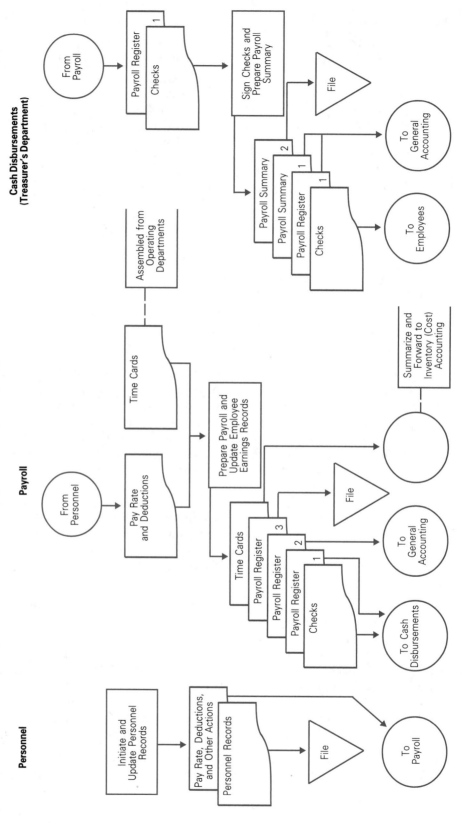

Figure 14-3:   Personnel and Payroll: Document Flow

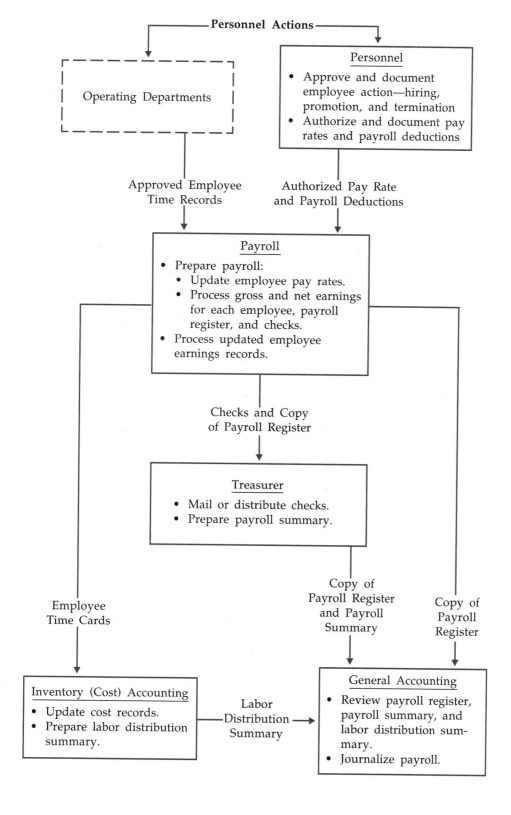

PERSONNEL MANAGEMENT

Without exception, all action taken by management in behalf of an employee—including hiring, promotion, transfer, and termination—should be approved both by department supervisors and by the personnel department, and should be documented in an employee's *personnel records*. Typically, personnel records also document:

- Salary or wage rates,
- Payroll deductions,
- Employee signatures,
- Job classification, and
- Performance evaluation.

To minimize the likelihood of fraud, personnel records should not be accessible to employees who are responsible for preparing, approving, or distributing payroll. For example, an employee who processed personnel records *and* prepared the payroll could destroy a salaried employee's termination records and abscond with (and forge endorsements for) subsequent paychecks.

When employees are terminated, the personnel department should determine the nature and terms of any related termination settlement, such as lump sum cash payments and accrued vacation pay. Immediately thereafter, the payroll department should be advised of the termination settlement and notified that further compensation has ceased.

PAYROLL PREPARATION AND DISTRIBUTION

Typically, the main source to prepare hourly wage employees' payroll and the *payroll register* is each employee's magnetic identification card: Employees "punch" in (out) at the beginning (end) of the workday on a time clock that interfaces directly with the company's computer, thereby creating an internally stored *time record* that software merges with pay rate and deduction data to compile payroll for the period. In addition, hours worked may also be accumulated in the manufacturing departments for each production project, thereby creating a second *time record*—for example, an *accumulated departmental labor charge report*—which Inventory (Cost) Accounting uses for charging direct labor hours to Work-in-Process Inventory.

From the information in the payroll register, facsimile-signed paychecks are printed and forwarded to the Treasurer's department along with a copy of the *payroll register*. A copy of the payroll register is also sent to General Accounting. As a control over payroll accuracy, the payroll register may be checked in detail by an employee not otherwise involved in payroll preparation. The payroll should also be reviewed for reasonableness by management. Each pay period, coincident with payroll preparation, cumulative *employee earnings records* are updated, providing a year-to-date summary of total earnings, taxes withheld, and deductions (e.g., for federal and state income taxes, union dues, health insurance, savings, etc.).

Paychecks forwarded to the Treasurer's department should be compared with listings in the payroll register. In small or middle-market entities, signed checks should be delivered to operating department supervisors for distribution to individual employees. However, in large entities, it's preferable that signed paychecks be distributed by a person independent of both the operating department and Payroll—called a paymaster in some companies—thereby removing opportunities for department supervisors to dismiss an employee, not report the dismissal to Payroll, and then divert the check for his or her own use. The *payroll register* and a copy of the payroll summary (e.g., total payroll by department, account distribution, etc.) prepared by Treasurer's Department personnel should be sent to General Accounting.

To obtain reasonable assurance that paychecks are distributed to bona fide employees only, an employee independent of payroll preparation sometimes compares, on a test basis, endorsements on canceled payroll checks, if returned by the bank, with employee signatures in personnel records. Differences could suggest errors or frauds, and should be investigated. At the end of the year, employee *W-2* forms should be prepared and mailed to employees. Mailed *W-2* forms that are returned by the postal service as undeliverable should be followed up—returned *W-2* forms could signal either incorrect addresses or, more serious, nonexistent employees.

A separate bank account (or accounts) should be maintained exclusively for payroll disbursements. Controls should limit access to blank checks and should assure that, if signed manually, checks are signed only by authorized officials.

INTERNAL CONTROL OBJECTIVES AND POTENTIAL ERRORS OR FRAUDS

In Chapter 12, which is also devoted to the expenditure/disbursement cycle, control objectives for purchasing and cash disbursements are discussed. The following sections focus on internal control over transaction authorization, execution, recording, and access to assets for personnel and payroll. The discussion identifies control objectives, examples of errors or frauds that may arise if objectives are not achieved, and examples of control procedures designed to prevent or detect errors or frauds. Figure 14-4 summarizes.

TRANSACTION AUTHORIZATION

Much as management should approve vendors (Chapter 12), management should also establish criteria for hiring line and staff employees. Otherwise, unqualified employees may be hired, potentially resulting in excessive training costs, unnecessary relocation costs, or penalties for violating equal opportunity laws, among other things. To control against unauthorized hiring, management should establish written hiring policies, verify all relevant information included in employment applications, and maintain updated personnel records for all employees.

Likewise, management should authorize compensation and payroll deductions, thereby protecting against excessive labor costs, violation of union contracts, and inaccurate accruals for pensions, vacations, or bonuses. Many companies control compensation and deductions by establishing procedures for reviewing and approving pay rates and deductions and by maintaining updated, authorized pay rates by job classification.

Although entry-level pay rates may be determined by authorized pay rate listings, management should authorize subsequent adjustments—for example, for promotions, transfers, and merit increases. Otherwise, unauthorized pay

Figure 14-4: Personnel and Payroll: Control Objectives, Potential Errors or Frauds, and Control Procedures

Control Objectives	Types of Errors or Frauds That Could Occur if Objective Not Met	Control Procedures Designed to Prevent or Detect Errors or Frauds
Transaction Authorization		
• Employees should be hired according to criteria authorized by management.	Unqualified employees may be hired, potentially resulting in excessive training costs, unnecessary relocation costs, or penalties for violating equal opportunity laws.	Establish written hiring policies and procedures. Maintain updated personnel records for all employees. Verify employment applications.
• Compensation and payroll deductions should be made in accordance with management's authorization.	Employees may be paid unauthorized amounts, potentially resulting in excessive labor costs or violation of union contracts. Accruals for pensions, vacations, or bonuses may be calculated from inaccurate information, potentially resulting in misstated accruals.	Maintain updated listings of authorized pay rates and deductions. Establish procedures for reviewing and approving pay rates and deductions.
• Adjustments to compensation or personnel records should be made in accordance with management's authorization.	Unauthorized adjustments may be processed to increase an employee's pay, potentially misappropriating cash and overstating labor costs.	Establish written statements of adjustment policies and procedures (e.g., pay rate adjustments).
Transaction Execution		
• Payroll and personnel procedures should be established in accordance with management's authorization.	Employees could process paychecks for terminated or fictitious employees, potentially resulting in misappropriated cash.	Establish personnel and payroll procedures manuals. Advertise available job openings widely throughout the entity.
• All payroll cash disbursements should be based upon a recognized liability.	Cash may be disbursed for services not performed, potentially resulting in misappropriated cash and overstated labor costs.	Prenumber and control time records, paychecks, and adjustment forms. Require manual dual signatories for all pay over a prespecified dollar amount.

Figure 14-4: *(continued)*

Control Objectives	Types of Errors or Frauds That Could Occur if Objective Not Met	Control Procedures Designed to Prevent or Detect Errors or Frauds
Recording • Amounts due to employees should be recorded at the proper amount, in the proper period, and be properly classified.	Payroll costs, labor costs, and related liabilities (e.g., federal tax withheld) may be inaccurate, potentially resulting in misstated expenses and liabilities. Summaries of detailed records (e.g., the payroll register and summary of labor costs) may not agree, potentially resulting in miscalculated payroll or misapplied labor costs.	Establish and document account distribution procedures. Reconcile appropriate ledgers and journals.
Access to Assets • Access to personnel and payroll records and to forms and documents should be restricted to personnel authorized by management.	Records, forms, or documents may be misused by unauthorized personnel, potentially resulting in misapplied cash or unauthorized labor costs.	Prenumber and establish physical controls over unused documents and forms. Segregate responsibilities for authorizing, executing, and recording payroll and personnel transactions. Maintain listings and samples of authorized signatories.

increases could be processed. Management could control unauthorized pay increases by establishing written policies for pay rate adjustments and communicating the policies to the personnel department and to operating department supervisors.

TRANSACTION EXECUTION

In labor-intensive businesses, such as the automotive industry, labor costs can be both extensive and subject to negotiated labor contracts, suggesting the need for controls that assure accurate payrolls. Otherwise, management could violate labor contracts, or employees could process paychecks for terminated or fictitious employees. As a result, most medium- to large-sized companies usually establish personnel and payroll procedures manuals and advertise available job openings widely throughout the company.

To control against disbursements for work not performed, all cash disbursements for payroll should be based on a recognized liability. Paychecks should reflect compensation for services actually rendered, just as disbursements to vendors should be based on goods and services actually received. Management can control unauthorized payroll disbursements by requiring a second, manual signature for all unusual or excessive paycheck amounts, prenumbered time cards, paychecks, and adjustment forms.

RECORDING

All amounts owed to employees should be recorded at the proper amounts and in the proper period, and should be classified properly. Otherwise, payroll and labor costs and related liabilities such as taxes withheld may be inaccurate, potentially resulting in misstated expenses, labor costs, and liabilities. In addition, summaries of detailed records, such as payroll summaries and registers, may not agree, which could result in miscalculated payroll or misapplied labor costs. In short, accurately calculated paychecks do not necessarily imply proper account distribution or properly applied labor costs. To control against improper recording, management could establish account distribution and labor cost allocation procedures, and reconcile appropriate ledgers, journals, and summaries.

ACCESS TO ASSETS

To control against misapplied cash and unauthorized labor costs, management should institute policies that restrict access to personnel and payroll records to authorized personnel only. For example, management could establish physical barriers over unused documents and forms (e.g., safes), prenumber documents, maintain listings of authorized signatories, and segregate responsibilities for authorizing, executing, and recording payroll and personnel transactions—essentially the same controls listed in Chapter 12 for purchases and cash disbursements.

SEGREGATION OF DUTIES

To assure adequate segregation of duties, Personnel Department responsibilities should be separated from payroll preparation, and both should be separated from cash disbursements and operating departments. Otherwise, an authorization function (personnel) would be combined with an execution function (payroll), thereby increasing opportunities for unauthorized employee action and for inflated pay rates. In addition, combining Payroll with operating departments, such as Production or Inventory Control, increases opportunities for unauthorized disbursements, because an employee would be responsible both for reporting hours worked and for calculating gross pay.

CONSIDERING INTERNAL CONTROL

Chapter 12 discusses the auditor's consideration of controls over three expenditure/disbursement cycle functions: purchasing, receiving, and cash disbursement. The following focuses on an auditor's consideration of controls over the cycle's personnel and payroll activities.

OBTAIN AN UNDERSTANDING

In the initial phase of considering internal control, an auditor attempts to determine how the system is supposed to work and whether control procedures have been prescribed by management to assure that the system is functioning as planned. Obtaining an understanding of the system includes:

1. Performing a *preliminary review,*
2. *Documenting* the system,
3. Performing a *transaction walk-through,* and
4. Determining whether existing *controls* are potentially reliable in assessing control risk below the maximum.

Preliminary Review

In a preliminary review, an auditor develops a general understanding of a client's *control environment,* of the *flow of transactions and records* through the accounting system, and of *control procedures* management has implemented to prevent or detect errors or frauds. For example, an auditor could obtain an understanding by reviewing the client's personnel and payroll procedures manual and by interviewing employees in Personnel and in Payroll. Assuming the preliminary review suggests that further consideration of internal control is likely to justify assessing control risk below the maximum and, thereby, restricting substantive tests of payroll balances, an auditor would proceed as follows.

System Documentation

Figure 14-2, discussed earlier, illustrates a flowchart for personnel and payroll. In turn, Figure 14-5 illustrates a questionnaire, a second method for presenting system documentation about personnel and payroll and about the distribution of payroll checks. Alternatively, an auditor could use a narrative to describe the payroll system either in whole or in part. For example, an auditor might prepare flowcharts and questionnaires to document payroll procedures for hourly employees and draft a narrative memorandum to document procedures for executive payroll, which typically involves fewer personnel and therefore fewer payroll checks.

Transaction Walk-Through

To confirm his or her understanding of the system flowcharted in Figure 14-2, the auditor could select a line item from a processed payroll register and trace the information: (1) to time reports summarized in the payroll department and filed in the inventory accounting department and (2) to records maintained in the personnel department. The purpose of the walk-through, however, is not necessarily to test control procedures, but to confirm the flowchart and completed questionnaire.

Identification of Control Procedures

An auditor completes the system documentation and continues the consideration of internal control in the same manner as outlined in Chapter 12 for purchases and cash disbursements.

- Identify the system's *control objectives.* The first column of Figure 14-4 identifies control objectives for personnel and payroll.

Figure 14-5:   Questionnaire: Personnel and Payroll

Question	Answer: Yes, No, or N/A	Remarks
Personnel and Payroll		
1. Are all employee changes—hiring, promotions, transfers, terminations—approved by operating department supervisors and by the personnel department?		
2. Are all employee changes documented in personnel records?		
3. Are all employee changes communicated promptly to the payroll department?		
4. Do employee personnel records include authorizations for all deductions and withholdings?		
5. Are guidelines established for determining account distribution for labor charges?		
6. Are employees who prepare or process payroll independent of hirings and terminations and excluded from distributing paychecks to employees?		
7. Is payroll approved by a responsible official independent of payroll preparation and processing?		
8. Is the preparation of employee time reports supervised to assure that hours reported are accurate?		
Cash Disbursement		
1. Are paychecks distributed by personnel independent of the personnel and payroll departments?		
2. Is the payroll bank account reconciled monthly by an employee independent of payroll preparation, processing, and distribution?		
3. Are employees required to provide identification before receiving a paycheck?		
4. Are unclaimed paychecks returned to an employee independent of payroll preparation, processing, and distribution?		
5. Are W-2 forms compared with payroll records and mailed by employees independent of payroll preparation, processing, and distribution?		
6. Are returned W-2 forms (e.g., marked "return to sender" by the U.S. Postal Service) investigated by employees who are independent of Payroll?		

- Consider the *potential errors or frauds* that might result if specific control objectives are not met. The second column of Figure 14-4 identifies examples of potential errors or frauds.
- Determine what *control procedures* are used by the entity to prevent or detect potentially material errors or frauds. The third column of Figure 14-4 identifies examples of potential controls.
- Design *tests of controls.*

Only those control procedures relevant to financial statement assertions are subjected to tests of controls, which are discussed next.

TESTS OF CONTROLS: PERSONNEL AND PAYROLL

Generally, internal evidence prepared by the client is the only persuasive audit evidence available for testing payroll. As a result, auditors often rely predominantly, if not exclusively, on tests of controls rather than substantive procedures when auditing payroll. If the results of tests of controls indicate that control procedures can be relied on in assessing control risk below the maximum, substantive testing focuses on analytical procedures such as ratio analysis. Some representative tests of controls for personnel and payroll and for the distribution of payroll checks are discussed below for the system flowcharted in Figure 14-2.

Personnel and Payroll

The payroll register is an entity's continuing record of employee compensation and provides the basis for preparing, distributing, and recording periodic payroll. Tests of controls follow.

Tests of Controls: Personnel and Payroll

1. Obtain the *payroll register* for a selected period (or periods) and verify the mathematical accuracy.
2. Obtain a related *payroll summary* and a *labor distribution summary*.
   a. Verify the mathematical accuracy of *payroll* and *labor distribution summaries* and compare with totals in the *payroll register*.
   b. Trace totals to postings in the general ledger and in cost accounting records.
3. Select a random sample of employees from the *payroll register* and obtain the personnel file for each employee selected.
   a. Examine files for completeness and review *employee action reports* for authorization.
   b. Compare pay rates and payroll deduction information in personnel records with entries in the payroll register; for hourly employees, obtain *time reports* and recompute gross earnings for the payroll period.
   c. Trace sampled entries in the *payroll register* to postings in individual employee cumulative earnings records.
   d. Trace selected employee names to a *payroll register* for a prior period and to a *payroll register* for a subsequent period; examine *employee action reports* for newly hired or terminated personnel.

As indicated in Step 1, the *payroll register* is the starting point for an auditor's tests of personnel and payroll. In Steps 1 and 2, the auditor addresses mathematical accuracy and postings by footing and cross-footing the *payroll register* and reconciling totals with related summary schedules and with the general ledger and inventory accounting records. Payroll accuracy and account distribution are of major concern to an auditor because of the significant impact of payroll on no less than seven financial statement accounts, including payroll expense, payroll taxes, work-in-process inventory, finished goods inventory, cost of sales, accrued payroll, and accrued payroll taxes.

In Step 3, an auditor selects a sample of entries in the *payroll register* as a basis for testing personnel records for completeness and proper authorization and for determining whether employee compensation accurately reflects authorized pay rates, payroll deductions, and hours worked. In addition, the auditor examines postings to individual employee cumulative earnings records, because these records provide the basis for preparing *W-2* forms and for calculating payroll tax expense.

Distribution of Employee Paychecks

Tests of payments to employees focus on the existence and authenticity of employees to whom disbursements are made, rather than cash disbursements per se. Representative tests follow.

Tests of Controls: Distribution of Paychecks

1. Obtain a sample of canceled payroll checks.
   a. Trace details of sampled checks (payee name, date, amount, and check number) to entries in the *payroll register*.
   b. Compare endorsements on checks with signatures in employee personnel records.
2. Take control of payroll checks just prior to distribution by department supervisors, and personally distribute checks to properly identified employees.

In Step 1a, the auditor traces details of sampled paychecks to entries in the *payroll register*, thereby addressing whether checks are recorded properly. Step 1b, sometimes called a "payroll payoff," focuses on the authenticity of employees, by comparing endorsements on canceled checks with signatures maintained in employee personnel records. The auditor also addresses the authenticity of employees in Step 2 by personally distributing paychecks to employees during work hours. This procedure normally requires that the auditor first examine an employee identification card with photo, if available, to assure that the employee is actually who he or she purports to be.

ASSESS CONTROL RISK

To complete the consideration of internal control for personnel and payroll, an auditor reviews system documentation and the results of tests of controls and determines whether existing controls are effective and can be relied on to assess control risk below the maximum, to assess detection risk above the minimum, and, therefore, to restrict substantive tests of payroll. The evaluation is based on the types of errors or frauds that could occur, control procedures that should prevent the errors or frauds, a determination of whether the necessary procedures exist and are followed, and any deficiencies in internal control.

Assuming control procedures are effective, auditors normally restrict year end substantive tests of payroll to analytical procedures. But if analytical procedures suggest that payroll-related balances are not reasonable, an auditor would increase the extent of year end testing by performing expanded substantive tests of details. The analytical procedures applied to payroll are discussed next.

SUBSTANTIVE TESTS: PAYROLL

As noted previously, substantive tests of payroll usually focus primarily or exclusively on analytical procedures. Representative year end procedures and related financial statement assertions are presented in Figure 14-6. If the results of tests of controls indicated that control risk cannot be assessed below the maximum, substantive procedures would be expanded accordingly. Also, if significant changes in control procedures or their method of application occurred subsequent to testing controls, the auditor would have to either reconsider internal control—for example, through additional tests of controls—or assess control risk at the maximum without reconsidering the controls.

ANALYTICAL PROCEDURES: PAYROLL EXPENSE AND ACCRUALS

In assessing the overall reasonableness of payroll expense and its distribution across accounts (for example, general and administrative expense, direct labor charged to inventory), an auditor might develop and analyze relationships among data. Selected items can be compared with corresponding items from prior years and/or with other items in the same period. Ratios are often useful in making comparisons, because relationships between accounts generally should not vary significantly over time in the absence of changes in the nature of an entity's business, production process, or accounting methods, among other things. Ratios can be calculated by an auditor to determine whether accounts relate to each other in the manner expected. For example, if total direct labor has approximated 35 percent of cost of sales for the previous two years, an auditor would expect the percentage for the current year to be close to 35 percent, unless changes have occurred that would be expected to alter the relationship. If relationships vary significantly from expected results, an auditor might conclude that additional substantive tests of account balances are necessary.

The reasonableness of payroll-related accruals can usually be determined with little detailed testing. For example, if employees are paid biweekly and one week's payroll is accrued at the end of the year, an auditor could simply determine whether the accrual is approximately equal to 50 percent of the total payroll for the most recent complete pay period. If different categories of

Figure 14-6:   Substantive Tests: Payroll

Assertions	Procedures
Occurrence Valuation	1. Determine by analytical procedures the reasonableness of payroll expense and account distribution.
Obligations Valuation Completeness	2. Determine the reasonableness of accruals for Wages, Salaries, and related accounts.

Presentation and
disclosure
	3. Review financial statements to determine whether:
	  a. Payroll and related accruals are properly classified and described.
	  b. Disclosures are adequate.

employees are paid at different intervals, an auditor might recalculate the accrual and examine subsequent payroll disbursements.

FINANCIAL STATEMENT DISCLOSURES

Finally, an auditor should review financial statements to determine that payroll and related accounts are properly classified and described and that all material information is disclosed. For example, information relating to stock options or deferred compensation plans should be included in the notes to the financial statements.

MANAGEMENT DISCRETION AND POSTRETIREMENT BENEFITS OTHER THAN PENSIONS

Payroll is an example of a financial statement caption auditors often "tie down" pretty much to the penny, since, like in the audit of Cash, an entity's payroll records should mirror the bank's records for paychecks cleared and, equally comforting to auditors, employees will complain loudly if paychecks are miscalculated. In short, there's little room for management to exercise discretion in recording current and accrued payroll. However, largely because of the bewildering uncertainty management faces in estimating *future* obligations, another personnel related cost leaves much more room for discretion and, therefore, requires far more of an auditor's critical attention: **postretirement benefits other than pensions**, in particular obligations for the discounted present value of future health care costs.[1]

A survey reported in *Business Week* estimates that postretirement health care benefits are offered by no less than 91 percent of the companies that employ over 5,000 people,[2] and Deloitte & Touche estimates that future health care costs range between a staggering $100 and $500 billion.[3] However, partly because the costs to fund postretirement health care benefits were neither tax-deductible nor, for that matter, binding obligations under prior definitions of liabilities, companies had largely ignored obligations for future health care costs in their current financial statements, electing instead to pay retirees' actual out-of-pocket health care costs as the costs were incurred, providing a penetrating example of off-balance-sheet financing and of a cash basis, "pay-as-you-go" system. In response, the FASB issued *Statement of Financial Accounting Standards No. 106*, "Employers' Accounting for Postretirement Benefits Other Than Pensions," a statement *The Wall Street Journal* called "one of the most significant changes to accounting ever . . . a rule on postretirement health benefits that could cut corporate profits by hundreds of billions of dollars,"[4] because, for the first time ever, the present value of future health care expenses and liabilities would be recognized in current financial statements.

---

1 Postretirement benefits also include life insurance, tuition assistance, and housing subsidies, among other things, all of which are important to retirees but none of which is usually as material to financial statements as the discounted present value of future health care costs.

2 "Now That Wasn't So Bad, Was It?" *Business Week* (December 2, 1991), p. 123.

3 "New FASB Rules on Accounting for Other Postretirement Benefits," *Deloitte & Touche Review* (December 1990).

4 "FASB Issues Rule Change on Benefits," *The Wall Street Journal* (December 20, 1990), p. A3.

MANAGEMENT AND AUDITOR INCENTIVES

Prior to *SFAS No. 106*, management was not required to report future liabilities for nonpension postretirement benefits and, as a consequence, none did. Although discretion over reporting the liability ceased with *SFAS No. 106*, management retains some discretion over the amount of the liability reported because, unlike future obligations for pensions, which generally require predictable payments to surviving retirees, future health care benefits are quite unpredictable both in timing (who will become ill when?) and in amount (who of the ill will be ill with what?). Clearly, management has incentives to understate the discounted present value of future health care obligations, largely because of the effect on reported income. For example, IBM's $2.3 billion charge to first quarter 1991 net income to adopt *SFAS No. 106* drove the company's first reported quarterly loss ever.[5] Auditors have incentives to assure that management's charge to income and reported liability are fairly presented in all material respects, since materially misstated amounts can affect current share prices and future health care payouts, and, as demonstrated in Chapter 5, auditors can be held liable for negligently failing to detect materially misstated financial statements. The following illustrates issues auditors confront when auditing an employer's accounting for postretirement health care.

HEALTH CARE OBLIGATIONS

Like pension benefits, postretirement health care benefits are a form of deferred compensation, the costs of which should be recognized over the *attribution period*, the period from the date an employee is hired to the date he or she is fully eligible to receive benefits (usually the retirement date). An employer is ultimately liable for the *expected postretirement benefit obligation*: the discounted present value of benefits expected to be paid in the future to employees and to their beneficiaries and eligible dependents. However, at any balance sheet date, the employer is liable for the *accumulated postretirement benefit obligation*: the portion of the expected obligation that employees have earned as of the balance sheet date. Under *SFAS No. 106*, an employer's *transition obligation*, the amount that should be reported on the balance sheet as a liability, is the amount by which the accumulated postretirement obligation exceeds the value of assets funded to date in the health care plan. As illustrated in the following partial footnote to the Boeing Company's December 31, 1992, financial statements, the transition obligation can be recognized as expense immediately and the plan may be unfunded:

In the fourth quarter of 1992, the Company adopted retroactive to January 1, 1992, the provisions of Statement of Financial Accounting Standards (SFAS) No. 106, "Employers' Accounting for Postretirement Benefits Other Than Pensions," using the immediate recognition transition option. SFAS No. 106 requires accrual of these benefits during an employee's service period. Prior to 1992, postretirement benefits consisting of retiree health care were accrued for eligible retirees and qualifying dependents. The effect of the immediate recognition of the transition obligation was a decrease to 1992 earnings on an after-tax basis of $1,002,000,000, or $2.95 per share based on the annual average shares outstanding. This accounting change increased 1992 pre-tax costs by $123,000,000. The retiree health care obligation is unfunded.

5   "IBM to Record Large Charge for New Rule," *The Wall Street Journal* (March 29, 1991), p. A3.

Immediate recognition of the transition obligation reduced earnings by a substantial amount. But notice that Boeing has not disclosed (nor was it required to disclose) the crucially important discount rate at which the present value of the obligation was calculated. What if an entity had chosen an abnormally high discount rate and thereby understated the present value of the obligation? Interestingly, research reveals that companies with relatively larger obligations and extreme price-earnings ratios are more likely to select reporting alternatives which, like high discount rates, more aggressively reduce health care obligations.[6] Consider the following case.

Ansonia Wire & Cable Company, an East Coast manufacturer and supplier of extruded copper wire products, employs over one thousand nonunion production and clerical employees, all of whom are eligible to participate in a defined benefit postretirement health plan. During year end audit work, Ansonia's chief executive and chief financial officers broach postretirement health care obligations with the auditor; management is concerned that a material transition obligation on their year end financial statements will:

- Endanger the success of an initial public offering of Class B common stock contemplated for the following year, and
- Raise the debt-to-equity ratio, causing the potential violation of a debt covenant on an existing commercial loan.

To maintain comparability with other wire & cable companies competing in the market for initial public offerings, management plans to expense immediately (rather than defer) the transition obligation. However, to minimize the amount of the obligation, management proposes that the discount rate used to calculate the present value of the accumulated postretirement obligation be equivalent to the high rate at which Ansonia's investment portfolio is performing.

AUDIT JUDGMENT: ACCOUNTING, LIABILITY, AND ETHICS

What management proposes runs dangerously close to deception; a clear violation of generally accepted accounting principles. If Ansonia's management insists on a high discount rate (even one that approximates the company's actual return on investment), the auditor has no alternative but to alert the client that:

- *SFAS No. 106* requires that the discount rate be based on the currently available rate of return on high-quality fixed-income investments, not a rate experienced otherwise by the reporting entity,
- Overstating the discount rate understates the transition obligation, thereby understating total liabilities,
- Understating total liabilities in this case effectively deceives the potential purchasers of the planned initial public offering and the bank whose debt covenants are apparently tied in part to the debt-equity ratio,
- An overstated discount rate, and the resulting understatement of liabilities, is a violation of generally accepted accounting principles, and

---

6   E. Amir and E. A. Gordon, "Firm's Choice of Estimation Parameters: Empirical Evidence from SFAS No. 106," *Journal of Accounting, Auditing & Finance* (Summer 1996), pp. 427-448.

- A departure from GAAP will cause the auditor to issue a qualified or adverse opinion, depending on materiality, and an explanatory paragraph that discloses the effect of the departure on reported earnings (Chapter 3, Figure 3-5).

If the auditor considers conspiring with Ansonia management to overstate the discount rate and understate the transition obligation, he or she risks serious legal and ethical implications. Assuming the initial public offering is effected, purchasers of the securities may take action under the Securities Act of 1933, Section 11 (Chapter 5), if any part of the registration statement contains an untrue statement of a material fact, in this case an untrue statement about existing liabilities. Further, the commercial bank holding Ansonia's long-term debt could bring an action under common law (Chapter 5) for losses, if any, on Ansonia's debt repayment, alleging that the bank relied on the financial statements in presuming that reported total debt, the numerator in the debt-to-equity ratio, was not misstated and, therefore, that the resulting ratio did not violate an existing debt convenant. As discussed in Chapter 5, the auditor could be liable for treble damages under the Racketeer Influenced and Corrupt Organizations (RICO) Act, since *Reves v. Arthur Young*, a 1993 U.S. Supreme Court case, does not provide the auditor relief from RICO when, as would be the case in Ansonia, he or she participated directly with management to perpetrate the fraud.

The case raises at least two ethical issues. First, the auditor violates the Code of Professional Conduct, Rule 203—Accounting Principles (Chapter 4), which provides that an AICPA member cannot issue an unqualified opinion if the financial statements contain a departure from generally accepted accounting principles. In the Ansonia case, the accounting principle violated is encompassed within an authoritative pronouncement: *SFAS No. 106*. Violating Rule 203 can result in an administrative reprimand, such as suspension to practice before the SEC, or revocation of a CPA's license to practice public accountancy. Second, conspiring with a client to deceive potential shareholders and commercial lenders raises serious questions about the auditor's ethical character, questions that far exceed the mere minimum standards of the AICPA's Code of Professional Conduct.

SUMMARY

In addition to purchases and cash disbursement transactions, the expenditure/ disbursement cycle also processes transactions and events related to personnel and payroll. Activities typically associated with personnel and payroll include the maintenance of personnel records, payroll preparation and account distri- bution, and cash disbursements to employees. Common documentation for personnel and payroll includes personnel records—the evidence supporting employee hirings, promotions, and terminations—and employee time records.

Audit tests of payroll usually focus on interim tests of controls; however, unlike most other audit areas, interim testing also includes procedures nor- mally associated with year end substantive tests of account balances. As a result, year end testing of payroll often focuses on analytical procedures de- signed to assess the reasonableness of recorded payroll expense and accruals.

If the consideration of internal control indicates control procedures are ineffective, or if analytical procedures suggest that payroll and payroll-related accounts appear unreasonable, an auditor would increase the extent of year end testing to include substantive tests of details.

Unlike payroll expense, which can be recalculated or estimated with some degree of certainty, the discounted present value of postretirement health care obligations is rather arduous to estimate, since it's not clear which employees will live to retirement, which of those who live will become ill, and, for that matter, what they'll be ill with and when. Although management must report postretirement health care obligations, there are opportunities to understate the obligations, among them the choice of an inappropriate discount rate.

KEY TERMS

Expenditure/disbursement cycle 504
Personnel records 505
Time records 505
Payroll register 505

Employee earnings records 505
Postretirement benefits other than
  pensions 518

REFERENCES

Auditing Standards

AICPA. *Codification of Statements on Auditing Standards*. New York: AICPA.

Accounting Standards

FASB. *Statement of Financial Accounting Standards No. 106*, "Employers' Accounting for Postretirement Benefits Other Than Pensions."

Books

Committee of Sponsoring Organizations of the Treadway Commission (COSO). *Internal Control: Integrated Framework. Executive Summary*. New York: COSO, 1992.
Committee of Sponsoring Organizations of the Treadway Commission (COSO). *Internal Control: Integrated Framework. Framework*. New York: COSO, 1992.
Committee of Sponsoring Organizations of the Treadway Commission (COSO). *Internal Control: Integrated Framework. Evaluation Tools*. New York: COSO, 1992.
Committee of Sponsoring Organizations of the Treadway Commission (COSO). *Internal Control: Integrated Framework. Reporting to External Parties*. New York: COSO, 1992.

QUESTIONS

1. Identify the major activities associated with a company's Payroll, Personnel, and Treasury Departments.
2. How can management assure that payroll checks are distributed only to bona fide employees?
3. How can management mitigate the likelihood of department managers processing payroll checks for terminated employees or processing unauthorized promotions and transfers?
4. Explain why Personnel employees should be separated from payroll preparation, and why Personnel and Payroll employees should be separated from cash disbursements.

5. How might an auditor perform a transaction walk-through when considering controls over personnel and payroll?

6. What source does an auditor use as the starting point for tests of personnel and payroll activities?

7. Why are payroll preparation accuracy and appropriate account distribution of major concern to an auditor?

8. How does an auditor test whether employees whose names appear on the payroll register are bona fide, i.e., actually employed by the company?

9. How can management control against paychecks being prepared for unauthorized or fictitious employees?

10. How can an auditor test the authenticity of employees to whom payroll checks are disbursed?

11. Why does the accounting for postretirement health care obligations create so much more difficulty for accountants and auditors than the accounting for and auditing of payroll expense?

MULTIPLE CHOICE QUESTIONS

1. Which of the following statements best explains why the accuracy of payroll calculations and of payroll account distribution is critical to an auditor?

a. Employees will complain to management if their paychecks do not reflect wages or salaries earned.

b. Payroll is paid in cash, an account that is highly susceptible to frauds.

c. Generally accepted auditing standards require that tests of Cash and payroll be coordinated.

d. Payroll impacts several balance sheet and income statement accounts.

2. Tests of controls over personnel and payroll focus on the preparation, distribution, and recording of earned salaries and wages. Which of the following is the primary source from which tests of personnel and payroll are derived?

a. Time cards.
b. Labor distribution summary.
c. Employee earnings records.
d. Payroll register.

3. Why does an auditor examine postings to employee cumulative earnings records?

a. Undetected errors would accumulate across years, making subsequent payroll accounts misstated.

b. Cumulative earnings records are the basis for preparing W-2 forms and for calculating payroll tax expense.

c. To detect unreported employee terminations.

d. To detect overstated wages paid to undeserving employees.

4. On a surprise basis, an auditor may elect to distribute paychecks to employees personally. What is the primary purpose of this audit procedure?

a. To assure that no extra payroll checks are prepared and distributed.

b. To test whether all paid employees exist.

c. To assure that paychecks are not distributed to an employee absent on the day the auditor distributes checks.

d. To test the procedures for distributing paychecks.

5. In determining whether control procedures are potentially reliable in assessing control risk below the maximum, an auditor performs four tasks, listed below in random order:
   1. Design tests of controls.
   2. Consider potential errors or frauds.
   3. Identify control objectives.
   4. Determine control procedures.
   In what order are these tasks performed in a financial statement audit?

   a. 1234
   b. 3241
   c. 2341
   d. 4312

6. After completing tests of controls, an auditor concludes from available evidence that control risk can be assessed below the maximum and detection risk above the minimum. Under these conditions:

   a. Substantive tests of controls can be eliminated.
   b. Substantive tests can be limited to analytical procedures.
   c. The extent of substantive tests of details can be restricted.
   d. Substantive tests of details can be performed at an interim date.

7. Which of the following financial statement assertions is of least concern to an auditor when testing payroll?

   a. Occurrence.
   b. Valuation.
   c. Completeness.
   d. Allocation.

8. Management has incentives to overstate the discounted present value of future health care obligations because the effect is to:

   a. Understate investment performance.
   b. Understate net income.
   c. Understate assets.
   d. Understate liabilities.

9. Current generally accepted accounting principles require that the discount rate for calculating the present value of future postretirement health care benefits be based on:

   a. The current rate of return on the reporting entity's investment portfolio.
   b. The current average rate of return on the investment portfolio of other companies operating in the reporting entity's industry.
   c. The current rate of return on plan assets held in similar health care plans.
   d. The current rate of return on high-quality fixed-income investments.

10. The transition obligation in accounting for postretirement health care benefits is the difference between:

   a. The accumulated postretirement obligation and the value of the assets funded to date.
   b. The accumulated postretirement obligation and the expected postretirement obligation.
   c. The unfunded future benefits and the value of the assets funded to date.
   d. The unfunded future benefits and the expected postretirement obligation.

PROBLEMS AND DISCUSSION CASES

14-1   *Controls Over Personnel and Payroll*
You are considering the controls over a client's personnel and payroll activities. System documentation was accomplished with a questionnaire and a narrative memorandum and, in conjunction with a transaction walk-through, indicated that the following potential errors or frauds may exist:
1. Several recent hirings violated equal opportunity laws.
2. A pay raise to employees in Department A was not approved by management.
3. An unauthorized, unapproved, and excessively high paycheck was cashed by a bona fide employee, but the check was for hours neither authorized nor worked.
4. Detailed payroll records sometimes do not agree with labor summaries or payroll tax accruals and go unnoticed.
5. When an employee's time card is not available, the employee obtains a new time card from an open bin outside the payroll office.

Required: For each potential error or fraud, indicate one or more control procedures that management could implement to prevent or detect the error or fraud.

14-2   *Identifying Deficiencies in Internal Control*
An auditor's audit working papers include the following narrative description of a segment of the Croyden, Inc., factory payroll system and the flowchart presented on the following two pages.

Narrative Memorandum
Internal control over the personnel department is effective and is not included in the accompanying flowchart.

At the beginning of each workweek, payroll clerk No. 1 reviews Payroll Department files to determine the employment status of factory employees, and prepares and distributes time cards as each individual arrives at work. The clerk verifies the identity of each payee before delivering signed checks to the factory supervisor. At the end of each workweek, the supervisor distributes payroll checks for the preceding workweek, reviews the current week's employee time cards, notes the regular and overtime hours worked on a summary form, and initials the time cards. The supervisor then delivers all time cards and unclaimed payroll checks to payroll clerk No. 2.

Required:
1. What are the deficiencies in internal control?
2. What inquiries should the auditor make to clarify whether additional deficiencies exist?

(AICPA Adapted)

14-3   *Errors, Fraud, and Control Procedures*
During your audit of Fletcher Corporation's June 30, 1999, financial statements, you become aware of the following control procedures over Fletcher's personnel and payroll activities:
1. All substantive information in employment applications is thoroughly checked and verified before offering an employment contract.
2. Authorized pay rates are maintained in personnel files for each employee.
3. All Personnel and Payroll Department procedures are clearly written in updated procedures manuals.
4. Dual signatories are required for all paychecks exceeding $1,200.
5. Procedures are established for charging direct labor hours to appropriate jobs.
6. Responsibility for authorizing, executing, and recording payroll is vested in separate personnel.

Problem 14-2:   Flowchart

Factory Employees	Factory Foreman	Personnel

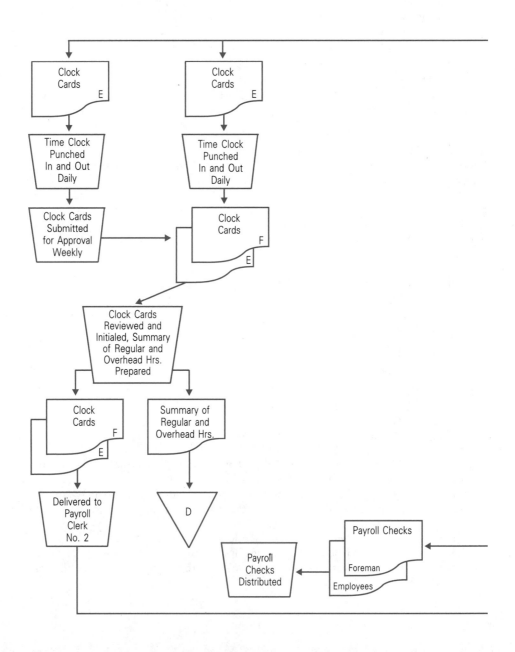

Problem 14-2: *(continued)*

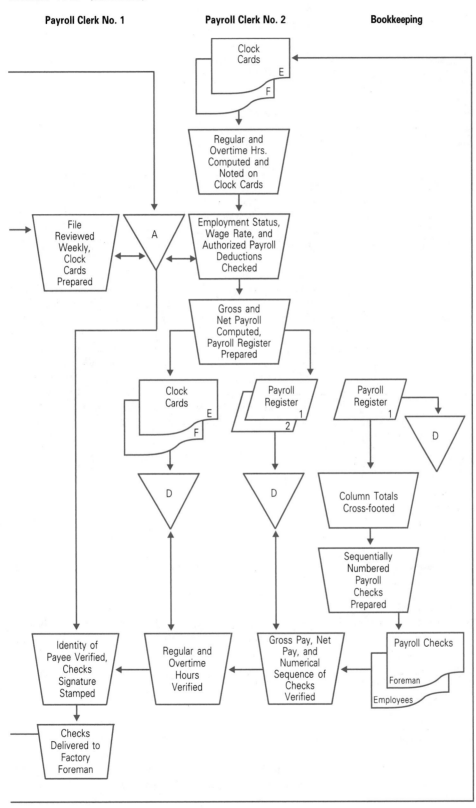

Required: For each control procedure, indicate: (a) a potential error or fraud that might be prevented or detected as a result of the control procedure, and (b) the control objective served by the control procedure. Organize your answer as follows:

Control Procedure	Potential Error or Fraud That Might Be Prevented or Detected	Control Objective
1.	(a)	(b)

14-4 *Improving Controls Over Hiring and Payroll*

The Linscott Supply Company employs about 50 production workers. Based on interviews, the factory supervisor hires or rejects job applicants. New hires prepare a W-4 form (Employee's Withholding Exemption Certificate) for the supervisor, who enters an hourly pay rate in the corner of the form and then passes the form on to a payroll clerk, thereby notifying Payroll that the worker has been employed. The supervisor advises Payroll of subsequent pay rate adjustments verbally.

A supply of blank time cards is kept in a box near the factory's front door entrance. Each worker takes a time card on Monday morning, writes in his or her name, and notes daily arrival and departure times in pencil. At the end of the week, workers drop the time cards in a box near the door. A payroll clerk collects completed time cards from the box on Monday morning. Two payroll clerks divide the cards alphabetically between them, one taking A to L, and the other M to Z. Each clerk is fully responsible for his or her portion of the payroll. The clerks compute gross pay, deductions, and net pay, post the details to each employee's earnings record, and prepare and number the payroll checks. Employees are deleted from the payroll when they fail to turn in a time card.

Payroll checks are signed manually by the chief accountant and given to the supervisor. The supervisor distributes the checks to the workers and arranges to deliver checks to workers who are absent. The payroll bank account is reconciled by the chief accountant, who also prepares quarterly and annual payroll tax returns.

Required: How might Linscott Supply Company improve controls over hiring and payroll?

14-5 *Designing Compensating Controls*

Early in your audit of the Kimberly Corporation, you note that the factory supervisor approves time cards for hours worked and for hourly rates and also distributes the payroll checks.

Required:
1. Design compensating controls you would pursue before concluding that an internal control deficiency exists.
2. If you find no compensating controls for the factory payroll, what audit procedures would test for errors or frauds?

14-6 *Why Not Substantive Tests?*

When auditing within the expenditure/disbursement cycle, auditors often rely predominantly on interim tests of controls rather than year end substantive tests of details. In fact, in many cases, year end procedures consist primarily of updating the auditor's understanding of the system, testing payroll activities, and performing analytical procedures to test the reasonableness of reported payroll balances.

Required: Explain why an auditor might rely predominantly on tests of controls, rather than substantive tests of details in auditing payroll.

14-7 *Drafting Tests of Controls From an Internal Control Questionnaire*

Following are selected questions from an internal control questionnaire relating to a company's personnel and payroll functions. A *Yes* response would indicate a potential strength of the system, and a *No* response, a potential weakness.

a. Do operating department supervisors and the personnel department approve all employee changes (hirings, transfers, promotions, terminations)?
b. Do employee personnel records include authorization for all deductions and withholdings?
c. Are employees who prepare payroll independent of payroll processing?
d. Does a responsible official independent of payroll preparation and processing approve the payroll?
e. Does an employee independent of payroll preparation, processing, and distribution reconcile the payroll bank account monthly?
f. Do employees independent of the payroll department forward for investigation returned W-2 forms?

Required: Assume that inquiries indicate the answer is *Yes* to each question. Design tests of controls that you believe would provide persuasive evidence that control risk is below the maximum.

14-8 *Selecting Audit Procedures*

An auditor is designing an audit program for a computerized payroll and is drafting procedures for payroll preparation, labor cost distribution, and paycheck distribution.

Required: For each of the following procedures, indicate whether the proposed audit step should or should not be included in the audit program. Justify each *No* response.

1. Review software that computes payroll.
2. Determine whether checks are delivered to department timekeepers for distribution.
3. Review workers' compensation claims.
4. Reconcile time card hours to hours recorded on production job cards.
5. Distribute checks to employees on a sample basis.
6. Obtain a certificate from the timekeeper for employees who were absent when the auditor distributed paychecks and who are to be paid later.
7. Verify documents in payroll files.
8. Review procedures for payroll check signing.

14-9 *Why a Separate Bank Account for Payroll?*

Many organizations maintain separate bank accounts for payroll, thereby segregating all payroll disbursements from general disbursements, such as payments for purchases, inventory, plant assets, and investments, among other things.

Required: Discuss why a separate bank account should be maintained for payroll and why one general bank account can be used for all other disbursements.

14-10 *Auditing Payroll*

James, who was engaged to audit the financial statements of Talbert Corporation, is about to audit payroll. Talbert uses a computer service center to process weekly payroll as follows:

Each Monday, Talbert's payroll clerk inputs data onto preprinted, service center-prepared input forms that are then faxed to the service center. The service center imports data from the input forms to master files. Weekly payroll is then processed. The weekly payroll register and payroll checks are printed and delivered by messenger to Talbert on Thursday. Part of the sample James selected includes the input form and payroll register shown on the following two pages.

Required:

1. Discuss how James could verify data on the payroll input form.
2. Discuss procedures James could follow to examine the November 26, 1999 payroll register.

(AICPA Adapted)

Talbert Corporation Payroll Input—Week Ending Friday, Nov. 26, 1999

| | | | | | Current Week's Payroll Data | | | | |
| | | | | | Hours | | | Special Deductions | | |
Name	Social Security No.	W-4	Information	Hourly Rate	Reg	OT	Bonds	Union	Other
A. Bell	999-99-9991	M-1		10.00	35	5	18.75		
B. Carr	999-99-9992	M-2		10.00	35	4			
C. Dawn	999-99-9993	S-1		10.00	35	6	18.75	4.00	
D. Ellis	999-99-9994	S-1		10.00	35	2		4.00	50.00
E. Frank	999-99-9995	M-4		10.00	35	1		4.00	
F. Gillis	999-99-9996	M-4		10.00	35			4.00	
G. Hugh	999-99-9997	M-1		7.00	35	2	18.75	4.00	
H. Jones	999-99-9998	M-2		7.00	35			4.00	25.00
I. King	999-99-9999	S-2		7.00	35	4		4.00	
New Employee									
J. Smith	999-99-9990	M-3		7.00	35				

Talbert Corporation Payroll Register—Nov. 26, 1999

Employee	Social Security No.	Hours		Payroll			Taxes Withheld				New Pay	Check No.
		Reg	OT	Reg	OT	Gross Payroll	FICA	Fed	State	Other Withheld		
A. Bell	999-99-9991	35	5	350.00	75.00	425.00	26.05	76.00	27.40	18.75	276.80	1499
B. Carr	999-99-9992	35	4	350.00	60.00	410.00	25.13	65.00	23.60		296.27	1500
C. Dawn	999-99-9993	35	6	350.00	90.00	440.00	26.97	100.90	28.60	22.75	260.78	1501
D. Ellis	999-99-9994	35	2	350.00	30.00	380.00	23.29	80.50	21.70	54.00	200.51	1502
E. Frank	999-99-9995	35	1	350.00	15.00	365.00	22.37	43.50	15.90	4.00	279.23	1503
F. Gillis	999-99-9996	35		350.00		350.00	21.46	41.40	15.00	4.00	268.14	1504
G. Hugh	999-99-9997	35	2	245.00	21.00	266.00	16.31	34.80	10.90	22.75	181.24	1505
H. Jones	999-99-9998	35		245.00		245.00	15.02	26.40	8.70	29.00	165.88	1506
I. King	999-99-9999	35	4	245.00	42.00	287.00	17.59	49.40	12.20	4.00	203.81	1507
J. Smith	999-99-9990	35		245.00		245.00	15.02	23.00	7.80		199.18	1508
Totals		350	24	3,080.00	333.00	3,413.00	209.21	540.90	171.80	159.25	2,331.84	

14-11   *Postretirement Benefits Other Than Pensions*

Nonunion production, clerical, and middle management employees of the Intersect Corporation participate in a postretirement benefit plan that encompasses health care, housing subsidies, and tuition benefits for surviving dependent children. Recent newspaper accounts indicate that the employment contract covering production employees will expire soon after the balance sheet date. In discussing the disclosures necessary to comply with *SFAS No. 106*, "Employers' Accounting for Postretirement Benefits Other Than Pensions," Intersect's chief financial officer tells the auditor that, although she plans to comply with *SFAS No. 106*, she does not plan to disclose that the health care plan is unfunded.

Required:

1. Explain why you think Intersect's chief financial officer would prefer not to disclose that the health care plan is unfunded.
2. Does failing to disclose that a health care plan is unfunded violate generally accepted accounting principles?

RESEARCH PROJECT

MANAGEMENT DISCRETION AND POSTRETIREMENT HEALTH CARE OBLIGATIONS

Owing in part to unprecedented controversy, the Financial Accounting Standards Board deliberated over ten years about the accounting for postretirement obligations other than pensions. The stakeholders in the controversy included some who predicted worldwide financial doom if the obligations were reported, others who claimed that reported liabilities overlooked significant off-balance-sheet financing if not reported, and still others who were daunted by the sheer complexity of the measurement issues involved. Other accounting issues have been controversial, but no other issue has involved such staggering dollar amounts.

Required: Using the newspaper and magazines file in NEXIS, Mead Data Central's automated data retrieval system, or newspapers and magazines in a library, select an article about the effect on a publicly traded company's financial statements of adopting FASB *Statement of Financial Accounting Standards No. 106*, "Employers' Accounting for Postretirement Benefits Other Than Pensions." Using the annual report file in the National Automated Accounting Research System (NAARS), or copies of annual reports in a library, select the annual report of the same company issued for the fiscal year referred to in the article. Draft a report that accomplishes the following:

1. Summarizes the article, indicating key issues, like management's or the financial community's reaction to the effect of the disclosure on reported income.
2. Lists and explains questions an auditor would likely pose to the management of the company you've selected.
3. Summarizes the company's disclosures about postretirement health care obligations from the balance sheet, the income statement (if separately disclosed), the footnote summarizing accounting policies (Note 1), and the footnote summarizing the health care obligation.

15

Tests of Controls and Substantive Tests in the Conversion Cycle: Inventory, Fixed Assets, and Management Discretion in Accounting for Impaired Assets

Major topics discussed in this chapter are:

- The nature of the conversion cycle.
- Assurance service opportunities related to the conversion cycle.
- An auditor's consideration of internal control in the conversion cycle.
- Substantive tests applicable to inventory and fixed assets.
- Applications of audit judgment to questions about management discretion and write-downs of impaired assets.
- Computer assisted audit techniques applicable to inventory and fixed assets.

Continuing the discussion of audit method, this chapter introduces tests of controls and substantive tests applicable to two major conversion cycle accounts: Inventory and Fixed Assets. Internal control is discussed first, and substantive tests of account balances are discussed thereafter. The chapter begins by summarizing the nature of the conversion cycle; introducing controls over an entity's inventory, inventory accounting, and fixed asset transactions; explaining an auditor's consideration of internal control within the conversion cycle; and suggesting assurance service opportunities. Next, the chapter explains specific substantive tests of details applicable to inventory and fixed assets. In turn, the chapter addresses accounting, legal, and ethical questions auditors face when auditing discretionary write-downs of impaired assets. Computer assisted substantive tests (Chapter 7) relevant to inventory and fixed assets are presented at the end of the chapter.

THE CONVERSION CYCLE

The conversion cycle encompasses the production of finished products for sale, and relates directly to two of the other cycles: It uses resources and information provided by the expenditure/disbursement cycle and provides resources and information to the revenue/receipt cycle. For example, the conversion cycle uses raw materials purchased from vendors through the expenditure/disbursement cycle and produces finished goods that are sold to customers through the revenue/receipt cycle.

Figure 15-1 summarizes the scope of the conversion cycle, listing primary business functions and related activities, journal entries, and forms. One major business function is captured by the cycle:

- Resources are held, used, or transformed.

Although stated simply, this one business function can be quite significant, because it relates both to inventory and to fixed assets, often two of the most significant assets in capital-intensive companies.

INVENTORY: AN INTRODUCTION

As noted in Chapter 12, when an entity purchases raw materials inventory, a *purchase order* is sent to the vendor, goods are received, and a liability is recorded. Assuming a perpetual inventory system, activities within the conversion cycle would include recording purchases in perpetual records, processing accumulated costs through a cost accounting system, and physically controlling the inventory.

Throughout the conversion cycle, journal entries are made to process inventory costs through production, to record the cost of goods sold, and to write down obsolete or damaged inventory. Paper or computer image documents include:

- **Labor charge report.** A summary of labor costs to be applied to work-in-process inventory.
- **Materials requisition.** An operating department's formal request for materials.
- **Perpetual inventory record.** A cumulative record of quantities on hand for an item or a class of inventory.

FIXED ASSETS: AN INTRODUCTION

Property, plant, and equipment—that is, fixed assets—are used both directly and indirectly to transform raw materials into finished products. For example, equipment might be used directly to extrude wire from copper, while a building would be used indirectly in the sense that wire extrusion equipment is housed within a manufacturing plant. As a result, fixed assets are related both to the conversion cycle and to inventory: to the conversion cycle because fixed assets transform inventory from raw materials to finished goods, and to inventory because some depreciation is applied to products as overhead.

Throughout the conversion cycle, journal entries are made to record depreciation and to apply overhead to inventory. Paper or computer image documents include:

- **Depreciation schedule.** A spreadsheet computing and summarizing depreciation.

Figure 15-1:   The Scope of the Conversion Cycle

Primary Business Function	Common Activities	Common Entries	Common Forms
Resources are held, used, or transformed	**INVENTORY** • Maintaining perpetual inventory records • Recording (cost accounting) • Physically controlling inventory	• Processing inventory costs through production (raw materials, work in process, finished goods) • Cost of goods sold • Write-down of obsolete or damaged inventory	• Labor charge reports • Materials requisition forms
	PLANT ASSETS • Additions • Disposals and retirements • Recording • Depreciation allocation	• Depreciation • Overhead applied • Addition, disposals, and retirements	• Depreciation schedules • Overhead application reports

- Overhead application report. A summary of overhead applied to work-in-process inventory.

The following section discusses the nature of the conversion cycle and related internal control considerations. The major activities and controls related to inventory—inventory control and inventory accounting—are discussed first, followed by fixed assets: records, additions, disposals, and depreciation.

INVENTORY AND INTERNAL CONTROL

Control procedures over inventory vary depending on whether the inventory is held by a nonmanufacturing or manufacturing company. In the case of a nonmanufacturing wholesaler or retailer, goods are acquired from vendors and sold to customers without alteration. Thus, the conversion cycle of a non-manufacturing entity accounts only for holding and physically controlling inventory prior to sale. But for a manufacturing company, the conversion cycle is more complex: Raw materials acquired from vendors must be transformed prior to sale, and the costs of transformation, such as direct labor and manufacturing overhead, must be accumulated and classified. The functional areas that control and record inventory are inventory control and inventory accounting, respectively.

INVENTORY CONTROL

Figure 15-2 illustrates the flow of inventory within a manufacturing company. The acquisition of inventory is part of the expenditure/disbursement cycle, and the distribution of finished goods is part of the revenue/receipt cycle. The conversion cycle encompasses movement of goods through the production process.

A *materials requisition* form is prepared by production personnel to request materials and supplies for use in production. Requisitions should be approved

Figure 15-2:   Inventory Flow

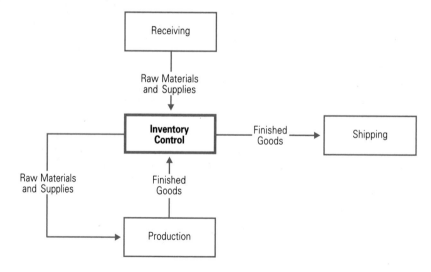

by a supervisor and forwarded to Inventory Control. Materials and supplies should not be released by Inventory Control personnel in the absence of an approved requisition.

Raw materials and finished goods should be controlled by Inventory Control personnel not involved in purchasing, receiving, shipping, production, or recording. Access to storage areas should be limited to authorized personnel. Physical safeguards are necessary within each of the production departments to protect work in process.

Inventory Control personnel should be responsible not only for controlling transfers of inventory in and out of storage areas, but also for monitoring inventory levels and for reporting slow-moving or damaged items. Inventory levels should be monitored to assure that they are neither too high, which would result in needlessly high carrying costs, nor too low, which could risk insufficient quantities on hand. Many companies monitor inventory levels through quantitative techniques such as *economic-order-quantity* models, which optimize the relationship between carrying costs and the risk of shortages, or *just-in-time*, an inventory management method that reduces carrying costs to zero because required supplies arrive "just in time." As a means for determining whether inventory is obsolete or otherwise unusable, slow-moving or damaged items should be reported to responsible officials and, if appropriate, removed from inventory; salable items should be written down to net realizable value and sold as scrap.

INVENTORY ACCOUNTING

Throughout the conversion cycle, entries are made to record the movement of inventory through the production process. Inventory (cost) accounting systems vary widely due to variations in the nature and complexity of production processes. Generally, though, an inventory accounting system involves two major sets of records: perpetual inventory records and cost records.

Perpetual Inventory Records

Inventory quantities, physical locations, and selected unit cost information usually are accumulated on perpetual inventory records maintained for a variety of major inventory classifications, including supplies, raw materials, and finished goods. Work-in-process inventory should also be controlled on perpetual records, though the records may take the form of progress reports, such as job-cost summaries.

As inventory flows through the production process, perpetual records should be updated continually, thereby providing a cumulative up-to-date record of quantities, physical location, and selected unit cost information. Updated information should be generated from formal source documents, such as requisitions, invoices, production reports, and shipping documents, which themselves should be controlled through sequential prenumbering and formal indications of approval (e.g., initials) or specific authorization, as discussed in Chapter 12.

In many companies, significant segments of inventory are stored off-premises in public warehouses or transferred either to dealers on consignment or to outside companies for processing. Off-premises inventory should be accounted for and controlled by the outside parties holding the goods.

Periodically, a company should confirm off-premises inventory, physically count quantities at off-premises locations, and reconcile confirmed or counted quantities with internal perpetual records.

Cost Records

Perpetual inventory records are used predominantly to account for inventory quantities throughout the production process. An inventory accounting system, however, must also account for inventory costs, which may be allocated on a FIFO, LIFO, average cost, or other acceptable basis. Whatever the cost-flow approach used, an inventory accounting system should be designed to account for and control inventory costs as they flow through the accounts illustrated in Figure 15-3.

Like perpetual inventory records, cost accounting records and reports should be updated continually, thereby providing an up-to-date record of accumulated costs. The updated information should be communicated to General Accounting personnel for summarizing and for recording journal entries in general ledger control accounts. If updated information is not communicated to the accounting department, accounts such as Raw Materials, Work in Process, and Finished Goods could be misstated. For example, if units of a particular raw material are physically transferred to production, the related inventory costs (for raw materials) should be transferred from raw materials to work-in-process inventory; otherwise, raw materials inventory would be overstated and work-in-process inventory understated, although total inventory would not be misstated. Thus, cost accounting records should be updated continually and agreed to, or periodically reconciled with, general ledger control accounts. To maintain effective segregation of duties, cost accounting records should be maintained by personnel independent of perpetual records, general accounting, purchasing, production, and inventory control.

INTERNAL CONTROL OBJECTIVES AND POTENTIAL ERRORS OR FRAUDS: INVENTORY

The following discussion, summarized in Figure 15-4, identifies some control objectives for inventory, describes examples of errors or frauds that may arise

Figure 15-3:   Inventory Cost Flow

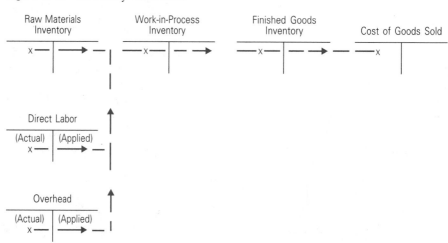

Figure 15-4: Inventory: Control Objectives, Potential Errors or Frauds, and Control Procedures

Control Objectives	Types of Errors or Frauds That Could Occur if Objective Is Not Met	Control Procedures Designed to Prevent or Detect Errors or Frauds
Transaction Authorization Production should be authorized in accordance with management's criteria.	Unauthorized quantities or products may be produced, potentially resulting in obsolete, excess, or otherwise unusable inventory and excess carrying costs.	Prepare statements of criteria for determining which products are to be produced and in what quantities.
Transaction Execution Procedures for using and physically transferring inventory should be established in accordance with management's authorization.	Unauthorized personnel may circumvent existing procedures, potentially resulting in stolen or misused inventory. Inventory may be misplaced, potentially resulting in unused assets.	Prepare inventory processing manuals, including procedures for controlling inventory movement. Restrict access to inventory to authorized personnel.
Recording Inventory used or transferred should be recorded at the correct amounts, be recorded in the proper period, and be properly classified.	Inventory placed in production may not be recorded, potentially resulting in misstated inventory and cost of sales.	Establish processing and recording procedures. Prenumber and control materials release forms and production orders. Maintain logs of inventory movement into and out of storerooms and production stages. Conduct periodic inventory counts, and investigate differences between recorded and actual quantities. Limit access to inventory and blank forms.
Inventory-related adjustments (e.g., to adjust recorded inventory to physical counts; to write down obsolete or unusable inventory) should be authorized in accordance with management's criteria.	Unauthorized adjustments may be recorded to conceal physical shortages, potentially resulting in misused and misstated inventory.	Establish policies for approving and recording adjustments. Prenumber and control inventory adjustment forms.

Figure 15-4: *(continued)*

Control Objectives	Types of Errors or Frauds That Could Occur if Objective Is Not Met	Control Procedures Designed to Prevent or Detect Errors or Frauds
Access to Assets Access to inventory should be restricted to personnel authorized by management.	Inventory could be stolen, lost, or diverted, potentially resulting in misapplied assets and misstated accounts.	Establish physical controls over inventory (e.g., fences, locks, inventory control clerks). Maintain insurance and fidelity bonds for personnel handling valuable inventory. Maintain adequate insurance coverage for assets. Segregate responsibility for handling inventory from inventory recording, cost accounting, and general accounting.
Access to production, cost accounting, and perpetual inventory records should be restricted to personnel authorized by management.	Inventory records could be misused, destroyed, or lost, potentially resulting in misstated and misused inventory.	Establish physical controls over unused forms and records. Maintain files of authorized signatures. Perform periodic compliance audits.

if an objective is not achieved, and offers examples of control procedures to prevent or detect errors or frauds in inventory. The objectives relate to transaction authorization, execution, recording, and access to assets.

Transaction Authorization

Before goods are produced, production should be authorized according to management's criteria. That is, no goods should be produced that are not specifically authorized by management. Otherwise, unauthorized products or quantities may be produced (perhaps, for example, for the express benefit of employees, rather than the company), potentially resulting in excess or otherwise unusable inventory and in excess carrying costs. To control against unauthorized production, management could prepare written statements of criteria for determining which products to produce and in what quantities. For example, management could require that no goods be produced unless quantities on hand have declined to a predetermined amount.

Transaction Execution

In order to avoid lost or misused inventory, management should authorize procedures for using and physically transferring inventory. For example, management could prepare inventory processing manuals, including procedures for controlling inventory movement, and could restrict access to inventory to authorized personnel.

Recording

Establishing procedures for using and transferring inventory, though, does not necessarily mean that inventory transfers and use will be recorded properly. Therefore, to avoid misplaced or misstated inventory, used or transferred inventory should be recorded at the correct amounts, be recognized in the proper period, and be classified properly. To control inventory recording, management could establish processing and recording procedures, prenumber and control materials release forms and production orders, and maintain logs of inventory movement into and out of storerooms and production stages.

Throughout, but most often at the end of, an accounting period, companies make journal entries to adjust recorded inventory to physical counts or to adjust carrying value for obsolete or unusable inventory. To avoid unauthorized adjustments—for example, adjustments to conceal physical shortages—management should require that all inventory adjustments be authorized in accordance with management's criteria. For example, management could establish policies for approving and recording adjustments and, in large companies, prenumber and control inventory adjustment documents.

Access to Assets

Inventory—particularly valuable consumer products, like portable appliances—can be stolen, lost, or diverted, potentially resulting in misapplied assets and misstated accounts. As a result, access to inventory should be restricted to personnel authorized by management. In practice, a variety of techniques are available to control inventory. For example, management could establish physical control over inventory (e.g., fences, locks, inventory control clerks); maintain insurance, both for inventory and for inventory personnel (i.e., fidelity bonds); and segregate responsibility for handling inventory from inventory recording, cost accounting, and general accounting.

In turn, management should also restrict access to production, cost accounting, and perpetual inventory records, thereby preventing misuse, destruction, or loss of inventory or inventory records. For example, management could establish physical controls over unused forms and records, maintain files of authorized signatures, and perform periodic compliance audits to assure that controls are complied with.

FIXED ASSETS AND INTERNAL CONTROL

Some companies use a separate cycle to process the acquisition, use, and disposition of fixed assets—land, buildings, machinery, and equipment. In others, the expenditure/disbursement cycle may process fixed asset additions, the revenue/receipt cycle may process disposals, and the conversion cycle may process transactions and events relating to the use of fixed assets. The latter is assumed in the following discussion, which focuses on controls applicable to fixed assets.

FIXED ASSET RECORDS

Land, buildings, machinery, and equipment should be documented in detailed records that account separately for each individual asset. For example, each detailed record might include the purchase date, historical cost, depreciation method, estimated useful life, salvage value, and accumulated depreciation. The records should be maintained by personnel not responsible for physically controlling fixed assets.

Periodically, but no less than annually, detailed records should be reconciled with fixed asset general ledger control accounts. Also, responsible personnel independent of fixed asset recording and physical control should periodically determine that recorded assets actually exist by observing machinery and equipment and by comparing identification numbers and general descriptions with detailed records.

Fixed assets should also be insured against fire or other potential casualties. As a result, assets should be appraised periodically to determine that insurance coverage reasonably approximates replacement cost. If coverage is inadequate, an entity could risk serious losses through both business interruption and an inability to replace productive assets. Clearly, the consequences of under-insurance can be devastating.

ADDITIONS

Unlike many other purchases, individual fixed asset additions are often material, necessitating specific authorization by the board of directors or by senior management. In many entities, formal authorization is also required for major repairs or improvements; since the expenditures may be large, management should assess the desirability of replacing, rather than repairing or improving, existing assets. Authorizations should be documented in writing and be sufficiently detailed to provide employees with a basis for executing fixed asset transactions. On a related note, additions should be reported to insurance companies, and coverage increased accordingly.

Unforeseen circumstances, such as vendor price increases, could raise the purchase price of an asset above amounts originally authorized, thereby requiring additional authorization (or approval). As a result, procedures should require that actual costs be compared with amounts authorized, and cost overruns reported to senior management for authorization. An entity should also assure that authorized additions are actually received and functioning as expected.

In addition to purchasing fixed assets, an entity might hire outside contractors to construct (or modify) buildings, machinery, or equipment. Constructed additions should also be authorized, and additional controls should be implemented that allow the entity to inspect and approve both actual production and detailed cost records as construction progresses. Inspection and approval privileges and cost records allow an entity to monitor progress continually, assuring that the project will meet specifications and cost ceilings authorized by senior management.

DISPOSALS

Fixed asset disposals, such as sales or retirements, should be authorized by senior management. Authorizations should be documented, and copies forwarded to accounting personnel to assure that assets disposed of are subsequently removed from fixed asset accounts.

Since insurance premiums are usually determined by the appraisal value of assets carried, asset disposals should be reported to insurance companies and premiums adjusted accordingly. Disposal of assets may result in gains or losses, measured by the difference between the asset's net book value and proceeds from the disposition. Controls should be established to assure that proceeds are deposited and gains or losses are recorded.

DEPRECIATION

Over time and through use, the future service potential of fixed assets (other than land) expires, and is recognized as depreciation expense. Depreciation expense for fixed assets used in production is assigned to work-in-process inventory as applied overhead and, as a result, flows through the conversion cycle. When finished goods are sold, depreciation expense is charged against revenue as part of the cost of sales.

Because of the significant impact depreciation expense can have on reported net income, an entity should maintain formal policies for determining depreciation methods, estimated useful lives, and salvage values. Periodically, the policies should be reviewed to determine whether they reasonably approximate actual experience. For example, if a particular type of machinery is depreciated over five years but normally lasts ten years, useful lives should be reconsidered.

INTERNAL CONTROL OBJECTIVES AND
POTENTIAL ERRORS OR FRAUDS: FIXED ASSETS

Earlier, control objectives for transaction authorization, execution, recording, and access to assets were discussed for inventory. The following discusses control objectives for fixed assets. The discussion, summarized in Figure 15-5, identifies control objectives, describes examples of errors or frauds that may arise if an objective is not achieved, and provides examples of controls often used by management to prevent or detect errors or frauds.

Transaction Authorization

Just as production should be authorized, fixed asset additions, disposals, and retirements should be authorized in accordance with management's criteria. Otherwise, assets such as machinery and equipment may be purchased or sold without management's knowledge, or assets may be disposed of at unfavorable prices, thereby sacrificing otherwise attainable resources. To control unauthorized transactions, management could develop written procedures for all additions, disposals, and retirements, and periodically compare scrap sale prices with published price lists.

Transaction Execution and Recording

Optimum operating capacity simply cannot be attained unless all fixed assets are accounted for, operating properly, and protected from misuse. For this

Figure 15-5: Fixed Assets: Control Objectives, Potential Errors or Frauds, and Control Procedures

Control Objectives	Types of Errors or Frauds That Could Occur if Objective Is Not Met	Control Procedures Designed to Prevent or Detect Errors or Frauds
Transaction Authorization Plant additions, disposals, and retirements should be authorized in accordance with management's criteria.	Assets may be purchased or sold without management's knowledge, potentially resulting in misapplied cash and misstated fixed asset records. Assets may be disposed of at unfavorable prices, potentially resulting in lost resources.	Prepare written procedures for all additions, disposals, and retirements. Periodically compare prices received for scrap with published prices.
Transaction Execution Procedures for operating, using, and physically moving fixed assets should be established in accordance with management's authorization.	Unauthorized personnel may circumvent existing procedures, potentially resulting in stolen or misused equipment. Equipment may be misplaced, potentially resulting in unused assets.	Establish procedures for operating, using, moving, and otherwise controlling fixed assets. Restrict access to movable fixed assets.
Recording Fixed assets added, disposed, or retired should be recorded at the correct amount, be recorded in the proper period, and be properly classified.	Fixed asset transactions may go unreported, potentially resulting in misstated balances.	Establish procedures for processing and recording fixed asset transactions. Establish procedures for identifying fixed assets eligible for disposal (e.g., sell as scrap) and retirement. Maintain detailed fixed asset records. Periodically reconcile fixed asset records with existing assets and investigate differences.
Depreciation and amortization should be calculated in accordance with management's authorization, be recorded in the proper period, and be properly classified.	Depreciation could be miscalculated or recognized on fixed assets not in service, potentially resulting in misstated depreciation expense and asset book values.	Establish policies for determining depreciation methods and for calculating depreciation on all categories of fixed assets.

Figure 15-5: *(continued)*

Control Objectives	Types of Errors or Frauds That Could Occur if Objective Is Not Met	Control Procedures Designed to Prevent or Detect Errors or Frauds
Access to Assets		
Access to fixed assets should be restricted to personnel authorized by management.	Fixed assets (e.g., equipment) could be stolen or lost, potentially resulting in misapplied assets and misstated accounts.	Establish physical controls over unused fixed assets (e.g., garages, secured fences). Maintain adequate insurance coverage. Segregate physical custody of fixed assets from fixed asset records and general accounting.
Access to asset and depreciation records should be restricted to personnel authorized by management.	Fixed asset and depreciation records could be misused, destroyed, or lost, potentially resulting in misstated assets.	Establish physical controls over unused forms and records. Perform periodic compliance audits, reconciling recorded assets with existing assets.

reason, management should establish procedures for operating, using, physically moving, and restricting access to movable fixed assets.

To avoid unreported transactions, fixed asset additions, disposals, and retirements should be recorded at the correct amount, be recognized in the proper period, and be classified properly. Unrecorded or improperly recorded transactions could result in misstated fixed asset accounts, and therefore in misstated financial statements. Management can control the recording function by establishing procedures for processing and recording fixed asset transactions and for identifying fixed assets eligible for sale or retirement. In addition, detailed fixed asset records should be maintained and periodically reconciled with existing assets.

The expiration of future service potential—depreciation and amortization—should be calculated in accordance with management's authorization and be recorded in the proper period. Otherwise, depreciation could be miscalculated or recognized on fixed assets not actually in service, either of which could result in misstated depreciation expense. As a result, management should establish policies for determining depreciation methods and for calculating depreciation on all fixed assets.

Access to Assets

To control against stolen or lost fixed assets, access should be restricted only to personnel authorized by management. Likewise, access to manufacturing areas and to production sites should be restricted, thereby reducing the likelihood of misused assets and, correspondingly, misstated accounts. Management should establish physical controls over unused assets (e.g., garages, secured fences), maintain adequate insurance coverage, and segregate the physical custody of fixed assets from recording and general accounting.

Just as access to fixed assets should be restricted, so should access to fixed asset records be restricted. Otherwise, fixed asset records could be altered to conceal shortages or be destroyed or lost, potentially resulting in misstated accounts. To control fixed asset records, management should establish controls over unused forms and records (e.g., locked cabinets or safes) or could perform periodic compliance audits, reconciling recorded assets with existing assets.

ASSURANCE SERVICES

Historical cost financial statements capture *financial* information about both inventory and fixed assets, but little about the *nonfinancial* information that also bears directly on investors', creditors', and suppliers' *information risk*. Consider, for example, the case of an institutional investor. Share prices represent the market's average estimate of the per share discounted present value of future cash flows likely to accrue to a company. The market arrives at an average share price by interpreting financial information, for which independent auditors reduce information risk, and nonfinancial information, for which no profession reduces information risk. In the industrial age, financial information was far more important than nonfinancial information, precisely because industrial assets, such as the inventory and fixed assets reported on the balance sheet, translated into future returns. For example, return was fairly highly correlated with the historical cost of industrial assets that produced product for sale.

However, in the information age, nonfinancial information, rather than industrial era assets, produces the lion's share of future returns. For example, if you were to buy a Motorola cellular phone today for say $100, about $10 or so would represent materials inventory cost (e.g., plastic, wire) and about $90 would be the value of the nonfinancial information—the knowledge assets—Motorola used to design and assemble the phone. Motorola's share price captures financial information made reliable by audited financial statements, and nonfinancial information about knowledge assets that is replete with uncontrolled information risk. The public accounting profession has a unique opportunity to react to the market's demand for nonfinancial information that supplements industrial era financial information and lends insight into the value of knowledge assets and management's capacity to innovate. A first step could be assurance services about production, back orders, and product quality—information that is already shared by some major vendors and suppliers. A second step could be assurance services that answer the question, "Where does value come from?" rather than, "Where does cost go?"—the question answered by GAAP-based historical cost financial statements.

Will companies supply the nonfinancial information that investors demand? The Information Technology Subcommittee of the AICPA *Special Committee on Assurance Services* (the Elliott Committee) responds: ". . . outsiders who seek corporate information (investors, creditors, regulators, environmental activists) are often able to obtain far more information than what is published in financial reports. Organizations find it beneficial to be responsive to information users' needs when trying to attract reasonably priced financing and strategic partners and to create or protect a positive public image. Some business purposes can be achieved only by supplying additional information."[1]

CONSIDERING INTERNAL CONTROL: INVENTORY

As explained in Chapter 7 and illustrated for the revenue/receipt and expenditure/disbursement cycles in Chapters 10, 12, and 14, an auditor's consideration of internal control involves obtaining an understanding of the system, testing controls, and assessing control risk. The following discussion focuses on an auditor's consideration of conversion cycle controls. Controls over inventory are addressed first, followed by controls over fixed assets.

OBTAIN AN UNDERSTANDING

An auditor's objective is to obtain an understanding of a client's internal controls: How is the system supposed to work and what controls have been prescribed by management to assure that the system does work? As discussed in Chapter 7, obtaining an understanding consists of: (1) performing a preliminary review, (2) documenting the system, (3) performing a transaction walk-through, and (4) determining whether existing controls are potentially reliable in assessing control risk below the maximum.

Preliminary Review

The purpose of the preliminary review is to determine whether further consideration of the controls is likely to justify restricting substantive tests of inventory. An auditor performs the preliminary review for inventory by reading the client's procedures manuals and by interviewing client personnel who are responsible for perpetual inventory records, cost records, and inventory accounting. Assuming that existing controls appear potentially reliable in assessing control risk below the maximum, an auditor proceeds by documenting the system.

System Documentation

An entity's inventory control and inventory accounting procedures can be documented with flowcharts, questionnaires, and/or narratives, although detailed flowcharts are less common in practice, particularly for small-to-medium-size companies. Figure 15-6 illustrates an internal control questionnaire for inventory, focusing on physical control, perpetual inventory records, and cost records, three areas critical to inventory control. A *no* response to any question would indicate a control procedure is not used and, therefore, that lacking compensating controls, a material error or fraud could result. Alternatively, or in conjunction with a flowchart or questionnaire, an auditor could use a narrative memorandum, for example to document materials transfer and recording procedures.

---

1   "The Effect of Information Technology on the Assurance Services Marketplace," Report of the Information Technology Subcommittee of the AICPA *Special Committee on Assurance Services* (1996) p. 9.

Figure 15-6: Questionnaire: Inventory

Performed by: _____
Date: _____

Question	*Answer: Yes, No, or N/A*	*Remarks*

Physical Control

1. Is inventory reasonably protected from physical deterioration and theft (e.g., fenced areas, restricted access storerooms)?
2. Are materials requisition forms required to obtain materials and supplies for use in production?
3. Are Inventory Control personnel segregated from purchasing, receiving, shipping, production, and recording functions?
4. Are Inventory Control personnel responsible for controlling transfers in and out of storage areas?
5. Are Inventory Control or other personnel responsible for monitoring inventory levels and reporting slow-moving or damaged items?
6. Is access to inventory restricted to authorized personnel?
7. Are physical inventory counts taken at least once a year for all inventories?
8. Is insurance coverage maintained and periodically reviewed for all inventory?

Perpetual Inventory Records

1. Are perpetual inventory records continually updated on a timely basis?
2. Are perpetual records maintained by employees independent of shipping, receiving, cost accounting, production, inventory control, and general accounting?
3. Are perpetual records reconciled with general ledger control accounts on a regular basis?
4. Are source documents (e.g., invoices, requisitions, bills of lading, etc.) that are related to perpetual records prenumbered, approved, and sent to General Accounting for entry in control accounts?
5. Are periodic inventory counts reconciled with perpetual records?

Cost Records

1. Are cost records continually updated on a timely basis?

Figure 15-6: *(continued)*

Performed by: _____
Date: _____

Question	Answer: Yes, No, or N/A	Remarks
2. Are cost records maintained by employees independent of perpetual records, production, inventory control, and general accounting?		
3. Are cost records reconciled with general ledger control accounts on a regular basis?		
4. Are cost accountants familiar with and continually updated about production processes?		
5. Are direct and indirect production costs accumulated in sufficient detail to enable accurate charges to work-in-process or finished goods inventory?		
6. Are all inventory transfers reported and recorded on a timely basis?		
7. Are Production personnel required to explain price and volume variances?		

Transaction Walk-Through

To confirm his or her understanding of the system, the auditor could trace one or several materials transfers from raw materials to work-in-process, to finished goods perpetual records, and to entries and postings in cost records, inventory accounting, and general accounting. Several transfers, rather than a single transfer, are often used for transaction walk-through, because individual units transferred (for example, from raw materials to work-in-process) are not likely to be identifiable as the same units transferred from work-in-process to finished goods.

Identification of Control Procedures

An auditor identifies controls to be relied on in assessing control risk below the maximum and designs tests of controls using the same approach outlined in Chapter 10 for the revenue/receipt cycle and in Chapters 12 and 14 for the expenditure/disbursement cycle:

- Identify the system's *control objectives*. The first column of Figure 15-4 identifies control objectives for inventory.
- Consider the *potential errors or frauds* that might result if specific control objectives are not met. The second column of Figure 15-4 identifies examples of potential errors or frauds.
- Determine which *control procedures* are used by the entity to prevent or detect potentially material errors or frauds. The third column of Figure 15-4 identifies examples of potential controls.
- Design *tests of controls*.

Tests of controls for inventory are described next.

TESTS OF CONTROLS: INVENTORY

Tests of controls over inventory focus on whether transfers of inventory through the production process are authorized and recorded. However, since tests of purchasing (Chapter 12) and selling (Chapter 10) may include tests of inventory records, an auditor should carefully coordinate tests to avoid duplication of effort.

Perpetual Records

Tests of controls over an entity's perpetual records focus on physical transfers of inventory to and from raw materials, work-in-process, and finished goods. The accuracy of recording transfers is important for at least two reasons. First, inaccurate recording of transfers could suggest that control procedures are neither complied with nor operating as planned, casting doubt on the reliability of the records. Second, inaccurate recording could suggest the possibility of double-counted inventory quantities. For example, if 100 units of raw materials inventory is transferred to work-in-process, perpetual records should reflect a 100-unit reduction in raw materials and a 100-unit increase in work-in-process; if, however, only the increase in work-in-process is recorded, raw materials would be overstated by 100 units, resulting in double counting. Correspondingly, if only the decrease in raw materials is recorded, work-in-process would be understated by 100 units. Some representative tests for perpetual records are presented below.

Tests of Controls: Perpetual Records

1. For sampled purchases of raw materials, compare quantities and unit costs from vendors' invoices with perpetual records, coordinating with tests of purchases in the expenditure/disbursement cycle.
2. For sampled transfers of raw materials from Inventory Control, trace to:
   a. Approved materials requisitions.
   b. Transfers to work-in-process perpetual records, comparing quantities and unit costs.
   c. Summary transfer entries in general ledger control accounts.
3. For sampled transfers from Work in Process, trace to:
   a. Transfers to finished goods perpetual records, comparing quantities and unit costs.
   b. Summary transfer entries in general ledger control accounts.
4. For sampled transfers from Finished Goods, trace to:
   a. Shipping documents, comparing quantities and unit costs, coordinating with tests of sales in the revenue/receipt cycle.
   b. Summary of cost of goods sold and sales entries.

In Step 1, the auditor is testing whether raw materials quantities and unit costs per the perpetual inventory records reflect actual purchases made during the period. Step 2, in contrast, tests transfers from raw materials to work-in-process perpetual records, but from three different perspectives. First, in Step 2(a), the auditor tests whether transfers were prompted by approved materials requisitions. That is, transfers to Work in Process should occur only when Production personnel request raw materials for specific jobs. Second, Step 2(b) tests whether quantities and unit costs on materials requisitions are reflected accurately in work-in-process perpetual records. Third, in Step 2(c), the auditor's focus shifts to the integrity of accounting records by tracing summary transfer entries from work-in-process perpetual records to Raw Materials and Work-in-Process Inventory, two general ledger control accounts.

In Step 3, the auditor focuses on transfers from work-in-process records to finished goods perpetual records. The logic and intent of Steps 3(a) and 3(b) are identical to Steps 2(b) and 2(c), respectively.

Step 4, the logical follow-up to Steps 2 and 3, focuses on transfers from finished goods perpetual records. Since transfers from finished goods inventory should result only from shipments, the auditor in Step 4(a) traces transfers out of finished goods perpetual records to shipping documents filed in the shipping department (see Figure 10-2). In Step 4(b), sampled finished goods transfers are traced to cost of goods sold and to sales entries, thereby assuring that the cost of finished goods shipped is matched with realized sales revenues.

Cost Records

Although crucial to an entity's inventory accounting system, perpetual records are intended primarily as a control over the location and flow of inventory *quantities*. Tests of controls must also be performed for the flow of inventory *costs* from raw materials to work-in-process, finished goods, and cost of goods sold.

Cost accounting systems differ significantly from company to company, depending on the products manufactured or processed. As a result, tests of controls also vary significantly from engagement to engagement. In many audits, though, an auditor focuses on accumulated labor and overhead charges to work-in-process inventory. Several tests follow.

Tests of Controls: Cost Records

1. Obtain summaries of charges to work-in-process inventory.
2. Test accumulated direct labor and overhead charges:
   a. For sampled direct labor charges, reconcile amounts with: (1) departmental labor charge reports, coordinating with tests of labor records in the expenditure/disbursement cycle, and (2) work-in-process perpetual records.
   b. For sampled overhead charges, reconcile rates with authorized standard costs, assuring that the basis for application (e.g., direct labor hours) is appropriate.
3. Review the basis for determining standard overhead rates, determining that:
   a. Expenses charged to overhead are reasonable and consistent with the prior period, and
   b. Standard rates reasonably approximate actual costs.
4. Determine the disposition of overapplied and underapplied overhead.

As indicated in Step 1, tests of cost records stem from a client's summary of charges (debits) to work-in-process inventory and, as suggested by Steps 2 through 4, focus on direct labor and overhead charges.

In Step 2(a), the auditor traces direct labor charges to two independent sources: departmental labor charge reports and work-in-process perpetual records (assuming labor charges are included in perpetual records, which in some companies may not be the case). Step 2(b) addresses whether overhead charges agree with authorized standard costs, and whether the basis for applying overhead—for example, direct labor hours, units of production, etc.—

is appropriate. In turn, Step 3 further addresses standard overhead costs, but from the viewpoint of whether overhead is applied consistently with the prior period and reasonably approximates actual costs.

Step 4 addresses how a client disposes of overapplied and underapplied overhead. Under generally accepted accounting principles, normal variances between actual and standard costs—the basis for determining overapplied and underapplied overhead—should be charged to the period incurred, usually through cost of sales. In contrast, abnormal variances, such as idle facilities expense or excessive spoilage, should be allocated between ending inventory and current operations, again through cost of sales.

ASSESS CONTROL RISK

An auditor reviews system documentation and the results of tests of controls to determine whether existing control procedures can be relied on to assess control risk below the maximum, assess detection risk above the minimum, and therefore to restrict substantive tests of inventory. The evaluation is based on four issues: (1) the types of errors or frauds that could occur, (2) necessary control procedures that should prevent or detect the errors or frauds, (3) whether the necessary procedures exist and are followed, and (4) any deficiencies in internal control. Substantive tests applicable to inventory are discussed later in the chapter. But first, the chapter considers internal controls over fixed assets.

CONSIDERING INTERNAL CONTROL: FIXED ASSETS

The following discussion addresses the auditor's consideration of controls over fixed assets.

OBTAIN AN UNDERSTANDING

Compared to inventory, fixed asset transactions are considerably less numerous, and individual transactions usually involve considerably larger dollar amounts. Thus, although the steps in a review of the system are identical (preliminary review, system documentation, transaction walk-through, and evaluation), an auditor's focus is different, since any one transaction alone could exceed the auditor's tolerable error for fixed assets.

Preliminary Review
The preliminary review is performed by reading the client's procedures manuals and by interviewing client personnel responsible for fixed asset additions, disposals and retirements, and recording. Assuming controls are potentially reliable in assessing control risk below the maximum, an auditor proceeds to system documentation.

System Documentation
Flowcharts are seldom used to document fixed asset systems, primarily because the number of transactions is not likely to justify extensive flowcharting. Rather, auditors often use internal control questionnaires similar to the one in Figure 15-7 to identify apparent deficiencies and narratives to document procedures for fixed asset additions, disposals and retirements, and recording.

Figure 15-7: Questionnaire: Fixed Assets

Performed by: _____
Date: _____

Question	Answer: Yes, No, or N/A	Remarks

Fixed Asset Records

1. Are detailed records maintained for each class of fixed assets (e.g., land, buildings, machinery, equipment)?
2. Is responsibility for maintaining fixed asset records segregated from responsibility for physically controlling fixed assets and from general accounting?
3. Are detailed records reconciled periodically with general ledger control accounts?
4. Are procedures followed to determine whether recorded fixed assets actually exist?
5. Is access to and the use of fixed assets restricted only to authorized personnel?
6. Is insurance coverage maintained and reviewed for all fixed assets?
7. Are fixed assets physically safeguarded from deterioration and theft?

Additions

1. Do procedures require authorization by the board of directors or senior management for fixed asset additions?
2. Are actual expenditures for fixed assets compared with amounts authorized?
3. Are procedures established to assure that fixed assets purchased are delivered in accordance with orders placed?
4. Are fixed asset additions promptly recorded in fixed asset records?
5. Are fixed asset additions promptly reported to General Accounting?
6. Are insurance companies notified of fixed asset additions in order to increase insurance coverage?
7. Is construction in progress—whether internally or externally contracted—authorized and periodically inspected?

Disposals and Retirements

1. Do procedures require authorization by the board of directors or senior management for fixed asset disposals and retirements?

Figure 15-7: *(continued)*

Performed by: _____
Date: _____

Question	Answer: Yes, No, or N/A	Remarks
2. Are procedures established to assure that the proceeds from fixed asset disposals are recorded properly and deposited?		
3. Are fixed asset disposals and retirements promptly recorded in fixed asset records?		
4. Are fixed asset disposals and retirements promptly reported to General Accounting for recording gains or losses?		
5. Are insurance companies notified of disposals and retirements to assure that insurance coverage is altered accordingly?		

Depreciation

1. Are procedures established to assure that additions are added to depreciation records and that disposals/retirements are deleted?
2. Are procedures established to assure that depreciation is recorded only for those fixed assets actually in service during the period?
3. Are procedures established for determining depreciation methods, estimated useful lives, and salvage values?

Transaction Walk-Through

To confirm her or his understanding of an entity's fixed asset system, an auditor could trace an addition transaction, a disposal transaction, and a retirement transaction through the system and examine depreciation schedules for conformity with prescribed procedures. Alternatively, some auditors ignore transaction walk-through altogether, electing instead to perform substantive tests of details on all fixed asset transactions at year end. In that case, tests of controls would also be ignored.

Identification of Control Procedures

Following system documentation, an auditor continues considering internal control exactly as outlined earlier in the chapter for inventory. Figure 15-5 identifies control objectives (column one), potential errors or frauds (column two), and control procedures (column three).

TESTS OF CONTROLS: FIXED ASSETS

When the number of fixed asset transactions is limited, an auditor may forego or limit tests of controls, electing instead to assess control risk at the maximum, assess allowable detection risk at the minimum, and rely on substantive tests of details. However, if the number of transactions is large, an auditor may elect to perform tests of controls over an entity's recording, addition, disposal, and depreciation activities.

Fixed Asset Records

Tests of fixed asset records focus on the relationship between detailed records and the general ledger and on the existence of, and insurance coverage for recorded assets. Some representative tests follow.

Tests of Controls: Fixed Asset Records

1. Reconcile total fixed assets per detailed records with the general ledger, and investigate any differences.
2. Physically inspect sampled fixed assets.
3. Review the adequacy of insurance coverage on recorded assets.

A company's detailed fixed asset records may take the form of a spreadsheet or a ledger, and as indicated in Step 1, should be reconciled in total with the general ledger. In Step 2, the auditor assures that the fixed assets—particularly additions for the current year—physically exist and have not been disposed of or retired. In Step 3, the auditor reviews the adequacy of fixed asset insurance coverage, since inadequate coverage may require financial statement disclosure.

Additions

An auditor's predominant concern in tests of fixed asset additions is that the related transactions are authorized and properly recorded. Several appropriate tests follow.

Tests of Controls: Additions

1. Obtain a summary of fixed asset additions from accounting personnel.
2. Foot the summary and reconcile total additions with total additions per the general ledger.
3. Randomly select a sample of additions, and for each sampled addition:
   a. Examine authorization(s), purchase order (or contract), receiving report, vendor's invoice, and other supporting documents.
   b. Examine evidence of cash payment (e.g., a canceled check) and trace to an entry in the voucher register (or other cash disbursements records).
   c. Examine evidence of an obligation for payment (e.g., a notes payable) and trace to subsidiary and general ledger accounts.
   d. Determine that classification as a fixed asset, rather than repairs and maintenance expense, is consistent with policy.

The company's summary of fixed asset additions, the basis for testing additions, may take the form of a spreadsheet or a detailed worksheet, among other things. Step 2 determines whether the summary is mathematically accurate, and reconciles the summary with the general ledger, the source for preparing financial statements.

   Step 3 addresses the substance of recorded fixed asset addition transactions. Additions can be sampled, as suggested in the program, or tested entirely, which is common when additions are not numerous. In Step 3(a), the auditor examines evidence that an addition was authorized and an asset received. Evidence of authorization could appear within the board of directors' minutes, particularly for substantial additions such as buildings, or could take the form of a division manager's memorandum. Receiving reports and invoices would indicate that the additions arrived and were billed by independent vendors.

Step 3(b), in contrast, determines whether the addition was paid for and was recorded properly as a cash disbursement. If a note or other obligation exists, the auditor would examine the document in Step 3(c), reconciling details with the subsidiary records and the general ledger. Step 3(d) assures that additions are classified properly as fixed assets rather than as repairs and maintenance expense. In addition, the step assures that classification as an asset or expense is consistent with company policy. For example, in some companies, additions of less than a predetermined dollar amount, say $1,000, might be charged to expense regardless of useful life, since the burden of record keeping is not necessarily justified for immaterial amounts.

Disposals

Like additions, an auditor is concerned that fixed asset disposals are authorized and properly recorded. Some representative tests follow.

Tests of Controls: Disposals

1. Obtain a summary of fixed asset disposals and retirements from accounting personnel.
2. Foot the summary and reconcile total disposals with total disposals per the general ledger.
3. Randomly select a sample of disposals, and for each sampled disposal:
   a. Examine authorization(s), the contract, the sales invoice, and other supporting documents.
   b. Examine entry in the cash receipts records.
   c. Examine the note receivable, if there is one, and trace to subsidiary and general ledger accounts.
   d. Calculate any gain or loss and trace to the general ledger.

A company's summary of fixed asset disposals and retirements—for example, a spreadsheet—is obtained in Step 1, tested for mathematical accuracy in Step 2, and agreed to the general ledger. As with additions, disposals and retirements may be sampled or tested entirely.

In Step 3(a), the auditor examines evidence that the transaction is authorized, for example, by reading the board of directors' minutes, and that the transaction occurred, as would be suggested by a signed contract and a sales invoice. Step 3(b) examines entries in the cash receipts records, thereby further supporting whether transactions occurred. If a note was received for a disposed asset, the auditor should examine the instrument and reconcile the transaction with the general ledger, as indicated in Step 3(c). In Step 3(d), the auditor recalculates any gain or loss from the disposal transaction, reconciling the amount with entries in the general ledger.

Depreciation

Tests of depreciation involve calculations and the review of recorded amounts, useful lives, and salvage values. Similar tests are performed for the amortization of intangible assets and the depletion of wasting assets. Several appropriate tests of depreciation follow.

Tests of Controls: Depreciation

1. Review depreciation methods by asset class and policies for useful lives and salvage values.
2. Randomly select a sample of fixed assets, and for each sampled asset:
   a. Determine whether the useful life and salvage value are consistent with policies.
   b. Recalculate depreciation expense and accumulated depreciation.

In Step 1, the auditor reviews methods and policies to assure that depreciation is calculated as planned. Step 2 tests sampled assets but could also be performed for all assets. Step 2(a) determines whether each asset's useful life and salvage value are consistent with company policy (Step 1), and Step 2(b) recalculates depreciation expense and accumulated depreciation.

ASSESS CONTROL RISK

The auditor assesses control risk for fixed assets in the same manner as discussed earlier for inventory.

FINANCIAL STATEMENT ASSERTIONS AND AUDIT PROCEDURES

Inventory and Fixed Assets are the most significant financial statement accounts processed through the conversion cycle. The following section provides an overview of how practicing auditors typically test each of the financial statement assertions introduced in Chapter 6: existence or occurrence, completeness, rights and obligations, valuation or allocation, and presentation and disclosure. Figure 15-8 summarizes the discussion by relating each assertion to specific audit procedures.

EXISTENCE OR OCCURRENCE

Within the conversion cycle, the existence or occurrence assertion addresses whether all recorded inventory and fixed assets existed at the balance sheet date and whether all recorded inventory and fixed asset transactions occurred during the period.

For inventory, existence or occurrence is tested by three separate but related procedures. First and foremost, the auditor observes the client's physical count of inventory, often at the balance sheet date, thereby assuring that recorded inventory exists. Second, for off-premises inventory, the auditor confirms recorded quantities with consignees or public warehouses. Finally, inventory cutoff is tested to assure that inventory-related transactions, such as purchases and sales, are recorded in the proper accounting period.

The existence of fixed asset balances and occurrence of transactions are tested by observing additions (and perhaps some previously existing assets), and by testing cutoff, to assure that additions and disposals are recorded in the proper accounting period.

Figure 15-8:   Relating Assertions and Audit Procedures: Inventory and Fixed Assets

Assertions	Audit Procedures	
	Inventory	Fixed Assets
Existence or occurrence	Observe physical inventory. Confirm off-premises inventory. Test cutoff.	Observe asset additions. Test cutoff.
Completeness	Observe physical inventory. Confirm off-premises inventory. Test cutoff. Perform analytical procedures.	Observe asset additions. Test cutoff. Perform analytical procedures.
Rights and obligations	Confirm off-premises inventory. Test cutoff. Review consignment and purchase commitments.	Test additions (and disposals). Test cutoff. Examine contracts and other documentation.
Valuation or allocation	Test final priced inventory. Review physical inventory for obsolete, slow-moving, or otherwise unsalable goods.	Verify accuracy of recorded fixed assets and depreciation expense. Test additions and disposals.
Presentation and disclosure	Compare statement presentation and disclosures with those required by GAAP.	Compare statement presentation and disclosures with those required by GAAP.

COMPLETENESS

The completeness assertion addresses whether all inventory and fixed asset transactions that should be presented in the financial statements are actually presented. That is, were all transactions recorded? To test completeness for inventory, an auditor observes the physical inventory and confirms off-premises inventory, to assure that all inventory is recorded. Cutoff tests assure that the recording of year end transactions is not postponed to the next accounting period. Analytical procedures also address completeness by testing whether recorded balances appear reasonable in relation to other accounts. Completeness for fixed assets is addressed by testing additions to assure they're all recorded, by testing cutoff, and by performing analytical procedures.

RIGHTS AND OBLIGATIONS

Within the conversion cycle, the rights assertion addresses whether an entity has property rights to inventory and to fixed assets. Rights to inventory are tested by confirming off-premises inventory quantities and by testing cutoff, which assures that rights to recorded inventory exist as of the balance sheet date. In addition, auditors also test current obligations for future commitments by reviewing any outstanding consignment or purchase agreements.

For fixed assets, rights are examined by testing additions (and disposals), by testing cutoff to determine whether rights exist at the balance sheet date, and by examining contracts or other supporting documentation, such as invoices for purchased assets and cost records for internally manufactured equipment.

VALUATION OR ALLOCATION

The valuation assertion addresses whether existing inventory and fixed assets are carried in the financial statements at appropriate amounts. For inventory, an auditor addresses carrying value primarily by testing the client's final priced inventory, but also by reviewing physical inventory for obsolete, slow-moving, or otherwise unsalable goods. The carrying value of fixed assets is tested by verifying the mathematical accuracy of recorded fixed assets and of the client's recorded depreciation expense. Valuation is also addressed when an auditor tests additions and disposals, since added fixed assets should be included in the current financial statements and disposed assets should not.

PRESENTATION AND DISCLOSURE

The presentation and disclosure assertion addresses whether recorded inventory and fixed assets are properly classified, described, and disclosed in the financial statements. Presentation and disclosure are tested by comparing a client's financial statement disclosures with generally accepted accounting principles for each reported account. Disclosure guidelines, such as the AICPA's annually updated *Accounting and Audit Manual*, among others, are used frequently by practicing auditors.

The following sections expand on this discussion by illustrating and further explaining each audit procedure. Substantive tests of inventory are discussed first, followed thereafter by tests of fixed assets.

SUBSTANTIVE TESTS OF INVENTORY

Substantive tests of inventory center on observing client personnel count inventory (and confirming off-premises inventory not observed), testing priced inventory (e.g., unit prices), testing cutoff, and performing analytical procedures. A program of substantive tests appears in Figure 15-9 and is keyed to, and discussed in the context of, the financial statement assertions presented earlier.

OBSERVE PHYSICAL INVENTORY

As discussed in Chapter 6, knowledge obtained directly by an auditor through observation can provide a highly persuasive form of evidence, and nowhere is observation more relevant than in testing inventory. Observation of a client's procedures for physically counting inventories contributes to no less than two assertions:

Figure 15-9:   Substantive Tests: Inventory

Assertions	Procedures
Existence Completeness	1. Observe physical inventory.
Existence Completeness Rights	2. Confirm inventory at off-premises locations.

Valuation	3. Obtain the final priced inventory records.
	   a. Extend, foot, and cross-foot the final priced inventory.
	   b. Test unit prices.
	   c. Agree total inventory per the final priced inventory with the general ledger.

Existence or occurrence Completeness Rights	4. Test cutoff, coordinating with tests performed for sales and receivables and for purchases and payables.
Completeness	5. Perform analytical procedures.

Presentation and
  disclosure
	6. Review financial statements to determine whether:
	   a. Inventories and cost of sales are properly classified and described.
	   b. Disclosures are adequate.

- *Existence.* Do inventories reported on the balance sheet physically exist?
- *Completeness.* Do inventories reported on the balance sheet include all materials, work-in-process, and finished goods?

Planning Inventory Counts

An auditor does not physically count inventory for a client, nor does the auditor physically participate as a counter. Rather, client personnel count and document inventory quantities, and the auditor observes the client's procedures. For periodic inventory systems, the physical counts serve as the only measure of quantities on hand; for perpetual systems, the counts serve as both a measure of quantities on hand and a test of the perpetual records.

Inventory quantities may be counted at interim rather than at year end. From an auditor's point of view, the appropriate timing of inventory counts depends on the type of inventory system—periodic or perpetual—and the effectiveness of internal control. Interim counts are more appropriate when well-kept perpetual records are maintained, internal control (including physical control over the movement of inventory) is effective, and perpetual records and financial statement accounts can be reconciled with year end balances. Otherwise, counts on or near the balance sheet date are more appropriate—for example, when a periodic inventory system is used, when perpetual records are not well-kept, or when internal control is ineffective.

Some time in advance of the count date, an auditor should plan for the inventory observation by reviewing management's proposed inventory counting procedures and their written instructions for employees who will count the inventory. The procedures should be well-planned and among other things might provide for:

- Controlling or eliminating stock movement on the count date.
- Stocking or arranging inventory in a manner convenient for counting (e.g., like-sized rows, clear separations between inventory classes).
- Pretesting counting devices such as weight scales.
- Segregating stock not to be included in the count, such as inventory held on consignment from suppliers.
- Identifying off-premises stock to be included in the count, such as inventory out on consignment with customers.
- Preparing preprinted count media, such as multipart tags, count sheets, or punched cards.
- Documenting damaged or obsolete inventory.

The employees who count inventory should be given written instructions which include information such as the:

- Count date and times.
- Names of supervisors and count teams by location.
- Count media.
- Procedures for counting and documenting quantities.
- Procedures for controlling and accounting for count media before, during, and after the physical counts.

The procedures and instructions should be complete, explicit, and reasonably adequate to facilitate accurate and reliable counts.

Observing Client Inventory Counts

Prior to, or on, the inventory count date, the in-charge auditor should coordinate with audit staff members assigned to the observation, providing them with duties, detailed instructions, and copies of the client's instructions. In general, most staff members' duties will include:

- Observing count teams.
- Making and documenting test counts.
- Noting damaged or slow-moving inventory.

An auditor observes client count teams in order to determine whether counters are adhering to the client's instructions and are counting and documenting quantities accurately. Count teams should proceed systematically, taking precautions to cover all, but not more than, their assigned areas; counting outside assigned areas could result in double-counting, thereby potentially overstating inventory.

In conjunction with observing count teams, an auditor should make and document test counts of some inventory items, agreeing quantities with count media compiled by client personnel. Test counts should be documented on working papers and indicate all details necessary to agree quantities subsequently with the final priced inventory, as illustrated in Figure 15-10. Documented details might include count media numbers (e.g., tag numbers), inventory stock numbers and descriptions, and quantities. In addition, an auditor should document any damaged or slow-moving goods, since these items may need to be adjusted to net realizable value in the accounts.

Information should be documented for goods shipped and received on the inventory count date. Assuming title passes on the count date, inventory

Figure 15-10:   Inventory Test Counts

C19
DN 1/27/00

The Wilson Company
Inventory Test Counts
December 31, 1999

Inventory Ticket Number	Location & Description	Count per:		Difference: Over (Under)
		Client	Audit	
	Warehouse A			
0462	Part A24-Copper cable	870 ft.	820 ft.[a]	50 ft.[b]
0163	Part A98-Rubber tubing	565 ft.	565 ft.[a]	—
0241	Part A99-Synthetic tubing	405 ft.	400 ft.[a]	5 ft.[b]
0328	Solder	125 lb.	125 lb.[a]	—
0612	3/8" Wire binding	600 ft.	600 ft.[a]	—
0761	3/4" Wire binding	298 ft.	295 ft.[a]	3 ft.[b]
0824	298 Engine oil	125 qts.	125 qts.[a]	—
0822	Bushings, 5/8"	625	625 [a]	—
	Department A—Finishing			
0014	Plating fluid	405 gal.	410 gal.[a]	(5 gal.)[b]
0129	Electrolyte solution	75 gal.	75 gal.[a]	–
0146	Oaklite 32	127 gal.	127 gal.[a]	–

a Reconciled with client's final priced inventory (work done 1/17/00—see C20-C24).

b Difference confirmed by client recount, and inventory tag corrected.

Conclusion

Based on test counts and observations, I am satisfied that the client's count procedures were reasonable, that counts were reasonably accurate, and that neither Warehouse A nor Dept. A.—Finishing contains significant quantities of obsolete, slow-moving, or otherwise nonsalable inventory.

shipments should be excluded from physical counts, and receipts should be included. Information documented for shipments and receipts on the count date is used in conjunction with other information in tests of cutoff.

Some goods on hand may represent consignments from suppliers and, therefore, are the supplier's inventory. An auditor should determine that all goods held on consignment are segregated from inventory prior to the physical counts. An auditor can further test for consignments by reviewing consignment agreements and making inquiries of client personnel.

Following completion of all inventory observation procedures, each audit staff member should prepare a working paper memorandum summarizing his or her observations, any significant departures from the client's preplanned instructions, and a conclusion about the accuracy of client counts.

CONFIRM OFF-PREMISES INVENTORY

Inventory held off-premises by consignees or in public warehouses need not necessarily be observed by an auditor, but should be confirmed. An example of a typical off-premises inventory confirmation request appears in Figure 15-11. If inventory in public warehouses is significant in relation to current or total assets, an auditor should also make supplemental inquiries, such as:

- Discussion about the client's control procedures for the preemployment investigation of warehouse managers, and tests of related evidence.
- Review of the client's control procedures to monitor the performance of warehouse managers and to test related evidence.
- Observation of physical counts whenever practical and reasonable.
- Confirmation from lenders (on a test basis, where appropriate) about pertinent details of warehouse receipts pledged as collateral.

TEST FINAL PRICED INVENTORY

Physical inventory counts provide information about quantities, but not about carrying values. Thus, after completed count media are summarized, employees not otherwise responsible for inventory record keeping or control should extend the quantities by unit costs in spreadsheets, resulting in a final priced

Figure 15-11: Confirmation Request for Off-Premises Inventory

The Wilson Company
15 Artubus Drive
Stony Brook, NY 11790

January 7, 2000

McGowen Warehousing
12456 Dartmouth Road
Indianapolis, IN 46298

Our auditors, Cheever & Yates, LLP, are auditing our financial statements for 1999. Will you please furnish them with the following information regarding merchandise held in your custody for us as of December 31, 1999:

- Quantities on hand, including:
  Lot number,
  Date received,
  Description of merchandise.
- A statement about whether the quantities were determined by physical count or represent your recorded amounts only.
- A list of negotiable or non-negotiable warehouse receipts issued, if any.
- A statement of any known liens against this merchandise.
- Indication of any damaged, spoiled, or deteriorated merchandise.

A prompt reply to our auditors will be appreciated. An envelope addressed to our auditors is enclosed.

Maxine Kuman
Controller

inventory by item number, product line, and inventory classification. To facilitate follow-up, each line item on the final priced inventory should identify the count media from which quantities were compiled. Quantities and the final priced inventory should be reconciled by client personnel with perpetual records and control accounts, respectively, and necessary adjustments should be recorded.

As part of year end substantive procedures, an auditor obtains the client's final priced inventory and performs tests of clerical accuracy. The auditor should extend (multiply quantities by unit costs), foot, and cross-foot the priced inventory, agreeing test counts with priced quantities, as illustrated in Figure 15-10 (tick mark *a*); dollar amounts to control accounts; and required adjustments to general ledger entries. Unit prices per the final priced inventory should be agreed with source documents on a sample basis, giving consideration to the cost flow methods adopted. For example, if raw materials costs are assigned to production on a first-in, first-out basis, unit costs should be agreed with the latest vendor invoices available for a period prior to the inventory count date, since the latest prices would be assigned to raw materials inventory and earlier costs would have been charged to work-in-process.

TEST CUTOFF

An auditor compiles inventory cutoff documentation during the physical inventory observation. The documentation includes shipping documents and receiving reports, and is used to test sales cutoff in conjunction with substantive tests for sales and accounts receivable (Chapter 11) and purchase cutoff in conjunction with substantive tests for purchases and accounts payable (Chapter 13).

The cutoff information, however, cannot necessarily be agreed with inventory account balances. For example, if goods are received (and title passes) on the count date, tracing related receiving reports to subsequent purchase and payable entries does not assure that the received goods were counted in inventory. Likewise, if goods are shipped (and title passes) on the count date, tracing related shipping documents to subsequent sales and receivables entries does not assure that the shipped goods were not counted in inventory. As a result, during the physical inventory observation, an auditor must assure that shipped and received goods are controlled to avoid both double-counting, as in the case of counting shipped goods in inventory, and undercounting, as in the case of failing to count received goods.

PERFORM ANALYTICAL PROCEDURES

An auditor uses analytical procedures—for example, comparing relationships between and among accounts—to address completeness and to determine whether conclusions drawn from substantive tests of details are reasonable. For example, inventory price tests might indicate that a client's inventory is priced accurately. But an auditor would not likely conclude that the priced sample was representative if other tests indicated that quantities at year end had dropped sharply since the prior year, and yet the general ledger book value of inventory had not.

For inventory, an auditor might use any of the following analytical tests, among others:

- Compare cost of sales divided by average inventory—inventory turnover—for the current year with that for prior years, thereby testing whether turnover is reduced, suggesting slow-moving or obsolete inventory.
- Compare the number-of-days-sales in inventory for the current year with that for prior years, again testing turnover.
- Compare gross profit margin for the current year with that for prior years, thereby testing whether inventory might possibly be understated or overstated.
- Compare volume-adjusted manufacturing costs for the current year with those for prior years, thereby testing whether unit costs might possibly be understated or overstated.

If any of the preceding tests reveal unusual relationships, an auditor would first make inquiries of management and then design additional detailed substantive tests or extend sample sizes if necessary. For example, in the above price testing illustration, the auditor might increase sample size, thereby performing additional price tests and attempting to control the risk of incorrect acceptance.

REVIEW FINANCIAL STATEMENT DISCLOSURES

An auditor reads financial statements to assess whether inventory and cost of sales are properly classified, described, and disclosed in accordance with generally accepted accounting principles. Inventories are usually stated at the lower of cost or market, according to a cost flow assumption (e.g., first-in, first-out), and may be classified as supplies, raw materials, work-in-process, and finished goods. Accrued losses should be disclosed for any purchase commitments made at unfavorable prices.

SUBSTANTIVE TESTS OF FIXED ASSETS

Fixed assets are less susceptible to frauds than some other assets, such as cash, securities, and some types of inventories. As a result, auditors often address some financial statement assertions at interim, when considering internal control. For example, an auditor addresses existence when physically inspecting fixed assets in conjunction with tests of controls over records. Thus, some substantive procedures are performed at interim, and follow-up or additional tests are done at year end for the intervening period since interim. Figure 15-12 presents a program of representative year end substantive tests for fixed assets and depreciation and is keyed to the assertions discussed earlier.

VERIFY ACCURACY OF RECORDED FIXED ASSETS

To test the mathematical accuracy of fixed asset records, an auditor obtains a client-prepared schedule summarizing detailed asset records. The schedule should include beginning balances, additions, disposals, and ending balances by fixed asset class, as illustrated in Figure 15-13. The auditor should reconcile beginning balances per the schedule with the prior year's financial statements. The accuracy of the summary schedule is checked by footing and cross-footing and by agreeing totals with general ledger accounts. Details for selected assets are then traced to the underlying detailed records.

Figure 15-12: Substantive Tests: Fixed Assets and Depreciation

Assertions	Procedures

Valuation	1. Verify mathematical accuracy of recorded fixed assets:
	  a. Obtain a year end summary schedule of detailed fixed asset records; foot and cross-foot the schedule.
	  b. Agree total fixed assets per the summary schedule with the general ledger.
	  c. Randomly select a sample of fixed assets from the summary schedule and trace to detailed fixed asset records.

Existence or
  occurrence
Completeness
Rights
Valuation
	2. Test additions and disposals since interim:
	  a. Examine supporting documentation and trace to entries in accounting records.
	  b. Observe (physically inspect) additions.

Existence or occurrence Completeness Rights	3. Test cutoff to determine whether fixed asset additions and disposals near year end are recorded in the appropriate accounting period.

Valuation	4. Verify mathematical accuracy of depreciation expense:
	  a. Obtain a summary schedule of depreciation expense organized by asset class from accounting personnel; foot and cross-foot the schedule.
	  b. Trace totals per the summary schedule to totals in the general ledger.
	  c. Randomly select a sample of fixed assets from the summary schedule and recalculate depreciation expense.

Completeness	5. Perform analytical procedures.

Presentation and
  disclosure
	6. Review financial statements to determine whether:
	  a. Fixed assets, accumulated depreciation, and depreciation expense are properly classified and described.
	  b. Disclosures are adequate.

TEST ADDITIONS AND DISPOSALS SINCE INTERIM

Additions and disposals since interim are tested in the same manner as discussed earlier under tests of controls. If relatively few fixed assets have been acquired since interim, an auditor may physically inspect all recorded additions. Otherwise, a randomly selected sample of additions should be observed.

While physically inspecting additions, an auditor should also be alert for other assets that appear to be new and, therefore, that may represent unrecorded additions. Likewise, he or she should be cognizant of areas where fixed assets may recently have been removed, suggesting the possibility of unrecorded disposals. For example, an area within a manufacturing plant may appear unusually clean and contain obvious floor markings that could suggest a machine was removed.

In addition, and closely related to the existence and rights assertions, an auditor also examines documents supporting fixed asset additions and traces

Figure 15-13: Schedule of Fixed Assets and Accumulated Depreciation

Schedule prepared by client.

E1
JB 1-18-00

The Wilson Company
Fixed Assets and Accumulated Depreciation
December 31, 1999

Fixed Assets

	Final Bal. 12-31-98	Additions	Retirements/ Disposals	Balance 12-31-99	Adjustments/ Reclass.	Adjusted Bal. 12-31-99
Land	$ 257,650 c	$ 15,200 E2		$ 272,850		$ 272,850 b
Buildings	3,461,520 c		$90,000 E2	3,371,520		3,371,520 b
Machinery & Equipment	1,590,850 c	175,000 E2		1,765,850		1,765,850 b
Furniture & Fixtures	621,420 c			621,420	$37,400	658,820 b
Automobiles	105,000 c			105,000		105,000 b
	$ 6,036,440 c	$190,200	$90,000	$ 6,136,640	$37,400	$ 6,174,040 b
	a	a	a	a, TB	a	a

Accumulated Depreciation

	Final Bal. 12-31-98	Expense	Retirements/ Disposals	Balance 12-31-99	Adjustments/ Reclass.	Adjusted Bal. 12-31-99
Buildings	$ 1,461,850 c	$138,000 d		$ 1,551,850	$24,000	$ 1,575,850 b
Machinery & Equipment	825,500 c	81,500 d	$48,000 E2	907,000		907,000 b
Furniture & Fixtures	242,100 c	26,500 d		268,600		268,600 b
Automobiles	68,250 c	13,200 d		81,450		81,450 b
	$ 2,597,700 c	$259,200	$48,000	$ 2,808,900	$24,000	$ 2,832,900 b
	a	a	a	a, TB	a	a

a Footed.
b Cross-footed.
c Agreed to 12-31-98 general ledger and financial statements.
d Recalculated for reasonableness.
TB Agreed to trial balance.

the additions to entries in the accounting records. Documentation may take several forms, depending on the nature of the asset, such as an invoice for purchased machinery or a contract for constructed buildings. Supporting documentation also addresses asset valuation, because supporting documents such as invoices, contracts, and canceled checks also represent evidence of an asset's historical cost.

TEST CUTOFF

Cutoff tests for fixed assets address whether additions and disposals near year end are recorded in the proper accounting period. Since acquisitions are processed through the expenditure/disbursement cycle and disposals through the revenue/receipt cycle, fixed asset cutoff can be tested in conjunction with cutoff tests for purchases and payables and for sales and receivables. Retired assets that are not sold, however, should be tested separately.

VERIFY ACCURACY OF DEPRECIATION EXPENSE

As part of an auditor's tests of valuation, he or she tests depreciation expense, since fixed assets are reported net of accumulated depreciation. Year end detailed tests may not be necessary, however, if interim tests of controls indicate that control over depreciation is adequate. Rather, an auditor might test the reasonableness of depreciation instead through analytical procedures.

   If an auditor decides to perform detailed substantive tests of depreciation expense at year end, a summary schedule of depreciation organized by asset class should be obtained from accounting personnel. The schedule should include beginning accumulated depreciation balances (which should be agreed with the prior year's financial statements), current year depreciation expense, reversals of accumulated depreciation for disposed assets, and ending accumulated depreciation balances, as illustrated in Figure 15-13. The auditor would test the schedule's accuracy by footing and cross-footing and by agreeing totals with general ledger accounts. Depreciation expense for selected assets should be recalculated.

PERFORM ANALYTICAL PROCEDURES

To address completeness, an auditor uses analytical procedures such as ratio and trend analysis and comparison of relationships between and among related accounts. For fixed assets, an auditor might use any of the following analytical tests, among others:

*   Compare repairs and maintenance costs for the current and prior years, thereby testing whether unusually large expenses signal potentially capitalizable assets.
*   Compare repairs and maintenance costs for the current year with budgeted amounts, again testing for signals of potentially capitalizable assets.
*   Compare depreciation expense divided by total depreciable assets for the current and prior years, thereby testing whether depreciable assets might be miscalculated.
*   Compare units of production divided by total productive assets, thereby testing whether assets may have been retired or disposed of without proper recording.

As in other analytical procedures, unusual items should be investigated by inquiries of management and then by additional substantive tests if necessary. For example, an auditor would likely recalculate depreciation if depreciation expense divided by productive assets declined significantly without a corresponding decline in total productive assets.

REVIEW FINANCIAL STATEMENT DISCLOSURES

The balance sheet should be read to determine whether fixed assets and related accumulated depreciation balances are properly classified and described. When a single net book value is reported for fixed assets in a condensed balance sheet, details should be included in the notes to the financial statements. Disclosures should include depreciation methods (including any differences between methods for tax and financial reporting purposes), useful lives employed for major asset categories, and other significant policies, such as policies for capitalizing major repairs and reporting gains and losses.

An entity may possess significant leasehold rights, though not ownership, to property and, as a result, may be required to capitalize the related asset. For example, a lease that transfers substantially all of the benefits and risks incident to property ownership should be accounted for as: (1) the acquisition of an asset and incurrence of an obligation by a lessee, and (2) the sale or financing arrangement by a lessor. An auditor should examine all lease agreements, assuring that the transactions are accounted for properly under FASB *Statement of Financial Accounting Standards No. 13*, "Accounting for Leases," and other related statements and interpretations. All leased assets requiring capitalization under generally accepted accounting principles should be properly classified and described in the balance sheet, and details of lease agreements should be disclosed in notes to the financial statements.

The income statement should be reviewed to determine whether depreciation expense is properly reported. Depreciation expense included in cost of sales should be disclosed separately in the income statement or in notes to the statements.

MANAGEMENT DISCRETION AND WRITE-DOWNS OF IMPAIRED ASSETS

For years, companies have written off the book value of fixed assets, natural resources, and intangibles disposed of voluntarily through sale or abandonment, or involuntarily through casualty or condemnation. However, only in the past decade have companies begun with any regularity to write off impaired assets—assets that continue in use but that have suffered an impairment of value as a result, for example, of corporate restructuring or slumping demand for uncompetitive products. For example, coincident with a restructuring, IBM wrote off over $2 billion in software investments and other assets[2] and, driven by technological advances, AT&T wrote off over $6 billion in obsolete telephone network equipment.[3] Owing in part to the potential for earnings manipulation, the Financial Accounting Standards Board added an

---

2   "IBM Announces Big Write-Off, Restructuring," *The Wall Street Journal* (December 6, 1989), p. A3.
3   "AT&T Reports Loss for Quarter and All of 1988," *The Wall Street Journal* (January 27, 1989), p. C20.

"impairment" project to its technical agenda in 1988, issued a "Discussion Memorandum" in 1990, and issued *Statement of Financial Accounting Standards No. 121*, "Accounting for the Impairment of Long-Lived Assets and for Long-Lived Assets to Be Disposed of" in 1995. But, despite *SFAS No. 121*, management continues to have some latitude on matters of measurement, among them estimates of future cash flows and of fair market values used to calculate the impairment loss recognized on assets written down.

MANAGEMENT AND AUDITOR INCENTIVES

The literature suggests that management could have two motives for manipulating the timing and the amount of impaired asset write-downs,[4] both of which relate to earnings management: "income smoothing" and "big baths." **Income smoothing** refers to a company's maintaining a steady rate of earnings growth over a series of years, thereby providing no reason for the financial markets to impute unexpected risk to the company or to expected stock prices. As a result, management could be motivated to recognize asset write-downs in otherwise high income periods, thereby maintaining steady growth and, correspondingly, diluting expectations of higher than expected income the following year. A **big bath**, in contrast, refers to the practice of timing asset write-downs to occur in an abnormally *unprofitable* year, signaling to the financial markets that bad times have long since passed. Interestingly, asset write-downs always result in higher reported future earnings, because future period depreciation expense is computed on lower fixed asset carrying values. Auditors have incentives to assure that the timing and amount of management's charge to current income is fairly presented in all material respects, since materially misstated amounts can affect current share prices, and, as demonstrated in Chapter 5, auditors can be held liable for negligently failing to detect materially misstated financial statements. The following addresses issues auditors confront when auditing discretionary write-downs of impaired assets.

DISCRETIONARY WRITE-DOWNS

Fixed assets are normally carried in the balance sheet at historical cost less accumulated depreciation—i.e., book value—unless events cause the value of the asset to decline permanently and significantly below book value. Typically, the events driving asset impairment relate to market forces not predicted when the assets were acquired. For example, as illustrated below, declining gold prices and a persistently weak gold market caused the Battle Mountain Gold Company to recognize asset impairment write-downs material to their financial statements:

Note 2: Asset Impairment
During the third quarter . . ., the Company recognized charges totaling approximately $23.3 million, net of $11 million income tax benefits . . ., for the impairment in value of certain of the Company's assets. The charges included: (1) a write-down of $17.6 million, net of a restated $9 million income tax benefit, of the Company's investment

---

4   For example, see L. J. Zucca and D. R. Campbell "A Closer Look at Discretionary Writedowns of Impaired Assets," *Accounting Horizons* (September 1992), pp. 28-41.

in the San Luis mine in Colorado to reduce the carrying value of the investment to a level which the Company believes will be recoverable under current market conditions (lower gold prices, compared with those at the time of project conception, and greater than anticipated capital expenditures resulting from a difficult start-up period led to the write-down), (2) a writeoff of $4 million, net of a restated $2 million income tax benefit, and (3) an impairment of $1.7 million, included as other income (expenses), net, to adjust to current market the value of certain equity securities acquired upon the previous disposition of a discontinued project.

Items (1) and (3) in the footnote relate to asset impairment write-downs, and Item (2) to a voluntary abandonment.

When a permanent and significant decline occurs, a company recognizes an **impairment loss**: the amount by which the carrying amount of the asset exceeds the fair value of the asset—fair value representing, for example, "net realizable value" if the asset is held for sale and the "present value of estimated expected future cash flows" if the asset is used internally. Judging the significance of an impairment loss is largely a matter of the loss's materiality to the financial statements. Judging permanence, however, is problematic, particularly when an auditor suspects income smoothing. Consider the following case.

Hawthorne Corporation, a publicly owned West Coast manufacturer of office products, rents a wide variety of mailing, shipping, copier, and facsimile equipment under short-term agreements, generally for periods of three to twelve months. Charges for equipment rental and maintenance contracts are billed in advance, and income is recognized when earned. Analysts have forecasted current earnings per share to be $4.80, an increase over the prior year that would maintain the company's 10 percent increase in each of the last five years. Through the close of the current fiscal year, but before year end audit work begins, unaudited net income from operations is $1,755,000, or $6.00 per share, although almost all of the net income is from mailing, shipping, and facsimile systems. At a conference with management, the chief financial officer (CFO) tells the auditors that, owing both to a retraction in the copier market and to Hawthorne's dwindling market share, the value of fixed assets used to manufacture the unprofitable line of copier products has been impaired. The CFO proposes that an impairment loss of $350,000 ($1.20 per share) be recognized currently, an amount reflecting the difference between recorded book value and fair value, measured by the CFO as the present value of predicted future cash flows discounted at 15 percent. Management argues that other competitors in the industry have recognized impairment losses.

AUDIT JUDGMENT: ACCOUNTING, LIABILITY, AND ETHICS

Although it's not clear that Hawthorne Corporation's proposed treatment of impaired copier-production assets necessarily departs from generally accepted accounting principles, there are at least three reasons to suspect earnings management. First, recognizing the impairment loss would be consistent with income smoothing, since earnings per share would fall to $4.80, an amount consistent with the company's five-year growth rate and, not coincidentally, with analysts' earnings forecasts. Second, the CFO's planned discount rate, 15 percent, exceeds most benchmarks of reasonable current discount rates (among them, the rate of return on fixed income investments) and could serve to understate the present value of future cash flows and, therefore, overstate the calculated impairment loss. Third, a search of the current annual report file in Mead Data Control Corporation's National Automated Accounting Research Service (NAARS) for the key words "asset impairment" reveals that, contrary to management's claim, no publicly traded competitors in the office products industry have recognized an asset impairment for copiers. If Hawthorne's management insists on booking an impairment loss, the auditor no has alternative but to alert the client that:

- Management will need to provide persuasive evidence that:
  - The claimed decline in copier production asset values is permanent (how does management know that the copier market has retracted?).
  - The rate used to discount future cash flows, and the amount of the future cash flows discounted, are reasonable.
- Lacking persuasive evidence that the impairment loss is reasonable, the auditor will conclude that the loss is materially misstated, a departure from GAAP.
- A departure from GAAP will cause the auditor to issue a qualified or adverse opinion, depending on materiality, and an explanatory paragraph that discloses the effect of the departure on reported earnings (Chapter 3, Figure 3-5).

If the auditor considers concurring with management about the impairment loss without persuasive evidence that the loss is reasonable, he or she risks serious legal and ethical implications. Since Hawthorne is publicly traded, statutory law applies and Sections 10(b) and 18 of the *Securities Exchange Act of 1934* (Chapter 5) provide shareholders with a means to recover losses resulting from false or misleading statements. In this case, shareholders could likely recover under Section 10(b) since the auditor knew, or should have known, that evidence supporting the impairment loss consisted of the CFO's oral claims, one of which (competitors' impairment losses) was not accurate. However, the plaintiff's basis for action—Section 10(b) or Section 18—would be judged by the plaintiff in consultation with an attorney. Further, as discussed in Chapter 5, the auditor could be liable for treble damages under the *Racketeer Influenced and Corrupt Organizations (RICO) Act*, since *Reves v. Arthur Young*, a 1993 U.S. Supreme Court case, does not provide relief from RICO when the auditor participated directly with management to perpetrate the fraud.

The case raises at least two ethical issues. First, the auditor's conduct may violate the *Code of Professional Conduct*, Rule 203—Accounting Principles (Chapter 4), which provides that an AICPA member cannot issue an unqualified opinion if the financial statements contain a departure from GAAP. In the Hawthorne case, the accounting principle violated is disclosure of a suspicious impairment loss that has not necessarily been realized. Violating Rule 203 can result in an administrative reprimand, such as suspension to practice before the SEC, or revocation of a CPA's license to practice public accountancy. Second, concurring with a disclosure based entirely on a client's oral claims raises serious questions about the auditor's ethical character, particularly when the client may have ulterior motives for booking the loss (i.e., income smoothing, meeting analysts' forecasts) and when available evidence disputes the client's claim.

COMPUTER ASSISTED SUBSTANTIVE
TESTS OF INVENTORY AND FIXED ASSETS

Although audit procedures can be performed effectively on data processed manually, computer systems allow an auditor to be just as effective and more reliable, because some audit tests can often be applied to entire audit populations rather than to samples, and because human processing errors are less likely. Thus, when part or all of a company's conversion cycle activities are recorded, classified, or summarized by computer, an auditor's year end procedures can be accomplished by computer assisted substantive and other tests of details. Figure 15-14 lists several computer assisted techniques for a series of audit procedures common to audits of inventory and fixed assets.

To illustrate computer assisted substantive tests, assume an auditor wishes to accomplish portions of the substantive tests in Figure 15-9 for inventory:

- Verify mathematical accuracy of the final priced inventory and perpetual records.
- Compare details in the final priced inventory with perpetual records.
- Perform price tests.
- Merge physical inventory counts with perpetual inventory records.

Any or all of these procedures can be accomplished using either generalized audit software or auditor-prepared software, although in either case the auditor's methodology would be identical to the procedures flowcharted in Figure 15-15.

As illustrated in Figure 15-15, the computer assisted tests require four data files: the perpetual inventory file, the physical inventory quantities file, the final priced inventory file, and the invoice price and terms file. The audit software would be designed to perform the following tasks for each of the above substantive tests:

Substantive Test	Computer Software Tasks
Verify mathematical accuracy.	Foot, cross-foot, and test extensions for the details constituting each stock number within the perpetual inventory file.
	Foot, cross-foot, and test extensions for each line item in the final priced inventory file.
	Print exceptions.
Compare details.	Compare quantities listed in the final priced inventory master file with quantities listed in the perpetual inventory file.
	Print exceptions.
Perform price tests.	Compare prices listed in the final priced inventory file with invoice prices contained within the invoice price and terms file.
	Print exceptions.

Figure 15-14: Computer Assisted Audit Tests: Inventory and Fixed Assets

| Audit Procedure | Computer Assisted Substantive Tests | |
	Inventory	Fixed Assets
Test mathematical accuracy.	Verify footings, cross-footings, and extensions of the final priced inventory and/or perpetual records.	Verify footings, cross-footings, and extensions of detailed fixed asset records. Recompute depreciation.
Summarize data for further testing or analysis.	Print listings of off-premises inventory for confirmation, and print confirmations. Array perpetual inventory records in descending order by dollar amounts to select target items for test counting. Access and print year end receipts and shipments for agreement with cutoff information obtained during the physical inventory observation.	Print fixed asset additions for observation. Print fixed asset disposals for agreement with recorded gain or loss.
Test accuracy of recorded data.	Trace details in final priced inventory to perpetual records. Perform price tests. Trace details in perpetual records to machine-readable source documents (e.g., receiving reports, production records).	Trace details in fixed asset records to machine-readable source documents.
Make a sample selection.	Select inventory items for price testing using internally stored random number generators and perpetual records.	Select additions for testing (or observation) from internally stored random number generators and detailed fixed asset records.
Compare similar data files.	Compare charges/credits in perpetual inventory records with the purchases/sales master files. Merge physical inventory counts with perpetual inventory records.	Agree fixed asset additions/disposals with the cash disbursements/cash receipts master files.

Substantive Test	Computer Software Tasks
Merge physical counts with perpetual records.	Update quantities within the perpetual inventory file for quantities counted on the physical inventory date and contained within the physical inventory quantities file.
	Print exceptions.

Auditors typically perform the tests listed above and illustrated in Figure 15-15 on their own laptop computers, although an auditor could arrange with client computer personnel to load and run the software on the client's computer. The software could be run either directly by the auditor or by client personnel under the auditor's supervision. Computer assisted tests would be documented within the audit working papers, and used in conjunction with other audit evidence to form judgments about whether the client's inventory is fairly stated at the balance sheet date.

Figure 15-15: Flowchart of Computer Assisted Tests

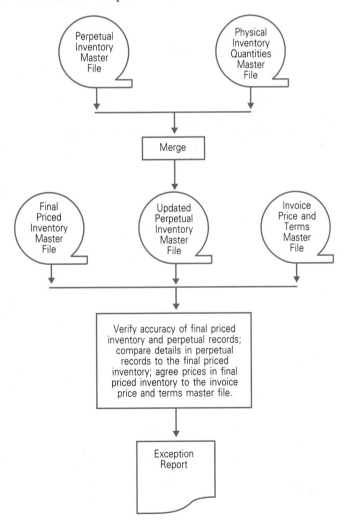

SUMMARY

The conversion cycle relates to the holding, use, or transformation of resources such as inventory and fixed assets. Internal controls over inventory focus primarily on the physical safeguarding of inventory and recorded accountability. Thus, tests of controls over inventory focus on whether transfers of inventory through production are properly authorized and recorded in perpetual records and cost records. Substantive tests of inventory and cost of sales include physical inventory observation, confirmation of off-premises inventory, verification of the accuracy of final priced inventory records, cutoff tests, analytical procedures, and review of financial statement presentation and disclosures.

Controls over fixed assets and tests of the controls focus on detailed asset records and on the proper authorization and recording of asset additions and disposals. Tests of controls over depreciation involve recalculations and reviewing depreciation methods, useful lives, and salvage values. Substantive tests of fixed assets and depreciation include verifying mathematical accuracy, testing additions and disposals, testing cutoff, analytical procedures, and reviewing financial statement presentation and disclosures.

Although writeoffs of fixed assets, natural resources, and intangibles are common when the assets are disposed of voluntarily or involuntarily, it has become common in the last decade to partially write off assets that, in the discretion of management, have suffered an impairment in value caused, for example, by slumping demand. Auditors should be cognizant of whether the impairment in value is permanent and significant, whether the timing of the writeoff is necessarily coincident with management's incentives to smooth income, and whether management's estimate of recoverable value is reasonable.

KEY TERMS

Labor charge report   534
Materials requisition   534
Perpetual inventory record   534
Depreciation schedule   534
Overhead application report   536

Impaired assets   569
Income smoothing   570
Big bath   570
Impairment loss   571

REFERENCES

Professional Standards

AICPA. *Codification of Statements on Auditing Standards.* New York: AICPA.
SAS No. 47, "Audit Risk and Materiality in Conducting an Audit."
SFAS No. 121, "Accounting for the Impairment of Long-Lived Assets and for Long-Lived Assets to Be Disposed of."

Books

Committee of Sponsoring Organizations of the Treadway Commission (COSO). *Internal Control: Integrated Framework.* Executive Summary. New York: COSO (1992).

Committee of Sponsoring Organizations of the Treadway Commission (COSO). *Internal Control: Integrated Framework*. Framework. New York: COSO (1992).

Committee of Sponsoring Organizations of the Treadway Commission (COSO). *Internal Control: Integrated Framework*. Evaluation Tools. New York: COSO (1992).

Committee of Sponsoring Organizations of the Treadway Commission (COSO). *Internal Control: Integrated Framework*. Reporting to External Parties. New York: COSO (1992).

Articles

D. Fried, M. Schiff, A. C. Sondhi. "Impairments and Writeoffs of Long-Lived Assets," *Management Accounting* (August 1989), pp. 48-50.

H. Nurnberg and N. W. Dittmar, Jr. "Auditing Considerations of FASB 121," *Journal of Accountancy* (July 1996), pp. 71-78.

M. Pearson and L. L. Okubara. "Restructuring and Impairment of Value: A Growing Controversy," *Accounting Horizons* (March 1987), pp. 35-41.

W. Schuetze. "Disclosure and the Impairment Question," *Journal of Accountancy* (December 1987), pp. 26-32.

M. G. Stevens. "When Impaired Assets Are a Drag," *Practical Accountant* (February 1994), pp. 52-54.

L. J. Zucca and D. R. Campbell. "A Closer Look at Discretionary Writedowns of Impaired Assets," *Accounting Horizons* (September 1992), pp. 30-41.

QUESTIONS

Inventory

1. Identify the major business function and activities common to the conversion cycle.
2. How does the conversion cycle of a manufacturing company differ from that of a retailer or wholesaler?
3. Describe the flow of inventory costs through the accounts of a manufacturer.
4. What is the major focus of tests of controls for perpetual records and for cost records?
5. How can management control against misplaced or misused inventory?
6. What procedure does an auditor use to determine whether recorded inventory exists?
7. For what reason does an auditor test a client's final priced inventory?
8. Identify and briefly describe the financial statement assertions that are relevant to physical inventory observations.
9. Under what conditions are interim, as opposed to year end, physical inventory counts appropriate?
10. Explain an auditor's role during a physical inventory observation.

Fixed Assets

11. Why should fixed assets be appraised periodically?
12. Identify some control procedures for fixed asset additions and disposals.
13. Why might an auditor elect to perform only limited or no tests of controls for fixed assets?
14. What is the focus of tests of controls for fixed asset records?
15. What is the focus of tests of controls for fixed asset additions and disposals?
16. How does an auditor test the valuation of fixed assets and depreciation?
17. Describe some substantive tests applicable to fixed asset additions and disposals.
18. Why would an auditor test cutoff for fixed asset transactions?
19. Given that write-downs decrease reported net income, why would management be motivated to write down impaired assets?
20. What incentives does an auditor have to assure that the timing and amount of discretionary write-downs for impaired assets is fairly presented in all material respects?

MULTIPLE CHOICE QUESTIONS

Inventory

1. Which of the following control procedures is most likely to prevent or detect errors or frauds resulting from the production of unauthorized products or unauthorized quantities of authorized products?

   a. State criteria for determining production.
   b. Establish procedures for processing and recording production.
   c. Conduct periodic inventory counts.
   d. Limit access to inventory and to unused forms.

2. Which of the following financial statement assertions are addressed by the physical observation of inventory counts?

   a. Existence and valuation.
   b. Rights and completeness.
   c. Presentation and disclosure.
   d. Completeness and existence.

3. To determine whether merchandise is included in ending inventory, an auditor could test:

   a. Open purchase orders.
   b. Purchase cutoff.
   c. Commitments made by Purchasing.
   d. Invoices received on or around year end.

4. From which of the following procedures would an auditor obtain evidence about the existence of inventory?

   a. Physical inventory observation.
   b. Written representations from management.
   c. Confirmation of inventories in a public warehouse.
   d. Recomputation of the final priced inventory.

5. Auditors usually trace the details of the test counts made during the physical inventory observation to the final priced inventory, a procedure that is done to provide evidence that items observed by the auditor at the physical inventory count date are:

   a. Owned by the client.
   b. Not obsolete.
   c. Physically present at the time the final priced inventory is prepared.
   d. Included in the final priced inventory.

Fixed Assets

6. What control objective is served by management implementing written procedures for all additions, disposals, and retirements?

   a. Procedures for operating, using, and physically moving plant assets should be established in accordance with management's criteria.
   b. Plant additions, disposals, and retirements should be authorized in accordance with management's criteria.
   c. Plant assets added, disposed, or retired should be recorded at the correct amounts, recorded in the proper period, and classified properly.
   d. Access to plant assets should be restricted to personnel authorized by management.

7. Which of the following financial statement assertions are addressed by testing the cutoff for plant asset additions?

   a. Existence and rights.
   b. Valuation or allocation.
   c. Completeness and valuation.
   d. Presentation and disclosure.

8. To control fixed asset additions, a company should establish control procedures that require:

   a. Capitalizing of the cost of fixed asset additions that exceeds a specified dollar amount.
   b. Restricting access to fixed assets.
   c. Classifying as investments fixed asset additions that are not used in the business.
   d. Authorizing and approving major fixed asset additions.

9. Which of the following would not likely motivate management to time the writeoff of impaired assets in the current period?

   a. Current unaudited net income is abnormally high in relation to prior years.
   b. The current rate of earnings growth is abnormally low in relation to prior years.
   c. Current unaudited earnings per share is abnormally high in relation to prior years.
   d. Current unaudited selling and administrative expenses are abnormally low in relation to prior years.

10. Which of the following provides management with some latitude in measuring the amount recognized in discretionary write-downs of impaired assets, even with the advent of an authoritative pronouncement?

   a. Estimated future cash flows.
   b. The date to which future cash flows are discounted.
   c. Fair market values.
   d. Impairment loss recognized.

PROBLEMS AND DISCUSSION CASES

Inventory

15-1 *Controls Over Inventory and Fixed Asset Records*
Assume you are considering internal control over a client's inventory and fixed asset records. System documentation was accomplished with a flowchart and questionnaire and, in conjunction with a transaction walk-through, revealed the following potential deficiencies in internal control:

a. Although immaterial in relation to the financial statements taken as a whole, employees sometimes use company assets and tools to build products for home use.
b. Inventory is sometimes misplaced, resulting in potentially time-consuming production delays.
c. During an interim month, the controller observed that inventory containing precious metals was stolen.
d. Delivery trucks were sold during the year without management's knowledge.
e. Scrap sales are sometimes executed but not recorded.
f. Depreciation for the first quarter was inaccurate, although not materially misstated.

g. Cash receipts personnel were observed making notations in fixed asset records.

Required: For each potential deficiency, indicate one or more control procedures that management could implement to reduce the likelihood of errors or frauds.

15-2 *Errors, Fraud, and Control Procedures*
While auditing Trowbridge Corporation's June 30, 1999 financial statements, you become aware of the following controls or procedures over Trowbridge's inventory control and inventory accounting activities:

a. No new products are produced without management's express written authorization.
b. Access to the warehouses is restricted to personnel named in a memorandum dated August 10, 1998.
c. Inventory movement into and out of storerooms and production sites is logged in journals maintained by inventory control personnel.
d. All personnel named in the August 10, 1998 memorandum (Item 2) are bonded for loss or theft.
e. Responsibility for handling inventory is segregated from inventory recording, cost accounting, and general accounting.
f. All materials release and production forms are maintained under lock and key and are distributed only to authorized personnel.

Required: For each control procedure, indicate: (a) a potential error or fraud that might be prevented or detected as a result of the control procedure, and (b) the control objective served by the control procedure. Organize your answer as follows:

Control Procedure	Potential Error or Fraud That Might Be Prevented or Detected	Control Objective

15-3 *Auditing Overapplied and Underapplied Overhead*
Denise Ondeyko, CPA is drafting an audit program to test controls over the Purdue Corporation's cost records.

Required:
1. Explain the importance of determining the disposition of overapplied and underapplied overhead. In your explanation, describe how overhead should be treated.
2. List and explain some items that should be included in overhead. What should not be included?

15-4 *Drafting Tests of Controls From an Internal Control Questionnaire*
Following are selected questions from an internal control questionnaire relating to a company's inventory control, perpetual inventory, and cost records. A *yes* response would indicate a potential strength, and a *no* response a potential weakness of the system.

a. Is inventory reasonably protected from physical deterioration and theft?
b. Are materials requisition forms required to request materials and supplies for use in production?
c. Are physical inventory counts taken at least once per year for all inventories?
d. Are perpetual inventory records continually updated on a timely basis?
e. Are perpetual records reconciled with general ledger control accounts on a regular basis?
f. Are all inventory transfers reported and recorded on a timely basis?
g. Are production personnel required to explain price and volume variances?

Required: Assume that inquiries indicate the answer is *yes* to each question. Draft tests of controls that you believe would provide persuasive evidence that the answer to each question, (a) through (g), is correct.

15-5 *Designing Tests of Controls*
Alicin Nagle, an in-charge auditor, is reviewing the inventory controls for the city of Carlton's vehicle maintenance facility. Nagle has learned the following:
a. Vehicle maintenance records indicate that, even though the total number of trucks is decreasing, the number of inoperative trucks waiting for spare parts is increasing.
b. Stockroom employees have been unable to find some parts, even though the perpetual inventory system shows the parts on hand.
c. The investment in spare parts inventory has remained at about the same level in each of the last three years.
d. Many of the spare parts can be used for passenger cars.
e. A clerk in the parts warehouse office maintains the perpetual inventory records.
    Required: Design tests of controls for each item listed.

15-6 *Relating Errors, Frauds, Audit Procedures, and Assertions in Substantive Tests of Inventory*
Following are errors, frauds, or other circumstances that an auditor might encounter as a result of applying year end substantive tests of details to inventory as of December 31, 1999:
a. Perpetual inventory records for selected products are not accurate.
b. A material amount of inventory is held in several public warehouses throughout the Midwest.
c. Unit prices for selected products on the final priced inventory appear low; the client uses the first-in, first-out cost flow assumption.
d. The final priced inventory reflects quantities from the perpetual inventory records.
e. Goods were received on December 31, but not recorded until January 2, 2000.
f. The client has begun to lag behind competitors in market share; the client is in the computer industry.
    Required: For each of the above items, indicate: (1) a specific substantive test or tests that might address the error, fraud, or circumstance, and (2) the financial statement assertion addressed by each test.

15-7 *Auditing Raw Materials Purchases*
During your audit of the financial statements of The Gary Manufacturing Company for the year ended December 31, 1999, you find that at January 1, 1999, the company had installed the following procedures for recording raw material purchases and payables:
a. Vendors' invoices are sent directly to the accounts payable department by the mail department.
b. All documents supporting the invoices are accumulated in the accounts payable department and attached to the invoices. After being checked and cash discounts computed, the invoices are entered on computers at workstations.
c. An invoice register is prepared from data compiled on-screen.
d. The general ledger control account is posted monthly from the totals shown in the invoice register and all other journals.
e. On due dates, the accounts payable are processed to prepare checks and remittance statements.
f. At the end of the month, unpaid accounts payable are compared with the general ledger control account.
    Required: List the procedures you would use to audit raw material purchases.

15-8 *Auditing Perpetual Inventory Records*
Decker is auditing the financial statements of Allright Wholesale Sales, Inc., for the year ended December 31, 1999. Allright has been in business for many years, although the company has never been audited. Decker is satisfied that ending inventory is fairly stated in all material respects and is considering alternative procedures to audit management's representations about the beginning inventory, which was not observed.

Allright sells only one product, bottled water, and maintains perpetual inventory records. In addition, Allright takes physical inventory counts monthly. Decker has already confirmed purchases with the supplier and has decided to concentrate on the reliability of perpetual inventory records and on analytical procedures to the extent that data within the prior years' unaudited records will allow.

Required: Design audit procedures, including analytical procedures, that Decker should apply to evaluate the reliability of perpetual inventory records and to audit the January 1, 1999 inventory.

(AICPA Adapted)

15-9 *Drafting Employee Instructions for a Physical Inventory Observation*
In connection with his audit of the financial statements of Knutson Products Co., an assembler of home appliances, for the year ended May 31, 1999, Ray Mendez is reviewing with Knutson's controller the plans for a physical inventory at the company warehouse on May 31, 1999.

Part A. Finished appliances, unassembled parts, and supplies are stored in the warehouse, which is attached to Knutson's assembly plant. The plant will operate during the count. On May 30, the warehouse will deliver to the plant the estimated quantities of unassembled parts and supplies required for May 31 production, but there may be emergency requisitions on May 31. During the count, the warehouse will continue to receive parts and supplies and to ship finished appliances. However, appliances completed on May 31 will be held in the plant until after the physical inventory.

Part B. Warehouse employees will join with Accounting Department employees in counting the inventory. The inventory takers will use a tag system.

Required: For Part A: What procedures should the company establish to assure that the inventory count includes all items that should be included and that nothing is counted twice? For Part B: What instructions should the company give to the inventory takers?

(AICPA Adpated)

15-10 *Identifying Problems in a Physical Inventory Observation*
Late in December 1999, your public accounting firm accepted an audit engagement at Fine Jewelers, Inc., a corporation that maintains a diamond wholesale store in New York City and retail jewelry stores in several Eastern cities. A buyer employed by the wholesale store purchases diamonds in the New York diamond market. The wholesale store carries a substantial inventory of diamonds that are set in rings and in other quality jewelry based on orders from the retail stores and from independent customers. The corporation values inventory by the specific identification cost method.

Required: Assume you are satisfied that Fine Jewelers, Inc. has no jewelry left by customers for repair or for sale on consignment and that no inventory owned by the corporation is in the possession of outsiders.

1. Discuss problems the auditor should anticipate confronting on the physical inventory as a result of the:
   a. Different locations of the inventories.
   b. Type of inventory.
2. a. Explain how your audit program for this inventory would differ from that used for most other inventories.
   b. Draft procedures for the audit of the corporation's diamond and diamond jewelry inventories, identifying any steps that you would apply only to the retail stores or to the wholesale store.
3. Assume that a shipment of diamond rings was in transit by messenger from the wholesale store to a retail store on the inventory date. What additional audit steps

would you take to satisfy yourself as to the gems that were in transit from the wholesale store on the inventory date?

(AICPA Adapted)

15-11 *Designing Procedures for a Physical Inventory Observation*
Your audit client, Household Appliances, Inc., operates a retail store in the center of town. Lacking sufficient storage space, Household keeps undisplayed inventory in a public warehouse outside of town. The warehouse receives inventory from suppliers and, on request from your client by a shipping advice or telephone call, delivers merchandise to customers or to the retail outlet. The accounts are maintained at the retail store by a bookkeeper. Each month the warehouse sends to the bookkeeper a quantity report indicating opening balance, receipts, deliveries, and ending balance. The bookkeeper compares book quantities on hand at month end with the warehouse report and adjusts the books to agree with the report. No physical counts of the merchandise at the warehouse were made by your client during the year. You are now preparing for your audit of the current year's financial statements. Last year you issued an unqualified opinion.
   Required:
1. Design audit procedures for observing the physical inventory of Household Appliances, Inc.:
   a.   At the retail outlet, and
   b.   At the warehouse.
2. As part of your tests, would you verify inventory quantities at the warehouse by:
   a.   A warehouse confirmation? Why?
   b.   Test counts of inventory at the warehouse? Why?
3. Since the bookkeeper adjusts the books to quantities shown on the warehouse report each month, what significance would you attach to the year end adjustments if they were substantial? Discuss.
4. Assume you are unable to satisfy yourself as to the inventory. Could you issue an unqualified opinion? Why?

(AICPA Adapted)

15-12 *Identifying Causes for Inventory Discrepancies*
Ashton Tate, an in-charge auditor, has completed the year end physical inventory observation at a large wholesaler of automotive parts. Tate reviewed management's inventory-taking instructions before the start of the physical inventory, made and recorded test counts, observed the controls over the inventory-taking process, and noted no significant exceptions. Tate's subsequent comparisons of the quantities shown on the count sheets with quantities listed on the perpetual inventory records disclosed numerous discrepancies.
   Required: Other than theft, what are the likely causes of the discrepancies?

15-13 *Shortages in Physical Inventory Quantities*
After observing a physical inventory, an auditor compared the physical inventory counts with the perpetual inventory records and noted apparent shortages that were materially larger than those found at the end of the previous year.
   Required:
1. Identify possible causes, other than theft, for the differences between the physical counts and the perpetual inventory records.
2. Briefly describe potential adverse effects the differences could cause.
3. Assuming that theft caused the differences, give recommendations to prevent theft.

15-14 *Inventory and Fixed Asset Disclosures*
LOC Container Corporation is preparing financial statements for the fiscal year ended April 30, 1999. Because all of LOC Container's shares are traded within state, the

company does not file reports with the Securities and Exchange Commission. The company manufactures plastic, glass, and paper containers for sale to food and drink manufacturers and to distributors. LOC maintains separate control accounts for raw materials, work-in-process, and finished goods inventories for each of the three types of containers. Inventories are valued at the lower of cost or market. The company's fixed assets are classified into the following major classes: land, office buildings, furniture and fixtures, manufacturing facilities, manufacturing equipment, and leasehold improvements. All fixed assets are carried at cost. Depreciation methods vary depending on the type of asset and acquisition date. LOC plans to present the inventory and fixed assets at April 30, 1999, as follows:

Inventories $1,659,609
Property, plant, and equipment (Net of Depreciation) $3,578,475

Required: What information must LOC Container Corporation disclose about inventories and fixed assets in audited financial statements issued to shareholders?
(CMA Adapted)

15-15 *Working Paper Review: Inventory Test Counts*
Following is an inventory test count working paper that documents Donald Schwab's physical inventory observations in the Hillsdale Company's roofing materials warehouse on December 31, 1999, the date of the physical inventory (and the last day of the fiscal year), including his follow-up work tracing test counted items to the client's final priced inventory on January 11, 2000.

Hillsdale Company, Inc.   C60
Inventory Test Counts: Roofing Materials Warehouse   DS
January 11, 2000

Ticket Number	Description	Count per: Client	Count per: Audit	Difference: Over (Under)
1245	Stock No. C10568: Shake shingle	1470 ct.	1430 ct.*	40 ct.
1324	Stock No. D56748: Tile shingle	1539 ct.	1539 ct.+	
1034	Stock No. E56849: Tenpenny nails	205 ft.	400 ft.*	5 ft.
1076	Stock No. L38271: Tar paper	125 ft.	120 ft.	
1089	Stock No. E56849: Edged Shake shingle	978 ct.	978 ct.*	
1090	Stock No. C84059: Facing glue	587 gal.	578 gal.+	
1099	Stock No. F57487: Carriage House shingle	798 ct.	798 ct.+	
0014	Stock No. G57849: Grand Manor shingle	1287 ct.	1292 ct.*	(5 ct.)
0129	Stock No. B77473: Sun Surf shingle	647 ct.	647 ct.*	
	Stock No. S75743: Classic Revival	547 ct.	547 ct.*	
0324	Stock No. T47383: Dimensional shingle	569 ct.	569 ct.*	

+ Agreed to client's corrected count sheet.
* Agreed to client's final priced inventory.

Conclusion
Based on test counts, I am satisfied that the client's count procedures were reasonable and that there are no significant quantities of otherwise nonsalable items.

Required: List the deficiencies in this working paper.

Fixed Assets

15-16 *Controls Over Fixed Assets*

You became aware of the following control procedures for Gatehouse & Company's fixed assets:

1. All scrapped assets are agreed with published price lists before being offered for sale and are never sold for amounts significantly below established prices.
2. Procedures for operating, using, moving, and controlling fixed assets are firmly established in periodically updated procedures manuals.
3. Procedures are established for identifying assets as potential scrap sale items, although actual sales must first be approved by division managers.
4. Physical custody over fixed assets is segregated from recording.
5. Fixed assets on the floor are reconciled periodically with fixed asset records, and vice versa.

Required: For each control procedure, indicate: (a) a potential error or fraud that might be prevented as a result of the control procedure, and (b) the control objective served by the control procedure. Organize your answer as follows:

Control Procedure	*Potential Error or Fraud That Might Be Prevented or Detected*	*Control Objective*

15-17 *Drafting Tests of Controls From an Internal Control Questionnaire*

Following are selected questions from an internal control questionnaire about a company's fixed asset records, additions, disposals, retirements, and depreciation functions. A *yes* response would indicate a potential strength of the system, a *no* response a potential weakness.

a. Are procedures followed to determine whether recorded fixed assets actually exist?
b. Is insurance coverage maintained and reviewed for all fixed assets?
c. Do procedures require authorization by the board of directors or senior management for fixed asset additions?
d. Are actual expenditures for fixed assets compared with amounts authorized?
e. Are procedures established to assure that the proceeds from fixed asset disposals are recorded properly and deposited?
f. Are fixed asset disposals and retirements promptly reported to General Accounting for recording gains and losses?
g. Are procedures established to assure that additions are added to depreciation records and disposals/retirements deleted?

Required: Assume that inquiries indicate the answer is *yes* to each question. Draft a test of controls that you believe would provide persuasive evidence that the answer to each question, (a) through (g), is correct.

15-18 *Relating Errors, Frauds, Audit Procedures, and Assertions in Substantive Tests of Fixed Assets*

Following are errors, frauds, or other circumstances that an auditor might encounter as a result of applying year end substantive tests of details to fixed assets as of December 31, 1999:

a. During the physical inventory observation, the auditor sees machinery not present during the December 31, 1998 physical inventory.
b. Separate detailed records are now maintained for all fixed assets.
c. New equipment was installed during late December and early January.
d. Depreciation expense is lower than in 1998, and yet additions far exceeded disposals and retirements in 1999.
e. Equipment may have been disposed of, but the disposal was not recorded.

Required: For each of the above items, indicate: (1) a specific substantive test or tests that might address the error, fraud, or circumstance, and (2) the financial statement assertion addressed by each test.

15-19 *Auditing Manufacturing Equipment, Depreciation, and Repairs*

In connection with a recurring audit of the financial statements of the Louis Manufacturing Company for the year ended December 31, you have been assigned the audit of these accounts: Manufacturing Equipment, Accumulated Depreciation, and Repairs to Manufacturing Equipment. Your review of Louis's policies and procedures has disclosed the following:

a. The manufacturing equipment account includes the net invoice price plus related freight and installation costs for all of the equipment in Louis's manufacturing plant.

b. The manufacturing equipment and accumulated depreciation accounts are supported by a subsidiary ledger that shows the cost and accumulated depreciation for each piece of equipment.

c. An annual budget for capital expenditures of $1,000 or more is prepared by the budget committee and approved by the board of directors. Capital expenditures over $1,000 that are not included in this budget must be approved by the board of directors, and variations of 20 percent or more must be explained to the board. Approval by the supervisor of production is required for capital expenditures under $1,000.

d. Company employees handle installation, removal, repair, and rebuilding of the machinery. Work orders are prepared for these activities and are subject to the same budgetary control as other expenditures. Work orders are not required for internal expenditures.

Required:

1. Identify the objectives of your audit of the manufacturing equipment, accumulated depreciation, and repairs to manufacturing equipment accounts.

2. Draft audit procedures for current year additions to the manufacturing equipment account.

(AICPA Adapted)

15-20 *Adjustments, Reclassifications, and the Audit of Fixed Assets*

Rivers is the auditor for a manufacturing company with a balance sheet that includes the caption "Property, Plant, and Equipment." Management has asked Rivers if audit adjustments or reclassifications are required for the following material items that have been included or excluded from "Property, Plant, and Equipment."

a. A tract of land was acquired during the year. The land is the future site of the client's new headquarters which will be constructed the following year. Commissions were paid to the real estate agent used to acquire the land, and expenditures were made to relocate the previous owner's equipment. The commissions and expenditures were expensed and are excluded from "Property, Plant, and Equipment."

b. Clearing costs were incurred to make the land ready for construction. The costs were included in "Property, Plant, and Equipment."

c. During the land clearing process, timber and gravel were recovered and sold. The proceeds from the sale were recorded as other income and are excluded from "Property, Plant, and Equipment."

d. A group of machines was purchased under a royalty agreement that provides royalty payments based on units of production from the machines. The cost of the machines, freight costs, unloading charges, and royalty payments were capitalized and are included in "Property, Plant, and Equipment."

Required:

1. Describe the general characteristics of assets, such as land, buildings, improvements, machinery, equipment, fixtures, etc., that should normally be classified as property, plant, and equipment, and identify audit objectives in connection with the audit of "Property, Plant, and Equipment."

2. Indicate whether each of the items (a) to (d) requires one or more audit adjustments or reclassifications, and explain why adjustments or reclassifications are required or not required.

Organize your answer as follows:

Item Number	Is Audit Adjustment or Reclassification Required? Yes or No	Reason Why Adjustment or Reclassification Is Required or Not Required

(AICPA Adapted)

15-21 *The Existence of and Title to Land Holdings*

Terra Land Development Corporation is a closely held family business engaged in purchasing large tracts of land, subdividing the tracts, and installing paved streets and utilities. The corporation does not construct buildings for the buyers of the land and does not have any affiliated construction companies. Undeveloped land is usually leased for farming until the corporation is ready to begin development. The corporation finances land acquisitions by mortgages; the mortgagers require audited financial statements. You have now begun your firm's initial audit of the financial statements for the year ended December 31, 1999. Your preliminary review of the accounts indicates that the corporation would have had a highly profitable year except that the corporate officers—all members of the family—were reimbursed for exceptionally large travel and entertainment expenses.

Required: The corporation has three tracts of land in various stages of development. List the audit procedures necessary to audit the physical existence of and title to the corporation's three land holdings.

(AICPA Adapted)

15-22 *Drafting Adjusting Journal Entries*

You are auditing the financial statements of the Ute Corporation for the year ended December 31, 1999. The client has prepared the following schedules for the fixed assets and depreciation accounts. You have agreed the opening balances with the general ledger and with your prior year's working papers.

Ute Corporation
Analysis of Fixed Assets and
Related Allowance for Depreciation Accounts
Year Ended December 31, 1999

Description	Final 12/31/98	Additions	Retirements	Per Books 12/31/99
Land	$ 22,500	$ 15,000		$ 37,500
Buildings	120,000	175,000		295,000
Machinery and Equipment	385,000	40,400	$26,000	399,400
	$527,500	$230,400	$26,000	$731,900

Allowance for Depreciation

Description	Final 12/31/98	Additions*	Retirements	Per Books 12/31/99
Buildings	$ 60,000	$ 8,300		$ 68,300
Machinery and Equipment	173,250	39,220		212,470
	$233,250	$ 47,520		$280,770

*Depreciation expense for the year.

Your audit reveals the following information:

a. All equipment is depreciated on the straight-line basis (no salvage value) based on the following estimated lives: buildings, 25 years; all other items, 10 years. Company policy is to take one-half year's depreciation on all asset acquisitions and disposals during the year.

b. On April 1, the company entered into a ten-year lease contract for a die-casting machine with annual rentals of $5,000 payable in advance every April 1. The lease is cancelable by either party (60 days written notice is required), and there is no option to renew the lease or to buy the equipment at the end of the lease. The estimated useful life of the machine is ten years with no salvage value. The company recorded the die-casting machine in the machinery and equipment account at $40,400, the discounted present value at the date of the lease, and $2,020, applicable to the machine, has been included in depreciation expense for the year.

c. The company completed the construction of a wing on the factory building on June 30, although the useful life of the building was not extended. The lowest construction bid received was $175,000, the amount recorded in the buildings account. Company personnel were used to construct the addition at a cost of $160,000 (materials, $75,000; labor, $55,000; and overhead, $30,000).

d. On August 18, $15,000 was paid for paving and fencing a portion of land owned by the company and used as a parking lot for employees. The expenditure was charged to the land account.

e. The amount shown in the machinery and equipment retirement column represents cash received on September 5 upon disposal of a machine purchased in July 1998 for $48,000. The accountant recorded depreciation expense of $3,500 on this machine in 1999.

f. Crux City donated land and a building, appraised at $100,000 and $400,000, respectively, to the Ute Corporation for a plant. On September 1, the company began operating the plant. Because no costs were involved, no entry was made for the transaction.

Required: Prepare the formal adjusting journal entries that you would suggest at December 31, 1999, to adjust the accounts for transactions (a) to (f). The books have not been closed. Round computations to the nearest dollar.

(AICPA Adapted)

15-23 *Drafting Audit Procedures for Depreciation*
You have been assigned to audit the fixed assets of the Johnson Corp., a manufacturer of janitorial supplies. The company maintains a detailed property ledger for all fixed assets. You prepare an audit program for the asset balances but have yet to prepare one for accumulated depreciation and depreciation expense.

Required: Draft audit procedures for accumulated depreciation and for depreciation expense.

15-24 *Earnings Manipulation and Impaired Assets*
The Sonora Company mines precious metals at excavation sites throughout North and South America. Although sales of copper and gold have flattened during the year and gold sales are well below the prior year, the company remains profitable, largely because of efficient mining technologies and a major company-wide cost containment program. No new sites have been discovered in the past two years and all existing mines have been depleted by no less than 50 percent. Sonora's chief executive officer is strongly considering a discretionary write-down of selected mines, arguing that the assets' values are significantly impaired.

Required: Identify, and explain the motive for, the key questions an auditor must ask to judge whether management's discretionary write-down of impaired assets is appropriate.

15-25 *Working Paper Review: Fixed Assets and Accumulated Depreciation*
Below is a client prepared schedule that captures fixed assets and accumulated depreciation for the Rock View Corporation, and for which Molly Giles has completed audit work.

Required: List the deficiencies in this working paper.

Schedule Prepared by Client

Rock View Corporation   E2
Fixed Assets and Accumulated Depreciation
December 31, 1999

Fixed Assets

	Final Balance 12-31-98	Additions	Retired/ Disposed	Balance 12-31-99	Adjust./ Reclass.	Adjusted Balance 12-31-99
Land	$ 657,908#	$24,965 **E6**	$110,000	$ 572,873	$ 21,000	$ 593,873
Buildings	989,602#	**E6**	46,000	943,602		943,602
Machinery/ Equipment	456,239#	55,000 &		511,239		511,239
Trucks	129,560#			129,560		129,560
	$2,233,309	$79,965	$156,000	$2,157,274	$ 21,000	$ 2,178,274

Accumulated Depreciation

	Final Balance 12-31-98	Expense	Retired/ Disposed	Balance 12-31-99	Adjust./ Reclass.	Adjusted Balance 12-31-99
Buildings	$ 345,876#	$ 78,453 @		$424,329		$424,329
Machinery/ Equipment	128,452#	34,983 @		163,435		163,435
Trucks	42,493#	12,873 @		55,366		55,366
	$ 516,821	$ 126,309		$643,130		$643,130

\# Agreed to prior year working papers.
& Observed new machine on plant floor.
@ Agreed to client depreciation spreadsheet.

RESEARCH PROJECT

DISCRETIONARY WRITE-DOWNS OF IMPAIRED ASSETS

Although once unusual, write-downs of impaired assets increased markedly in the first half of the 1980s. For example, D. Fried, M. Schiff, and A. C. Sondhi, in "Impairments and Writeoffs of Long-Lived Assets," *Management Accounting* (August 1989), pp. 48-50, report that of 702 companies studied during the period 1980-1985, writeoffs increased in number from 38 to 207 and in pretax amount from $28.3 million to $117.5 million. Reports of asset write-downs are quite common in the financial press today.

Required: Using the newspaper and magazines file in NEXIS, Mead Data Central's automated data retrieval system, or newspapers and magazines in a library, select an article about the effect on a publicly traded company of a discretionary write-down of impaired assets. Using the annual report file in the National Automated Accounting Research System (NAARS) or copies of annual reports in a library, select the annual report of the same company issued for the fiscal year referred to in the article. Draft a report that accomplishes the following:

1. Summarizes the article, indicating key issues—like management's or the financial community's reaction to the effect of the disclosure on reported income.
2. Lists and explains questions an auditor would likely pose to the management of the company you've selected.
3. Summarizes the company's disclosures about asset write-downs that appear in the footnotes (i.e., the footnote summarizing the write-down and the footnote summarizing accounting policies—Note 1—if separately explained) and the income statement (if disclosed as a separate line item).

16

Tests of Controls and Substantive Tests in the Financing Cycle: Investments, Debt, Equity, and Management Discretion in Accounting for Financial Instruments

Major topics discussed in this chapter are:

- **The nature of the financing cycle.**
- **Controls over the custody, recording, valuation, acquisition, and sale of investments and over the issuance and retirement of long-term debt and equity securities.**
- **Assurance and consulting service opportunities related to investments.**
- **An auditor's consideration of internal control in the financing cycle.**
- **Substantive tests of investments, long-term debt, and equity balances.**
- **Application of audit judgment to questions about management discretion in accounting for financial instruments.**

This chapter introduces tests of controls and substantive tests applicable to three major financing cycle accounts: Investments, Long-Term Debt, and Equity. The chapter begins by summarizing the nature of the financing cycle and by introducing controls over the custody, recording, valuation, acquisition, and sale of investments and over the issuance and retirement of debt instruments and equity securities. In turn, the chapter offers examples of assurance and consulting service opportunities related to investments. Next, an auditor's consideration of internal control in the financing cycle is introduced, and detailed substantive tests are explained. Finally, the chapter addresses accounting, legal, and ethical questions auditors face when auditing financial instruments.

THE FINANCING CYCLE

The financing cycle processes transactions and events that generate capital funds, and is directly related to two other cycles, since it uses resources and information provided by the expenditure/disbursement cycle and provides resources and information to the revenue/receipt cycle. For example, the financing cycle might process a cash disbursement (expenditure/disbursement cycle) to retire long-term debt and process a cash receipt (revenue/receipt cycle) from the sale of capital stock.

Figure 16-1 summarizes the scope of the financing cycle, listing the cycle's primary business functions and common activities, journal entries, and forms. Two major business functions are associated with the cycle:

- Capital funds are received from investors and creditors.
- Capital funds are used for operations or temporarily invested until needed for operations.

The cycle begins with management's decisions about the optimum sources of capital funds from debt and equity financing and the optimum allocation of funds between internal operations and outside investments. In turn, the cycle encompasses the payment of dividends on capital stock and interest on debt, and the redemption of capital stock (treasury stock transactions) and the retirement of debt.

Throughout the financing cycle, journal entries are made for the issuance and retirement of debt and capital stock and the acquisition and sale of investments. Common forms and documents include:

- **Bond certificate.** A debt security document representing a stated amount of corporate debt. Bond certificates are frequently issued in denominations of $1,000.
- **Commercial paper.** A general category of commercial loan instruments, due and payable in accordance with terms described on the instrument.
- **Stock certificate.** An equity security document representing ownership of a stated number of shares of capital stock.
- **Treasury bill.** A debt instrument issued by the U.S. Treasury Department.

Following are internal control considerations for the three major groups of transactions underlying the financing cycle:

- Investments in marketable securities,
- Issuance of long-term debt securities, and
- Issuance of equity securities.

Investments are discussed first, followed by debt, and then equity.

INVESTMENTS

Depending on cash position and operating cash requirements, an entity may invest resources in:

1. Marketable debt instruments and marketable equity securities, such as: (a) instruments representing ownership (e.g., common and preferred stock) or (b) rights to acquire ownership (e.g., warrants, rights, and call options), or (c) rights to dispose of ownership (e.g., put options), or
2. Government obligations, such as U.S. Treasury bills.

Figure 16-1: The Scope of the Financing Cycle

Primary Business Function		Common Activities	Common Entries	Common Forms
• Capital funds are received from investors and creditors	DEBT	• Recording • Incurrence and retirement • Interest	• Debt incurrence • Debt retirement • Interest expense	• Bond certificates • Notes
	EQUITY	• Recording • Issuance and retirement • Dividends	• Stock issuance • Stock retirement • Dividends	• Stock certificates
• Capital funds are used for operations or temporarily invested until needed for operations	INVESTMENTS	• Custody • Recording • Valuation • Acquisitions and sales • Income	• Investment acquisitions • Investment sales • Interest income • Interest income • Dividend income	• Bond certificates • Commercial paper • Stock certificates • Treasury bills

The financing cycle processes current and noncurrent investments, directing resources into other private- and public-sector equity and debt instruments, with the objective of optimizing financial return on idle cash. In short, the financing cycle processes transactions that convert internal resources into external investments, liquidating when necessary to convert investments into cash either for internal working capital needs or for alternative investments.

The major functions and controls related to investments are discussed in the following sections. Custody, recording, and valuation are addressed first, followed by acquisitions, sales, and income.

Custody, Recording, and Valuation

Generally, an entity's investment securities are held in the custody of either internal officials or independent external custodians, such as stock brokerage firms. Although less common, internal custody is required by law in some towns and municipalities. If securities are maintained internally, at least two officials should be held jointly responsible, thereby minimizing the likelihood of unauthorized sales (in the absence of collusion). Securities maintained by internal parties should be counted periodically on a surprise basis by employees who do not otherwise have custody or access.

An employee independent of the custodial function should maintain detailed records for securities held, compiling information such as certificate numbers and quantities. Detailed records offer a control over securities that should be in the custody of either external custodians or internal officials. If maintained externally, securities listings should be prepared by the custodian at least monthly, mailed to the company, and reconciled with internal records.

Acquisitions, Sales, and Income

All acquisitions and sales of current and noncurrent securities should be authorized by the board of directors or an authorized investment committee. Periodically, recorded acquisition and selling prices should be compared with published price quotations, such as those in *The Wall Street Journal*, assuring that transactions were recorded at accurate prices.

Debt and equity securities yield income in the form of interest and dividends, respectively, and result in gains or losses when sold. Dividend income should be recognized when declared, interest income accrued when earned, and gains and losses recorded when the securities are sold. Periodically, recorded income, gains, and losses should be recalculated by employees not otherwise responsible for the custody, acquisition, or sale of securities.

DEBT

Long-term debt, such as a bond or a commercial bank loan, is incurred to raise capital funds for internal investment, potentially yielding a rate of return greater than the cost of financing the debt. For example, an entity would issue 7 percent, ten-year bonds only if the internal rate of return is expected to be higher than 7 percent; otherwise, the debt would not be economically feasible.

Generally, debt incurrence and retirement transactions are relatively few in number, but are usually accompanied by extensive supporting documents, such as SEC filings and bond issuance authorizations from shareholders and the board of directors. The financing cycle processes debt incurrence and retirement transactions, directing resources through the revenue/receipt and expenditure/disbursement cycles, respectively. Following are specific control procedures for several of the more common debt-related financing cycle activities: recording, incurrence, retirement, and interest.

All long-term debt, such as bonds and loans, should be authorized by the board of directors. Authorizations should be expressly documented in the board's minutes, clearly indicating maximum indebtedness and the names of officers authorized to negotiate each transaction.

Typically, debt instruments such as loan agreements contain restrictive covenants that, if violated by a debtor, could result in the debt becoming due immediately. For example, a restrictive covenant might cause a loan to become due if a debtor's current ratio falls below a predetermined level, say 1 to 1. Interestingly, even if a debtor violates a restrictive covenant, the creditor is not likely to know without investigating. As a result, creditors often require that debtors submit annual reports from their auditors on compliance with contractual provisions. (This type of report is illustrated in Chapter 18.)

Bonds and notes present additional control problems, since unissued instruments are held by the entity and are therefore susceptible to frauds. Unissued bonds and notes should be prenumbered consecutively and controlled by an employee who neither maintains detailed debt records nor has access to general accounting records. Periodically, an independent employee should physically inspect unissued debt instruments and account for the numerical sequence.

When retired, debt instruments should either be canceled—for example, by perforation—or be destroyed. Records should be kept for canceled instruments, and affidavits from witnesses should be kept for destroyed instruments.

All debt instruments should be accounted for in detailed records, often called *bond* or *note registers*. The registers should be maintained by an employee not otherwise responsible for the custody, incurrence, or redemption of long-term debt. Periodically, an independent employee should reconcile the registers with the general ledger. An authorized employee should calculate interest expense in accordance with the terms of each instrument, and the resulting payments should be processed through the expenditure/disbursement cycle.

EQUITY

Equity securities (common and preferred stock) are issued by a company in order to raise capital funds for internal investment, such as capital expansion. Like long-term debt incurrence and retirement, equity issuance and retirement transactions are generally not numerous, but are usually supported by extensive documentation, such as authorizations and SEC registration statements. The financing cycle processes equity issuance and retirement transactions, directing resources through the revenue/receipt and expenditure/disbursement cycles, respectively. Following are specific control procedures for several common activities: recording, issuance, retirement, and dividends.

All transactions relating to equity securities, including issuance, retirement, and dividend distributions, should be formally authorized by the board of directors and should be documented. Some transactions may also require shareholder approval in accordance with state laws or corporation bylaws. All issuances and retirements should be approved both in price and in quantity by the board of directors either specifically or generally, as in the case of authorized stock option plans.

Stock certificates should be prenumbered consecutively, signed by authorized officers when issued, and promptly canceled when surrendered for retirement. Unissued certificates should be physically safeguarded with access limited to authorized individuals. Treasury shares that have not been retired and canceled should be accounted for and controlled.

Many companies enhance control over equity securities by utilizing independent *registrars* and *transfer agents* (e.g., investment bankers) to assure that securities are issued, recorded, and transferred properly. In some small companies, however, detailed equity securities records are maintained internally by employees, necessitating particularly effective internal controls, since in many cases securities can be easily converted into cash. If records are maintained internally, the custody of stock certificates, processing of stock transactions, and detailed record keeping should each be performed by separate officials or employees.

Depending on the materiality and volume of stock transactions, a company's detailed records might include a *shareholders' ledger* to account for outstanding shares and owners, a *transfer journal* to record shares transferred, and *certificate control records* to account for the numbers of issued and unissued shares. The shareholders' ledger should be up-to-date, particularly as of dividend record dates, and periodically reconciled with the transfer journal and certificate control records. The reconciliations should be performed by an employee not otherwise responsible for the records. If an entity has stock option plans or convertible securities (e.g., convertible preferred stock or bonds) outstanding, adequate records of equity shares reserved for potential issuance should also be maintained. A company should maintain adequate procedures and policies to assure that all applicable SEC filing requirements are met and that stock exchange regulations and securities laws are not violated. Some of these filing requirements, regulations, and laws are discussed in Chapter 5.

Unlike interest on long-term debt that must be paid in accordance with debt instruments outstanding, dividends on capital stock are paid only if declared by the board of directors. Cash dividends to individual shareholders should be computed from record date information in the shareholders' ledger and paid from a special bank account reserved for dividend payments. The dividend bank account should be reconciled periodically by an independent employee not otherwise responsible for maintaining shareholder records or processing dividend payments. Although not usually a significant problem, unclaimed dividend checks, resulting for example from incorrect shareholder mailing addresses, should be returned to an independent official and controlled until resolved.

INTERNAL CONTROL OBJECTIVES AND POTENTIAL ERRORS OR FRAUDS: INVESTMENTS, DEBT, AND EQUITY

The following discussion focuses on internal control over investments, debt, and equity. As in previous chapters, the discussion identifies control objectives for transaction authorization, execution, recording, and access to assets. Examples of potential errors or frauds are described, along with examples of control procedures often used to prevent or detect the errors or frauds. Figure 16-2 summarizes the discussion.

Figure 16-2: Investments, Debt, and Equity: Control Objectives, Potential Errors or Frauds, and Control Procedures

Control Objectives	Types of Errors ors Frauds That Could Occur if Objective Is Not Met	Control Procedures That Should Prevent or Detect Errors or Frauds
Transaction Authorization and Execution		
• Investment transactions (marketable securities, long-term debt, and equity investments) should be made in accordance with management's authorization.	Investments could be made in violation of company policies (e.g., an investment portfolio that includes more debt instruments than allowed by the board of directors), potentially resulting in more risk on investments than desired.	Establish policies for selecting and approving investment transactions. Prepare lists of authorized investments.
• Sources of capital funds—debt and equity—should be authorized in accordance with management's criteria.	Capital funds could be obtained at unfavorable terms/cost or with overly restrictive covenants, potentially resulting in uneconomical financing.	Establish policies for obtaining capital funds.
• Adjustments of investments (e.g., adjustment of carrying value), debt (e.g., adjustment of debt obligations after renegotiation), and equity (e.g., changes to par or stated value of stock) should be authorized in accordance with management's criteria.	Unauthorized or incorrect adjustments could be made, potentially resulting in misstated accounts and violations of loan covenants.	Establish policies for approving investment, debt, and equity adjustments. Prenumber and control adjustment forms. Require specific authorization for adjustments exceeding pre-established dollar amounts.
Recording		
• Investment, debt, and equity transactions should be recorded at the correct amounts, in the proper period, and be properly classified.	Detailed or subsidiary records may be inaccurate, potentially resulting in inaccurate account balances and misstated financial statements.	Establish processing and recording procedures. Review board minutes regularly for directives related to dividend, long-term debt, and treasury transactions. Prepare schedules of interest and loan payment due dates.

Figure 16-2: *(continued)*

Control Objectives	Types of Errors or Frauds That Could Occur if Objective Is Not Met	Control Procedures That Should Prevent or Detect Errors or Frauds
Access to Assets • Access to securities should be restricted to personnel authorized by management.	Securities may be lost, stolen, destroyed, or diverted, potentially resulting in misapplied resources and misstated accounts.	Establish physical barriers over investment securities (e.g., locked safes), or place them with independent parties, such as brokers. Carry insurance and fidelity bonds. Maintain files of authorized signatures. Segregate investment approval from accounting and from custody of securities.
• Access to investment-, debt-, and equity-related records and forms should be restricted to personnel authorized by management.	Records may be lost or stolen, potentially resulting in the reporting of inaccurate carrying values. Forms could be used to sell securities and divert the cash proceeds, potentially resulting in misappropriated assets and misstated financial statements.	Establish physical barriers over forms and records. Prenumber critical forms. Carry insurance and fidelity bonds. Account for all unissued, issued, and retired securities by an official independent of physically controlling securities, accounting, and cash activities.

Transaction Authorization and Execution

Before trading securities on the capital markets, all investment acquisitions and sales should be authorized in accordance with management's criteria. Lacking authorization, investments could be made in violation of company policies. For example, bonds could be purchased without regard for the fact that the board of directors resolved to restrict investment in non-AAA bonds to 5 percent of the total investment portfolio. In addition, capital funds could be obtained at excessive interest rates or with overly restrictive debt covenants, resulting in uneconomical financing. To control these potential errors, management could establish policies for selecting and approving investment transactions and for obtaining capital funds, and prepare lists of authorized investments if necessary.

Journal entries that adjust investment carrying values and debt obligations should be authorized in accordance with management's criteria; otherwise, unauthorized or incorrect adjustments could be made, potentially resulting in misstated accounts and violations of loan covenants. To control adjustments, management could establish processing procedures, prenumber and control adjustment forms, and require specific authorization for adjustments exceeding pre-established amounts.

Recording

If detailed or subsidiary records are inaccurate, then account balances may be inaccurate and financial statements misstated. As a result, all investment, debt, and equity transactions should be recorded at the correct amounts, in the proper period, and be classified properly. Management could control against inaccurate records by establishing processing and recording procedures, regularly reviewing board minutes for financing cycle resolutions, and preparing schedules of interest and loan payment due dates.

Access to Assets

Apart from cash, few other assets are more susceptible to frauds than investment securities: There is a ready market for them and, as a result, they can be converted into cash easily. Therefore, access to securities should be restricted to personnel authorized by management. Otherwise, securities may be lost or stolen, potentially resulting in misapplied resources and misstated accounts. Management can help control securities by establishing physical barriers, such as fireproof safes, although more often securities are held by independent custodians such as brokerage houses. In addition, personnel responsible for approving investments should not also be responsible for recording or for maintaining custody of the securities.

To protect capital funds, access to accounting records and forms should be restricted to personnel authorized by management. If access is not restricted, records may be lost or stolen, or forms could be used to sell securities and divert the cash proceeds. Management could control access by establishing physical barriers over prenumbered forms and records and by carrying insurance and fidelity bonds. Also, officials responsible for unissued, issued, and retired securities should not also be responsible for physically controlling securities or for performing accounting and cash activities.

ASSURANCE AND CONSULTING SERVICES RELATED TO INVESTMENTS

One lesson learned from the savings and loan crisis of the 1980s was that public accounting firms had not adequately assessed the quality of bank loan portfolios in independent financial statement audits. In short, auditors had not determined whether default risk was captured in loan loss reserves. In response, some firms now offer a new service—often called a *loan collateral review*—to provide banks with comfort about problem borrowers and misstated collateral. Most loan collateral reviews report on a borrower's collateral assets and internal control, and are performed using agreed-upon procedures (Chapter 18) by the practitioner and a bank loan officer. For example, the lead bank in a large multibank financing arrangement in the semiconductor and telecommunications industry might engage a public accounting firm to perform a quarterly loan collateral review, thereby offering more comfort to the participating banks than the lead bank's internal review might hold.

In the past several years, public accounting firms have leveraged heavily in the investment and financial services markets. Two examples: First, although the *Investment Advisors Act of 1940* has long allowed certified public accountants to offer investment advice that is incidental to their practices, few firms responded until recently. In 1996, Coopers & Lybrand became the last Big Six public accounting firm to register with the Securities and Exchange Commission (SEC) as an investment advisor.[1] The practice, called Coopers & Lybrand Financial Advisors LLC, operates out of major city offices, such as New York and Los Angeles, and offers reviews of investment managers' performance rather than buy/sell investment advice. Interestingly, the market is large and growing. For example, investments in employee benefit plans, such as retirement assets—estimated roughly at $3 trillion—are managed largely by investment managers.

Second, Price Waterhouse's financial services industry practice introduced an Electronic Financial Services Consulting Group to help financial institutions develop electronic products and services.[2] The proliferation of Internet shopping and a joint electronic payment security agreement among IBM, MasterCard, Microsoft, and Visa, translate into a growing market in electronic financial consulting, since downsized banks no longer have the luxury of excess employee capacity to manage technology, electronic commerce, and new product development. As with many other assurance and consulting service opportunities, technology is driving change.

However, the Securities and Exchange Commission, among others in the financial community, has questioned the advisability of a public accounting firm serving both as an *independent* auditor and as an investment or consulting advisor. For example, KPMG Peat Marwick resigned as independent auditor for Communication Intelligence Corp., a software developer, to ward off SEC criticisms of the firm's strategic partnership in KPMG BayMark Capital, an independent investment banking venture that advised Communication Intelligence. *The Wall Street Journal* reported that ". . . in SEC filings and interviews, Communication Intelligence said the SEC was concerned that the two roles might conflict, and that KPMG's auditing responsibilities might be influenced by KPMG BayMark's efforts to find deals for Communication Intelligence."[3] As the SEC's criticism and KPMG's resignation suggest, some ventures into lucrative consulting services may leave firms with little choice but to serve a client either as a consultant *or* as independent auditor. In the case of Communication Intelligence, KPMG Peat Marwick chose the former.

CONSIDERING INTERNAL CONTROL IN THE FINANCING CYCLE

As discussed in Chapter 7, an auditor considers an entity's internal controls as a basis for assessing control risk. However, in some instances, an auditor may conclude that the volume of investment, debt, and equity transactions is

---

1   S. Hook. "Coopers Investor Unit Shows Change in Profession," *Accounting Today* (April 22-May 5, 1996), pp. 3, 37.
2   "PW Targets Remote Banking Market," *Public Accounting Report* (February 29, 1996), p. 4.
3   C. McCoy. "KPMG Quits as Software Firm's Auditor as SEC Questions Dual Relationship," *The Wall Street Journal* (August 12, 1996), p. B4.

not sufficiently large to justify either the cost of performing tests of controls or the resulting reduction in control risk below the maximum. In these instances, the auditor would obtain an understanding of the system sufficient to plan the audit, omit tests of controls, and design substantive tests of account balances assuming allowable detection risk is at the minimum. In short, the auditor relies exclusively on substantive testing.

If an entity's investments and financing (i.e., issuance of bonds, stock, etc.) are maintained by an independent custodian, such as a broker or underwriter, the auditor's review of the system will consist primarily of obtaining an understanding of how the transactions are authorized and how documentation from the custodian is recorded in the general ledger. As a result, when custodians are used, transaction execution—the purchase, sale, issuance, and retirement of securities—and access to assets are of less concern to the auditor, because they are handled by independent external parties. In contrast, if securities are maintained by internal officials, such as a corporate secretary, the auditor would be concerned with control procedures over transaction authorization, execution, recording, and access to assets, because all aspects of the entity's investment and financing transactions are handled internally, and inadequate segregation of duties could lead to frauds.

Flowcharts are not often used to document an entity's investment, debt, and equity accounting systems. More often, auditors use questionnaires—for example, Figure 16-3 for investments, Figure 16-4 for debt, and Figure 16-5 for equity—to identify deficiencies, and narratives to document procedures for the custody, recording, valuation, acquisition, and sale of investments.

FINANCIAL STATEMENT ASSERTIONS AND AUDIT PROCEDURES

Within the financing cycle, Investments, Long-Term Debt, and Capital Stock are typically the most material financial statement account balances. Each account is discussed below in the context of the audit procedures commonly used by auditors to address each of the financial statement assertions introduced in Chapter 6: existence or occurrence, completeness, rights and obligations, valuation or allocation, and presentation and disclosure. Figure 16-6 relates each assertion to specific audit procedures and summarizes the discussion that follows.

EXISTENCE OR OCCURRENCE

Within the financing cycle, the existence or occurrence assertion addresses whether all recorded investments, debt, and capital stock exist at the balance sheet date and whether all recorded investment, debt, and capital stock transactions occurred during the period.

Testing the existence or occurrence assertion for investments depends on whether securities are maintained externally by an independent trustee/broker or internally by authorized personnel. If securities are maintained externally, the auditor would confirm balances with the independent trustee or broker; if held internally, the auditor would physically inspect and count all securities on hand. In turn, cutoff testing also addresses existence or occurrence by assuring that all investment transactions are recorded in the proper accounting period.

Figure 16-3:   Questionnaire: Investments

| | Performed by: _____ |
| | Date: _____ |

Question	Answer: Yes, No, or N/A	Remarks

Custody, Recording, and Valuation

1. Are securities and other negotiable instruments in the custody of an independent custodian? If not, are they adequately secured (e.g., locked in a safe)?
2. Are at least two officials responsible for internally held securities?
3. Is a detailed record of securities maintained by an official independent of officials responsible for custody?
4. Is the listing of investments periodically reconciled with investment records?
5. Are securities in the name of the client (or restrictively endorsed in the name of the client)?
6. Are independent officials responsible for reviewing and reporting changing securities' values?
7. Are adequately detailed investment records and general ledger control accounts maintained for the various investment classifications?

Acquisitions, Sales, and Income

1. Are acquisitions and sales of investment securities authorized by the board of directors or a duly authorized investment committee?
2. Are brokers, custodians, or other intermediaries authorized or designated by the board of directors?
3. Are brokers' advices promptly compared with documented acquisition and sales authorizations?
4. Is an independent check made to determine whether acquisition or sales prices are fair and objective?
5. Is investment income (e.g., interest, dividends) periodically recalculated and verified?

The existence or occurrence of long-term debt can be tested three ways: First, all recorded loans and other notes payable, including terms, due dates, and accrued interest, are confirmed with creditors. Second, to support the results of confirmation procedures, the auditor physically examines all bond indentures and other long-term indebtedness agreements, thereby determining

Figure 16-4:   Questionnaire: Debt

Performed by: _____
Date: _____

Question	Answer: Yes, No, or N/A	Remarks
1. Are all long-term debt and other borrowings authorized by the board of directors?		
2. Is an officer responsible for determining whether all debt covenants are complied with?		
3. Are unissued bonds and notes prenumbered consecutively and controlled by an official independent of recording?		
4. Are all retired debt instruments canceled or destroyed?		
5. Are adequately detailed bond and note registers and general ledger accounts maintained for the various debt classifications?		
6. Are interest payments and accruals periodically recalculated?		

whether all outstanding debt was confirmed. Third, the auditor physically inspects unissued instruments, thereby testing whether all issued securities are recorded as long-term debt. That is, long-term debt could be understated if a debt instrument were neither on hand nor recorded.

For capital stock, an auditor tests existence or occurrence by verifying recorded shareholders' equity balances. That is, the auditor would foot and cross-foot the client's schedule of changes in shareholders' equity balances, account for unissued or retired shares, and, if detailed records and stock certificates are maintained externally, confirm shares outstanding with registrars and transfer agents. In addition, the auditor would also examine supporting documentation and authorizations for any stock issuances, stock dividends, and stock splits occurring during the year. Of course, if securities transactions are executed by independent registrars or transfer agents, the auditor would confirm capital stock transactions and balances directly with the registrar or agent.

COMPLETENESS

The completeness assertion addresses whether all investments, long-term debt, and capital stock that should be presented in the financial statements are actually presented. That is, were all transactions recorded?

For investments, completeness is addressed by testing cutoff, which tests whether otherwise bona fide transactions are recorded in the proper accounting period, and by analytical procedures, which help determine whether recorded investment balances are reasonable or, in contrast, appear unusual, thereby requiring inquiries of management and/or additional substantive tests.

Analytical procedures also constitute a primary test of completeness for long-term debt and capital stock, because unusual relationships—for example,

Figure 16-5:   Questionnaire: Equity

	Performed by: _____	
	Date: _____	
Question	*Answer: Yes, No, or N/A*	*Remarks*
1. Are all capital stock issuances, retirements, and dividend distributions authorized by the board of directors?		
2. Are capital stock transactions authorized by stockholder vote, where required by state law?		
3. Are unissued stock certificates prenumbered consecutively and safeguarded?		
4. Are independent registrars and transfer agents authorized by the board of directors?		
5. Are detailed capital stock records, such as a stockholders' ledger, transfer journal, certificate control records, and general ledger control accounts maintained for the various capital stock classifications?		
6. Are detailed capital stock records maintained by officials independent of the custody of securities?		
7. Are treasury shares adequately controlled and accounted for?		
8. Are procedures established to assure that the entity is complying with stock exchange and securities laws?		
9. Are dividend payments and accruals periodically recalculated?		

widely varying ratios in comparison with prior years—may signal unrecorded or improperly recorded transactions. However, for long-term debt, the auditor should also inspect and account for unissued instruments, and for capital stock, the auditor would also verify recorded shareholders' equity balances.

RIGHTS AND OBLIGATIONS

Within the financing cycle, the rights assertion addresses whether an entity has property rights to investments, and the obligations assertion addresses whether long-term debt and capital stock represent bona fide obligations.

Rights to investments are tested by confirming securities held by external trustees/brokers and/or by physically inspecting securities on hand, depending on whether the securities are maintained internally or externally.

For long-term debt, obligations are tested by confirming loans and other notes with creditors, by examining bond indentures and other indebtedness agreements, and by confirming bond and serial note balances and interest with trustees. In turn, because issued capital stock is held by many shareholders, auditors typically test obligations by verifying recorded shareholders' equity balances, as discussed earlier, rather than by confirming with shareholders.

Figure 16-6:   Relating Financial Statement Assertions and Audit Procedures: Investments, Long-Term Debt, and Capital Stock

Assertions	Audit Procedures		
	Investments	Long-Term Debt	Capital Stock
Existence or occurrence	Confirm securities held by trustees/ brokers.	Confirm loans and other notes payable with creditors.	Verify recorded stockholders' equity balances.
	Physically inspect securities held internally.	Examine bond indentures and other long-term indebtedness agreements.	Examine supporting documentation and authorizations for stock issuances, stock dividends, and stock splits.
	Test cutoff.	Physically inspect unissued instruments.	
Completeness	Test cutoff.	Perform analytical procedures.	Perform analytical procedures.
	Perform analytical procedures.	Physically inspect and account for unissued instruments.	Verify recorded stockholders' equity balances.
Rights and obligations	Confirm securities held by trustees/ brokers.	Confirm loans and other notes payable with creditors.	Verify recorded stockholders' equity balances.
	Physically inspect securities held internally.	Examine bond indentures and other long-term indebtedness agreements.	
		Confirm bond and serial note balances and interest payments directly with trustees.	
Valuation	Verify securities transactions.	Verify debt-related transactions.	Verify recorded stockholders' equity balances.
	Confirm securities held by trustees/ brokers.	Confirm loans and other notes payable with creditors.	
	Check quoted securities prices.	Recalculate interest and premium/ discount amortizations.	
Presentation and disclosure	Compare statement presentation and disclosures with those required by GAAP.	Compare statement presentation and disclosures with those required by GAAP.	Compare statement presentation and disclosures with those required by GAAP.

VALUATION

The valuation assertion addresses whether investments, debt, and capital stock balances are carried in the financial statements at appropriate dollar amounts.

For investments, valuation is addressed by verifying securities transactions and unit prices—i.e., market values—at the balance sheet date, and by confirming securities held by trustees. For debt, auditors test valuation by verifying debt-related transactions, by confirming loans and other notes payable with creditors, and by recalculating interest and amortizations of premiums and discounts. The carrying value of capital stock is tested by verifying recorded shareholders' equity balances, which is also a primary test of existence or occurrence, completeness, and rights and obligations.

PRESENTATION AND DISCLOSURE

The presentation and disclosure assertion addresses whether recorded investments, debts, and capital stock are properly classified, described, and disclosed in the financial statements. As indicated in earlier chapters, presentation and disclosure are tested by comparing a client's financial statement disclosures with generally accepted accounting principles for each reported account. Disclosure guidelines, such as the AICPA's annually updated *Accounting and Audit Manual*, are often used by practicing auditors to assure that disclosures are complete.

SUBSTANTIVE TESTS OF INVESTMENTS IN MARKETABLE SECURITIES

A program of representative substantive tests applicable to investments is presented in Figure 16-7 along with the related financial statement assertions.

VERIFY MATHEMATICAL ACCURACY AND EXAMINE DOCUMENTATION

An auditor's tests of clerical accuracy relate primarily to a schedule of securities transactions that summarizes investment activity for the entire year, as illustrated in Figure 16-8. The working paper for securities trading activity is the auditor's primary source for testing acquisitions, sales, and the recognition of dividend and interest income. Because the schedule is the primary source for testing, the auditor tests the schedule's mathematical accuracy and reconciles balances with the general ledger, thereby assuring that detailed records accurately represent the investment account's recorded general ledger balance.

In Step 2, the auditor samples or tests all investment transactions for board of directors' or other authorization (e.g., from an investment committee), for brokers' advices, for published market quotations, and for properly calculated dividend and interest accruals, premium and discount amortizations, and gains and losses on sales. Thus, the focus of Step 2 is on whether recorded transactions are authorized and, equally important, whether they actually occurred.

CONFIRM OR PHYSICALLY INSPECT SECURITIES

For securities held off-premises by a custodian, such as a brokerage house, an auditor confirms details with the custodian and compares confirmation

Figure 16-7: Substantive Tests: Investments and Investment Revenue

Assertions	Procedures

Valuation	1. Obtain a schedule of securities transactions from client personnel and verify mathematical accuracy:
	  a. Foot and cross-foot the schedule.
	  b. Reconcile security balances with the general ledger.
	2. For sampled (or all) transactions:
	  a. Examine board of directors' or other appropriate authorization.
	  b. Examine broker's advice or other documentation.
	  c. Compare price with published market quotations.
	  d. Test calculations for dividend and interest income and accruals, for premium and discount amortizations, and for gains and losses on sales.

Existence Valuation Rights	3. Confirm securities held by trustees or physically inspect and count securities on hand.
Existence Completeness	4. Test cutoff to determine whether acquisitions, sales, and investment revenue are recorded in the proper accounting period.
Valuation	5. Review the valuation of securities.
Completeness	6. Perform analytical procedures.

Presentation
  and disclosure
	7. Review financial statements to determine whether:
	  a. Investments, gains and losses, and investment revenue are properly classified and described.
	  b. Disclosures are adequate.

responses with management's records. The auditor should also determine whether the custodian is trustworthy, and therefore whether a client's investments are secure. Normally, though, this procedure is not performed when the custodian is well-known and insured, such as a national or regional brokerage house.

For securities held internally, an auditor should physically inspect and count the securities on hand and compare the certificate numbers, quantity, and description of securities with detailed records. In addition, an auditor should determine if a client's balance sheet valuation procedures for infrequently traded securities are reasonable and reliable. Infrequently traded securities are of particular concern to the auditor, because there may not be objective, balance sheet date price quotations for the securities, thereby necessitating that the auditor consult an investee's audited financial statements and credit ratings in order to assess the reasonableness of carrying values.

TEST CUTOFF

Cutoff tests are performed to determine that securities transactions near the balance sheet date are recorded in the proper accounting period. Supporting documentation may be examined for all or a sample of the acquisitions and

Figure 16-8: Investments: Marketable Equity Securities

D2
AP 1/10/00

The Wilson Company
Investments: Marketable Equity Securities
December 31, 1999

Description	Date Acquired/ Sold	No. Shares	Price per Share	Balance 12/31/98	Transactions: at Cost — Acquired	Transactions: at Cost — (Sold)	Balance 12/31/99	Realized Gain (Loss)	Divided Income	Market Value 12/31/99 — Per Share	Market Value 12/31/99 — Total
Trading Securities											
ABC Corp.—											
Common	5/20/96	700	$23	$16,100[a]			$16,100[d,j]		$ 725[f]	$25.50[g]	$17,850[h]
Albion Co.—	6/30/97	800	32	25,600[a]					1,050[f]	35.00[g]	35,000[h]
Common	7/15/99	200	34		$ 6,800[b]		32,400[d,j]				
Elston Inc.—	8/12/98	500	19	9,500[a]							
Common	9/30/99	300	17			$ (5,700)[c]	3,800[d,j]	$(600)[e]	550[f]	16.00[g]	3,200[h]
Merton Inc.—											
Common	11/15/92	800	18	14,400[a]			14,400[d,j]		1,100[f]	23.00[g]	18,400[h]
				$65,600[a]	$ 6,800	$ (5,700)	$66,700[d,j]	$(600)	$ 3,425		$74,450[h]
				i			i		i		i

(continued)

Figure 16-8:   *(continued)*

Description	Date Acquired/ Sold	No. Shares	Price per Share	Balance 12/31/98	Transactions: at cost Acquired	(Sold)	Balance 12/31/99	Realized Gain (Loss)	Divided Income	Market Value 12/31/99 Per Share	Total
Available-for-sale Securities											
Carter, Rice— Common	12/01/95	1,000	28	$28,000a			$ 28,000d,j		$2,050f	33.00g	$ 33,000h
Ling Inc.— Common	10/09/97	1,500	13	19,500a			19,500d,j			18.00g	27,000h
Winston Corp.— Common	5/10/97	800	15	12,000a						—	—
	12/30/99	800	17			$(12,000)c	—	$ 1,600e	875f		
				$59,500a		$(12,000)c	$ 47,500	$ 1,600	$2,925		$ 60,000
				i			i		i		i

a   Traced to general ledger and prior year working papers.
b   Agreed with broker's advice, cash disbursements records, and board of directors' authorization.
c   Agreed with broker's advice, cash receipts records, and board of directors' authorization.
d   Traced to general ledger.
e   Calculated and agreed with general ledger.
f   Agreed with dividend rates in *Standard & Poor* and calculated; traced proceeds to cash receipts records.
g   Agreed with 12/31/99 market quotations in 1/2/00 *The Wall Street Journal.*
h   Calculated.
i   Footed.
j   Cross-footed.

sales shortly before and after the balance sheet date. Transaction dates and amounts for each transaction reviewed should be agreed with detailed records and entries in the general ledger. The auditor should recalculate gains and losses for each sales transaction examined and agree the calculations with recorded amounts. Tests of cutoff should also be performed for investment revenue transactions near the balance sheet date, and accruals for interest revenue should be reviewed for reasonableness.

REVIEW VALUATION

An auditor tests valuation by examining documentation supporting transactions recorded and by recalculating dividend and interest income. Examining supporting documentation, however, substantiates historical cost only. Thus, an auditor examines market quotations to assure that marketable equity securities are reported at the lower of aggregate cost or market, and that marketable debt securities are reported at the lower of cost or cost less permanent declines in market value.

PERFORM ANALYTICAL PROCEDURES

An auditor can use analytical procedures to test completeness and to determine whether conclusions drawn from substantive tests are reasonable. Several representative analytical procedures follow:

- Compare current year purchase and sales transactions to those of prior years and to the entity's stated investment plans.
- Compare current year dividends, interest, and other investment income with those of prior years.
- Calculate the percentage of accrued investment income to total investments and estimate total accrued income based on current investments.

Any unusual or unexpected relationships should be investigated further through inquiries of management and additional substantive tests of details.

REVIEW FINANCIAL STATEMENT DISCLOSURES

Financial statements are read to determine that investments are properly classified and described in the balance sheet and that gains and losses and investment revenue are properly presented in the income statement. Under *Statement of Financial Accounting Standards No. 115,* "Accounting for Certain Investments in Debt and Equity Securities," debt held to maturity and debt or equity that is either held in a trading portfolio or made available for sale should be reported separately in the balance sheet. And, disclosures for each classification vary: Debt held to maturity is stated in the balance sheet at cost; debt or equity in a trading portfolio or available for sale is marked to market.

SUBSTANTIVE TESTS OF LONG-TERM DEBT

For most companies, long-term debt transactions are likely to be relatively infrequent but highly material, resulting in extensive—if not exclusive—reliance on substantive procedures. A representative program of substantive tests applicable to debt is presented in Figure 16-9 and is tied to financial statement assertions.

VERIFY MATHEMATICAL ACCURACY AND EXAMINE DOCUMENTATION

To test mathematical accuracy, an auditor examines a schedule that summarizes debt transactions for the year. Figure 16-10 illustrates.

The auditor foots and cross-foots the schedule, reconciling totals with balances in the general ledger, and, as illustrated in Figure 16-10, examines documentation supporting each debt-related transaction. For example, new debt would be reconciled with cash receipts records and with the board of directors' authorization, and the auditor would examine the debt instrument, determining which assets, if any, had been pledged as collateral. In turn,

Figure 16-9: Substantive Tests: Debt and Interest Expense

Assertions	Procedures
Existence or occurrence Valuation Completeness Obligations	1. Obtain a schedule of bonds, notes payable, and other long-term indebtedness from accounting personnel and verify mathematical accuracy: a. Foot and cross-foot the schedule. b. Reconcile totals with balances in the general ledger. c. Examine documentation supporting debt-related transactions. d. If debt instruments are maintained internally, review a sample of entries in detailed bond records and physically inspect and account for unissued instruments.
Existence Obligations Valuation	2. Confirm bonds outstanding and interest payments directly with trustees, and loans and notes payable directly with creditors, coordinating with bank confirmations where appropriate (Chapter 11).
Existence or occurrence Obligations	3. Obtain bond indentures and other long-term indebtedness agreements: a. Examine documentation and board of directors' authorizations. b. Determine that proceeds are recorded properly and used as intended by the board. c. Review for compliance with restrictive covenants.
Valuation	4. Recalculate interest paid or accrued and amortizations of premiums or discounts.
Existence or occurrence Completeness	5. Perform analytical procedures.
Presentation and disclosure	6. Review financial statements to determine whether: a. Debt obligations are properly classified and described in the balance sheet and interest expense is properly reported in the income statement. b. Disclosures are adequate.

Figure 16-10: Long-Term Debt, Bonds, and Related Interest

The Wilson Company
Long-Term Debt: Bonds, Notes Payable, and Related Interest
December 31, 1999

Description	Principal				Interest			
	Balance 12/31/98	Additions	Payments	Balance 12/31/99	Balance 12/31/98	Expense	Payments	Balance 12/31/99
8% bonds, due 12/31/06; due $1,000,000 per year; 10-yr. Bond; issued 1/1/94; face—$1,000,000; qtrly. interest.	$ 800,000[a,i]	—	$100,000[c]	$ 700,000[d,e]	$20,000[a]	$ 80,000[f]	$ 80,000[g]	$20,000[d,e]
9% note to First Nat'l Bank; due 12/31/01; 3-yr. Note; incurred 1/1/99; face—$360,000; semiannual interest; due $60,000 every six months.		$360,000[b,k]	120,000[c]	240,000[d,e]	—	32,400[f]	—	32,400[d,e]
10% note to Nat'l Bank; due 6/30/01; 3-yr. Note; incurred 7/01/98; face—$300,000; qtrly. interest; due $50,000 every six months.	250,000[a,j]	—	100,000[c]	150,000[d,e]	15,000[a]	30,000[f]	30,000[g]	15,000[d,e]
	$1,050,000	$360,000	$320,000	$1,090,000	$35,000	$142,400	$110,000	$67,400[d,e]
	h	h	h	h	h	h	h	h

(continued)

Figure 16-10:   *(continued)*

a   Traced to general ledger and prior year working papers.
b   Examined note, agreed with cash receipts records and board of directors' authorization.
c   Agreed amount with bond/note, and agreed with cash disbursements records.
d   Traced to general ledger.
e   Cross-footed.
f   Calculated.
g   Calculated and agreed with cash disbursements records.
h   Footed.
i   Land and buildings at 1001 Dexter St. pledged as collateral.
j   Investment in Carter, Rice (see D2) pledged as collateral.
k   Land and buildings at 131 Japonica Street pledged as collateral.

payments would be reconciled in amount with bonds or notes and with cash disbursements records. If debt instruments are maintained internally, an auditor would review a sample of entries in detailed bond records and physically inspect and account for unissued instruments. Otherwise—that is, if debt is handled by independent trustees—the auditor would confirm, as indicated next.

CONFIRM BONDS, LOANS, AND NOTES PAYABLE

Bonds and interest payments should be confirmed directly with trustees, thereby determining whether the debt exists, is valued properly, and represents a bona fide obligation. In turn, loans and other notes payable are confirmed directly with creditors. All returned confirmations should be examined in detail and agreed with recorded balances, and differences should be investigated.

EXAMINE BOND INDENTURES AND OTHER LONG-TERM INDEBTEDNESS AGREEMENTS

All long-term indebtedness agreements should be examined by the auditor to determine that transactions were executed in accordance with board of directors' authorizations, including the subsequent use of borrowed funds. If funds are not used as stipulated in indebtedness agreements, the entity may be in violation of state or federal laws, because monies would have been expended in violation of agreements with creditors. When examining debt instruments, the auditor should note all restrictive covenants and determine that the company is in compliance for the current period. For example, if a long-term note in the amount of $1,000,000 carries a debt covenant specifying that the borrower's current ratio may not fall below 3 to 2, lack of compliance at the balance sheet date could result in the creditor calling the loan immediately, thereby requiring that the auditor propose a journal entry to reclassify the principal from a long-term to a current liability.

RECALCULATE INTEREST AND AMORTIZATIONS

Interest paid or accrued for the year should be recalculated by the auditor and reconciled with the general ledger, as illustrated in Figure 16-10. In addition, any related interest payments should be reconciled with cash disbursements records. If outstanding bonds were issued originally at more or less than face value, the related premium or discount amortization should be recalculated by the auditor and compared with entries in the general ledger.

PERFORM ANALYTICAL PROCEDURES

To test existence or occurrence and completeness, and to confirm the results of detailed substantive tests of details, the auditor performs analytical procedures such as ratio analysis and comparisons of relationships among related accounts or transactions. For example, analytical procedures for long-term debt could include any or all of the following tests:

*   Compare current amortization amounts with prior actual amounts and current budgeted amounts.

- Compare current interest costs with prior actual costs and current budgeted costs.
- Compare current and noncurrent debt obligations with prior actual obligations and current budgeted obligations.
- Compare debt issue costs and premiums/discounts to prospectuses and other internal debt reports.

Although no one of the above analytical procedures will necessarily detect misstatements, they could direct an auditor's attention to accounts or balances requiring additional tests of details or inquiries.

REVIEW FINANCIAL STATEMENT DISCLOSURES

Financial statement classifications, descriptions, and disclosures relating to debt and interest expense should be read by the auditor. The currently maturing portion of long-term debt should generally be classified as a current liability in the absence of refinancing agreements. Disclosures should include information regarding maturities, interest rates, and other terms and conditions; assets pledged as collateral; debt conversion features; and troubled debt restructurings.

SUBSTANTIVE TESTS OF CAPITAL STOCK, RETAINED EARNINGS, AND EARNINGS PER SHARE

Figure 16-11 presents a program of substantive tests for capital stock, retained earnings, and earnings per share and, like the other audit programs, is tied to the assertions introduced earlier. The procedures listed in Figure 16-11 encompass all the major types of transactions that normally affect shareholders' equity. However, it is unlikely that all these transactions would occur within a single year for any given audit client. In fact, in many cases, changes in shareholders' equity are attributable solely to changes in retained earnings resulting from net earnings or losses and from dividend payments.

VERIFY SHAREHOLDERS' EQUITY BALANCES

To address the valuation of shareholders' equity from the standpoint of mathematical accuracy, an auditor should obtain a client-prepared schedule summarizing changes in shareholders' equity accounts, including capital stock and related premium accounts for each class of stock outstanding, treasury stock accounts, and retained earnings. The schedule is footed and cross-footed by the auditor and the totals are reconciled with the general ledger, as illustrated in Figure 16-12. Other procedures for verifying shareholders' equity depend on whether equity transactions are executed through independent parties or internally as described in Figure 16-11.

REVIEW STOCK ISSUANCES, STOCK DIVIDENDS, AND SPLITS

If the number of shares outstanding has increased during the year as a result of stock issuances, stock dividends, or stock splits, the supporting documentation and authorizations should be examined for each transaction. For stock

Figure 16-11: Substantive Tests: Capital Stock, Retained Earnings, and Earnings per Share

Assertions	Procedures

Existence or occurrence
Valuation
Completeness
Obligations
	1. Verify recorded stockholders' equity balances:
	  a. Obtain a schedule of changes in stockholders' equity accounts from accounting personnel.
	  b. Foot and cross-foot the schedule, reconciling balances with the general ledger.
	  c. If detailed records and stock certificates are maintained internally:
	    (1) Examine a sample of entries in the stockholders' ledger, the transfer journal, and certificate control records.
	    (2) Foot the stockholders' ledger and reconcile with the general ledger.
	    (3) Account for unissued certificates, examine retired shares for evidence of cancellation, and count treasury shares on hand.
	  d. If detailed records and stock certificates are maintained externally, confirm shares outstanding, unissued shares, and treasury shares directly with registrars and transfer agents.

Occurrence
Valuation
	2. Review stock issuances, stock dividends, and stock splits:
	  a. Examine supporting documentation and authorizations.
	  b. For issuances, compare the authorized number of shares and price per share with entries in the general ledger, and compare proceeds from issuance with cash receipts records.
	  c. For stock dividends, compare the authorized number of shares and value per share and determine that stock dividends are recorded in accordance with GAAP.
	  d. For stock splits, examine memorandum entries and compare with authorized number of shares and assigned value per share.

Occurrence
Valuation
	3. Review treasury stock transactions:
	  a. Examine supporting documentation and authorizations.
	  b. Compare authorized number of shares and price per share with entries in the general ledger.
	  c. Compare disbursements for purchases and receipts for sales with cash records.
	  d. Determine that the basis of accounting is appropriate.

Occurrence
Valuation
	4. Verify recorded dividends.
	  a. Examine supporting documentation and authorization.
	  b. Recalculate dividends and agree with entries in general ledger.
	  c. Reconcile recorded dividends with cash records.

Figure 16-11:   *(continued)*

Assertions	Procedures
Valuation	5. Recalculate earnings per share.
Completeness	6. Perform analytical procedures.
Presentation and disclosure	7. Review financial statements to determine whether: a. Capital stock, retained earnings, and earnings per share are properly classified and described. b. Disclosures are adequate.

issuances (sales of previously unissued stock), an auditor should determine through recalculation that the general ledger entries accurately reflect the number of shares and selling price per share authorized by the board of directors. In the case of par or stated value stock, the auditor should determine that the selling price is properly allocated to capital stock and related premium accounts. Proceeds from the issuance of stock should be traced to cash receipts records.

When dividends are issued to shareholders in the form of additional shares of stock, an auditor should determine that entries in the general ledger reflect the number of shares and value per share authorized by the board of directors. The auditor should also review the assigned value per share to determine whether the value is appropriate relative to the number of shares issued.

Figure 16-12:   Capital Stock and Additional Paid-In Capital

J2
AP 1/12/00

The Wilson Company
Capital Stock and Additional Paid-In Capital
December 31, 1999

	Authorized	Issued & Outstanding	Amount (at Par)	Additional Paid-In Capital
Balance, Dec. 31, 1998, $5 par. Issued 6/1/99 at par (proceeds in cash).	15,000 Shs.[a]	12,000 Shs.[b] 2,000 Shs.[c]	$60,000[b] 10,000[d]	$5,000[b] —
Balance, Dec. 31, 1999	15,000 Shs.	14,000 Shs.	$70,000	$5,000
		e	e	

a Agreed with corporate charter.
b Traced to general ledger and prior year working papers.
c Agreed with board of directors' authorization.
d Agreed with cash receipts records.
e Footed.

Although stock splits have no effect on total shareholders' equity, they do increase the number of shares outstanding. An auditor should review underlying documentation and related memorandum entries to determine that stock splits were authorized and that the change in shares outstanding is recorded properly.

REVIEW TREASURY STOCK TRANSACTIONS

Many entities, particularly large publicly traded corporations, frequently buy and sell shares of their own stock. Shares may be acquired directly from shareholders in a stock redemption, or may be bought and sold on the open market. Treasury stock transactions may be undertaken for a variety of reasons including, for example, the acquisition of shares needed for distribution to employees under employee stock option plans. An auditor should review documentation and authorizations for treasury stock transactions and examine related entries in the general ledger and cash records. The auditor should determine that the accounting method used to record treasury stock transactions complies with generally accepted accounting principles and that general ledger entries accurately reflect the method used by the company.

VERIFY RECORDED DIVIDENDS

Supporting documentation and authorizations should be reviewed by an auditor for all dividends declared during the year under audit. The mathematical accuracy of dividends should be verified through recalculation and comparing totals with the general ledger and cash records.

RECALCULATE EARNINGS PER SHARE

An auditor should recalculate earnings per share to determine that all increases and decreases in shares outstanding are reflected properly in earnings per share. In some cases, entities with complex capital structures may report more than one earnings per share amount. An auditor should review the terms of all outstanding stock rights, warrants, options, and convertible securities to determine whether reported earnings per share are consistent with generally accepted accounting principles.

PERFORM ANALYTICAL PROCEDURES

Analytical procedures are not typically used for equity accounts unless the volume and breadth of transactions are extensive. When transactions are extensive, any or all of the following analytical procedures, among others, may be informative:

- For the current year, compute the return on shareholders' equity, the book value per share, and the dividend payout ratio, and compare figures with those of prior years.
- Compare current year dividend amounts with those of prior years.
- Compute current year balances for common and preferred stock and additional paid-in capital, and compare with balances of prior years.
- Compare current year treasury shares with those of prior years.

Of course, the auditor would investigate any unusual or unexpected relationships.

REVIEW FINANCIAL STATEMENT DISCLOSURES

An entity's financial statements should be read to determine whether all shareholders' equity balances are properly classified and described in the balance sheet and whether earnings per share are properly reported in the income statement. Notes to the financial statements should be reviewed to determine that disclosures are adequate. Frequently, disclosures relating to shareholders' equity are fairly extensive and include detailed schedules of changes in capital stock balances and retained earnings.

MANAGEMENT DISCRETION IN ACCOUNTING FOR FINANCIAL INSTRUMENTS

Dominated by historical cost accounting, traditional financial statements provide little information about the value of a company. The accounting profession in general, and the Financial Accounting Standards Board (FASB) in particular, have long been handcuffed in responding to this criticism since current value, unlike historical cost, is neither objective nor wholly verifiable. Interestingly, the objectivity and verifiability arguments make sense for many assets, but not for those assets that have a readily determinable market value, like investments in debt and equity securities.

Prior to 1993, the authoritative literature on investments was inconsistent across industries, and the generally accepted, though contradictory, lower-of-cost-or-market rule treated differently the accounting for unrealized gains and losses on debt held for sale and on noncurrent equity securities: Reductions in value (unrealized losses) were recognized, but appreciations (unrealized gains) were not. In response, the FASB added a far-reaching financial instruments project to its agenda that has since resulted in several pronouncements, among them *Statement of Financial Accounting Standards No. 115*, "Accounting for Certain Investments in Debt and Equity Securities," which requires that debt and equity securities be accounted for in three separate portfolios: "held to maturity," "trading securities," and "available for sale." **Held-to-maturity securities** are debt and equity investments an entity has both the positive intent and the ability to hold till maturity. **Trading securities** are debt and equity investments held for sale in the near term. **Available-for-sale securities** are debt and equity investments not classified as either held-to-maturity or trading. Note from Figure 16-13 that unrealized gains and losses on trading securities—that is, "paper" gains (and losses)—are recognized as current earnings on the income statement, but that gains and losses on securities held-to-maturity or available-for-sale are recognized only when an actual sale occurs.

MANAGEMENT AND AUDITOR INCENTIVES

The differential treatment of unrealized gains and losses across investment portfolios provides management with opportunities to manage reported earnings. Two examples: First, management could shift securities to or from a

Figure 16-13:   Investment Securities Portfolios

Investment Portfolio	Securities Included	Unrealized Gains and Losses	Balance Sheet Disclosure
Held-to-Maturity Securities	Debt and equity that an entity has both the positive intent and ability to hold till maturity.	Not recognized.	Amortized cost: Current or noncurrent assets.
Trading Securities	Debt and equity held for sale in the near term.	Recognized in current earnings.	Fair value: Current assets.
Available-for-Sale Securities	Debt and equity not classified as held-to-maturity or trading.	Excluded from earnings; reported in shareholders' equity.	Fair value: Current or noncurrent assets.

trading securities portfolio, thereby managing the recognition of unrealized gains and losses. In a period of declining (or excessively rising) earnings but rising (or declining) share prices in selected available-for-sale securities, management could boost (or reduce) earnings by reclassifying available-for-sale securities to trading securities and accounting for the resulting unrealized gains (or losses) in current earnings. Second, within the available-for-sale portfolio, management could selectively sell securities that would result in gains, and hold securities that would result in losses. In a dissent to *SFAS No. 115*, two FASB members pointed out that "an impressive amount of empirical evidence indicates that many financial institutions" had selectively sold or held securities, and that selective trading "undermines the relevance and reliability of accounting information."[4] Auditors, in turn, have incentives in general to assure that management complies with the requirements of *SFAS No. 115* and in particular to monitor management's intent, as the case below illustrates.

ACCOUNTING FOR FINANCIAL INSTRUMENTS: A CASE STUDY

Owing to several cost-effective design changes in their truck filter product line, Provident Corporation, a publicly traded company, dominates the automotive filter aftermarket. To meet analysts' forecasts of projected annual earnings, fourth quarter income from operations will have to exceed both the company's expectations and all prior years' fourth quarter results. The company has considerable debt and equity security holdings partitioned within trading, available-for-sale, and held-to-maturity portfolios.

Late in the fourth quarter, management hosts a meeting with the auditors, ostensibly to plan the timing of, and the company's involvement in, year end audit work. During the meeting, Provident's chief executive officer (CEO)

---

4   *Statement of Financial Accounting Standards No. 115*, "Accounting for Certain Investments in Debt and Equity Securities," par. 25.

alerts the auditors about securities trades planned for the last month of the fiscal year. The CEO claims that, although management had the undisputed intent to hold selected debt instruments to maturity, the likelihood of failing to meet analysts' earnings projections suggests the company no longer has the ability to hold the securities. As a result, the CEO plans to transfer debt securities from the held-to-maturity portfolio into the trading securities portfolio, and to sell all available-for-sale securities for which the realized gain will exceed by 15 percent the original purchase price. The CEO believes that meeting analysts' forecasts is crucially important to Provident's shareholders. The auditor believes that the company's fourth quarter trading strategy is driven partly by shareholder expectations, and mostly by the CEO's executive compensation contract, which is tied to the magnitude of reported earnings and to Provident's share price.

AUDIT JUDGMENT: ACCOUNTING, LIABILITY, AND ETHICS

Provident's fourth quarter trading strategy raises three questions. First, has the CEO planned trades that either circumvent or violate generally accepted accounting principles, specifically *SFAS No. 115*? Rather than circumvent *SFAS No. 115*, management's trading strategy actually takes advantage of earnings management opportunities provided by the pronouncement. Selectively selling appreciated available-for-sale securities while simultaneously holding depreciated securities is not precluded by *SFAS No. 115*, even though the motive clearly is to inflate earnings with recognized gains on selective securities trades. Shifting debt securities from the held-to-maturity portfolio into the trading securities portfolio allows management to recognize unrealized gains in current earnings, which is not precluded by *SFAS No. 115* either, although in this case the auditor would likely be skeptical that the CEO's argument—earnings may fall below analysts' projections—is necessarily a reason to conclude that the company is no longer able to hold debt securities to maturity. After all, the company is neither about to suffer a net loss nor in any apparent danger of bankruptcy.

Second, what is the auditor's potential legal liability? And third, what are the ethical implications to the auditor? Interestingly, the answer to both questions likely is "none." The CEO's trading strategy does not render the auditor culpable under either Section 10(b) or Section 18 of the *Securities Exchange Act of 1934*, since there is no intent by management to do any more than what a literal reading of *SFAS No. 115* would allow. There is no violation of generally accepted accounting principles, no violation of the *Code of Professional Conduct*, no false or misleading disclosures (Section 18), and no intent to deceive [Section 10(b)]. In fact, the CEO's behavior is actually consistent with the interests of Provident's shareholders: The wealth of the CEO (executive compensation) and of the company's shareholders are both tied to Provident's share price. However, the auditor would be responsible to determine whether other stakeholders, apart from Provident shareholders, were necessarily deceived. For example, the CEO may have a hidden agenda: If the switch from held-to-maturity to trading securities increases current assets (recall from Figure 16-13 that trading securities are carried as current assets at fair value rather than at amortized cost), the CEO may be masking a debt covenant violation tied to maintaining a prespecified current ratio.

SUMMARY

The financing cycle involves an entity's business functions for generating and using capital funds and investing funds not currently needed for operations. Common activities related to equity and debt financing include the issuance and retirement of equity and debt securities, payment of dividends and interest to investors and creditors, and recording of equity and debt transactions. In turn, these functions lead to three major balance sheet accounts: Investments, Long-Term Debt, and Capital Stock, each of which is discussed in this chapter in the context of substantive tests of details. When performing substantive tests of investments, long-term debt, and capital stock, an auditor's major objectives are to determine that each account exists, represents all transactions that should be presented, represents rights and obligations of the entity, is valued properly, and is presented and disclosed properly within the financial statements.

Accounting for financial instruments, an attempt by the accounting profession to mark assets—in this case, trading securities and available-for-sale securities—to market, is a major departure from historical cost, the measure that has long dominated financial accounting and reporting. Although an authoritative pronouncement guides the accounting for financial instruments, the pronouncement nevertheless provides management with opportunities to manage earnings by transferring securities among portfolios and by timing the sale of selected securities. Auditors have incentives to assure that management complies with the authoritative pronouncement on financial instruments and, in addition, to be cognizant of management's intent.

KEY TERMS

Bond certificate 592	Held-to-maturity securities 619
Commercial paper 592	Trading securities 619
Stock certificate 592	Available-for-sale securities 619
Treasury bill 592	

REFERENCES

Auditing Standards

AICPA. *Codification of Statements on Auditing Standards.* New York: AICPA.
SAS No. 47, "Audit Risk and Materiality in Conducting an Audit."

Accounting Standards

SFAS No. 115, "Accounting for Certain Investments in Debt and Equity Securities."

Books

Committee of Sponsoring Organizations of the Treadway Commission (COSO). *Internal Control: Integrated Framework.* Executive Summary. New York: COSO (1992).
Committee of Sponsoring Organizations of the Treadway Commission (COSO). *Internal Control: Integrated Framework.* Framework. New York: COSO (1992).
Committee of Sponsoring Organizations of the Treadway Commission (COSO). *Internal Control: Integrated Framework.* Evaluation Tools. New York: COSO (1992).

Committee of Sponsoring Organizations of the Treadway Commission (COSO). *Internal Control: Integrated Framework.* Reporting to External Parties. New York: COSO (1992).

QUESTIONS

1. Identify the business functions associated with the financing cycle.
2. Describe some control procedures applicable to capital stock.
3. What is a restrictive debt covenant?
4. Why should unissued bonds be prenumbered consecutively?
5. Explain how an auditor tests the existence of investments recorded within a client's financial statements.
6. How does an auditor test the valuation of investment securities?
7. Why does an auditor typically examine market quotations for a client's investments?
8. What procedures can be used to determine whether all transactions that should be recorded are recorded?
9. Briefly describe the procedures an auditor might use to test long-term debt and interest expense at year end.
10. Why do auditors frequently rely predominantly or exclusively on substantive tests in auditing shareholders' equity and long-term debt?
11. How does an auditor verify recorded shareholders' equity balances?
12. Identify the specific types of transactions relating to shareholders' equity that are tested by an auditor at year end.
13. How and why does an auditor test earnings per share?
14. How should unrealized gains and losses on investments in equity securities be accounted for?
15. Briefly, why did the Financial Accounting Standards Board add the financial instruments project to its technical agenda?

MULTIPLE CHOICE QUESTIONS

1. Assuming that one of management's control objectives is to restrict access to securities, which of the following would *not* be appropriate to satisfy the objective?

a. Establish physical barriers over forms and records.
b. Establish physical barriers over investment securities.
c. Maintain files of authorized signatures.
d. Segregate investment approval from custody of the securities.

2. What control objective is served by management's establishing policies for selecting and approving investment transactions?

a. Sources of capital funds should be authorized in accordance with management's criteria.
b. Investment transactions should be made in accordance with management's criteria.
c. Investment transactions should be recorded at the correct amounts and in the proper accounting period.
d. Access to securities should be restricted to authorized personnel.

3. Which financial statement assertions are served by testing cutoff over investment transactions?

a. Existence and completeness.
b. Rights and valuation.
c. Existence and rights.
d. Presentation and disclosure.

4. Which financial statement assertion is served by confirming bonds, notes, and interest payments directly with trustees?

a. Completeness.
b. Valuation.
c. Rights.
d. Presentation and disclosure.

5. Why is it less common for auditors to perform extensive tests of controls over investments, debt, and equity?

a. It is customary to assess control risk at the maximum for these accounts.
b. Physical custody of securities is often vested in outside trustees.
c. The volume of transactions is not often large enough to justify the cost of tests of controls.
d. These transactions are not supported by extensive documentation.

6. How can an auditor test the assertion of completeness for capital stock?

a. Verify stockholders' equity balances.
b. Test supporting documentation for stock issuances, stock dividends, and stock splits.
c. Confirm transactions with independent trustees.
d. Perform analytical procedures.

7. Which of the following are debt investments an entity has both the positive intent and the ability to hold till maturity?

a. Trading securities.
b. Call options.
c. Available-for-sale securities.
d. Held-to-maturity securities.

8. For which of the following portfolios are unrealized gains and losses not recognized?

a. Trading securities.
b. Call options.
c. Available-for-sale securities.
d. Held-to-maturity securities.

9. Which of the following would not likely motivate management to selectively sell available-for-sale securities?

a. Market share declined 5 percent this year.
b. A new product has not been well-received.
c. Like each of the prior five years, current year earnings are likely to increase by 10 percent.
d. Management compensation is tied to earnings.

10. Which portfolio of debt and equity securities is always reported as a current asset in the balance sheet?

a. Treasury shares.
b. Held-to-maturity securities.
c. Available-for-sale securities.
d. Trading securities.

PROBLEMS AND DISCUSSION CASES

16-1 *Errors, Fraud, and Control Procedures*
In your audit of the Whitestable Company's December 31, 1999 financial statements, you become aware of the following controls or procedures over investments, debt, and equity:
a. On June 15, 1999, the board of directors established criteria for selecting debt and equity investments.
b. Policies have been established for selecting debt or equity financing.
c. On a monthly basis, interest and loan payment amounts are prepared or updated.
d. All internally held securities are maintained under lock and key in a fireproof vault within the treasurer's office.
e. All unissued securities are maintained and periodically checked by personnel independent of cash activities.
Required: For each control procedure, indicate: (a) a potential error or fraud that might be prevented or detected as a result of the control procedure and (b) what control objective is served by the control procedure. Organize your answer as follows:

Control Procedure	*Potential Error or Fraud That Might Be Prevented or Detected*	*Control Objective*

16-2 *Drafting Tests of Controls From an Internal Control Questionnaire: Investment Transactions*
Following are selected questions from an internal control questionnaire for a company's investment transactions. The questions relate to the custody, recording, and valuation of investments, and to acquisitions, sales, and income. A *yes* response to any question would indicate a potential strength of the system, and a *no* response a potential weakness.
a. Is a detailed record of securities maintained by an official who is independent of officials responsible for custody?
b. Is the listing of investments periodically reconciled with investment records?
c. Are securities in the name of the entity (or restrictively endorsed in the name of the entity)?
d. Are acquisitions and sales of investment securities authorized by the board of directors or by an authorized investment committee?
e. Are brokers' advices promptly compared with documented acquisition and sales authorizations?
f. Is an independent check made to determine whether acquisition or sales prices are fair and objective?
g. Is investment income periodically recalculated and verified?
Required: Assume that inquiries indicate no apparent weaknesses in internal control. Draft a test of controls you believe would provide persuasive evidence that no deficiencies exist.

16-3 *Relating Errors, Frauds, Audit Procedures, and Assertions in Substantive Tests of Investments*
Following are errors, frauds, or other circumstances that an auditor might encounter as a result of applying audit tests to investments as of the balance sheet date:

a. The client does not maintain detailed records for investments.
b. All debt securities are maintained in a locked, fireproof vault in the treasurer's office.
c. All equity securities are held by independent brokers.
d. The client traded heavily in marketable securities near the end of the year.
e. The market value of selected equity securities fluctuated widely throughout the year.

Required: For each of the above, indicate: (1) a specific substantive test or tests that might address the error, fraud, or circumstance and (2) the financial statement assertion addressed by each test.

16-4   *Planning the Audit of Marketable Securities*

In an audit of the financial statements of Belasco Chemicals, Inc., Karen Mack is deciding whether to inspect marketable securities on the balance sheet date, May 31, 1999, or at some other date. The marketable securities held by Belasco include negotiable bearer bonds, which are kept in a safe in the treasurer's office, and miscellaneous stocks and bonds, which are kept in a safe-deposit box at The Merchants Bank. Both the negotiable bearer bonds and the miscellaneous stocks and bonds are material to Belasco's financial statements.

Required:
1. What are the factors that Mack should consider when deciding whether to inspect securities on May 31, 1999, as opposed to other dates?
2. Assume that Mack plans to have a member of her staff inspect securities at Belasco's offices and at The Merchants Bank on May 31, 1999. What instructions should she give to the staff member about inspecting and including evidence in the working papers?
3. Assume Mack believes that sending a staff member to Belasco's offices and to The Merchants Bank on May 31, 1999 is impractical. What alternative procedures might she use to assure herself that the company physically possesses marketable securities on May 31, 1999, if the securities are inspected: (a) May 28, 1999? (b) June 5, 1999?

(AICPA Adapted)

16-5   *Auditing an Investment Portfolio*

As a result of highly profitable operations over a number of years, Eastern Manufacturing Corporation has accumulated a substantial investment portfolio. In auditing the financial statements for the year ended December 31, 1999, the following information came to the auditor's attention:

a. Continuing manufacturing operations resulted in an operating loss for the year.
b. In 1999, the corporation placed the securities in their investment portfolio with a financial institution that will serve as custodian of the securities. Formerly the securities were kept in a safe-deposit box at a local bank.
c. On December 22, 1999, the corporation sold and then repurchased on the same day a number of securities that had appreciated greatly in value. Management stated that the purpose of the sale and repurchase was to establish a higher cost and book value for the securities and to avoid reporting a loss for the year.

Required:
1. List the objectives of the auditor's tests of the investment account.
2. Under what conditions would the auditor accept a confirmation of the securities from the custodian rather than personally inspecting and counting the securities?
3. What disclosure, if any, of the sale and repurchase of securities would the auditor recommend for the financial statements? What impact, if any, would the sale and repurchase have on the auditor's opinion on the financial statements if the client accepts the auditor's disclosure recommendations? Discuss.

(AICPA Adapted)

16-6 *Working Paper Review*
An audit client prepared the schedule on the next page. After completing the procedures listed at the bottom of the schedule, an audit assistant initialed, dated, and indexed the working paper.
   Required: List the deficiencies in this working paper.

16-7 *Auditing Secured Notes and Equity Securities*
You have been engaged to audit the financial statements of the Elliott Company for the year ended December 31, 1999. You also audited the December 31, 1998 financial statements. Following is the December 31, 1999 trial balance:

	Dr. (Cr.)
Cash	$ 128,000
Interest Receivable	47,450
Dividends Receivable	1,750
14 Percent Secured Note Receivable	730,000
Investments at Cost: Bowen Common Stock	322,000
Investments at Equity: Woods Common Stock	284,000
Land	185,000
Accounts Payable	(31,000)
Interest Payable	(6,500)
16 Percent Secured Note Payable to Bank	(275,000)
Common Stock	(480,000)
Paid-In Capital in Excess of Par	(800,000)
Retained Earnings	(100,500)
Dividend Revenue	(3,750)
Interest Revenue	(47,450)
Equity in Earnings of Investments Carried at Equity	(40,000)
Interest Expense	26,000
General and Administrative Expense	60,000

You have obtained the following data:
a.   The 14 percent note receivable is due from Tysinger Corporation and is secured by a first mortgage on land sold to Tysinger by Elliott on December 21, 1998. The note was to have been paid in 20 equal quarterly payments beginning March 31, 1999, plus interest. Tysinger, however, is in very poor financial condition and has not made any principal or interest payments to date.
b.   The Bowen common stock was purchased for cash on September 21, 1998, in the market where the stock is traded actively. The stock is used as security for the note payable and is held by the bank. Elliott's investment in Bowen represents approximately 1 percent of Bowen's total outstanding shares.
c.   Elliott's investment in Woods represents 40 percent of the outstanding common stock that is actively traded. Woods is audited by another auditor and has a December 31 year end.
d.   Elliott neither purchased nor sold any equity investments during the year other than what's noted above.
   Required: For the following account balances, discuss: (1) the types of evidence you should obtain and (2) the audit procedures you should perform.
1.   14 Percent Secured Note Receivable.
2.   Bowen Common Stock.
3.   Woods Common Stock.
4.   Dividend Revenue.

(AICPA Adapted)

Problem 16-6

Williston & May
Marketable Securities
December 31, 1999

Description of Security											Dividend & Interest		
Corp. Bonds	%	Year Due	Serial No.	Face Value of Bonds	Gen. Ledger 1/1	Purch. in 1999	Sold in 1999	Cost	Gen. Ledger 12/31	12/31 Market	Pay Date(s)	Amount Rec.	Accruals 12/31
A	6	2003	21-7	$ 10,000	$ 9,400ᵃ				$ 9,400	$ 9,100	1/15	$ 300^{b,d}	$ 275
D	4	2004	73-0	30,000	27,500ᵃ				27,500	26,220	7/15	300^{b,d}	100
G	9	2005	16-4	5,000	4,000ᵃ				4,000	5,080	12/1	1,200^{b,d}	188
Rc	5	2006	08-2	70,000	66,000ᵃ		$57,000^{b,c}	66,000			8/1	450^{b,d}	
Sc	10	2007	07-4	100,000		$100,000^{c,e}			100,000	101,250	7/1	5,000^{b,d}	5,000
					$106,900	$100,000	$57,000	$66,000	$140,900	$141,650		$7,250	$5,563
					a, f	f	f	f	f, g	f		f	f
Stocks													
P 1,000 shs.— Common			1044		$ 7,500ᵃ				$ 7,500	$ 7,600	3/1	$ 750^{b,d}	
											6/1	750^{b,d}	
											9/1	750^{b,d}	
											12/1	750^{b,d}	$ 250
U 50 shs.— Common			8530		9,700ᵃ				9,700	9,800	2/1	800^{b,d}	
											8/1	800^{b,d}	667
					$ 17,200				$ 17,200	$ 17,400		$4,600	$ 917
					a, f				f, g	f		f	f

a   Beginning balances reconciled with 1998 working papers.
b   Traced to cash receipts.
c   Minutes examined (purchase and sales approved by the board of directors).
d   Reconciled with 1099.
e   Confirmed by tracing to broker's advice.
f   Total footed.
g   Reconciled with general ledger.

16-8 *Auditing Noncurrent Investments*

Harold Brodkey is engaged in the audit of the Longview Corporation's financial statements for the year ended December 31, 1999, and is about to begin auditing noncurrent investment securities. Longview's records indicate the company owns various bearer bonds, as well as 25 percent of the outstanding common stock of Industrial National Inc. Brodkey is satisfied with evidence supporting the presumption that Longview exercises significant influence over Industrial National. The various securities are at two locations:

- Recently acquired securities are in the company's safe in the custody of the treasurer.
- All other securities are in the company's bank safe-deposit box.

All the securities in Longview's portfolio are actively traded in a broad market.

Required:
1. Assuming that control procedures for securities may be relied on in assessing control risk below the maximum, what are the objectives of the audit of these noncurrent investment securities?
2. What audit procedures should Brodkey perform to audit Longview's noncurrent investment securities?

16-9 *Drafting Tests of Controls From an Internal Control Questionnaire: Debt and Equity Transactions*

Following are selected questions from an internal control questionnaire relating to a company's debt and equity transactions. A *yes* response to any question indicates a potential strength of the system, and a *no* response indicates a potential weakness.

a. Are all long-term debt and other borrowings authorized by the board of directors?
b. Is an officer responsible for determining whether all debt covenants are complied with?
c. Are unissued bonds and notes prenumbered consecutively and controlled by an official independent of recording?
d. Are interest payments and accruals recalculated periodically?
e. Are unissued stock certificates prenumbered consecutively and safeguarded?
f. Are treasury shares adequately controlled and accounted for?
g. Are dividend payments and accruals recalculated periodically?

Required: Assume that inquiries indicate no apparent deficiencies in internal control. Draft tests of controls that you believe would provide persuasive evidence that no deficiencies exist.

16-10 *Relating Errors, Frauds, Audit Procedures, and Assertions in Substantive Tests of Long-Term Debt*

Following are errors, frauds, or other circumstances that an auditor might encounter as a result of applying audit tests to long-term debt as of the balance sheet date:

a. Detailed long-term debt records may not be accurate.
b. All debt instruments are held by banks.
c. There is no documentation supporting a bond indenture.
d. Proceeds from the bond issuance have all been expended.
e. Various debt instruments required interest payments on the last day of all but two months.

Required: For each of the above, indicate: (1) a specific substantive test or tests that might address the error, fraud, or circumstance and (2) the financial statement assertion addressed by each test.

16-11 *Internal Controls Over Investments, Debt, and Capital Stock*

Ronald Ondeyko, CPA, is considering the LaSalle Company's internal controls over investments, long-term debt, and capital stock. System documentation was accomplished with a questionnaire and a narrative memorandum and, in conjunction with a transaction walk-through, revealed the following potential deficiencies in internal control:

a. The historical cost of all long-term debt exceeds company policies for debt to equity ratios.

b. The company entered into a long-term debt agreement requiring a 2 to 1 current ratio at year end, yet the current ratio when the agreement was signed was approximately 1.5 to 1.

c. Internally held securities have been misplaced occasionally, though in all cases the securities were recovered.

d. In an open letter to the board of directors, a group of shareholders criticized the company for investing in a domestic corporation alleged to have violated human rights in a foreign country.

e. Signatures on investment authorizations vary from the chairman of the board's investment committee to the treasurer and controller.

Required: For each potential deficiency, indicate a control procedure or procedures that management could implement to reduce the likelihood of errors or frauds.

16-12 *Auditing Debt Covenants*

The following covenants are extracted from the indenture of a bond issue. Although the bond due date is 2016, failure to comply with any covenant automatically advances the due date of the loan to the date of noncompliance:

a. The debtor company shall maintain a working capital ratio of 2 to 1 at all times, and, in any fiscal year following a failure to maintain said ratio, the company shall restrict compensation of officers to a total of $250,000. Officers for this purpose shall include chairman of the board of directors, president, all vice presidents, secretary, and treasurer.

b. The debtor company shall keep all property which is security for this debt insured against loss by fire to the extent of 100 percent of actual value. Policies of insurance constituting this protection shall be filed with the trustee.

c. The debtor company shall pay all taxes legally assessed against property which is security for this debt within the time provided by law for payment without penalty, and shall deposit receipted tax bills or equally acceptable evidence of payment with the trustee.

d. A sinking fund shall be deposited with the trustee by semiannual payments of $300,000, from which the trustee shall, at his or her discretion, purchase bonds of this issue.

Required:

1. Draft audit procedures for each covenant.
2. Comment on any disclosures you think necessary.

(AICPA Adapted)

16-13 *Auditing Long-Term Debt*

You were engaged to audit the financial statements of Ronlyn Corporation for the year ended June 30, 1999. On May 1, 1999, the corporation borrowed $500,000 from Second National Bank to finance plant expansion. The agreement provided for annual payments of principal and interest over five years. The existing plant was pledged as security for the loan. Due to unexpected difficulties in acquiring the new building site, plant expansion had not begun at June 30, 1999. To make use of the borrowed funds, management decided to invest in stocks and bonds, and on May 16, 1999, the $500,000 was invested in securities.

Required:

1. What are the audit objectives in the audit of long-term debt?
2. Prepare an audit program for the audit of the long-term note agreement between Ronlyn and Second National Bank.

3.   How could you verify the security position of Ronlyn at June 30, 1999?
4.   In your audit of investments, how would you:
     a.   Verify the dividend or interest income recorded?
     b.   Determine market value?
     c.   Establish the authority for security purchases?

(AICPA Adapted)

16-14   *Relating Errors, Frauds, Audit Procedures, and Assertions in Substantive Tests of Capital Stock*

Following are errors, frauds, or other circumstances that an auditor might encounter as a result of applying audit tests to capital stock as of December 31, the balance sheet date:

a.   Shareholders' equity accounts are not accurate.
b.   Stock dividends were issued during the year.
c.   Treasury stock was purchased in December.
d.   Dividends were declared and paid before the end of the year.
e.   The client's common stock is traded actively on a national stock exchange.

Required: For each of the above, indicate: (1) a specific substantive test or tests that might address the error, fraud, or circumstance and (2) the financial statement assertion addressed by each test.

16-15   *Auditing Shareholders' Equity*

On May 1, 1999 you were engaged by a committee of shareholders to perform a special audit as of December 31, 1998, of the shareholders' equity of the Major Corporation, whose stock is actively traded on a stock exchange. The shareholders who engaged you believe that information in the shareholders' equity section of the published annual report for the year ended December 31, 1998 is incorrect. If your conclusions confirm their suspicions, they intend to use the report in a proxy fight. Management agrees to permit your audit but refuses to permit any direct confirmation with shareholders. To secure cooperation in the audit, the committee of shareholders has agreed to this limitation, and you have been instructed to limit your audit accordingly. You have been instructed also to exclude the audit of revenue and expense accounts for the year.

   Required:
1.   Prepare an audit program to audit shareholders' equity, assuming no scope limitations.
2.   Describe any special auditing procedures you would undertake given the limitations and other special circumstances you confront in the Major Corporation engagement.
3.   Discuss the content of your report for the special engagement, including comments on the opinion that you would issue.

(AICPA Adapted)

16-16   *Auditing Shareholders' Equity*

You are engaged in an audit of the financial statements of Pate Corporation for the year ended December 31, 1999. The financial statements and records of Pate Corporation have not been audited by another auditor in prior years. The shareholders' equity section of Pate Corporation's balance sheet at December 31, 1999, follows:

Shareholders' equity:	
Capital stock—10,000 shares of $10 par value	
authorized; 5,000 shares issued and outstanding	$ 50,000
Capital contributed in excess of par value	32,580
Retained earnings	47,320
Total shareholders' equity	$ 129,900

Founded in 1997, Pate Corporation has ten shareholders and serves as its own registrar and transfer agent. There are no capital stock subscription contracts in effect.

Required:
1. Prepare a program to audit the three accounts constituting the Pate Corporation's shareholders' equity section.
2. Why do auditors audit retained earnings?

(AICPA Adapted)

16-17 *Discrepancies Between Authorized and Outstanding Shares*
The Eaton Company was incorporated July 10, 1999, with authorized capital as follows:
a. Common stock, Class A, 20,000 shares, par value $25 per share.
b. Common stock, Class B, 100,000 shares, par value $5 per share.
The capital stock account in the general ledger is credited with only one item in the year 1999—capital stock sold for cash, at par—as follows:
a. Class A, 12,000 shares.
b. Class B, 60,000 shares.
The sum of open certificate stubs in the stock certificate books at December 31, 1999 indicates that 82,000 shares of stock were outstanding.

Required:
1. Explain the discrepancy.
2. What procedures would you perform to determine the cause of the discrepancy?

(AICPA Adapted)

16-18 *Earnings Manipulation and Financial Instruments*
The Signet Corporation management is transferring securities across their held-to-maturity, trading, and available-for-sale portfolios. Within the industry, management has the reputation of being aggressive, both in operating the business and in securities trading. In prior years, income from investments has exceeded 10 percent of reported earnings.

Required: Identify, and explain the motive for, the key questions an auditor must ask to judge whether management's accounting for financial instruments is appropriate.

RESEARCH PROJECT

MANAGEMENT DISCRETION IN ACCOUNTING FOR FINANCIAL INSTRUMENTS

In September 1990, the chairman of the Securities Exchange Commission criticized carrying investments at amortized cost and argued that, in the banking and savings & loan industries, "serious consideration must be given to reporting all investment securities at market value." Following several years of inconsistent accounting practices across industries, and calls to mark selected assets to market, the Financial Accounting Standards Board issued *Statement of Financial Accounting Standards No. 115*, "Accounting for Certain Investments in Debt and Equity Securities," which responds largely to the issue of consistency, partly to the issue of market value, and, in the process, leaves some room for management discretion in managing earnings.

Required: Using the newspaper and magazines file in NEXIS, Mead Data Central's automated data retrieval system, or newspapers and magazines in a library, select an article about a publicly traded company's accounting for financial instruments. Using the annual report file in the National Automated Accounting Research System (NAARS), or copies of annual reports in a library, select the annual report of the same company issued for the fiscal year referred to in the article. Draft a report that accomplishes the following:

1. Summarizes the article, indicating key issues, like management's or the financial community's reaction to the effect of disclosures about financial instruments on reported income.
2. Lists and explains questions an auditor would likely pose to the management of the company you've selected.
3. Summarizes the company's disclosures about financial instruments that appear in the footnotes (e.g., the footnote summarizing accounting policies, usually Note 1).

17

Completing an Engagement

Major topics discussed in this chapter are:

- **Substantive tests of revenue and expense accounts.**
- **Procedures for auditing accounting estimates, including loss contingencies.**
- **Review for related party transactions.**
- **Subsequent events.**
- **Inquiries of a client's legal counsel.**
- **Role and content of a management representation letter.**
- **Process of forming an opinion.**
- **Responsibility for communicating with the audit committee.**
- **Subsequent discovery of facts existing at the report date.**
- **Consideration of omitted procedures after the report date.**

Completing an assurance, attestation, or audit engagement poses for the practitioner some of the same questions: What risks are imposed by related parties? Are management's assertions dependent on estimates or legal interpretations? Which of management's oral representations should we ask be cast in writing? How shall we go about forming an opinion on management's assertions? What ought we say to directors or trustees that we might not say in our report? and What risks do we incur after issuing a report for facts we learn later about our client or work? This chapter addresses these and other questions a practitioner confronts when "wrapping up" an engagement, although most of the illustrations relate to the service for which the profession has collected the most experience: financial statement auditing.

The chapter begins by distinguishing between, and illustrating, tests of details and analytical procedures commonly used to test revenue and expense accounts. Next, the chapter addresses procedures for auditing accounting estimates and for "wrapping up" an engagement: reviewing for related party transactions, reviewing for events that occur subsequent to the balance sheet date, making inquiries of a client's lawyer, and obtaining a management representation letter. In turn, the chapter discusses how and why an auditor performs overall analytical procedures, reviews working papers in detail, and arranges for an independent technical review of working papers by an audit partner not otherwise assigned to the engagement—each of which is an integral part of the auditor's process of formulating an opinion on an entity's financial statements taken as a whole. Finally, the chapter discusses an auditor's responsibility to communicate with the audit committee, and two issues related to the period after the auditor issues an audit report: the subsequent discovery of facts existing at the report date, and the consideration of procedures unknowingly omitted during the engagement.

SUBSTANTIVE TESTS OF REVENUE AND EXPENSE ACCOUNTS

A financial statement audit performed in accordance with *generally accepted auditing standards* encompasses all the basic financial statements, not just the balance sheet. Yet the discussion of substantive procedures in Chapters 10 through 16 focuses primarily on balance sheet accounts, and only secondarily on income statement accounts. Although focusing on the balance sheet is not uncommon in practice, an auditor must also perform substantive tests of revenue and expense accounts, because: (1) an audit report extends not only to the balance sheet, but also to the income statement, and (2) some financial statement users are compelled equally if not more by results of operations, which are measured by the income statement, than by financial position, which is measured in part by the balance sheet.

Not all of the financial statement assertions introduced in Chapter 6 are necessarily relevant to revenue and expense accounts. Rather, the most relevant assertions are occurrence, valuation and allocation, completeness, and presentation and disclosure, each of which can be tested either by direct tests of details or by analytical procedures, or both. The following discusses and illustrates each type of test.

TESTS OF DETAILS

Extensive tests of details, rather than analytical procedures, are appropriate when:

- Control risk is at the maximum,
- Transaction volume is low,
- Analytical procedures reveal unusual or unexpected results, or
- An account(s) requires special attention.

Analytical procedures applied during the final stages of an audit are usually intended as tests of the reasonableness of an account balance or disclosure. But their value to an auditor depends highly on the effectiveness of an entity's internal controls, since poorly designed or ineffective controls could result in misstated accounts and, therefore, in relationships—for example, ratios or trends—that are neither reasonable nor reliable. Thus, when *control risk is at the maximum*, an auditor should apply direct tests of details, rather than risk being misled by analytical procedures that produce unreliable measures.

Although analytical procedures are appropriate regardless of transaction volume, very low volume accounts are better tested by direct tests of details, since all of the recorded transactions can likely be tested, thereby minimizing uncertainty about whether an account is presented fairly. In fact, analytical procedures are not particularly informative for *low-volume accounts* because the information content of minor account balance fluctuations is often trivial.

As indicated throughout the book, tests of details are particularly appropriate when analytical procedures reveal *unusual or unexpected results*. For example, declining receivables balances coupled with steady collections and rising sales could signal overstated sales and would prompt an auditor to design detailed tests of recorded sales.

Some income statement accounts require *special attention*, thereby rendering analytical procedures inappropriate. For example, charitable contributions must be listed in detail on income tax returns, and executive compensation must be disclosed separately in Securities and Exchange Commission filings. Thus, for these among other accounts, auditors typically opt for direct tests of details rather than rely exclusively on analytical procedures.

The nature and extent of direct tests of details for revenue and expense accounts will vary depending on the circumstances, but in all cases the auditor must address the financial statement assertions listed earlier. For example, an auditor might address occurrence—i.e., determine whether recorded revenue and expense transactions actually occurred—by comparing recorded revenue with underlying documents such as deposits and contracts, as illustrated in the analysis of other income in Figure 17-1, or by physically examining evidence

Figure 17-1:   Direct Tests of Details: Other Income

BB6
AP 1/10/00

The Wilson Company
Analysis of Other Income
December 31, 1999

Date	Received From	Description	Amount
April 30	Weil & White, Inc. Los Angeles, California	Royalty Income: Annual royalty due by April 30 of each year for Weil & White's use of Wilson patents on centrifuge machines. Royalty based on Weil & White production through March 31.	$7,430[a]
December 31	Sansibar & Company Chicago, Illinois	Rent Income: Initial month's rent for property at 6204 Mitchell Street, Chicago, rented for 12 months to Sansibar.	850[b]
			$8,280
			c

a   Reconciled with royalty report (see workpaper BB9), with royalty contract, and with cash receipts journal.
b   Reconciled with rent agreement and with cash receipts journal; agreement expires November 30, 2000.
c   Footed and reconciled with general ledger.

of expenditures, such as advertising copy in a local newspaper, as illustrated in Figure 17-2. Typically, valuation is tested by extending, footing, and cross-footing detail schedules prepared by the client to support recorded revenues and expenses and reconciling totals with balances in the general ledger. In addition, an auditor might trace recorded amounts for a sample of transactions to supporting documents, such as deposit slips and bank statement clearings. An auditor can test completeness by performing tests of cutoff for transactions occurring near the balance sheet date.

The occurrence, valuation, and completeness of revenue that has been earned but not yet received, or expenses incurred but not yet paid, could be tested by recalculations that match incurred costs with earned revenue in accordance with the accounting concept of matching.

ANALYTICAL PROCEDURES

In lieu of or in addition to tests of details, an auditor can test the reasonableness of recorded revenue and expense balances by **analytical procedures** that focus

Figure 17-2: Direct Tests of Details: Advertising Expense

BB12
AP 1/13/00

The Wilson Company
Analysis of Advertising Expense
December 31, 1999

Date	Payee	Description	Amount
March 30	Wire & Cable Monthly Chicago, Illinois	Full-page advertisement for cable-extruding machinery.	$ 950[a]
May 15	Chemical Weekly New York, New York	Half-page advertisement for recently introduced chemical centrifuge machinery. Ad ran for six weekly issues, beginning June 1.	1,500[b]
August 10	St. Louis Post-Dispatch St. Louis, Missouri	Full-page color ad in paper's Sunday Supplement, advertising Wilson's support and involvement in youth job-training program.	400[a]
			$2,850
			c

a Examined ad copy and invoice; traced to cash disbursements journal.
b Examined ad copy and contract; traced to cash disbursements journal.
c Footed and reconciled with general ledger.

on relationships over time and between accounts. Relationships over time provide evidence about the fluctuation of account balances from one period to the next. For example, an auditor might compare the balances of current year revenue and expense accounts with balances for the prior year, obtaining explanations from management for unusual fluctuations. In turn, relationships between accounts provide evidence about whether the balance of one account is reasonable in relation to another account.

An example of analytical procedures for payroll appears in the audit program in Figure 14-6 and the related discussion. Note that the payroll tests emphasize analytical procedures and, therefore, assume that controls over payroll are reliable and that transaction volume is relatively high—otherwise, direct tests of details would have been more appropriate.

AUDITING ACCOUNTING ESTIMATES

Most transactions and events can be readily tested by an auditor because the audit population is known with certainty, supporting evidence generally exists, and there are no uncertainties about the existence of an asset, liability, income, or expense. However, auditors must also apply audit procedures to **accounting estimates**, which are financial statement elements, items, or accounts that have been *approximated by management* in order to disclose them in the accounting period that gave rise to their economic substance. Accounting estimates are often necessary because the valuation of some accounts, or the measurement of some amounts, may be uncertain pending the outcome of future events, or because data about past events cannot be accumulated on a timely, cost-effective basis. Examples include:

- Airline passenger revenue,
- Warranty claims,
- Allowance for uncollectible receivables,
- Obsolete inventory,
- Depreciation and amortization,
- Accrued property taxes,
- Pension costs,
- Subscription income,
- Percentage of completion income on construction contracts, and
- Loss contingencies.

Although management is responsible to make accounting estimates, auditors are responsible under *Statement on Auditing Standards No. 57*, "Auditing Accounting Estimates" (AU Sec. 342), to evaluate the reasonableness of management's estimates.

EVALUATING ACCOUNTING ESTIMATES

Accounting estimates are more susceptible to material misstatement than factual data, partly because estimates involve uncertainty and subjectivity, and partly because controls over estimates are more difficult for management to establish than controls over factual data. An auditor's objectives in evaluating accounting estimates are to:

- Provide reasonable assurance that management developed all material estimates, and
- Assure that the estimates are reasonable and are presented in the financial statements in accordance with GAAP.

The risk of material misstatement for accounting estimates will vary depending on the controls established by management, the complexity and subjectivity of the estimation process, the availability and reliability of relevant evidence, and the nature and uncertainty of assumptions made by management. In evaluating the reasonableness of accounting estimates, an auditor should obtain an understanding of how management developed the estimate and then, based on his or her understanding, consider:

- Reviewing and testing the process used by management,
- Developing an independent estimate for comparison, and/or
- Reviewing relevant transactions or events that occurred subsequent to the balance sheet date.

LOSS CONTINGENCIES

One among the accounting estimates listed above, a **loss contingency**, is defined in *Statement of Financial Accounting Standards No. 5*, "Accounting for Contingencies," as ". . . an existing condition, situation, or set of circumstances involving uncertainty as to possible gain or loss to an enterprise that will ultimately be resolved when one or more future events occurs or fails to occur." When completing an engagement, auditors are particularly concerned with the existence of unrecorded loss contingencies, because failure to recognize a material loss contingency would result in overstated income and understated liabilities and, therefore, in materially misstated financial statements. As a result, one of the procedures typically performed when completing an audit is a review for potential contingent liabilities. Examples of loss contingencies include:

- Pending or threatened litigation for patent infringements, product warranties, or product defects,
- Guarantees of third-party obligations,
- Discounted notes receivable or factored accounts receivable, and
- Disputed income tax deductions.

Loss contingencies should be recognized and a liability recorded in the accounts if: (1) it is *probable* that a liability had been incurred at the balance sheet date, and (2) the amount of the loss can be *reasonably estimated*. However, if the loss is either probable or estimable—that is, either (1) or (2) but not both—or if there is a *reasonable possibility* that a liability may have been incurred, then the financial statements should include a footnote explaining the nature of the contingency and an estimate of the possible loss, or range of loss, or a statement that an estimate cannot be made.

Searching for Loss Contingencies

Searching for potential loss contingencies requires that auditors exercise not only keen judgment but some creativity, since the existence of contingent liabilities is not always readily apparent. At a minimum, auditors usually perform the following procedures to search for unrecorded loss contingencies:

- Ask management about the possibility of unrecorded contingencies.
- Read minutes of the board of directors' and shareholders' meetings.
- Read contracts, loan agreements, lease agreements, and similar documents.
- Review reports prepared by agents of the Internal Revenue Service and other taxing authorities.
- Analyze legal expenses for the year, and examine documentation (e.g., invoices) from attorneys that may suggest litigation is pending or in progress.
- Review current year working papers for indications of potential contingencies.

Importantly, auditors are also responsible for loss contingencies that occur or are discovered *after* the balance sheet date, because they could be material subsequent events, as discussed later in the chapter.

COMPLETING AN AUDIT

After completing the audit procedures discussed in Chapters 10 through 16 and in this chapter, an auditor performs additional procedures that are designed to "wrap up" the engagement and to generate additional evidence that may affect either the conclusions reached for individual accounts or the auditor's report. These procedures are:

- Reviewing for related party transactions,
- Reviewing for subsequent events,
- Making inquiries of a client's legal counsel,
- Obtaining a management representation letter, and
- Forming an opinion.

Importantly, an auditor's responsibility for audited financial statements does not end either on the report date or when an audit report is physically communicated to the client. Rather, an auditor continues to be responsible for the:

- Communication with the audit committee,

and, under certain circumstances, for the

- Subsequent discovery of facts existing at the date of the auditor's report, and
- Consideration of omitted procedures after the report date.

All these procedures and responsibilities are discussed separately below.

REVIEW FOR RELATED PARTY TRANSACTIONS

In most cases, parties to a transaction are unrelated and independent, thereby increasing the likelihood that the transaction is at "arm's length"—that is, a bargained exchange. Occasionally, however, parties to a transaction are not independent. Rather, they are related and may include the reporting entity; its affiliates; principal owners, managers, and their immediate family members; and others in a position to influence or to be influenced. The significance of a **related party transaction** is that disclosing the legal form of the transaction may not accurately reflect its economic substance. *Statement on Auditing Standards No. 45*, "Omnibus Statement on Auditing Standards: 1983" (AU Sec. 334), addresses related party transactions.

A relationship between or among related parties does not necessarily mean a transaction is not at arm's length. But an auditor should be aware, nevertheless, that the *likelihood* of a related party transaction not being at arm's length increases when management has incentives to manipulate earnings. For example, the likelihood would increase if management demonstrates an unusual urgency to maintain a favorable earnings trend in the hope of supporting the company's stock price, if management made an overly optimistic earnings forecast at the beginning of the year, if the entity depends wholly or primarily on a single or relatively few products for the ongoing success of the business, if the entity operates in a declining industry characterized by a large number of business failures, or if there is significant pending litigation, especially litigation between shareholders and management. Any of these situations could be sufficient motivation for a client to engage in a related party transaction that is not at arm's length.

Certain relationships, such as parent-subsidiary or investor-investee, are obvious to an auditor, and any material transactions between these parties should be investigated. However, to determine the existence of less obvious related parties, the auditor needs to follow specific procedures. For example, apart from evaluating management's procedures for identifying related parties, the auditor could: (1) review filings with the SEC and other regulatory agencies for the names of related parties and for other businesses in which the entity's officers and directors occupy directorship or management positions, (2) determine the names of all pensions and trusts established for the benefit of employees and the names of their officers and trustees, (3) review the shareholder listings of closely held companies to identify principal shareholders, and (4) review material investment transactions to determine whether the nature and extent of investments during the period creates related parties.

Once related parties have been identified, the auditor then examines any material transactions management entered into with these parties. But, how does the auditor distinguish related party transactions from others, particularly those that are unrecorded and/or not at arm's length? The following procedures provide guidance for identifying these transactions:

- Provide the audit team with the names of known related parties.
- Review the minutes of meetings of the board of directors and executive or operating committees for information about material transactions authorized or discussed.
- Review proxy material filed with the SEC for information about material transactions with related parties.
- Review conflict-of-interests statements obtained from management.
- Review the extent and nature of business transacted with major customers, suppliers, borrowers, and lenders for indications of previously undisclosed relationships.
- Review invoices from law firms for indications of the existence of related parties or related party transactions.
- Review confirmations of loans receivable and payable for indications of guarantees.

After identifying related party transactions, an auditor should apply the audit procedures necessary to assess the purpose, nature, and extent of the transactions and their effect on the financial statements. In general, the procedures should extend beyond simply making inquiries of management and might include obtaining an understanding of the business purpose of the transactions, examining documentation (such as invoices or contracts), and determining whether the transactions were approved by the board of directors. The accounting considerations and required disclosures for related party transactions are discussed in FASB *Statement of Financial Accounting Standards No. 57*, "Related Party Disclosures."

REVIEW FOR SUBSEQUENT EVENTS

An auditor is primarily concerned with the balance sheet as of a particular date, such as December 31, 1999, and related statements of earnings, retained earnings, and cash flows for a particular period, such as January 1 through December 31, 1999. However, events sometimes occur or become known subsequent to the balance sheet date but before issuance of the audit report—the **subsequent period**—that have an effect on financial statement disclosures. An independent auditor's responsibility for subsequent events and related audit procedures is addressed in AU Sections 560 and 561 of the AICPA's *Codification of Statements on Auditing Standards*.

Subsequent events are classified into two major types:

- *Type I Events.* Subsequent events that reveal or confirm conditions *existing at or before* the balance sheet date and that require *adjustment* to the financial statements.
- *Type II Events.* Subsequent events that reveal conditions *arising after* the balance sheet date and that require *disclosure*, but not financial statement adjustment.

Type I Events

Type I subsequent events relate to conditions existing at or before the balance sheet date that affect estimates inherent in the process of preparing financial statements. Accordingly, the financial statements should be adjusted for any material changes in estimates. Examples include:

- Collection of receivables or settlement of liabilities in amounts substantially different from amounts recorded at the balance sheet date,
- Realization of a loss on the sale of investments, inventories, or properties held for sale when the subsequent sale merely confirms a previously existing unrecognized loss, and
- Discontinuance, at an estimated loss, of operations of a subsidiary where the contributing circumstances unfolded over a period of time prior to the balance sheet date.

Some Type I subsequent events require only a reclassification of amounts, rather than adjustment, and therefore do not affect recorded net income or loss. A common example is reclassifying long-term liabilities to short-term when an expected refinancing arrangement did not occur before the liabilities became due.

Type II Events

Type II subsequent events relate to conditions that did not exist at or before the balance sheet date, yet are disclosed because they may be of such significance that the financial statements would be misleading if the events are not disclosed. Normally, financial statements are supplemented with pro forma information giving retroactive effect to Type II events. Examples include:

- Business combinations,
- Issuance of new notes, bonds, or other indebtedness,
- Changes in capital structure,
- Declaration of unusual cash or stock dividends or omission of a regular dividend, and
- Damage from fire, flood, or other casualty.

Borderline Cases

In some cases, it's not altogether clear whether an event should be classified as Type I or Type II. For example, the sale or abandonment of significant manufacturing facilities typically results from careful management studies that, if not documented, are at least substantially contemplated over a somewhat lengthy period of time. Even if not contemplated, certainly the conditions leading to the motive for sale or abandonment (e.g., significant losses over several periods) would have arisen prior to the balance sheet date. Thus, in the case of a sale or abandonment, an argument could be made for either Type I or Type II treatment: Type I because conditions giving rise to the event probably occurred before year end, or Type II because the economic impact of the event did not occur until after year end.

A related question is the decision about whether adjustment or disclosure is really necessary at all. For example, declaring a regular quarterly dividend after year end may not be considered worthy of disclosure if the entity has paid dividends for several years. That is, if a dividend is normally paid, disclosure may not be informative. On the other hand, a first-time dividend declared after year end certainly would represent useful information and should be disclosed.

Procedures in the Subsequent Period

During the subsequent period, an auditor performs the majority of, if not all, year end substantive tests but is also responsible to detect and, if warranted, disclose material subsequent events. Some year end substantive procedures, such as cutoff testing, partly address subsequent events, but are insufficient to discharge an auditor's responsibility for detecting and disclosing subsequent events. As a result, auditors typically perform the following procedures at or near the completion of field work to detect subsequent events:

- Read the latest available interim financial statements (e.g., the quarter ending March 31, 2000) and compare them with the financial statements being reported on (e.g., December 31, 1999).
- Inquire of management:
  - Whether the interim statements have been prepared on the same basis as the statements being audited,
  - Whether any substantial contingent liabilities or commitments existed at the date of the balance sheet,
  - Whether there was any significant change in the capital stock, long-term debt, or working capital to the date of inquiry,

- Whether there were any significant changes in estimates for amounts included or disclosed in the financial statements, and
- Whether any unusual adjustments were made during the period from the balance sheet date to the date of inquiry.
- Read the available minutes of meetings of shareholders, directors, and appropriate committees, such as the finance committee.
- Assemble pertinent findings resulting from inquiries of legal counsel (discussed later in this chapter) and other auditing procedures for litigation, claims, and assessments.
- Obtain a letter of representation from management (discussed later in this chapter) as of the date of the auditor's report.

In addition, the auditor would make any additional inquiries or design and perform additional procedures to address any questions or uncertainties arising from the above procedures. Disclosures would be handled as follows.

Disclosure

Although they require adjustments to financial statements, Type I subsequent events generally need not also be disclosed in notes to the financial statements. Type II events, in contrast, should be fully disclosed in any of the following alternative forms:

- Explanatory note.
- Parenthetical explanation.
- Reference in the financial statements to pro forma information.
- If warranted, a qualified opinion, adverse opinion, or disclaimer of opinion.

To illustrate an *explanatory note*, assume The Wilson Company incurred a contingent liability on February 5, 2000, and the auditor's report is dated February 7, 2000. The information could be disclosed in an explanatory note as follows:

Note 12: Contingent liabilities.

On February 5, 2000, management was advised by the U.S. Attorney located in New York City that a federal grand jury in New York had indicted the company on charges of conspiracy and fraud in the 1999 sale of the company's common stock to First Source Investment Company. Management has not had sufficient time to evaluate the effect this indictment will have on the company; however, management believes that the fine, if any, that could be levied against the company if found guilty of the actions charged, would not exceed $225,000.

Parenthetical explanations are simply brief comments next to the accounts affected in the financial statements. For example, liquidation of a material note payable after the balance sheet date could be disclosed in parentheses aside Notes Payable on the balance sheet.

Pro forma information—that is, disclosing what the financial statements would have looked like if the event had occurred on or before year end—may be appropriate if any Type II subsequent events are so material that historical financial statements alone would be misleading. Pro forma statements, however, can be misleading if certain events are included and other significant events are not.

Issuing a *qualified or adverse opinion, or disclaiming an opinion* is typically done only as a last resort, when all other efforts to persuade the client to use alternative disclosure methods have failed. The wording of these reports is discussed in Chapter 3.

MAKE INQUIRIES OF CLIENT'S LEGAL COUNSEL

Occasionally, an economic event can impact an entity's financial position more heavily than a transaction, a prominent example being loss contingencies, discussed earlier. A loss contingency that arises from litigation, claims, and assessments, though, is not only an accounting and disclosure matter, but also a legal matter, since the probability and amount of loss is determined by arbitration, administrative proceedings, or the courts. Thus, determining the existence of a loss contingency is often a legal question, requiring that an auditor communicate directly with a client's attorney about liabilities arising from litigation, claims, and assessments.

Because of their own potential legal exposure for disclosing inaccurate or confidential information, attorneys are cautious about furnishing auditors with letters divulging legal matters, sometimes called legal letters, particularly matters involving unasserted claims—that is, claims for which a plaintiff may have a legal right but has not yet taken action. For example, an attorney may be aware that a client has infringed on another company's patent and therefore that a suit could be brought by the injured party. Consider the attorney's precarious position: If the attorney divulges the unasserted claim to the auditor, and the claim is then disclosed in the audited financial statements, the disclosure may well result in a claim being asserted against the client.

Following extensive correspondence between the AICPA and the American Bar Association about the attorney's position and the auditor's needs, the Auditing Standards Board issued *Statement on Auditing Standards No. 12*, "Inquiry of a Client's Lawyer Concerning Litigation, Claims, and Assessments" (AU Sec. 337). *SAS No. 12* requires that a list of legal issues be prepared by the client's *management*, rather than the client's attorney, and then sent to the attorney, requesting information about: (1) pending or threatened litigation, claims, and assessments, and (2) unasserted claims and assessments.

As illustrated in Figure 17-3, the attorney is requested to furnish the following information for all pending or threatened litigation, claims, and assessments, and to comment on differences between the attorney's and management's views:

- A description of the nature of the matter, progress to date, and action the client intends to take.
- An evaluation of the likelihood of an unfavorable outcome and an estimate, if one can be made, of the amount or range of potential loss.
- A statement that management's list of pending or threatened claims is complete, or identification of any omissions.

As also illustrated in Figure 17-3, for unasserted claims, an attorney is requested to identify any differences between management's and his or her views. Thus, *SAS No. 12* requires that an attorney respond to management's representations about pending or threatened litigation and unasserted claims

Figure 17-3:   Inquiry Letter to Legal Counsel

THE WILSON COMPANY
15 Artubus Drive
Stony Book, NY 11790

February 14, 2000

John O'Hara
Attorney at Law
126 East 57th Street
New York, New York 10025

Dear Mr. O'Hara:

In connection with an audit of our financial statements at December 31, 1999, and for the period then ended, management has prepared and furnished to our auditors, Cheever & Yates LLPs, a description and evaluation of certain contingencies, including those set forth below, involving matters with respect to which you have been engaged and to which you have devoted substantive attention on behalf of The Wilson Company in the form of legal consultation or representation. These contingencies are regarded by management as material for this purpose. Your response should include matters that existed at December 31, 1999, and during the period from that date to the date of your response.

Pending or Threatened Litigation

[In this section, management would list all pending or threatened litigation, including the following information for each: (1) the nature of the litigation, (2) the progress of the case, (3) the way management is responding or intends to respond, and (4) an evaluation of the likelihood of an unfavorable outcome and an estimate, if one can be made, of the amount or range of potential loss.]

Please furnish to our auditors such explanation, if any, that you consider necessary to supplement the foregoing information, including an explanation of those matters about which your views may differ from those stated and an indication of the omission of any pending or threatened litigation, claims, and assessments or a statement that the list of such matters is complete.

Unasserted Claims and Assessments

[In this section, management would list all probable unasserted claims and assessments, including the following for each: (1) the nature of the matter, (2) the way management intends to respond if the claim is asserted, and (3) an evaluation of the likelihood of an unfavorable outcome and an estimate, if one can be made, of the amount or range of potential loss.]

Please furnish to our auditors such explanation, if any, that you consider necessary to supplement the foregoing information, including an explanation of those matters about which your views may differ from those stated.

We understand that whenever, in the course of performing legal services for us with respect to a matter recognized to involve an unasserted possible claim that may call for financial statement disclosure, you have formed a professional conclusion that we should disclose or consider disclosure concerning such possible claim

Figure 17-3:   *(continued)*

or assessment, as a matter of professional responsibility to us, you will so advise us and will consult with us concerning the question of such disclosure and the applicable requirements of *Statement of Financial Accounting Standards No. 5*. Please specifically confirm to our auditors that our understanding is correct.

Please specifically identify the nature of and reasons for any limitation on your response.

Very truly yours,
The Wilson Company

Raymond Carver
President

(but does not require that the attorney prepare a list). If an attorney fails to respond or responds insufficiently, a significant uncertainty may exist about the recording and disclosure of loss contingencies, requiring that an auditor modify the audit report, as discussed in Chapter 3.

OBTAIN A MANAGEMENT REPRESENTATION LETTER

Throughout an engagement, an auditor obtains numerous representations from management. In fact, much of the evidence obtained during an audit consists of management's oral representations (among them statements about errors, frauds, and related parties), and written representations (such as journals, ledgers, and other documents). Although written representations are tangible, oral representations are not, thereby requiring that an auditor obtain a **management representation letter** documenting management's most significant representations.

Statement on Auditing Standards No. 19, "Client Representations" (AU Sec. 333), requires that the letter be addressed to the auditor and dated as of the audit report date, since the auditor is concerned with events occurring through that date. The letter should be signed by appropriate members of management, normally the chief executive officer and the chief financial officer, and should specifically state management's understanding that the financial statements are management's representations and primary responsibility, and that the auditors relied on management's representations in forming an opinion on the financial statements.

The specific representations obtained for an audit engagement vary depending on the circumstances, but ordinarily include:

- Management's acknowledgment of responsibility for the financial statements.
- Availability of all financial records and related data.
- Completeness and availability of all minutes of meetings of shareholders, directors, and committees of directors.
- Absence of errors in financial statements and of unrecorded transactions.

- Information about related party transactions.
- Information about subsequent events.
- Disclaimer of fraud involving management or employees.
- Plans or intentions that may affect the carrying value or classification of assets or liabilities.
- Satisfactory title to assets, liens on assets, and assets pledged as collateral.

A management representation letter is so critical to an audit that management's refusal to furnish a written letter would preclude an auditor from issuing an unqualified opinion, regardless of the audit results otherwise. A sample representation letter appears in Figure 17-4.

Figure 17-4:   Management Representation Letter

THE WILSON COMPANY
15 Artubus Drive
Stony Brook, NY 11790

February 14, 2000

Cheever & Yates LLPs
345 Park Avenue
New York, New York 10154

Dear Mr. Cheever:

In connection with your audit of the financial statements of The Wilson Company as of December 31, 1999, and for the year ended December 31, 1999, for the purpose of expressing an opinion about whether the financial statements present fairly the financial position, results of operations, and cash flows of The Wilson Company in conformity with generally accepted accounting principles, we confirm, to the best of our knowledge and belief, the following representations made to you during your audit:

We are responsible for the fair presentation in the financial statements of financial position, results of operations, and cash flows in conformity with generally accepted accounting principles.

We have made available to you all financial records and related data; minutes of the meetings of stockholders, directors, and committees of directors; or summaries of actions of recent meetings for which minutes have not yet been prepared.

There have been no irregularities involving management or employees who have significant roles in the internal control structure; frauds involving other employees that could have a material effect on the financial statements; or communications from regulatory agencies concerning noncompliance with, or deficiencies in, financial reporting practices that could have a material effect on the financial statements.

We have no plans or intentions that may materially affect the carrying value or classification of assets and liabilities.

The following data have been properly recorded or disclosed in the financial statements:

Figure 17-4: *(continued)*

1. Related party transactions and related amounts receivable or payable, including sales, purchases, loans, transfers, leasing arrangements, and guarantees.
2. Capital stock repurchase options or agreements, or capital stock reserved for options, warrants, conversions, or other requirements.
3. Arrangements with financial institutions involving compensating balances or other arrangements involving restrictions on cash balances and line-of-credit or similar arrangements.
4. Agreements to repurchase assets previously sold.

There are no violations or possible violations of laws or regulations whose effects should be considered for disclosure in the financial statements or as a basis for recording a loss contingency, nor are there other material liabilities, or gain or

loss contingencies that are required to be accrued or disclosed by *Statement of Financial Accounting Standards No. 5.*

There are no unasserted claims or assessments that our lawyer has advised us are probable of assertion and must be disclosed in accordance with *Statement of Financial Accounting Standards No. 5.*

There are no material transactions that have not been properly recorded in the accounting records underlying the financial statements.

Provision has been made to reduce excess or obsolete inventories, when material, to their estimated net realizable value.

The company has satisfactory title to all owned assets, and there are no liens or encumbrances on such assets, nor has any asset been pledged.

Provision has been made for any material loss to be sustained in the fulfillment of, or from inability to fulfill, any sales commitments.

Provision has been made for any material loss to be sustained as a result of purchase commitments for inventory quantities in excess of normal requirements or at prices in excess of the prevailing market prices.

We have complied with all aspects of contractual agreements that would have a material effect on the financial statements in the event of noncompliance.

No events have occurred subsequent to the balance sheet date that would require adjustment to, or disclosure in, the financial statements.

Raymond Carver
President

Maxine Kuman
Controller

FORMING AN OPINION

In a public accounting firm, an audit partner, sometimes called the *engagement partner*, is responsible for reaching an overall opinion on an entity's financial position, results of operations, and cash flows, but only after:

- Performing an overall review of the financial statements through analytical procedures,
- Reviewing audit working papers in detail, and
- Obtaining a technical review of the working papers by an audit partner not assigned to the engagement.

Each is discussed below.

ANALYTICAL PROCEDURES AS AN OVERALL REVIEW

Statement on Auditing Standards No. 56, "Analytical Procedures," requires that an auditor apply analytical procedures when completing an engagement to test whether the relationships among recorded account balances appear reasonable, the intent being to identify issues that might otherwise have gone undetected during detailed testing. For example, unlike detailed tests, analytical procedures applied to the relationship between recorded Sales and Accounts Receivable would not offer evidence that the accounts are misstated, but if sales were to decrease in the current period by 50 percent, an auditor might reasonably expect receivables to decrease by a comparable percentage. If receivables did not decrease, the auditor might consider several potential explanations, among them:

- Allowance for Doubtful Accounts might be understated,
- Accounts Receivable might be overstated, or
- Sales might be understated.

If the relationship between account balances appears unreasonable, as in this illustration (sales decrease by 50 percent, but receivables don't), the auditor should make inquiries of management and then: (1) evaluate the reasonableness of management's replies in relation to the auditor's knowledge of the client's business and information obtained during the audit, and (2) consider the need to corroborate management's replies through additional procedures, such as further substantive tests of sales, receivables, and/or the allowance for doubtful accounts.

REVIEW OF WORKING PAPERS

After documenting audit procedures for an individual financial statement account, an auditor drafts his or her conclusion about the account in the audit working papers. The conclusion should state whether, in the auditor's judgment, the account is presented fairly, the account is not presented fairly, or evidence is insufficient or inadequate to reach a conclusion. For example, a conclusion that an account is presented fairly might be worded:

Based upon audit procedures performed, I am satisfied that Accounts Receivable is presented fairly in all material respects at December 31, 1999.

A conclusion should be included on the working paper lead schedule for each major financial statement account audited. Thereafter, typically on or about the last day of field work, the audit partner reviews the entire set of working papers, all of which should have been reviewed previously by the manager and the senior accountant who acted in a supervisory capacity during the engagement. The partner's review is intended to determine whether the working papers demonstrate and document compliance with *generally accepted auditing standards* and the firm's standards of performance. Figure 17-5 illustrates a partner's review checklist, categorizing the procedures as: those related to the mechanical accuracy of the working papers and those related to audit scope.

Figure 17-5: Working Papers Review Checklist

Mechanical Accuracy

- Trace supporting balances on individual working paper schedules to lead schedules.
- Trace lead schedule balances to working trial balances.
- Trace trial balance amounts to the financial statements.
- Review compliance with restrictive loan covenants.
- Review indexing of working papers.
- Review cross-referencing within the working papers.
- Test significant calculations in the working papers, such as:
    Accruals for interest income and expense.
    Accruals for state, local, and federal income taxes.
    Accruals for pension and profit-sharing plans.
    Depreciation.
    Inventory price testing.
    Lease calculations.
    Earnings per share.
- Determine that all audit working papers are complete, properly headed, and dated.

Audit Scope

- Determine that the consideration of internal control is adequate and that the scope of year end substantive tests of details is justified given the level of control risk.
- Determine that audit programs were appropriate for the circumstances.
- Determine that audit procedures adequately addressed the audit assertions of existence or occurrence, completeness, rights and obligations, valuation or allocation, and presentation and disclosure.
- Determine that the scope and results of the accounts receivable confirmations were reasonable.
- Determine that the physical inventory observation procedures were adequate.
- Determine that management representation letters are accurate, complete, and signed by management.
- Determine that legal letters are appropriate and signed.
- Determine that related party transactions are disclosed as necessary.
- Review all proposed adjusting journal entries.
- Determine that the audited financial statements are properly presented in accordance with generally accepted accounting principles.
- Determine that the opinion expressed in the audit report (unqualified, qualified, adverse, or disclaimer of opinion) is justified by evidence documented within the working papers.
- Determine that all exceptions and review notes within the working papers have been cleared.

The audit partner reaches an overall opinion on the financial statements taken as a whole by considering the propriety of all audit conclusions documented within the working papers. If the conclusions indicate the accounts and disclosures are presented fairly in all material respects, the partner would issue an unqualified opinion on the financial statements taken as a whole. Otherwise (or if a conclusion is not reached for a specific account) the partner would consider the need to issue a qualified opinion, an adverse opinion, or a disclaimer of opinion, all of which are discussed in detail and illustrated in Chapter 3.

OBTAIN AN INDEPENDENT TECHNICAL REVIEW

Before an audit report is communicated to the client, an audit partner or partners not otherwise assigned to the engagement should perform a technical review of the audit working papers (sometimes called a *cold review*), determining whether *generally accepted auditing standards* were followed and whether the working papers support the conclusions and opinion reached. The technical review is the final step in the process of reviewing audit working papers and, therefore, is the final check before an audit report is released.

COMMUNICATION WITH THE AUDIT COMMITTEE

Throughout an engagement, auditors acquire information that does not necessarily require disclosure in the financial statements, but that may be helpful to the board of directors' audit committee in discharging their responsibility for overseeing the entity's financial reporting function. Some professional pronouncements require that auditors communicate specific matters to the audit committee, among them *SAS No. 60*, "The Communication of Internal Control Structure Related Matters Noted in an Audit," discussed in Chapter 7, and *SAS No. 54*, "Illegal Acts by Clients," discussed in Chapter 5. Given the responsibility assumed by audit committees as the sole intermediary between independent auditors and the full board of directors, the Auditing Standards Board issued *Statement on Auditing Standards No. 61*, "Communication with Audit Committees" (AU Sec. 380), which requires that auditors communicate to the audit committee additional information not specifically addressed otherwise in professional pronouncements but that may assist the committee in overseeing the financial reporting and disclosure process for which management is responsible.

The statement requires communication with the audit committee but does not preclude communication with management or others within the entity who may benefit, like internal auditors or the chief financial officer. The matters to be communicated include:

- The auditor's responsibility under generally accepted auditing standards.
- Significant accounting policies.
- Management's judgments and accounting estimates.
- Significant audit adjustments.
- Other information in documents containing audited financial statements (e.g., annual reports to shareholders).
- Disagreements with management.

- Management's consultation with other accountants about accounting and auditing matters.
- Major issues discussed with management prior to retaining the auditor for the next audit.
- Difficulties encountered in performing the audit.

The communications typically are incidental to the audit and therefore need not be made before issuing the audit report. In addition, the communications may either be oral or written, although oral communications should be documented by written memoranda in the working papers.

SUBSEQUENT DISCOVERY OF FACTS EXISTING AT THE REPORT DATE

After an audit report has been issued, an auditor is generally under no obligation to make further inquiries or to perform additional audit procedures. Sometimes, however, new information may surface which bears on one or more of management's assertions, and which would have affected the audited financial statements or the audit report had the information come to the auditor's attention on or before the report date. For example, the auditor may become aware from reliable news releases that technological advances have rendered inventory obsolete, suggesting that the carrying value of inventory is overstated, thereby affecting management's valuation assertion. Regardless of whether the new information could have (or should have) been known as of the report date, the auditor is responsible to discuss the matter with appropriate levels of management, including the board of directors, and to take additional action if:

- The information is reliable,
- The facts existed at the report date,
- The audit report would have been affected if the information had been known, and
- Persons are currently relying or are likely to rely on the financial statements and would attach importance to the information.

The additional action taken by an auditor would depend on whether the client makes appropriate disclosure of the newly discovered information, as discussed below. However, in either case—whether the client makes, or refuses to make, additional disclosures—the auditor's overriding concern is to assure that current and potential financial statement users no longer rely on the original audit report.

CLIENT MAKES DISCLOSURE

When a client agrees to disclose, the method and form of disclosure will depend on the circumstances. For example, if the effect of the newly discovered information can be determined promptly, disclosure would consist of revised financial statements and a revised audit report. The reasons for revision should be described in a note to the financial statements and referred to in the auditor's report. Further, the revised statements and report should be communicated to all persons known to be (or likely to be) relying on them. However, if the effect of the newly discovered information cannot be determined without a prolonged investigation, the issuance of revised statements and a revised report would necessarily be delayed. In this case, appropriate disclosure would consist of the client notifying all persons known or likely to be relying on the original statements that the report should no longer be relied on, and that revised financial statements and a revised audit report are forthcoming.

CLIENT REFUSES DISCLOSURE

In contrast, if the client refuses to disclose, the auditor should notify each member of the board of directors and, barring legal advice to the contrary, should formally notify management, each regulatory agency having jurisdiction over the client, and each person known to be relying on the financial statements that the original audit report can no longer be relied on. For publicly traded clients, notification to each person known to be relying on the report is an ominous, time-consuming task. As a result, notification to the regulatory agencies will usually be the only practical method for the auditor to provide notification.

CONSIDERATION OF OMITTED PROCEDURES AFTER THE REPORT DATE

The previous section deals with the subsequent discovery of *facts* existing at the report date. But what if a public accounting firm's peer review (Chapter 4) or internal quality control inspection reveals that a client's previously issued financial statements are fairly stated but that one or more necessary *auditing procedures* were omitted during the audit engagement? *Statement on Auditing Standards No. 46*, "Consideration of Omitted Procedures After the Report Date" (AU Sec. 390) addresses this situation.

As with the subsequent discovery of facts, an auditor is under no obligation either to perform audit procedures after the report is issued or to conduct a retrospective review of previously completed audit work. However, because of potential legal liability for due diligence (Chapter 5), an auditor should consider consulting an attorney and, with the attorney's advice and assistance, determine a course of action when omitted procedures come to his or her attention.

In most cases, the auditor would assess the importance of the omitted procedures to the financial statements taken as a whole by reviewing the completed working papers, discussing the circumstances with assigned audit staff and, from this information, reevaluating overall audit scope. That is, was the extent of the auditing procedures applied adequate even in the absence of the procedures omitted? For example, an auditor might conclude that confirming loans and other long-term notes payable was adequate to partially address the assertions of existence, obligations, and valuation, even though the audit working papers reveal that bond indentures and other long-term indebtedness agreements were not examined. However, if the auditor believes that a previously issued report is no longer supported absent the procedures, and that persons are either relying or likely to rely on the report, he or she should promptly undertake to apply the omitted procedures. If the auditor concludes by performing omitted procedures that the previously issued report is no longer supported, he or she should assure that current and potential financial statement users no longer place reliance on the previously issued report—for example, by following procedures discussed earlier for the subsequent discovery of facts existing at the report date.

SUMMARY

This chapter, which concludes the discussion of detailed procedures, addresses substantive tests of revenue and expense accounts and introduces procedures necessary to complete a financial statement audit. In general, substantive tests of revenue and expense accounts take the form of detailed tests or reasonableness tests (analytical procedures), both of which can provide complete or partial support for the financial statement assertions of occurrence, valuation or allocation, completeness, and presentation and disclosure.

When completing an engagement, an auditor must review both for material subsequent events and for contingent liabilities. Each requires considerable judgment because, unlike many other audit areas, neither is recorded in the financial statements. An auditor also makes inquiries of a client's legal counsel about pending or threatened litigation and unasserted claims, and he or she obtains a representation letter from management about assertions made during the engagement.

To form an overall opinion on the financial statements taken as a whole, auditors review the entire set of working papers and perform overall analytical procedures. In turn, before an audit report is issued, an independent review should be performed by an audit partner not otherwise assigned to the engagement. The purpose of the independent review is to provide assurance that members of the audit team, most of whom have been involved in the details of the engagement, have not overlooked an issue central to either the audited financial statements or the audit report.

Even after communicating with the audit committee and after an audit report is issued, the auditor maintains responsibility for the subsequent discovery of facts existing at the date of the auditor's report and for considering the omission of procedures during the engagement, both of which are critical to an auditor's potential legal liability.

KEY TERMS

Analytical procedures   637
Accounting estimates   638
Loss contingency   639
Related party transaction   640
Subsequent period   642
Subsequent events   642

Type I subsequent events   642
Type II subsequent events   642
Legal letters   645
Unasserted claims   645
Management representation letter   647

REFERENCES

Professional Standards

AICPA. *Codification of Statements on Auditing Standards* (AU Sec. 333, 334, 337, 342, 380, 390, 560, 561); New York: AICPA.

SAS No. 12, "Inquiry of a Client's Lawyer Concerning Litigation, Claims, and Assessments" (AU Sec. 337).

SAS No. 19, "Client Representations" (AU Sec. 333).

SAS No. 45, "Omnibus Statement on Auditing Standards: 1983" (AU Sec. 334).

SAS No. 46, "Consideration of Omitted Procedures After the Report Date" (AU Sec. 390).

SAS No. 57, "Auditing Accounting Estimates" (AU Sec. 342).

SAS No. 61, "Communication with Audit Committees" (AU Sec. 380).

QUESTIONS

1. Identify and briefly discuss the two types of substantive tests an auditor performs for revenue and expense accounts.
2. Subsequent events occur after the last day of an entity's fiscal year and on or before the report date. Why would an auditor be concerned about transactions and events occurring in this time period?
3. What is the difference between Type I and Type II subsequent events?
4. Identify the alternative types of disclosure appropriate for Type II subsequent events.
5. What is the purpose of a management representation letter?
6. What information should an auditor request from a client's legal counsel in a letter of audit inquiry?
7. What is the relationship between audit conclusions reached for individual financial statement accounts and an auditor's overall opinion on the financial statements taken as a whole?
8. In general, what procedures does an auditor apply during the subsequent period to identify significant subsequent events?
9. Under what conditions would an auditor take action for the subsequent discovery of facts existing at the report date?
10. How should an auditor proceed if a client refuses to disclose the subsequent discovery of facts existing at the report date?
11. How should an auditor proceed in the event he or she becomes aware, after the report date, that audit procedures were omitted during the engagement?

MULTIPLE CHOICE QUESTIONS

1. Tests of details, rather than analytical procedures, are appropriate when:

a. Control risk is below the maximum.
b. Transaction volume for the account or class of transactions is high.
c. Analytical procedures reveal unexpected results.
d. The account does not require special attention.

2. Comparing current and prior year revenues and expenses and investigating all changes exceeding 10 percent would most likely reveal that:

a. Management's capitalization policy for small tools changed in the current year.
b. Declining economic conditions caused an inadequate provision for uncollectible receivables.
c. Fourth quarter payroll taxes were not paid.
d. Higher current rates were not recognized in property tax accruals.

3. Under *Statement on Auditing Standards No. 57*, "Auditing Accounting Estimates," an auditor is responsible for:

a. Making accounting estimates.
b. Evaluating the reasonableness of management's estimates.
c. Auditing transactions in the subsequent period that lend insight into estimates recorded at the balance sheet date.
d. Including accounting estimates within the letter of audit inquiry sent to all attorneys of record.

4. Which of the following would not likely be a related party transaction?

a. Sales to another corporation with a similar name.
b. Purchases from an entity controlled by the purchasing entity's majority shareholder.
c. Loan from an entity to a major shareholder.
d. Sale of land to an entity by a director's spouse.

5. Subsequent events occur after the:

a. Balance sheet date.
b. Date of the auditor's report.
c. Balance sheet date, but on or before the date of the auditor's report.
d. Date of the auditor's report, but on or before the date of a registration statement.

6. The following events occurred after the end of the fiscal year but before the auditor issued a report. Which event would not require disclosure in the financial statements?

a. Sale of a bond or issuance of capital stock.
b. Loss of plant or inventories from a fire or flood.
c. A major decline in the trade price of the corporation's common shares.
d. Settlement of litigation when the event giving rise to the claim took place after the balance sheet date.

(AICPA Adapted)

7. Of the following, which would likely be classified as a Type II subsequent event?

a. Collection of receivables in amounts substantially different from amounts recorded at the balance sheet date.
b. Realization of a loss on the sale of an investment when the subsequent sale confirms a previously existing unrecognized loss.
c. Discontinuance, at an estimated loss, of operations of a subsidiary where the contributing circumstances developed prior to year end.
d. A business combination accounted for as a pooling of interests.

8. Although an attorney's letter reveals no significant disagreements with management's assessment of contingent liabilities, the attorney resigns shortly thereafter, suggesting:

a. The auditor must begin anew the audit of contingent liabilities.
b. Undisclosed unasserted claims.
c. The attorney was unable to conclude about the significance of litigation, claims, and assessments.
d. An adverse opinion is necessary.

9. The date of a management representation letter coincides with the:

a. Date of the auditor's report.
b. Balance sheet date.

c. Date of the latest subsequent event referred to in notes to the financial statements.
d. Date of the engagement letter.

10. A final independent review of the audit working papers is normally done by:

a. The engagement partner.
b. The chief technical partner of the office conducting the audit.
c. A partner not otherwise assigned to the engagement.
d. The engagement manager.

11. Under *Statement on Auditing Standards No. 61,* "Communication with Audit Committees," which of the following would an auditor typically communicate to the audit committee?

a. Difficulties encountered in performing the audit.
b. Turnover in the staff assigned to the audit.
c. Matters included within an attorney's letter.
d. The contents of the management representation letter.

PROBLEMS AND DISCUSSION CASES

17-1   *Why Coordinate Tests of Balance Sheet and Income Statement Accounts?*
In a properly planned financial statement audit, auditors typically coordinate tests of balance sheet and income statement accounts. For example, in practice auditors often coordinate tests of accounts receivables and sales, and of accounts payable and purchases.

Required: Discuss reasons for coordinating the tests of balance sheet and income statement accounts, illustrating by examples.

17-2   *Independent Working Paper Review*
Nicole Lutes, a partner in a regional public accounting firm, is conducting the independent technical review—the "cold" review—of working papers for the December 31, 1999, year end audit of Singer Corporation. In 1996, two years before Lutes was admitted to the partnership, she was the audit manager on the Singer engagement. One of the working papers, a schedule of ratios and an analysis of account balance changes from 1998 to 1999, reveals that advertising expense, stated at $150,000 on December 31, 1998, increased to $180,000 in 1999, an increase of $30,000, or 20 percent. Sales and cost of goods sold in both years were relatively stable. Lutes reviews a working paper schedule, "Analysis of Advertising Expense," which reveals that for $20,000 of the 1999 advertising expense balance, the audit staff examined advertising copy and invoices and traced payments to the cash disbursements records. Interim tests of controls indicated that control procedures over advertising transactions are not particularly reliable. The working papers provide no explanation of the $30,000 increase in advertising.
    Required:
1. Explain the purpose of an independent technical review of working papers.
2. Is Lutes a reasonable choice to perform the 1999 independent technical review given that she was the manager on the 1996 Singer Corporation engagement? Explain.
3. In your judgment, were the nature and scope of the audit of advertising expense reasonable? Explain.

17-3   *Related Party Transactions*
In any audit engagement, an auditor is concerned that financial statements reflect properly the economic substance of material related party transactions. To achieve this

objective, auditors attempt to determine the existence of related parties and the nature of transactions entered into between the audit client and the related parties. During the course of an audit engagement, you have identified two potential related party transactions. The first involves a significant shareholder who has borrowed cash to purchase a new home. The second is an affiliated company that has agreed to supply your audit client with raw materials.

Required: Describe how each of the two potential related party transactions should be structured so that the legal form of the transaction accurately reflects the economic substance. Include the items an auditor would review to assure that the transactions were made at "arm's length."

17-4   *Drafting a Related Parties Footnote*

Subsidiaries of First of America, a major commercial bank, have made loans to First of America directors and executive officers. The loans totaled $56,965,000 at December 31, 1999 (3.6 percent of total shareholders' equity) and $42,405,000 at December 31, 1998. During 1999, $39,201,000 of new loans were made, and repayments and other reductions totaled $24,641,000. Management believes that the loans do not affect materially the financial condition of First of America, that the loans are consistent with sound business practice in the banking industry, and that the loans do not impose more than the normal risk of collectibility. There is every reason to believe the loans were made at nonpreferential terms and rates, and no reason to believe the loans were made to immediate members of the directors' families or violated either corporate policy or applicable laws and regulations.

Required: Draft a related parties footnote for First of America's December 31, 1999 financial statements.

17-5   *Responsibility for Subsequent Events*

Michael is auditing the financial statements of the Diannah Corporation as of and for the period ended September 30, 1999. Michael plans to complete field work and sign the auditor's report on November 15, 1999. Michael's audit work is designed primarily to obtain evidence that will provide a reasonable degree of assurance that the Diannah Corporation's September 30, 1999, financial statements present fairly the financial position, results of operations, and cash flows in accordance with generally accepted accounting principles. Michael is concerned, however, about events and transactions of the Diannah Corporation that occur after September 30, 1999, since he does not have the same degree of assurance for these events as for those that occurred in the period ending September 30, 1999.

Required: Define what is commonly referred to in auditing as a "subsequent event" and describe the two general types of subsequent events that require consideration by the management of Diannah Corporation and evaluation by Michael.

(AICPA Adapted)

17-6   *Identifying Subsequent Events*

Although an auditor reaches an opinion on financial statements as of the last day of a client's fiscal year—for example, December 31—the auditor is also responsible for material transactions or events occurring through the last day of field work that provide additional evidence about financial statement disclosures as of the balance sheet date.

Required: Describe the procedures an auditor should apply at or near the completion of field work to identify material subsequent transactions or events.

17-7   *Disclosing Subsequent Events*

Jason Hirsch, engagement partner for the December 31, 1999 Flowmeter, Inc. financial statement audit, is aware that events and transactions which took place after December 31, 1999 (but before he issues his report dated February 28, 2000) may affect the company's financial statements. The following material events or transactions have come to Hirsch's attention:

a. On January 3, 2000, Flowmeter, Inc. received a shipment of raw materials from Canada. The materials had been ordered in October 1999, and shipped FOB shipping point in November 1999.

b. On January 15, 2000, the company settled and paid a personal injury claim of a former employee as the result of an accident that occurred in March 1995. The company had not previously recorded a liability for the claim.

c. On January 25, 2000, the company agreed to purchase for cash the outstanding stock of Porter Electrical Co. The acquisition is likely to double the sales volume of Flowmeter, Inc.

d. On February 1, 2000, a plant owned by Flowmeter, Inc. was damaged by a flood, resulting in an uninsured loss of inventory.

e. On February 5, 2000, Flowmeter, Inc. issued and sold to the general public $2,000,000 in convertible bonds.

Required: For each of the above events or transactions, discuss audit procedures that should have brought the item to the auditor's attention, and the form of (and reasons for) disclosure in the financial statements.

(AICPA Adapted)

17-8 *Detecting and Distinguishing Between Type I and Type II Events*
Windek is nearing completion of an audit of the financial statements of Jubilee, Inc. for the year ended December 31, 1999. Windek is currently concerned that subsequent events may require adjustment to or disclosure in the financial statements.

Required:
1. Briefly explain what is meant by a "subsequent event."
2. How do those subsequent events that require financial statement adjustment differ from those that require financial statement disclosure?
3. What are the procedures that should be performed in order to identify subsequent events?

(AICPA Adapted)

17-9 *Detecting Loss Contingencies*
An independent auditor has completed substantive tests of balance sheet and income statement accounts, and now plans to begin procedures designed to determine whether there are any loss contingencies arising from litigation, claims, or assessments. Thus far, the auditor has inquired of (and discussed with) management the policies and procedures they have adopted for identifying, evaluating, and accounting for litigation, claims, and assessments.

Required: What procedures should the auditor follow to detect loss contingencies arising from litigation, claims, and assessments?

17-10 *Responsibilities for Management Representation Letters*
Statement on Auditing Standards No. 19, "Client Representations," requires that an independent auditor obtain a written representation letter from management, and precludes the auditor from issuing an unqualified opinion if management—in particular, the chief executive officer—refuses to sign the letter.

Required:
1. What are the objectives of obtaining a management representation letter?
2. Who should prepare and sign the letter?
3. When should a representation letter be obtained?
4. Why should a representation letter be prepared for each year in which an audit is performed?

17-11   *Drafting a Management Representation Letter*
L. B. Feldman is completing the June 30, 1999, audit of Carter, Rice, Storrs & Bement, a manufacturer and supplier of paper products. The company has operated successfully since 1948, when it was founded by Charles Carter, still the chief executive officer. The last day of field work is August 2, 1999. During the engagement, Feldman received numerous oral representations, but is particularly concerned with representations relating to:

* Potential irregularities involving management and employees.
* Related party transactions.
* Compensating balances involving restrictions on cash balances.
* Possible violations of state law.
* Loss contingencies.
* Potential unasserted claims or assessments.

Feldman has no evidence to suggest that any of the items listed is necessarily a problem in the Carter, Rice engagement, but she is concerned that the client may not sign a management representation letter because of the potential legal implications if some of the items listed were to occur without management's knowledge.

Required:
1. Draft a management representation letter, including the proper date, addressee, and signatory. The letter should cover only the items listed.
2. How should Feldman proceed if management fails to sign the representation letter?

17-12   *What to Include in a Management Representation Letter*
During the audit of the financial statements of Amis Manufacturing, Inc., the company's president, R. Alderman, and E. K. Luddy, the auditor, reviewed matters that were supposed to be included in a written representation letter. Upon receiving the following client representation letter, Luddy contacted Alderman to state that the letter was incomplete.

To: E. K. Luddy, CPA

In connection with your audit of the balance sheet of Amis Manufacturing, Inc., as of December 31, 1999, and the related statements of income, retained earnings, and cash flows for the year then ended, for the purpose of expressing an opinion as to whether the financial statements present fairly the financial position, results of operations, and cash flows of Amis Manufacturing, Inc., in conformity with generally accepted accounting principles, we confirm, to the best of our knowledge and belief, the following representations made to you during your engagement. There were no:

* Plans or intentions that may materially affect the carrying value or classification of assets and liabilities.
* Communications from regulatory agencies concerning noncompliance with, or deficiencies in, financial reporting practices.
* Agreements to repurchase assets previously sold.
* Violations or possible violations of laws or regulations whose effects should be considered for disclosure in the financial statements or as a basis for recording a loss contingency.
* Unasserted claims or assessments that our lawyer has advised are probable of assertion and must be disclosed in accordance with *Statement of Financial Accounting Standards No. 5.*
* Capital stock repurchase options or agreements, or capital stock reserved for options, warrants, conversions, or other requirements.

- Compensating balances or other arrangements involving restrictions on cash balances.

R. Alderman, President
Amis Manufacturing, Inc.

March 14, 2000

Required: Identify the other matters that Alderman's representation letter should confirm.

(AICPA Adapted)

RESEARCH PROJECTS

1. ANNUAL REPORTS AND THE AUDIT PROCESS

Throughout an engagement, the independent auditor makes observations, documents evidence, confirms transactions, tests accounting data, compares recorded amounts, and makes many inquiries, all with an eye toward the engagement's two major end products: audited financial statements and the auditor's report, both of which are printed within a corporation's annual report to shareholders. In short, the engagement proceeds forward to a discernible end. But much like a crime scene lends leads to a crime, so too does the annual report lend insight into the audit process. Much can be learned about audit practice from little more than management's annual report.

Required: Select an annual report for a publicly traded corporation and, from disclosures contained within the auditor's report, management's statement of responsibility for the financial statements, and the audited financial statements, draft a report that responds to each of the following:

1. For those expense captions identified explicitly on the income statement, which would likely have been audited by tests of details and which would likely have been subjected to analytical procedures only? Why?
2. Explain the accounting and disclosure issues likely underlying each reported accounting estimate and loss contingency.
3. Explain the disclosures, if any, made for related party transactions. What likely motivated the transactions?
4. Explain the disclosures, if any, made for subsequent events, distinguishing between those that were Type I events and those that were Type II events.
5. Identify the transactions or events, if any, that likely were included in a legal letter. Explain information the auditor would have required from a lawyer to disclose the transactions or events adequately.
6. What disclosures included within the financial statements were likely included in management's representation letter?

2. IS THIS A SUBSEQUENT EVENT?

The daily financial press is replete with newsworthy releases that bear on the financial operations of publicly traded corporations. Not coincidentally, some of the releases translate to significant subsequent event disclosures in corporate financial statements since, after leaving the field, an auditor's first clue to a subsequent event often comes from news clippings.

Required: Using the annual report file in the National Automated Accounting Research System (NAARS), the AICPA's *Accounting Trends and Techniques,* or copies of annual reports in a library, select a report for a publicly traded corporation that discloses a material subsequent event. Using the newspaper file in NEXIS, Mead Data Central's automated data retrieval system, or recent copies of *The Wall Street Journal*, select an article you believe may translate into a material subsequent event for a publicly traded corporation. Draft a report that accomplishes the following:

1. For the annual report selected, explain the intuition underlying the subsequent event and whether the event is a Type I or Type II subsequent event.
2. For the article selected:
   a. Explain why you believe the article may translate into a Type I or Type II subsequent event.
   b. If you believe a footnote is appropriate, draft the subsequent event footnote, using as a guide the language in the disclosure you discuss in (1), among other disclosures you may locate in NAARS, *Accounting Trends and Techniques,* or the library.

PART 4

ATTESTATION ENGAGEMENTS, COMPLIANCE AND INTERNAL AUDITING

18

Assurance and Attestation Services

Major topics discussed in this chapter are:

- The AICPA's Special Committee on Assurance Services' (the Elliott Committee's) recommendations for assurance service opportunities.
- Assurance services for:
  Electronic commerce.
  Health care providers.
- Attestation services for:
  Compilations and reviews of financial statements.
  Interim financial information.
  Comprehensive bases of accounting other than GAAP.
  Specified elements, accounts, or items of a financial statement and nonfinancial statement assertions: applying GAAS or agreed-upon procedures.
  Compliance with contractual requirements.
  Letters for underwriters.
  Financial forecasts and projections.
  Personal financial statements.
  Applications of accounting principles.

Prior chapters introduced assurance services offered by Consumers Union (Chapters 1, 3, and 5), Underwriters Laboratories (Chapters 2 and 5), and public accounting firms (Chapters 1-4, 7, 10, 12, 15, and 16). In addition, prior chapters illustrated a number of attestation services offered by public accounting firms—including services by Coopers & Lybrand for Wilson Sporting Goods' Ultra golf ball assertions (Chapters 1 and 2), Price Waterhouse for Stanley H. Kaplan's SAT improvement assertions (Chapter 1), KPMG Peat Marwick on ethics management (Chapter 4), Ernst & Young for CoreStates Financial's internal control assertions (Chapter 7), and the Deloitte & Touche/ Gradient Technologies partnered service on Internet security (Chapter 7), among others. This chapter outlines recommendations of the AICPA's *Special Committee on Assurance Services* (the Elliott Committee), introduces industry-specific assurance services offered by the public accounting profession for electronic commerce and for health care providers, and illustrates several common attestation services for which the profession has issued professional guidance.

Recall from Chapter 1 the distinction between assurance and attestation services: Assurance services improve (or report on) the quality of information. In contrast, attestation services are a type of assurance service in which the attester—typically, a public accounting firm—offers assurance about another party's written assertions. However, as the work of the AICPA's Special Committee on Assurance Services (Chapter 1) becomes more influential and the collected experience of practitioners in new markets increases, the distinction is likely to be less important. In fact, another equally useful way to think about assurance and attestation services in the public accounting profession is this: While attestation services have long been offered (for example, the AICPA's eleven attestation standards date back to 1986), other assurance services are rather new.

ASSURANCE SERVICES

Professional Growth Through New Assurance Services, the Special Committee on Assurance Services' (the Elliott Committee's) interim report to the AICPA Council, forecasts that the power to decide information content will shift from the producers of information (for example, auditors) to the consumers of information (such as investors, creditors, and managers, among other informed decision makers), and that information technology will enable dramatic change both in what decision makers demand and in what practitioners provide. What's more, although certified public accountants hold a regulated monopoly in the market for financial statement audit services, other professionals, such as niche consultants (Chapter 1), will likely compete to provide nonregulated, consumer-driven assurance services. Make no mistake about it, public accounting firms have compelling economic incentives to enter—rather than ignore—the assurance services market, since the growth of individual firms may depend crucially on which firms succeed when the market clears. For example, as the Elliott Committee observes, "Over the past six years inflation-adjusted accounting and auditing services have been flat for the 60 largest firms. In fact, revenue from those services now accounts for less than half of total revenue for the firms . . . And since gross domestic product has risen 28 percent in real terms over the past six years, accounting and auditing revenue represents a declining portion of GDP."[1] Does this mean that audited financial statements have no value? No, it means that in the information age, audited financial statements are only one part of the information mix that decision makers seek. It's no coincidence that the "auditing" departments of many public accounting firms are now called "assurance service" departments.

The well-respected services of Consumers Union and Underwriters Laboratories aside, what new industry-specific value-added assurance services are likely to be demanded from public accounting firms? Figure 18-1 outlines six assurance services the Elliott Committee recommended (from hundreds the Committee considered) and concluded could "double or even triple the current $7 billion market for assurance services."[2] *Electronic commerce* services assure

---

1   AICPA Special Committee on Assurance Services (the Elliott Committee). *Professional Growth Through New Assurance Services*. New York: AICPA (1995), pp. 1-2.
2   "Billions in Assurance Opportunity Await, Elliott Says," *Public Accounting Report* (October 31, 1996), p. 5.

Figure 18-1: AICPA Special Committee on Assurance Services' Recommended Assurance Service Opportunities

Electronic Commerce
Assuring the authenticity and security of electronic transactions and communication.

Health Care
Assuring the effectiveness of health care organizations and reporting on systems and controls.

Risk Assessment
Assuring the quality of information about the likelihood and magnitude of adverse events.

Systems Reliability
Assuring information integrity and controls.

Entity Performance
Assuring the relevance and reliability of performance measures.

Elder Care
Assuring the financial transactions and care of the elderly.

the authenticity and security of electronic transactions and communication, including digital bank electronic payment cards, encryption systems, wide-area computer networks, and electronic systems software. *Health care* services assure the quality—and the outcomes—of services offered by health care organizations, including reports on information systems and controls. *Risk assessment* assurances report on the likelihood and magnitude of risks that entities bear (for example, in environmental practices) which, as the Elliott Committee speculates, "could amount to 10%-20% of annual financial auditing fees."[3] *Systems reliability* services—arguably the most similar to the portfolio of professional services offered by public accounting firms in the past (see Chapter 7)—assure the integrity of information and controls. *Entity performance* services assure the relevance and reliability of performance measures such as product market share, product warranty and quality guarantees, and benchmarking against leading competitors. Finally, *elder care* services assure the financial transactions of the elderly and monitor, for example, home health care contracts and nursing home services. The following two sections of the chapter offer illustrations for two of these services: electronic commerce and health care.

ELECTRONIC COMMERCE ASSURANCES

Introduced in Chapter 7, electronic commerce and Internet technology have revolutionized the way that information is exchanged and business is transacted. The industrial age has given way to the information age and, correspondingly, to electronic commerce. For example, in the 1980s large companies such as General Motors and Sears required that trading partners use *electronic*

---

3   "AICPA Unveils New Assurance Services," *The Practical Accountant* (December 1996), p. 6.

data integration (EDI: Chapter 6) to order and bill, marking the first evidence of electronic commerce actually ruling out paper transactions. EDI standards, developed in 1988 by the American National Standards Institute and called *ANSI X12,* allow trading partners to communicate in common electronic formats to accomplish an assortment of tasks without paper, including order entry, invoicing, claims filing, just-in-time inventory management, and rapid response to customer order patterns.

In the 1990s, electronic commerce penetrated dramatically larger markets, becoming available both to small companies and to retail customers in the form of electronic shopping, banking, entertainment, education, and financial networks on the Internet. Virtually any business transaction can be executed electronically and settled in digital cash, essentially eliminating the need for paper documents. However, the anonymity of electronic commerce also increases the risk of unauthorized surveillance and transmission failures, opening a new market for *data-integrity* assurance services (e.g., do processing systems alter transactions?) and *data-security* assurance services (e.g., do processing systems preclude unauthorized disclosure?), both of which the profession is well-positioned to offer. For example, consider the case of data security:

In a data-security assurance service, a practitioner offers assurances that:

- Parties to a transaction are authentic, and
- Transactions and documents are protected.

However, like the attestation and audit service engagements introduced earlier in the text, a practitioner needs a set of *criteria* against which to measure authenticity and protection. For example, in an attestation service for internal control (Chapter 7), the measurement criteria appear in the Committee of Sponsoring Organizations' *(COSO)* report, "Internal Control: Integrated Framework," which provides evaluation tools for the control environment, risk assessment, control activities, information and communication, and monitoring. In contrast, there are no generally accepted data-security measurement criteria to date, suggesting that the profession could either develop—or partner with other professions to develop—say, *Data-Security Standards in Telecommunications.*

Assuming measurement criteria are available and data-security risk drives sufficient demand, the profession could offer assurances on digital electronic bank payment cards ("smart cards"), on EDI security, on Internet commerce software and transactions, and on digital authorization and signature verification, among a host of other things. Interestingly, some practitioners within the profession already offer some of these services. For example, Deloitte & Touche and Thurston Group, Inc., a private merchant bank in Chicago, have entered into a joint venture, called NetDox, Inc. NetDox uses Internet capability and encryption technology to transmit documents electronically, including legal briefs, insurance forms, financial documents, and other confidential information that had been delivered typically by overnight mail to avoid data surveillance and to ensure confirmation of receipt.[4] NetDox bundles transmission software with e-mail services that enable subscribers to route electronic documents through NetDox and that enables NetDox to track delivery, retain

---

4   D. Bank. "Deloitte & Touche Auditors to Account for E-Mail Delivery with NetDox, Inc.," *The Wall Street Journal* (January 30, 1997), p. B2.

an electronic thumbprint of the transmission, and assure the security of the transmission. Joint ventures, such as NetDox, offer public accounting firms an important means to overcome competition and to enjoy economies of scale. For example, barriers to the profession's entry into the data-security assurance service market could likely come from several formidable sources, among them competition from major electronic service providers such as Microsoft.

HEALTH CARE ASSURANCES AND CORE COMPETENCIES

Interestingly, public accounting firms of all sizes—from Big Six to local firms—are designing and marketing creative assurance services, and some are offering value-added services in conjunction with financial statement audits. Three examples follow from the health care industry—two that have been done and another that's likely to be demanded:

First, owing to accusations about three doctors' irregular research and billing practices, the University of California at San Diego engaged KPMG Peat Marwick to lend assurance about the quality of the university's fertility research program.[5] Among other things, the firm investigated whistle-blowers' allegations of false insurance claims, unjustifiable billings for physicians in training, and whether viable embryos were used illegally in clinical research. The university could have relied on an internal investigation, but leveraged instead on the credibility of a Big Six public accounting firm to win back public confidence.

Second, Moss Adams, a prominent regional firm identified in Chapter 1, offers a variety of benchmarking assurances to health care providers through-out the country.[6] For example, Moss Adams compiles financial and productivity data and then benchmarks the relative performance of physicians' groups for health maintenance organizations. Interestingly, Moss Adams enjoys a presence in other industry-specific assurance markets as well—for example, performance measurement in the apparel, forest products, and financial institutions industries—making them an important example of a regional firm that demonstrates leadership in new product development.

Third, have you ever had need for a health care provider: a hospital, a specialist, managed care? How did you—how does anybody—select among them? Most rely on word of mouth or on published reports of local data, such as *The Cleveland Area Hospital Quality Outcome Measurements and Patient Satisfaction Report.* Some others have benefit of large employers who rate the quality of employee health care. For example, Marriott, Pepsico, and Xerox demand and rate outcome data from health maintenance organizations (HMOs); GTE prepares an elaborate report card from employee medical records and physician interviews; and USAir compiles and compares employee and national treatment data.[7] What's clear is that there is a need for health care provider assurances, and a demand is likely soon to follow, since over $3 trillion is spent annually on health care in the U.S.

---

5   L. Berton. "Accountants Expand Scope of Audit Work," *The Wall Street Journal* (June 17, 1996), pp. B1, B8.
6   G. Cheney. "Regional Firm Hits National Market with New Assurance Services," *Accounting Today* (January 6-19, 1997), pp. 3, 9.
7   *Business Week* (April 8, 1996), p. 74.

Two decades ago, certified public accountants came to the table armed with a well-defined set of competencies, among them knowledge of generally accepted accounting principles and generally accepted auditing standards, a facility in the ways of evaluating evidence, a deft sense of how to manage risk, and tact in engaging and retaining clients. The next two decades will require this *plus* a much broader set of core competencies that make clear the CPA's capability to contribute value. Adapted from the report of the Special Committee on Assurance Services' Subcommittee on Competencies, Figure 18-2 lists some core competencies for the 21st century. Although some of the competencies are attained in preprofessional curricula, the bulk are attained from nothing short of a concentrated commitment to lifelong learning.

Figure 18-2: Core Competencies for Assurance Services

Administrative Capability
Possess an understanding of practice economics, financial management, staffing and staff development, and managing financial return on professional engagements.

Analytical Skills
Use search and research skills, perform systems analysis and review, use analytical models to support professional judgment, recognize and understand anomalies, and know "what should be there" and sense what is not.

Business Advisory Skills
Apply technical knowledge to insightful recommendations, see solutions to complex problems, and take intellectual risks to create ideas that help clients achieve their objectives.

Capacity for Work
Maintain a strong work ethic; stay calm in the face of demanding pressure.

Communication Skills
Express ideas clearly and unambiguously, collaborate on decision-making teams, lead discussion, and inspire confidence.

Intellectual Capability
Challenge conventional thinking, show imagination, and use diagnostic thinking.

Marketing and Selling
Develop credentials in a market or industry, draft compelling service proposals, offer value, and close.

Model Building and Technology
Understand methods and databases to measure performance and outcomes unambiguously; master relevant technologies.

People Development
Offer coaching and feedback, allocate tasks to capable staff, and project a positive role model for subordinates and peers.

Relationship Management
Understand client needs, leverage relationships through coordination and interaction, and establish and maintain credibility with key decision makers.

ATTESTATION SERVICES

Although most of the attestation services introduced in earlier chapters were performed under the profession's attestation standards (Chapter 2), only one had the advantage of a professional pronouncement: Ernst & Young's attestation (Chapter 7) for CoreStates Financial's assertions about internal control (*SSAE No. 2,* "Reporting on an Entity's Internal Control Structure Over Financial Reporting," as amended by *SSAE No. 6).* Following are several common attestation services for which the profession has issued professional guidance, including *Statements on Standards for Attestation Engagements* and *Statements on Auditing Standards.*

COMPILATIONS AND REVIEWS OF UNAUDITED FINANCIAL STATEMENTS

What assurances can a practitioner offer about *unaudited* financial statements? Actually, the level of assurances has changed over the years. Prior to the 1980s, despite guidance in the now-superseded *Statement on Auditing Procedure No. 38,* "Unaudited Financial Statements," and an AICPA *Guide for Engagements to Prepare Unaudited Financial Statements,* services for unaudited statements confused both users and practitioners. Some users, such as small lending institutions, believed that practitioners must have applied "some" procedures to prepare unaudited statements: maybe not enough to issue an opinion, but certainly enough to offer minimum assurances. And some practitioners were uncertain about the extent of procedures to apply: Should they apply any at all, and what could they say about what they had done?

The confusion led to two problems: First, some small companies were denied access to the commercial-capital market, since they were unable to afford the audits that lending institutions demanded. Second, some users placed more reliance on the unaudited statements than practitioners intended, resulting in a considerable number of legal liability cases, among them *1136 Tenants' Corp. v. Max Rothenberg & Co.* (Chapter 5). In response, the AICPA held meetings with the American Bankers Association, prompting two new financial statement services: a *review* of financial statements (introduced in Chapter 1) which provides less assurance than an audit, and a *compilation* of financial statements which provides no assurance at all (and, therefore, is not an attestation service). The *Accounting and Review Services Committee's* (Chapter 1) *Statements on Standards for Accounting and Review Services* (SSARS), particularly *SSARS No. 1,* provide guidance for performing compilation and review services for nonpublic companies.

In a **review engagement**, an attestation service performed under the AICPA's attestation standards (Chapter 2), the independent accountant performs analytical procedures, makes inquiries of management, and issues a report that provides *negative assurance,* using language that states the accountant is "not aware of any material modifications that should be made to the financial statements in order for them to be in conformity with GAAP." Note the subtle difference between an audit report and a review report: An audit report (Chapter 3) gives *positive assurance* (". . . the financial statements present fairly . . . in conformity with GAAP"), whereas a review report gives only *negative assurance* (". . . not aware of . . . modifications that should be made"). Because review engagements require less work (that is, analytical procedures and inquiries, rather than audit procedures), reviews are less costly and are usually requested by small, owner-managed companies. For example, when evaluating commercial loan applications, banks will often rely on the negative assurance provided by a review report, rather than demand that an applicant produce the positive assurance of a far more expensive audit report, a demand they made freely prior to *SSARS No. 1*.

In a **compilation engagement**, the accountant compiles financial statements from management's unaudited and unreviewed accounts, and issues a report that provides literally no assurance. The service merely compiles financial statements in proper form, but is useful to rather small owner-managed companies that elect to outsource the preparation of financial statements rather than to employ accounting personnel internally. Specifically, a compilation report states that the accountant "has not audited or reviewed the financial statements and, accordingly, does not express an opinion or any form of assurance." Compilation services are less costly than reviews and are often selected by small companies that have neither the expertise to prepare financial statements nor the need for assurances.

As with a financial statement audit, a practitioner needs to be independent to perform a review engagement, but need not be to perform a compilation. Each service is discussed more fully next.

COMPILATION OF FINANCIAL STATEMENTS

A **compilation of financial statements** consists of "presenting in the form of financial statements information that is the representation of management *without undertaking to express any assurance* on the statements."[8] In a compilation engagement, an accountant compiles unaudited financial statements but offers no assurances about whether the statements are presented in conformity with generally accepted accounting principles (GAAP). Even though compilations require no audit procedures and no expression of assurance, *SSARS No. 1*, "Compilation and Review of Financial Statements," recognizes that because of potential liability, an accountant might feel uncomfortable compiling financial statements unless he or she also performs other accounting services for the client, like general ledger bookkeeping.

When engaged to compile financial statements, an accountant develops:

- Knowledge about accounting principles and practices in the entity's industry, and
- An understanding of the entity's transactions, accounting records, and the qualifications of accounting personnel.

Although an accountant is not required to perform any audit procedures, he or she may become aware of errors, omissions, or other deficiencies in information that management supplies. For example, a remarkably high gross margin may suggest a company did not record the companion cost-of-sales entry for each recorded sale, thereby requiring that the accountant obtain additional information. If the client refuses to provide necessary information, the accountant should withdraw from the engagement.

---

8   Accounting and Review Services Committee. *Statement on Standards for Accounting and Review Services No. 1*, "Compilation and Review of Financial Statements." New York: AICPA (1978), par. 4.

Compiled financial statements are accompanied by an accountant's report dated as of the day the compilation was completed. The report describes the scope of the accountant's work, includes a statement about the nature and limitations of a compilation, and states explicitly that an audit was not performed and an opinion is not expressed. A standard compilation report follows:

Accountant's Compilation Report

The accompanying balance sheet of Tolman Company as of December 31, 1999, and the related statements of income, retained earnings, and cash flows for the year then ended have been compiled by us.

A compilation is limited to presenting in the form of financial statements information that is the representation of management (owners). We have not audited or reviewed the accompanying financial statements and, accordingly, do not express an opinion or any other form of assurance on them.

Source: SSARS No. 1.

Each page of the compiled financial statements should include a reference such as "See Accountant's Compilation Report." If not independent of a client, an accountant may still compile statements, although the last paragraph of the report should read, "We are not independent with respect to X Company."

Even though a compilation does not require determining whether financial statements conform with GAAP, an accountant may nevertheless become aware of material departures. For example, a client may have capitalized research and development costs even though FASB *Statement No. 2,* "Accounting for Research and Development Costs," requires they be charged as period expenses. If a client does not revise the statements to conform with GAAP, the accountant considers revising the standard compilation report. To illustrate, assume the Fallon Company's financial statements disclose land at appraised value rather than cost. The second paragraph should be expanded and a new paragraph added to the standard compilation report as follows:

Independent Accountant's Compilation Report:
Departure from GAAP

. . . However, we did become aware of a departure from generally accepted accounting principles that is described in the following paragraph.

As disclosed in note 2 to the financial statements, generally accepted accounting principles require that land be stated at cost. Management has informed us that the Fallon Company has stated its land at appraised value and that, if GAAP had been followed, the land account and stockholders' equity would have been decreased by $_____.

Source: SSARS No. 1.

REVIEW OF FINANCIAL STATEMENTS

A **review of financial statements** consists of "performing inquiry and analytical procedures that provide the accountant with a reasonable basis for expressing negative assurance that there are no material modifications that should be made to the statements in order for them to be in conformity with generally accepted accounting principles or, if applicable, with another comprehensive basis of accounting."[9] Thus, on the basis of inquiry and analytical procedures, an accountant expresses negative assurance: more assurance than a compilation report, but less than an audit report. Owing to the potential for legal liability, an accountant might feel uncomfortable reviewing financial statements unless he or she also performs a compilation or another accounting service for a review client.

Ordinarily, an accountant's analytical procedures and inquiries consist of the following:

1. Analytical procedures that may identify unusual matters, such as:
   a. Comparing current with comparable prior period financial statements,
   b. Comparing financial statements with budgets and forecasts, and
   c. Studying relationships between financial statement elements expected to conform with predictable patterns (e.g., Sales and Accounts Receivable).
2. Inquiries about the entity's accounting principles and practices, and about procedures for recording, classifying, summarizing, and disclosing transactions in the financial statements.
3. Inquiries about actions taken at meetings of shareholders and the board of directors.
4. Considering whether the financial statements appear to conform with GAAP.
5. Obtaining reports from other accountants engaged to audit or review a subsidiary's financial statements.
6. Inquiries of persons responsible for financial and accounting matters concerning:
   a. Whether the financial statements have been prepared in accordance with GAAP,
   b. Changes in the entity's business or accounting principles,
   c. Questions that arose when performing inquiry and analytical procedures, and
   d. Subsequent events that have a material effect on the financial statements.

As with compilations, reviewed financial statements should be accompanied by an accountant's report dated as of the day the review was completed. The report should state that a review was performed in accordance with AICPA standards and that the financial statements are the representations of management. The nature of a review should be described, and the report should expressly state that the scope of a review is substantially less than the scope of an audit. A standard review report follows:

Independent Accountant's Review Report

We have reviewed the accompanying balance sheet of Goff Company as of December 31, 1999, and the related statements of income, retained earnings, and cash flows for the year then ended, in accordance with Statements on Standards for Accounting

---

9   *Ibid.*

and Review Services issued by the American Institute of Certified Public Accountants. All information included in these financial statements is the representation of management of the Goff Company.

A review consists principally of inquiries of company personnel and analytical procedures applied to financial data. It is substantially less in scope than an audit in accordance with generally accepted auditing standards, the objective of which is the expression of an opinion regarding the financial statements taken as a whole. Accordingly, we do not express such an opinion.

Based on our review, we are not aware of any material modifications that should be made to the accompanying financial statements in order for them to be in conformity with generally accepted accounting principles.

Source: SSARS No. 1 and SSARS No. 7.

Each page of the reviewed financial statements should include a reference such as "See Accountant's Review Report."

A review does not provide a basis for determining whether financial statements conform with GAAP. But, when an accountant becomes aware of material departures from GAAP, the financial statements are revised or the report is modified. The following illustrates a modified review report assuming a departure from GAAP:

Independent Accountant's Review Report:
Departure from GAAP

(First two paragraphs unchanged.)

Based on our review, with the exception of the matter described in the following paragraph, we are not aware of any material modifications. . . .

As disclosed in note 3 to the financial statements, generally accepted accounting principles require that inventory cost consist of material, labor, and overhead. Management has informed us that the inventory of finished goods and work-in-process is stated in the accompanying financial statements at material and labor cost only, and that the effects of this departure from generally accepted accounting principles on financial position, results of operations, and changes in financial position have not been determined.

Source: SSARS No. 1.

INTERIM FINANCIAL STATEMENTS

No regulations require that interim financial statements be audited or reviewed before release to the public. However, regulators have repeatedly called for mandatory quarterly reviews and the SEC both encourages reviews for *Form 10-Q* (the quarterly report to the SEC) and permits retroactive fourth-quarter reviews prior to submitting *Form 10-K* (the annual report to the SEC). If not required, why would a publicly traded company elect voluntarily to purchase quarterly reviews from independent attesters? Which companies report voluntarily? Based on data from 238 companies that voluntarily purchased *10-Q* quarterly reviews and 133 companies that had *10-K* reviews, a study found that purchasers tend to be larger (total assets), have more business segments, spend more on internal auditing, and have more shares owned by officers and directors.[10]

Statement on Auditing Standards No. 71, "Interim Financial Information," provides guidance on interim review procedures and on reporting, but allows a practitioner to express negative assurance only, not an opinion, on interim financial information. That is, the accountant states whether he or she is *aware of any material modifications necessary to conform the information with GAAP*, not whether the statements actually do conform with GAAP, since the limited inquiries and analytical procedures prescribed by *SAS No. 71* are not adequate to form an opinion on the quarterly financial statements.

INTERIM REVIEW PROCEDURES

Compared to annual financial statement audits, practitioners typically have far less time available to assemble **interim financial statements**. As a result, costs, expenses, deferrals, and accruals are often estimated to a greater extent in interim than in annual financial statements.

A review of interim financial information under *SAS No. 71* consists primarily of analytical procedures and inquiries that include:

1. Analytical procedures that may identify unusual matters, including:
   a. Comparing interim financial information with the immediate preceding interim period and with corresponding prior periods,
   b. Considering plausible relationships between both financial data (e.g., sales to cost of sales) and nonfinancial data (e.g., payroll expense to number of employees), and
   c. Comparing recorded amounts, or ratios calculated from recorded amounts, to budgets, forecasts, and industry gross margin information.
2. Inquiries about internal control, including significant changes.
3. Reading the minutes of shareholders' and board of directors' meetings to identify actions that may affect the interim financial information.
4. Considering whether the interim financial information conforms with GAAP.
5. Obtaining reports from other accountants engaged to review a subsidiary's financial information.
6. Inquiries of personnel responsible for financial and accounting matters concerning:
   a. Whether the interim financial information has been prepared in accordance with GAAP,
   b. Changes in business activities and accounting principles,
   c. Matters about which questions have arisen, and
   d. Events subsequent to the date of interim financial information that would have a material effect on the information.
7. Obtaining written representations from management.

---

10   M. Ettridge, D. Simon, D. Smith, and M. Stone. "Why Do Companies Purchase Timely Quarterly Reviews?" *Journal of Accounting and Economics* (September 1995).

Note that these procedures are substantially less in scope and require far less work than an audit: The auditor's effort is limited to analytical procedures and inquiries, rather than to search and verification procedures.

REPORTING ON A SEPARATE INTERIM PERIOD

An accountant's report accompanies reviewed interim financial information and includes a statement that the review was made in accordance with AICPA standards. The report identifies the interim financial information reviewed, describes the nature of procedures performed, and states that the scope of a review is substantially less than an audit. Interestingly, the three paragraphs of the interim review report communicate a similar message in substantially similar language to that of an *SSARS No. 1* review report, illustrated earlier, but note carefully that the interim review procedures required by *SAS No. 71* are actually somewhat more extensive than those required in a *SSARS No. 1* review.[11] For example, unlike *SSARS No. 1*, *SAS No. 71* requires inquiries about an entity's internal controls, and analytical procedures that compare recorded amounts (or ratios calculated from recorded amounts) to expectations developed by the accountant. A standard review report for interim period information follows:

**Independent Accountant's Report on
Interim Financial Information**

We have reviewed the accompanying financial statements of the Jenks Company and consolidated subsidiaries for the three-month period ended September 30, 1999. These financial statements are the responsibility of the company's management.

We conducted our review in accordance with standards established by the American Institute of Certified Public Accountants. A review of interim financial information consists principally of applying analytical procedures to financial data and making inquiries of persons responsible for financial and accounting matters. It is substantially less in scope than an audit conducted in accordance with generally accepted auditing standards, the objective of which is the expression of an opinion regarding the financial statements taken as a whole. Accordingly, we do not express such an opinion.

Based on our review, we are not aware of any material modifications that should be made to the accompanying financial statements for them to be in conformity with generally accepted accounting principles.

Source: SAS No. 71.

As in compilations and reviews under *SSARS No. 1*, a review of interim financial information may reveal a material departure from GAAP, even though no audit procedures are performed. If a client does not revise the interim financial information, the accountant should consider revising the standard review report, describing the nature of the departure and the effect on interim information. For example, assume a client excludes certain lease obligations from assets and liabilities that should be capitalized in accordance with FASB

Statement No. 13, "Accounting for Leases." Modifications to the standard review report follow:

**Independent Accountant's Report on
Interim Financial Information:
Departure from GAAP**

(First two paragraphs unchanged.)

Based on information furnished to us by management, we believe that the Company has excluded from property and debt in the accompanying balance sheet certain lease obligations that should be capitalized in order to conform with generally accepted accounting principles. This information indicates that if lease obligations were capitalized at September 30, 1999, property would be increased by $_____, long-term debt by $_____, and net income and earnings per share would be increased (decreased) by $_____, $_____, $_____, and $_____, respectively, for the three-month and nine-month periods then ended.

Based on our review, with the exception of the matter described in the preceding paragraph, we are not aware of any material modifications. . .

Source: SAS No. 71.

INTERIM INFORMATION ACCOMPANYING AUDITED STATEMENTS

SAS No. 71 also addresses the effect on a standard audit report when interim financial information accompanies audited financial statements. SEC *Regulation S-K, Item 302(a)* requires that quarterly sales, income, and earnings per share data be presented as supplementary information outside the audited financial statements or in an unaudited note to the statements. An independent auditor should review the interim information in accordance with the procedures outlined earlier. However, a separate report is not issued, and a standard audit report need not refer to the quarterly information unless the information is either omitted or not reviewed, in which case the audit report should be modified (called "exception reporting").

COMPREHENSIVE BASES OF ACCOUNTING OTHER THAN GAAP

For some entities, financial statements prepared in accordance with GAAP may be less telling than statements prepared on another comprehensive basis of accounting. For example, not-for-profit philanthropic organizations may be better served by the cash basis of accounting, and utility rate-making commissions may consider themselves better served when state-regulated utilities prepare financial statements in conformity with the commission's prescribed chart of accounts. *Statement on Auditing Standards No. 62,* "Special Reports" (AU Sec. 623), identifies four generally accepted, comprehensive bases of accounting (other than GAAP):

1. Cash receipts and disbursements basis of accounting.
2. A basis of accounting used to comply with a regulatory agency's requirements.

3. A basis of accounting used to file income tax returns.
4. A set of criteria having substantial support (e.g., price-level adjusted financial statements).

These are the only four generally accepted comprehensive bases of accounting. Stated another way: Any other bases of accounting, among them bases designed to portray a wholly unrealistic financial position, should be interpreted by an auditor as a departure from GAAP, thereby requiring that the auditor issue a qualified opinion or, if materiality warrants, an adverse opinion (Chapter 3).

If an entity's financial statements are presented on a generally accepted comprehensive basis other than GAAP, an accountant's report should include:

1. A title that includes the word *independent*, and
2. Separate paragraphs stating the:
    a. Statements were audited and are management's responsibility.
    b. Audit complied with GAAS.
    c. Comprehensive basis of accounting.
    d. Auditor's opinion on whether the financial statements conform to the comprehensive basis of accounting.

A report on cash basis financial statements follows:

**Independent Auditor's Report on
Cash Basis Financial Statements**

We have audited the statements of assets and liabilities arising from cash transactions of the Slater Company as of December 31, 1999, and the related statement of revenue collected and expenses paid for the year then ended. These financial statements are the responsibility of the Company's management. Our responsibility is to express an opinion on these statements based on our audit.

We conducted our audit in accordance with generally accepted auditing standards. Those standards require that we plan and perform the audit to obtain reasonable assurance about whether the financial statements are free of material misstatement. An audit includes examining, on a test basis, evidence supporting the amounts and disclosures in the financial statements. An audit also includes assessing the accounting principles used and significant estimates made by management, as well as evaluating the overall financial statement presentation. We believe that our audit provides a reasonable basis for our opinion.

As described in note 1, these financial statements were prepared on the basis of cash receipts and disbursements, which is a comprehensive basis of accounting other than generally accepted accounting principles.

In our opinion, the financial statements referred to above present fairly, in all material respects, the assets and liabilities arising from cash transactions of the Slater Company as of December 31, 1999, and the revenue collected and expenses paid during the year then ended, on the basis of accounting described in note 1.

Source: SAS No. 62.

SPECIFIED ELEMENTS, ACCOUNTS, OR ITEMS OF A FINANCIAL STATEMENT AND NONFINANCIAL STATEMENT ASSERTIONS

An independent accountant may be engaged to attest to specified financial statement elements, accounts, or items within an entity's financial statements, as opposed to an entire set of financial statements taken as a whole. Generally, these engagements either:

1. Apply *generally accepted auditing standards* and express an *opinion*, or
2. Apply *agreed-upon procedures* and express *limited assurance.*

GAAS

Compliance with contractual agreements sometimes requires that an entity provide an opinion, rather than a review or compilation report, on a specified financial statement item, such as gross sales. For example, a retailer's lease agreement with a shopping mall may tie rental payments to gross sales (e.g., 2 percent of sales), thereby requiring that the retailer engage an independent auditor to report on gross sales, only, rather than financial position, results of operations, and cash flows, as in a typical financial statement audit. When an independent accountant is engaged to express an opinion on specified financial statement items, the report should describe the scope of the engagement; identify the elements, accounts, or items audited; and state the auditor's opinion. The following illustrates a report expressing an unqualified opinion on gross sales:

Independent Auditor's Report on Gross Sales for the Purpose of Computing Rental Payments

We have audited the accompanying schedule of gross sales (as defined in the lease agreement dated March 4, 1999, between Fain & Company, as lessor, and Anderson Little Stores Corporation, as lessee) of Anderson Little Stores Corporation at its North Main Street store, Pawtucket, Rhode Island, for the year ended December 31, 1999. This schedule is the responsibility of Anderson Little Stores Corporation's management. Our responsibility is to express an opinion on the schedule based on our audit.

We conducted our audit in accordance with generally accepted auditing standards. Those standards require that we plan and perform the audit to obtain reasonable assurance about whether the schedule of gross sales is free of material misstatement. An audit includes examining, on a test basis, evidence supporting the amounts and disclosures in the schedule. An audit also includes assessing the accounting principles used and significant estimates made by management, as well as evaluating the overall schedule presentation. We believe that our audit provides a reasonable basis for our opinion.

In our opinion, the schedule of gross sales referred to above presents fairly, in all material respects, the gross sales of Anderson Little Stores Corporation at its North Main Street store, Pawtucket, Rhode Island, for the year ended December 31, 1999, in conformity with the basis specified in the lease agreement referred to above.

This report is intended solely for the information and use of the boards of directors and managements of Anderson Little Stores Corporation and Fain & Company, and should not be used for any other purpose.

Source: SAS No. 62.

AGREED-UPON PROCEDURES

In contrast, an independent accountant may be engaged to apply agreed-upon procedures—that is, procedures that are insufficient for expressing an opinion either on the item or, for that matter, on the financial statements from which the item was taken. For example, the *Federal Depository Insurance Corporation (FDIC) Improvement Act of 1991*, a response to the savings and loan industry debacle of the 1980s, requires insured depository institutions to have independent accountants perform agreed-upon procedures that test a bank's compliance with the FDIC's "safety and soundness" laws and regulations. The FDIC laws and regulations relate primarily to loans made to insiders and to dividend requirements. The agreed-upon procedures were developed jointly by representatives of both the AICPA and the banking profession. However, in most other agreed-upon procedures engagements, the procedures are engagement-specific and are drafted by the independent accountant, and by what the profession calls the "specified users" (the client and other beneficiaries of the accountant's report).

Practitioners today offer two types of agreed-upon procedures services, distinguished by what the procedures are applied to and by the applicable professional pronouncement:

Agreed-Upon Procedures Applied to	Pronouncement
1. Specified elements, accounts, or items of a financial statement	SAS No. 75, "Engagements to Apply Agreed-Upon Procedures to Specified Elements, Accounts, or Items of a Financial Statement"
2. Nonfinancial statement assertions	SSAE No. 4, "Agreed-Upon Procedures Engagements"

Practitioners provide *limited*, but not *negative*, assurance in both types of engagements. *Limited assurance* means the accountant makes a direct positive statement—for example, "We found no difference," or "We found no exceptions." In contrast, *negative assurance* means the accountant makes a negative statement—for example, "We are not aware . . .," or "Nothing came to our attention . . ." In practice, negative assurance is reserved for review-level engagements.

Under *SAS No. 75*, agreed-upon procedures are applied to specified elements, accounts, or items of a financial statement—that is, to accounting information which is part of, but significantly less than, a financial statement. For example, the procedures might be applied to receivables that a corporation records in accordance with GAAP, or property and equipment that a municipality records in an enterprise fund under a modified accrual basis of accounting. Under *SSAE No. 4*, agreed-upon procedures are applied to management's written, nonfinancial statement assertions, such as "All investment securities owned by the Hendriken Corporation during 1999 were traded on exchanges specified in the company's investment policy," or "Employee evaluations included in personnel files as of September 30, 1999 are dated within the time frame prescribed by the company and the United Auto Workers, Local 317."

Reports issued under *SAS No. 75* and *SSAE No. 4* are roughly equivalent. For example, a report on agreed-upon procedures applied to specified elements, accounts, or items of a financial statement includes:

1. A title that includes the word *independent*.
2. Reference to the specified elements, accounts, or items and to the basis of accounting.
3. The names of the specified users and a statement that the users agreed to the procedures.
4. Reference to standards established by the AICPA.
5. A statement that the sufficiency of the procedures is solely the responsibility of the specified users and a disclaimer of responsibility for the sufficiency of the procedures.
6. A list of the procedures performed and the findings.
7. A statement that the accountant was not engaged to perform an audit, and a statement restricting the use of the report.

An illustration follows:

Independent Accountant's Report on Agreed-Upon Procedures

We have performed the procedures described below, which were agreed-upon by the Trustee of the LaSalle Company, with respect to the claims of creditors to determine the validity of claims of the LaSalle Company as of May 31, 1999, as set forth in Schedule A. This engagement to apply agreed-upon procedures was performed in accordance with standards established by the American Institute of Certified Public Accountants. The sufficiency of these procedures is solely the responsibility of the Trustee of the LaSalle Company. Consequently, we make no representations regarding the sufficiency of the procedures described below either for the purpose for which this report has been requested or for any other purpose.

The procedures and associated findings are as follows:

1. Compare the total of the trial balance of accounts payable at May 31, 1999, prepared by the LaSalle Company, to the balance in the related general ledger account.

The total of the accounts payable trial balance agreed with the balance in the related general ledger account.

2. Compare the amounts for claims received from creditors (as shown in claim documents provided by the LaSalle Company) to the respective amounts shown in the trial balance of accounts payable. Using the data included in the claims documents and in the LaSalle Company's accounts payable detail records, reconcile any differences found to the accounts payable trial balance.

All differences noted are presented in column 3 of Schedule A. Except for those amounts shown in column 4 of Schedule A, all differences were reconciled.

3. Examine the documentation submitted by creditors in support of the amounts claimed and compare to the following documentation in the LaSalle Company's files: invoices, receiving reports, and other evidence of receipt of goods or services.

No exceptions were found as a result of these comparisons.

We were not engaged to, and did not, perform an audit, the objective of which would be the expression of an opinion on the specified elements, accounts, or items. Accordingly, we do not express such an opinion. Had we performed additional procedures, other matters might have come to our attention that would have been reported to you.

This report is intended solely for the use of the Trustee of the LaSalle Company and should not be used by those who have not agreed to the procedures and taken responsibility for the sufficiency of the procedures for their purposes.

Source: SAS No. 75.

REPORTS ON COMPLIANCE WITH CONTRACTUAL AGREEMENTS OR REGULATORY REQUIREMENTS

An audit client may also engage an auditor to attest to management's compliance with contractual agreements such as bond indentures, loan agreements, or government grant reporting requirements. An engagement to report on compliance with contractual agreements usually arises when an audit client has borrowed funds and entered into a contractual arrangement that imposes a requirement on the borrower to make payments into a sinking fund, to maintain a minimum current ratio, or to restrict dividend payments to shareholders. An auditor's reporting obligation under *Statement on Auditing Standards No. 62*, "Special Reports" (AU Sec. 623), is to provide assurance either in a separate report or in a paragraph within the standard audit report, although the auditor should not express assurance unless the financial statements have been audited. A separate report on compliance with a contractual agreement follows:

Independent Auditor's Report on
Compliance with a Contractual Agreement

We have audited, in accordance with generally accepted auditing standards, the balance sheet of Potter Company as of December 31, 1998, and the related statements of income, retained earnings, and cash flows for the year then ended, and have issued our report thereon dated February 16, 1999.

In connection with our audit, nothing came to our attention that caused us to believe that the Company failed to comply with the terms, covenants, provisions, or conditions of Sections 12 to 17, inclusive, of the Indenture dated July 21, 1997, with Citizens Bank, insofar as they relate to accounting matters. However, our audit was not directed primarily toward obtaining knowledge of such noncompliance.

This report is intended solely for the information and use of the boards of directors and managements of Potter Company and Citizens Bank and should not be used for any other purpose.

Source: SAS No. 62.

LETTERS FOR UNDERWRITERS

Less than five months after AT&T announced their decision to split into three separate companies, securities in Lucent Technologies—comprised of Bell Laboratories and AT&T's telecommunications equipment segment—were sold on the New York Stock Exchange in the single biggest initial public offering of securities in U.S. history, $3.1 billion. Consistent with the *Securities Act of 1933*, AT&T first filed a registration statement with the Securities and Exchange Commission (Chapter 5) before offering Lucent securities for sale to the public. As is typical, an investment bank and other financial institutions served as AT&T's underwriters by purchasing some of the securities for investment or resale and by selling the bulk of the securities to the public. (An underwriter is an intermediary between an offering entity and the investing public and, as a result, is a primary party to the registration process.)

The *Securities Act of 1933* holds an underwriter responsible to perform a "reasonable investigation" of all financial and accounting data before participating in the filing. To fulfill their responsibility to investigate financial and accounting matters they were not expert in, the underwriters for the Lucent Technologies offering engaged Coopers & Lybrand,[12] AT&T's independent auditors, to prepare what is often called a **comfort letter** in accordance with *Statement on Auditing Standards No. 72*, "Letters for Underwriters and Certain Other Requesting Parties." In general, the letter reports:

1. An *opinion* on whether the latest audited financial statements comply with the Act's accounting requirements, and
2. *Negative assurance* on unaudited interim financial information for the period between the date of the latest audited financial statements and the date of the registration statement.

The unaudited interim financial information is subjected to the inquiries and analytical procedures prescribed by *Statement on Auditing Standards No. 71*, "Interim Financial Information," introduced earlier in the chapter.

Comfort letters vary in content depending on an underwriter's needs. For example, an underwriter's needs will vary for foreign offerings, including Eurodollar and other off-shore offerings, or for acquisition transactions, including exchanges of stock rather than stock-for-cash offerings. The purpose of the accountant's comfort letter is to provide assurance to the underwriter, not to the SEC. As a result, the letter is not filed with the SEC as part of the registration statement. Rather, the letter is held by the underwriter and produced only as a defense against claims by securities purchasers. Because of the variety and, in particular, the length of comfort letters prepared in practice, a sample letter is not illustrated here. However, an appendix to *SAS No. 72* includes sixteen sample letters covering a wide range of circumstances, among them Example A, a typical letter.

FINANCIAL FORECASTS AND PROJECTIONS

Most all of the reports issued by independent accountants and auditors attest to financial information compiled from transactions and events that occurred

12   "C&L Reaps Profits from Largest-Ever IPO," *Public Accounting Report* (March 31, 1996), p. 3.

in the past. Reports on forecasts and projections, in contrast, are a break from tradition: Attestations are made about transactions and events that not only haven't yet happened but that may never happen at all. This change in direction—attesting to the past v. the future—does not preclude an independent accountant from assisting an entity in preparing published forecasts and projections. But, an accountant should never allow an entity to use his or her name in a manner that may lead users to believe the accountant vouches for the achievability of a financial forecast or projection. The ASB's *Statement on Standards for Attestation Engagements No. 1,* "Attestation Standards" (AT Section 200, entitled "Financial Forecasts and Projections") defines a *financial forecast* and a *financial projection,* and sets forth standards and guidance for engagements to compile, examine, or apply agreed-upon procedures to prospective financial statements.

FORECASTS AND PROJECTIONS

Financial forecasts and projections are referred to as **prospective financial statements.** A **financial forecast** is a prospective financial statement that presents an entity's expected financial position, results of operations, and cash flows. Unlike audited, compiled, or reviewed financial statements, all of which are based on past transactions and events, forecasts are based on expected transactions and events, and reflect assumptions the reporting entity expects to exist and the course of action management expects to take. A financial forecast may be expressed in single monetary amounts or as a range of amounts.

In contrast, a **financial projection** is also a prospective financial statement that presents an entity's expected financial position, results of operations, and cash flows, but is based on one or more hypothetical assumptions. For example, a financial projection may be prepared to evaluate one or more hypothetical courses of action—that is, it addresses "What would happen if . . . ?" Like a forecast, a financial projection may contain a range of monetary amounts.

COMPILATION OF PROSPECTIVE FINANCIAL STATEMENTS

A compilation of prospective financial statements involves:

1. Assembling prospective financial statements based on management's assumptions, and
2. Performing compilation procedures, including comparing the prospective financial statements with the summary of significant assumptions and accounting policies.

The summary of significant assumptions is essential to a reader's understanding of the prospective financial statements. An accountant should not compile prospective financial statements that omit the summary of assumptions or, in the case of a financial projection, that fail to disclose the hypothetical assumptions.

To illustrate a compilation report on prospective financial statements, assume that the Curtis Corporation engages an independent accountant to prepare projected financial statements that will be used in negotiating a plant expansion loan from the Industrial National Bank. A compilation report follows:

Accountant's Compilation Report on a Financial Projection

We have compiled the accompanying projected balance sheet, statements of income, retained earnings, and cash flows of the Curtis Corporation as of December 31, 2000, and for the year then ending, in accordance with standards established by the American Institute of Certified Public Accountants.

The accompanying projection and this report were prepared for the Industrial National Bank for the purpose of negotiating a plant expansion loan and should not be used for any other purpose.

A compilation is limited to presenting in the form of a projection information that is the representation of management and does not include evaluation of the support for the assumptions underlying the projection. We have not audited the projection and, accordingly, do not express an opinion or any other form of assurance on the accompanying statements or assumptions. Furthermore, even if the loan is granted and the physical plant is expanded, there will usually be differences between the projected and actual results, because events and circumstances frequently do not occur as expected, and those differences may be material. We have no responsibility to update this report for events and circumstances occurring after the date of this report.

Source: SSAE No. 1, AT Section 218.

Note in this case that there was only one hypothetical assumption: that the loan was granted.

EXAMINATION OF PROSPECTIVE FINANCIAL STATEMENTS

In an examination of prospective financial statements, an independent accountant expresses an opinion. But unlike an opinion on audited financial statements, which provides assurance about whether the statements conform with GAAP, an opinion on prospective financial statements provides assurance on whether: (1) the prospective financial statements conform with AICPA guidelines, i.e., *SSAE No. 1*, "Attestation Standards" (AT Section 200), and (2) the assumptions provide a reasonable basis for a forecast or projection. The following illustrates a standard report on the examination of a financial forecast:

**Independent Accountant's Report on
an Examination of a Financial Forecast**

We have examined the accompanying forecasted balance sheet, statements of income, retained earnings, and cash flows of the McCabe Company as of December 31, 2000, and for the year then ending. These forecasted financial statements are the responsibility of the company's management. Our responsibility is to express an opinion on these forecasted financial statements based on our examination made in accordance with standards for an examination of a forecast established by the American Institute of Certified Public Accountants.

In our opinion, the accompanying forecast is presented in conformity with guidelines for presentation of a forecast established by the American Institute of Certified Public Accountants, and the underlying assumptions provide a reasonable basis for management's forecast. However, there will usually be differences between the forecasted and actual results, because events and circumstances frequently do not occur as expected, and those differences may be material. We have no responsibility to update this report for events and circumstances occurring after the date of this report.

Source: SSAE No. 1, AT Section 232.

Like the compilation report on a financial projection illustrated earlier, the above report alerts readers that assumptions may not mirror future events and circumstances, and that the accountant is under no obligation to update the report if future information casts doubt on earlier assumptions.

APPLYING AGREED-UPON PROCEDURES TO PROSPECTIVE FINANCIAL STATEMENTS

Accountants are sometimes engaged to apply agreed-upon procedures to prospective financial statements for the express benefit of a specific third party, such as a commercial bank. However, these engagements may be accepted only if: (1) the specified users have participated in establishing the nature and scope of the engagement and take responsibility for the procedures performed, (2) the report is distributed only to the specified users, and (3) the statements include a summary of significant assumptions. The agreed-upon procedures may be limited or extensive, but responsibility for their adequacy rests with the user.

A report on the results of applying agreed-upon procedures should:

1.   Indicate the prospective financial statements covered.
2.   Indicate that use of the report is limited to the specified user(s).
3.   Describe the procedures performed.
4.   Disclaim an opinion on the statements and assumptions if the procedures are less than those usually performed in an audit.
5.   State the accountant's findings.
6.   State that the prospective results may not be achieved.
7.   State that the accountant assumes no responsibility to update the report.

PERSONAL FINANCIAL STATEMENTS

Much like businesses, individuals or families may also require audited financial statements, though for different reasons. For example, a political candidate may elect to disclose publicly his or her personal financial position, or an individual may need personal statements to acquire bank credit when organizing a business. Interestingly, **personal financial statements** differ markedly from financial statements prepared in accordance with GAAP. For example, assets are reported at estimated current values in personal financial statements, thereby requiring that the accountant attest to current value—a more challenging task than attesting to historical cost.

The AICPA's *Statement of Position 82-1,* "Accounting and Financial Reporting for Personal Financial Statements," and the *Personal Financial Statements Guide,* provide guidance to auditors and accountants for audit and nonaudit engagements on personal financial statements. The *Guide* illustrates an unqualified report on the personal financial statements of a married couple:

**Independent Auditor's Report
on Personal Financial Statements**

We have audited the statement of financial condition of Mr. and Mrs. Robert V. Bracken as of December 31, 1999, and the related statement of changes in net worth for the year then ended. These statements are the responsibility of Mr. and Mrs. Bracken. Our responsibility is to express an opinion on these statements based on our audit.

In our opinion, the financial statements referred to above present fairly, in all material respects, the financial position of Mr. and Mrs. Robert V. Bracken as of December 31, 1999, and the changes in their net worth for the year then ended, in conformity with generally accepted accounting principles.

Source: AICPA's Personal Financial Statements Guide.

REPORTS ON THE APPLICATION OF ACCOUNTING PRINCIPLES

Occasionally, an accountant will report to a nonclient about the application of accounting principles. For example, entities sometimes engage an independent accountant (called the "reporting accountant") to report on the application of an accounting principle proposed by the entity's independent auditor (called the "continuing accountant")—that is, a second opinion. *Statement on Auditing Standards No. 50*, "Reports on the Application of Accounting Principles," provides guidance when an auditor reports in writing or orally on: (1) the application of accounting principles, or (2) a nonclient's audit opinion. A sample report follows:

**Independent Accountant's Report
on the Application of Accounting Principles**

We have been engaged to report on the appropriate application of generally accepted accounting principles to the specific transaction described below. This report is being issued to the Prospect Company for assistance in evaluating accounting principles for the described specific transaction. Our engagement has been conducted in accordance with standards established by the American Institute of Certified Public Accountants.

The facts, circumstances, and assumptions relevant to the specific transaction as provided to us by management of the Prospect Company are as follows:

[Text describing facts, circumstances, and assumptions.]

[Text discussing accounting principles.]

The ultimate responsibility for the decision on the appropriate application of generally accepted accounting principles for an actual transaction rests with the preparers of financial statements, who should consult with their continuing accountants. Our judgment of the appropriate application of generally accepted accounting principles for the described transaction is based solely on the facts provided to us as described above; should these facts and circumstances differ, our conclusion may change.

Source: SAS No. 50.

Because the request for a second opinion may have been motivated by a disagreement between the client and the continuing accountant, the reporting accountant should consult with the continuing accountant to assure that all relevant facts have been revealed. In short, if there are disagreements, the continuing accountant should be privy to both sides of the story.

SUMMARY

Although an emerging rather than a mature product line, assurance services are being offered currently by several public accounting firms and are being encouraged by the prominent work and recommendations of the AICPA's Special Committee on Assurance Services (the Elliott Committee). Importantly, the potential for assurance services is far more vast than the electronic commerce and health care assurances illustrated in this chapter. As Jim Naus, managing partner of Crowe Chizek has said, "The methods that accountants use to check data and information can be spread to almost any field and can provide valuable information for a wide range of clients."[13]

More mature, but also promising, attestation services have long been offered by the profession and guided by the Auditing Standards Board's attestation standards (Chapter 2). For example, attestation services are offered commonly for compilations and reviews of financial statements, interim financial information, comprehensive bases of accounting other than GAAP, agreed-upon procedures, compliance with contractual requirements, letters for underwriters, financial forecasts and projections, personal financial statements, and applications of accounting principles.

KEY TERMS

Review engagement 673
Compilation engagement 674
Compilation of financial statements 674
Review of financial statements 675
Interim financial statements 678

Comfort letter 686
Prospective financial statements 687
Financial forecast 687
Financial projection 687
Personal financial statements 689

REFERENCES

Statements on Auditing Standards (SASs)

AICPA. *Codification of Statements on Auditing Standards*. New York: AICPA.
SAS No. 50, "Reports on the Application of Accounting Principles."
SAS No. 62, "Special Reports."
SAS No. 71, "Interim Financial Information."
SAS No. 72, "Letters for Underwriters and Certain Other Requesting Parties."
SAS No. 75, "Engagements to Apply Agreed-Upon Procedures to Specified Elements, Accounts, or Items of a Financial Statement."
SAS No. 76, "Amendments to SAS No. 72, Letters for Underwriters and Certain Other Requesting Parties."

13 L. Berton. "Accountants Expand Scope of Audit Work," *The Wall Street Journal* (June 17, 1996), p. B8.

Statements on Standards for Accounting and Review Services (SSARSs)

AICPA. *Codification of Statements on Standards for Accounting and Review Services.* New York: AICPA.
SSARS No. 1, "Compilation and Review of Financial Statements."
SSARS No. 7, "Omnibus Statement on Standards for Accounting and Review Services—1992."

Statements on Standards for Attestation Engagements (SSAEs)

SSAE No. 1, "Attestation Standards" [includes "Attestation Standards" (AT 100), "Financial Forecasts and Projections" (AT 200), and "Reporting on Pro Forma Financial Information" (AT 300)].
SSAE No. 2, "Reporting on an Entity's Internal Control Structure Over Financial Reporting."
SSAE No. 3, "Compliance Attestation."
SSAE No. 4, "Agreed-Upon Procedures Engagements."

Professional Report

AICPA Special Committee on Assurance Services (the Elliott Committee). *Professional Growth Through New Assurance Services.* New York: AICPA (1995).

Web Site

AICPA, Special Committee on Assurance Services (the Elliott Committee): http://www.aicpa.org/assurance/pre/index.htm.

Articles, Books

Bogan, W. T., and W. T. Conn, Jr. "The Meaning of Compliance Attestation," *Journal of Accountancy* (April 1994), pp. 59-64.

Brackney, K. S., and G. L. Helms. "A Survey of Attestation Practices," *Auditing: A Journal of Practice & Theory* (Fall 1996), pp. 85-98.

Chan, S., M. Govindan, J. Y. Picard, G. S. Takach, and B. Wright. *EDI Control, Management, and Audit Issues.* New York: AICPA (1995).

Cheney, G. "Creating the Firms of the 21st Century," *Accounting Today* (December 16, 1996-January 5, 1997), pp. 1, 70.

Cheney, G. "Regional Firm Hits National Market with New Assurance Services," *Accounting Today* (January 6-19, 1997).

Craig, J. "Preserving the Profession's Assurance Function: An Interview with AICPA Vice President Dan Guy," *The CPA Journal* (January 1994), pp. 36-40.

Elliott, R. K. "The Third Wave Breaks on the Shores of Accounting," *Accounting Horizons* (June 1992), pp. 62-85.

Elliott, R. K. "The Future of Audits," *Journal of Accountancy* (September 1994), pp. 74-82.

Elliott, R. K. "Confronting the Future: Choices for the Attest Function," *Accounting Horizons* (September 1994), pp. 106-124.

Elliott, R. K. "AICPA Assurance Services Committee: What is the Future of Auditing?" *Journal of Corporate Accounting and Finance* (Winter 1994-95), pp. 87-97.

Elliott, R. K. "The Future of Assurance Services: Implications for Academia," *Accounting Horizons* (December 1995), pp. 118-127.

Mancino, J. M., and D. M. Guy. "Reviews of Financial Statements: SAS No. 71 vs. SSARS," *Journal of Accountancy* (March 1993), pp. 61-67.

Read, W., and S. Tomczyk. "An Examination of Changes in Scope of Services Performed by CPA Firms," *Accounting Horizons* (September 1992), pp. 42-51.

Williamson, A. L. "The Mirror Standards," *Journal of Accountancy* (December 1995), pp. 87-91.

QUESTIONS

1. Compare and contrast assurance and attestation services.
2. Discuss why entry into the assurance services market is important to public accounting firms.
3. Explain what is meant by a compilation and by a review of financial statements.
4. Describe the purpose of, and give examples of analytical procedures performed in, a review of financial statements.
5. In what situations might an independent accountant review interim financial information?

6. Why are costs, expenses, deferrals, and accruals often estimated to a greater extent in interim than in annual financial statements?

7. What is a "comprehensive basis of accounting other than GAAP"?

8. To what does an auditor's opinion relate when an entity's financial statements are prepared on a comprehensive basis of accounting other than GAAP?

9. Explain the purpose of letters for underwriters.

10. Explain the difference between a financial forecast and a financial projection.

11. What does a report on personal financial statements typically address?

12. Under what conditions might an independent accountant report on the application of accounting principles?

MULTIPLE CHOICE QUESTIONS

1. Which of the following would not be considered an attestation engagement under *SSAE No. 1*, "Attestation Standards"?

a. A compilation of financial statements.
b. A letter for an underwriter.
c. A report on the application of an accounting principle.
d. A report on financial statements that are prepared on a comprehensive basis of accounting other than GAAP.

2. In a review engagement, the independent accountant's procedures include:

a. Examining bank reconciliations.
b. Confirming accounts receivable with debtors.
c. Reading the financial statements to consider whether they appear to conform with GAAP.
d. Obtaining a letter of audit inquiry from all attorneys of record.

3. Which of the following is correct about the AICPA's attestation standards?

a. The attestation standards supersede generally accepted auditing standards.
b. The attestation standards supersede generally accepted auditing standards only for financial statement audits of publicly traded corporations.
c. The attestation standards apply to all attestation engagements.
d. The attestation standards derive their authority from general acceptance among practitioners.

4. Which of the following procedures is not appropriate to a review of interim financial information?

a. Confirm cash balances with all banks and depositories.
b. Make inquiries concerning the accounting system and any significant changes in the internal control structure.
c. Perform analytical procedures to identify and provide a basis for inquiry about relationships and individual items that appear unusual.
d. Read the minutes of meetings of stockholders, the board of directors, and committees of the board.

5. When engaged to express an opinion on one or more specified elements, accounts, or items of a financial statement, an auditor:

a. May not describe auditing procedures applied.
b. Should advise that professional standards preclude anything other than a piecemeal opinion.

   c. May assume that the first standard of reporting concerning generally accepted accounting principles does not apply.

   d. Should perform the engagement only if the specified elements, accounts, or items constitute a major portion of the financial statements.

6. *Statement on Auditing Standards No. 62,* "Special Reports," is explicit about what is meant by a comprehensive basis of accounting other than GAAP. Of the following, which is not a comprehensive basis of accounting according to *SAS No. 62*?

   a. Cash receipts and disbursements basis of accounting.

   b. A basis of accounting used to comply with a regulatory agency's requirements.

   c. Historical cost adjusted for the current value of tangible assets.

   d. A basis of accounting used to file income tax returns.

7. Which of the following would not be appropriate to a report on an engagement to apply agreed-upon procedures to specified financial statement items?

   a. Indicate the intended distribution of the report.

   b. Provide an opinion on the specified elements, accounts, or items.

   c. Enumerate the procedures performed.

   d. State that the report relates only to the elements, accounts, or items specified.

8. What is meant by a financial forecast under *Statement on Standards for Attestation Engagements No. 1,* "Attestation Standards" (AT Section 200, entitled "Financial Forecasts and Projections")?

   a. A prospective financial statement that predicts an entity's expected financial position, results of operations, and cash flows.

   b. A prospective financial statement that presents an entity's expected financial position, results of operations, and cash flows.

   c. A prospective financial statement that presents an entity's expected financial position, results of operations, and cash flows based on one or more hypothetical assumptions.

   d. A prospective financial statement that predicts an entity's expected financial position, results of operations, and cash flows based on one or more hypothetical assumptions.

9. Which of the following is not appropriate for the accountant's report on the results of applying agreed-upon procedures to prospective financial statements?

   a. State the accountant's opinion on the results of applying the agreed-upon procedures.

   b. Indicate the prospective financial statements reported on.

   c. Indicate that the use of the report is limited to the specified user(s).

   d. Indicate that the prospective results may not be achieved.

10. Under *Statement on Auditing Standards No. 50,* "Reports on the Application of Accounting Principles," an independent accountant may give a second opinion on matters relating to a financial statement audit performed by another independent accountant. Which of the following is not appropriate to the accountant's report?

   a. Indicate that the ultimate responsibility for deciding on the appropriate accounting principles rests with the continuing accountant.

   b. State the facts, circumstances, and assumptions relevant to the transaction.

   c. State that the engagement has been conducted in accordance with standards established by the AICPA.

   d. State that the accountant's judgment of the appropriate application of accounting principles is based solely on the facts provided by the client.

PROBLEMS AND DISCUSSION CASES

18-1 *Proposing an Assurance Service Engagement*

VAN Technologies, a value-added network service provider, links subscribing electronic data integration (EDI) networks, receives network transmissions from trading partners, translates transmissions into an ANSI 12 format, and functions as an electronic post office by transmitting and acknowledging orders electronically. Owing to widespread reports of data-security problems in EDI networks, several subscribers have approached management, questioning VAN's controls over hacker attacks, transmission failures, identification authentication, and infiltration of confidential data files. In response, management asks an engagement partner in Settles & Weick, LLP to propose on offering assurances that would quiet subscribers' fears.

Required:

1. Is the engagement an assurance service engagement or an attestation service engagement? Explain.
2. Discuss the barriers the engagement partner ought to consider before proposing on the engagement.

18-2 *Compilation of Financial Statements*

A compilation of financial statements involves presenting management's assertions in the form of financial statements without expressing any degree of assurance. Nevertheless, even though no assurance is expressed, an independent accountant must comply with the provisions of *SSARS No. 1*, "Compilation and Review of Financial Statements."

Required:

1. Identify the type of knowledge and understanding that an independent accountant should obtain in a compilation engagement.
2. How does an accountant inform users of the nature and limitations of a compilation?
3. What actions should an independent accountant take when he or she becomes aware of a material departure from GAAP in financial statements compiled?

18-3 *Review of Financial Statements*

Christopher Rossi, CPA has been engaged by the Barrington Company, a nonpublicly held manufacturer of children's toys, to review Barrington's December 31, 1999 financial statements. Rossi accepts the engagement, and performs inquiries and analytical procedures sufficient to provide a reasonable basis for expressing negative assurance that no material modifications are necessary to conform the statements with generally accepted accounting principles. While making inquiries of Barrington's chief financial officer, Rossi discovers that land is carried at appraised value rather than historical cost, and that the company refuses to adjust the December 31, 1999 statements. All inquiries and analytical procedures are completed on January 28, 2000.

Required: Prepare the review report Rossi would present to Barrington's board of directors, assuming the effect on financial statements of carrying land at appraised value has not been determined by management.

18-4 *Interim Financial Statements*

Richard Bernstein, who has audited the financial statements of the Century Group, Inc., a publicly held company, for the year ended December 31, 1999, has been asked to perform a limited review of the unaudited interim financial statements of the Century Group for the quarter ending March 31, 2000. The engagement letter states that a limited review does not provide a basis for expressing an opinion.

Required:

1. Explain why Bernstein's limited review will not provide a basis for expressing an opinion.

2. What are the review procedures that Bernstein should perform, and what is the purpose of each procedure? Structure your response as follows:

Procedure   *Purpose of Procedure*

(AICPA Adapted)

18-5 *Minimizing Misunderstandings About Unaudited Financial Statements*
The limitations on a practitioner's professional responsibilities when associated with unaudited financial statements are often misunderstood, although the risk of misunderstanding can be reduced substantially by carefully following professional pronouncements and by taking other appropriate measures.

Required: The following are situations a practitioner may encounter in his or her association with unaudited financial statements. Briefly discuss the extent of the practitioner's responsibilities and, if appropriate, the actions he or she should take to minimize any misunderstandings.

1. A group of investors who own a farm managed by an independent agent engage an independent accountant to prepare quarterly unaudited financial statements. The accountant prepares the financial statements from information supplied by the independent agent. Subsequently, the investors find that the statements are inaccurate because the agent embezzled funds. The investors refuse to pay the accountant's fee and blame the accountant for allowing the embezzlement to go undetected, contending that representations from the independent agent should not have been relied on.

2. In comparing the trial balance with the general ledger, an accountant finds an account labeled "Audit Fees" in which the client has accumulated the accountant's quarterly billings for accounting services, including the preparation of quarterly unaudited financial statements.

3. To determine appropriate account classification, an accountant reviewed a number of the client's invoices. The accountant noted in the working papers that some invoices were missing, but felt they did not affect the unaudited financial statements, and thus did nothing further. The client subsequently discovered that invoices were missing and contended that the accountant should not have ignored the missing invoices when preparing the financial statements, but had a responsibility to at least inform the client that they were missing.

4. An accountant is engaged to review the financial statements prepared by a client's controller. During the review, the accountant learns of several items that by generally accepted accounting principles would require adjustment to the statements and notes. The controller agrees to make the recommended adjustments but refuses to add the notes because the statements are unaudited.

(AICPA Adapted)

18-6 *Comprehensive Bases of Accounting Other Than GAAP*
Rose & Co., LLP, has completed the audit of the financial statements of Bale & Booster, a partnership, for the year ended December 31, 1999. The financial statements were prepared on the income tax (cash) basis and include footnotes indicating that the partnership was involved in continuing litigation for alleged infringement of a competitor's patent. Damages, if any, resulting from the litigation could not be estimated as of the last day of field work. Prior year financial statements were not presented.

Required: Draft an audit report.

18-7 *An Opinion Based on Agreed-Upon Procedures*
Management often calls for an independent auditor's assistance. For example, an audit client's management might request that their auditor apply agreed-upon procedures to some, but not all, of the financial statement accounts of a company that management

considers a serious candidate for acquisition. Assume that U-Clean Corporation, an audit client, has requested that your firm perform agreed-upon procedures at the Ajax Corporation. At the completion of the engagement, an audit assistant prepares the following report for your review:

We have applied certain agreed-upon procedures, as discussed below, to accounting records of Ajax Corporation as of December 31, 1999, solely to assist U-Clean Corporation in connection with the proposed acquisition of Ajax Corporation.

We have examined the cash in banks and accounts receivable of Ajax Corporation as of December 31, 1999, in accordance with generally accepted auditing standards and, accordingly, included such tests of the accounting records and such other auditing procedures as we considered necessary in the circumstances.

In our opinion, the cash and receivables referred to above are presented fairly, in all material respects, as of December 31, 1999, in conformity with generally accepted accounting principles. We therefore recommend that U-Clean Corporation acquire Ajax Corporation pursuant to the proposed agreement.

Required: Comment on the proposed report, describing those assertions that are:
1.   Incorrect or should otherwise be deleted.
2.   Missing and should be inserted.

(AICPA Adapted)

18-8   *Describing Findings in an Agreed-Upon Procedures Engagement*
Agreed-upon procedures engagements on elements, accounts, or items of a financial statement and on nonfinancial statement assertions require that the independent accountant describe both the procedures and the findings in his or her report. Following are two agreed-upon procedures—one for cash, and another for invoices—and two alternative means of reporting findings for each procedure.

1.   *Agreed-Upon Procedure: Cash*
     Trace all outstanding checks appearing on a bank reconciliation as of a certain date to checks cleared in the bank statement as of the subsequent month.
     a.   *Description of Findings: A*
          "All outstanding checks appearing on the bank reconciliation were cleared in the subsequent month's bank statement."
     b.   *Description of Findings: B*
          "Nothing came to my attention as a result of applying the procedure."
2.   *Agreed-Upon Procedure: Invoices*
     Compare the amounts of the invoices included in the over-ninety-days column of an identified schedule of aged accounts receivable of a specific customer (as of a certain date) to the amounts and invoice dates shown on the outstanding invoices, and determine whether or not the amounts agree, and whether or not the invoice dates precede the date indicated on the schedule by more than ninety days.
     a.   *Description of Findings: A*
          "All outstanding invoice amounts agreed with the amounts shown on the schedule in the over-ninety-days column, and the dates shown on such invoices preceded the date indicated on the schedule by more than ninety days."
     b.   *Description of Findings: B*
          "The outstanding invoice amounts agreed within an approximation of the amounts shown on the schedule in the over-ninety-days column, and nothing came to our attention to indicate that the dates shown on the invoices preceded the date indicated on the schedule by more than ninety days."
Required: For each agreed-upon procedure, explain which description of findings, *A* or *B*, is appropriate, and why.

18-9 *Financial Statement v. Nonfinancial Statement Assertions in Agreed-Upon Procedures Engagements*

Understanding whether agreed-upon procedures relate to a specified element, account, or item of a financial statement or to a nonfinancial statement assertion is important because the professional pronouncements used for the two situations differ. *SAS No. 75,* "Engagements to Apply Agreed-Upon Procedures to Specified Elements, Accounts, or Items of a Financial Statement" applies in the first case, and *SSAE No. 4,* "Agreed-Upon Procedures Engagements" applies in the second case. Following are a series of items for which an independent accountant might apply agreed-upon procedures:

1. The cash accounts included in an entity's general ledger maintained for the purpose of preparing financial statements represented as being in accordance with generally accepted accounting principles.
2. A schedule of accounts receivable that reflects the accounts receivable is presented in conformity with generally accepted accounting principles.
3. An entity maintained an effective internal control over financial reporting based on established criteria.
4. The accounts included in the caption "Property and Equipment" identified in a Statement of Assets, Liabilities, and Capital presented on an income tax basis.
5. An entity complied with requirements of specified laws, regulations, rules, contracts, and grants.
6. Investment securities were traded on approved exchanges.
7. The gross income component of a Statement of Operations was presented in accordance with the rules of a regulatory agency.
8. Statistical production data complied with policy.

Required: For each item (1) though (8), indicate whether the item is a specified element, account, or item of a financial statement or a nonfinancial statement assertion.

18-10 *Personal Financial Statements*

Roger Francoeur, a candidate for town council, is campaigning on a platform of open government and fiscal responsibility. During his campaign, Francoeur requests that you prepare personal financial statements, fully disclosing his financial position for the twelve-month period ended June 30, 1999. Unfamiliar with the nature of personal financial statements, Francoeur asks that you explain the major similarities and differences between the financial statements and audit reports that are issued for personal and corporate financial statements.

Required: Describe the major similarities and differences alluded to by Francoeur, indicating the rationale underlying each difference. Ignore differences related to the titles of financial statements.

18-11 *Inappropriate Behavior in a Nonattest Engagement*

Brown received a telephone call from Calhoun, the sole owner and manager of a small company, asking Brown to prepare financial statements for the company. Calhoun told Brown that the statements were needed in two weeks, but was vague when Brown asked about the intended use of the statements. Brown was convinced that Calhoun thought Brown's work would constitute an audit. To avoid confusion, Brown decided not to explain to Calhoun that the engagement would be to prepare the financial statements only. Brown understood that a substantial fee would be paid if the work were completed in two weeks, accepted the engagement, and started work at once.

Brown discovered an accrued expense account labeled "Professional Fees" and learned that the balance in the account represented an accrual for the cost of Brown's services. Brown suggested to Calhoun's bookkeeper that the account name be changed to "Fees for Limited Audit Engagement." Brown also reviewed several invoices to determine whether accounts were being classified properly. Some invoices were missing. Brown listed the missing invoice numbers in the working papers with a note indicating that they should be followed up during the next engagement. Brown also discovered that fixed assets were carried at estimated current replacement costs. Based on available records, Brown prepared a balance sheet, income statement, and statement of shareholders' equity. In addition, Brown drafted the notes but decided that any mention of the replacement costs would only mislead the readers. Brown suggested to Calhoun that readers of the financial statements would be better informed if they received a separate letter from Calhoun explaining the meaning and effect of the estimated replacement costs of the fixed assets. Brown mailed the financial statements to Calhoun with the following note included on each page:

> *The accompanying financial statements are submitted to you without complete audit verification.*

Required: Identify the inappropriate actions of Brown and indicate what Brown should have done to avoid each inappropriate action. Structure your response as follows:

Inappropriate Action	*What Brown Should Have Done to Avoid Inappropriate Action*

(AICPA Adapted)

RESEARCH PROJECTS

1. ASSURANCE SERVICES AND RETAIL ELECTRONIC COMMERCE

Woolford Marketing, an Internet marketing organization, estimates that by the year 2000, no fewer than 500 million subscribers will access Internet browser services to purchase goods and services electronically. Like the 1990s, most subscribers are expected to use a single, primary transaction media: credit cards. Given that most people willingly pay annual credit card fees averaging say $35, there's reason to believe the same people would be willing to pay say $5 annually to purchase assurances against invasion of privacy and harassment from unwanted solicitors. This translates into a $2.5 billion assurance service market (500 million subscribers $5) for data-security assur - ances alone. For perspective, consider that currently the Fortune 500 companies pay less to public accounting firms for financial statement audits. There's every reason to believe that information technology could create considerable demand for data-security assurances, but no reason to doubt that demand could create ferocious competition from assurance service providers far removed from the public accounting profession.

  Required: Using a browser service, like Netscape's Navigator or Microsoft's Explorer, link to a Web site that offers retail, business, entertainment, or education purchases. Draft a report that describes the Web site's offerings and identifies assurances you think consumers (or the Web site manager) would be willing to purchase (or supply). For example, what assurances would *you* want about credit card number security and freedom from unwanted solicitation?

2. THE MOTIVATION FOR PROFESSIONAL STANDARDS

This chapter referenced a number of *Statements on Auditing Standards* (*SASs*), *Statements on Standards for Accounting and Review Services* (*SSARSs*), and *Statements on Standards for Attestation Engagements* (*SSAEs*), since all of the attestation services introduced in the chapter are guided by professional pronouncements. Like many professional standards in public accounting, the issues that drove some of the pronouncements addressed in this chapter were somewhat controversial—in fact, they likely would not have reached the Auditing Standards Board's technical agenda otherwise. For example, *SSARS No. 1,* "Compilation and Review of Financial Statements," resulted largely because the price of an audit, the only attest service independent accountants were empowered to perform on financial statements, raised the cost of capital beyond the means of many small owner-managed companies. The review services introduced in *SSARS No. 1* offered lending institutions the negative assurance they needed, and provided a cost-effective attestation alternative for players in the commercial-capital market.

Required: Select any *SAS, SSARS,* or *SSAE* referenced at the end of any chapter in this text, and draft a report that identifies the stakeholders and the issue(s) that likely drove the pronouncement. Sources include *In Our Opinion*, a publication of the Auditing Standards Board; the Board's letter to the profession included in exposure drafts for *SASs, SSARSs,* or *SSAEs*; the financial press (e.g., *The Wall Street Journal, Business Week*); the professional literature (e.g., *Journal of Accountancy, The CPA Journal, Accounting Today*); and magazines published by state societies of CPAs, such as *The Michigan CPA*.

19

Compliance Auditing and Internal Auditing

Major topics discussed in this chapter are:

Compliance auditing:
- Distinguishing among financial statement, compliance, and internal auditing.
- Auditing compliance with laws and regulations under generally accepted auditing standards.
- Auditing under the GAO's *Government Auditing Standards*.
- Auditing under the *Single Audit Act Amendment of 1996* and OMB *Circular A-133*, "Audits of States, Local Governments, and Non-profit Organizations."

Internal auditing:
- The role of independence in internal auditing.
- The nature and types of internal operational audits.
- How internal auditors perform operational audits.
- The relationship between internal and independent financial statement auditing.

Financial statement, compliance, and internal auditing are distinctly different types of audit activities, each providing unique professional responsibilities, opportunities, and challenges to its practitioners. Figure 19-1 distinguishes among these three types of audits and indicates the professional standards governing each. This chapter, devoted exclusively to compliance auditing and to internal auditing, serves as a basis for comparing financial statement auditing with two other dominant audit activities practiced in the United States. Governmental compliance auditing is discussed first, followed thereafter by internal auditing.

COMPLIANCE AUDITING

Annually, the U.S. government grants over $100 billion in federal financial assistance to the states and to over 80,000 local governmental units for transportation, welfare, education, health services, and job training programs, among other things. However, responding to a 1984 letter from a subcommittee of the U.S. House of Representatives' Committee on Government Operations, the U.S.

Figure 19-1: Distinguishing Among Financial Statement, Compliance, and Internal Auditing

	Type of Audits	*Standards*
Financial statement auditing	Financial statement audit	AICPA: *Generally Accepted Auditing Standards*
Compliance auditing	Financial audit, Performance audit	GAO: *Government Auditing Standards*
Internal auditing	Operational audit	IIA: *Standards for the Professional Practice of Internal Auditing*

General Accounting Office (GAO) conducted two studies of the quality of governmental audits. In much-publicized reports,[1] the GAO revealed that certified public accountants repeatedly failed to comply with applicable laws and regulations, failed to consider internal control, and failed to follow generally accepted auditing standards. In response, an AICPA task force[2] recommended that the Auditing Standards Board provide guidance to practitioners about testing and reporting on the laws and regulations that govern a governmental entity. In 1991, the Board issued a statement on auditing standards which, owing to changes in federal law, was superseded by today's *SAS No. 74,* "Compliance Auditing Applicable to Governmental Entities and to Other Recipients of Governmental Financial Assistance." *SAS No. 74* documents an auditor's responsibilities for complying with:

- Laws and regulations under *generally accepted auditing standards,*
- The GAO's *government auditing standards,* and
- The *Single Audit Act.*

Other types of compliance audits are also performed in the United States. For example, public accounting firms offer audits of a company's compliance with minimum wage laws, employee benefits programs, and commercial bank lending agreements. However, the discussion here focuses on governmental compliance audits, since they're so topical, having captured the attention of Congress, the GAO, the Auditing Standards Board, and the financial press. The next three sections of the chapter discuss each of an auditor's threefold responsibilities under *SAS No. 74.*

RESPONSIBILITIES UNDER GENERALLY ACCEPTED AUDITING STANDARDS

Governmental entities are subject to a variety of laws and regulations not generally applicable to private sector, profit-making entities. For example, local

---

1   U.S. General Accounting Office. *CPA Audit Quality: Inspectors General Find Significant Problems.* Washington, D.C.: U.S. GAO (1985); U.S. General Accounting Office. *CPA Audit Quality: Many Governmental Audits Do Not Comply with Professional Standards.* Washington, D.C.: U.S. GAO (1986).

2   AICPA. *Report of the Task Force on the Quality of Audits of Governmental Units.* New York: AICPA (1987).

laws may restrict the authority of a municipality to assess taxes or issue debt, state laws may require that proceeds received from a tax assessment be accounted for in a special revenue fund, and federal laws may restrict the disbursement of social service payments to eligible applicants. Violations of any of these, among other laws and regulations, could have a direct and material effect on a reporting entity's financial statements. For example, if a state receives a federal allocation for state welfare payments, disbursements to ineligible recipients may require that the state's department of health and human services disclose a contingent liability for potential fines and penalties payable to the federal government.

Under *SAS No. 74*, an auditor's responsibility for detecting violations of laws and regulations is identical to the auditor's responsibility for client errors, for fraud, and for illegal acts, all of which were introduced in Chapter 5. That is, the auditor should assess the risk that violations of laws and regulations may cause the financial statements to contain a direct and material misstatement and should consider this assessment in designing the audit procedures to be performed. In practice, this responsibility imposes two specific requirements on the auditor: to understand the effects of laws and regulations on a governmental entity's financial statements and to assess risk, both of which are discussed next.

THE EFFECTS OF LAWS AND REGULATIONS AND THE ASSESSMENT OF RISK

In planning a compliance audit, an auditor assesses whether management has identified laws and regulations that have a direct and material effect on the financial statements. The auditor also performs the procedures in Figure 19-2 to assess whether management has overlooked relevant laws or regulations and to develop an understanding of potential effects on the financial statements.

Having identified relevant laws and regulations, the auditor next assesses the risk of material misstatement arising from violations, based on two points.

Figure 19-2: Identifying Laws and Regulations

- Consider knowledge obtained in prior year audits.
- Discuss laws and regulations with the entity's chief financial officer, legal counsel, or grant administrators.
- Obtain written representation from management that they:
  - Are responsible for compliance with laws and regulations, and
  - Have identified and disclosed to the auditor all laws and regulations that have a direct and material effect on the financial statements.
- Review relevant portions of grant and loan agreements.
- Review minutes of meetings of the legislative bodies having jurisdiction over the entity (e.g., elected state legislature) for enactment of laws and regulations affecting the entity.
- Inquire of the program administrators of governmental entities that provided grants to the entity about restrictions, limitations, terms, and conditions under which grants were provided to the entity.
- Review information about compliance requirements available from state societies of CPAs or associations of government accountants.

First, the auditor considers the nature, cause, and amount of known and likely misstatements detected in prior audits. Second, the auditor considers the competence of client personnel responsible for complying with applicable laws and regulations, and the organizational structure of management. For example, an auditor is likely to assess risk at the maximum for a governmental entity that is decentralized and lacks adequate monitoring over responsible employees.

INTERNAL CONTROL

As explained in Chapter 7, the second standard of field work requires that an auditor obtain an understanding of an entity's internal controls sufficient to plan the audit and to assess control risk. Obtaining an understanding in a compliance audit also requires that the auditor obtain knowledge about the design—and performance—of internal control policies and procedures relevant to assertions affected by compliance with laws and regulations. For example, in obtaining an understanding of the components of internal control—the control environment, risk assessment, control activities, information and communication, and monitoring (Chapter 7)—the auditor may learn that the control environment is affected significantly by management's lack of awareness about applicable laws and regulations. Deficiencies like these should affect the auditor's assessment of control risk and should be reported to the governmental entity's oversight authority (e.g., city council) under *SAS No. 60*, "Communication of Internal Control Structure Related Matters Noted in an Audit" (Chapter 7).

GOVERNMENT AUDITING STANDARDS

Headed by the Comptroller General of the United States, the U.S. GAO is a nonpolitical federal agency responsible for conducting audits in behalf of Congress. The GAO publishes *Government Auditing Standards*[3] (often called the "Yellow Book"), an authoritative document that defines generally accepted **government auditing standards** (sometimes referred to by the acronym "GAGAS"). GAGAS include all ten of the AICPA's generally accepted auditing standards (Chapter 2) plus additional standards related, for example, to quality control, working papers, and legal and regulatory requirements. The Yellow Book identifies two types of generally accepted governmental audits: financial audits and performance audits.

Financial audits include financial statement audits and financial related audits, defined as follows:

Financial statement audits determine (1) whether the financial statements of an audited entity present fairly the financial position, results of financial operations, and cash flows in accordance with generally accepted accounting principles, and (2) whether the entity has complied with laws and regulations for those transactions that may have a material effect upon the financial statements.[4]

---

3   U.S. General Accounting Office. *Government Auditing Standards: Standards for Audit of Governmental Organizations, Programs, Activities and Functions.* Washington, D.C.: U.S. Government Printing Office (1994).
4   *Ibid.*, p. 2-1.

Financial related audits include determining (1) whether financial reports and related items, such as elements, accounts, or funds are fairly presented, (2) whether financial information is presented in accordance with established or stated criteria, and (3) whether the entity has adhered to specific financial compliance requirements.[5]

In turn, *performance audits* include economy and efficiency audits and program audits, defined as follows:

Economy and efficiency audits include determining (1) whether the entity is acquiring, protecting, and using its resources (such as personnel, property, and space) economically and efficiently, (2) the causes of inefficiencies or uneconomical practices, and (3) whether the entity has complied with laws and regulations concerning matters of economy and efficiency.[6]

Program audits include determining (1) the extent to which the desired results or benefits established by the legislature or other authorizing body are being achieved, (2) the effectiveness of organizations, programs, activities, or functions, and (3) whether the entity has complied with laws and regulations applicable to the program.[7]

Although performance audits are conducted frequently in practice, *SAS No. 74* and this chapter focus on financial audits, the type of governmental audit that is most similar to financial statement audits of business entities. Note carefully that the main difference between a financial statement audit for a business and a governmental financial audit is that a governmental financial audit requires that an auditor assume *more* responsibility. The additional responsibility relates to reporting on compliance with laws and regulations and on internal control, each of which is addressed separately next.

REPORTING ON COMPLIANCE WITH LAWS AND REGULATIONS

In a governmental financial audit, the auditor is required to test an entity's compliance with applicable laws and regulations and to prepare a written report that provides:

- Positive assurance on the results of tests for noncompliance, and
- A description of material instances of noncompliance, if any.

For example, assume that, coincident with tests designed to determine whether a governmental entity's financial statements are free of material misstatement, an auditor tests items subject to laws or regulations but detects no material instances of noncompliance. In this case, the auditor provides positive assurance using language such as, "The results of our tests disclosed no instances of noncompliance . . ." Figure 19-3 illustrates a separate report for an entity in which the auditor detects material instances of noncompliance.

REPORTING ON INTERNAL CONTROL

As discussed in Chapter 7, *SAS No. 60*, "Communication of Internal Control Structure Related Matters Noted in an Audit" requires in a financial statement audit that an auditor communicate reportable conditions to the board of

5   *Ibid.*, p. 2-2.
6   *Ibid.*, p. 2-3.
7   *Ibid.*, p. 2-3.

Figure 19-3:   Reporting on Compliance with Laws and Regulations: Material Instances of Noncompliance

We have audited the financial statements of the City of Pawtucket, Rhode Island, as of and for the year ended June 30, 1999, and have issued our report thereon dated August 15, 1999.

We conducted our audit in accordance with generally accepted auditing standards and Government Auditing Standards, issued by the Comptroller General of the United States. Those standards require that we plan and perform the audit to obtain reasonable assurance about whether the financial statements are free of material misstatement.

Compliance with laws, regulations, contracts, and grants applicable to the City of Pawtucket, Rhode Island, is the responsibility of the City's management. As part of obtaining reasonable assurance about whether the financial statements are free of material misstatement, we performed tests of the City's compliance with certain provisions of laws, regulations, contracts, and grants. However, the objective of our audit of the financial statements was not to provide an opinion on the overall compliance with such provisions. Accordingly, we do not express such an opinion.

Material instances of noncompliance are failures to follow requirements, or violations of prohibitions, contained in statutes, regulations, contracts, or grants that cause us to conclude that the aggregation of the misstatements resulting from those failures or violations is material to the financial statements. The results of our tests of compliance disclosed the following material instances of noncompliance, the effects of which have been corrected in the City of Pawtucket, Rhode Island's 1999 financial statements.

[Include paragraphs describing the material instances of noncompliance.]

We considered these material instances of noncompliance in forming our opinion on whether the City of Pawtucket, Rhode Island's 1999 financial statements are presented fairly, in all material respects, in conformity with generally accepted accounting principles, and this report does not affect our report dated August 15, 1999, on those financial statements.

This report is intended for the information of the audit committee, management, and the city council. This is not intended to limit the distribution of this report, which is a matter of public record.

directors' audit committee (or to individuals with equivalent responsibility and authority). Government auditing standards go further. Whereas *SAS No. 60* requires a report only when an auditor detects reportable conditions, government auditing standards require a report on internal control in *all* governmental financial audits, even when reportable conditions are not detected. In addition, government auditing standards require a report on internal control that is far more comprehensive than the *SAS No. 60* report illustrated in Chapter 7. For example, a report under government auditing standards: (1) describes the costs, benefits, objectives, and limitations of internal control, (2) states that the auditor assessed control risk, and (3) describes deficiencies in internal control not significant enough to be considered reportable conditions under *SAS No. 60*. Figure 19-4 illustrates a report on internal control when an auditor has noted reportable conditions.

Figure 19-4: Reporting on Internal Control: Reportable Conditions

We have audited the financial statements of the City of Lexington, Kentucky, as of and for the year ended June 30, 1999, and have issued our report thereon dated August 15, 1999.

We conducted our audit in accordance with generally accepted auditing standards and Government Auditing Standards, issued by the Comptroller General of the United States. Those standards require that we plan and perform the audit to obtain reasonable assurance about whether the financial statements are free of material misstatement.

The management of the City of Lexington, Kentucky, is responsible for establishing and maintaining an internal control structure. In fulfilling this responsibility, estimates and judgments by management are required to assess the expected benefits and related costs of internal control structure policies and procedures. The objectives of an internal control structure are to provide management with reasonable, but not absolute, assurance that assets are safeguarded against loss from unauthorized use or disposition and that transactions are executed in accordance with management's authorization and are recorded properly to permit the preparation of financial statements in accordance with generally accepted accounting principles. Because of inherent limitations in any internal control structure, errors or irregularities may nevertheless occur and not be detected. Also, projection of any evaluation of the structure to future periods is subject to the risk that procedures may become inadequate because of changes in conditions or that the effectiveness of the design and operation of policies and procedures may deteriorate.

In planning and performing our audit of the financial statements of the City of Lexington, Kentucky, as of and for the year ended June 30, 1999, we obtained an understanding of the design of relevant policies and procedures and whether they had been placed in operation, and we assessed control risk in order to determine our auditing procedures for the purpose of expressing our opinion on the financial statements, and not to provide an opinion on internal control. Accordingly, we do not express an opinion.

We noted certain matters involving the internal control structure and its operation that we consider to be reportable conditions under standards established by the American Institute of Certified Public Accountants. Reportable conditions involve matters coming to our attention relating to significant deficiencies in the design or operation of the internal control structure that, in our judgment, could adversely affect the City's ability to record, process, summarize, and report financial data consistent with the assertions of management in the financial statements.

[Include paragraphs to describe the reportable conditions noted.]

A material weakness is a reportable condition in which the design or operation of one or more of the internal control structure elements does not reduce to a relatively low level the risk that errors or irregularities in amounts that would be material in relation to the financial statements being audited may occur and not be detected within a timely period by employees in the normal course of performing their assigned functions.

Our consideration of the internal control structure would not necessarily disclose all matters in the internal control structure that might be reportable conditions and, accordingly, would not necessarily disclose all reportable conditions that are also considered to be material weaknesses as defined above. However, we believe none of the reportable conditions described above is a material weakness.

We also noted other matters involving the internal control structure and its operation that we have reported to the management of the City of Lexington, Kentucky, in a separate letter dated August 15, 1999.

This report is intended for the information of the audit committee, management, and city council. This is not intended to limit the distribution of this report, which is a matter of public record.

THE SINGLE AUDIT ACT AMENDMENT OF 1996

Financial audits and performance audits are performed annually by governmental or independent auditors for the states, for state agencies, and for local governmental units such as cities, towns, counties, school districts, fire districts, housing authorities, and port authorities, among others. To assure accountability for federal grant funds received by these entities, the federal government previously required periodic audits of each grant received. For example, if a governmental unit participated in ten federal grant programs, then ten individual grant audits were required.

Because there was little coordination among federal, state, and local auditors, and because the requirements of each grant audit varied widely, the GAO and the Joint Management Improvement Program (JMIP) reported in 1979 that grant-by-grant audits often resulted in considerable duplication of effort: The same internal controls were studied and evaluated, and the same accounting records were audited. In short, grant-by-grant audits were not cost-effective. As a result, both the GAO and the JMIP recommended that grant-by-grant audits be abandoned and be replaced by a single audit of each governmental unit receiving federal assistance—that is, one audit of the recipient entity rather than a separate audit of each grant received by the entity. In response, Congress enacted the **Single Audit Act** of 1984, which was intended to: (1) improve the financial management of state and local governments receiving federal funds, (2) establish uniform audit requirements for federal grant recipients, (3) promote efficient and effective use of audit resources, and (4) ensure that federal departments and agencies rely on one audit report only: the single audit report. In 1996, the Act was amended by the *Single Audit Act Amendment*.

AUDIT COVERAGE

The *Single Audit Act* (and *Amendment*) apply to all governmental units that receive *any* federal assistance, although the reporting requirements of the Act apply generally to governments receiving over $300,000 in grant funds per year. Although far-reaching, the *Single Audit Act* does not limit the authority of federal agencies to conduct additional audits as deemed necessary. However, the single audit is *the* definitive audit of federal assistance programs and, as a result, additional audits must be done at the cost of the federal agency requiring the audit, not at the cost of the grant recipient.

REPORTS

In addition to a report on the general purpose financial statements required by generally accepted auditing standards, and reports on compliance with laws and regulations and on internal control required by *government auditing standards*, the *Single Audit Act* of 1984, the *Single Audit Act Amendment of 1996,* and U.S. Office of Management and Budget (OMB) *Circular A-133,* "Audits of States, Local Governments, and Non-profit Organizations" require no less than five additional reports:

1. Report on Compliance with General Requirements.
2. Report on Major Program Compliance with Specific Requirements.
3. Report on Nonmajor Program Compliance with Specific Requirements.
4. Report on the Schedule of Federal Financial Assistance.
5. Report on Internal Controls over Federal Financial Assistance.

Thus, a governmental entity subject to the *Single Audit Act* may require as many as eight separate reports (nine, if illegal acts are detected).

Report on Compliance with General Requirements

The OMB's "Compliance Supplement for Single Audits of States, Local Governments, and Non-profit Organizations," an interpretive supplement to *OMB A-133,* identifies nine "general requirements" that, according to the Supplement, involve significant national policy and that could have a material effect on an entity's financial statements. Figure 19-5 lists the general requirements. An auditor is responsible to test an entity's compliance with the nine general requirements using procedures suggested within the Compliance Supplement and to report—not give an opinion—on the results of the procedures performed. Figure 19-6 illustrates a report.

Report on Major Program Compliance with Specific Requirements

SAS No. 74 requires that an auditor perform auditing procedures designed to provide reasonable assurance of detecting material noncompliance with *specific*

Figure 19-5: The Single Audit Act: General Requirements

- *Political Activity*: Prohibits the use of federal funds for partisan politics.
- *Davis-Bacon Act*: Requires that laborers working on federally financed construction projects be paid a wage not less than the prevailing regional wage established by the Secretary of Labor.
- *Civil Rights*: Prohibits violation of anyone's civil rights in a program funded by the federal government.
- *Cash Management*: Requires recipients of federal financial assistance to minimize the time lapsed between receipt and disbursement of assistance.
- *Relocation Assistance and Real Property Acquisition*: Prescribes how real property should be acquired with federal financial assistance and how recipients must help relocate displaced people.
- *Federal Financial Reports*: Prescribes federal financial reports that must be filed.
- *Allowable Cost/Cost Principle*: Prescribes the direct and indirect costs allowable for federal reimbursement.
- *Drug-Free Workplace*: Prescribes that grantees must certify that they provide a drug-free workplace.
- *Administrative Requirements*: Prescribes additional administrative requirements.

Figure 19-6: The Single Audit Act: Compliance with General Requirements

We have audited the financial statements of the City of South Bend, Indiana, as of and for the year ended June 30, 1999, and have issued our report thereon dated August 15, 1999.

We have applied procedures to test compliance with the following requirements applicable to its federal financial assistance programs, which are identified in the schedule of federal financial assistance, for the year ended June 30, 1999.

[List the general requirements from Figure 19-5 that were tested.]

Our procedures were limited to the applicable procedures described in the Office of Management and Budget's "Compliance Supplement for Single Audits of States, Local Governments, and Non-profit Organizations." Our procedures were substantially less in scope than an audit, the objective of which is the expression of an opinion on the City of South Bend's compliance with the requirements listed in the preceding paragraph. Accordingly, we do not express such an opinion.

With respect to the items tested, the results of those procedures disclosed no material instances of noncompliance with the requirements listed in the second paragraph of this report. With respect to items not tested, nothing came to our attention that caused us to believe that the City of South Bend, Indiana, had not complied, in all material respects, with those requirements. However, the results of our procedures disclosed immaterial instances of noncompliance with those requirements, which are described in the accompanying schedule of findings and questioned costs.

This report is intended for the information of the audit committee, management, and city council. This is not intended to limit the distribution of this report, which is a matter of public record.

requirements applicable to *major* financial assistance programs. Unlike the nine general requirements noted previously, specific requirements vary across federal financial assistance programs, although they involve five categories of requirements, listed in Figure 19-7. Also unlike the report on general requirements, which relates to all federal financial assistance programs, the report on specific requirements relates only to major federal financial assistance programs. The distinction between major and nonmajor programs is based on risk. In general, a major program is determined from risk factors such as the auditee's prior compliance violations and from cash and noncash (e.g., food stamps) expenditures. For example, the threshold for determining a major program is about $300,000 in expenditures for the period audited, and increases as the total federal financial assistance expenditures increase. An auditor is responsible to test an entity's compliance with major program specific requirements using procedures suggested in the Compliance Supplement and to express an opinion on the entity's compliance. Figure 19-8 illustrates an unqualified opinion on an entity's compliance with specific requirements.

Report on Nonmajor Program Compliance with Specific Requirements

In a financial audit of a state or local governmental entity, an auditor may have tested transactions selected from nonmajor federal financial assistance programs. The *Single Audit Act Amendment of 1996* and OMB *Circular A-133* require that the transactions tested for this purpose also be tested for compliance with

Figure 19-7: The Single Audit Act: Specific Requirements

- *Types of Services Allowed or Not Allowed*: Specifies the types of goods or services entities may purchase with financial assistance.
- *Eligibility*: Specifies the characteristics of individuals or groups to whom entities may give financial assistance.
- *Matching, Level of Effort, or Earmarking*: Specifies amounts entities should contribute from their own resources toward projects for which financial assistance is provided.
- *Reporting*: Specifies reports entities must file in addition to those required by the general requirements.
- *Special Tests and Provisions*: Other provisions for which federal agencies have determined that noncompliance could materially affect the program.

Figure 19-8: The Single Audit Act: Major Program Compliance with Specific Requirements

(Unqualified Opinion)

We have audited the financial statements of the City of Portland, Oregon, as of and for the year ended June 30, 1999, and have issued our report thereon dated August 15, 1999.

We also audited the City of Portland's compliance with the requirements governing [list requirements tested] that are applicable to each of its major federal financial assistance programs, which are identified in the accompanying schedule of federal financial assistance, for the year ended June 30, 1999. The management of the City of Portland is responsible for the City's compliance with those requirements. Our responsibility is to express an opinion on compliance with those requirements based on our audit.

We conducted our audit of compliance with those requirements in accordance with generally accepted auditing standards; Government Auditing Standards, issued by the Comptroller General of the United States; and OMB Circular A-133, "Audits of States, Local Governments, and Non-profit Organizations." Those standards and OMB Circular A-133 require that we plan and perform the audit to obtain reasonable assurance about whether material noncompliance with the requirements referred to above occurred. An audit includes examining, on a test basis, evidence about the City of Portland's compliance with those requirements. We believe that our audit provides a reasonable basis for our opinion.

In our opinion, the City of Portland, Oregon, complied, in all material respects, with the requirements governing [list requirements tested] that are applicable to each of its major federal financial assistance programs for the year ended June 30, 1999.

This report is intended for the information of the audit committee, management, and city council. This is not intended to limit the distribution of this report, which is a matter of public record.

applicable federal laws and regulations. Generally, auditors test these transactions for the allowability of the program expenditure and for the eligibility of the individuals or groups to whom the entity disbursed financial assistance. Figure 19-9 illustrates a report on testing compliance with the requirements applicable to nonmajor federal financial assistance programs.

Figure 19-9: The Single Audit Act: Nonmajor Program Compliance with Specific Requirements

We have audited the financial statements of Michiana Regional Airport as of and for the year ended June 30, 1999, and have issued our report thereon dated August 15, 1999.

In connection with our audit of the financial statements of Michiana Regional Airport and with our consideration of the Michiana Regional Airport's internal control structure used to administer federal financial assistance programs, and as required by Office of Management and Budget Circular A-133, "Audits of States, Local Governments, and Non-profit Organizations," we selected certain transactions applicable to certain nonmajor federal financial assistance programs for the year ended June 30, 1999. As required by Circular A-133, we have performed auditing procedures to test compliance with the requirements governing [list requirements tested] that are applicable to those transactions. Our procedures were substantially less in scope than an audit, the objective of which is the expression of an opinion on the Michiana Regional Airport's compliance with these requirements. Accordingly, we do not express such an opinion.

With respect to the items tested, the results of those procedures disclosed no material instances of noncompliance with the requirements listed in the preceding paragraph. With respect to items not tested, nothing came to our attention that caused us to believe that Michiana Regional Airport had not complied, in all material respects, with those requirements.

This report is intended for the information of the audit committee and management. This is not intended to limit the distribution of this report, which is a matter of public record.

Report on the Schedule of Federal Financial Assistance

To comply with the *Single Audit Act Amendment of 1996*, all federal grant recipients prepare a schedule of federal financial assistance for purposes of additional analysis, not as a required part of the general purpose financial statements. Among other things, the schedule is required to identify all federal agencies granting funds to the governmental agency, all major programs, the expenditures for each major program, and total federal financial assistance. The auditor's report on the schedule provides an opinion on whether the schedule is fairly presented in all material respects in relation to the general purpose financial statements, not in relation to the schedule itself. That is, the auditor is not responsible for errors or frauds material to the schedule but rather for errors or frauds material to the financial statements.

Report on Internal Controls over Federal Financial Assistance

Governmental entities subject to the *Single Audit Act Amendment* receive not one, but two separate reports on internal control: a report on internal controls considered by the auditor when auditing the general purpose financial statements under *Government Auditing Standards* (as illustrated in Figure 19-4) and a separate report (required by the *Single Audit Act Amendment*) on the entity's internal controls over federal financial assistance programs. The auditor does not express an opinion on controls over federal financial assistance. Rather, he or she reports on weaknesses material to federal financial assistance programs. Note carefully the difference between the two reports: The report on internal control required by *Government Auditing Standards* reports weaknesses material to the financial statements; the report required by the *Single Audit Act Amendment of 1996* reports weaknesses material to federal financial assistance programs.

INTERNAL AUDITING

In 1941, the first definitive internal auditing book was published, Victor Z. Brink's *Modern Internal Auditing*, and the Institute of Internal Auditors was founded, two landmark events in the rise of internal auditing as a profession. The Institute of Internal Auditors has grown from 24 charter members in 1941 to over 40,000 members worldwide today. In half a century, the Institute has done many things to enhance the professional stature of internal auditors, among them approving a statement of responsibilities, developing a common body of knowledge and a code of ethics, establishing continuing education and professional certification (Certified Internal Auditor) programs, and adopting standards for the professional practice of internal auditing.

Throughout the 1940s and 1950s, internal auditing in many organizations focused solely on financial auditing, and internal audit departments were heavily involved in the analysis of financial statements for management. Today, internal auditing takes on a much broader range of responsibility, as suggested in the Institute of Internal Auditors' *Statement of Responsibilities of Internal Auditors*:

The objective of internal auditing is to assist all members of management in the effective discharge of their responsibilities by furnishing them with analyses, appraisals, recommendations, and pertinent comments concerning activities reviewed. Internal auditors are concerned with any phase of business activity in which they may be of service to management. This involves going beyond the accounting and financial records to obtain a full understanding of the operations under review.

Given this objective, the Statement identifies several major internal audit activities, such as appraising and recommending improvements for the:

1. Adequacy and application of financial and operating controls.
2. Extent of compliance with established policies, plans, and procedures.
3. Extent to which assets are accounted for and safeguarded from loss.
4. Reliability of information reported by management.
5. Performance of employees and management.

The objective and the five related activities describe the scope of **operational auditing**, the dominant activity of contemporary internal audit practice. Internal auditing is no longer confined to financial matters—instead, it's much more creative, an opportunity to lend insight into issues not readily apparent to management, like projected cost savings on regional distribution centers for nationally marketed consumer products.

INDEPENDENCE IN INTERNAL AUDITING

Although the term "independent auditor" typically refers to auditors in independent public accounting firms, an internal auditor's effectiveness depends crucially on his or her independence from the *personnel* and the *activities* of an organization. Otherwise, the integrity of an internal auditor's conclusions and recommendations would lack credibility. For example, would you find credible a glowing report on a financial vice president's projected financing strategy prepared by an internal auditor who reports to the vice president of finance? The Institute of Internal Auditors' *Codification of Standards for the Professional Practice of Internal Auditing* underscores the significance of independence in a statement that identifies organizational status and objectivity as the primary means for achieving independence from personnel and activities, respectively: "Independence permits internal auditors to render the impartial and unbiased judgments essential to the proper conduct of audits. It is achieved through organizational status and objectivity."

ORGANIZATIONAL STATUS

The *Codification of Standards for the Professional Practice of Internal Auditing* discusses organizational status in part as follows:

The director of the internal auditing department should be responsible to an individual in the organization with sufficient authority to promote independence and to ensure broad audit coverage, adequate consideration of audit reports, and appropriate action on audit recommendations.[8]

Internal auditors should report to an organizational level above the levels audited—otherwise, they may not be inclined to criticize peers or superiors. For example, an internal auditor who reports to the chief financial officer (CFO) may be reluctant to report weaknesses in the CFO's activities and support staff, weaknesses that may be counterproductive to the organization's goals. On the other hand, an internal auditor who reports to the board of directors would not likely be reluctant to report weaknesses in staff levels below the board of directors. The higher the organizational level reported to, the greater the range of an internal auditor's potential effectiveness.

In practice, internal auditors in most organizations have traditionally reported to a financial executive, such as the vice president of finance. In recent years, however, internal auditing has become increasingly oriented toward operational control, oversight, and protection, all of which are major responsibilities of the board of directors. As a result of the increased emphasis on serving the needs of the board of directors, rather than management, internal auditing has moved further away from financial auditing, its traditional role, and closer to operational auditing, its emerging role. This trend, and the resulting effect on the internal auditor's organizational status, is illustrated in the following excerpt from an article in *The Wall Street Journal*:

Worries about foreign payoffs and corporate accountability prompt more firms to expand the clout of internal audit staffs. About a third of internal audit managers now report to boards of directors, instead of to controllers, says a poll by John Stork & Partners, a search firm.

---

8   Institute of Internal Auditors. *Codification of Standards for the Professional Practice of Internal Auditing.* Altamonte Springs, FL (1989), p. 9.

OBJECTIVITY

The *Codification of Standards for the Professional Practice of Internal Auditing* discusses objectivity as follows:

The internal auditor's objectivity is not adversely affected when the auditor recommends standards of control for systems or reviews procedures before they are implemented. Designing, installing, and operating systems are not audit functions. Also, the drafting of procedures for systems is not an audit function. Performing such activities is presumed to impair audit objectivity.[9]

Thus, internal auditors are not simply one of the organization's controls—they are a control over all other controls. For this reason, while internal auditors can recommend controls, they should not design and implement the controls. Rather, to maximize their objectivity, internal auditors should serve the organization as independent appraisers of existing controls. To design, implement *and* audit controls could result in a conflict of interests: Could an internal auditor objectively audit controls that he or she designed and implemented?

THE NATURE OF OPERATIONAL AUDITING

Just as a financial statement audit was described in Chapter 1 as a special application of the scientific method of inquiry, so too is an operational audit a special application of the scientific method. The objectives of internal and independent auditors differ, but the logic underlying their audit activities is similar.

In general, internal operational audits are conducted for any one or more of six different purposes, all of which derive from the major internal audit activities listed earlier from the Institute of Internal Auditors' *Statement of Responsibilities*:

1. Appraisal of controls.
2. Compliance.
3. Protection of assets.
4. Verification.
5. Appraisal of performance.
6. Recommendations for operating improvements.

Each is discussed below.

APPRAISAL OF CONTROLS

Entities implement internal controls to assure compliance with management's goals and objectives. The controls may take the form of policies, programs, and/or procedures. For example, a company may institute a *program* of recording and monitoring inventory spoilage in manufacturing plants as an *operating control* to achieve the *organizational objective* of reducing costs company-wide. Although specific individual controls will vary, they all maintain a common framework:

9   *Ibid.*, p. 14.

Framework	*Example*
1. An objective.	1. Reduce inventory spoilage costs.
2. Techniques for determining compliance with the objective.	2. Order raw materials just-in-time to minimize inventory levels and, therefore, control spoilage costs.

3. Action regarding noncompliance.	3. If spoilage costs increase, consider:
	  a. Reassessing the variables in the order quantity model.
	  b. Alternative methods of inventory storage.

When appraising controls, the internal auditor's purpose is to determine whether control activities are adequate. That is, are the controls satisfactory in light of the objectives for which they were designed? Appraisal of controls is a particularly significant operational audit activity, because internal auditing itself is an organizational control designed to measure and evaluate the effectiveness of other controls.

COMPLIANCE

Controls are meaningless unless the controls are complied with. Thus, the purpose of an operational audit for compliance is to determine whether specific control policies, programs, or procedures are operating satisfactorily. The focus of compliance reviews, however, is not necessarily on dealing with the potential results of noncompliance (e.g., excess inventory spoilage), but on preventing further instances of noncompliance.

PROTECTION OF ASSETS

Closely related to compliance reviews are organizational audits designed to determine whether assets are properly accounted for and safeguarded from losses. Asset protection reviews may be conducted both for liquid assets (e.g., cash and marketable securities) and for nonliquid assets (e.g., inventory and property, plant, and equipment), although the focus of each may differ since liquid assets are much more susceptible to frauds. In either case, however, the internal auditor is concerned primarily with testing the effectiveness of those accounting, financial, and operating controls that were designed to account for and safeguard assets.

VERIFICATION

Unless accurate and reliable, the data used by management to make decisions is likely to lead to poor decisions. Thus, operational audits can be designed to verify the accuracy and reliability of data used in internal management reports. As is the case with compliance reviews, the focus of verification reviews is not necessarily on responding to the results of inaccurate or unreliable data but, rather, on promoting accuracy and reliability.

Management information systems are intended to provide input for management decisions. Thus, the information system should generate the most relevant, or useful, data for a particular type of decision. As a result, verification reviews are often designed to evaluate the relevance and usefulness of data as well as accuracy and reliability.

APPRAISAL OF PERFORMANCE

Employee performance is much more difficult to quantify than accounting or financial control compliance. As a result, interpretations and appraisals of employee performance can be tenuous at best. For example, employee performance is often influenced by variables other than extrinsic economic rewards, such as an employee's job satisfaction and acceptance among peers. Interpreting the effect of these and other variables on an employee's motivation to discharge his or her responsibilities adequately can be difficult, thereby suggesting that appraising employee performance can also be particularly difficult. Nevertheless, as a major organizational control over operational effectiveness, internal auditors are frequently called on to appraise employee performance. Employee performance reviews, however, can represent the one operational audit activity least consistent with the boundaries of an internal auditor's professional expertise.

RECOMMENDATIONS FOR IMPROVEMENTS

Each of an internal auditor's operational audit activities should be designed to generate recommendations for improvements. When a reportable condition, error, fraud, or illegal act is discovered, its effects should be corrected and recommendations made to improve accountability. Although not itself an audit activity, recommending improvements as a result of any of the operational audit activities is a most significant by-product of the internal auditor's professional role. It is not enough for internal auditors to criticize; they must also be creative in developing recommendations for improvements.

PERFORMING OPERATIONAL AUDITS

Although actual operational audits may vary depending on the circumstances, most include several basic characteristics, each of which is related to the scientific method of inquiry (introduced in Chapter 1), as illustrated in Figure 19-10 and discussed in the following sections.

Figure 19-10: Relating the Scientific Method of Inquiry and Operational Audits

Scientific Method	Operational Audit Function
1. Observe and recognize a problem.	Management requests an operational audit. Auditor familiarization with the operational activity to be reviewed.
2. Formulate a hypothesis.	Overall hypothesis: The accounting, financial, or operating control is operating properly and is relevant to the control's objective.
3. Gather relevant, verifiable evidence to test the hypothesis.	Select appropriate operational audit procedures and gather sufficient competent evidential matter.
4. Evaluate evidence.	Evaluate evidential matter to determine if the hypothesis is supported, refuted, or inconclusive.
5. Develop conclusions.	Report to the appropriate organizational level.

MANAGEMENT REQUESTS AN OPERATIONAL AUDIT

Management may request operational audits for any one or more of the six purposes discussed in the previous section. More specifically, however, management may request that these six reviews be applied to the organization's:

- Computer facilities.
- Financial management practices.
- Quality control activities.
- Research and development efforts.
- Social responsibility.
- Financial statement accounts.

This list is by no means exhaustive. In fact, potential applications of internal audit activities are almost limitless.

AUDITOR FAMILIARIZATION

Soon after an operational audit is assigned, an internal auditor and his or her staff should attempt to familiarize themselves with the specific operational activity to be reviewed. An operational audit should not be conducted in a vacuum; rather, to maximize efficiency, preliminary information should be gathered and the audit planned in advance. Several preliminary considerations for familiarization follow:

- Review internal audit working paper files and reports from prior operational audits.
- Discuss and coordinate the timing and scope of the review with the manager of the activity to be audited.
- Coordinate staff requirements with the director of internal auditing to assure that the operational audit can be completed on time.

FORMULATING A HYPOTHESIS

Developing an overall hypothesis requires careful consideration of the objectives of the operational audit. For example, if the purpose is to appraise controls, the internal auditor should determine the type of control policies, programs, and procedures to be reviewed and the purpose for which each control was designed. The operational audit hypothesis is then stated in terms of whether a control is desirable and potentially effective under the circumstances.

SELECTING PROCEDURES AND GATHERING EVIDENCE

Operational audit procedures are selected in light of the overall hypothesis of the audit. Specific considerations in selecting procedures may include:

- The formality of the reviewed activity's information system; an informal system may preclude the internal auditor from reviewing all relevant information.
- Considering whether the control is designed to provide overall reasonableness or detailed compliance; more detailed compliance usually requires more detailed audit work.

- Overt evidence of problems, such as verbal admittance by employees of noncompliance with a prescribed control.

The internal auditor should attempt to gather the most appropriate evidence for the audit procedures selected. Evidence should be gathered in sufficient quantity to promote logical conclusions and should be of the highest quality available—for example, written documents are generally of higher quality (though sometimes less informative) than informal verbal suppositions.

EVALUATING EVIDENCE AND REPORTING RESULTS

In auditing, evidence is the only basis for drawing conclusions. Thus, the evidence gathered should be evaluated objectively and in light of the overall hypothesis. In turn, audit conclusions should be communicated to appropriate levels of management and within a reasonable time period. Unlike audit reports for financial statement audits (Chapter 3), standardized internal audit reports are not common, since the reports are not intended for use by third parties. Thus, the form and content of an internal audit report is usually left to the discretion of the internal auditor.

RELATING INTERNAL AND INDEPENDENT AUDITING

Although internal and independent auditors use roughly the same audit methods, they have *different objectives* when performing audits. The objective of internal auditing is to assist management and the board of directors concerning the activities reviewed, and the objective of independent auditing is to express an opinion on the financial statements audited. In addition, internal and independent auditors serve the needs of *different user groups*. The needs of external users are not served by internal operational audits, and the needs of internal users are not served wholly by financial statement audits. Thus, internal and independent auditing are separate and distinct independent appraisal activities.

Despite these differences, however, there is a relationship between internal and independent auditing, as illustrated in Figure 19-11. Both groups of auditors rely on the same database. Also, internal users rely on both internal and

Figure 19-11:   The Relationships Among Auditors and Users

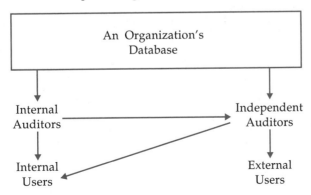

independent auditors, and external users rely on independent auditors only. Importantly, independent auditors can and often do rely on an internal auditor's work when the internal audit function is effective. As a result, an organization's internal audit function can have a significant effect on the nature, timing, and extent of audit procedures applied by an independent auditor in a financial statement audit. *Statement on Auditing Standards No. 65*, "The Auditor's Consideration of the Internal Audit Function in an Audit of Financial Statements" provides guidance on considering the work of internal auditors and on using internal auditors to provide direct assistance to the independent auditor.

OBTAINING AN UNDERSTANDING OF THE INTERNAL AUDIT FUNCTION

Under the second standard of field work (Chapter 7), an independent auditor obtains an understanding of an entity's internal controls sufficient to plan the audit. Because internal auditors are responsible to monitor the performance of an entity's controls, the auditor should obtain an understanding of the internal audit function sufficient to identify internal audit activities that are relevant to planning the audit. In obtaining an understanding, the independent auditor should make inquiries of management about the internal audit department's:

- Organizational status within the entity.
- Adherence to professional standards.
- Audit plan, including the nature, timing, and extent of audit work.
- Access to records, and whether there are limitations on the scope of their activities imposed by management.
- Charter, mission statement, or similar directive from management or the board of directors.

The auditor's inquiries should be directed only toward those internal audit activities relevant to a financial statement audit. For example, the internal auditor's role in operational audits about the timeliness of management's decision-making process would not be relevant to the independent auditor, but the internal auditor's role in implementing controls to safeguard assets would be relevant.

ASSESSING THE COMPETENCE AND OBJECTIVITY OF INTERNAL AUDITORS

The *Codification of Statements on Auditing Standards* states that achieving an organization's control objectives ". . . depends on the competence and integrity of personnel, the independence of their assigned functions, and their understanding of the prescribed procedures." Consistent with this language, *SAS No. 65* requires that independent auditors review the competence and objectivity of internal auditors before their work is relied on. Competence can be reviewed by considering, for example:

- The internal auditors' educational levels, professional experience, professional certification, and continuing education;
- Audit policies, programs, and procedures;
- Practices for assigning internal auditors;
- Supervision and review of internal auditors' work; and

- The quality of working paper documentation, reports, and recommendations.

Objectivity, in turn, can be reviewed by considering the organizational level to which internal auditors report and policies used to maintain internal auditors' objectivity about the areas or departments audited. As discussed earlier, objectivity and organizational status are closely related to an internal auditor's independence. Internal auditors cannot be considered independent from organizational levels at or above those to which they report. Thus, independent auditors cannot rely on internal audit work performed for organizational levels at or above those to which an internal auditor reports—the internal auditor's objectivity and independence would be suspect. For example, assuming competence and objectivity, an independent auditor may request that an internal auditor examine additions to property, plant, and equipment, thereby reducing the time required by an independent auditor to examine the property, plant, and equipment account.

EFFECT OF THE INTERNAL AUDITOR'S WORK ON THE AUDIT

The effectiveness of an organization's internal audit function is one among a series of variables considered by an independent auditor when planning and conducting a financial statement audit. Other variables, discussed more fully in earlier chapters, include materiality and audit risk. Independent auditors consider these other variables to determine their effect on the scope of a financial statement audit. Importantly, the scope of an independent audit can be reduced if an organization's internal audit function is effective. Thus, the effectiveness of an entity's internal audit function and the scope of an independent audit are inversely related: As the effectiveness of internal auditing increases, the scope of an independent audit can decrease.

In practice, independent auditors rely on internal auditors in addressing three issues relevant to a financial statement audit:

1. Understanding internal control.
2. Assessing risk.
3. Performing substantive procedures.

Understanding Internal Control

Procedures performed by internal auditors may provide information relevant to the independent auditor's assessment of control risk, since a primary purpose of internal auditing is to monitor an entity's control activities. For example, assuming the internal auditors are competent and objective, their flowcharts of an entity's accounting system could be used to obtain information about the design of related policies and procedures, thereby reducing the time required by an independent auditor to assess control risk.

Assessing Risk

As discussed in Chapter 2, the independent auditor assesses risk at both the financial statement level and the account balance level, and the effectiveness of an entity's internal audit function may affect both. For example, at the financial statement level, if the internal auditor's audit plan includes relevant audit work at various locations throughout the country or around the world, the independent auditor may coordinate his or her work with the internal auditors, thereby reducing the number of locations at which the independent auditor would otherwise need to perform auditing procedures. At the account balance level, the scope of the internal audit function may include tests of controls for selected financial statement assertions, such as completeness for sales and receivables, thereby reducing the scope of the independent auditor's tests.

Substantive Tests

Many internal audit departments also perform substantive tests of details, which, as discussed in Chapter 6, are the independent auditor's primary means of detecting material misstatements in financial statement accounts. As a result, some procedures performed by internal auditors may provide the independent auditor with direct evidence about material misstatements. For example, as part of their normal audit function, the internal auditors may confirm accounts receivable and observe the counting of physical inventories—two procedures typically performed by independent auditors. Assuming the internal audit function is competent and objective, substantive tests performed by internal auditors may provide important evidence to the independent auditor in restricting detection risk for some financial statement assertions.

EVALUATING AN INTERNAL AUDITOR'S WORK

Although independent auditors often rely on the work of competent and objective internal auditors, the responsibility to report on the financial statements rests solely with the independent auditor. Unlike opinions based partly on the report of another independent auditor, discussed in Chapter 3, the responsibility for an audit cannot be shared with an internal auditor. Even though internal auditors may provide information for the independent auditor's judgments about the assessment of control risk and inherent risk (Chapter 7), about the materiality of misstatements, and about the sufficiency of tests performed, those judgments are the independent auditor's responsibility.

Despite reviews of an internal auditor's competence and objectivity, an independent auditor should not accept an internal auditor's work "on blind faith." The internal auditor's work should be evaluated before it is fully relied on. An internal auditor's documented evidence should be examined on a test basis to provide an independent auditor with a basis for judging the adequacy and appropriateness of:

- The scope of internal audit work.
- Audit programs.
- Working paper documentation.
- Conclusions reached.
- Any reports prepared.

In addition, the independent auditor should perform tests on some of the internal auditor's work. For example, if an internal auditor examined evidence in support of 25 additions to property, plant, and equipment, an independent auditor may examine evidence in support of a small number of the same additions, comparing the results with those reached by the internal auditor.

KEY TERMS

COMPLIANCE AUDITING

Government auditing standards 704   Program audits 705
Economy and efficiency audits 705   Single Audit Act 708

INTERNAL AUDITING

Operational auditing 713

REFERENCES

COMPLIANCE AUDITING

Professional Standards

AICPA. *Codification of Statements on Auditing Standards.* New York: AICPA (AU Sec. 316, 317, 319, 325, 801).
AICPA. *Audits of State and Local Governmental Units: Audit and Accounting Guide.* New York: AICPA (1994).
SAS No. 54, "Illegal Acts by Clients" (AU Sec. 317).
SAS No. 74, "Compliance Auditing Applicable to Governmental Entities and to Other Recipients of Governmental Financial Assistance" (AU Sec. 801).
U.S. General Accounting Office (GAO). *Government Auditing Standards.* Washington, D.C.: U.S. Government Printing Office (1994).
U.S. Office of Management and Budget (OMB). *Circular A-133* "Audits of States, Local Governments, and Non-profit Organizations." Washington, D.C.: EOP Publications.

Articles, Books

Broadus, W. A., Jr., and J. D. Comtois. "The Single Audit Act: A Needed Reform," *Journal of Accountancy* (April 1985), pp. 62-70.
Brown, C. D., and P. Burnaby. "The Evolution of the Single Audit Act: A 20 Year Process," *Accounting Horizons* (June 1988), pp. 47-52.
Forrester, R. "Are Your Not-for-Profit Clients Ready for Compliance Auditing?" *Journal of Accountancy* (July 1990), pp. 70-76.
Hay, L. E., and F. F. Antonio. "What Users Want in Governmental Financial Reports," *Journal of Accountancy* (August 1990), pp. 91-98.
Jackson, N. J., Jr., and J. C. Skeely. "Auditing Federal Awards: A New Approach," *Journal of Accountancy* (November 1996), pp. 53-60.
Miller, J. R., and F. D. Wolf. "A Look at the New Yellow Book: Tomorrow's Government Audits," *Journal of Accountancy* (November 1988), pp. 64-80.
Ramsey, T., and C. Satterwaite. "Is Government Practice for You?—Understanding the Single Audit," *The Practical Accountant* (May 1992), pp. 34-43.

INTERNAL AUDITING

Professional Standards

SAS No. 55, "Consideration of the Internal Control Structure in a Financial Statement Audit" (AU Sec. 319).
SAS No. 65, "The Auditor's Consideration of the Internal Audit Function in an Audit of Financial Statements."
SAS No. 78, "Consideration of Internal Control in a Financial Statement Audit: An Amendment to SAS No. 55."
Institute of Internal Auditors (IIA). *Codification of Standards for the Professional Practice of Internal Auditing.* Altamonte Springs, FL: The Institute of Internal Auditors, Inc.
SIAS (Statement on Internal Auditing Standards) No. 1, "Control: Concepts and Responsibilities."

SIAS No. 2, "Communicating Results."

SIAS No. 3, "Deterrence, Detection, Investigation, and Reporting of Fraud."

SIAS No. 4, "Quality Assurance."

SIAS No. 5, "Internal Auditors' Relationships with Independent Outside Auditors."

SIAS No. 6, "Audit Working Papers."

Articles, Books

Brink, V. Z., J. A. Cashin, and H. Witt. *Modern Internal Auditing: An Operational Approach*, 3rd ed. New York: The Ronald Press Company (1973).

Colbert, J. L. "How to Make the Most of Your Client's Internal Auditors," *The Practical Accountant* (November 1990), pp. 66-75.

Elifoglu, I. H., A. P. Fitzsimons, and M. H. Levine. "SAS 65 Provides New Guidance for Independent Auditors Who Rely on Internal Auditors," *The Practical Accountant* (May 1992), pp. 64-73.

Ratliff, R. L., W. A. Wallace, J. K. Loebbecke, and W. G. McFarland. *Internal Auditing: Principles and Techniques*. Altamonte Springs, FL: The Institute of Internal Auditors, Inc. (1988).

Sawyer, L. B. *The Practice of Modern Internal Auditing*. Altamonte Springs, FL: The Institute of Internal Auditors, Inc. (1973).

QUESTIONS

COMPLIANCE AUDITING

1. Distinguish between financial statement auditing, compliance auditing, and internal auditing.

2. What three responsibilities do generally accepted auditing standards impose in compliance audits of governmental entities?

3. What is the auditor's responsibility under generally accepted auditing standards to detect direct and material violations of laws and regulations?

4. What types of audits are addressed in the GAO's *Government Auditing Standards*?

5. In reporting on compliance with laws and regulations, what does the GAO's *Government Auditing Standards* require an auditor to report?

6. To whom are reports on compliance with laws and regulations typically distributed?

7. In what ways does reporting on internal control in an audit under the GAO's *Government Auditing Standards* differ from reporting on internal control under *SAS No. 60*, "Communication of Internal Control Structure Related Matters Noted in an Audit," the statement governing reports under generally accepted auditing standards?

8. Which governmental entities are required to have a single audit?

9. What responsibilities are imposed on the auditor by the Single Audit Act Amendment and by OMB *Circular A-133*, "Audits of States, Local Governments, and Non-profit Organizations."

10. Identify the general and specific laws and regulations addressed in the Single Audit Act Amendment and OMB *Circular A-128*, "Audits of States, Local Governments, and Non-profit Organizations."

INTERNAL AUDITING

11. Cite several significant events in the development of contemporary internal auditing in the U.S.

12. What are the major internal audit activities identified in the Institute of Internal Auditors' *Statement of Responsibilities of Internal Auditors*?

13. What are the primary sources of an internal auditor's independence as identified in the Institute of Internal Auditors' *Statement of Responsibilities of Internal Auditors*?

14. Outline the overall approach to an internal operational audit. How is this approach similar to other types of audit activities?

15. How are internal auditing and independent auditing related?
16. What requirements does *SAS No. 65*, "The Auditor's Consideration of the Internal Audit Function in an Audit of Financial Statements" impose upon independent auditors regarding internal auditors?
17. What information should the independent auditor consider when assessing the competence of the internal auditors?
18. What information should the independent auditor consider when assessing the objectivity of the internal auditors?
19. The work of internal auditors may affect the nature, timing, and extent of a financial statement audit. What audit areas are most likely to be affected by the work of the internal auditors?
20. When evaluating the effectiveness of an internal auditor's work, what should the independent auditor consider about the internal auditor?

MULTIPLE CHOICE QUESTIONS

COMPLIANCE AUDITING

1. A governmental auditor is performing an audit of the city of Pawtucket, Rhode Island. The auditor's objective is to determine whether the city's financial statements are presented fairly in all material respects and whether the city has complied with laws and regulations that may have a bearing on the financial statements. This is an example of which of the following types of audits?

   a. Financial audit.
   b. Program audit.
   c. Financial and compliance audit.
   d. Economy and efficiency audit.

2. Which of the following procedures is not appropriate for identifying laws and regulations that management may have overlooked?

   a. Discussing laws and regulations with the entity's chief financial officer, legal counsel, or grant administrators.
   b. Reviewing grant and loan agreements.
   c. Reviewing information about compliance requirements available from state societies of CPAs.
   d. Confirming violations with agencies granting federal financial assistance to the entity.

3. Which of the following procedures would likely lend insight into the risk of material misstatement arising from violations of laws and regulations?

   a. Confirming receivables balances with debtors.
   b. Observing the procedures used by grant administrators to detect violations of laws and regulations.
   c. Considering the competence of client personnel responsible for complying with applicable laws and regulations.
   d. Interviewing recipients of grant funds disbursed by the entity.

4. In a financial audit under the GAO's *Government Auditing Standards*, an auditor is not responsible for which of the following?

   a. Determining whether the financial statements present fairly financial position, results of operations, and cash flows in conformity with GAAP.
   b. Planning the audit with due professional care.

c. Determining whether the entity has complied with applicable laws and regulations.
d. Determining whether the entity is acquiring, protecting, and using resources economically and efficiently.

5. In reporting on compliance with laws and regulations under the GAO's *Government Auditing Standards*, which of the following procedures is not appropriate?

a. Providing positive assurance on items tested.
b. Providing a description of material instances of noncompliance.
c. Providing an opinion on management's responsibility for instances of noncompliance.
d. Providing negative assurance on items not specifically tested.

6. In reporting on internal control, the GAO's *Government Auditing Standards* imposes more responsibility on an auditor than *SAS No. 60*, "Communication of Internal Control Structure Related Matters Noted in an Audit," the standard under generally accepted auditing standards. How do the GAO's standards differ from *SAS No. 60*?

a. *SAS No. 60* does not require communication of reportable conditions.
b. A report under the GAO's standards describes deficiencies in internal control that are not significant enough to be considered reportable conditions under *SAS No. 60*.
c. *SAS No. 60* requires that the auditor identify internal control categories.
d. The GAO's standards require a report on compliance with laws and regulations.

7. The *Single Audit Act* evolved because:

a. The GAO was overburdened with grant audits.
b. Congress preferred that governmental auditors emphasize grant contracts rather than financial statements.
c. There was a need for audits that de-emphasized grants that were immaterial to the financial statements.
d. Grant-by-grant audits were not cost-effective.

8. Under the *Single Audit Act*, specific requirements include:

a. Political activity.
b. Federal financial reports.
c. Eligibility.
d. Administrative requirements.

INTERNAL AUDITING

9. The independence of an internal auditing department will most likely be assured if it reports to the:

a. President.
b. Controller.
c. Treasurer.
d. Board of directors.

10. A major responsibility of internal auditing is to:

a. Install sound accounting, financial, and operating controls at reasonable cost.
b. Determine the extent of compliance with established policies, plans, and procedures.
c. Account for the company's assets and safeguard them from losses.
d. Develop reliable management data.

11. In comparison to the independent auditor, an internal auditor is more likely to be concerned with:

   a. Legal and regulatory compliance.
   b. Cost accounting procedures.
   c. Operational auditing.
   d. Internal control.

12. Taylor Sales Corp. maintains a large, full-time internal audit staff that reports directly to the chief accountant. Audit reports prepared by the internal auditors indicate that the system is functioning as it should and that the accounting records are reliable. The independent auditor will probably:

   a. Eliminate tests of controls.
   b. Increase the depth of the assessment of control risk.
   c. Avoid duplicating the work performed by the internal audit staff.
   d. Place limited reliance on the work performed by the internal audit staff.

13. When an independent auditor decides that the work performed by internal auditors may have a bearing on the nature, timing, and extent of planned audit procedures, the independent auditor should evaluate the objectivity of the internal auditors. Relative to objectivity, the independent auditor should:

   a. Consider the organizational level to which internal auditors report.
   b. Review the quality control program in effect for the internal audit staff.
   c. Examine the quality of the internal audit reports.
   d. Consider the qualifications of the internal audit staff.

14. Operational audits generally have been performed by internal auditors but may be performed by independent accountants. A primary purpose of an operational audit is to provide:

   a. A means of assuring that internal controls are functioning as planned.
   b. Aid to the independent auditor, who is auditing the financial statements.
   c. The results of internal examinations of financial and accounting matters to an entity's top-level management.
   d. A measure of management performance in meeting organizational goals.

15. When an independent auditor relies on the work of an internal auditor, he or she should examine the internal auditor's work to provide a basis for judging the:

   a. Qualifications of the internal auditor.
   b. Integrity of the internal auditor.
   c. Scope of the internal auditor's work.
   d. Importance of the internal audit function to the board of directors' audit committee.

PROBLEMS AND DISCUSSION CASES

COMPLIANCE AUDITING

19-1 *Responsibility for Tax Assessments in a Special Revenue Fund*
Jayne Phillips, CPA has been engaged by the town council of Granger to perform an audit of the town's June 30, 1999 financial statements in accordance with generally accepted auditing standards. By referendum, the town in November 1998 approved a special tax assessment to be used in constructing an addition to the local high school and in purchasing temporary freestanding classrooms for the middle school. The referendum called for the assessment to be accounted for in a special revenue fund.

Required: What is Phillips's responsibility regarding the accounting for the special tax assessment?

19-2 *Responsibilities Under GAAS and Government Auditing Standards*
The City of Central Falls has engaged Robert Cohen, CPA to audit the June 30, 1999 financial statements of the City's Water Department under the GAO's *Government Auditing Standards*. Cohen's report will be used by the City and by the state's legislative auditors who, under laws passed by the General Assembly, will perform an audit of the City for the fiscal year ended June 30, 1999. The Water Department generates revenue from two sources: a water use tax and a budgetary allocation from the City's general fund.
Required:
1. How does Cohen's responsibility in auditing the Water Department's financial statements under the GAO's *Government Auditing Standards* differ from his responsibility under generally accepted auditing standards?
2. In reporting on the Water Department's compliance with laws and regulations, what specifically must Cohen report about transactions tested during the audit?

19-3 *Reporting on Internal Control Under Government Auditing Standards*
Michael Cunningham, CPA is preparing a report on internal control in conjunction with an audit of the City of Warwick's June 30, 1999 financial statements. The audit is being conducted in accordance with the GAO's *Government Auditing Standards*. The City of Warwick has two transaction cycles: a revenue/receipt cycle and an expenditure/disbursement cycle. During the engagement, Cunningham noted one reportable condition: Policies and procedures have not been implemented to subject material purchases to competitive bids. An experienced auditor, Cunningham has frequently reported on internal control under *SAS No. 60*, "Communication of Internal Control Structure Related Matters Noted in an Audit," but has never before performed an audit for a governmental entity.
Required:
1. How does Cunningham's responsibility for reporting on internal control under the GAO's *Government Auditing Standards* differ from his responsibility under *SAS No. 60*?
2. From the facts above, draft a report on internal control.

19-4 *The Single Audit Act Amendment and OMB Circular A-133*
Owing to a small federal grant from the Department of Housing and Urban Development (HUD) to the Town of Stillman, Nadine Gordimer, CPA has performed grant audits for the town in each of the past five years. The town has received no other federal financial assistance. However, in 1999, the town applied for and received an additional one-year HUD grant for the minimum amount subjecting Stillman to the requirements of the *Single Audit Act* and OMB *Circular A-133*, "Audits of States, Local Governments, and Non-profit Organizations." The grant funds were received and disbursed for low-income housing refurbishing in 1999. Not having performed a single audit previously, Gordimer seeks your advice.
Required:
1. Does the HUD grant to the Town of Stillman represent a major program or a nonmajor program under the *Single Audit Act*?
2. Explain the town's reporting responsibilities under the Single Audit Act.

19-5 *Governmental Financial Audits and Financial Statement Audits*
Wil Stevens is executive vice president of a major automobile manufacturing company. Stevens was recently elected Mayor of Detroit. Prior to assuming office, he calls on you, his independent auditor, for advice. He asks you to explain the major similarities and

differences between a financial audit for a large city and a financial statement audit for an industrial corporation.

Required: Describe the major similarities and differences between a governmental financial audit and a financial statement audit of a business enterprise.

19-6 *Auditing a Federally Funded Housing Allowance Program*

A public accounting firm has been engaged to perform the audit of a local, federally funded Housing Allowance Program. The objective of the program is to increase the housing standards of Agana County through subsidized rent payments. The program, however, has been criticized by local authorities for failing to achieve significant results during its two years of existence. You have been assigned to plan an audit.

Required:
1. What matters should you take into consideration when planning the Housing Allowance engagement?
2. Apply the scientific method of inquiry (Chapter 1) to the engagement, giving examples of procedures and measurement criteria the firm should deem appropriate.

19-7 *Auditing a Department of Education School Breakfast Program*

As a GAO auditor, you have been assigned to perform an audit of a Department of Education School Breakfast Program. The Department had instructed all schools to order commodities in economical institutional-size packages to the extent possible. In eight of the 22 schools covered by the review, you have found purchases in smaller-size packages. You estimate that additional costs total $10,000 per month, per school. Considering the escalation in food prices, it was evident that bulk purchasing was essential due to favorable quantity discounts. But Department of Education officials stated that although bulk purchases were encouraged, they were not mandated.

Required:
1. What type of audit is contemplated by the description above? Explain.
2. Draft a paragraph summarizing the recommendations you would include in a report to the Department of Education.

INTERNAL AUDITING

19-8 *Developing a New Internal Audit Department*

Bird Machine Company is considering developing an internal audit department. A few years ago, the company began an expansion program that included acquiring new businesses, some of which are located quite far from the home office. Bird Machine retained the prior managements after most acquisitions and expects to continue to do so. The corporate organization is decentralized, and the parent company (Bird Machine) sets general policies. Division and subsidiary managements are quite autonomous—their performance is measured against budgets and return-on-investment targets established at the beginning of each year. The separate units of Bird Machine manufacture and market their own products. Current sales volume is $150,000,000.

Bird Machine has been audited by the public accounting firm in which you are a manager. You have supervised the audit for the past three years and have now been asked by Bird Machine Company to prepare a report on activities that could be assumed by an internal audit department.

Required:
1. Draft a report that describes:
   a. The objectives of independent and internal auditors.
   b. The types of audits an internal audit department might be expected to perform.
   c. The relationship between the internal and the independent auditor.
2. The company has offered you the position of director of internal auditing. Describe changes in your audit philosophy and in your relationship to Bird Machine's management if you were to take the job.

19-9 *Why Both Internal Auditing and a Financial Statement Audit?*

Amy Baat, a local real estate broker, has been appointed to the board of directors of the PennMed Corporation. At a recent board meeting, Baat discovered two planned expenditures for auditing: The controller's budget included an amount for internal auditing, and the treasurer's budget included an amount for the 1999 financial statement audit by a major public accounting firm.

Baat didn't understand the need for two different expenditures for auditing. Since the fee for the financial statement audit was less than the cost of internal auditing, she proposed eliminating the internal audit function.

Required:

1. Explain to Baat the purposes served by internal auditing and by a financial statement audit.
2. What benefits does the public accounting firm performing an audit derive from internal auditing?

19-10 *An Internal Auditor's Objectivity and Independence*

Many internal audit departments report to a level of authority below either the board of directors or the chief executive officer. But these cases raise some doubt about the internal auditors' objectivity and independence. The organization chart below is an example.

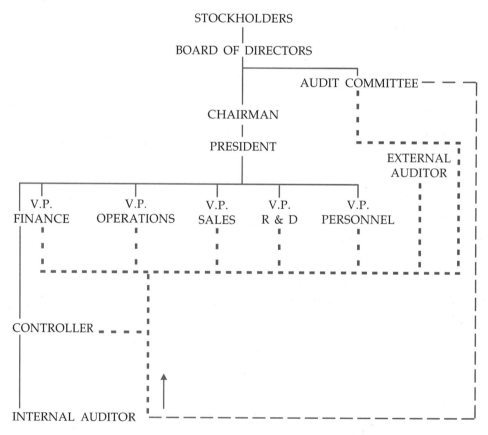

LEGEND

——————— Administrative responsibility

— — — Functional responsibility

▪ ▪ ▪ ▪ Report of internal audit findings as appropriate

Required: Cite the advantages and disadvantages to the internal audit department of having the responsibilities depicted in the chart.

(IIA Adapted)

19-11 *Initial Steps in Establishing an Internal Audit Function*
A consulting professional in a public accounting firm, you have been engaged to establish an internal audit function in the Newman Crosby Corporation, a commercial manufacturer of fabricated steel fittings that employs thousands in four Midwest states. The company markets to wholesale, manufacturing, and warehousing businesses in the U.S. and abroad.

Required: Describe the initial steps you would take to familiarize yourself with the company before establishing the internal audit function.

19-12 *Modifying Internal Auditing to Accommodate External Auditing*
Over the past several years, Hobble, Inc. has expanded, diversified, and grown both in sales and in profits. Two years ago Hobble's management established an internal audit department that is responsible for evaluating and recommending modifications in control activities, reviewing operations to promote efficiency and economy, and conducting special inquiries at management's direction.

As in prior years, Hobble, Inc. has engaged Plautz & Associates, LLP as independent auditors for the current year, 1999. The partner in charge of the Hobble audit has made an appointment with the manager of Hobble's internal audit department to discuss the progress of the department, including new personnel and new activities. The partner needs this information to plan the scope of the audit and to determine the amount of assistance that will be needed from the internal audit department.

Required: The scope of an independent audit can be modified if a competent internal audit department exists. What characteristics of Hobble's internal audit department and of its work should Plautz & Associates evaluate when establishing the scope of the financial statement audit?

(IMA Adapted)

19-13 *Criticizing an Internal Auditor's Objectivity*
The internal auditing department of a large service entity is responsible to the controller who, in turn, is responsible to the president. As part of the internal audit responsibility, regular audits are performed of payroll, general accounting, accounts receivable, and accounts payable. Because these activities also report to the controller, criticism is frequently made that the internal auditor cannot be objective.

Required: Following are two solutions that might eliminate the criticism. Describe briefly the advantages and disadvantages of each.
1. The internal auditing department could send audit reports about activities under the controller's supervision directly to the president.
2. The director of internal auditing could discuss the organizational problem with the independent auditors and ask them to make a recommendation that would eliminate the criticism.

19-14 *Stock Shortages and Internal Auditing*
During the audit of purchasing and inventory operations, an internal auditor discovers that significant quantities of purchased materials are neither in stock nor accounted for. Stock records, controlled by the warehouse supervisor, do not reflect shortages and the inventory reports appear to have been altered. The internal auditor suspects that the warehouse supervisor altered the reports, since he has the greatest opportunity to remove materials for personal gain.

The auditor notifies the department manager and together they confront the suspected supervisor. The supervisor offers no explanation for the shortages and denies any wrongdoing. The department manager immediately suspends the supervisor, pending further investigation, and informs the warehouse employees. Since no adequate explanation for the shortages was obtained, the auditor contacts security for assistance.

Required: List actions the auditor and the department manager might take that could hinder a successful investigation and could subject the company to legal proceedings. Briefly discuss the possible adverse effect of each action.

(IIA Adapted)

19-15   *Coordinating Internal and External Auditors*
The agenda of a forthcoming meeting of the audit committee of a board of directors indicates that you are to discuss coordination between independent and internal auditors.

Required:
1. What are the advantages of coordination between independent and internal auditors?
2. What are the essential ingredients to establishing effective coordination between independent and internal auditors?

RESEARCH PROJECTS

1.   ONE AUDIT, SEVERAL REPORTS

The report on a *nongovernmental* entity's audited financial statements captures an independent auditor's opinion on financial position, results of operations, and cash flows in a single, critical phrase known well to the users of financial statements: ". . . present fairly in all material respects . . ." (Chapter 3). One audit, one audit report. But in the array of reports on a state or local governmental entity's single audit, auditors report on a variety of matters crucial to compliance with the *Single Audit Act Amendment* and with the Office of Management and Budget (OMB) *Circular A-133*, among them the entity's general purpose financial statements, compliance with laws and regulations, and participation in federal financial assistance programs. One audit, several reports.

Required: Select the audit reports issued for a single audit of a state or local governmental unit either from the National Automated Accounting Research System (NAARS), a computerized data bank that includes several hundred governmental reports (among others), or from another source such as a governmental unit near you.

1. Draft a report that interprets the meaning of each paragraph (i.e., why do you think professional standards require auditors to say what they're saying?) and indicates the conclusions reached by the auditor (i.e., what is the critical phrase users anchor on?) in each of the five reports introduced in this chapter that are applicable to the reporting entity:
   a.   Report on compliance with general requirements.
   b.   Report on major program compliance with specific requirements.
   c.   Report on nonmajor program compliance with specific requirements.
   d.   Report on the schedule of federal financial assistance.
   e.   Report on internal controls over federal financial assistance.
2. Explain why you think that a single audit report may not include one or more of the reports listed above.

2.   INTERNAL AUDITING IN SELECTED INDUSTRIES

Just as financial statement auditing varies by industry, so too does internal auditing, in part because the risks vary from industry to industry. For example, the risks related to accounting estimates are quite different in the airline industry (i.e., frequent-flier liabilities), the construction industry (i.e., percentage of completion), and the health care industry (i.e., third-party reimbursements). However, although the professional literature is replete with guidance about financial statement audits in several major industries—for example, the AICPA's *Audit and Accounting Guides*—the literature is less forthcoming about industry-specific operational auditing.

Required: Select an AICPA *Audit and Accounting Guide* for an industry that interests you (e.g., airlines, casinos, construction contractors, finance companies, property and liability insurance companies, providers of health care) and a recent annual report for a publicly traded company within the industry. Draft a report that:

1. Discusses how a public accounting firm could use the company's internal audit department to accomplish the audit of audit-and-accounting issues identified within the *Audit Guide.*
2. Discusses the company's internal audit department using information accessed from:
    a. The company's World Wide Web home page, or
    b. The company directly (a mailing address and telephone number are typically included in an annual report).

Glossary

Accounting and Review Services Committee (ARSC). The senior technical committee of the AICPA responsible for promulgating pronouncements on accounting and review services.

accounting estimates. Financial statement elements, items, or accounts that have been approximated by management.

accounting system. Methods and records established by management to record and report transactions and events and to maintain accountability for assets and liabilities.

adjusting entries (AJEs). Journal entries proposed by the independent auditor that correct a client's books.

adverse opinion. A communication within an attestation report or an audit report indicating, respectively, that management's assertion is *not presented fairly* in conformity with established criteria, or that management's financial statements are *do not present fairly* the financial position, results of operations, and cash flows in conformity with generally accepted accounting principles.

AICPA Code of Professional Conduct. The principles, rules of conduct, interpretations, and rulings governing an AICPA member's ethical responsibilities to the public, to clients, and to colleagues in the profession.

allowance for sampling risk. The auditor's allowance for the risk that a sample may contain disproportionately more or less monetary misstatement than exists within the population.

American Institute of Certified Public Accountants (AICPA). The national, voluntary membership organization of certified public accountants.

analytical procedures. Evaluations of financial information made by a study of plausible relationships among financial and nonfinancial data.

area franchise fee. The up-front, lump sum fee a franchisee pays a franchisor for the exclusive right to market the franchisor's product or service.

assurance services. Three-party contracts that improve the quality of information.

attestation services. A communicated statement of opinion, based upon convincing evidence, by an independent, competent, authoritative person concerning the degree of correspondence in all material respects of accounting information communicated by an entity with established criteria.

attestation (attest) engagement. A professional services engagement in which a practitioner issues a written communication that expresses a conclusion about the reliability of a written assertion made by the client.

attestation report. A letter communicating the assertion attested to, management's and the attestor's responsibilities, what an attestation engagement entails, and the attestor's opinion.

attestation risk. The probability that an attestor may unknowingly fail to appropriately modify a conclusion on a written assertion that is materially misstated.

attestation (attest) standards. Eleven general, fieldwork, and reporting standards for attestation engagements.

attribute. A characteristic of a control procedure.

attribute estimation sampling. A statistical sampling plan for tests of controls that reaches conclusions about a rate of deviation from a prescribed control procedure.

attributes sampling plan. An audit sampling plan designed to test the rate of deviation from a prescribed control procedure.

audit committee. A committee of an entity's board of directors that serves as an intermediary between the independent auditor and the full board.

audit evidence. The underlying accounting data and corroborating information used by auditors to test management's financial statement assertions.

audit hooks. A computer assisted audit technique in which an auditor reserves exits in a client's application software to insert at will commands for audit processing.

audit modules. A computer assisted audit technique in which an auditor places generalized audit software within a client's application software for the purpose of selecting data for subsequent testing, such as the selection and printing of accounts receivable confirmations.

audit population (population). All of the items within a class of transactions or account balance.

audit procedures. Detailed methods or techniques used by an independent auditor, such as observation, documentation, confirmation, mechanical tests of accounting data, comparisons, and inquiries, to discharge his or her responsibilities under generally accepted auditing standards.

audit program. A detailed list of audit procedures to be performed for a particular aspect of a financial statement audit.

audit report. A letter communicating what was audited, management's and the auditor's responsibilities, what an audit entails, and the auditor's opinion.

audit risk. The probability that an auditor may unknowingly fail to appropriately modify an opinion on financial statements that are materially misstated.

audit services (auditing). A systematic process of objectively obtaining and evaluating evidence regarding assertions about economic actions and events to ascertain the degree of correspondence between those assertions and established criteria and to communicate the results to interested users. *See* financial statement auditing.

audit trail. Records and documents that support executed transactions.

Auditing Standards Board (ASB). The senior technical committee of the AICPA responsible for promulgating auditing standards and procedures since 1978.

Auditing Standards Executive Committee (AudSEC). The senior technical committee of the AICPA responsible for promulgating auditing standards and procedures during the years 1972-1978.

available-for-sale securities. Debt and equity securities not classified as held-to-maturity securities or trading securities.

B

base case system evaluation (BCSE). A computer assisted audit technique in which an auditor prepares test data to test every possible condition that a client's software will confront.

big baths. Refers to the practice of a company timing asset write-downs to occur in an abnormally *un*profitable year, signaling to the financial markets that bad times have long since passed by.

bill of lading. A Uniform Commercial Code shipping document.

bond certificate. A document (debt security) representing a stated amount of debt owed by an entity.

breach of contract. Violation of the terms of a contract.

business risk. The probability that a practitioner may incur damages despite issuing an appropriate report.

C

Certified public accountants (CPAs). Individuals who have passed the Uniform CPA Examination and have satisfied all the education and experience requirements of their respective state boards of accountancy.

collusion. An irregularity perpetrated by two or more employees, each of whose job responsibilities is necessary to complete the irregularity. (Collusion is controlled by adequate segregation of duties.)

comfort letter. In an initial public offering of securities, a written communication from the independent accountant to an underwriter about procedures the accountant performed on the unaudited financial statements and schedules accompanying a client's registration statement.

commercial paper. A general category of commercial loan instruments, due and payable in accordance with terms described on the instrument.

Committee on Auditing Procedure (CAP). The senior technical committee of the AICPA responsible for promulgating auditing standards and procedures during the years 1939-1972.

common law. Law evolving from precedent-setting court cases; based in the doctrine of *stare decisis:* principles of law that are established in precedent-setting cases are handed down to succeeding cases within the jurisdiction.

compilation of financial statements. A nonattest service in which the accountant prepares financial statements from a client's unaudited and unreviewed accounts and issues a report that provides no assurance, using language that states the accountant "has not audited or reviewed the financial statements and, accordingly, does not express an opinion or any form of assurance."

completeness. An assertion within financial statements that all transactions and accounts that should be presented in the financial statements are included.

compliance audit. An audit designed to assess whether a not-for-profit entity's financial statements are presented fairly in accordance with generally accepted accounting principles and whether the entity has complied with applicable laws and regulations. Compliance audits are performed either by independent auditors or by governmental auditors.

consulting services. Two-party contracts that recommend uses for information.

contingent monetary effects. In responding to detected illegal acts, payments such as fines, penalties, and damages that in some circumstances, such as the *Foreign Corrupt Practices Act*, may be quite substantial.

control activities (control procedures). Policies and procedures established by management in addition to the control environment and the accounting system to provide reasonable assurance that specific objectives are achieved.

control environment. Management's and the board of directors' attitude toward, awareness of, and corrective actions concerning internal control.

control risk. The risk that error could occur and not be prevented or detected by the internal controls.

conversion cycle. The policies and procedures encompassing the production of finished products for sale.

credit memoranda. Documents indicating that a customer's account will be credited for goods returned by the customer.

customer order. A written (or unwritten, in the case of a telephone order) request from a customer to purchase goods.

customer remittance advice. A document that accompanies a sales invoice and is intended to be returned with a customer's cash remittance (payment) for handling and recording.

cutoff bank statement. A seven- to ten-day bank statement for a period usually beginning the first day after the balance sheet date (e.g., January 1). A cutoff bank statement is used to verify deposits in transit and outstanding checks appearing on the year end bank reconciliation.

D

database management (DBM) system. In computer systems, an integrated collection of stored data that can be accessed for processing wholly or in part, by authorized access codes.

depreciation schedule. A work sheet computing and summarizing depreciation.

detection risk. The risk that error could occur and not be detected by the auditor's procedures.

deviation. In a control procedure, the absence of an attribute.

difference estimation. A classical variables sampling plan designed to estimate the amount of monetary misstatement in a population—called the difference estimate—from the difference between recorded and audited amounts observed in a sample.

disclaimer of opinion. A one-paragraph letter communicating that an attestor or an auditor, respectively, does not express an opinion on management's assertion or on management's financial statements.

discovery sampling. A sampling plan designed to calculate the sample size required to achieve a desired probability of observing at least one deviation in a sample if the population deviation rate equals or exceeds a specified critical rate of deviation.

dual-purpose tests. Auditing procedures designed to provide evidence about both control risk and likely monetary error.

E

earnings manipulation. Management's altering of reported earnings (either upward to inflate earnings or downward to deflate earnings)—typically occurs when the accounting for a transaction or event allows management some discretion over the timing or the amount of earnings to be reported.

economy and efficiency audit. A governmental audit under the GAO's *Government Auditing Standards;* an economy and efficiency audit includes determining (1) whether the entity is acquiring, protecting, and using its resources economi-

cally and efficiently, (2) the causes of inefficiencies or uneconomical practices, and (3) whether the entity has complied with laws and regulations concerning matters of economy and efficiency.

employee earnings record. A record maintained for each employee that provides a cumulative, year-to-date summary of total earnings, withholdings, and deductions.

end user computing. Computer information systems in which management empowers end users to develop task-specific application software.

engagement letter. A written agreement between an independent auditor and an audit client that describes the terms of the audit engagement and the role of the auditor.

environmental liability. An actual or contingent liability arising from the violation by an entity of environmental laws and regulations, such as the Congressional Comprehensive Environmental Response, Compensation, and Liability Act of 1980 ("CERCLA" or, more popularly, the "Superfund" legislation); the Superfund Amendment and Reauthorization Act of 1986; and the Clean Air Act of 1990.

errors. Unintentional mistakes or omissions of amounts or of disclosures in financial statements.

ethics rulings. Issued by the AICPA's professional ethics division and intended to summarize the applicability of Rules of Conduct and Interpretations to specific situations.

evidential matter. The accounting data that underlie financial statements (e.g., journals, ledgers) and the corroborating information that underlies accounting data (e.g., contracts, canceled checks).

existence or occurrence. An assertion within financial statements that all recorded assets, liabilities, and equities exist at a given date, and all recorded transactions occurred during a given period.

expenditure/disbursement cycle. The policies and procedures encompassing the acquisition and purchase of goods and services.

F

financial forecast. A prospective financial statement that presents an entity's expected financial position, results of operations, and cash flows.

financial projection. A prospective financial statement that presents an entity's expected financial position, results of operations, and cash flows, and is based on one or more assumptions.

financial statement assertions. Explicit and implicit representations embodied within financial statements and related to existence or occurrence, completeness, rights and obligations, valuation or allocation, and presentation and disclosure.

financial statement audit. An audit of an entity's four basic financial statements—balance sheet (statement of financial position), income statement, statement of cash flows, and (if applicable) statement of retained earnings—the purpose of which is to form an opinion on whether the statements present fairly in all material respects the entity's financial position, results of operations, and cash flows in conformity with generally accepted accounting principles.

financing cycle. The policies and procedures encompassing the acquisition of capital funds.

flowchart. Interrelated symbols that diagram the flow of transactions and events through an accounting system.

Foreign Corrupt Practices Act (FCPA). Federal statutory law preventing payments or gifts to foreign governments or officials and requiring compliance with recordkeeping and internal-control provisions.

foreseen third parties. Under common law, third parties not specifically identified by name to the auditor as beneficiaries of an entity's audited financial state-

ments, but whose general identity and purpose for relying on the audited statements are known by the auditor.

fraud. An intentional misrepresentation of a material fact that includes *fraudulent financial reporting* (an intentional misstatement or omission of amounts or disclosures in financial statements) and *misappropriation of assets* (theft of an entity's assets).

G

general standards. The first three of the ten generally accepted auditing standards are (1) requiring adequate technical training and proficiency, (2) having an independence in mental attitude, and (3) using due professional care.

generally accepted accounting principles (GAAP). The consensus at any point in time about which resources and obligations should be recorded as assets and liabilities, which changes in assets and liabilities should be recorded, when changes should be recorded, how assets and liabilities and changes in them should be measured, and what should be disclosed in financial statements.

generally accepted auditing standards (GAAS). Ten authoritative statements that represent the guidelines and measures of quality for a financial statement audit.

government auditing standards. Standards for the audit of governmental entities, contained in the GAO's *Governmental Auditing Standards* (sometimes called "generally accepted governmental auditing standards" [GAGAS]).

governmental auditors. Auditors employed by governmental entities such as state legislative audit departments and the U.S. General Accounting Office (GAO).

gross negligence. A lack of even minimum care in performing professional services; for example, a reckless departure from generally accepted auditing standards.

H

held-to-maturity securities. Debt that an entity has the positive intent and ability to hold to maturity.

I

illegal acts. Violations of laws or governmental regulations.

impaired assets. Assets an entity continues to use but that have suffered a decline in value as a result of, for example, corporate restructuring or slumping demand for uncompetitive products.

impairment loss. In accounting for the discretionary write-down of impaired assets, the amount by which the asset's carrying amount exceeds the asset's fair amount.

income smoothing. Refers to a company's maintaining a steady rate of earnings growth over a series of years, thereby providing no reason for the financial markets to impute unexpected risk in the company or in expected stock prices.

independent auditors. Certified public accountants within public accounting firms who perform independent financial statement audits.

inherent risk. The susceptibility of an account balance to error, assuming there are no related control procedures.

integrated test data. A computer assisted audit technique in which fictitious test data are integrated with actual client data without the computer department's knowledge, thus allowing the auditor to compare the client's output with the results expected by the auditor.

interim financial statements. Financial statements reflecting financial position, results of operations, and cash flows for a period less than a fiscal year (e.g., quarterly financial statements).

internal auditors. Employees of an entity whose job is to conduct operational audits among other audit activities for the entity. Internal audit reports are not made available to the public.

internal control. A process, effected by an entity's board of directors, management, and other personnel, designed to provide reasonable assurance that the entity achieves objectives about the effectiveness and efficiency of operations, the reliability of financial reporting, and compliance with applicable laws and regulations.

Interpretations of the Rules of Conduct. Issued by the AICPA's professional ethics division and intended to interpret the scope and applicability of the Rules of Conduct.

introductory paragraph. The first paragraph of an attestation or audit report, intended to communicate the assertion attested to or the financial statements audited, that the assertion or statements are management's responsibility, and that the attestor/auditor is responsible only for the opinion communicated, not for the assertion or financial statements.

J

joint-and-several liability. In legal liability, a plaintiff in an action against an auditor can potentially recover all damages from the auditor alone, even though the auditor's report may have contributed only partially to the plaintiff's loss.

K

kiting. An intentional fraud that conceals cash shortages by (1) transferring funds from one bank to another and (2) recording the receipt on or before the balance sheet date and the disbursement after the balance sheet date.

L

labor charge report. A summary of labor costs to be applied to work-in-process inventory.

lapping. An intentional irregularity that conceals cash shortages resulting from delays in recording cash collections.

legal (lawyer's) letter. A written representation to the independent auditor from a client's lawyer about the entity's pending and threatened litigation, claims, and assessments.

limited liability partnership (LLP) or limited liability company (LLC). A form of organization that provides a CPA firm with the benefits of taxation as a partnership, thereby avoiding double taxation (i.e., corporate taxes to the professional corporation and individual taxes to the shareholders), and limited liability, thereby providing relief from vicarious liability.

local area network (LAN). Llinked microcomputers that access data files and software from a central file server and that direct print jobs from a central print server.

loss contingencies (contingencies). An existing condition, situation, or set of circumstances involving uncertainty as to possible gain or loss that will ultimately be resolved when one or more future events occur or fail to occur (e.g., pending litigation for a patent infringement suit).

M

management (client) representation letter. Written representations from management to the independent auditor about assertions made by management (e.g., management has made available to the auditor all financial records) and about management's responsibility for the financial statements.

materiality. The magnitude of an omission or misstatement that would have changed or influenced the judgment of a reasonable person relying on an assertion.

material weakness. A subset of reportable conditions, a material weakness is a condition in which the design or operation of the specific internal control elements do not reduce to a relatively low level the risk that errors or irregularities in amounts that would be material in relation to the financial statements being audited may occur and not be detected within a timely period by employees in the normal course of performing their assigned functions.

materials requisition. A formal request for materials by an operating department.

mean-per-unit estimation. A classical variables sampling plan designed to estimate the average audited value for each population item from the average observed in the sample.

N

narrative memorandum. A written description of a particular phase or phases of an accounting system.

negative confirmation. A written confirmation requesting that a customer respond directly to the auditor only if the account receivable balance is incorrect according to the customer's accounts payable records.

nonsampling risk. All aspects of audit risk not attributable to sampling.

nonstatistical sampling plan. An audit sampling plan that does not apply the laws of probability.

O

operational audit. An audit performed by an entity's internal auditors (or by independent auditors) to assess the efficiency and effectiveness of management's operating procedures.

opinion paragraph. A paragraph within an attestation or audit report intended to communicate the attestor's or auditor's opinion on whether management's assertion is reliable or on whether management's financial statements present fairly in all material respects the financial position, results of operations, and cash flows in conformity with generally accepted accounting principles.

ordinary negligence. A lack of reasonable care in performing professional services; for example, violating one of the generally accepted auditing standards.

overhead application report. A summary of overhead applied to work-in-process inventory.

P

parallel simulation. A computer assisted audit technique in which an auditor prepares software to process client-prepared input on the client's or the auditor's computer.

payroll register. A record prepared each pay period, listing all employees and indicating the gross pay, withholdings, deductions, and net pay for each employee during the period.

peer (quality) review. An independent outside review of a public accounting firm's quality control procedures performed by CPAs not otherwise employed by the reviewed firm.

perpetual inventory record. A cumulative record of quantities on hand for a particular item or class of inventory.

personal financial statements. Financial statements that present the financial position of an individual or family.

personnel records. Documents maintained for each employee by the personnel department that provide a permanent record of all essential information pertaining to the employee, including date of employment, job classification, salary or hourly pay rate, promotions, payroll deductions, terminations, etc.

positive confirmation. A written confirmation requesting that a customer respond directly to the auditor about whether the account receivable balance is correct or incorrect according to the customer's accounts payable records.

postretirement benefits other than pensions. An entity's obligations to retirees for health care, life insurance, tuition assistance, and housing subsidies, among other things.

potentially responsible party. In environmental law, a party, usually an alleged industrial polluter, identified by the U.S. Environmental Protection Agency (EPA) as potentially responsible for cleaning up hazardous waste.

predecessor auditor. In a change of auditors, the independent auditor being replaced.

presentation and disclosure. An assertion within financial statements stating that all components of the statements are properly classified, described, and disclosed.

primary beneficiaries. Under common law, third parties specifically identified by name to the auditor as beneficiaries of an entity's audited financial statements.

principal auditor. One among two or more auditors in a multisite (i.e., more than one location) or multientity (e.g., parent and subsidiaries) audit that is responsible for reporting on financial statements. The decision as to which auditor is the principal auditor is based on the revenues and assets audited by each auditor, the extent of each auditor's knowledge of the overall financial statements, and the significance of the sites or entities audited by each auditor in relation to the combined entity's activities taken as a whole.

principles of the Code of Professional Conduct. Positively worded goals in the form of declarative statements about an AICPA member's responsibilities as professionals; obligation to the public interest; sense of integrity, objectivity, and independence; and observance of professional and technical standards.

privity. A relationship between parties to a contract; for example, the parties named to a professional services contract are "in privity."

probability-proportional-to-size (PPS) sampling. A sampling plan based in attributes sampling theory.

program audit. A governmental audit under the GAO's *Government Auditing Standards*. A program audit includes determining (1) the extent to which the desired results or benefits established by the legislature or other authorizing body are being achieved, (2) the effectiveness of organizations, programs, activities, or functions, and (3) whether the entity has complied with laws and regulations applicable to the program.

proportionate liability. In legal liability, a plaintiff in an action against an auditor can potentially recover only the portion of awarded damages that are attributed to the auditor's proportionate share of responsibility.

prospective financial statements. Financial statements that present an entity's expected—or expected under one or more assumptions—financial position, results of operations, and cash flows.

Public Oversight Board (POB). An autonomous body that monitors the performance of those public accounting firms that audit publicly traded companies.

purchase order. A written request to a vendor to purchase goods.

purchase requisition. A written request to supervisory personnel from an employee or department requesting that goods be purchased.

Q

qualified opinion. A communication within an attestation report or an audit report indicating that except for the effects of a matter, respectively, management's assertion is presented fairly in all material respects in conformity with established criteria, or management's financial statements present fairly in all material respects the financial position, results of operations, and cash flows in conformity with generally accepted accounting principles.

quality control. Internal policies and procedures designed to assure consistent performance and achievement within an individual public accounting firm.

questionnaire. In the independent auditor's consideration of internal control, a series of questions designed to detect deficiencies in an entity's control procedures.

R

Racketeer Influenced and Corrupt Organizations Act (RICO). Passed as part of the Organized Crime Control Act of 1970, this federal statutory law prevents the movement of organized crime into legitimate business.

ratio estimation. A classical variables sampling plan designed to estimate the amount of monetary misstatement in a population—called the ratio estimate—from the ratio between recorded and audited amounts observed in the sample.

receiving report. A document containing information about goods received.

reclassification entries (RJEs). Journal entries made within the independent auditor's working papers to reclassify a client's account classifications for financial statement reporting purposes.

registration statement. A statement filed with the SEC, usually on Form S-1, to offer securities for sale to the public under the Securities Act of 1933.

related party transaction. A transaction that, because it is between an entity and another party related to the entity (e.g., a principal owner, a director, a manager, or his/her immediate family), increases substantially the risk that the transaction is not at arm's length.

remittance advice. *See* customer remittance advice.

reportable conditions. Significant deficiencies in the design or operation of internal control that could adversely affect an entity's ability to record, process, summarize, and report financial data consistent with management's financial statement assertions.

revenue/receipt cycle. The policies and procedures encompassing the sale of goods or services to customers and the collection of cash.

review of financial statements. An attest service in which the independent accountant performs analytical procedures, makes inquiries of client personnel, and issues a report that provides limited (sometimes called negative) assurance, using language that states the accountant is "not aware of any material modifications that should be made to the financial statements in order for them to be in conformity with GAAP."

rights and obligations. An assertion within financial statements that all assets are the rights of the entity and liabilities are the obligations of the entity at a given date.

risk. The probability that management's assertions may contain material omissions or misstatements

risk of assessing control risk too high. The risk that a sample deviation rate supports assessing control risk at the maximum when, unbeknown to the auditor, the true deviation rate in the population supports assessing control risk below the maximum.

risk of assessing control risk too low. The risk that a sample deviation rate supports assessing control risk below the maximum when, unbeknown to the auditor, the true deviation rate in the population supports assessing control risk at the maximum.

risk of incorrect acceptance. The risk that a sample supports the conclusion that a recorded account balance is not materially misstated when, unbeknown to the auditor, the account is materially misstated.

risk of incorrect rejection. The risk that a sample supports the conclusion that a recorded account balance is materially misstated when, unbeknown to the auditor, the account is not materially misstated.

Rules of Conduct. Eleven rules of the Code of Professional Conduct that are enforceable against AICPA members for all professional services, including financial statement auditing. The Rules are about independence, integrity and objectivity, general standards, compliance with standards, accounting principles, confidential client information, contingent fees, acts discreditable to the profession, advertising, and the form and name of an accounting practice.

S

sales invoice. A document containing information about goods sold and representing formal notice to a customer about the amount and terms of payment.

sales order. A document describing goods ordered by a customer, including all relevant information about price, quantity, and payment terms.

sample deviation rate (sample rate of deviation). The auditor's estimate of the true but unknown population deviation rate.

sampling. Applying procedures to less than 100 percent of the items that constitute an audit population.

sampling plan. The procedures a practitioner uses to accomplish an audit sampling application.

sampling risk. The risk that the conclusions drawn from testing a sample might be different if the entire population were tested—that is, a sample might not be representative in the sense that the sample may contain disproportionately more or fewer control deviations or monetary differences than exist in the population.

sampling unit. Any of the individual items constituting a population.

scope paragraph. A paragraph within an audit report (usually the second) intended to communicate (1) that the audit was conducted in accordance with generally accepted auditing standards and (2) what an audit entails.

search for unrecorded liabilities. A substantive audit test designed to determine whether an audit client's liabilities are understated.

Securities Act of 1933. Federal statutory law regulating the inital public offering and sale of securities.

Securities and Exchange Commission (SEC). An agency of the U.S. government created by Congress in 1934 to regulate the registration and exchange of securities under the Securities Act of 1933 and the Securities Exchange Act of 1934.

Securities Exchange Act of 1934. Federal statutory law regulating the trading of previously issued securities.

segregation of duties. The separation of employee responsibilities to prevent any one employee, acting alone, from committing and concealing irregularities.

sequential (stop-or-go) sampling. A statistical sampling plan for tests of controls in which the sample is selected in steps, with each step conditional on the results of the previous step.

shipping document. A document containing information about goods shipped and representing a contract between the seller and carrier (e.g., trucking company).

Single Audit Act. Enacted by Congress in 1984, the Act was intended to improve the financial management of state and local governments receiving federal funds, establish uniform audit requirements for federal grant recipients, promote efficient and effective use of audit resources, and ensure that federal departments and agencies rely on one audit only: the single audit.

standard report. A letter communicating what was audited, management's and the auditor's responsibilities, what an audit entails, and an unqualified opinion.

standard deviation. A measure of the variation or dispersion among the items in a population.

standards of field work. The fourth, fifth, and sixth of the ten generally accepted auditing standards are (1) requiring adequate planning and supervision, (2)

consideration of an entity's internal controls, and (3) gathering sufficient competent evidential matter.

standards of reporting. The last four of the ten generally accepted auditing standards are (1) requiring that an entity's financial statements conform to generally accepted accounting principles, (2) consistently applying accounting principles, (3) using informative disclosures, and (4) expressing an opinion on the financial statements taken as a whole.

Statements on Auditing Procedures (SAPs). Auditing pronouncements issued by the Committee on Auditing Procedure from 1939-1972; fifty-four SAPs were issued and some remain effective today, codified within the AICPA's Codification of Statements on Auditing Standards.

Statements on Auditing Standards (SASs). Auditing pronouncements issued from 1972-1978 by the Auditing Standards Executive Committee and, since 1978, by the Auditing Standards Board; the statements interpret generally accepted auditing standards.

Statements on Standards for Accounting and Review Services (SSARSs). Accounting and review services pronouncements issued by the Accounting and Review Services Committee.

Statements on Standards for Attestation Engagements (SSAEs). Attestation engagement standards issued by the Auditing Standards Board.

statistical sampling plan. An audit sampling plan that applies the laws of probability to select a sample and to evaluate the results of testing the sample.

statutory law. Law in written statutes enacted by Congress and by elected state legislatures.

stock certificate. A document (equity security) representing ownership of a stated number of shares of capital stock.

subsequent events. Events (or transactions) occurring during the subsequent period (defined next) that lend hindsight to amounts and information disclosed in financial statements as of the balance sheet date.

subsequent period. In subsequent events, the period after the balance sheet date and on or before the last day of field work.

substantive tests. Tests of details and analytical procedures performed to detect material misstatements in the account balance, transaction class, and disclosure components of financial statements.

successor auditor. In a change of auditors, the newly appointed independent auditor.

systems control audit review files (SCARFs). Logs that collect transaction information for review subsequently by the auditor.

T

telecommunications. The transmission of alphanumeric, voice, video, facsimile, and other data by wire, fiber optics, microwave, laser, or other means of transmission.

test data. A computer assisted audit technique in which the auditor processes data planted with errors to test the ability of a client's software to detect them.

tests of controls. Tests directed toward the design or operation of an internal control policy or procedure to assess its effectiveness in preventing or detecting material misstatements in a financial statement assertion.

tests of details. Substantive tests intended to detect material misstatements in the financial statements.

time records. A record of hours worked by an employee during a particular pay period.

tolerable error. The maximum monetary error that may exist in an account balance without causing the financial statements to be misstated materially.

tolerable rate of deviation (tolerable deviation rate). The maximum population rate of deviation from a prescribed

control procedure that an auditor will tolerate without modifying the assessed level of control risk.

tort. A wrongful act, other than breach of contract, that results in injury to another person.

trading securities. Debt and equity securities held for sale in the near term.

transaction cycle. A vehicle through which similar repetitive transactions are processed by an entity's accounting system; examples include the revenue/receipt cycle, the expenditure/disbursement cycle, the financing cycle, and the conversion cycle.

transaction tagging. A computer assisted audit technique in which a transaction record is "tagged" and then "traced" through critical control points in an information system.

treasury bill. A debt instrument issued by the U.S. Treasury Department.

type I subsequent events. Subsequent events that reveal or confirm conditions existing at or before the balance sheet date and that require adjustment to the financial statements.

type II subsequent events. Subsequent events that reveal conditions arising after the balance sheet date and that require disclosure in, but not adjustment to, the financial statements.

U

unasserted claims. Claims for which a plaintiff may have a legal right but has not yet begun proceedings.

unqualified opinion. A communication within an attestation or audit report indicating, respectively, that management's assertion is presented fairly in all material respects in conformity with established criteria, or that management's financial statements present fairly in all material respects the financial position, results of operations, and cash flows in conformity with generally accepted accounting principles.

V

valuation or allocation. An assertion within financial statements that all assets, liabilities, equities, revenues, and expenses have been included in the statements at appropriate amounts.

variables sampling plan. An audit sampling plan designed to test whether a recorded account balance is misstated materially.

vendor's invoice. A document containing information about goods purchased, representing formal notice to a purchaser about the terms and due date of payment.

voucher package. A set of documents (usually the purchase requisition, purchase order, receiving report, and invoice) relating to a purchase transaction.

W

working papers. The principal written record of the work performed and the conclusions reached by an auditor during a financial statement audit.

Index

T